CLINTON MILK CO
NEWARK, N.J

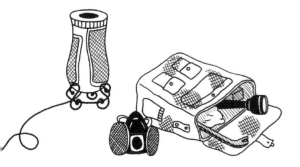

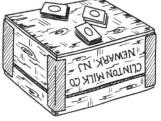

BLACK DOG & LEVENTHAL PUBLISHERS
HACHETTE BOOK GROUP
1290 AVENUE OF THE AMERICAS
NEW YORK, NY 10104

WWW.HACHETTEBOOKGROUP.COM
WWW.BLACKDOGANDLEVENTHAL.COM

FIRST EDITION: MAY 2023

BLACK DOG & LEVENTHAL PUBLISHERS IS AN IMPRINT OF PERSEUS BOOKS, LLC, A SUBSIDIARY OF HACHETTE BOOK GROUP, INC. THE BLACK DOG & LEVENTHAL PUBLISHERS NAME AND LOGO ARE TRADEMARKS OF HACHETTE BOOK GROUP, INC.

THE PUBLISHER IS NOT RESPONSIBLE FOR WEBSITES (OR THEIR CONTENT) THAT ARE NOT OWNED BY THE PUBLISHER.

THE HACHETTE SPEAKERS BUREAU PROVIDES A WIDE RANGE OF AUTHORS FOR SPEAKING EVENTS. TO FIND OUT MORE, GO TO WWW.HACHETTESPEAKERSBUREAU.COM OR CALL (866) 376-6591.

PRINT BOOK INTERIOR DESIGN BY KATIE BENEZRA

LCCN: 2022937224

ISBNS: 978-0-7624-6825-6 (HARDCOVER);
978-0-7624-6823-2 (EBOOK)

PRINTED IN CHINA

APS

10 9 8 7 6 5 4 3 2 1

CinaMoon Restaurant
MANHATTAN AVE
stokrotkd
BEAUTY PRODUCTS
WWW.STOKROTKD.COM
662 MANHATTAN AV.
660 MANHATTAN Ave.
BROOKLYN INDUSTRIES
ARMY & NAVY
PAWN SHOP
SINCE 1989
WE BUY GOLD

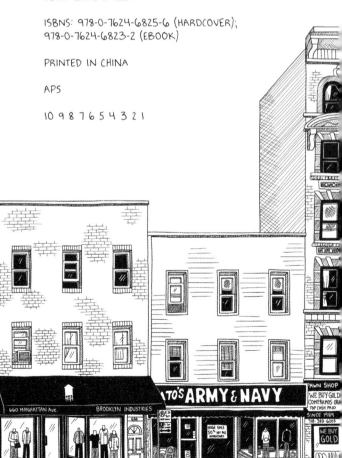

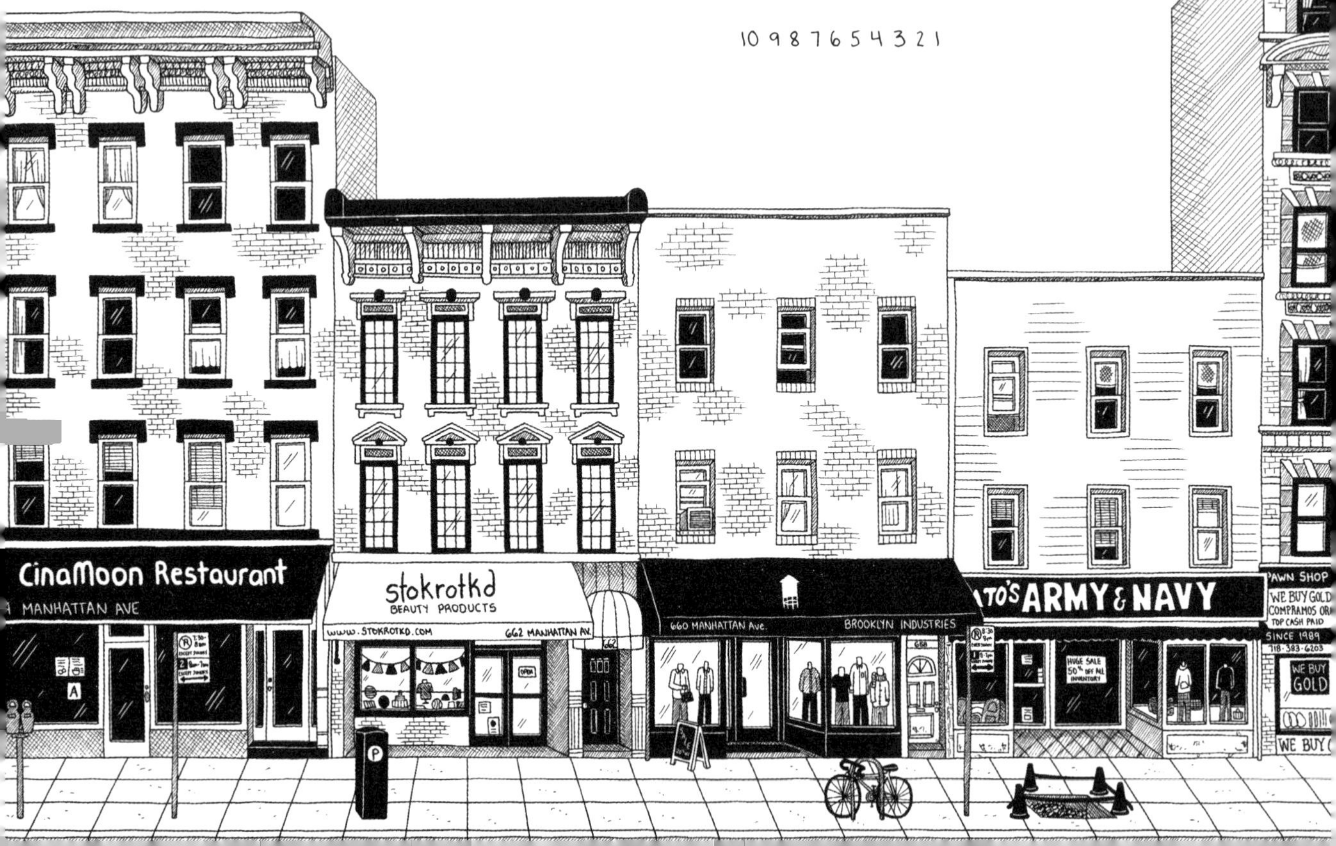

IMPOSSIBLE PEOPLE

A COMPLETELY AVERAGE RECOVERY STORY

JULIA WERTZ

BLACK DOG
& LEVENTHAL
PUBLISHERS
NEW YORK

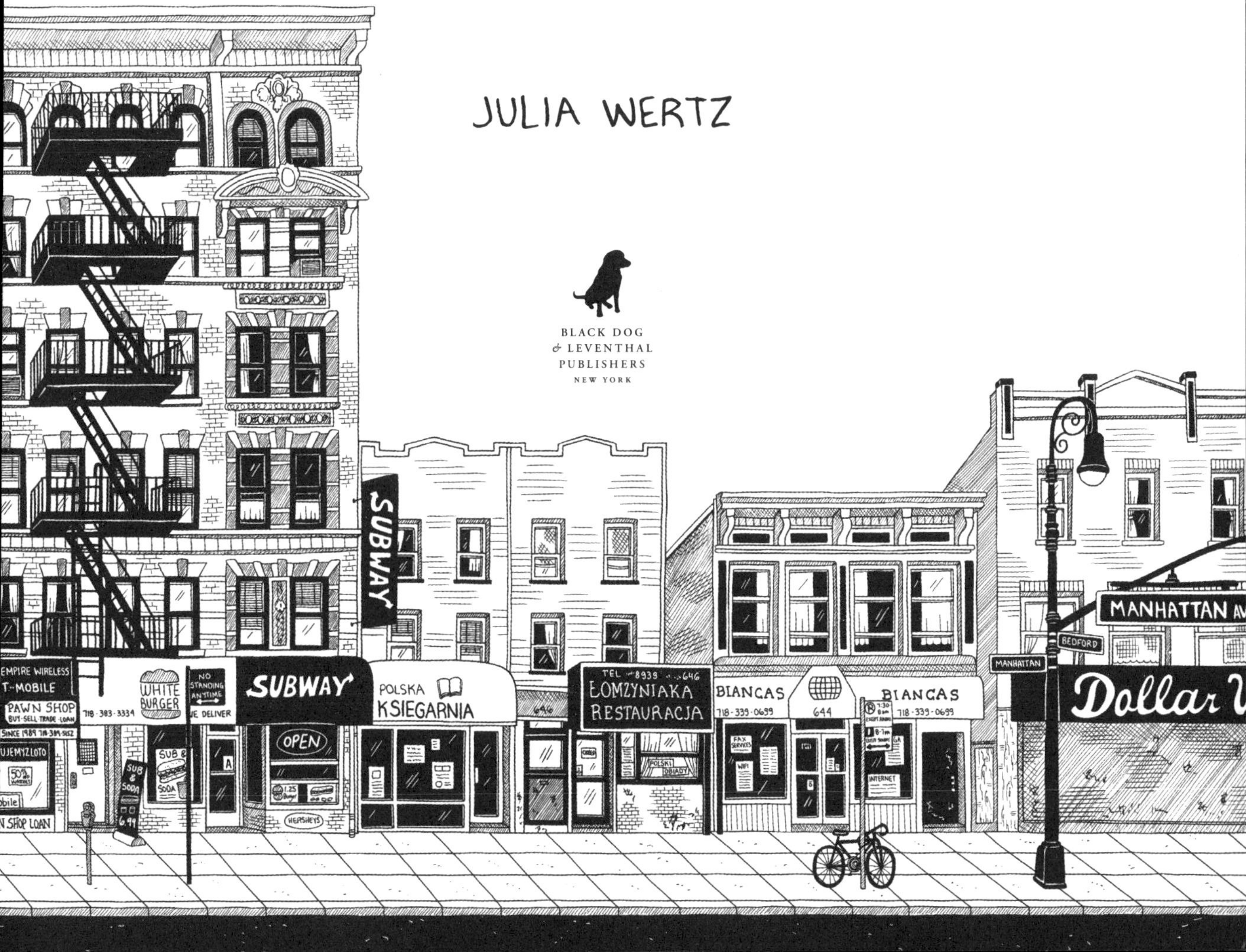
SUBWAY
EMPIRE WIRELESS
T-MOBILE
PAWN SHOP
WHITE BURGER
NO STANDING ANYTIME
SUBWAY
OPEN
POLSKA KSIEGARNIA
ŁOMZYNIAKA RESTAURACJA
BIANCAS
644
BIANCAS
MANHATTAN
BEDFORD
MANHATTAN AV
Dollar

FOR JENNIFER PHIPPEN AND SARAH GLIDDEN.
I LOVE YOU BOTH SO MUCH.

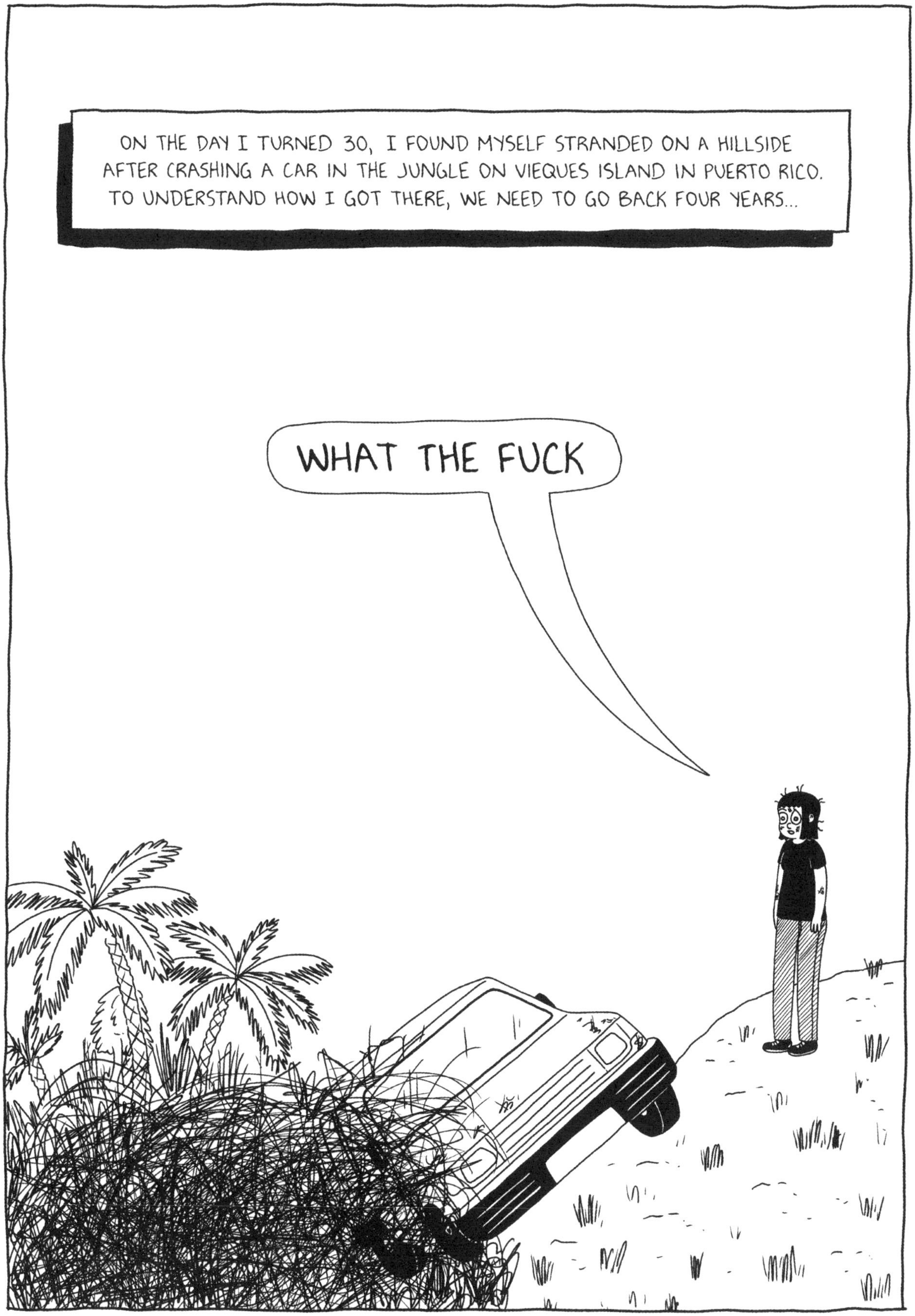
ON THE DAY I TURNED 30, I FOUND MYSELF STRANDED ON A HILLSIDE AFTER CRASHING A CAR IN THE JUNGLE ON VIEQUES ISLAND IN PUERTO RICO. TO UNDERSTAND HOW I GOT THERE, WE NEED TO GO BACK FOUR YEARS...
WHAT THE FUCK

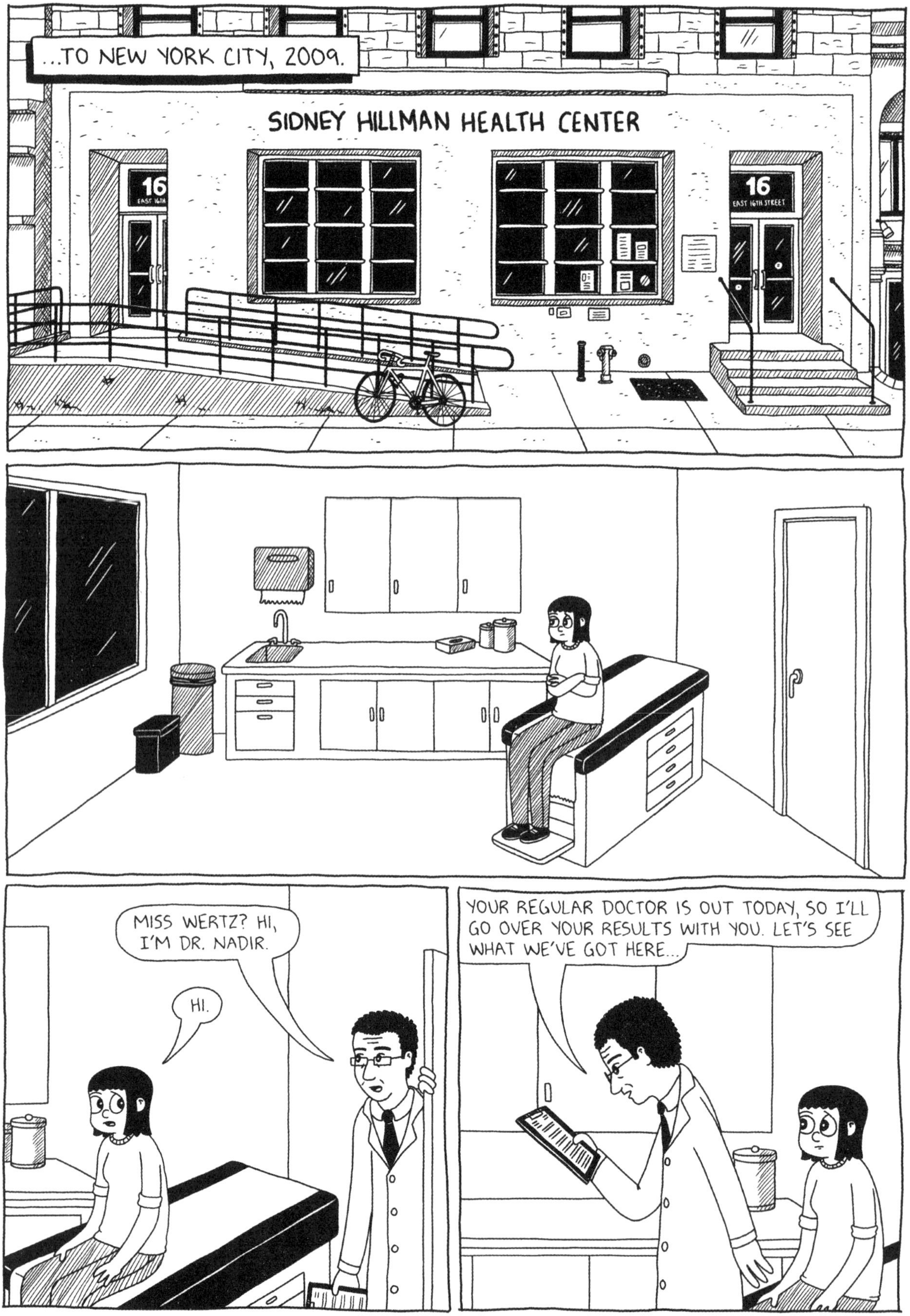
...TO NEW YORK CITY, 2009.
SIDNEY HILLMAN HEALTH CENTER
16
EAST 16TH STREET
MISS WERTZ? HI, I'M DR. NADIR.
HI.
YOUR REGULAR DOCTOR IS OUT TODAY, SO I'LL GO OVER YOUR RESULTS WITH YOU. LET'S SEE WHAT WE'VE GOT HERE...

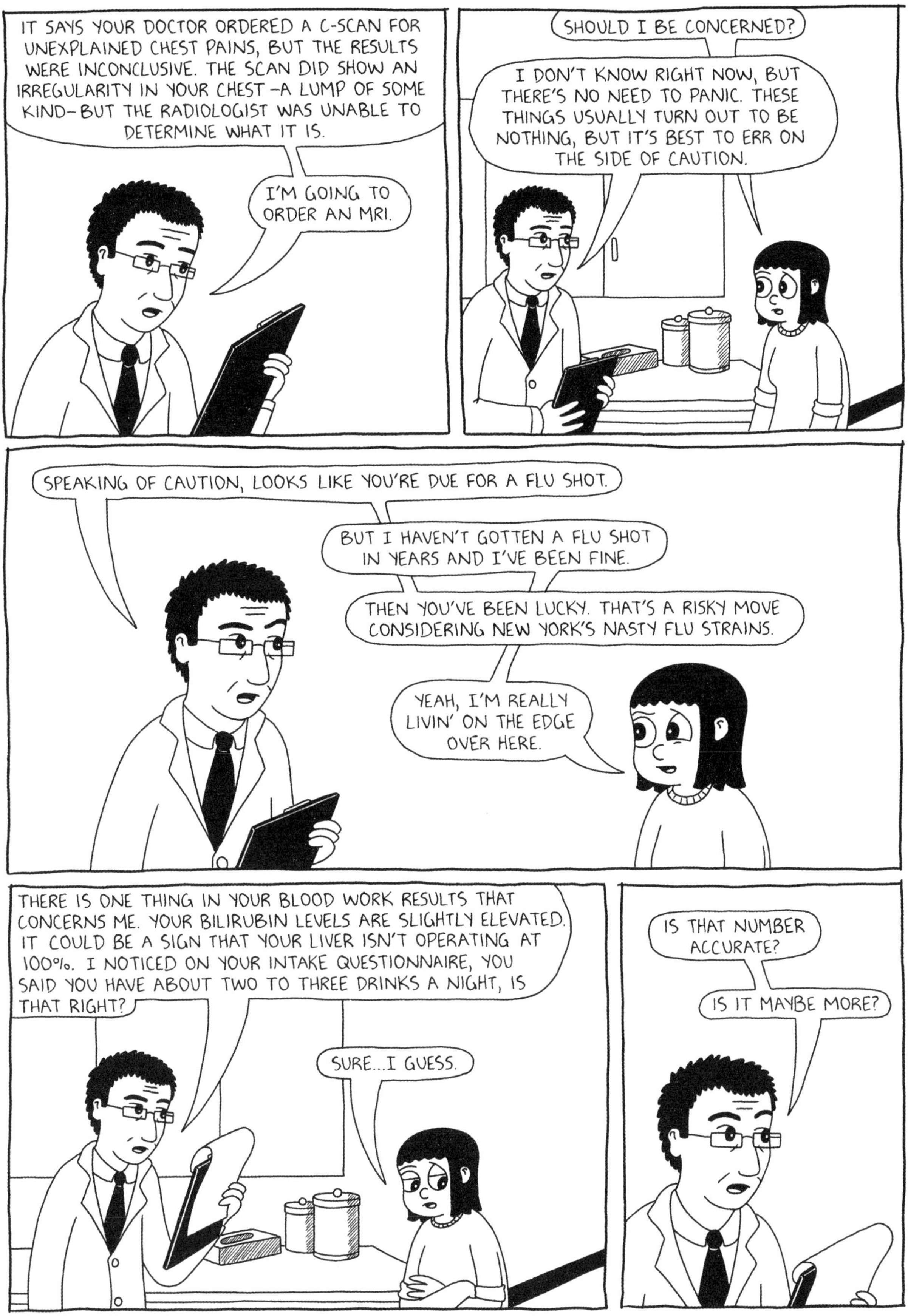
IT SAYS YOUR DOCTOR ORDERED A C-SCAN FOR UNEXPLAINED CHEST PAINS, BUT THE RESULTS WERE INCONCLUSIVE. THE SCAN DID SHOW AN IRREGULARITY IN YOUR CHEST–A LUMP OF SOME KIND–BUT THE RADIOLOGIST WAS UNABLE TO DETERMINE WHAT IT IS.
I'M GOING TO ORDER AN MRI.
SHOULD I BE CONCERNED?
I DON'T KNOW RIGHT NOW, BUT THERE'S NO NEED TO PANIC. THESE THINGS USUALLY TURN OUT TO BE NOTHING, BUT IT'S BEST TO ERR ON THE SIDE OF CAUTION.
SPEAKING OF CAUTION, LOOKS LIKE YOU'RE DUE FOR A FLU SHOT.
BUT I HAVEN'T GOTTEN A FLU SHOT IN YEARS AND I'VE BEEN FINE.
THEN YOU'VE BEEN LUCKY. THAT'S A RISKY MOVE CONSIDERING NEW YORK'S NASTY FLU STRAINS.
YEAH, I'M REALLY LIVIN' ON THE EDGE OVER HERE.
THERE IS ONE THING IN YOUR BLOOD WORK RESULTS THAT CONCERNS ME. YOUR BILIRUBIN LEVELS ARE SLIGHTLY ELEVATED. IT COULD BE A SIGN THAT YOUR LIVER ISN'T OPERATING AT 100%. I NOTICED ON YOUR INTAKE QUESTIONNAIRE, YOU SAID YOU HAVE ABOUT TWO TO THREE DRINKS A NIGHT, IS THAT RIGHT?
SURE...I GUESS.
IS THAT NUMBER ACCURATE?
IS IT MAYBE MORE?

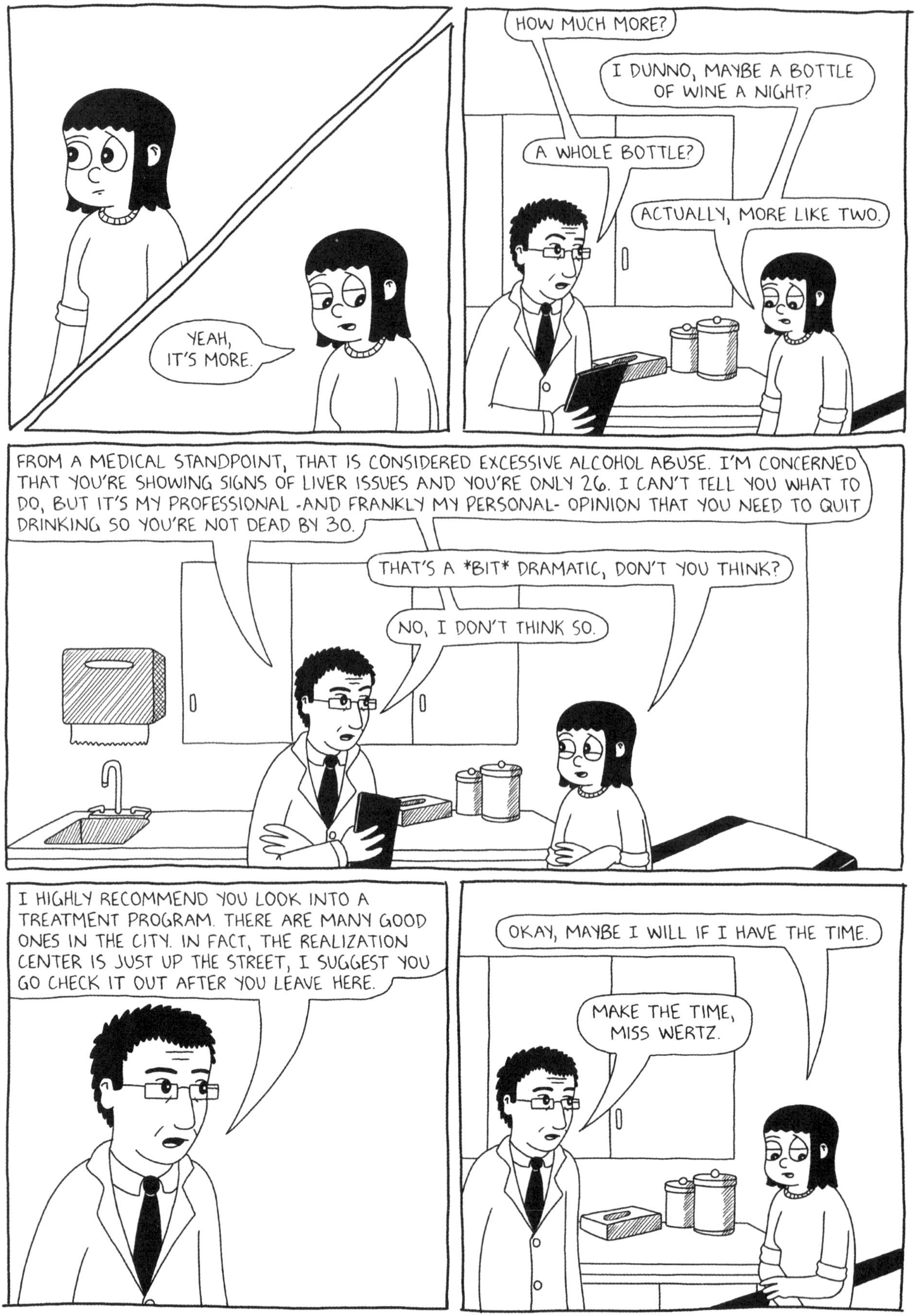
YEAH, IT'S MORE.
HOW MUCH MORE?
I DUNNO, MAYBE A BOTTLE OF WINE A NIGHT?
A WHOLE BOTTLE?
ACTUALLY, MORE LIKE TWO.
FROM A MEDICAL STANDPOINT, THAT IS CONSIDERED EXCESSIVE ALCOHOL ABUSE. I'M CONCERNED THAT YOU'RE SHOWING SIGNS OF LIVER ISSUES AND YOU'RE ONLY 26. I CAN'T TELL YOU WHAT TO DO, BUT IT'S MY PROFESSIONAL -AND FRANKLY MY PERSONAL- OPINION THAT YOU NEED TO QUIT DRINKING SO YOU'RE NOT DEAD BY 30.
THAT'S A *BIT* DRAMATIC, DON'T YOU THINK?
NO, I DON'T THINK SO.
I HIGHLY RECOMMEND YOU LOOK INTO A TREATMENT PROGRAM. THERE ARE MANY GOOD ONES IN THE CITY. IN FACT, THE REALIZATION CENTER IS JUST UP THE STREET, I SUGGEST YOU GO CHECK IT OUT AFTER YOU LEAVE HERE.
OKAY, MAYBE I WILL IF I HAVE THE TIME.
MAKE THE TIME, MISS WERTZ.

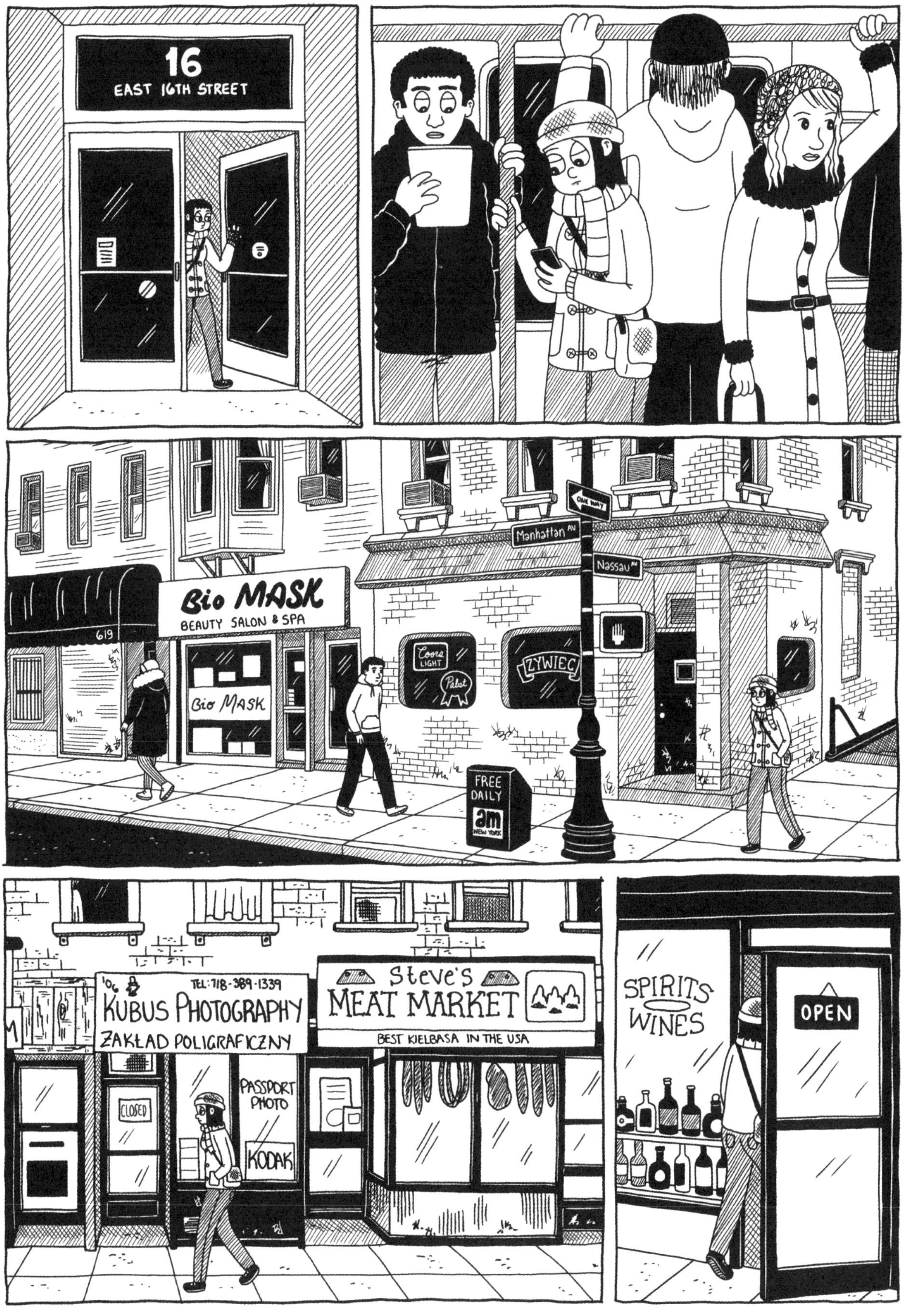
16
EAST 16TH STREET
ONE WAY
Manhattan AV
Nassau AV
Bio MASK
BEAUTY SALON & SPA
619
Bio MASK
Coors LIGHT
Pabst
ZYWIEC
FREE DAILY
am
NEW YORK
106
TEL: 718-389-1339
KUBUS PHOTOGRAPHY
ZAKŁAD POLIGRAFICZNY
CLOSED
PASSPORT PHOTO
KODAK
Steve's
MEAT MARKET
BEST KIELBASA IN THE USA
SPIRITS
WINES
OPEN

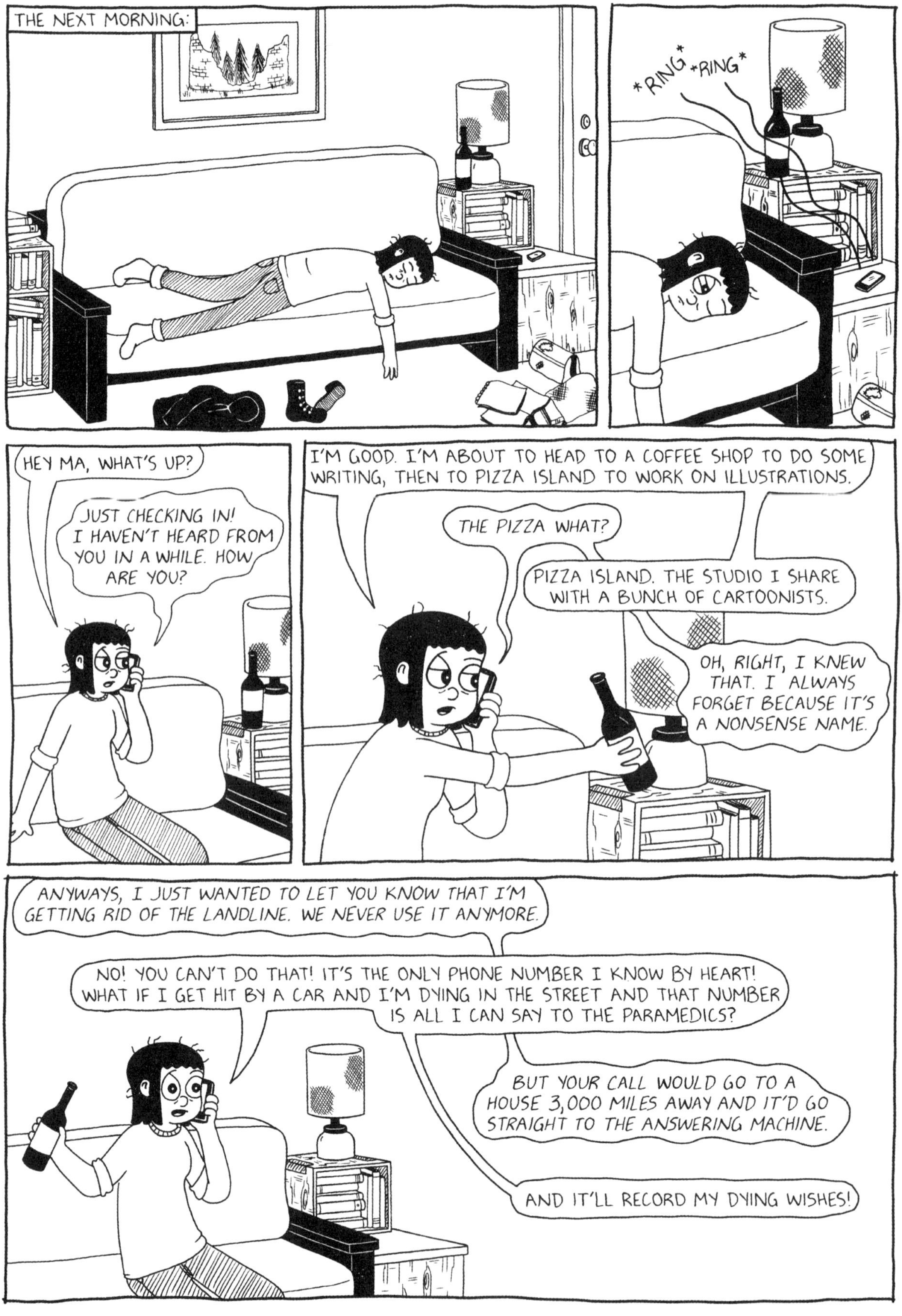
THE NEXT MORNING:
RING *RING*
HEY MA, WHAT'S UP?
JUST CHECKING IN! I HAVEN'T HEARD FROM YOU IN A WHILE. HOW ARE YOU?
I'M GOOD. I'M ABOUT TO HEAD TO A COFFEE SHOP TO DO SOME WRITING, THEN TO PIZZA ISLAND TO WORK ON ILLUSTRATIONS.
THE PIZZA WHAT?
PIZZA ISLAND. THE STUDIO I SHARE WITH A BUNCH OF CARTOONISTS.
OH, RIGHT, I KNEW THAT. I ALWAYS FORGET BECAUSE IT'S A NONSENSE NAME.
ANYWAYS, I JUST WANTED TO LET YOU KNOW THAT I'M GETTING RID OF THE LANDLINE. WE NEVER USE IT ANYMORE.
NO! YOU CAN'T DO THAT! IT'S THE ONLY PHONE NUMBER I KNOW BY HEART! WHAT IF I GET HIT BY A CAR AND I'M DYING IN THE STREET AND THAT NUMBER IS ALL I CAN SAY TO THE PARAMEDICS?
BUT YOUR CALL WOULD GO TO A HOUSE 3,000 MILES AWAY AND IT'D GO STRAIGHT TO THE ANSWERING MACHINE.
AND IT'LL RECORD MY DYING WISHES!

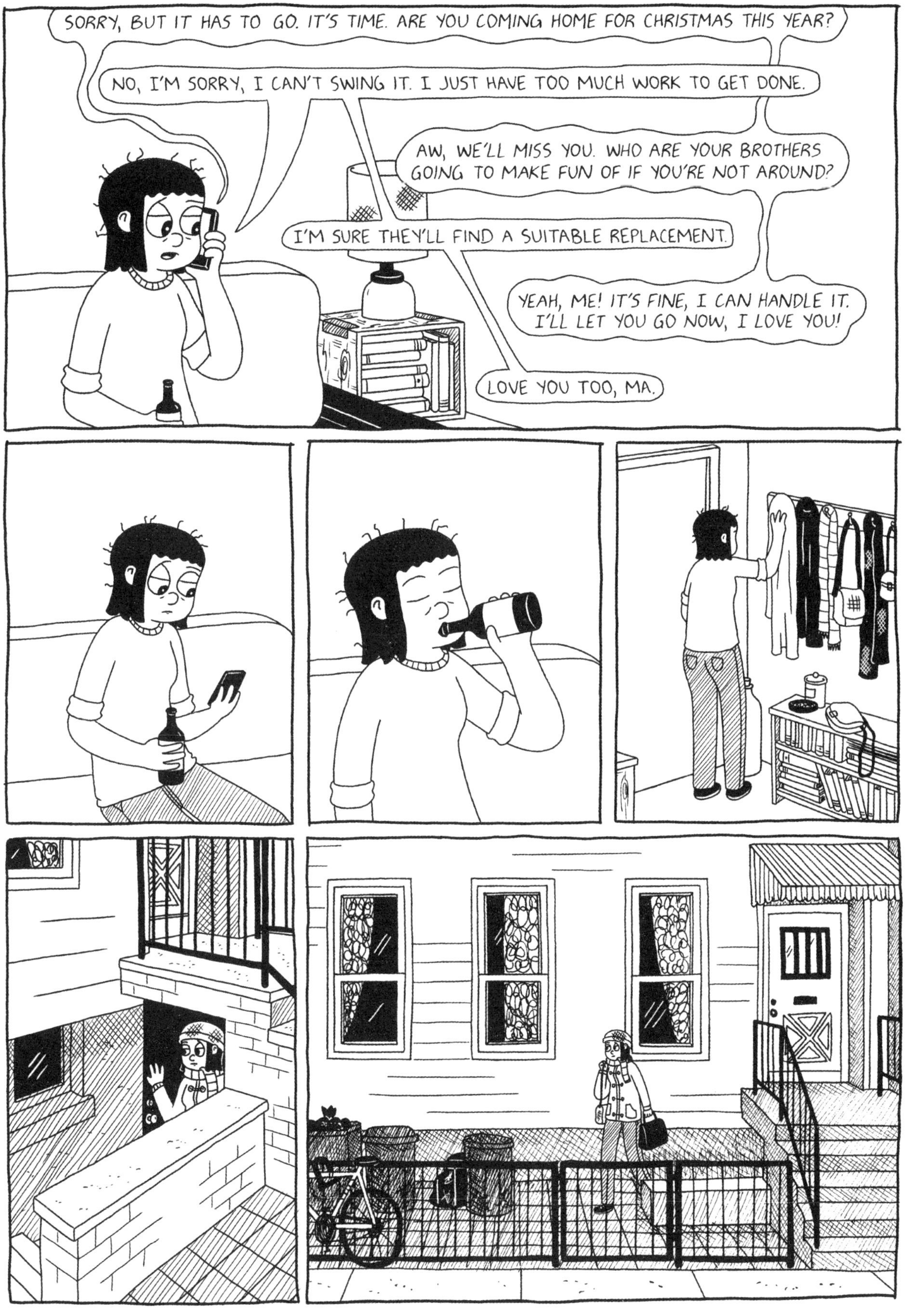
SORRY, BUT IT HAS TO GO. IT'S TIME. ARE YOU COMING HOME FOR CHRISTMAS THIS YEAR?
NO, I'M SORRY, I CAN'T SWING IT. I JUST HAVE TOO MUCH WORK TO GET DONE.
AW, WE'LL MISS YOU. WHO ARE YOUR BROTHERS GOING TO MAKE FUN OF IF YOU'RE NOT AROUND?
I'M SURE THEY'LL FIND A SUITABLE REPLACEMENT.
YEAH, ME! IT'S FINE, I CAN HANDLE IT. I'LL LET YOU GO NOW, I LOVE YOU!
LOVE YOU TOO, MA.

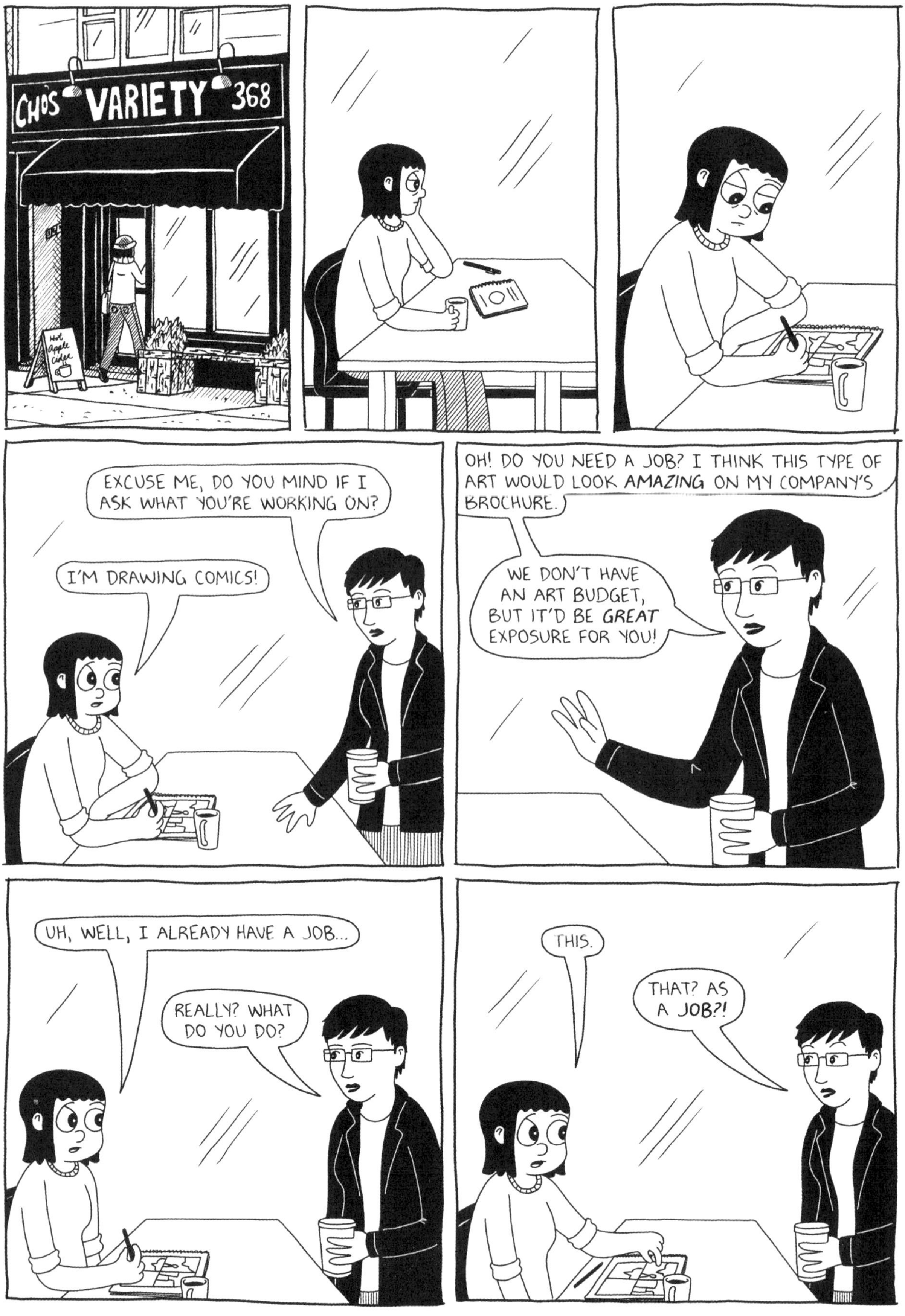
CHO'S VARIETY 368
Hot Apple Cider
EXCUSE ME, DO YOU MIND IF I ASK WHAT YOU'RE WORKING ON?
I'M DRAWING COMICS!
OH! DO YOU NEED A JOB? I THINK THIS TYPE OF ART WOULD LOOK AMAZING ON MY COMPANY'S BROCHURE.
WE DON'T HAVE AN ART BUDGET, BUT IT'D BE GREAT EXPOSURE FOR YOU!
UH, WELL, I ALREADY HAVE A JOB...
REALLY? WHAT DO YOU DO?
THIS.
THAT? AS A JOB?!

LATER THAT MORNING, SARAH, WHO LIVED A FEW BLOCKS AWAY, STOPPED BY TO PICK ME UP ON HER WAY TO THE STUDIO.

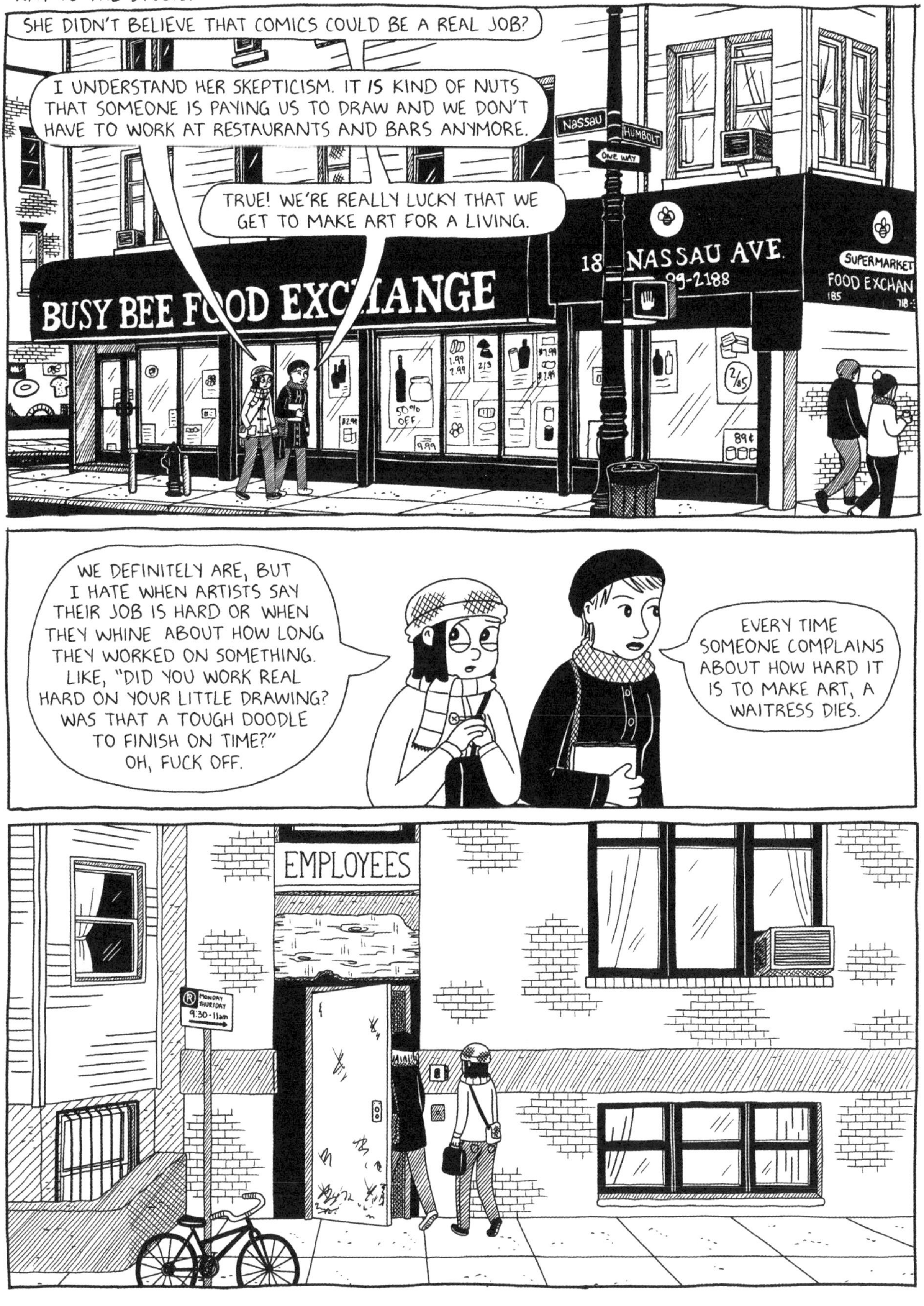
SHE DIDN'T BELIEVE THAT COMICS COULD BE A REAL JOB?
I UNDERSTAND HER SKEPTICISM. IT IS KIND OF NUTS THAT SOMEONE IS PAYING US TO DRAW AND WE DON'T HAVE TO WORK AT RESTAURANTS AND BARS ANYMORE.
TRUE! WE'RE REALLY LUCKY THAT WE GET TO MAKE ART FOR A LIVING.
NASSAU
HUMBOLT
ONE WAY
BUSY BEE FOOD EXCHANGE
NASSAU AVE.
SUPERMARKET
FOOD EXCHAN
WE DEFINITELY ARE, BUT I HATE WHEN ARTISTS SAY THEIR JOB IS HARD OR WHEN THEY WHINE ABOUT HOW LONG THEY WORKED ON SOMETHING. LIKE, "DID YOU WORK REAL HARD ON YOUR LITTLE DRAWING? WAS THAT A TOUGH DOODLE TO FINISH ON TIME?" OH, FUCK OFF.
EVERY TIME SOMEONE COMPLAINS ABOUT HOW HARD IT IS TO MAKE ART, A WAITRESS DIES.
EMPLOYEES

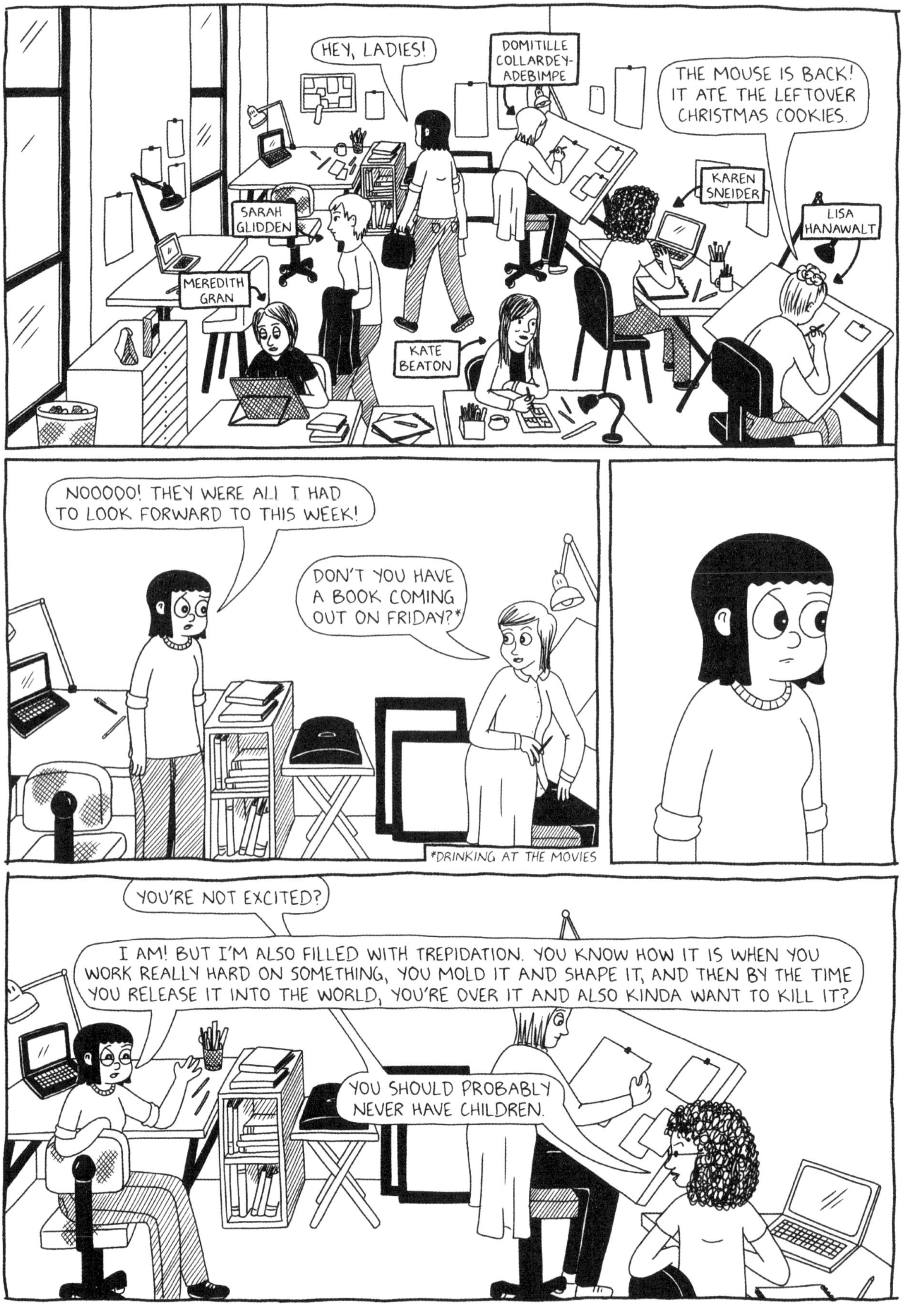
HEY, LADIES!
DOMITILLE COLLARDEY-ADEBIMPE
THE MOUSE IS BACK! IT ATE THE LEFTOVER CHRISTMAS COOKIES.
KAREN SNEIDER
SARAH GLIDDEN
LISA HANAWALT
MEREDITH GRAN
KATE BEATON
NOOOOO! THEY WERE ALL I HAD TO LOOK FORWARD TO THIS WEEK!
DON'T YOU HAVE A BOOK COMING OUT ON FRIDAY?*
*DRINKING AT THE MOVIES
YOU'RE NOT EXCITED?
I AM! BUT I'M ALSO FILLED WITH TREPIDATION. YOU KNOW HOW IT IS WHEN YOU WORK REALLY HARD ON SOMETHING, YOU MOLD IT AND SHAPE IT, AND THEN BY THE TIME YOU RELEASE IT INTO THE WORLD, YOU'RE OVER IT AND ALSO KINDA WANT TO KILL IT?
YOU SHOULD PROBABLY NEVER HAVE CHILDREN.

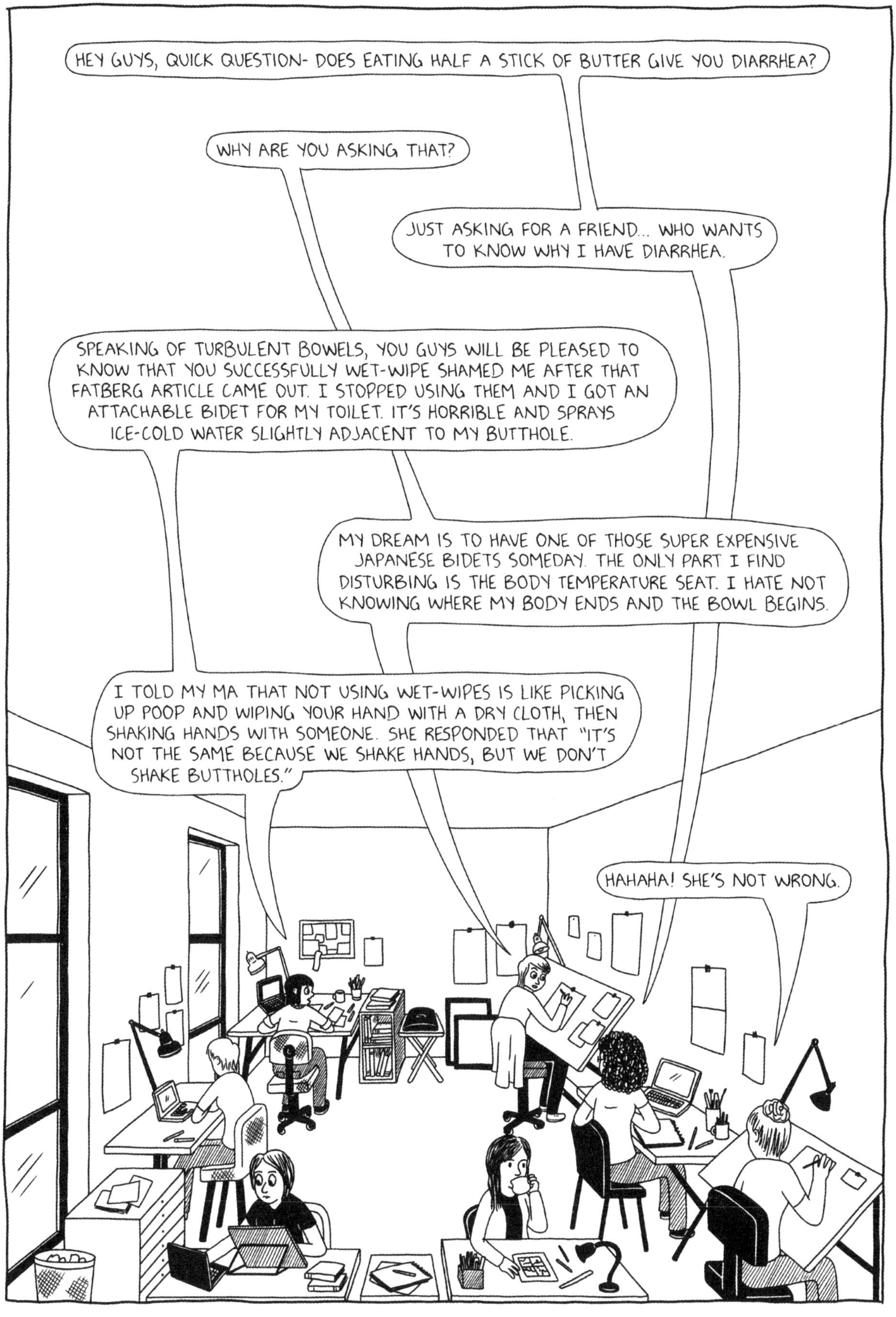
HEY GUYS, QUICK QUESTION- DOES EATING HALF A STICK OF BUTTER GIVE YOU DIARRHEA?
WHY ARE YOU ASKING THAT?
JUST ASKING FOR A FRIEND... WHO WANTS TO KNOW WHY I HAVE DIARRHEA.
SPEAKING OF TURBULENT BOWELS, YOU GUYS WILL BE PLEASED TO KNOW THAT YOU SUCCESSFULLY WET-WIPE SHAMED ME AFTER THAT FATBERG ARTICLE CAME OUT. I STOPPED USING THEM AND I GOT AN ATTACHABLE BIDET FOR MY TOILET. IT'S HORRIBLE AND SPRAYS ICE-COLD WATER SLIGHTLY ADJACENT TO MY BUTTHOLE.
MY DREAM IS TO HAVE ONE OF THOSE SUPER EXPENSIVE JAPANESE BIDETS SOMEDAY. THE ONLY PART I FIND DISTURBING IS THE BODY TEMPERATURE SEAT. I HATE NOT KNOWING WHERE MY BODY ENDS AND THE BOWL BEGINS.
I TOLD MY MA THAT NOT USING WET-WIPES IS LIKE PICKING UP POOP AND WIPING YOUR HAND WITH A DRY CLOTH, THEN SHAKING HANDS WITH SOMEONE. SHE RESPONDED THAT "IT'S NOT THE SAME BECAUSE WE SHAKE HANDS, BUT WE DON'T SHAKE BUTTHOLES."
HAHAHA! SHE'S NOT WRONG.

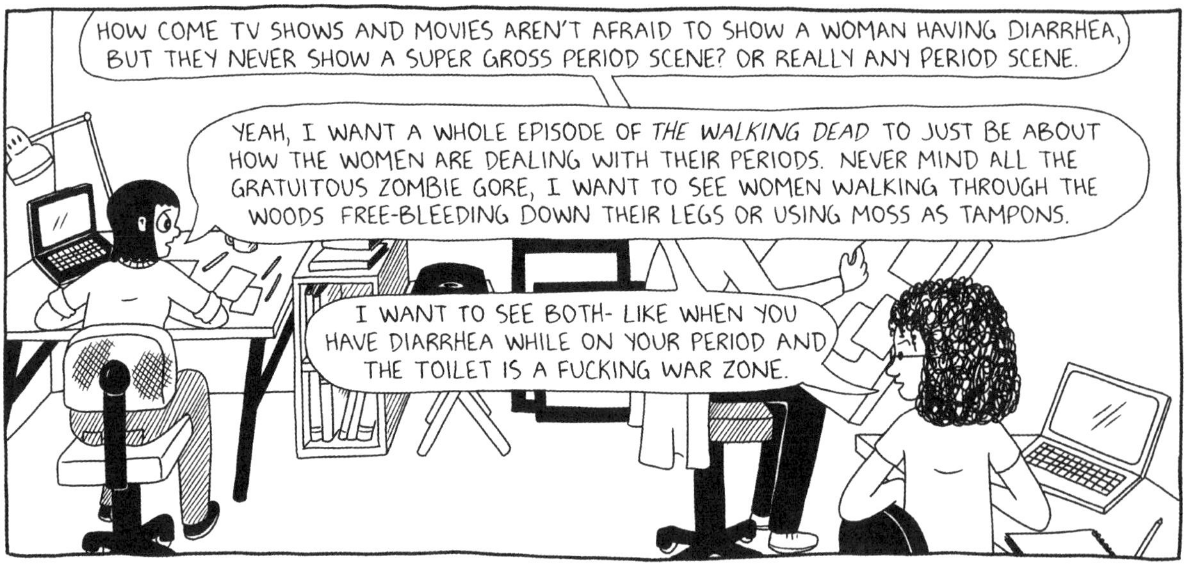
HOW COME TV SHOWS AND MOVIES AREN'T AFRAID TO SHOW A WOMAN HAVING DIARRHEA, BUT THEY NEVER SHOW A SUPER GROSS PERIOD SCENE? OR REALLY ANY PERIOD SCENE.
YEAH, I WANT A WHOLE EPISODE OF *THE WALKING DEAD* TO JUST BE ABOUT HOW THE WOMEN ARE DEALING WITH THEIR PERIODS. NEVER MIND ALL THE GRATUITOUS ZOMBIE GORE, I WANT TO SEE WOMEN WALKING THROUGH THE WOODS FREE-BLEEDING DOWN THEIR LEGS OR USING MOSS AS TAMPONS.
I WANT TO SEE BOTH- LIKE WHEN YOU HAVE DIARRHEA WHILE ON YOUR PERIOD AND THE TOILET IS A FUCKING WAR ZONE.

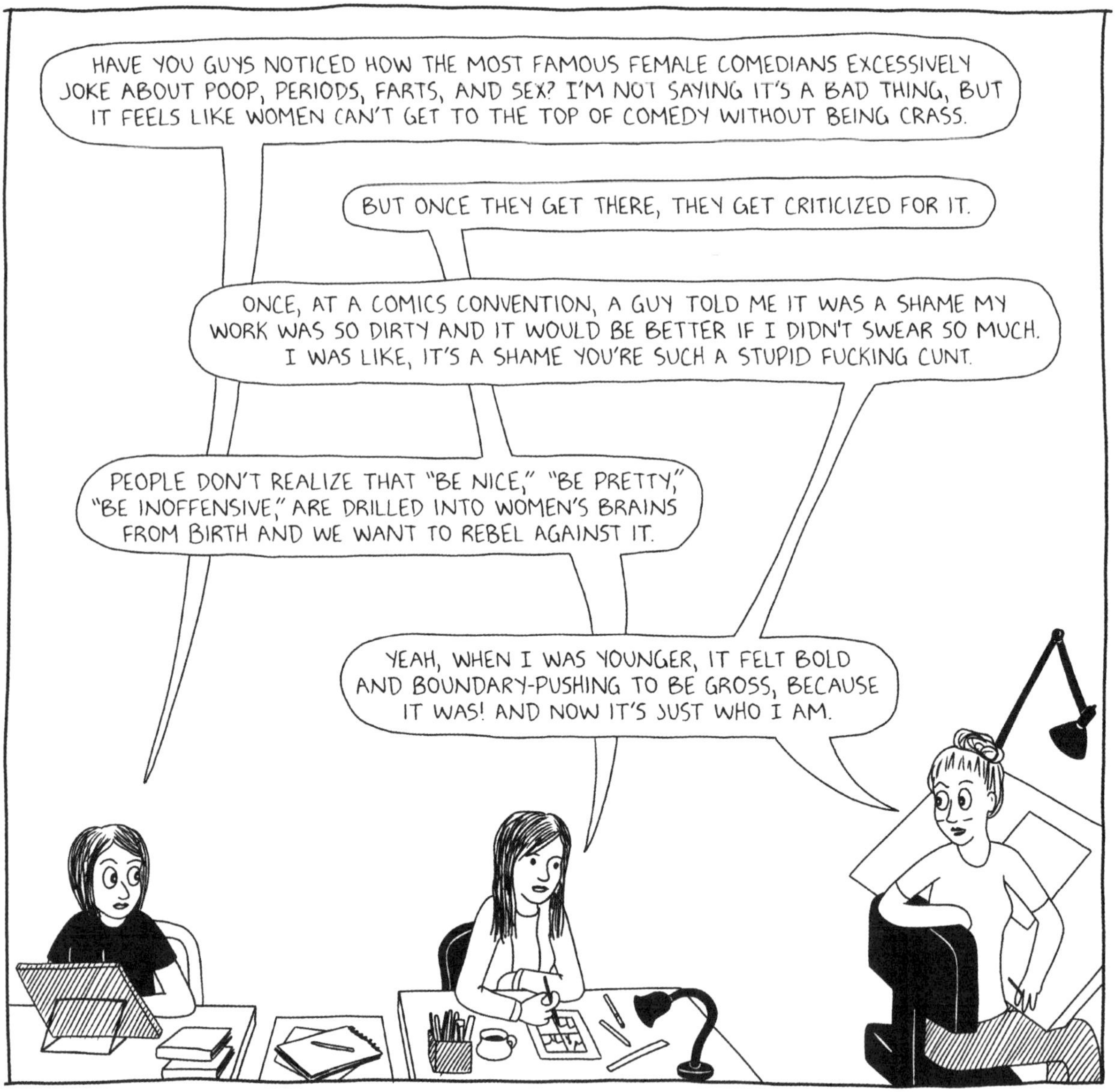
HAVE YOU GUYS NOTICED HOW THE MOST FAMOUS FEMALE COMEDIANS EXCESSIVELY JOKE ABOUT POOP, PERIODS, FARTS, AND SEX? I'M NOT SAYING IT'S A BAD THING, BUT IT FEELS LIKE WOMEN CAN'T GET TO THE TOP OF COMEDY WITHOUT BEING CRASS.
BUT ONCE THEY GET THERE, THEY GET CRITICIZED FOR IT.
ONCE, AT A COMICS CONVENTION, A GUY TOLD ME IT WAS A SHAME MY WORK WAS SO DIRTY AND IT WOULD BE BETTER IF I DIDN'T SWEAR SO MUCH. I WAS LIKE, IT'S A SHAME YOU'RE SUCH A STUPID FUCKING CUNT.
PEOPLE DON'T REALIZE THAT "BE NICE," "BE PRETTY," "BE INOFFENSIVE," ARE DRILLED INTO WOMEN'S BRAINS FROM BIRTH AND WE WANT TO REBEL AGAINST IT.
YEAH, WHEN I WAS YOUNGER, IT FELT BOLD AND BOUNDARY-PUSHING TO BE GROSS, BECAUSE IT WAS! AND NOW IT'S JUST WHO I AM.

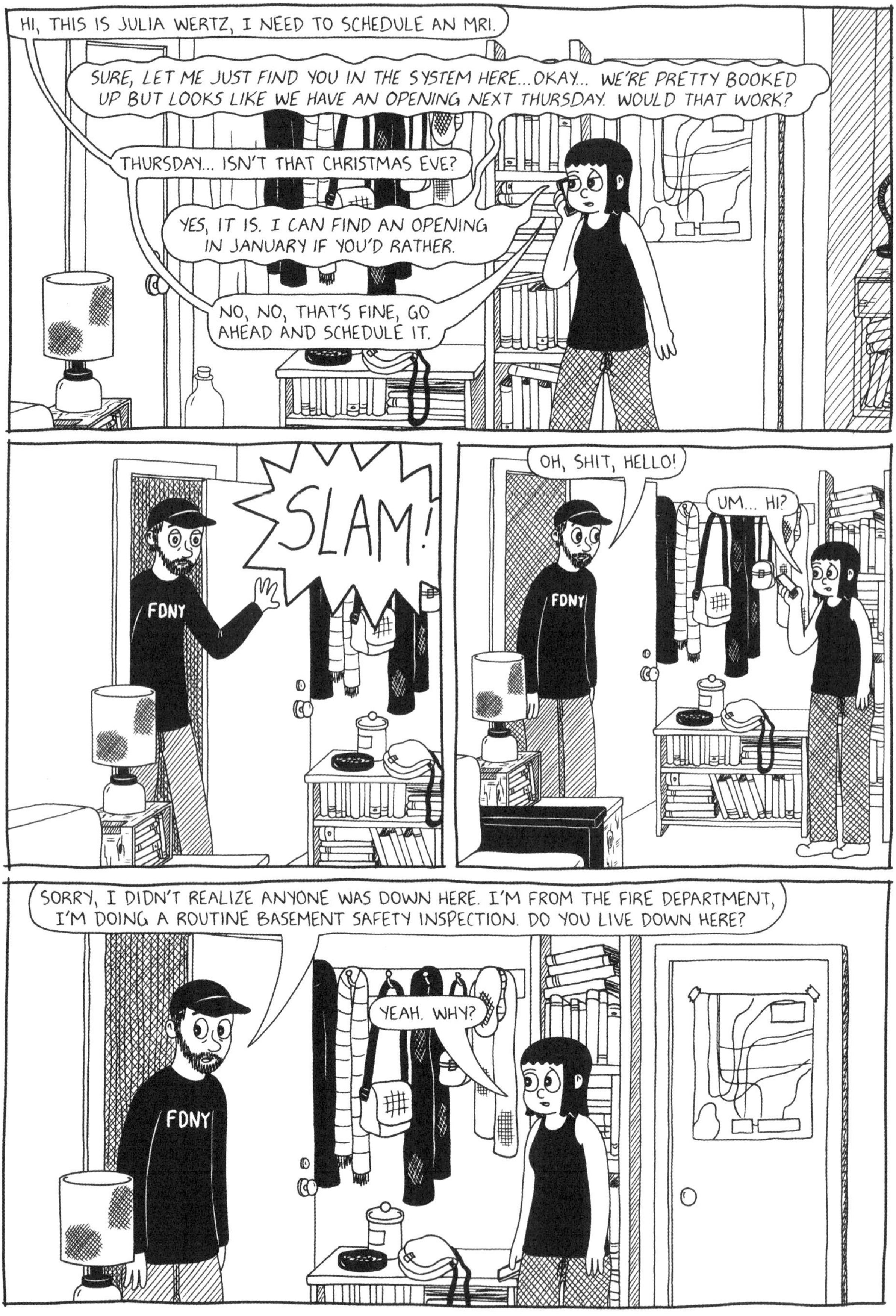
HI, THIS IS JULIA WERTZ, I NEED TO SCHEDULE AN MRI.
SURE, LET ME JUST FIND YOU IN THE SYSTEM HERE...OKAY... WE'RE PRETTY BOOKED UP BUT LOOKS LIKE WE HAVE AN OPENING NEXT THURSDAY. WOULD THAT WORK?
THURSDAY... ISN'T THAT CHRISTMAS EVE?
YES, IT IS. I CAN FIND AN OPENING IN JANUARY IF YOU'D RATHER.
NO, NO, THAT'S FINE, GO AHEAD AND SCHEDULE IT.
FDNY
SLAM!
OH, SHIT, HELLO!
UM... HI?
FDNY
SORRY, I DIDN'T REALIZE ANYONE WAS DOWN HERE. I'M FROM THE FIRE DEPARTMENT, I'M DOING A ROUTINE BASEMENT SAFETY INSPECTION. DO YOU LIVE DOWN HERE?
YEAH. WHY?
FDNY

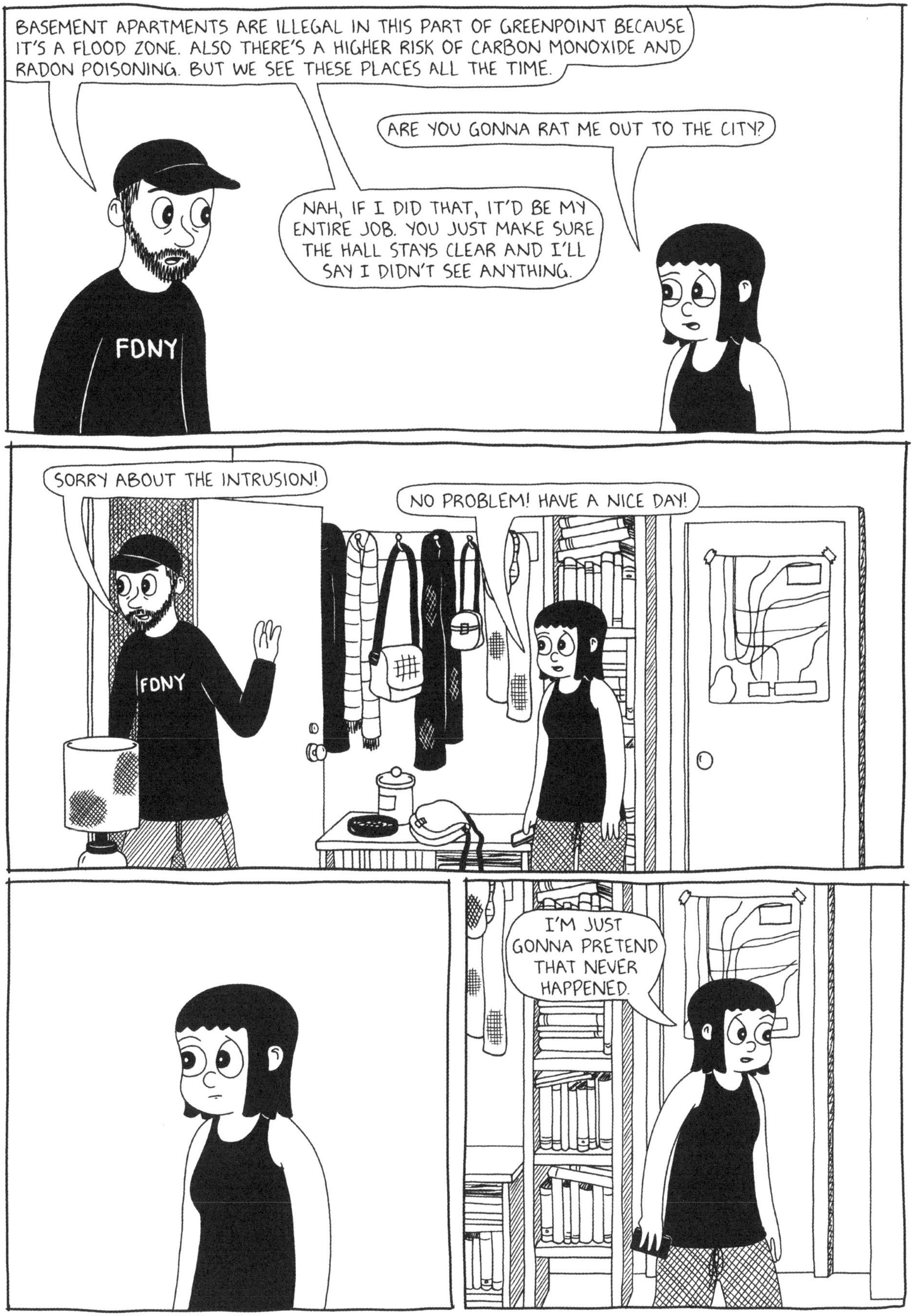
BASEMENT APARTMENTS ARE ILLEGAL IN THIS PART OF GREENPOINT BECAUSE IT'S A FLOOD ZONE. ALSO THERE'S A HIGHER RISK OF CARBON MONOXIDE AND RADON POISONING. BUT WE SEE THESE PLACES ALL THE TIME.
ARE YOU GONNA RAT ME OUT TO THE CITY?
NAH, IF I DID THAT, IT'D BE MY ENTIRE JOB. YOU JUST MAKE SURE THE HALL STAYS CLEAR AND I'LL SAY I DIDN'T SEE ANYTHING.
FDNY
SORRY ABOUT THE INTRUSION!
NO PROBLEM! HAVE A NICE DAY!
FDNY
I'M JUST GONNA PRETEND THAT NEVER HAPPENED.

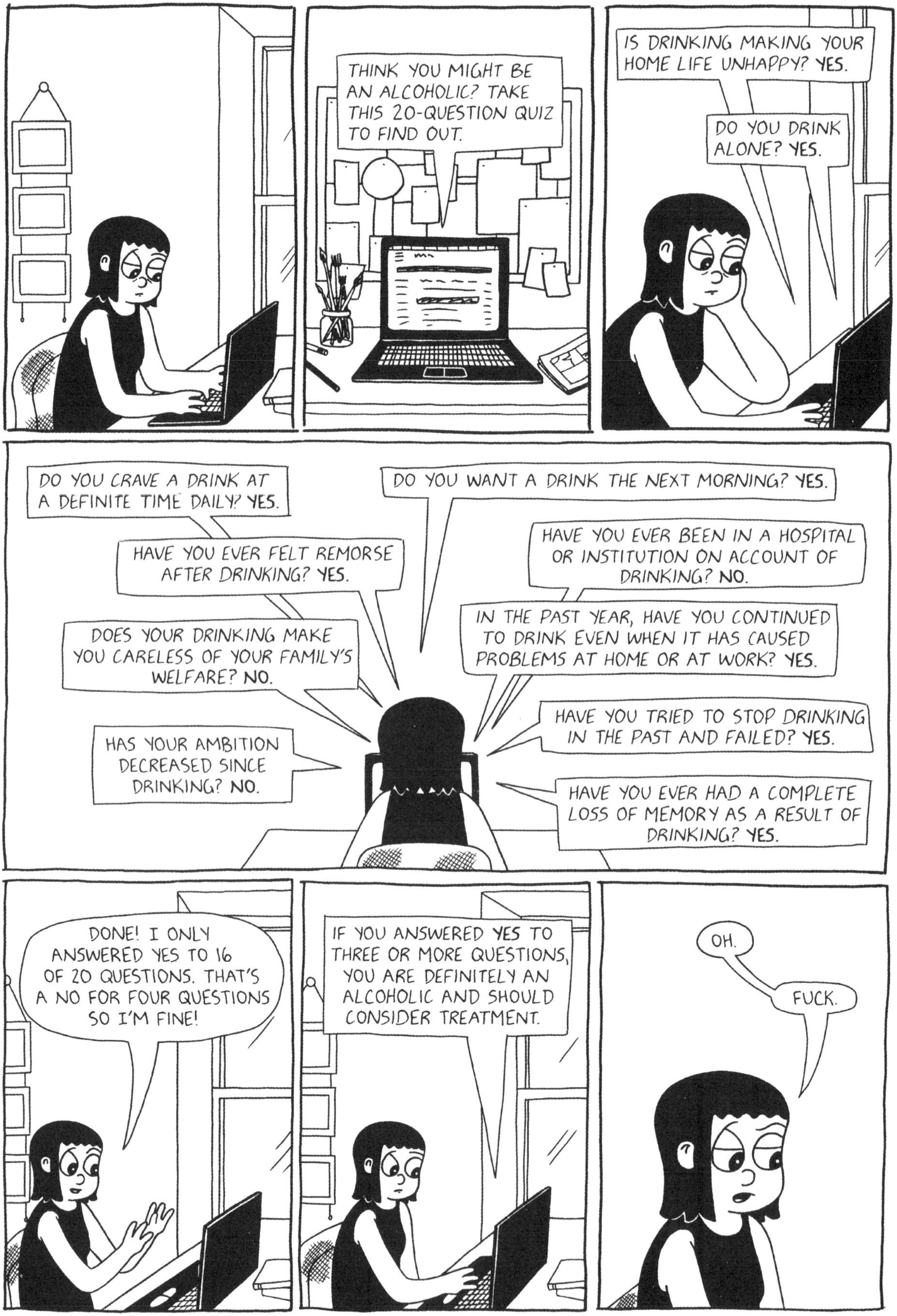

THINK YOU MIGHT BE AN ALCOHOLIC? TAKE THIS 20-QUESTION QUIZ TO FIND OUT.
IS DRINKING MAKING YOUR HOME LIFE UNHAPPY? YES.
DO YOU DRINK ALONE? YES.
DO YOU CRAVE A DRINK AT A DEFINITE TIME DAILY? YES.
HAVE YOU EVER FELT REMORSE AFTER DRINKING? YES.
DOES YOUR DRINKING MAKE YOU CARELESS OF YOUR FAMILY'S WELFARE? NO.
HAS YOUR AMBITION DECREASED SINCE DRINKING? NO.
DO YOU WANT A DRINK THE NEXT MORNING? YES.
HAVE YOU EVER BEEN IN A HOSPITAL OR INSTITUTION ON ACCOUNT OF DRINKING? NO.
IN THE PAST YEAR, HAVE YOU CONTINUED TO DRINK EVEN WHEN IT HAS CAUSED PROBLEMS AT HOME OR AT WORK? YES.
HAVE YOU TRIED TO STOP DRINKING IN THE PAST AND FAILED? YES.
HAVE YOU EVER HAD A COMPLETE LOSS OF MEMORY AS A RESULT OF DRINKING? YES.
DONE! I ONLY ANSWERED YES TO 16 OF 20 QUESTIONS. THAT'S A NO FOR FOUR QUESTIONS SO I'M FINE!
IF YOU ANSWERED YES TO THREE OR MORE QUESTIONS, YOU ARE DEFINITELY AN ALCOHOLIC AND SHOULD CONSIDER TREATMENT.
OH.
FUCK.

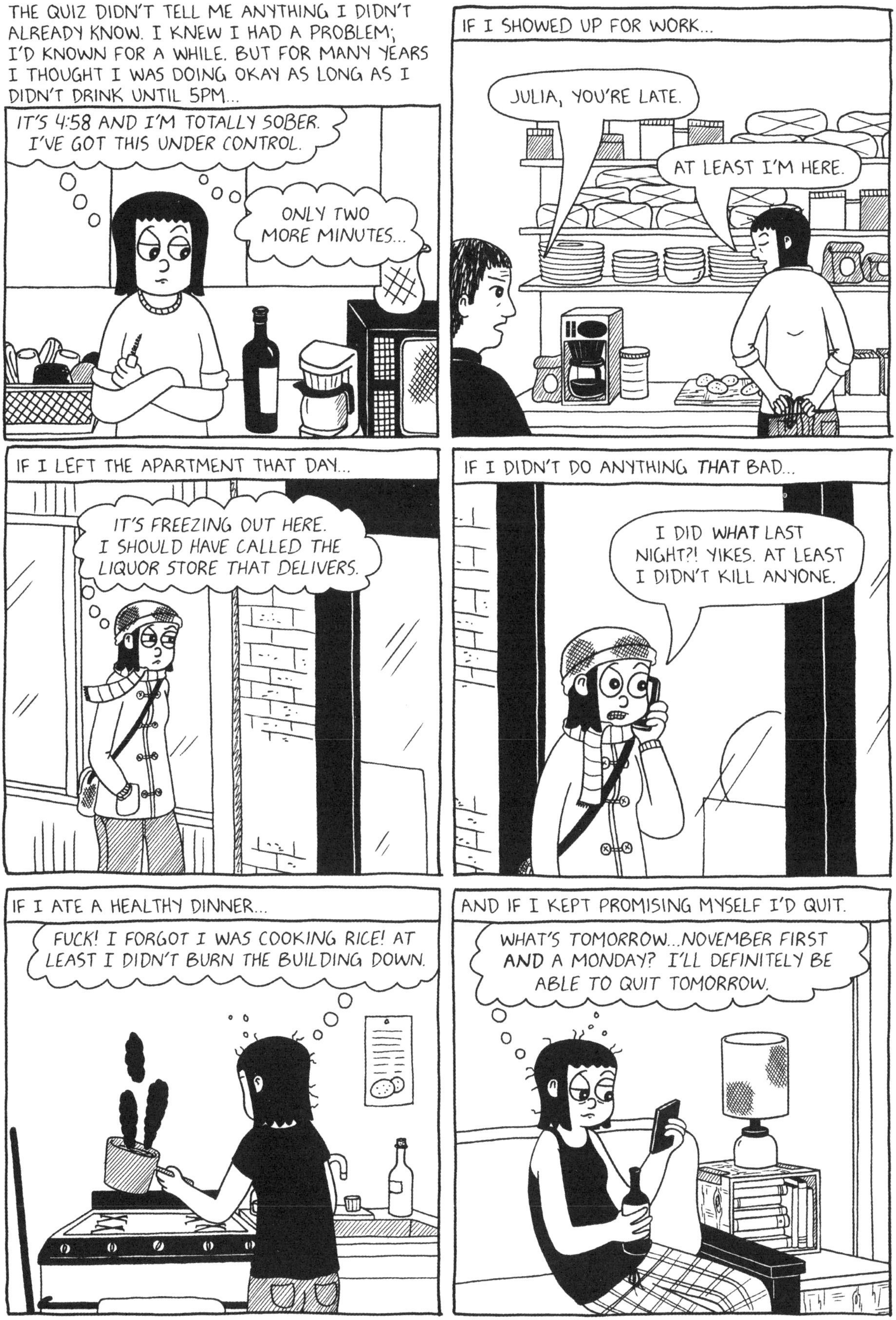
THE QUIZ DIDN'T TELL ME ANYTHING I DIDN'T ALREADY KNOW. I KNEW I HAD A PROBLEM; I'D KNOWN FOR A WHILE. BUT FOR MANY YEARS I THOUGHT I WAS DOING OKAY AS LONG AS I DIDN'T DRINK UNTIL 5PM...
IT'S 4:58 AND I'M TOTALLY SOBER. I'VE GOT THIS UNDER CONTROL.
ONLY TWO MORE MINUTES...
IF I SHOWED UP FOR WORK...
JULIA, YOU'RE LATE.
AT LEAST I'M HERE.
IF I LEFT THE APARTMENT THAT DAY...
IT'S FREEZING OUT HERE. I SHOULD HAVE CALLED THE LIQUOR STORE THAT DELIVERS.
IF I DIDN'T DO ANYTHING THAT BAD...
I DID WHAT LAST NIGHT?! YIKES. AT LEAST I DIDN'T KILL ANYONE.
IF I ATE A HEALTHY DINNER...
FUCK! I FORGOT I WAS COOKING RICE! AT LEAST I DIDN'T BURN THE BUILDING DOWN.
AND IF I KEPT PROMISING MYSELF I'D QUIT.
WHAT'S TOMORROW...NOVEMBER FIRST AND A MONDAY? I'LL DEFINITELY BE ABLE TO QUIT TOMORROW.

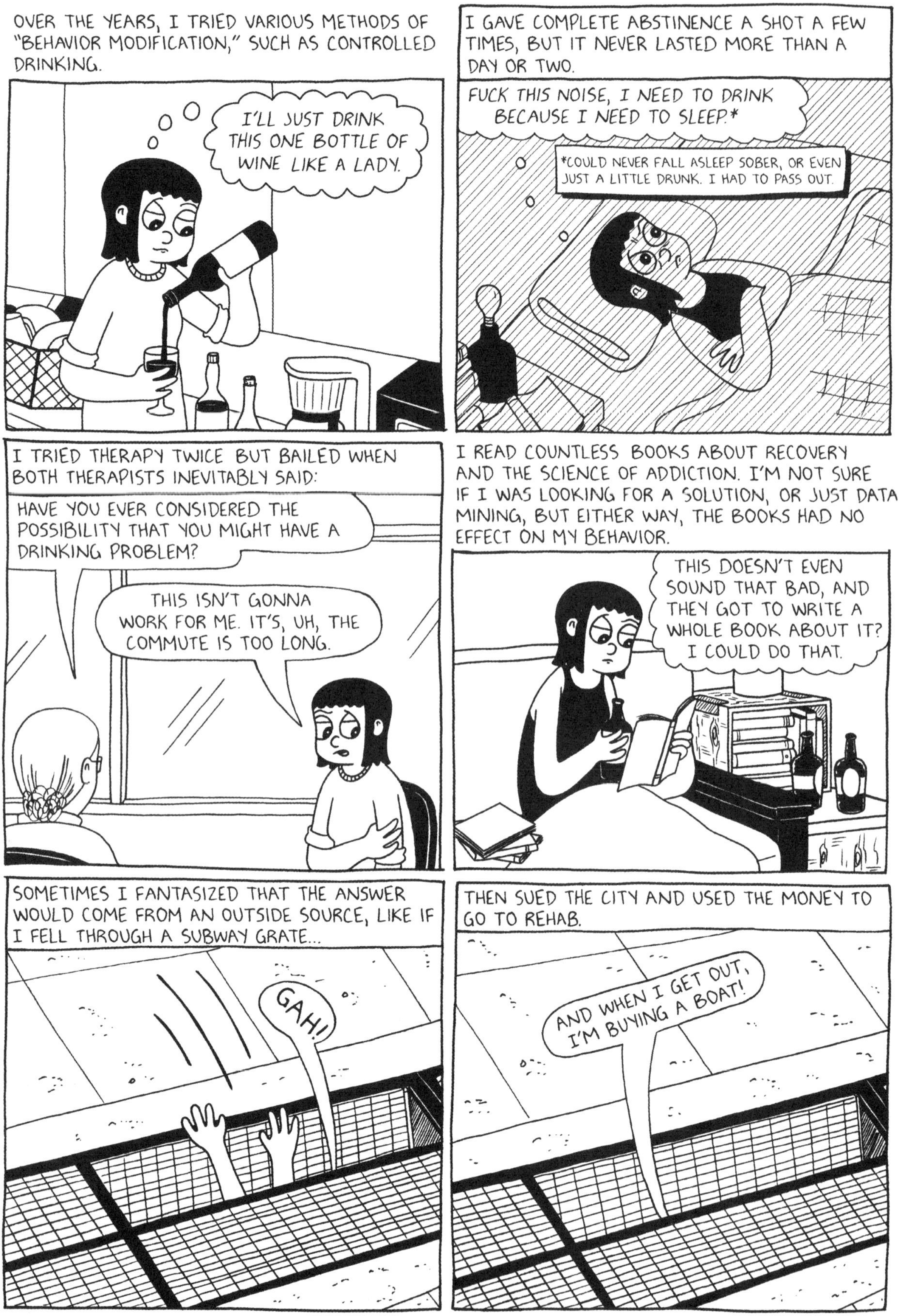
OVER THE YEARS, I TRIED VARIOUS METHODS OF "BEHAVIOR MODIFICATION," SUCH AS CONTROLLED DRINKING.
I'LL JUST DRINK THIS ONE BOTTLE OF WINE LIKE A LADY.
I GAVE COMPLETE ABSTINENCE A SHOT A FEW TIMES, BUT IT NEVER LASTED MORE THAN A DAY OR TWO.
FUCK THIS NOISE, I NEED TO DRINK BECAUSE I NEED TO SLEEP.*
*COULD NEVER FALL ASLEEP SOBER, OR EVEN JUST A LITTLE DRUNK. I HAD TO PASS OUT.
I TRIED THERAPY TWICE BUT BAILED WHEN BOTH THERAPISTS INEVITABLY SAID:
HAVE YOU EVER CONSIDERED THE POSSIBILITY THAT YOU MIGHT HAVE A DRINKING PROBLEM?
THIS ISN'T GONNA WORK FOR ME. IT'S, UH, THE COMMUTE IS TOO LONG.
I READ COUNTLESS BOOKS ABOUT RECOVERY AND THE SCIENCE OF ADDICTION. I'M NOT SURE IF I WAS LOOKING FOR A SOLUTION, OR JUST DATA MINING, BUT EITHER WAY, THE BOOKS HAD NO EFFECT ON MY BEHAVIOR.
THIS DOESN'T EVEN SOUND THAT BAD, AND THEY GOT TO WRITE A WHOLE BOOK ABOUT IT? I COULD DO THAT.
SOMETIMES I FANTASIZED THAT THE ANSWER WOULD COME FROM AN OUTSIDE SOURCE, LIKE IF I FELL THROUGH A SUBWAY GRATE...
GAH!
THEN SUED THE CITY AND USED THE MONEY TO GO TO REHAB.
AND WHEN I GET OUT, I'M BUYING A BOAT!

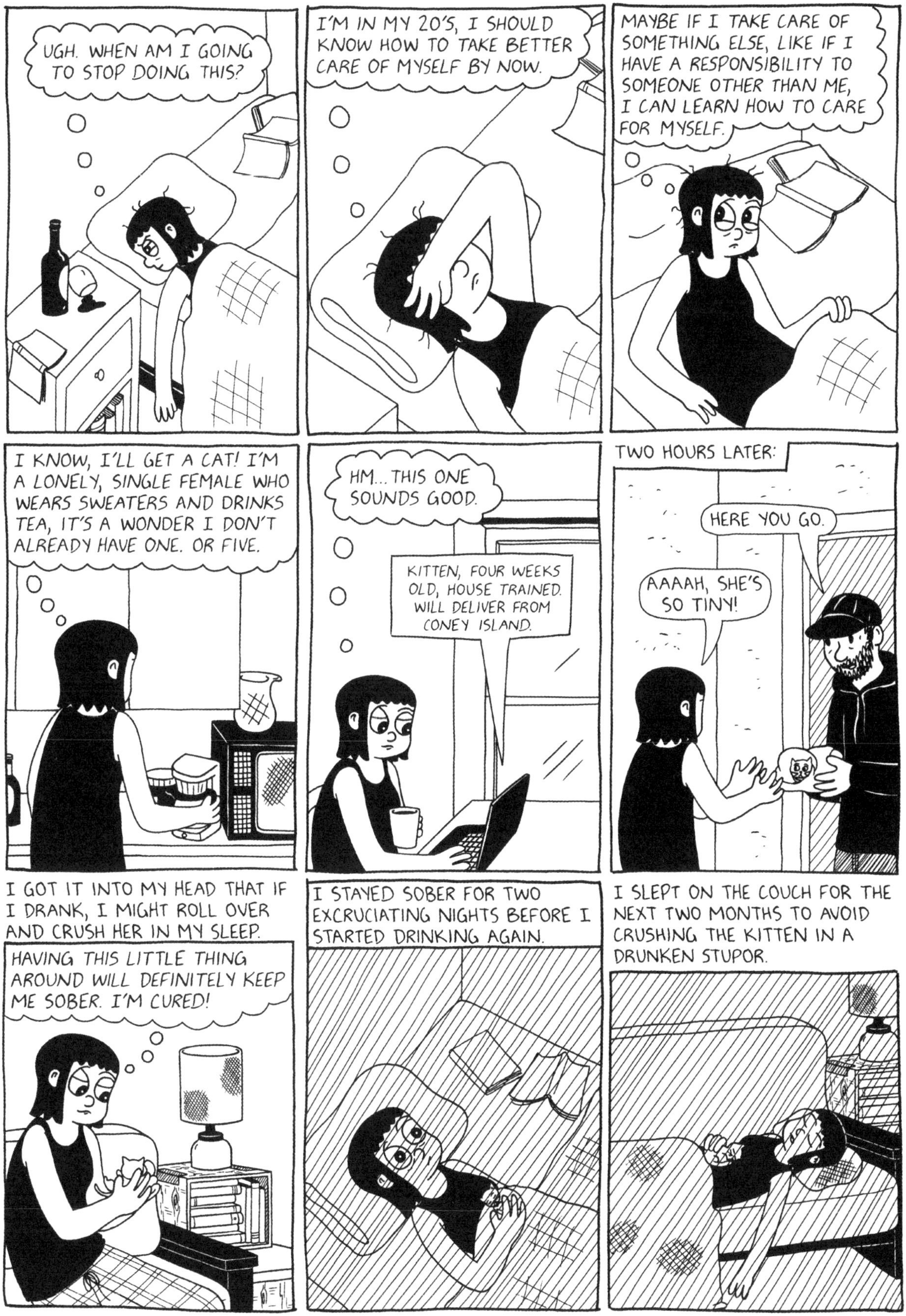
UGH. WHEN AM I GOING TO STOP DOING THIS?
I'M IN MY 20'S, I SHOULD KNOW HOW TO TAKE BETTER CARE OF MYSELF BY NOW.
MAYBE IF I TAKE CARE OF SOMETHING ELSE, LIKE IF I HAVE A RESPONSIBILITY TO SOMEONE OTHER THAN ME, I CAN LEARN HOW TO CARE FOR MYSELF.
I KNOW, I'LL GET A CAT! I'M A LONELY, SINGLE FEMALE WHO WEARS SWEATERS AND DRINKS TEA, IT'S A WONDER I DON'T ALREADY HAVE ONE. OR FIVE.
HM... THIS ONE SOUNDS GOOD.
KITTEN, FOUR WEEKS OLD, HOUSE TRAINED. WILL DELIVER FROM CONEY ISLAND.
TWO HOURS LATER:
HERE YOU GO.
AAAAH, SHE'S SO TINY!
I GOT IT INTO MY HEAD THAT IF I DRANK, I MIGHT ROLL OVER AND CRUSH HER IN MY SLEEP.
HAVING THIS LITTLE THING AROUND WILL DEFINITELY KEEP ME SOBER. I'M CURED!
I STAYED SOBER FOR TWO EXCRUCIATING NIGHTS BEFORE I STARTED DRINKING AGAIN.
I SLEPT ON THE COUCH FOR THE NEXT TWO MONTHS TO AVOID CRUSHING THE KITTEN IN A DRUNKEN STUPOR.

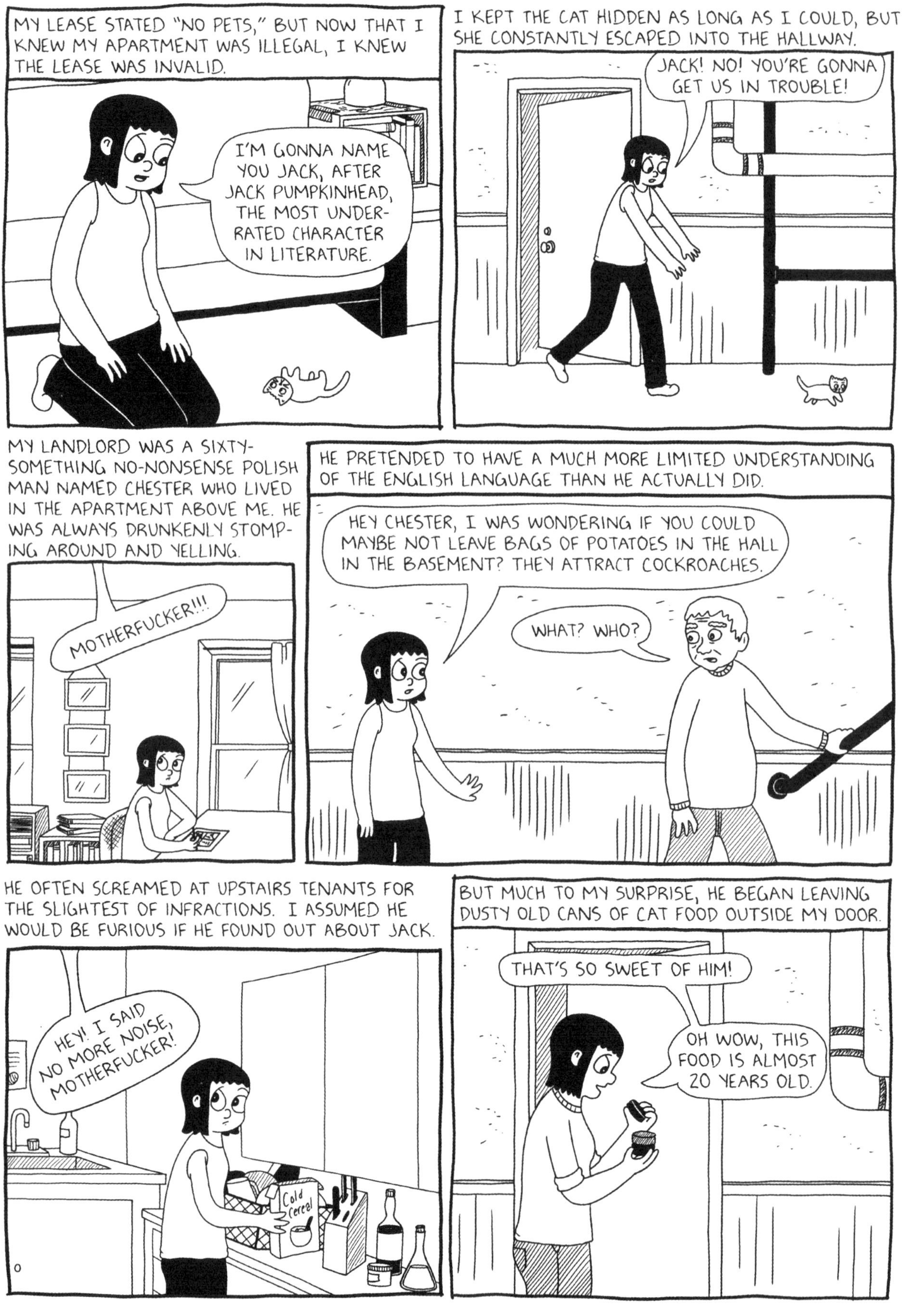
MY LEASE STATED "NO PETS," BUT NOW THAT I KNEW MY APARTMENT WAS ILLEGAL, I KNEW THE LEASE WAS INVALID.
I'M GONNA NAME YOU JACK, AFTER JACK PUMPKINHEAD, THE MOST UNDER-RATED CHARACTER IN LITERATURE.
I KEPT THE CAT HIDDEN AS LONG AS I COULD, BUT SHE CONSTANTLY ESCAPED INTO THE HALLWAY.
JACK! NO! YOU'RE GONNA GET US IN TROUBLE!
MY LANDLORD WAS A SIXTY-SOMETHING NO-NONSENSE POLISH MAN NAMED CHESTER WHO LIVED IN THE APARTMENT ABOVE ME. HE WAS ALWAYS DRUNKENLY STOMPING AROUND AND YELLING.
MOTHERFUCKER!!!
HE PRETENDED TO HAVE A MUCH MORE LIMITED UNDERSTANDING OF THE ENGLISH LANGUAGE THAN HE ACTUALLY DID.
HEY CHESTER, I WAS WONDERING IF YOU COULD MAYBE NOT LEAVE BAGS OF POTATOES IN THE HALL IN THE BASEMENT? THEY ATTRACT COCKROACHES.
WHAT? WHO?
HE OFTEN SCREAMED AT UPSTAIRS TENANTS FOR THE SLIGHTEST OF INFRACTIONS. I ASSUMED HE WOULD BE FURIOUS IF HE FOUND OUT ABOUT JACK.
HEY! I SAID NO MORE NOISE, MOTHERFUCKER!
Cold Cereal
BUT MUCH TO MY SURPRISE, HE BEGAN LEAVING DUSTY OLD CANS OF CAT FOOD OUTSIDE MY DOOR.
THAT'S SO SWEET OF HIM!
OH WOW, THIS FOOD IS ALMOST 20 YEARS OLD.

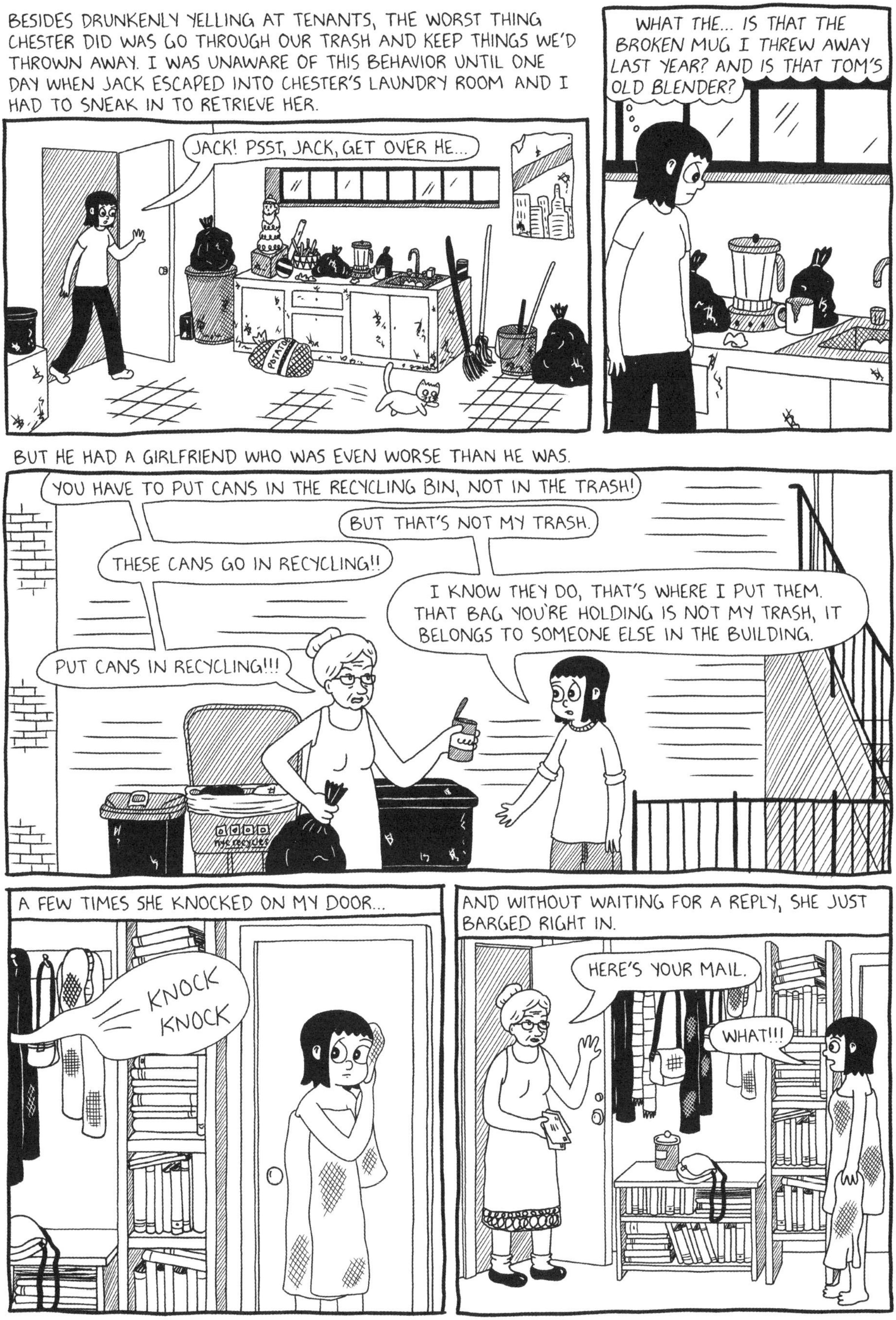
BESIDES DRUNKENLY YELLING AT TENANTS, THE WORST THING CHESTER DID WAS GO THROUGH OUR TRASH AND KEEP THINGS WE'D THROWN AWAY. I WAS UNAWARE OF THIS BEHAVIOR UNTIL ONE DAY WHEN JACK ESCAPED INTO CHESTER'S LAUNDRY ROOM AND I HAD TO SNEAK IN TO RETRIEVE HER.
JACK! PSST, JACK, GET OVER HE...
WHAT THE... IS THAT THE BROKEN MUG I THREW AWAY LAST YEAR? AND IS THAT TOM'S OLD BLENDER?
BUT HE HAD A GIRLFRIEND WHO WAS EVEN WORSE THAN HE WAS.
YOU HAVE TO PUT CANS IN THE RECYCLING BIN, NOT IN THE TRASH!
BUT THAT'S NOT MY TRASH.
THESE CANS GO IN RECYCLING!!
I KNOW THEY DO, THAT'S WHERE I PUT THEM. THAT BAG YOU'RE HOLDING IS NOT MY TRASH, IT BELONGS TO SOMEONE ELSE IN THE BUILDING.
PUT CANS IN RECYCLING!!!
A FEW TIMES SHE KNOCKED ON MY DOOR...
KNOCK KNOCK
AND WITHOUT WAITING FOR A REPLY, SHE JUST BARGED RIGHT IN.
HERE'S YOUR MAIL.
WHAT!!!

AS SOON AS CHESTER KNEW THAT I KNEW MY APARTMENT WAS ILLEGAL, OUR RELATIONSHIP CHANGED. SINCE NEITHER OF US HAD ANY LEGAL RECOURSE SHOULD SOMETHING GO WRONG, WE FORMED AN UNSPOKEN TRUCE. I NEVER COMPLAINED ABOUT THE OVERFLOWING SINK, THE YELLING, HIS BOUNDARY-CHALLENGED GIRLFRIEND, THE OCCASIONAL BATHROOM FLOODING, OR ANY OTHER MYRIAD OF QUIRKS THE BUILDING CONTAINED, AND HE NEVER RAISED MY RENT. IT WAS A GOOD ARRANGEMENT. LIFE IN MY TINY BASEMENT APARTMENT WAS COMFORTABLE, COZY, AND MOST IMPORTANTLY, CHEAP AS HELL (BY NEW YORK CITY STANDARDS).

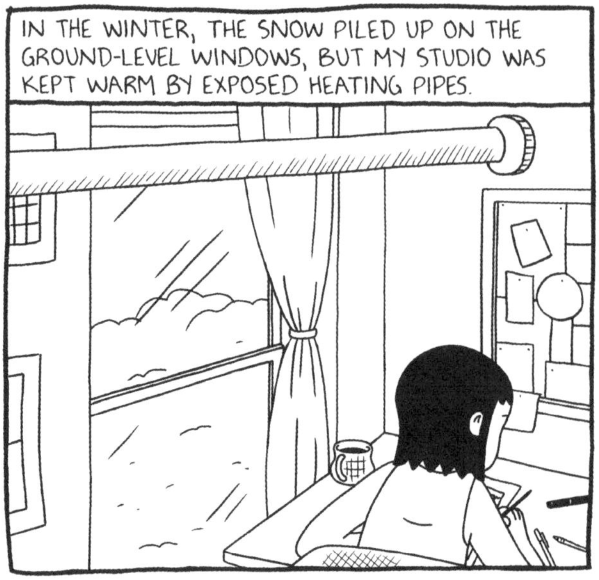
IN THE WINTER, THE SNOW PILED UP ON THE GROUND-LEVEL WINDOWS, BUT MY STUDIO WAS KEPT WARM BY EXPOSED HEATING PIPES.

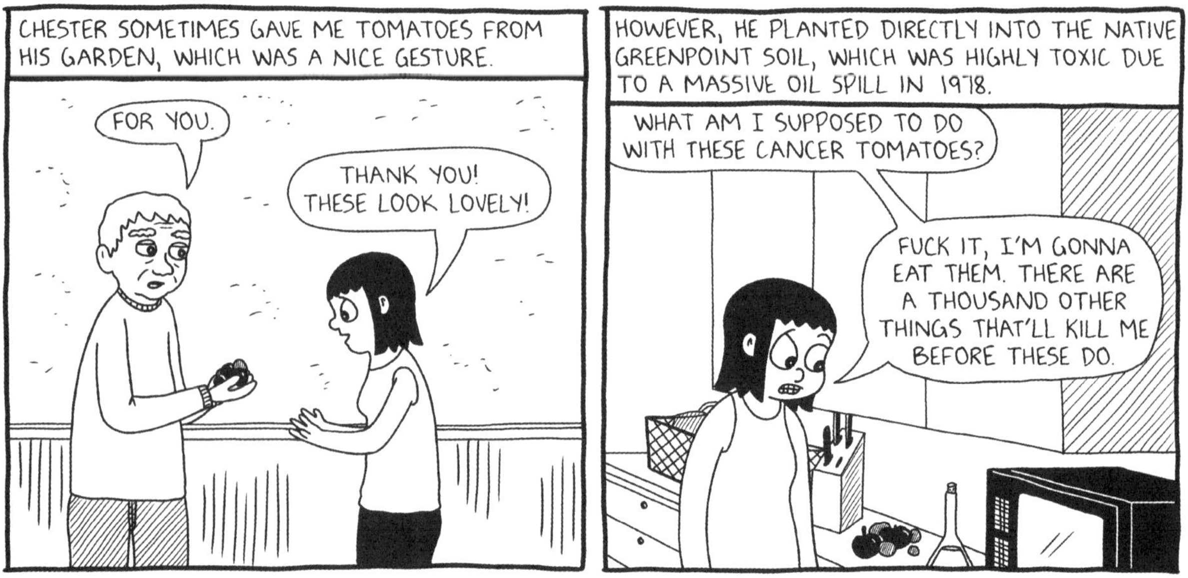
CHESTER SOMETIMES GAVE ME TOMATOES FROM HIS GARDEN, WHICH WAS A NICE GESTURE.
FOR YOU.
THANK YOU! THESE LOOK LOVELY!
HOWEVER, HE PLANTED DIRECTLY INTO THE NATIVE GREENPOINT SOIL, WHICH WAS HIGHLY TOXIC DUE TO A MASSIVE OIL SPILL IN 1978.
WHAT AM I SUPPOSED TO DO WITH THESE CANCER TOMATOES?
FUCK IT, I'M GONNA EAT THEM. THERE ARE A THOUSAND OTHER THINGS THAT'LL KILL ME BEFORE THESE DO.

EVERY AUGUST, HE STRUNG UP CUCUMBER VINES OUTSIDE MY WINDOWS. IT FILLED THE STUDIO WITH A COOL GREEN LIGHT THAT WAS A WELCOME RESPITE FROM THE RELENTLESS SUMMER HEAT.

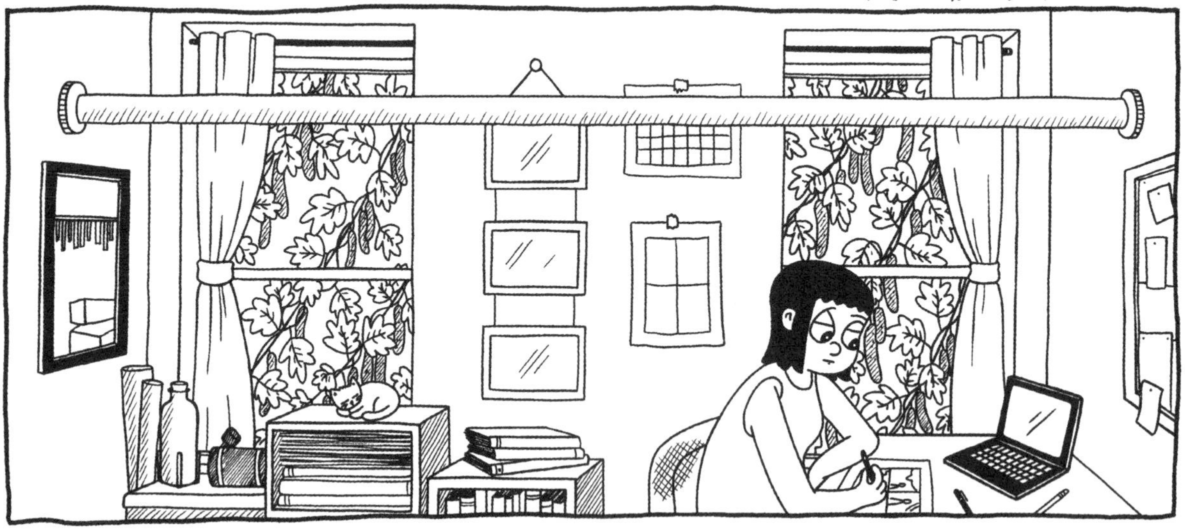

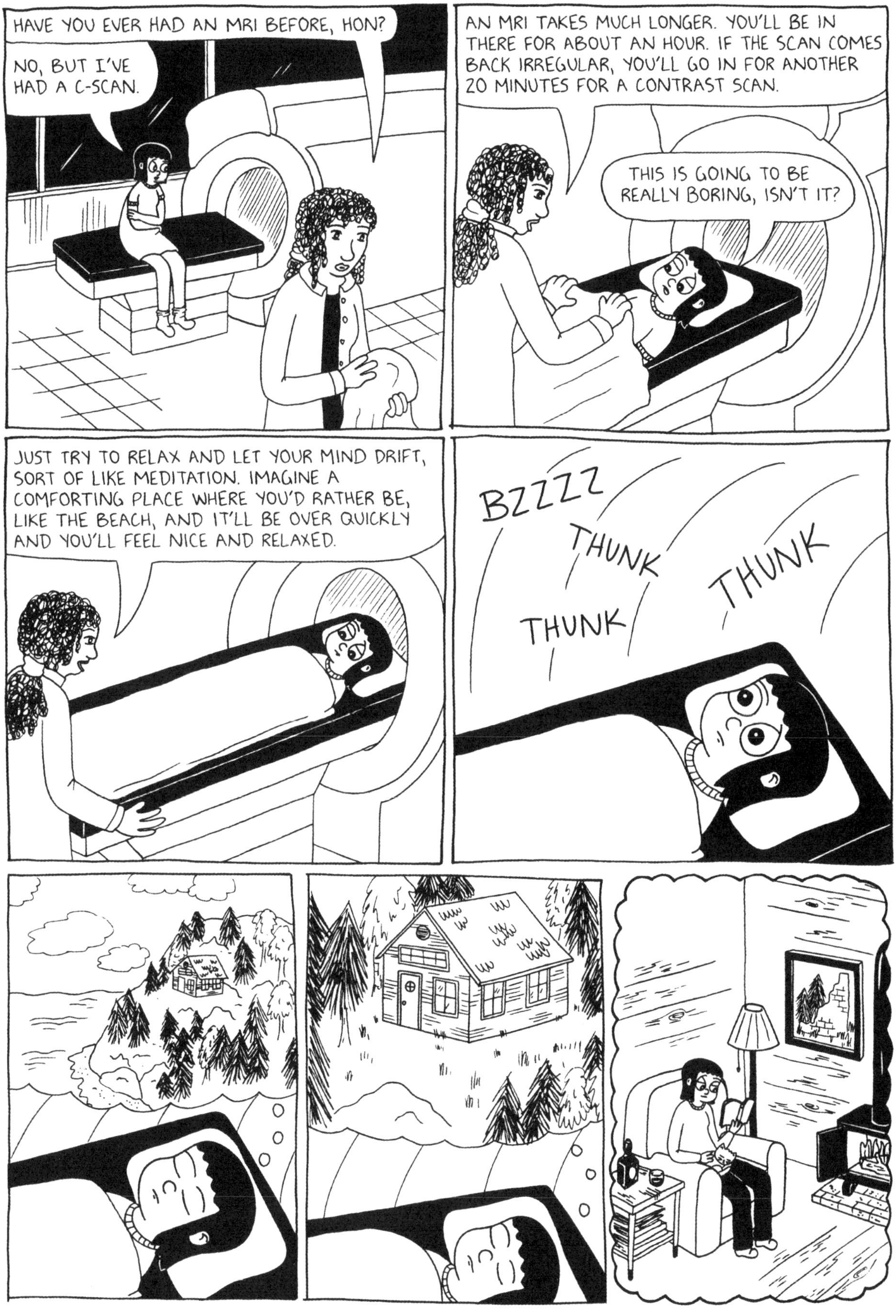
HAVE YOU EVER HAD AN MRI BEFORE, HON?
NO, BUT I'VE HAD A C-SCAN.
AN MRI TAKES MUCH LONGER. YOU'LL BE IN THERE FOR ABOUT AN HOUR. IF THE SCAN COMES BACK IRREGULAR, YOU'LL GO IN FOR ANOTHER 20 MINUTES FOR A CONTRAST SCAN.
THIS IS GOING TO BE REALLY BORING, ISN'T IT?
JUST TRY TO RELAX AND LET YOUR MIND DRIFT, SORT OF LIKE MEDITATION. IMAGINE A COMFORTING PLACE WHERE YOU'D RATHER BE, LIKE THE BEACH, AND IT'LL BE OVER QUICKLY AND YOU'LL FEEL NICE AND RELAXED.
BZZZZ
THUNK
THUNK
THUNK

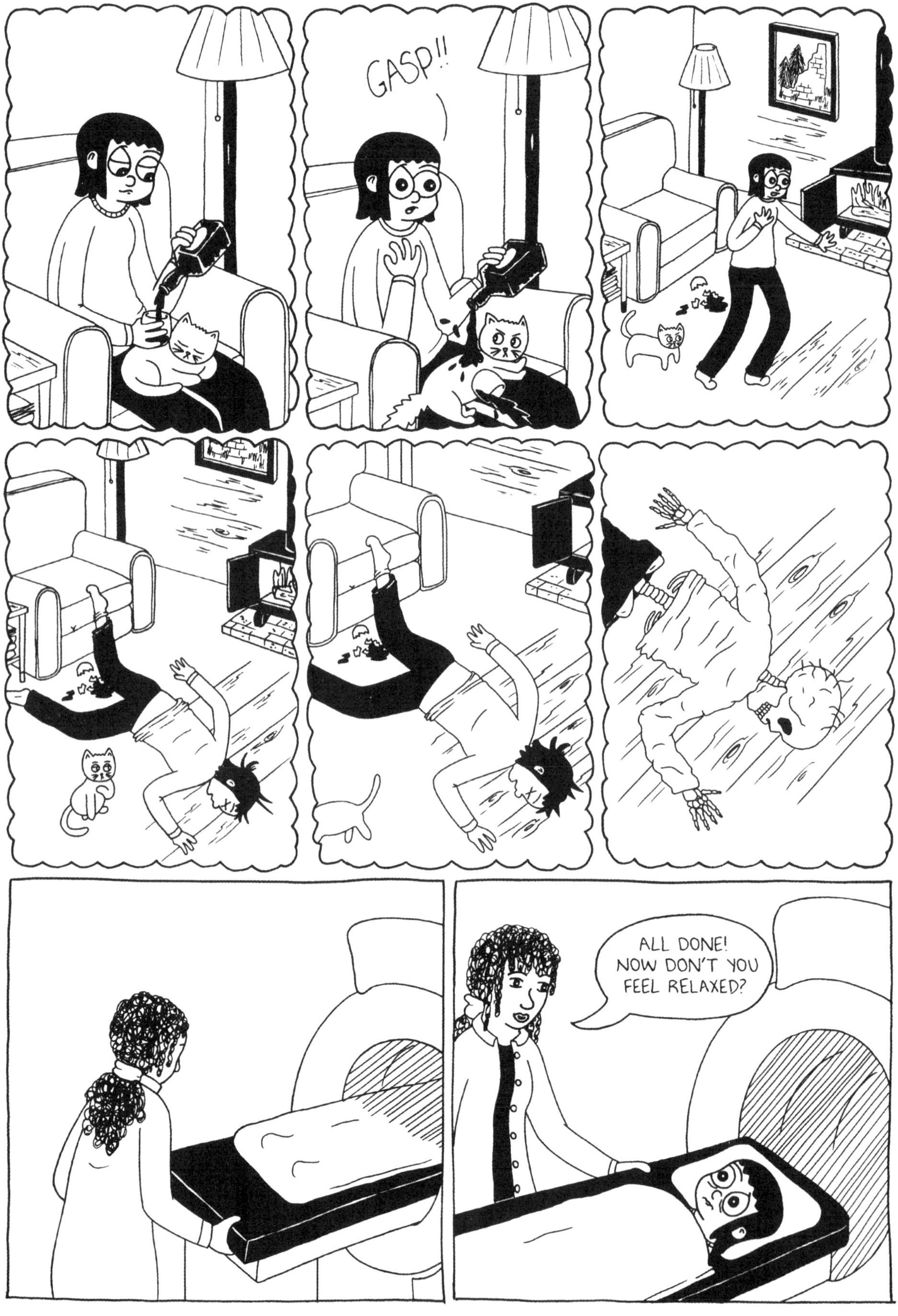
GASP!!
ALL DONE! NOW DON'T YOU FEEL RELAXED?

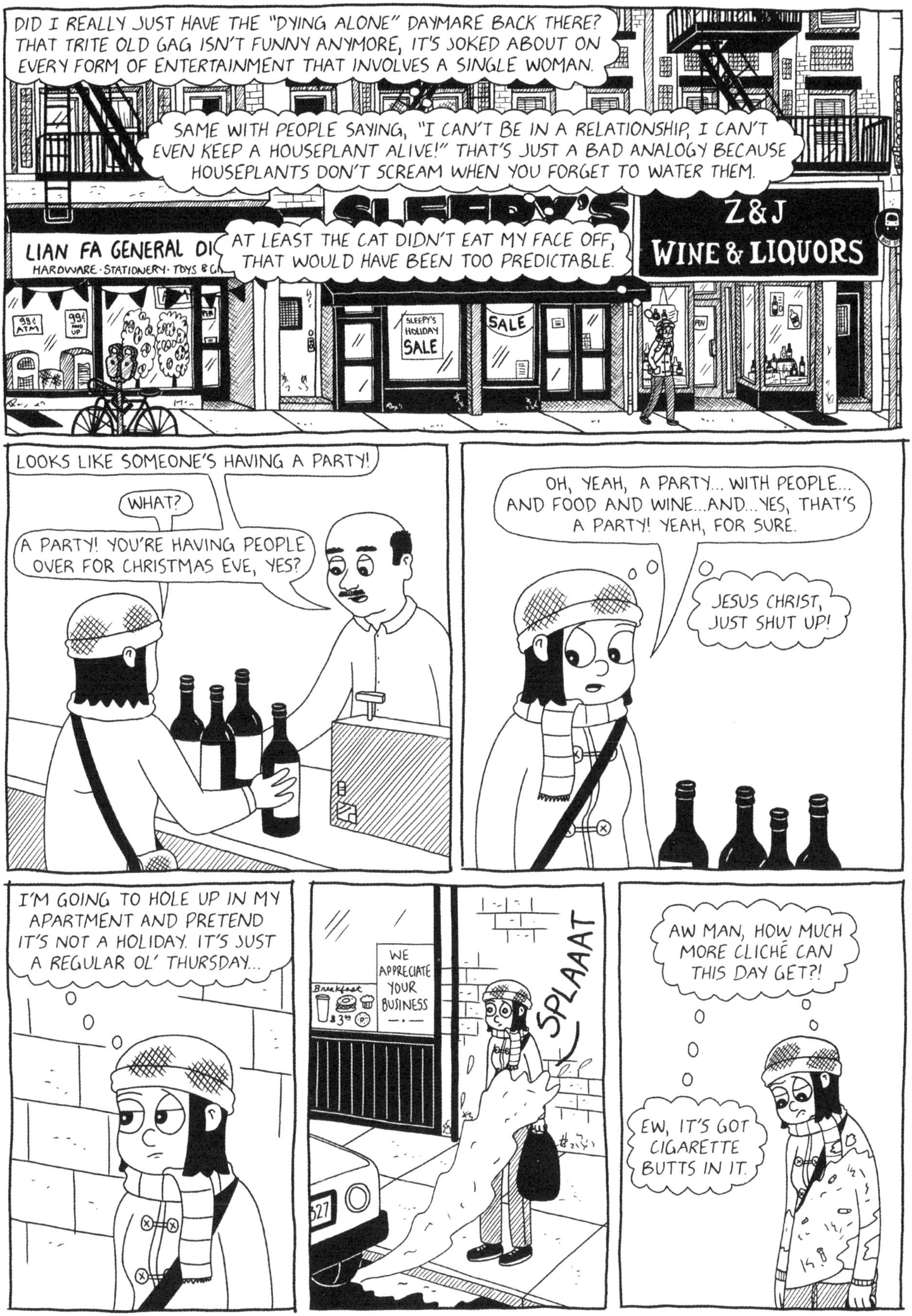
DID I REALLY JUST HAVE THE "DYING ALONE" DAYMARE BACK THERE? THAT TRITE OLD GAG ISN'T FUNNY ANYMORE, IT'S JOKED ABOUT ON EVERY FORM OF ENTERTAINMENT THAT INVOLVES A SINGLE WOMAN.
SAME WITH PEOPLE SAYING, "I CAN'T BE IN A RELATIONSHIP, I CAN'T EVEN KEEP A HOUSEPLANT ALIVE!" THAT'S JUST A BAD ANALOGY BECAUSE HOUSEPLANTS DON'T SCREAM WHEN YOU FORGET TO WATER THEM.
AT LEAST THE CAT DIDN'T EAT MY FACE OFF, THAT WOULD HAVE BEEN TOO PREDICTABLE.
SLEEPY'S
Z&J WINE & LIQUORS
LIAN FA GENERAL DI
HARDWARE · STATIONERY · TOYS &
SLEEPY'S HOLIDAY SALE
SALE
LOOKS LIKE SOMEONE'S HAVING A PARTY!
WHAT?
A PARTY! YOU'RE HAVING PEOPLE OVER FOR CHRISTMAS EVE, YES?
OH, YEAH, A PARTY... WITH PEOPLE... AND FOOD AND WINE...AND...YES, THAT'S A PARTY! YEAH, FOR SURE.
JESUS CHRIST, JUST SHUT UP!
I'M GOING TO HOLE UP IN MY APARTMENT AND PRETEND IT'S NOT A HOLIDAY. IT'S JUST A REGULAR OL' THURSDAY...
WE APPRECIATE YOUR BUSINESS
Breakfast
SPLAAAT
AW MAN, HOW MUCH MORE CLICHÉ CAN THIS DAY GET?!
EW, IT'S GOT CIGARETTE BUTTS IN IT.

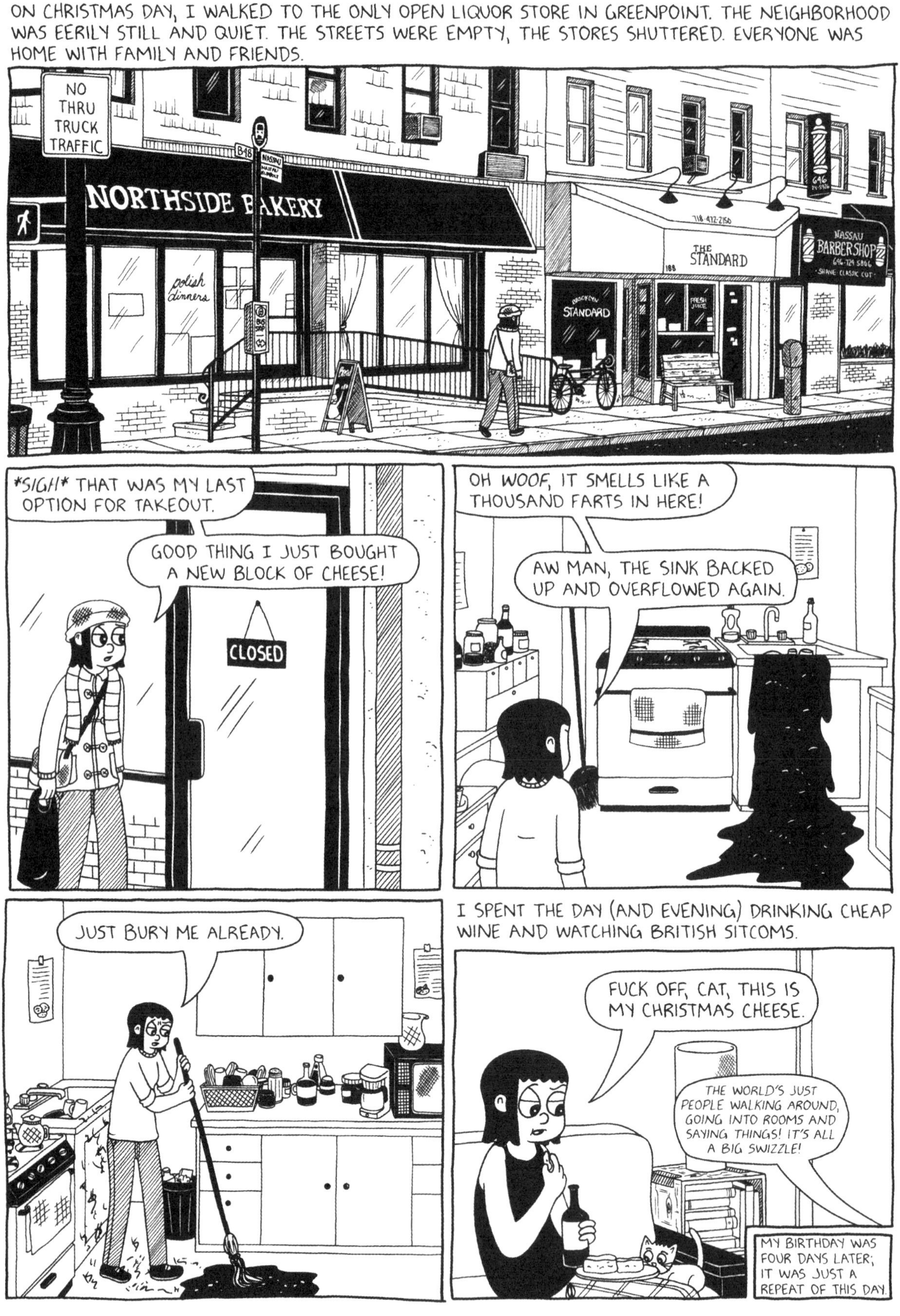
ON CHRISTMAS DAY, I WALKED TO THE ONLY OPEN LIQUOR STORE IN GREENPOINT. THE NEIGHBORHOOD WAS EERILY STILL AND QUIET. THE STREETS WERE EMPTY, THE STORES SHUTTERED. EVERYONE WAS HOME WITH FAMILY AND FRIENDS.
NO THRU TRUCK TRAFFIC
NORTHSIDE BAKERY
polish dinners
THE STANDARD
NASSAU BARBERSHOP
SIGH THAT WAS MY LAST OPTION FOR TAKEOUT.
GOOD THING I JUST BOUGHT A NEW BLOCK OF CHEESE!
CLOSED
OH WOOF, IT SMELLS LIKE A THOUSAND FARTS IN HERE!
AW MAN, THE SINK BACKED UP AND OVERFLOWED AGAIN.
JUST BURY ME ALREADY.
I SPENT THE DAY (AND EVENING) DRINKING CHEAP WINE AND WATCHING BRITISH SITCOMS.
FUCK OFF, CAT, THIS IS MY CHRISTMAS CHEESE.
THE WORLD'S JUST PEOPLE WALKING AROUND, GOING INTO ROOMS AND SAYING THINGS! IT'S ALL A BIG SWIZZLE!
MY BIRTHDAY WAS FOUR DAYS LATER; IT WAS JUST A REPEAT OF THIS DAY.

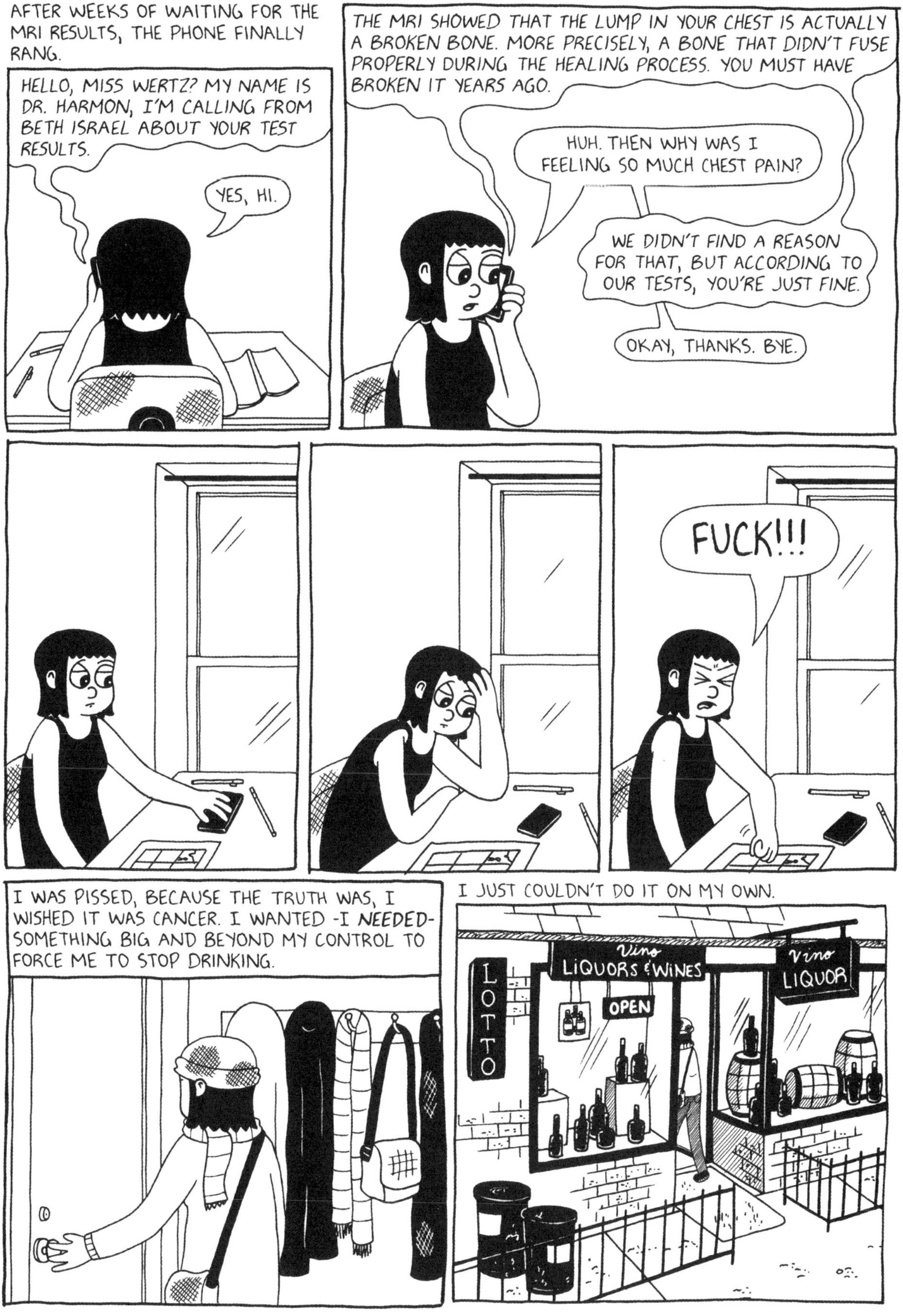
AFTER WEEKS OF WAITING FOR THE MRI RESULTS, THE PHONE FINALLY RANG.
HELLO, MISS WERTZ? MY NAME IS DR. HARMON, I'M CALLING FROM BETH ISRAEL ABOUT YOUR TEST RESULTS.
YES, HI.
THE MRI SHOWED THAT THE LUMP IN YOUR CHEST IS ACTUALLY A BROKEN BONE. MORE PRECISELY, A BONE THAT DIDN'T FUSE PROPERLY DURING THE HEALING PROCESS. YOU MUST HAVE BROKEN IT YEARS AGO.
HUH. THEN WHY WAS I FEELING SO MUCH CHEST PAIN?
WE DIDN'T FIND A REASON FOR THAT, BUT ACCORDING TO OUR TESTS, YOU'RE JUST FINE.
OKAY, THANKS. BYE.
FUCK!!!
I WAS PISSED, BECAUSE THE TRUTH WAS, I WISHED IT WAS CANCER. I WANTED -I NEEDED- SOMETHING BIG AND BEYOND MY CONTROL TO FORCE ME TO STOP DRINKING.
I JUST COULDN'T DO IT ON MY OWN.
LOTTO
Vino
LIQUORS & WINES
OPEN
Vino
LIQUOR

AFTER THE HEALTH SCARE AND THE CAT FAILED TO KEEP ME SOBER, I DECIDED TO TRY THERAPY.

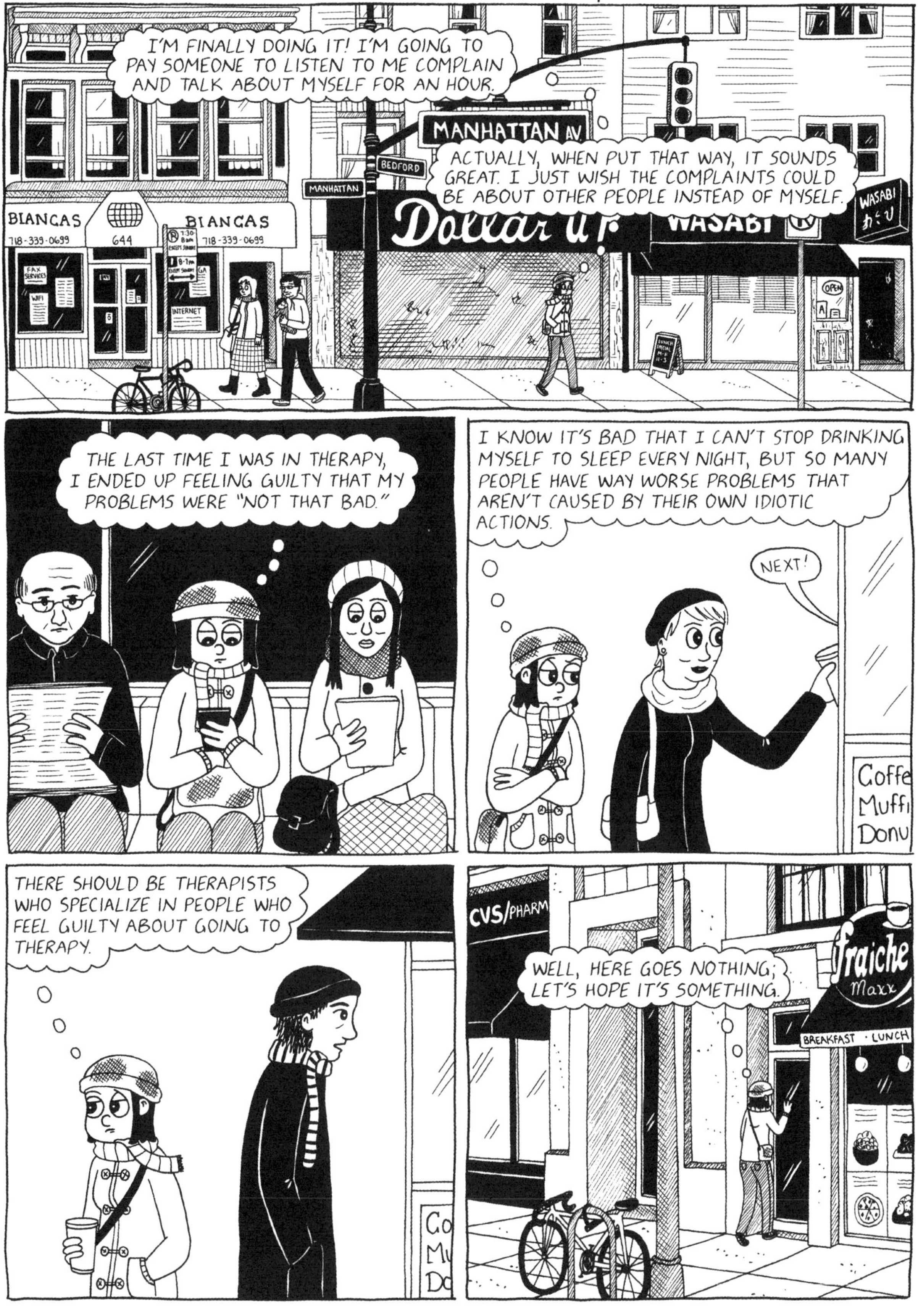

I'M FINALLY DOING IT! I'M GOING TO PAY SOMEONE TO LISTEN TO ME COMPLAIN AND TALK ABOUT MYSELF FOR AN HOUR.
MANHATTAN AV
BEDFORD
MANHATTAN
ACTUALLY, WHEN PUT THAT WAY, IT SOUNDS GREAT. I JUST WISH THE COMPLAINTS COULD BE ABOUT OTHER PEOPLE INSTEAD OF MYSELF.
BIANCAS
718-339-0699
644
BIANCAS
718-339-0699
Dollar up
WASABI
WASABI
OPEN
THE LAST TIME I WAS IN THERAPY, I ENDED UP FEELING GUILTY THAT MY PROBLEMS WERE "NOT THAT BAD."
I KNOW IT'S BAD THAT I CAN'T STOP DRINKING MYSELF TO SLEEP EVERY NIGHT, BUT SO MANY PEOPLE HAVE WAY WORSE PROBLEMS THAT AREN'T CAUSED BY THEIR OWN IDIOTIC ACTIONS.
NEXT!
Coffe
Muffi
Donu
THERE SHOULD BE THERAPISTS WHO SPECIALIZE IN PEOPLE WHO FEEL GUILTY ABOUT GOING TO THERAPY.
CVS/PHARM
WELL, HERE GOES NOTHING; LET'S HOPE IT'S SOMETHING.
fraiche
Maxx
BREAKFAST · LUNCH

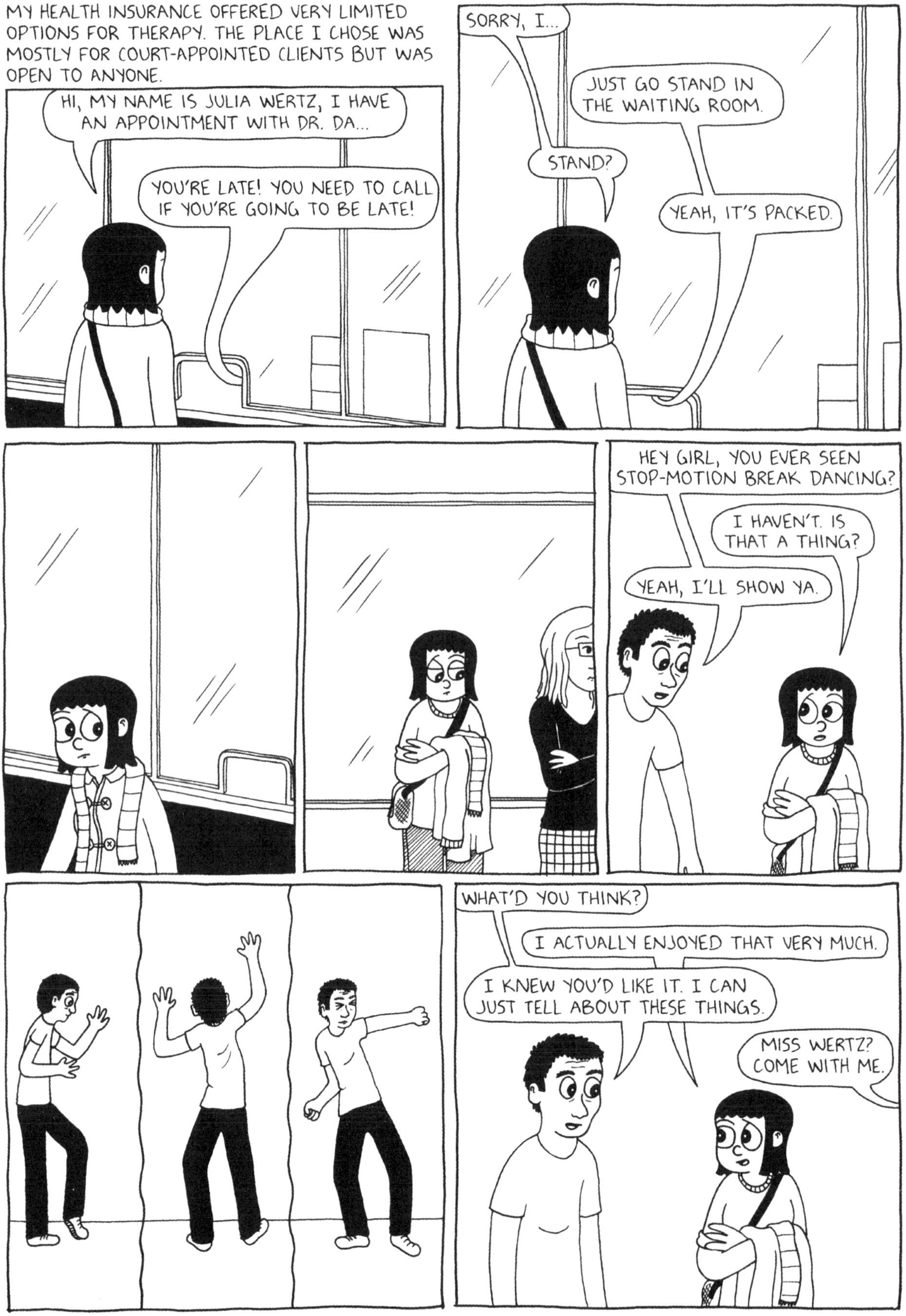
MY HEALTH INSURANCE OFFERED VERY LIMITED OPTIONS FOR THERAPY. THE PLACE I CHOSE WAS MOSTLY FOR COURT-APPOINTED CLIENTS BUT WAS OPEN TO ANYONE.
HI, MY NAME IS JULIA WERTZ, I HAVE AN APPOINTMENT WITH DR. DA...
YOU'RE LATE! YOU NEED TO CALL IF YOU'RE GOING TO BE LATE!
SORRY, I...
JUST GO STAND IN THE WAITING ROOM.
STAND?
YEAH, IT'S PACKED.
HEY GIRL, YOU EVER SEEN STOP-MOTION BREAK DANCING?
I HAVEN'T. IS THAT A THING?
YEAH, I'LL SHOW YA.
WHAT'D YOU THINK?
I ACTUALLY ENJOYED THAT VERY MUCH.
I KNEW YOU'D LIKE IT. I CAN JUST TELL ABOUT THESE THINGS.
MISS WERTZ? COME WITH ME.

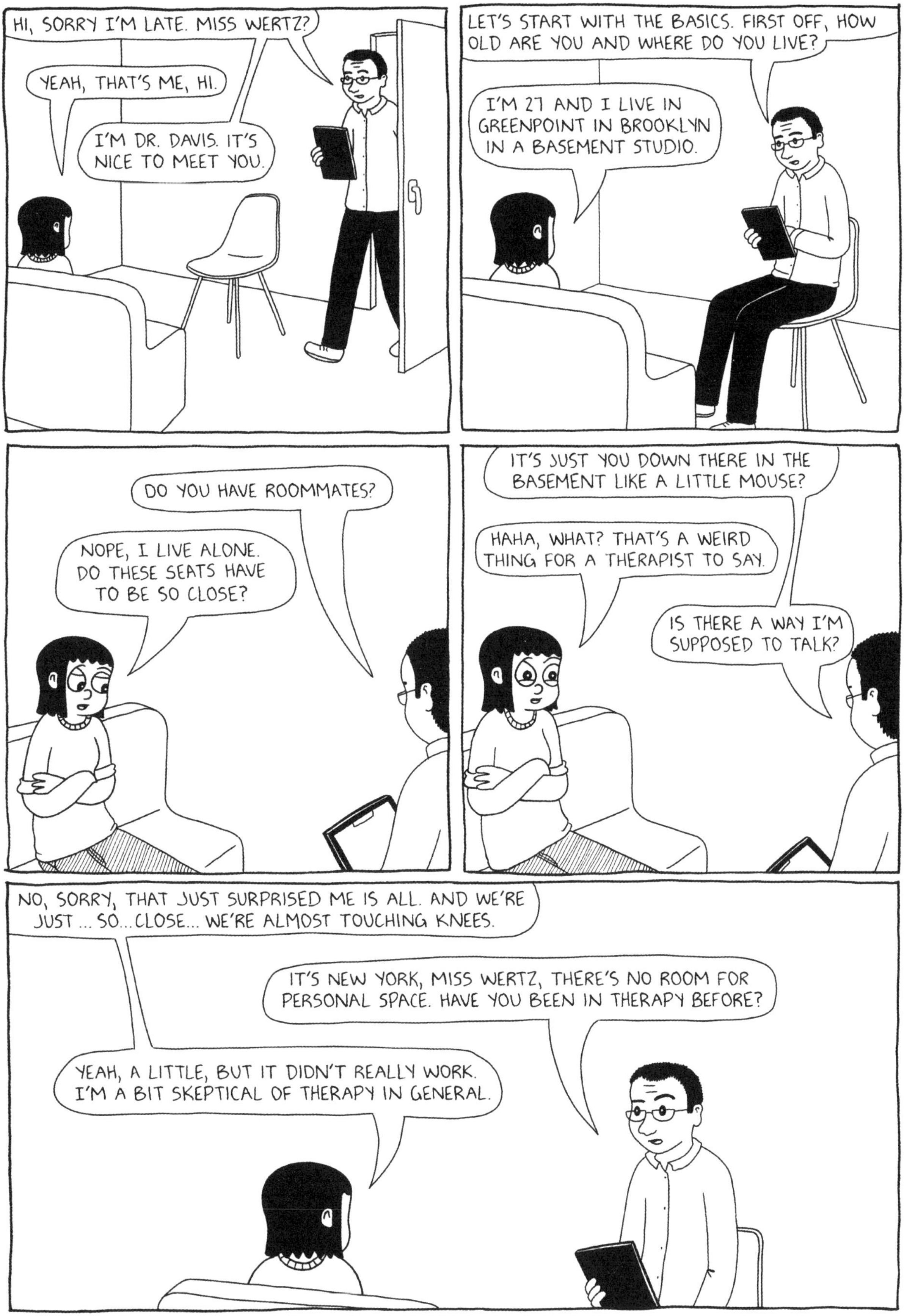
HI, SORRY I'M LATE. MISS WERTZ?
YEAH, THAT'S ME, HI.
I'M DR. DAVIS. IT'S NICE TO MEET YOU.
LET'S START WITH THE BASICS. FIRST OFF, HOW OLD ARE YOU AND WHERE DO YOU LIVE?
I'M 27 AND I LIVE IN GREENPOINT IN BROOKLYN IN A BASEMENT STUDIO.
DO YOU HAVE ROOMMATES?
NOPE, I LIVE ALONE. DO THESE SEATS HAVE TO BE SO CLOSE?
IT'S JUST YOU DOWN THERE IN THE BASEMENT LIKE A LITTLE MOUSE?
HAHA, WHAT? THAT'S A WEIRD THING FOR A THERAPIST TO SAY.
IS THERE A WAY I'M SUPPOSED TO TALK?
NO, SORRY, THAT JUST SURPRISED ME IS ALL. AND WE'RE JUST ... SO... CLOSE... WE'RE ALMOST TOUCHING KNEES.
IT'S NEW YORK, MISS WERTZ, THERE'S NO ROOM FOR PERSONAL SPACE. HAVE YOU BEEN IN THERAPY BEFORE?
YEAH, A LITTLE, BUT IT DIDN'T REALLY WORK. I'M A BIT SKEPTICAL OF THERAPY IN GENERAL.

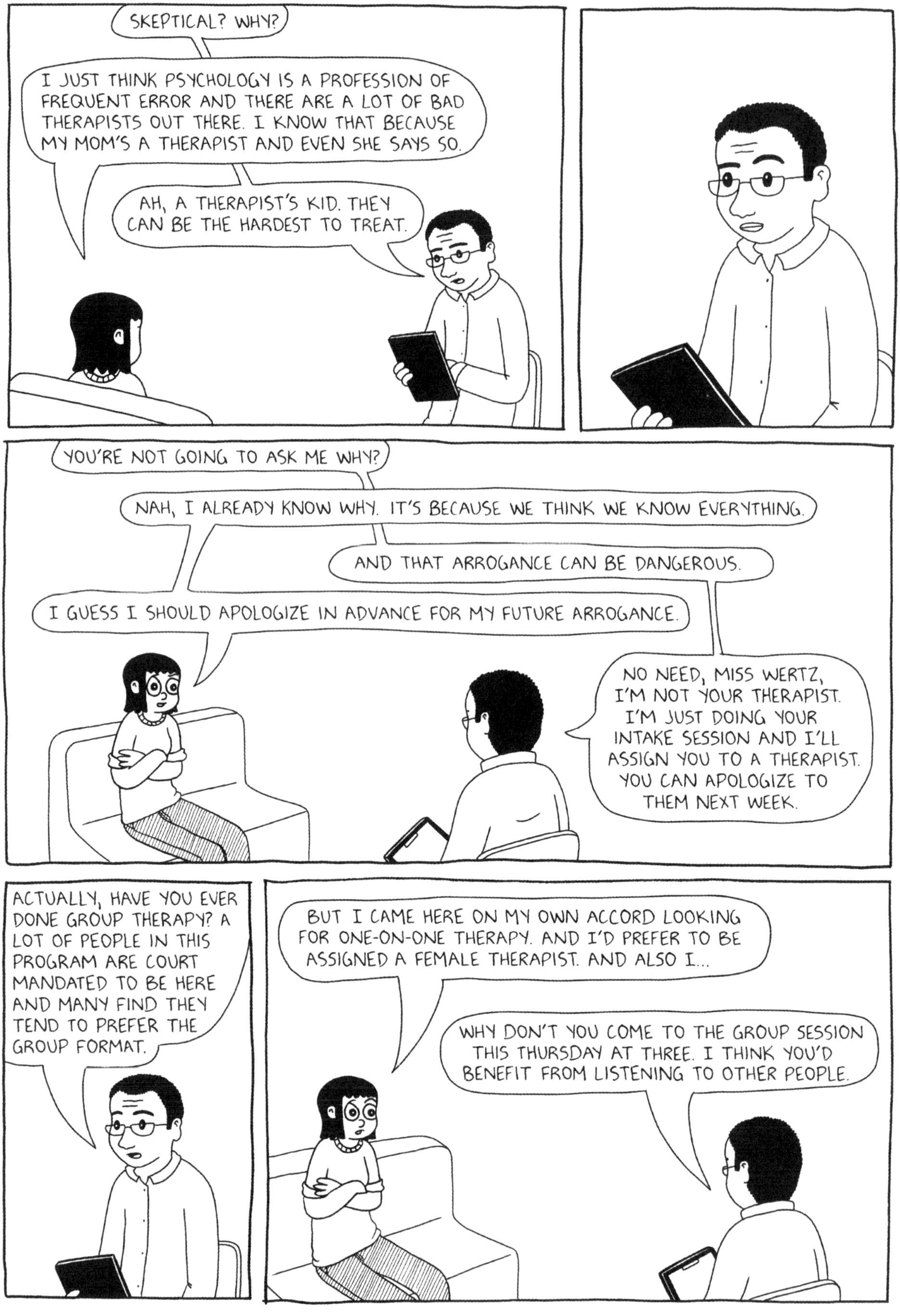
SKEPTICAL? WHY?
I JUST THINK PSYCHOLOGY IS A PROFESSION OF FREQUENT ERROR AND THERE ARE A LOT OF BAD THERAPISTS OUT THERE. I KNOW THAT BECAUSE MY MOM'S A THERAPIST AND EVEN SHE SAYS SO.
AH, A THERAPIST'S KID. THEY CAN BE THE HARDEST TO TREAT.
YOU'RE NOT GOING TO ASK ME WHY?
NAH, I ALREADY KNOW WHY. IT'S BECAUSE WE THINK WE KNOW EVERYTHING.
AND THAT ARROGANCE CAN BE DANGEROUS.
I GUESS I SHOULD APOLOGIZE IN ADVANCE FOR MY FUTURE ARROGANCE.
NO NEED, MISS WERTZ, I'M NOT YOUR THERAPIST. I'M JUST DOING YOUR INTAKE SESSION AND I'LL ASSIGN YOU TO A THERAPIST. YOU CAN APOLOGIZE TO THEM NEXT WEEK.
ACTUALLY, HAVE YOU EVER DONE GROUP THERAPY? A LOT OF PEOPLE IN THIS PROGRAM ARE COURT MANDATED TO BE HERE AND MANY FIND THEY TEND TO PREFER THE GROUP FORMAT.
BUT I CAME HERE ON MY OWN ACCORD LOOKING FOR ONE-ON-ONE THERAPY. AND I'D PREFER TO BE ASSIGNED A FEMALE THERAPIST. AND ALSO I...
WHY DON'T YOU COME TO THE GROUP SESSION THIS THURSDAY AT THREE. I THINK YOU'D BENEFIT FROM LISTENING TO OTHER PEOPLE.

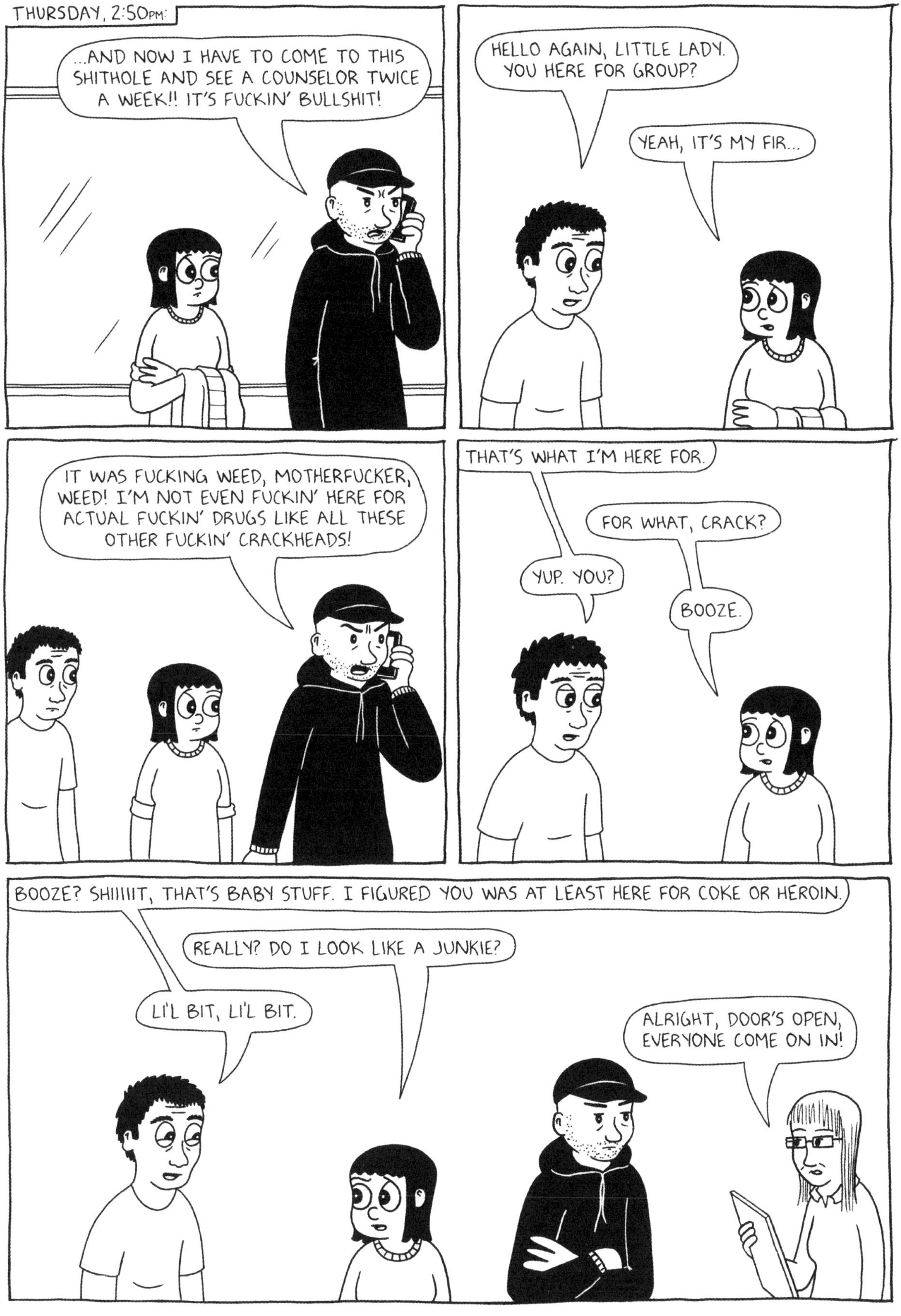
THURSDAY, 2:50PM:
...AND NOW I HAVE TO COME TO THIS SHITHOLE AND SEE A COUNSELOR TWICE A WEEK!! IT'S FUCKIN' BULLSHIT!
HELLO AGAIN, LITTLE LADY. YOU HERE FOR GROUP?
YEAH, IT'S MY FIR...
IT WAS FUCKING WEED, MOTHERFUCKER, WEED! I'M NOT EVEN FUCKIN' HERE FOR ACTUAL FUCKIN' DRUGS LIKE ALL THESE OTHER FUCKIN' CRACKHEADS!
THAT'S WHAT I'M HERE FOR.
FOR WHAT, CRACK?
YUP. YOU?
BOOZE.
BOOZE? SHIIIIIT, THAT'S BABY STUFF. I FIGURED YOU WAS AT LEAST HERE FOR COKE OR HEROIN.
REALLY? DO I LOOK LIKE A JUNKIE?
LI'L BIT, LI'L BIT.
ALRIGHT, DOOR'S OPEN, EVERYONE COME ON IN!

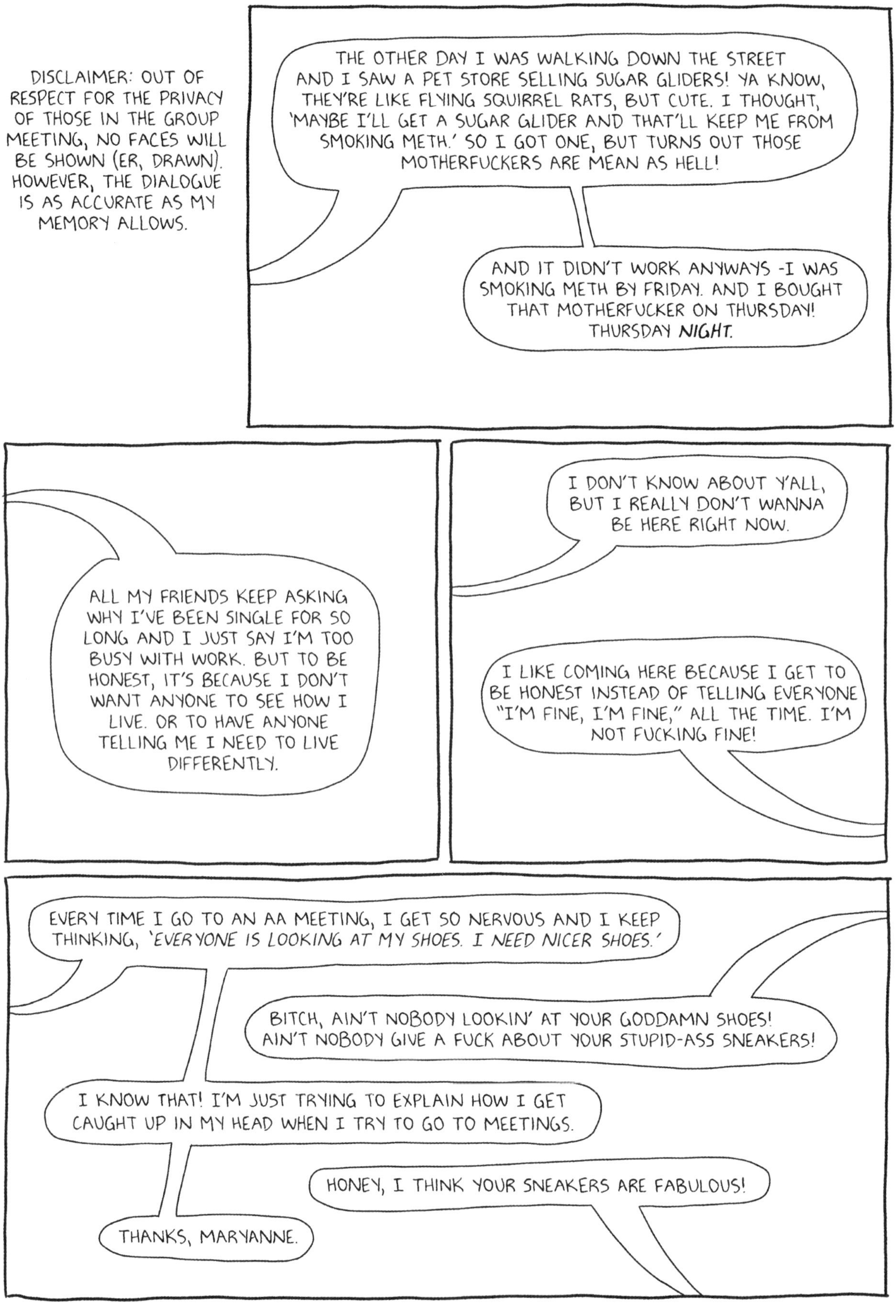
DISCLAIMER: OUT OF RESPECT FOR THE PRIVACY OF THOSE IN THE GROUP MEETING, NO FACES WILL BE SHOWN (ER, DRAWN). HOWEVER, THE DIALOGUE IS AS ACCURATE AS MY MEMORY ALLOWS.
THE OTHER DAY I WAS WALKING DOWN THE STREET AND I SAW A PET STORE SELLING SUGAR GLIDERS! YA KNOW, THEY'RE LIKE FLYING SQUIRREL RATS, BUT CUTE. I THOUGHT, 'MAYBE I'LL GET A SUGAR GLIDER AND THAT'LL KEEP ME FROM SMOKING METH.' SO I GOT ONE, BUT TURNS OUT THOSE MOTHERFUCKERS ARE MEAN AS HELL!
AND IT DIDN'T WORK ANYWAYS -I WAS SMOKING METH BY FRIDAY. AND I BOUGHT THAT MOTHERFUCKER ON THURSDAY! THURSDAY **NIGHT.**
ALL MY FRIENDS KEEP ASKING WHY I'VE BEEN SINGLE FOR SO LONG AND I JUST SAY I'M TOO BUSY WITH WORK. BUT TO BE HONEST, IT'S BECAUSE I DON'T WANT ANYONE TO SEE HOW I LIVE. OR TO HAVE ANYONE TELLING ME I NEED TO LIVE DIFFERENTLY.
I DON'T KNOW ABOUT Y'ALL, BUT I REALLY DON'T WANNA BE HERE RIGHT NOW.
I LIKE COMING HERE BECAUSE I GET TO BE HONEST INSTEAD OF TELLING EVERYONE "I'M FINE, I'M FINE," ALL THE TIME. I'M NOT FUCKING FINE!
EVERY TIME I GO TO AN AA MEETING, I GET SO NERVOUS AND I KEEP THINKING, '*EVERYONE IS LOOKING AT MY SHOES. I NEED NICER SHOES.*'
BITCH, AIN'T NOBODY LOOKIN' AT YOUR GODDAMN SHOES! AIN'T NOBODY GIVE A FUCK ABOUT YOUR STUPID-ASS SNEAKERS!
I KNOW THAT! I'M JUST TRYING TO EXPLAIN HOW I GET CAUGHT UP IN MY HEAD WHEN I TRY TO GO TO MEETINGS.
HONEY, I THINK YOUR SNEAKERS ARE FABULOUS!
THANKS, MARYANNE.

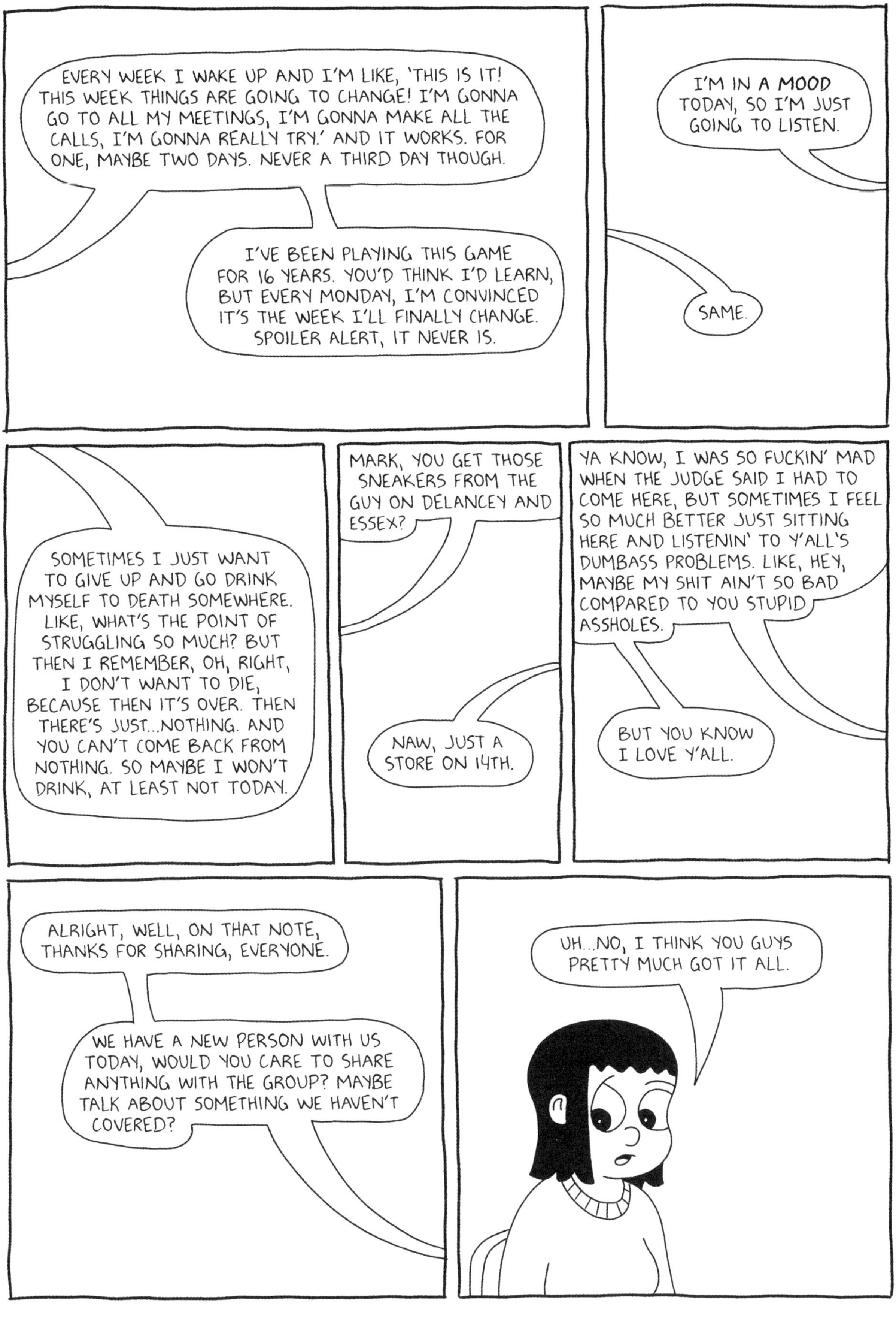
EVERY WEEK I WAKE UP AND I'M LIKE, 'THIS IS IT! THIS WEEK THINGS ARE GOING TO CHANGE! I'M GONNA GO TO ALL MY MEETINGS, I'M GONNA MAKE ALL THE CALLS, I'M GONNA REALLY TRY.' AND IT WORKS. FOR ONE, MAYBE TWO DAYS. NEVER A THIRD DAY THOUGH.
I'VE BEEN PLAYING THIS GAME FOR 16 YEARS. YOU'D THINK I'D LEARN, BUT EVERY MONDAY, I'M CONVINCED IT'S THE WEEK I'LL FINALLY CHANGE. SPOILER ALERT, IT NEVER IS.
I'M IN A **MOOD** TODAY, SO I'M JUST GOING TO LISTEN.
SAME.
SOMETIMES I JUST WANT TO GIVE UP AND GO DRINK MYSELF TO DEATH SOMEWHERE. LIKE, WHAT'S THE POINT OF STRUGGLING SO MUCH? BUT THEN I REMEMBER, OH, RIGHT, I DON'T WANT TO DIE, BECAUSE THEN IT'S OVER. THEN THERE'S JUST...NOTHING. AND YOU CAN'T COME BACK FROM NOTHING. SO MAYBE I WON'T DRINK, AT LEAST NOT TODAY.
MARK, YOU GET THOSE SNEAKERS FROM THE GUY ON DELANCEY AND ESSEX?
NAW, JUST A STORE ON 14TH.
YA KNOW, I WAS SO FUCKIN' MAD WHEN THE JUDGE SAID I HAD TO COME HERE, BUT SOMETIMES I FEEL SO MUCH BETTER JUST SITTING HERE AND LISTENIN' TO Y'ALL'S DUMBASS PROBLEMS. LIKE, HEY, MAYBE MY SHIT AIN'T SO BAD COMPARED TO YOU STUPID ASSHOLES.
BUT YOU KNOW I LOVE Y'ALL.
ALRIGHT, WELL, ON THAT NOTE, THANKS FOR SHARING, EVERYONE.
WE HAVE A NEW PERSON WITH US TODAY, WOULD YOU CARE TO SHARE ANYTHING WITH THE GROUP? MAYBE TALK ABOUT SOMETHING WE HAVEN'T COVERED?
UH...NO, I THINK YOU GUYS PRETTY MUCH GOT IT ALL.

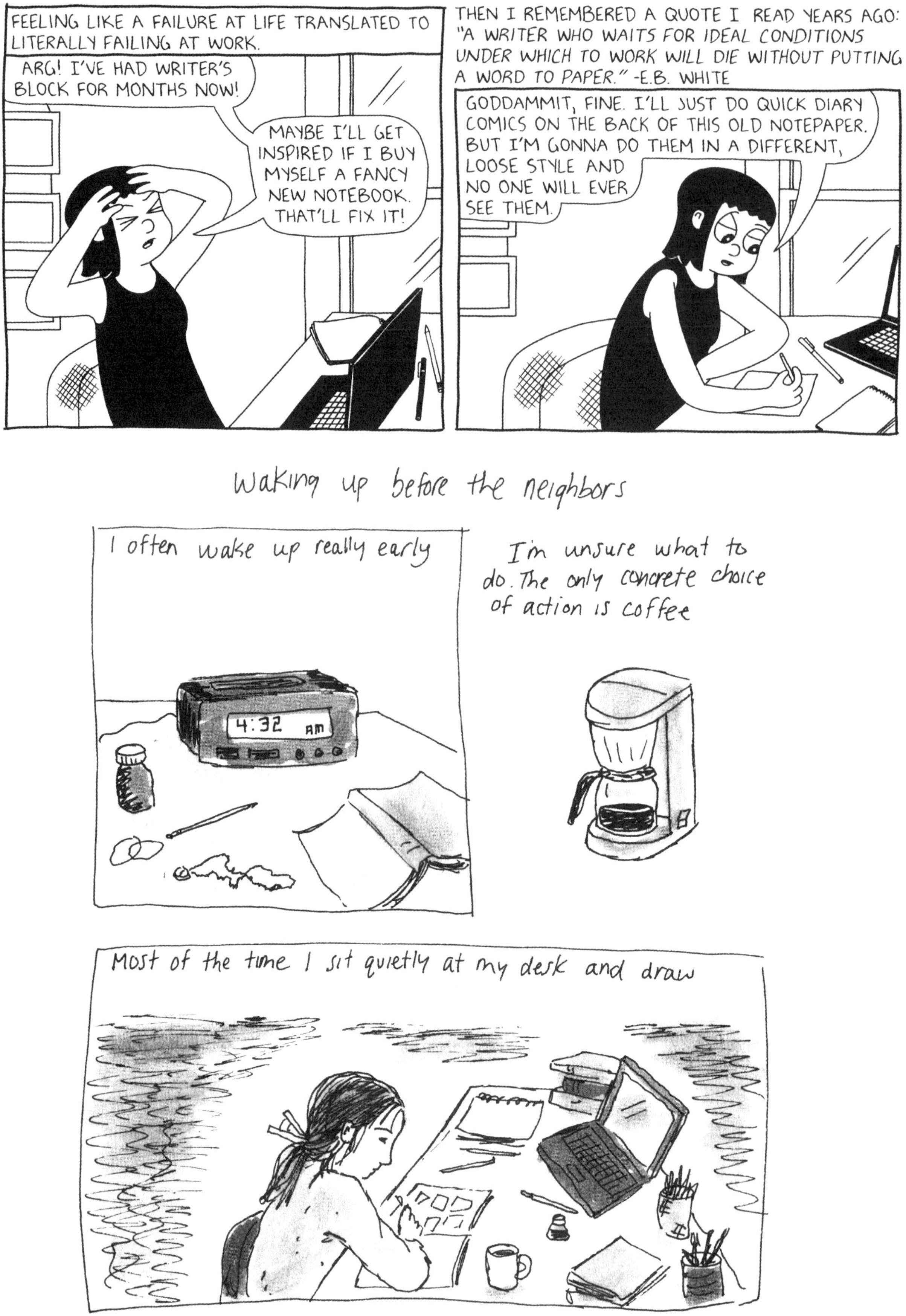
FEELING LIKE A FAILURE AT LIFE TRANSLATED TO LITERALLY FAILING AT WORK.
ARG! I'VE HAD WRITER'S BLOCK FOR MONTHS NOW!
MAYBE I'LL GET INSPIRED IF I BUY MYSELF A FANCY NEW NOTEBOOK. THAT'LL FIX IT!
THEN I REMEMBERED A QUOTE I READ YEARS AGO: "A WRITER WHO WAITS FOR IDEAL CONDITIONS UNDER WHICH TO WORK WILL DIE WITHOUT PUTTING A WORD TO PAPER." -E.B. WHITE
GODDAMMIT, FINE. I'LL JUST DO QUICK DIARY COMICS ON THE BACK OF THIS OLD NOTEPAPER. BUT I'M GONNA DO THEM IN A DIFFERENT, LOOSE STYLE AND NO ONE WILL EVER SEE THEM.
waking up before the neighbors
I often wake up really early
4:32 AM
I'm unsure what to do. The only concrete choice of action is coffee
Most of the time I sit quietly at my desk and draw

I don't turn on the radio or the computer. I don't listen to music or do any "real" work.

So from the time I awake until the sun rises is like a no-man's-land. It doesn't really exist.

Sometimes when I wake up too early, I sit on the couch and read.

I try to sit on my couch as much as possible (I often sleep on it)...

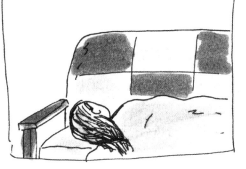

because I feel like it's some great accomplishment to own my own couch...

Even though it's really just an old futon.

I CONTINUED TO GO TO GROUP THERAPY, BUT MOSTLY JUST TO LISTEN. EVENTUALLY, I WAS GIVEN A ONE-ON-ONE THERAPIST I SAW TWICE A MONTH.

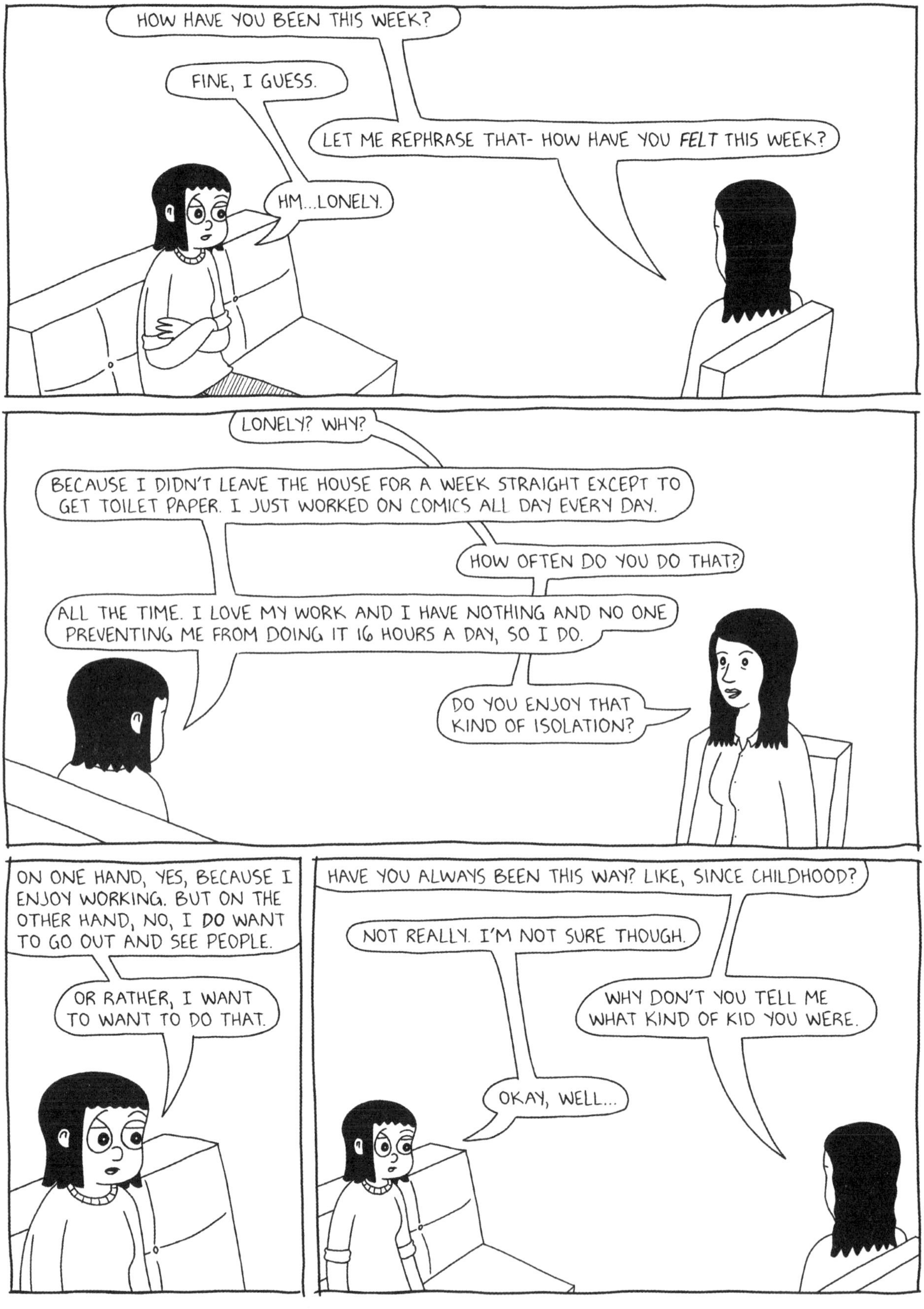
HOW HAVE YOU BEEN THIS WEEK?
FINE, I GUESS.
LET ME REPHRASE THAT- HOW HAVE YOU *FELT* THIS WEEK?
HM...LONELY.
LONELY? WHY?
BECAUSE I DIDN'T LEAVE THE HOUSE FOR A WEEK STRAIGHT EXCEPT TO GET TOILET PAPER. I JUST WORKED ON COMICS ALL DAY EVERY DAY.
HOW OFTEN DO YOU DO THAT?
ALL THE TIME. I LOVE MY WORK AND I HAVE NOTHING AND NO ONE PREVENTING ME FROM DOING IT 16 HOURS A DAY, SO I DO.
DO YOU ENJOY THAT KIND OF ISOLATION?
ON ONE HAND, YES, BECAUSE I ENJOY WORKING. BUT ON THE OTHER HAND, NO, I **DO** WANT TO GO OUT AND SEE PEOPLE.
OR RATHER, I WANT TO WANT TO DO THAT.
HAVE YOU ALWAYS BEEN THIS WAY? LIKE, SINCE CHILDHOOD?
NOT REALLY. I'M NOT SURE THOUGH.
WHY DON'T YOU TELL ME WHAT KIND OF KID YOU WERE.
OKAY, WELL...

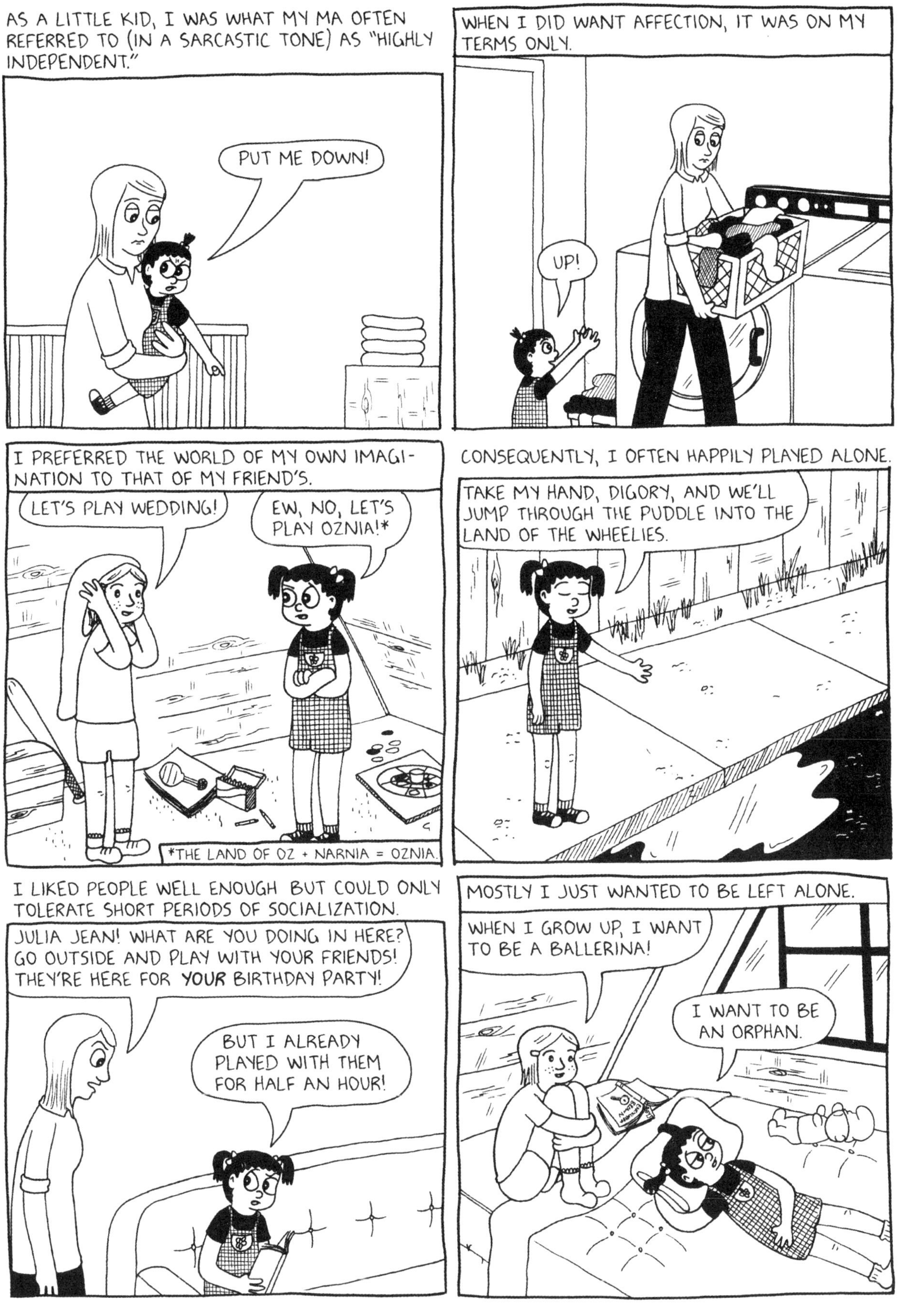
AS A LITTLE KID, I WAS WHAT MY MA OFTEN REFERRED TO (IN A SARCASTIC TONE) AS "HIGHLY INDEPENDENT."
PUT ME DOWN!
WHEN I DID WANT AFFECTION, IT WAS ON MY TERMS ONLY.
UP!
I PREFERRED THE WORLD OF MY OWN IMAGINATION TO THAT OF MY FRIEND'S.
LET'S PLAY WEDDING!
EW, NO, LET'S PLAY OZNIA!*
*THE LAND OF OZ + NARNIA = OZNIA.
CONSEQUENTLY, I OFTEN HAPPILY PLAYED ALONE.
TAKE MY HAND, DIGORY, AND WE'LL JUMP THROUGH THE PUDDLE INTO THE LAND OF THE WHEELIES.
I LIKED PEOPLE WELL ENOUGH BUT COULD ONLY TOLERATE SHORT PERIODS OF SOCIALIZATION.
JULIA JEAN! WHAT ARE YOU DOING IN HERE? GO OUTSIDE AND PLAY WITH YOUR FRIENDS! THEY'RE HERE FOR YOUR BIRTHDAY PARTY!
BUT I ALREADY PLAYED WITH THEM FOR HALF AN HOUR!
MOSTLY I JUST WANTED TO BE LEFT ALONE.
WHEN I GROW UP, I WANT TO BE A BALLERINA!
I WANT TO BE AN ORPHAN.

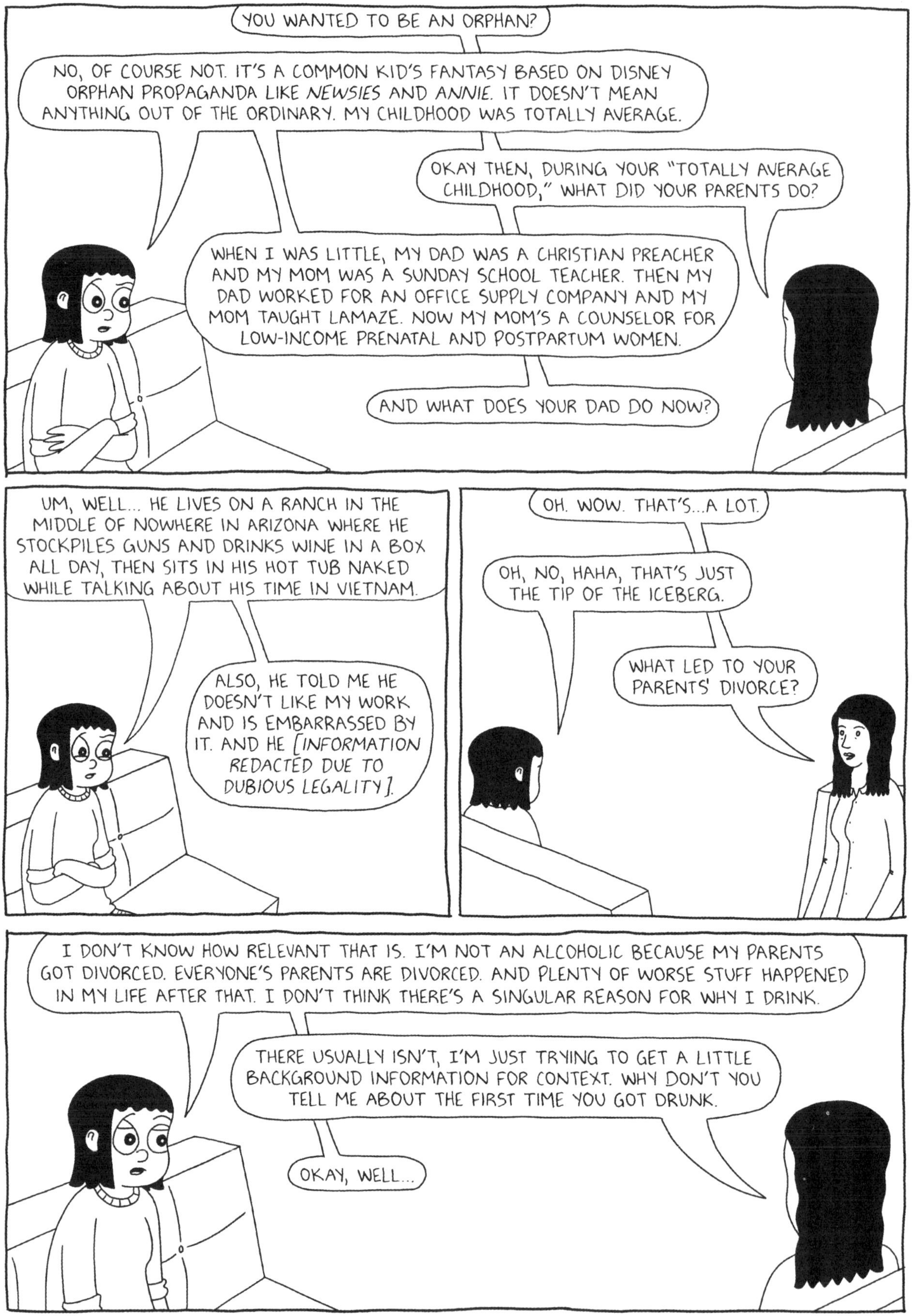
YOU WANTED TO BE AN ORPHAN?
NO, OF COURSE NOT. IT'S A COMMON KID'S FANTASY BASED ON DISNEY ORPHAN PROPAGANDA LIKE *NEWSIES* AND *ANNIE*. IT DOESN'T MEAN ANYTHING OUT OF THE ORDINARY. MY CHILDHOOD WAS TOTALLY AVERAGE.
OKAY THEN, DURING YOUR "TOTALLY AVERAGE CHILDHOOD," WHAT DID YOUR PARENTS DO?
WHEN I WAS LITTLE, MY DAD WAS A CHRISTIAN PREACHER AND MY MOM WAS A SUNDAY SCHOOL TEACHER. THEN MY DAD WORKED FOR AN OFFICE SUPPLY COMPANY AND MY MOM TAUGHT LAMAZE. NOW MY MOM'S A COUNSELOR FOR LOW-INCOME PRENATAL AND POSTPARTUM WOMEN.
AND WHAT DOES YOUR DAD DO NOW?
UM, WELL... HE LIVES ON A RANCH IN THE MIDDLE OF NOWHERE IN ARIZONA WHERE HE STOCKPILES GUNS AND DRINKS WINE IN A BOX ALL DAY, THEN SITS IN HIS HOT TUB NAKED WHILE TALKING ABOUT HIS TIME IN VIETNAM.
ALSO, HE TOLD ME HE DOESN'T LIKE MY WORK AND IS EMBARRASSED BY IT. AND HE [*INFORMATION REDACTED DUE TO DUBIOUS LEGALITY*].
OH. WOW. THAT'S...A LOT.
OH, NO, HAHA, THAT'S JUST THE TIP OF THE ICEBERG.
WHAT LED TO YOUR PARENTS' DIVORCE?
I DON'T KNOW HOW RELEVANT THAT IS. I'M NOT AN ALCOHOLIC BECAUSE MY PARENTS GOT DIVORCED. EVERYONE'S PARENTS ARE DIVORCED. AND PLENTY OF WORSE STUFF HAPPENED IN MY LIFE AFTER THAT. I DON'T THINK THERE'S A SINGULAR REASON FOR WHY I DRINK.
THERE USUALLY ISN'T, I'M JUST TRYING TO GET A LITTLE BACKGROUND INFORMATION FOR CONTEXT. WHY DON'T YOU TELL ME ABOUT THE FIRST TIME YOU GOT DRUNK.
OKAY, WELL...

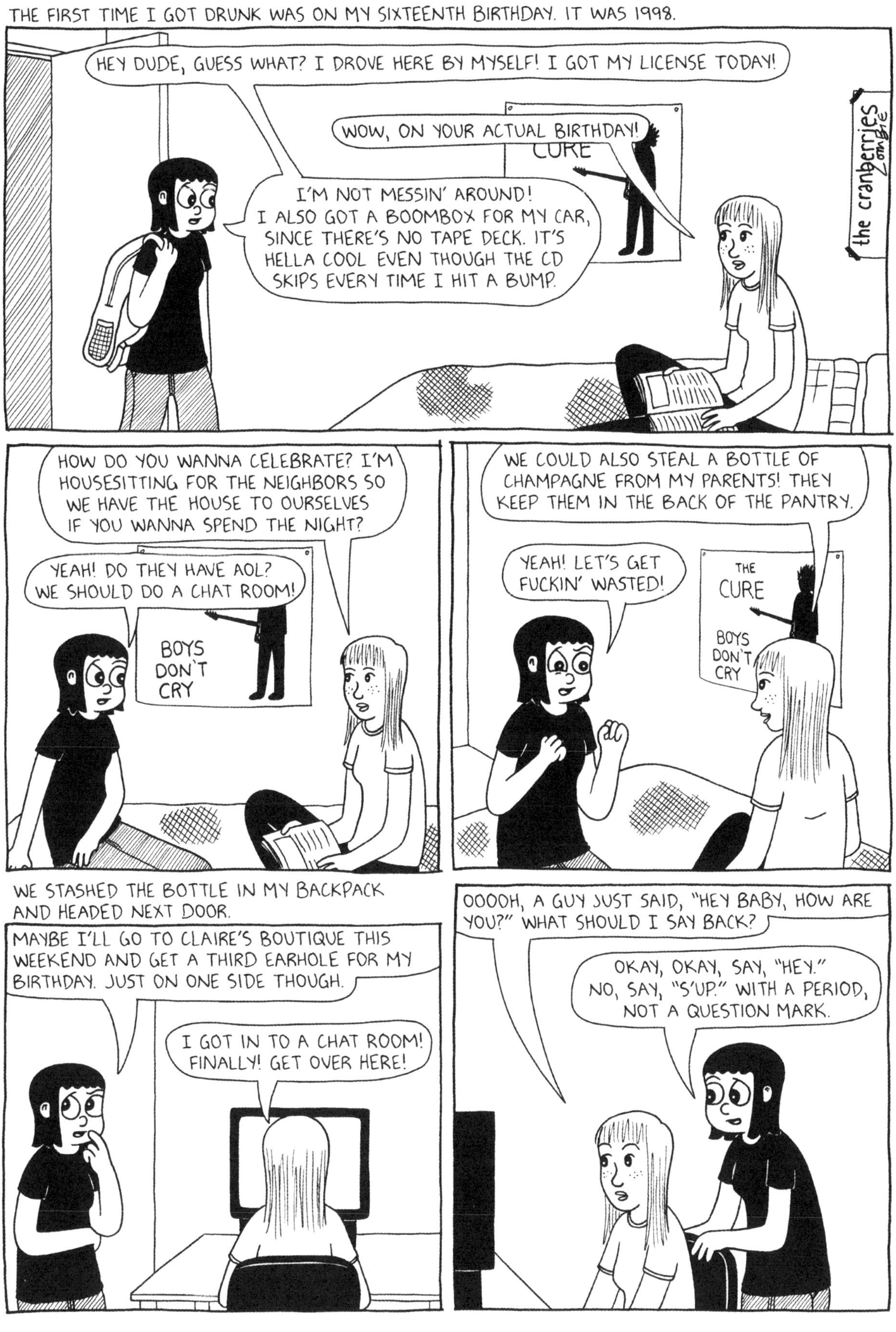
THE FIRST TIME I GOT DRUNK WAS ON MY SIXTEENTH BIRTHDAY. IT WAS 1998.
HEY DUDE, GUESS WHAT? I DROVE HERE BY MYSELF! I GOT MY LICENSE TODAY!
WOW, ON YOUR ACTUAL BIRTHDAY!
I'M NOT MESSIN' AROUND! I ALSO GOT A BOOMBOX FOR MY CAR, SINCE THERE'S NO TAPE DECK. IT'S HELLA COOL EVEN THOUGH THE CD SKIPS EVERY TIME I HIT A BUMP.
CURE
the cranberries Zombie
HOW DO YOU WANNA CELEBRATE? I'M HOUSESITTING FOR THE NEIGHBORS SO WE HAVE THE HOUSE TO OURSELVES IF YOU WANNA SPEND THE NIGHT?
YEAH! DO THEY HAVE AOL? WE SHOULD DO A CHAT ROOM!
BOYS DON'T CRY
WE COULD ALSO STEAL A BOTTLE OF CHAMPAGNE FROM MY PARENTS! THEY KEEP THEM IN THE BACK OF THE PANTRY.
YEAH! LET'S GET FUCKIN' WASTED!
THE CURE
BOYS DON'T CRY
WE STASHED THE BOTTLE IN MY BACKPACK AND HEADED NEXT DOOR.
MAYBE I'LL GO TO CLAIRE'S BOUTIQUE THIS WEEKEND AND GET A THIRD EARHOLE FOR MY BIRTHDAY. JUST ON ONE SIDE THOUGH.
I GOT IN TO A CHAT ROOM! FINALLY! GET OVER HERE!
OOOOH, A GUY JUST SAID, "HEY BABY, HOW ARE YOU?" WHAT SHOULD I SAY BACK?
OKAY, OKAY, SAY, "HEY." NO, SAY, "S'UP." WITH A PERIOD, NOT A QUESTION MARK.

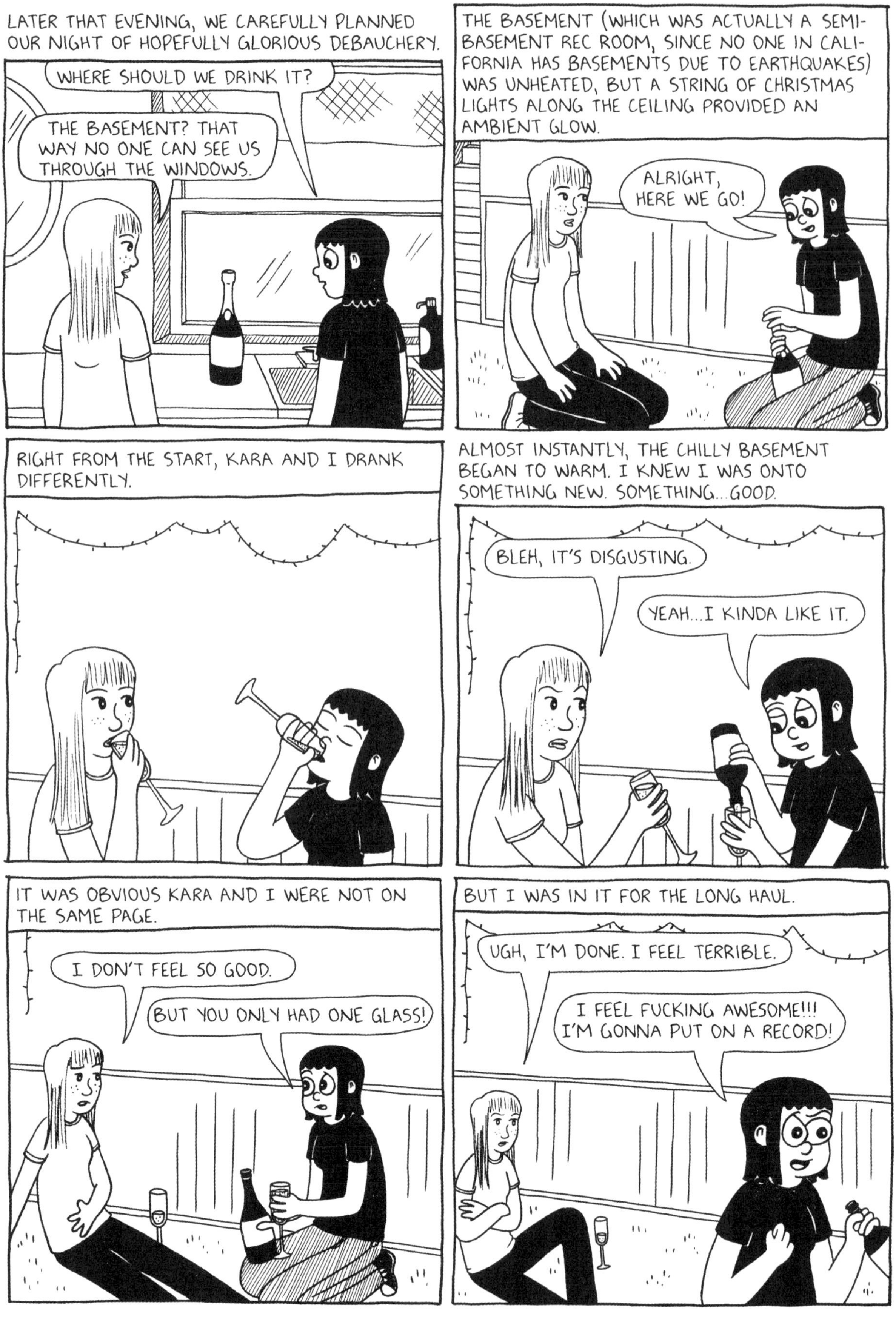
LATER THAT EVENING, WE CAREFULLY PLANNED OUR NIGHT OF HOPEFULLY GLORIOUS DEBAUCHERY.
WHERE SHOULD WE DRINK IT?
THE BASEMENT? THAT WAY NO ONE CAN SEE US THROUGH THE WINDOWS.
THE BASEMENT (WHICH WAS ACTUALLY A SEMI-BASEMENT REC ROOM, SINCE NO ONE IN CALIFORNIA HAS BASEMENTS DUE TO EARTHQUAKES) WAS UNHEATED, BUT A STRING OF CHRISTMAS LIGHTS ALONG THE CEILING PROVIDED AN AMBIENT GLOW.
ALRIGHT, HERE WE GO!
RIGHT FROM THE START, KARA AND I DRANK DIFFERENTLY.
ALMOST INSTANTLY, THE CHILLY BASEMENT BEGAN TO WARM. I KNEW I WAS ONTO SOMETHING NEW. SOMETHING...GOOD.
BLEH, IT'S DISGUSTING.
YEAH...I KINDA LIKE IT.
IT WAS OBVIOUS KARA AND I WERE NOT ON THE SAME PAGE.
I DON'T FEEL SO GOOD.
BUT YOU ONLY HAD ONE GLASS!
BUT I WAS IN IT FOR THE LONG HAUL.
UGH, I'M DONE. I FEEL TERRIBLE.
I FEEL FUCKING AWESOME!!! I'M GONNA PUT ON A RECORD!

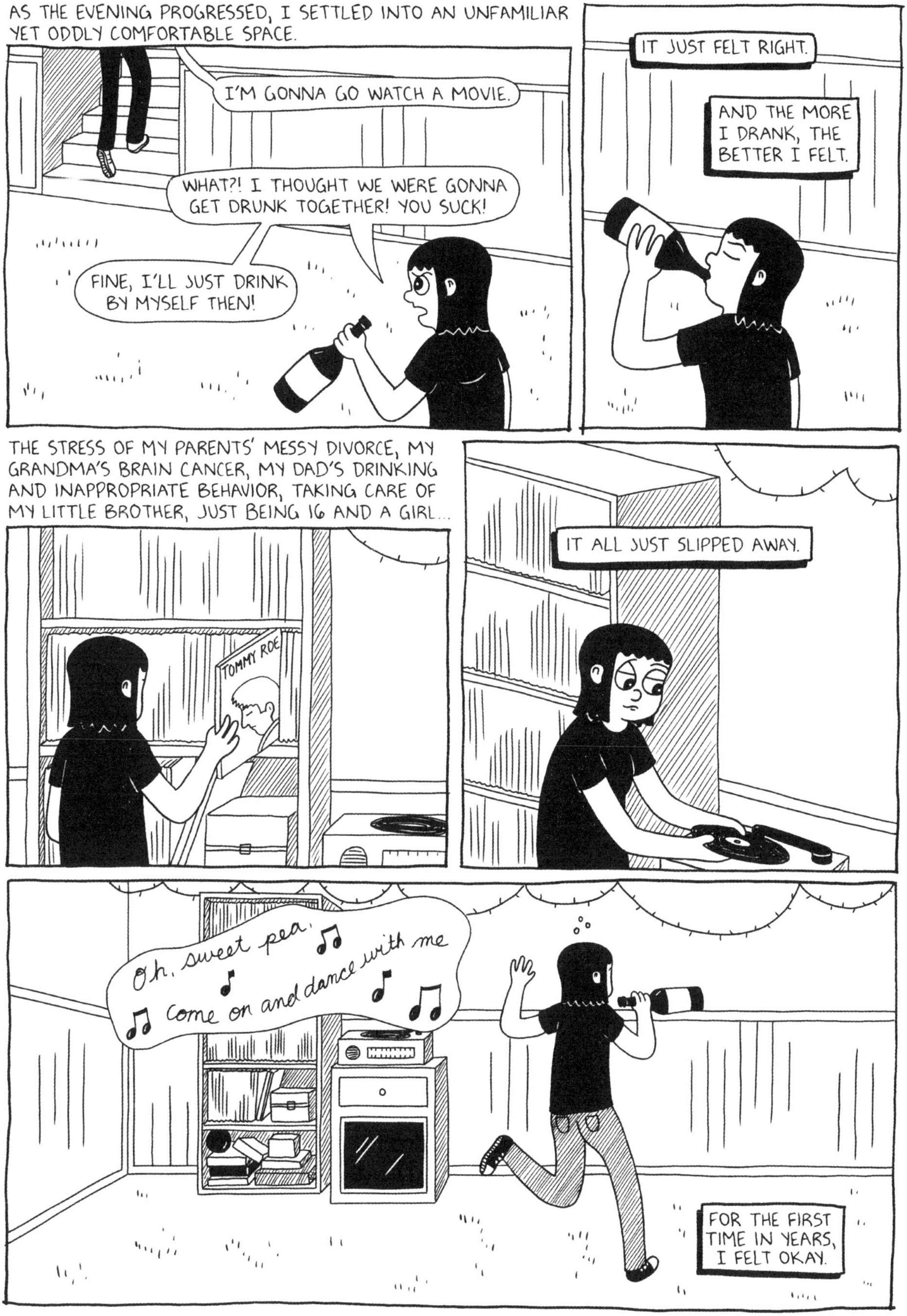
AS THE EVENING PROGRESSED, I SETTLED INTO AN UNFAMILIAR YET ODDLY COMFORTABLE SPACE.
I'M GONNA GO WATCH A MOVIE.
WHAT?! I THOUGHT WE WERE GONNA GET DRUNK TOGETHER! YOU SUCK!
FINE, I'LL JUST DRINK BY MYSELF THEN!
IT JUST FELT RIGHT.
AND THE MORE I DRANK, THE BETTER I FELT.
THE STRESS OF MY PARENTS' MESSY DIVORCE, MY GRANDMA'S BRAIN CANCER, MY DAD'S DRINKING AND INAPPROPRIATE BEHAVIOR, TAKING CARE OF MY LITTLE BROTHER, JUST BEING 16 AND A GIRL...
TOMMY ROE
IT ALL JUST SLIPPED AWAY.
Oh, sweet pea, come on and dance with me
FOR THE FIRST TIME IN YEARS, I FELT OKAY.

I SPENT THE REST OF THE EVENING CYCLING THROUGH THE STEREOTYPICAL PHASES OF A GOOD OLD-FASHIONED DRUNK, DESPITE HAVING NO PREVIOUS EXPERIENCE. IT CAME NATURALLY TO ME.

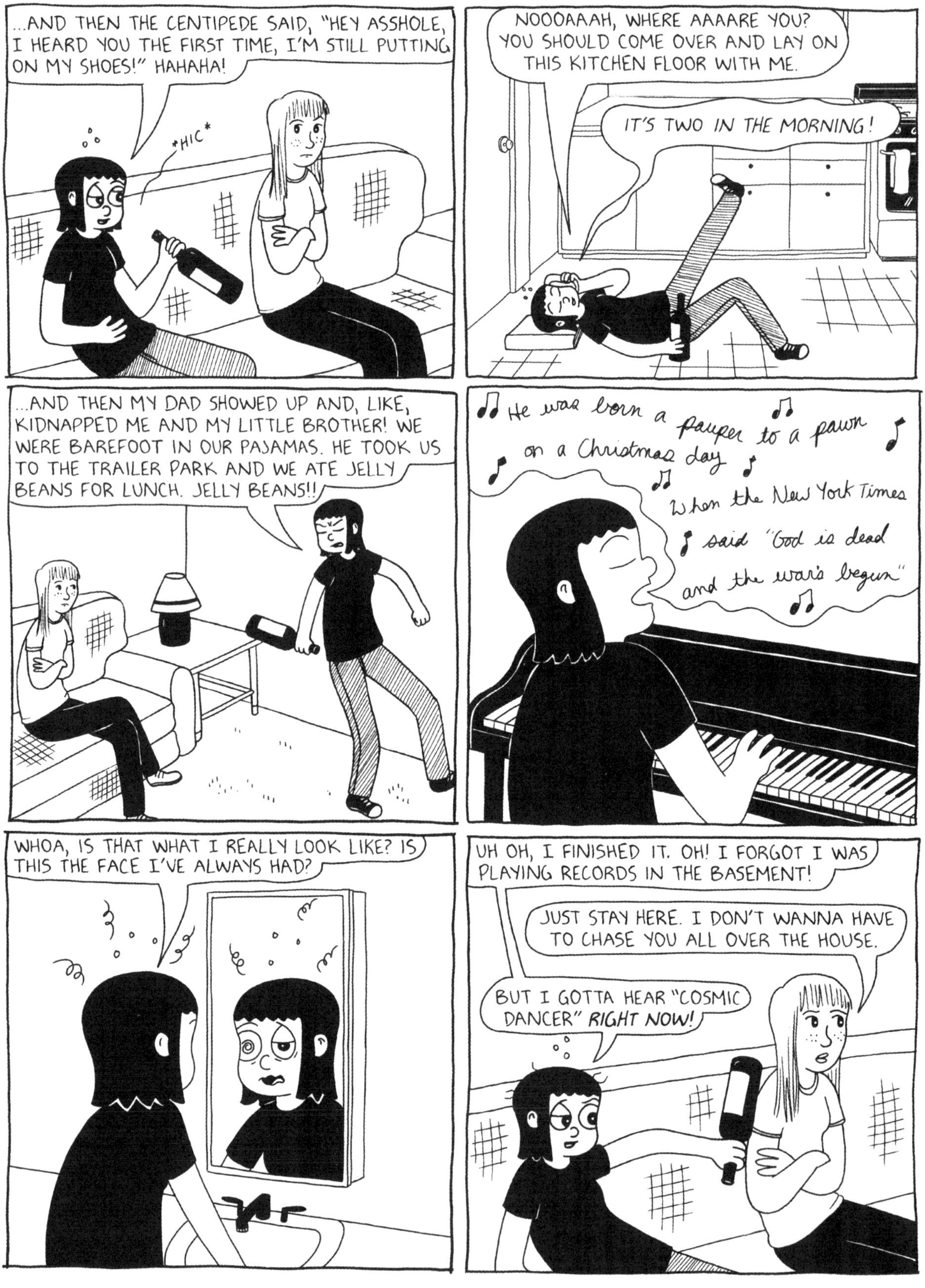
...AND THEN THE CENTIPEDE SAID, "HEY ASSHOLE, I HEARD YOU THE FIRST TIME, I'M STILL PUTTING ON MY SHOES!" HAHAHA!
HIC
NOOOAAAH, WHERE AAAARE YOU? YOU SHOULD COME OVER AND LAY ON THIS KITCHEN FLOOR WITH ME.
IT'S TWO IN THE MORNING!
...AND THEN MY DAD SHOWED UP AND, LIKE, KIDNAPPED ME AND MY LITTLE BROTHER! WE WERE BAREFOOT IN OUR PAJAMAS. HE TOOK US TO THE TRAILER PARK AND WE ATE JELLY BEANS FOR LUNCH. JELLY BEANS!!
He was born a pauper to a pawn on a Christmas day
When the New York Times said "God is dead and the war's begun"
WHOA, IS THAT WHAT I REALLY LOOK LIKE? IS THIS THE FACE I'VE ALWAYS HAD?
UH OH, I FINISHED IT. OH! I FORGOT I WAS PLAYING RECORDS IN THE BASEMENT!
JUST STAY HERE. I DON'T WANNA HAVE TO CHASE YOU ALL OVER THE HOUSE.
BUT I GOTTA HEAR "COSMIC DANCER" RIGHT NOW!

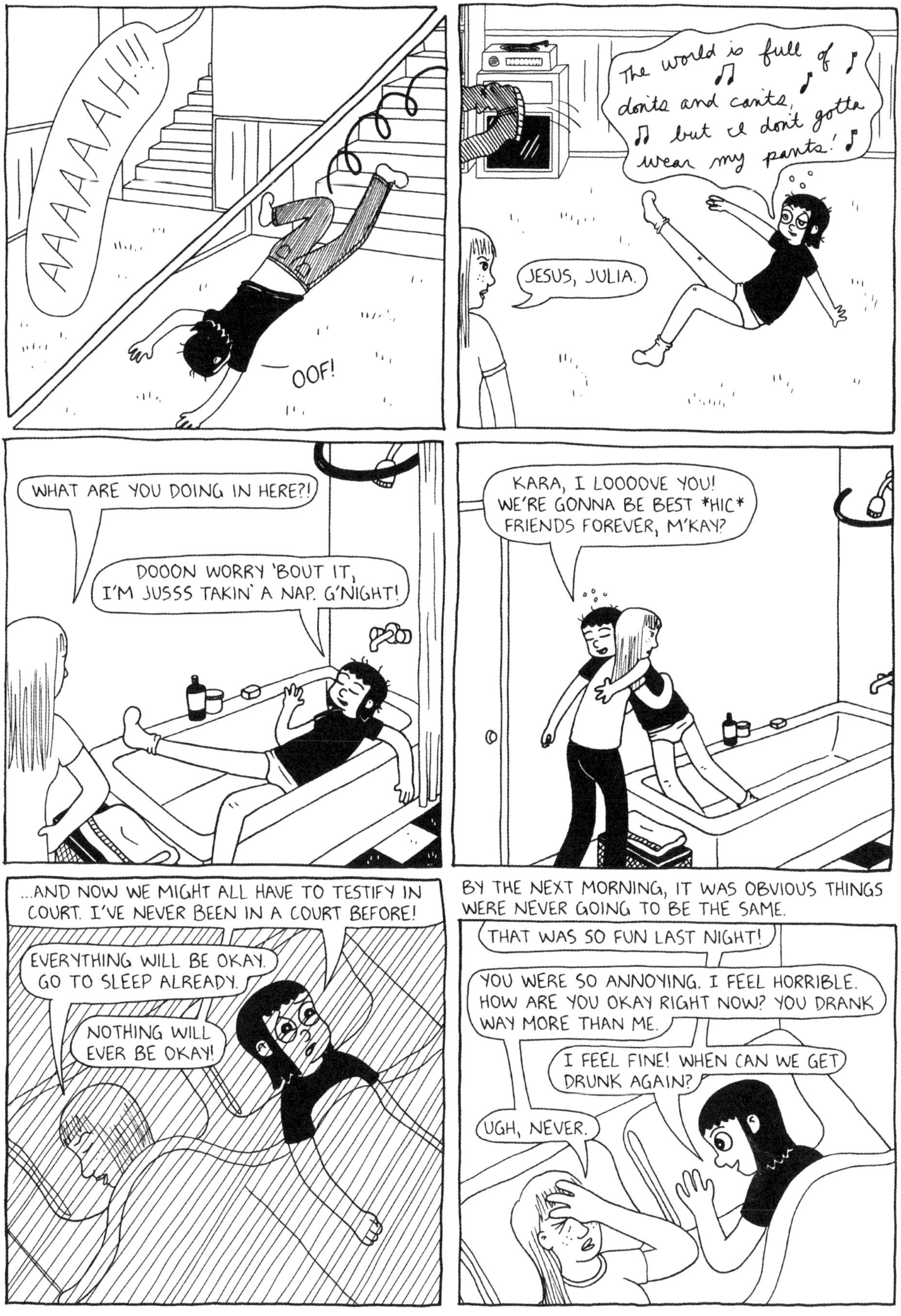
AAAAAAH!!!
OOF!
The world is full of donts and cants, but I dont gotta wear my pants!
JESUS, JULIA.
WHAT ARE YOU DOING IN HERE?!
DOOON WORRY 'BOUT IT, I'M JUSSS TAKIN' A NAP. G'NIGHT!
KARA, I LOOOOVE YOU! WE'RE GONNA BE BEST *HIC* FRIENDS FOREVER, M'KAY?
...AND NOW WE MIGHT ALL HAVE TO TESTIFY IN COURT. I'VE NEVER BEEN IN A COURT BEFORE!
EVERYTHING WILL BE OKAY. GO TO SLEEP ALREADY.
NOTHING WILL EVER BE OKAY!
BY THE NEXT MORNING, IT WAS OBVIOUS THINGS WERE NEVER GOING TO BE THE SAME.
THAT WAS SO FUN LAST NIGHT!
YOU WERE SO ANNOYING. I FEEL HORRIBLE. HOW ARE YOU OKAY RIGHT NOW? YOU DRANK WAY MORE THAN ME.
I FEEL FINE! WHEN CAN WE GET DRUNK AGAIN?
UGH, NEVER.

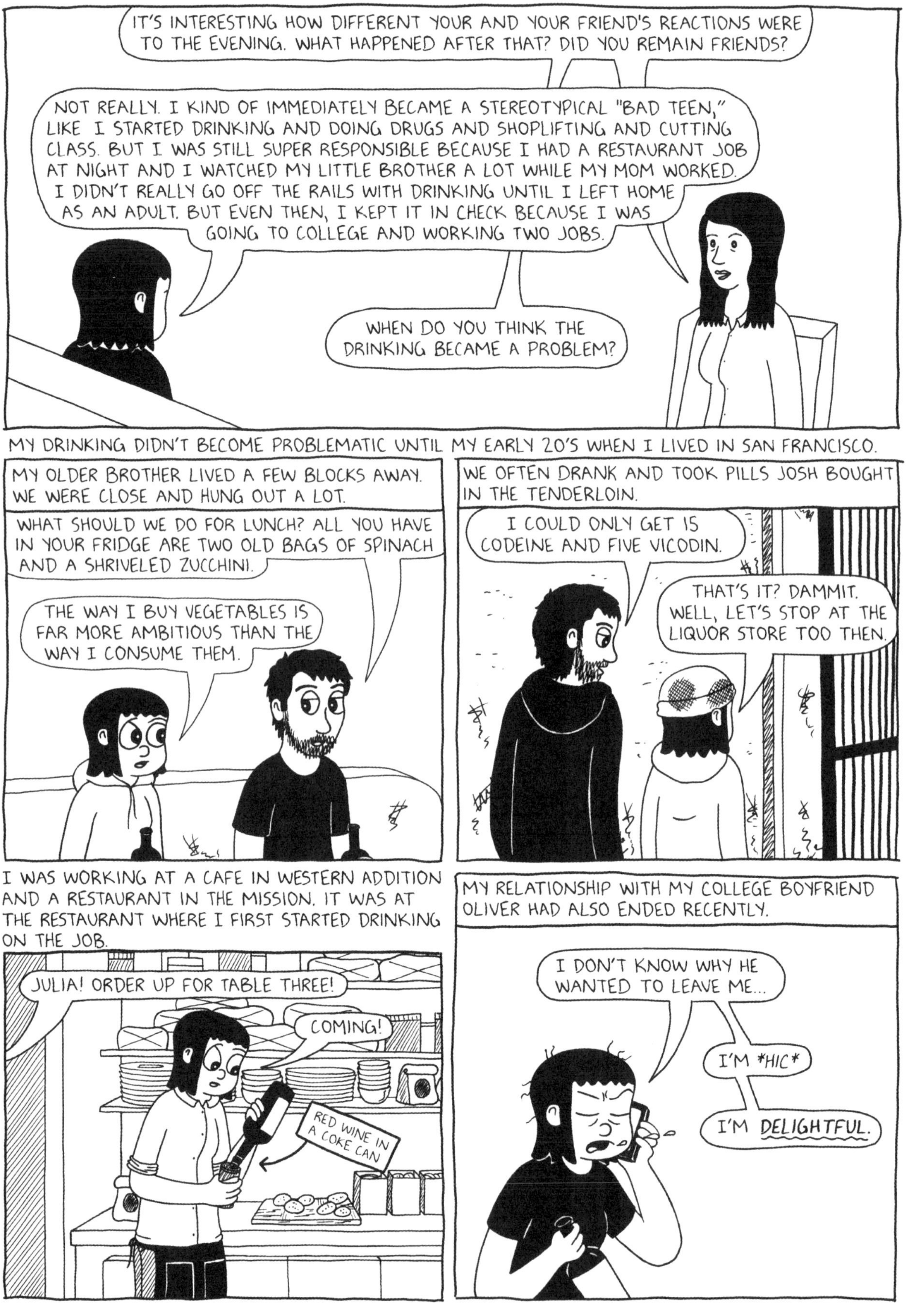
IT'S INTERESTING HOW DIFFERENT YOUR AND YOUR FRIEND'S REACTIONS WERE TO THE EVENING. WHAT HAPPENED AFTER THAT? DID YOU REMAIN FRIENDS?
NOT REALLY. I KIND OF IMMEDIATELY BECAME A STEREOTYPICAL "BAD TEEN," LIKE I STARTED DRINKING AND DOING DRUGS AND SHOPLIFTING AND CUTTING CLASS. BUT I WAS STILL SUPER RESPONSIBLE BECAUSE I HAD A RESTAURANT JOB AT NIGHT AND I WATCHED MY LITTLE BROTHER A LOT WHILE MY MOM WORKED. I DIDN'T REALLY GO OFF THE RAILS WITH DRINKING UNTIL I LEFT HOME AS AN ADULT. BUT EVEN THEN, I KEPT IT IN CHECK BECAUSE I WAS GOING TO COLLEGE AND WORKING TWO JOBS.
WHEN DO YOU THINK THE DRINKING BECAME A PROBLEM?
MY DRINKING DIDN'T BECOME PROBLEMATIC UNTIL MY EARLY 20'S WHEN I LIVED IN SAN FRANCISCO.
MY OLDER BROTHER LIVED A FEW BLOCKS AWAY. WE WERE CLOSE AND HUNG OUT A LOT.
WHAT SHOULD WE DO FOR LUNCH? ALL YOU HAVE IN YOUR FRIDGE ARE TWO OLD BAGS OF SPINACH AND A SHRIVELED ZUCCHINI.
THE WAY I BUY VEGETABLES IS FAR MORE AMBITIOUS THAN THE WAY I CONSUME THEM.
WE OFTEN DRANK AND TOOK PILLS JOSH BOUGHT IN THE TENDERLOIN.
I COULD ONLY GET IS CODEINE AND FIVE VICODIN.
THAT'S IT? DAMMIT. WELL, LET'S STOP AT THE LIQUOR STORE TOO THEN.
I WAS WORKING AT A CAFE IN WESTERN ADDITION AND A RESTAURANT IN THE MISSION. IT WAS AT THE RESTAURANT WHERE I FIRST STARTED DRINKING ON THE JOB.
JULIA! ORDER UP FOR TABLE THREE!
COMING!
RED WINE IN A COKE CAN
MY RELATIONSHIP WITH MY COLLEGE BOYFRIEND OLIVER HAD ALSO ENDED RECENTLY.
I DON'T KNOW WHY HE WANTED TO LEAVE ME...
I'M *HIC*
I'M DELIGHTFUL.

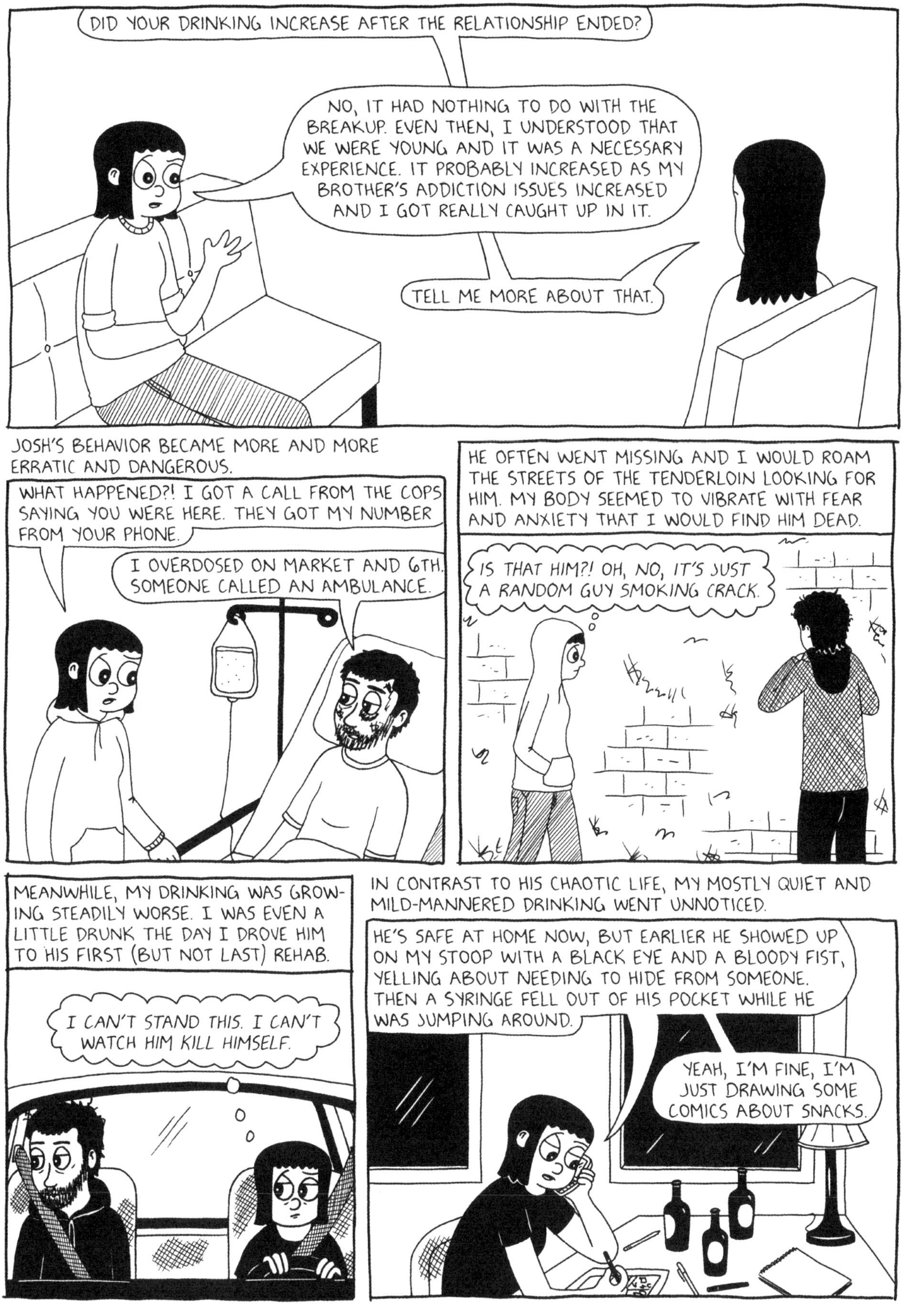
DID YOUR DRINKING INCREASE AFTER THE RELATIONSHIP ENDED?
NO, IT HAD NOTHING TO DO WITH THE BREAKUP. EVEN THEN, I UNDERSTOOD THAT WE WERE YOUNG AND IT WAS A NECESSARY EXPERIENCE. IT PROBABLY INCREASED AS MY BROTHER'S ADDICTION ISSUES INCREASED AND I GOT REALLY CAUGHT UP IN IT.
TELL ME MORE ABOUT THAT.
JOSH'S BEHAVIOR BECAME MORE AND MORE ERRATIC AND DANGEROUS.
WHAT HAPPENED?! I GOT A CALL FROM THE COPS SAYING YOU WERE HERE. THEY GOT MY NUMBER FROM YOUR PHONE.
I OVERDOSED ON MARKET AND 6TH. SOMEONE CALLED AN AMBULANCE.
HE OFTEN WENT MISSING AND I WOULD ROAM THE STREETS OF THE TENDERLOIN LOOKING FOR HIM. MY BODY SEEMED TO VIBRATE WITH FEAR AND ANXIETY THAT I WOULD FIND HIM DEAD.
IS THAT HIM?! OH, NO, IT'S JUST A RANDOM GUY SMOKING CRACK.
MEANWHILE, MY DRINKING WAS GROWING STEADILY WORSE. I WAS EVEN A LITTLE DRUNK THE DAY I DROVE HIM TO HIS FIRST (BUT NOT LAST) REHAB.
I CAN'T STAND THIS. I CAN'T WATCH HIM KILL HIMSELF.
IN CONTRAST TO HIS CHAOTIC LIFE, MY MOSTLY QUIET AND MILD-MANNERED DRINKING WENT UNNOTICED.
HE'S SAFE AT HOME NOW, BUT EARLIER HE SHOWED UP ON MY STOOP WITH A BLACK EYE AND A BLOODY FIST, YELLING ABOUT NEEDING TO HIDE FROM SOMEONE. THEN A SYRINGE FELL OUT OF HIS POCKET WHILE HE WAS JUMPING AROUND.
YEAH, I'M FINE, I'M JUST DRAWING SOME COMICS ABOUT SNACKS.

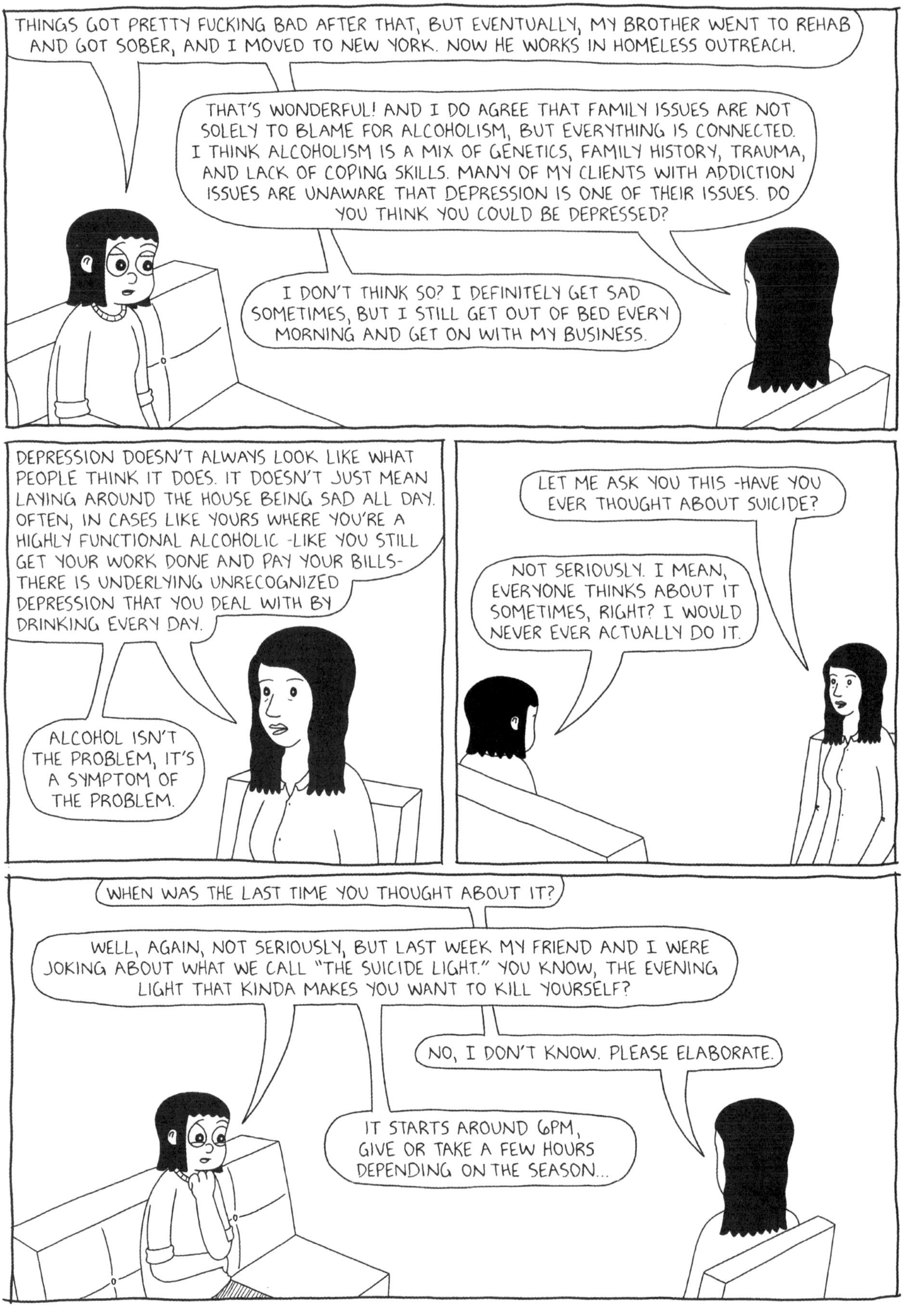
THINGS GOT PRETTY FUCKING BAD AFTER THAT, BUT EVENTUALLY, MY BROTHER WENT TO REHAB AND GOT SOBER, AND I MOVED TO NEW YORK. NOW HE WORKS IN HOMELESS OUTREACH.
THAT'S WONDERFUL! AND I DO AGREE THAT FAMILY ISSUES ARE NOT SOLELY TO BLAME FOR ALCOHOLISM, BUT EVERYTHING IS CONNECTED. I THINK ALCOHOLISM IS A MIX OF GENETICS, FAMILY HISTORY, TRAUMA, AND LACK OF COPING SKILLS. MANY OF MY CLIENTS WITH ADDICTION ISSUES ARE UNAWARE THAT DEPRESSION IS ONE OF THEIR ISSUES. DO YOU THINK YOU COULD BE DEPRESSED?
I DON'T THINK SO? I DEFINITELY GET SAD SOMETIMES, BUT I STILL GET OUT OF BED EVERY MORNING AND GET ON WITH MY BUSINESS.
DEPRESSION DOESN'T ALWAYS LOOK LIKE WHAT PEOPLE THINK IT DOES. IT DOESN'T JUST MEAN LAYING AROUND THE HOUSE BEING SAD ALL DAY. OFTEN, IN CASES LIKE YOURS WHERE YOU'RE A HIGHLY FUNCTIONAL ALCOHOLIC -LIKE YOU STILL GET YOUR WORK DONE AND PAY YOUR BILLS- THERE IS UNDERLYING UNRECOGNIZED DEPRESSION THAT YOU DEAL WITH BY DRINKING EVERY DAY.
ALCOHOL ISN'T THE PROBLEM, IT'S A SYMPTOM OF THE PROBLEM.
LET ME ASK YOU THIS -HAVE YOU EVER THOUGHT ABOUT SUICIDE?
NOT SERIOUSLY. I MEAN, EVERYONE THINKS ABOUT IT SOMETIMES, RIGHT? I WOULD NEVER EVER ACTUALLY DO IT.
WHEN WAS THE LAST TIME YOU THOUGHT ABOUT IT?
WELL, AGAIN, NOT SERIOUSLY, BUT LAST WEEK MY FRIEND AND I WERE JOKING ABOUT WHAT WE CALL "THE SUICIDE LIGHT." YOU KNOW, THE EVENING LIGHT THAT KINDA MAKES YOU WANT TO KILL YOURSELF?
NO, I DON'T KNOW. PLEASE ELABORATE.
IT STARTS AROUND 6PM, GIVE OR TAKE A FEW HOURS DEPENDING ON THE SEASON...

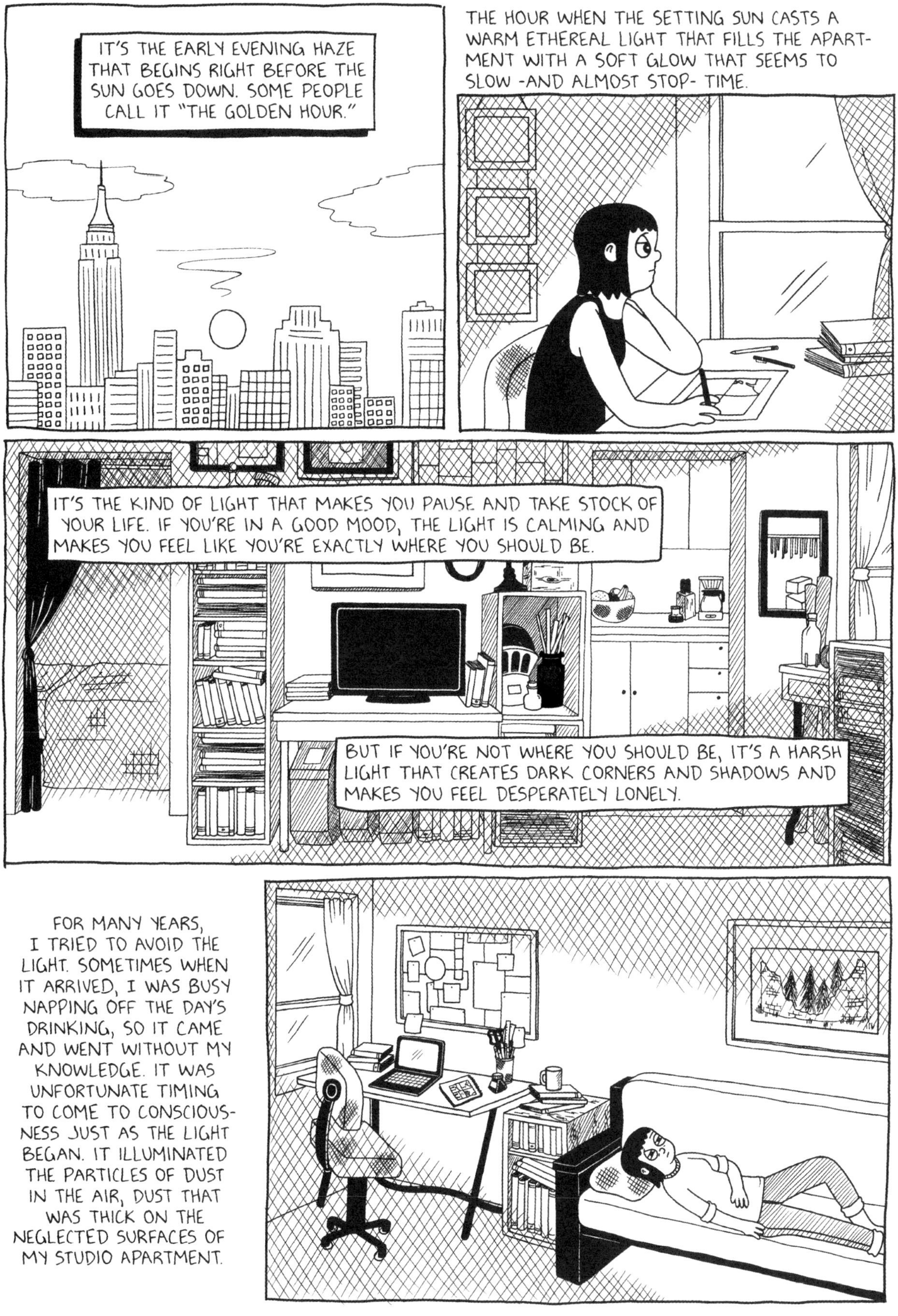
IT'S THE EARLY EVENING HAZE THAT BEGINS RIGHT BEFORE THE SUN GOES DOWN. SOME PEOPLE CALL IT "THE GOLDEN HOUR."
THE HOUR WHEN THE SETTING SUN CASTS A WARM ETHEREAL LIGHT THAT FILLS THE APARTMENT WITH A SOFT GLOW THAT SEEMS TO SLOW -AND ALMOST STOP- TIME.
IT'S THE KIND OF LIGHT THAT MAKES YOU PAUSE AND TAKE STOCK OF YOUR LIFE. IF YOU'RE IN A GOOD MOOD, THE LIGHT IS CALMING AND MAKES YOU FEEL LIKE YOU'RE EXACTLY WHERE YOU SHOULD BE.
BUT IF YOU'RE NOT WHERE YOU SHOULD BE, IT'S A HARSH LIGHT THAT CREATES DARK CORNERS AND SHADOWS AND MAKES YOU FEEL DESPERATELY LONELY.
FOR MANY YEARS, I TRIED TO AVOID THE LIGHT. SOMETIMES WHEN IT ARRIVED, I WAS BUSY NAPPING OFF THE DAY'S DRINKING, SO IT CAME AND WENT WITHOUT MY KNOWLEDGE. IT WAS UNFORTUNATE TIMING TO COME TO CONSCIOUSNESS JUST AS THE LIGHT BEGAN. IT ILLUMINATED THE PARTICLES OF DUST IN THE AIR, DUST THAT WAS THICK ON THE NEGLECTED SURFACES OF MY STUDIO APARTMENT.

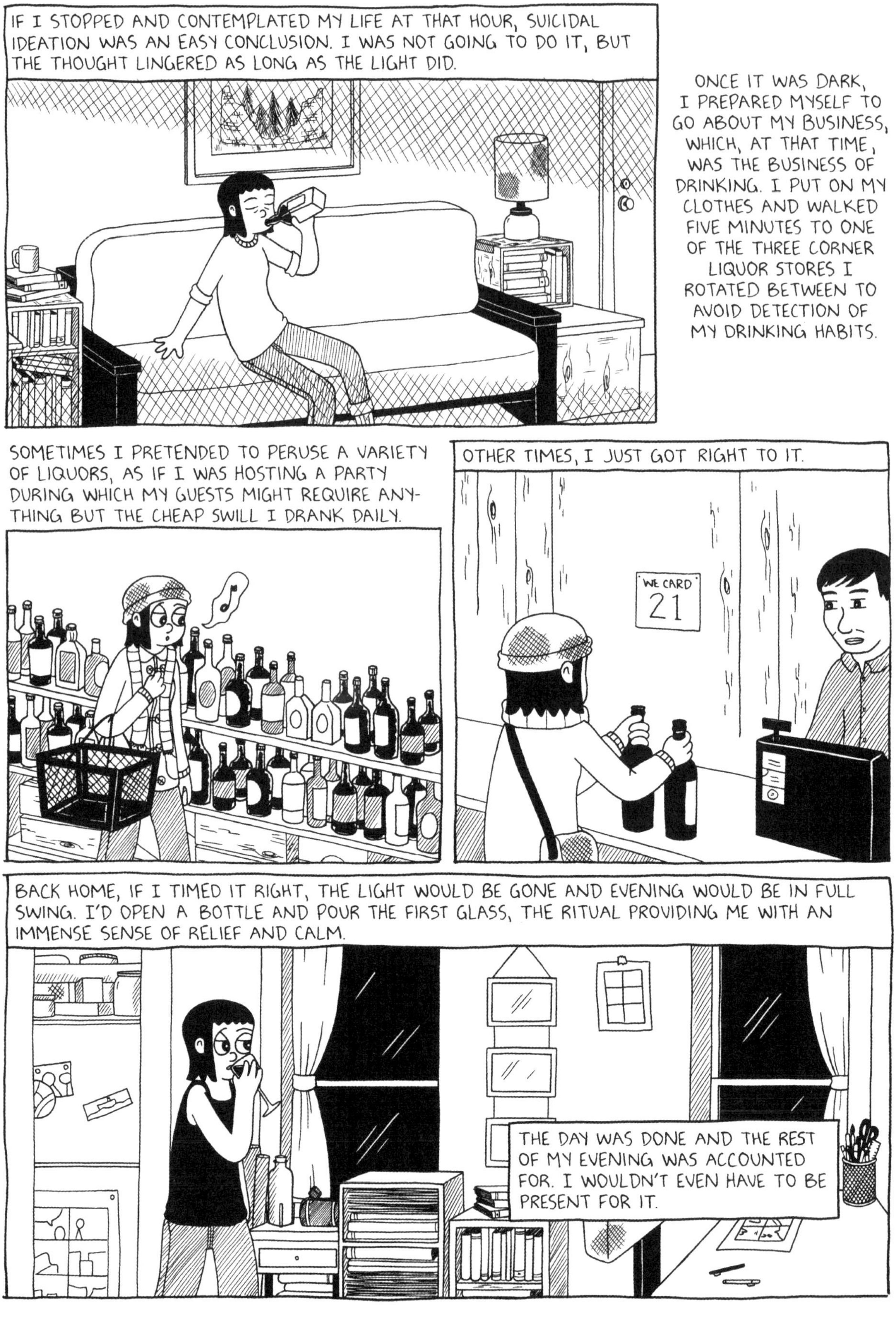
IF I STOPPED AND CONTEMPLATED MY LIFE AT THAT HOUR, SUICIDAL IDEATION WAS AN EASY CONCLUSION. I WAS NOT GOING TO DO IT, BUT THE THOUGHT LINGERED AS LONG AS THE LIGHT DID.
ONCE IT WAS DARK, I PREPARED MYSELF TO GO ABOUT MY BUSINESS, WHICH, AT THAT TIME, WAS THE BUSINESS OF DRINKING. I PUT ON MY CLOTHES AND WALKED FIVE MINUTES TO ONE OF THE THREE CORNER LIQUOR STORES I ROTATED BETWEEN TO AVOID DETECTION OF MY DRINKING HABITS.
SOMETIMES I PRETENDED TO PERUSE A VARIETY OF LIQUORS, AS IF I WAS HOSTING A PARTY DURING WHICH MY GUESTS MIGHT REQUIRE ANYTHING BUT THE CHEAP SWILL I DRANK DAILY.
OTHER TIMES, I JUST GOT RIGHT TO IT.
WE CARD 21
BACK HOME, IF I TIMED IT RIGHT, THE LIGHT WOULD BE GONE AND EVENING WOULD BE IN FULL SWING. I'D OPEN A BOTTLE AND POUR THE FIRST GLASS, THE RITUAL PROVIDING ME WITH AN IMMENSE SENSE OF RELIEF AND CALM.
THE DAY WAS DONE AND THE REST OF MY EVENING WAS ACCOUNTED FOR. I WOULDN'T EVEN HAVE TO BE PRESENT FOR IT.

I SPENT THE FIRST FEW HOURS OF THE EVENING DRINKING AND FINISHING UP WORK TASKS THAT REQUIRED MINIMAL CONCENTRATION- MOSTLY SCANNING AND EDITING. AFTER A CERTAIN NUMBER OF DRINKS, I WOULDN'T BE ABLE TO WORK ANYMORE, BUT I'M NOT SURE WHAT I DID AFTER THAT. I WAS A BLACKOUT DRINKER, THE EVENING EVENTS UNFOLDED WITHOUT MY CONSCIOUS KNOWLEDGE.

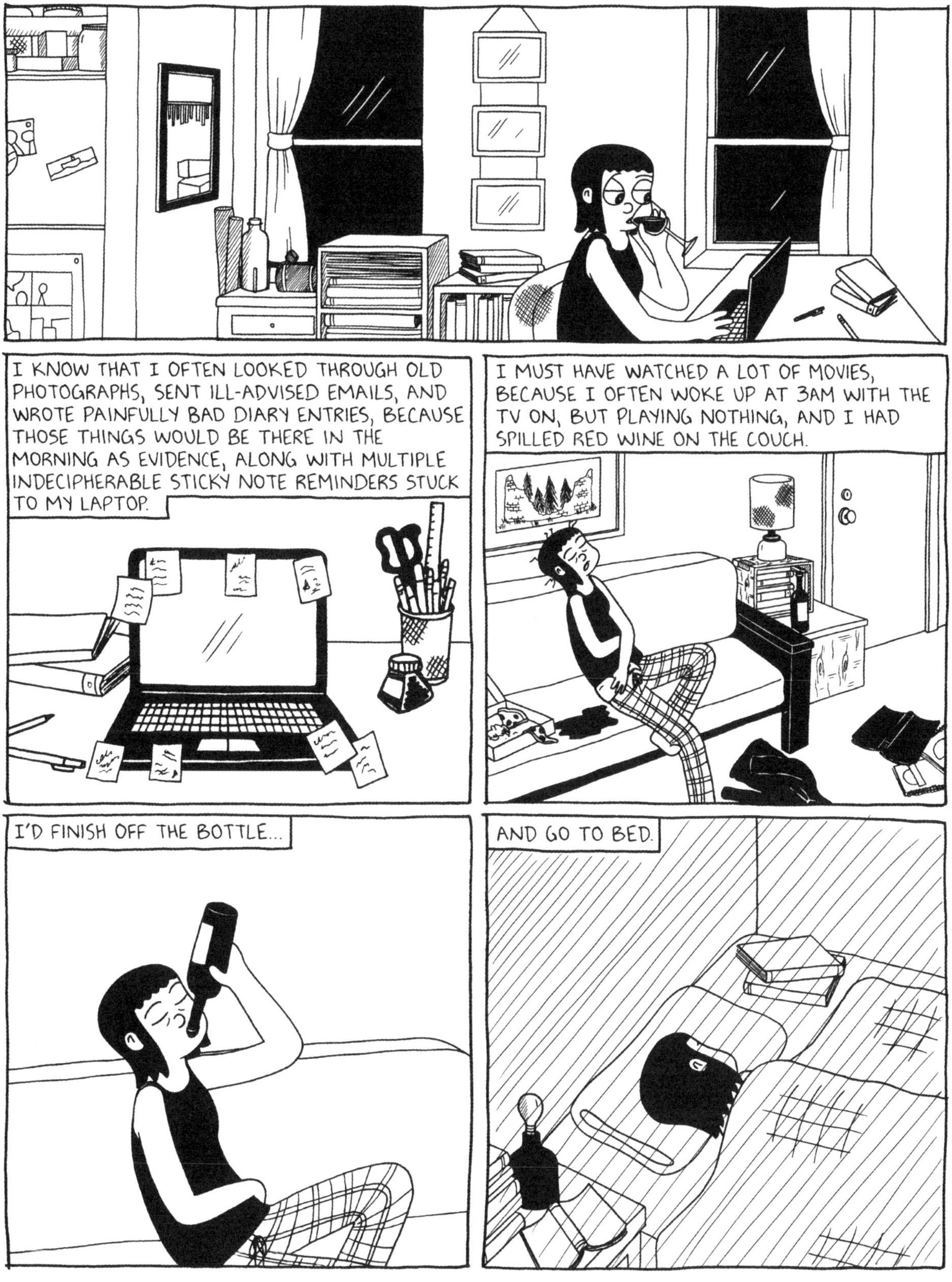
I KNOW THAT I OFTEN LOOKED THROUGH OLD PHOTOGRAPHS, SENT ILL-ADVISED EMAILS, AND WROTE PAINFULLY BAD DIARY ENTRIES, BECAUSE THOSE THINGS WOULD BE THERE IN THE MORNING AS EVIDENCE, ALONG WITH MULTIPLE INDECIPHERABLE STICKY NOTE REMINDERS STUCK TO MY LAPTOP.
I MUST HAVE WATCHED A LOT OF MOVIES, BECAUSE I OFTEN WOKE UP AT 3AM WITH THE TV ON, BUT PLAYING NOTHING, AND I HAD SPILLED RED WINE ON THE COUCH.
I'D FINISH OFF THE BOTTLE...
AND GO TO BED.

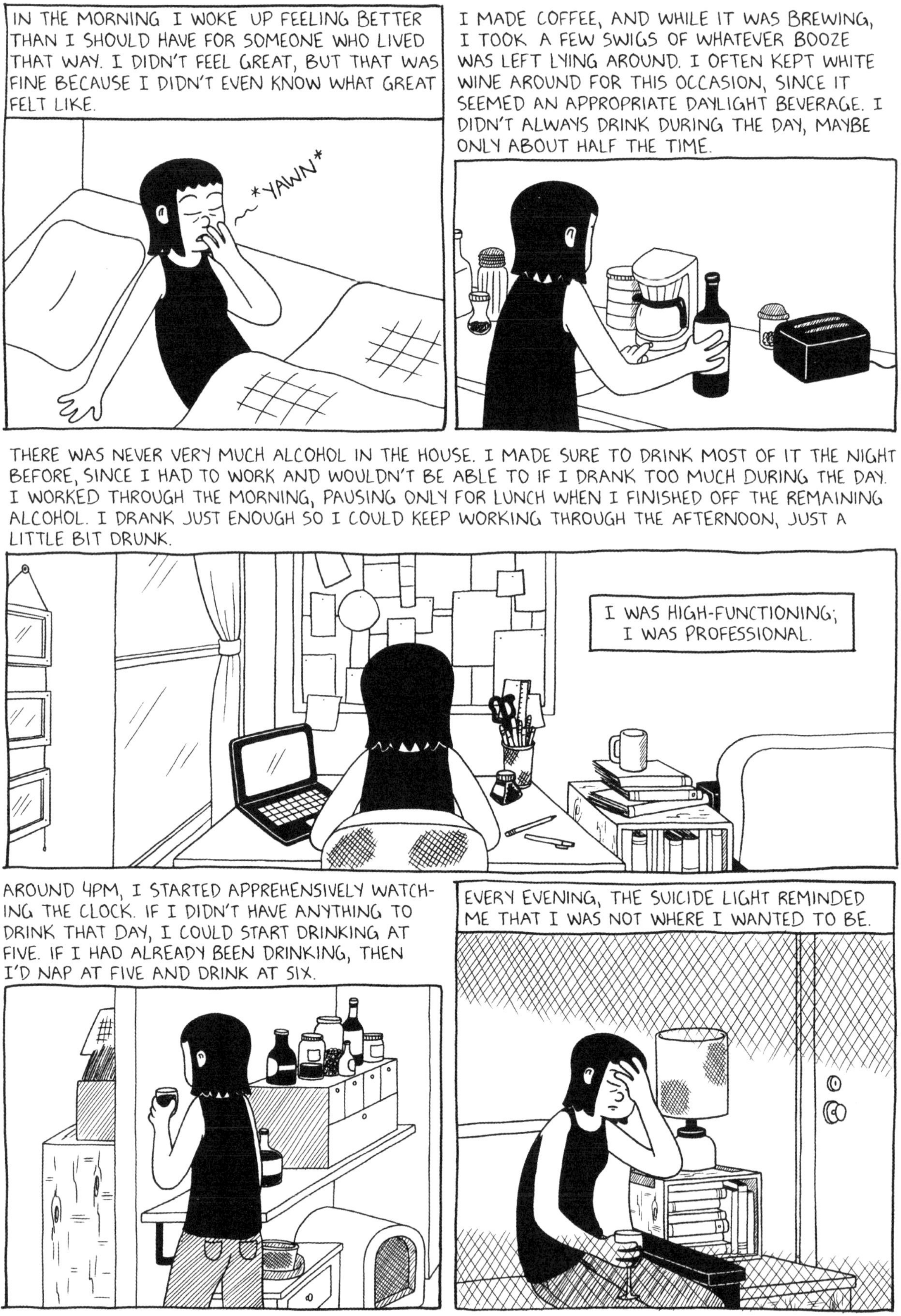
IN THE MORNING I WOKE UP FEELING BETTER THAN I SHOULD HAVE FOR SOMEONE WHO LIVED THAT WAY. I DIDN'T FEEL GREAT, BUT THAT WAS FINE BECAUSE I DIDN'T EVEN KNOW WHAT GREAT FELT LIKE.
YAWN
I MADE COFFEE, AND WHILE IT WAS BREWING, I TOOK A FEW SWIGS OF WHATEVER BOOZE WAS LEFT LYING AROUND. I OFTEN KEPT WHITE WINE AROUND FOR THIS OCCASION, SINCE IT SEEMED AN APPROPRIATE DAYLIGHT BEVERAGE. I DIDN'T ALWAYS DRINK DURING THE DAY, MAYBE ONLY ABOUT HALF THE TIME.
THERE WAS NEVER VERY MUCH ALCOHOL IN THE HOUSE. I MADE SURE TO DRINK MOST OF IT THE NIGHT BEFORE, SINCE I HAD TO WORK AND WOULDN'T BE ABLE TO IF I DRANK TOO MUCH DURING THE DAY. I WORKED THROUGH THE MORNING, PAUSING ONLY FOR LUNCH WHEN I FINISHED OFF THE REMAINING ALCOHOL. I DRANK JUST ENOUGH SO I COULD KEEP WORKING THROUGH THE AFTERNOON, JUST A LITTLE BIT DRUNK.
I WAS HIGH-FUNCTIONING; I WAS PROFESSIONAL.
AROUND 4PM, I STARTED APPREHENSIVELY WATCHING THE CLOCK. IF I DIDN'T HAVE ANYTHING TO DRINK THAT DAY, I COULD START DRINKING AT FIVE. IF I HAD ALREADY BEEN DRINKING, THEN I'D NAP AT FIVE AND DRINK AT SIX.
EVERY EVENING, THE SUICIDE LIGHT REMINDED ME THAT I WAS NOT WHERE I WANTED TO BE.

SOME DAYS, THE LIGHT FELT SO HARSH THAT IT DROVE ME OUT OF THE HOUSE. OCCASIONALLY I'D MEET UP WITH FRIENDS OR ATTEND A SOCIAL EVENT, BUT OFTEN I JUST WANDERED THE NEIGHBORHOOD.

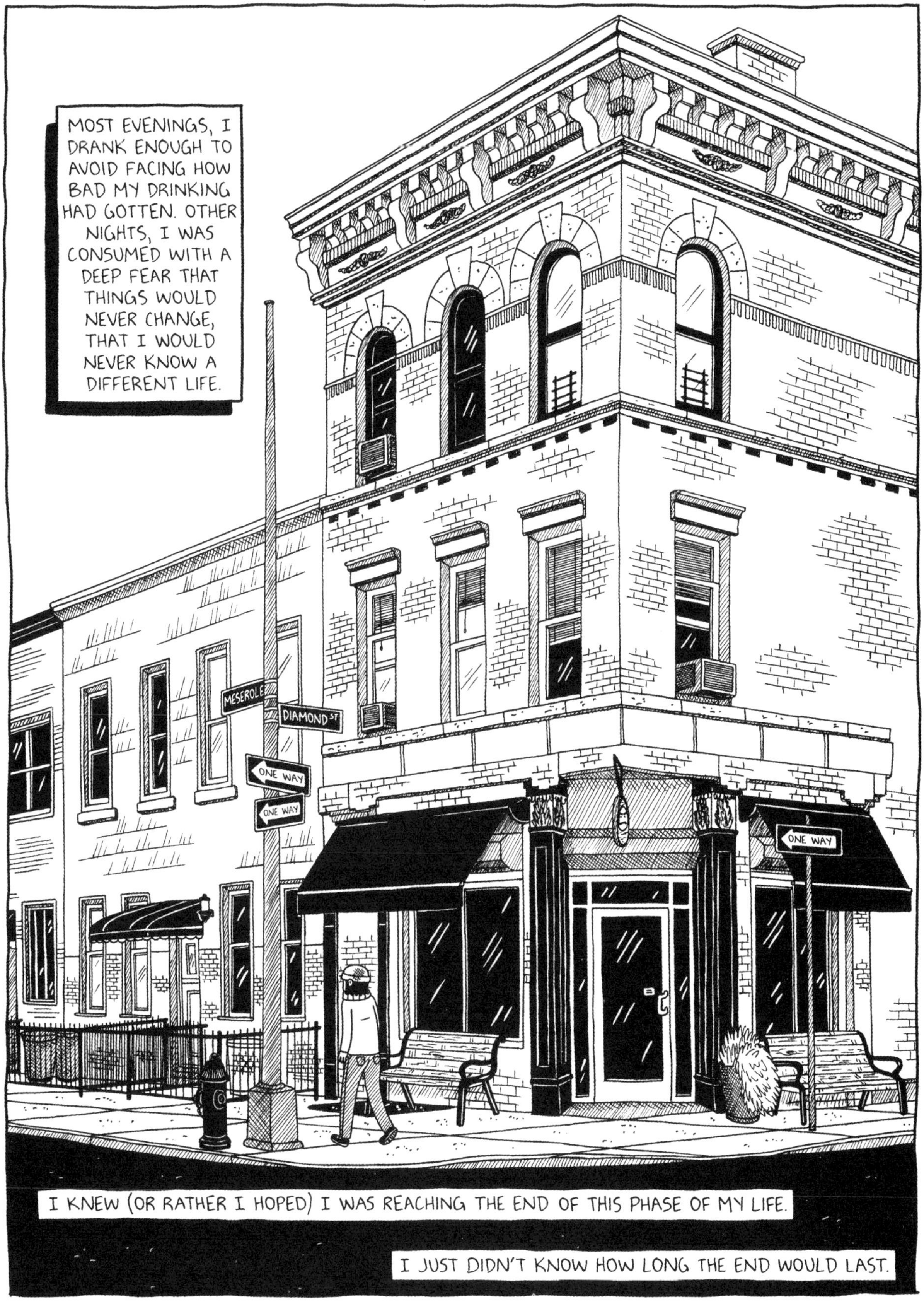
MOST EVENINGS, I DRANK ENOUGH TO AVOID FACING HOW BAD MY DRINKING HAD GOTTEN. OTHER NIGHTS, I WAS CONSUMED WITH A DEEP FEAR THAT THINGS WOULD NEVER CHANGE, THAT I WOULD NEVER KNOW A DIFFERENT LIFE.
MESEROLE
DIAMOND ST
ONE WAY
ONE WAY
ONE WAY
I KNEW (OR RATHER I HOPED) I WAS REACHING THE END OF THIS PHASE OF MY LIFE.
I JUST DIDN'T KNOW HOW LONG THE END WOULD LAST.

January

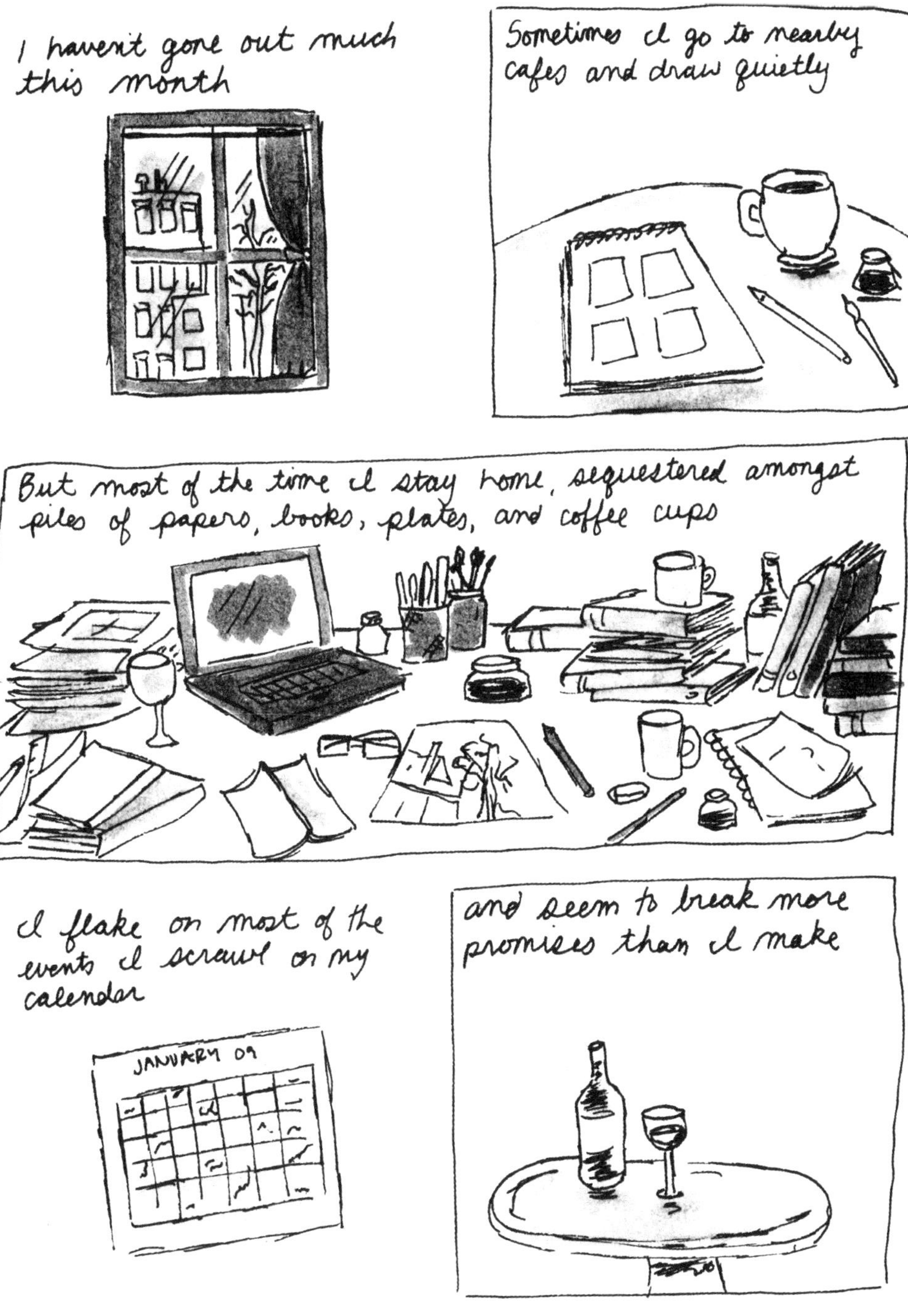

I haven't gone out much this month
Sometimes I go to nearby cafes and draw quietly
But most of the time I stay home, sequestered amongst piles of papers, books, plates, and coffee cups
I flake on most of the events I scrawl on my calendar
JANUARY 09
and seem to break more promises than I make

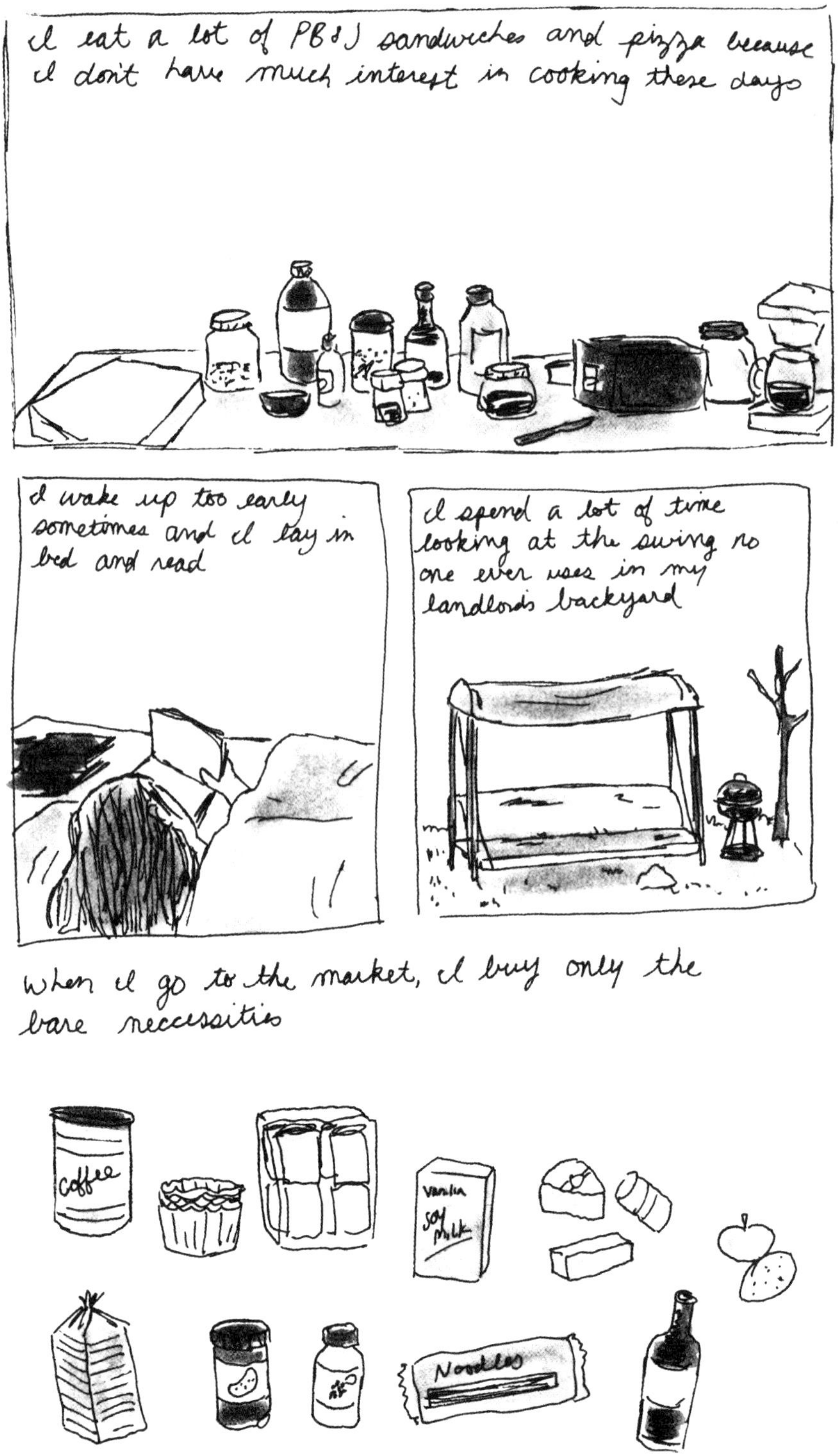
I eat a lot of PB&J sandwiches and pizza because I don't have much interest in cooking these days
I wake up too early sometimes and I lay in bed and read
I spend a lot of time looking at the swing no one ever uses in my landlord's backyard
When I go to the market, I buy only the bare neccessities
Coffee
Vanilla Soy Milk
Noodles

My hair is getting long & unruly - I clip it back with clips I got at the dollar store to hold back the curtains on the window

I wear the same ugly sweater every day

I start books and don't finish them - they pile up on the side of my bed that I don't sleep on

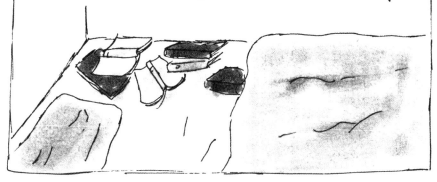

I don't keep mirrors in my studio and when I catch a glimpse of myself in the window, I'm surprised at how young I look...

... as though I expect a much older face to be looking back

I find things on the street and bring them home to my tiny studio

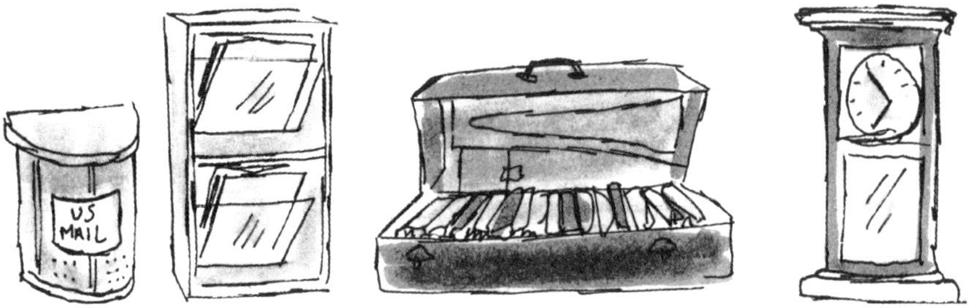
US MAIL

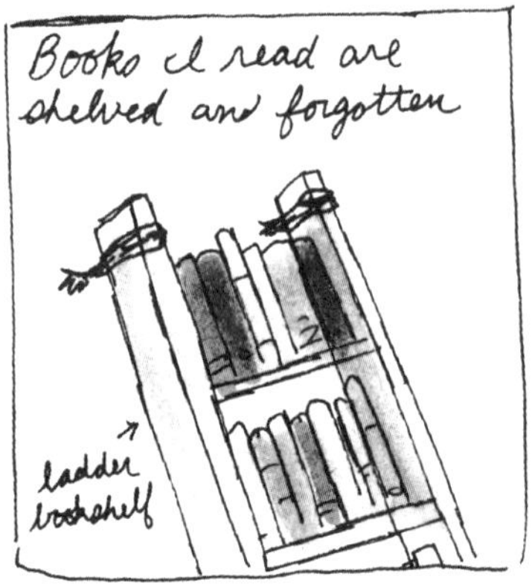
Books I read are shelved and forgotten
ladder bookshelf

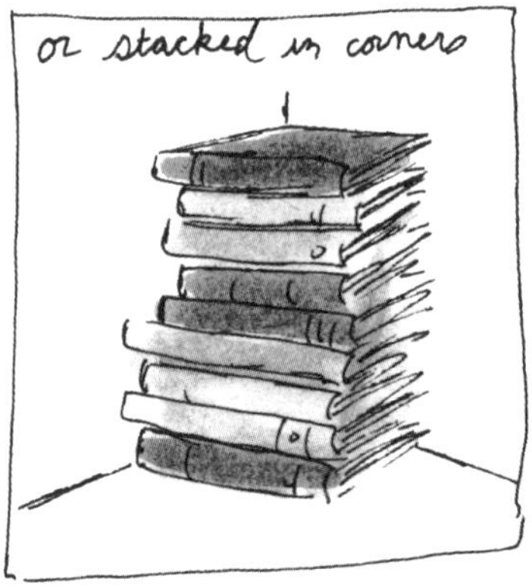
or stacked in corners

Sometimes I think I surround myself with these things so I'll feel less alone

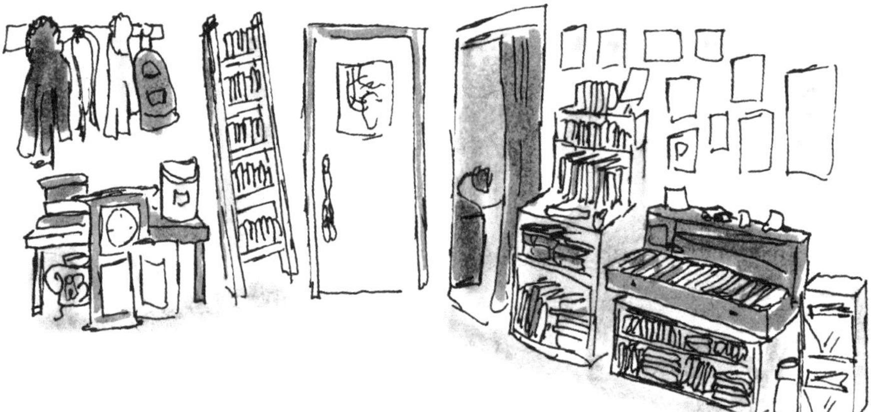

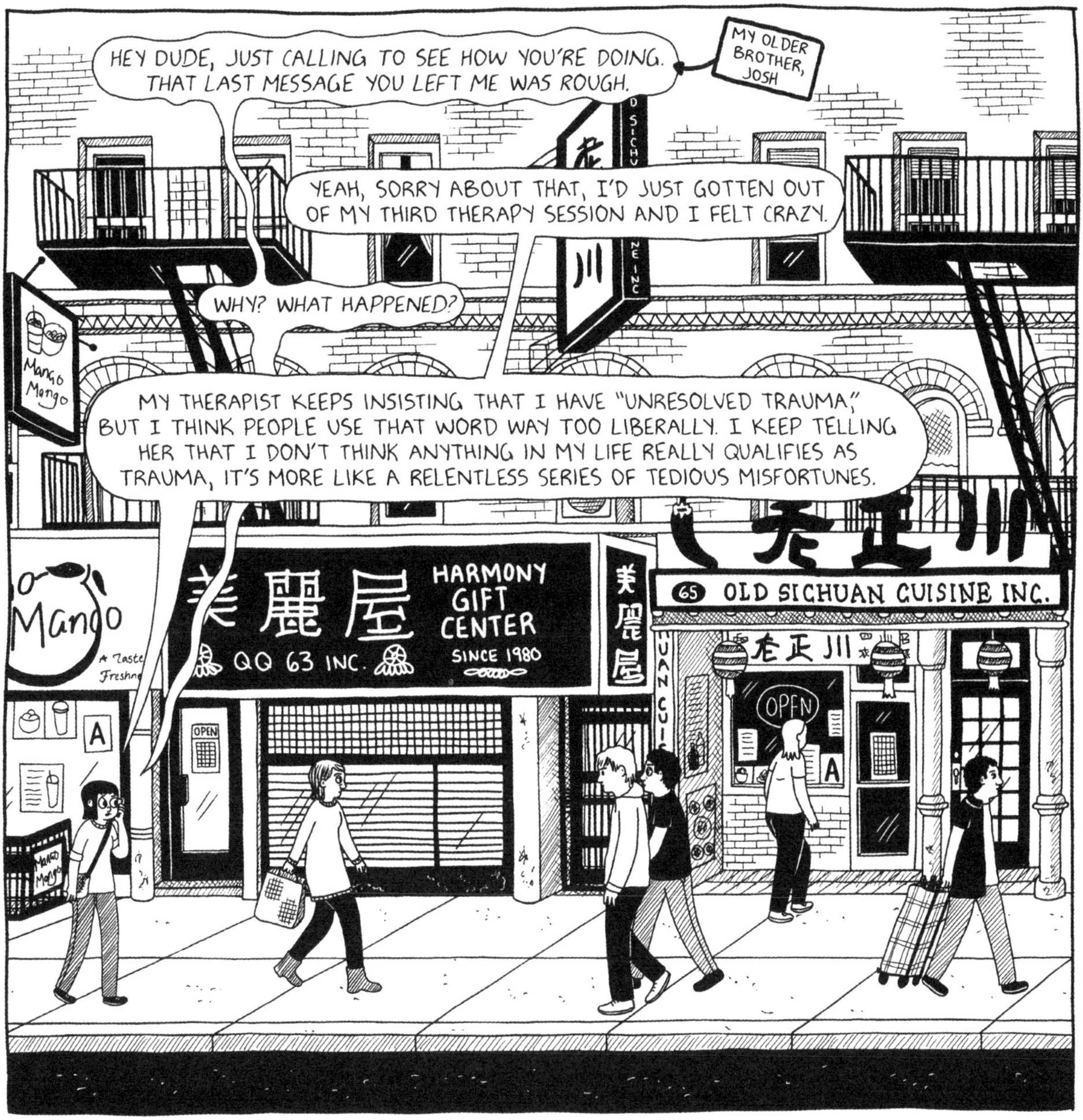
HEY DUDE, JUST CALLING TO SEE HOW YOU'RE DOING. THAT LAST MESSAGE YOU LEFT ME WAS ROUGH.
MY OLDER BROTHER, JOSH
YEAH, SORRY ABOUT THAT, I'D JUST GOTTEN OUT OF MY THIRD THERAPY SESSION AND I FELT CRAZY.
WHY? WHAT HAPPENED?
MY THERAPIST KEEPS INSISTING THAT I HAVE "UNRESOLVED TRAUMA," BUT I THINK PEOPLE USE THAT WORD WAY TOO LIBERALLY. I KEEP TELLING HER THAT I DON'T THINK ANYTHING IN MY LIFE REALLY QUALIFIES AS TRAUMA, IT'S MORE LIKE A RELENTLESS SERIES OF TEDIOUS MISFORTUNES.
Mango Mango
美麗屋
HARMONY GIFT CENTER
QQ 63 INC.
SINCE 1980
65 OLD SICHUAN CUISINE INC.
OPEN

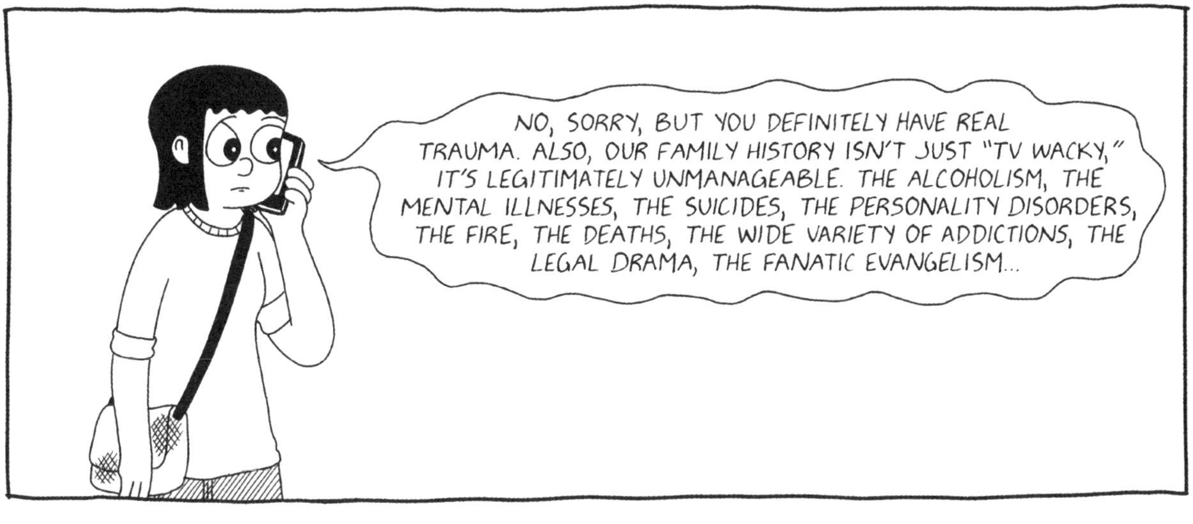
NO, SORRY, BUT YOU DEFINITELY HAVE REAL TRAUMA. ALSO, OUR FAMILY HISTORY ISN'T JUST "TV WACKY," IT'S LEGITIMATELY UNMANAGEABLE. THE ALCOHOLISM, THE MENTAL ILLNESSES, THE SUICIDES, THE PERSONALITY DISORDERS, THE FIRE, THE DEATHS, THE WIDE VARIETY OF ADDICTIONS, THE LEGAL DRAMA, THE FANATIC EVANGELISM...

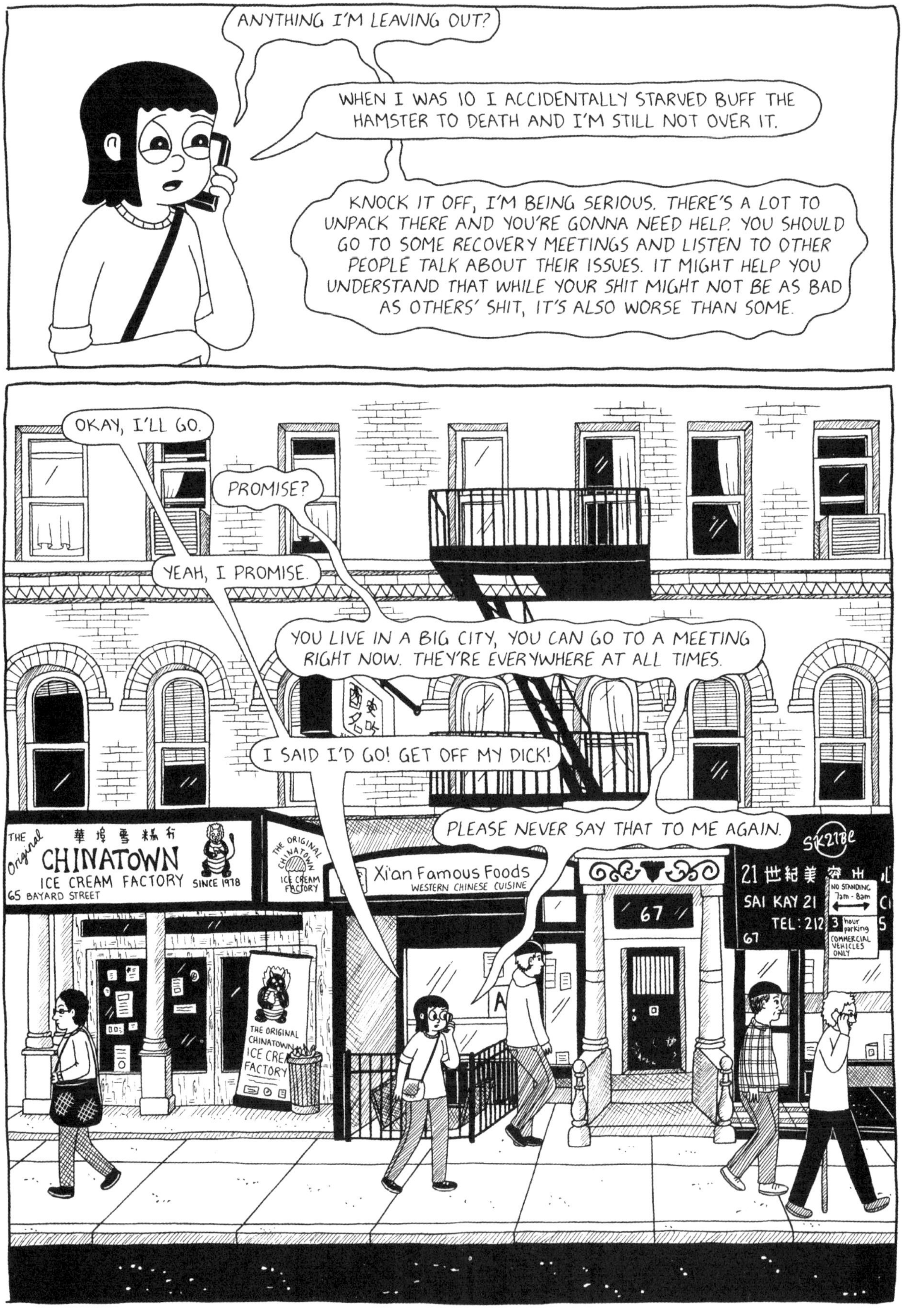
ANYTHING I'M LEAVING OUT?
WHEN I WAS 10 I ACCIDENTALLY STARVED BUFF THE HAMSTER TO DEATH AND I'M STILL NOT OVER IT.
KNOCK IT OFF, I'M BEING SERIOUS. THERE'S A LOT TO UNPACK THERE AND YOU'RE GONNA NEED HELP. YOU SHOULD GO TO SOME RECOVERY MEETINGS AND LISTEN TO OTHER PEOPLE TALK ABOUT THEIR ISSUES. IT MIGHT HELP YOU UNDERSTAND THAT WHILE YOUR SHIT MIGHT NOT BE AS BAD AS OTHERS' SHIT, IT'S ALSO WORSE THAN SOME.
OKAY, I'LL GO.
PROMISE?
YEAH, I PROMISE.
YOU LIVE IN A BIG CITY, YOU CAN GO TO A MEETING RIGHT NOW. THEY'RE EVERYWHERE AT ALL TIMES.
I SAID I'D GO! GET OFF MY DICK!
PLEASE NEVER SAY THAT TO ME AGAIN.
THE Original CHINATOWN ICE CREAM FACTORY
65 BAYARD STREET
SINCE 1978
THE ORIGINAL CHINATOWN ICE CREAM FACTORY
Xi'an Famous Foods
WESTERN CHINESE CUISINE
THE ORIGINAL CHINATOWN ICE CREAM FACTORY
67
SAI KAY 21
TEL: 212
67
NO STANDING 7am - 8am
3 hour parking
COMMERCIAL VEHICLES ONLY

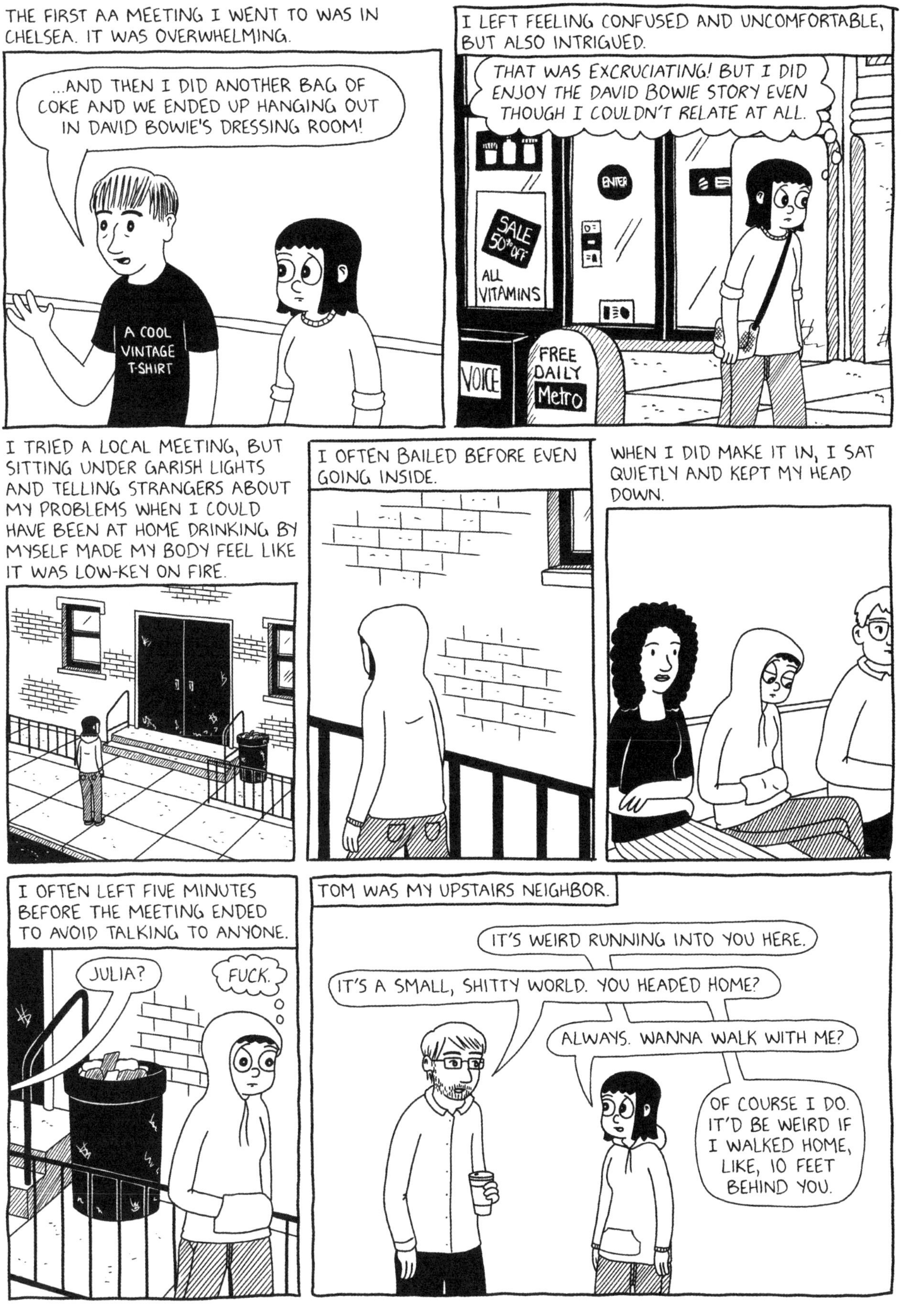
THE FIRST AA MEETING I WENT TO WAS IN CHELSEA. IT WAS OVERWHELMING.
...AND THEN I DID ANOTHER BAG OF COKE AND WE ENDED UP HANGING OUT IN DAVID BOWIE'S DRESSING ROOM!
A COOL VINTAGE T-SHIRT
I LEFT FEELING CONFUSED AND UNCOMFORTABLE, BUT ALSO INTRIGUED.
THAT WAS EXCRUCIATING! BUT I DID ENJOY THE DAVID BOWIE STORY EVEN THOUGH I COULDN'T RELATE AT ALL.
ENTER
SALE 50% OFF
ALL VITAMINS
FREE DAILY Metro
VOICE
I TRIED A LOCAL MEETING, BUT SITTING UNDER GARISH LIGHTS AND TELLING STRANGERS ABOUT MY PROBLEMS WHEN I COULD HAVE BEEN AT HOME DRINKING BY MYSELF MADE MY BODY FEEL LIKE IT WAS LOW-KEY ON FIRE.
I OFTEN BAILED BEFORE EVEN GOING INSIDE.
WHEN I DID MAKE IT IN, I SAT QUIETLY AND KEPT MY HEAD DOWN.
I OFTEN LEFT FIVE MINUTES BEFORE THE MEETING ENDED TO AVOID TALKING TO ANYONE.
JULIA?
FUCK.
TOM WAS MY UPSTAIRS NEIGHBOR.
IT'S WEIRD RUNNING INTO YOU HERE.
IT'S A SMALL, SHITTY WORLD. YOU HEADED HOME?
ALWAYS. WANNA WALK WITH ME?
OF COURSE I DO. IT'D BE WEIRD IF I WALKED HOME, LIKE, 10 FEET BEHIND YOU.

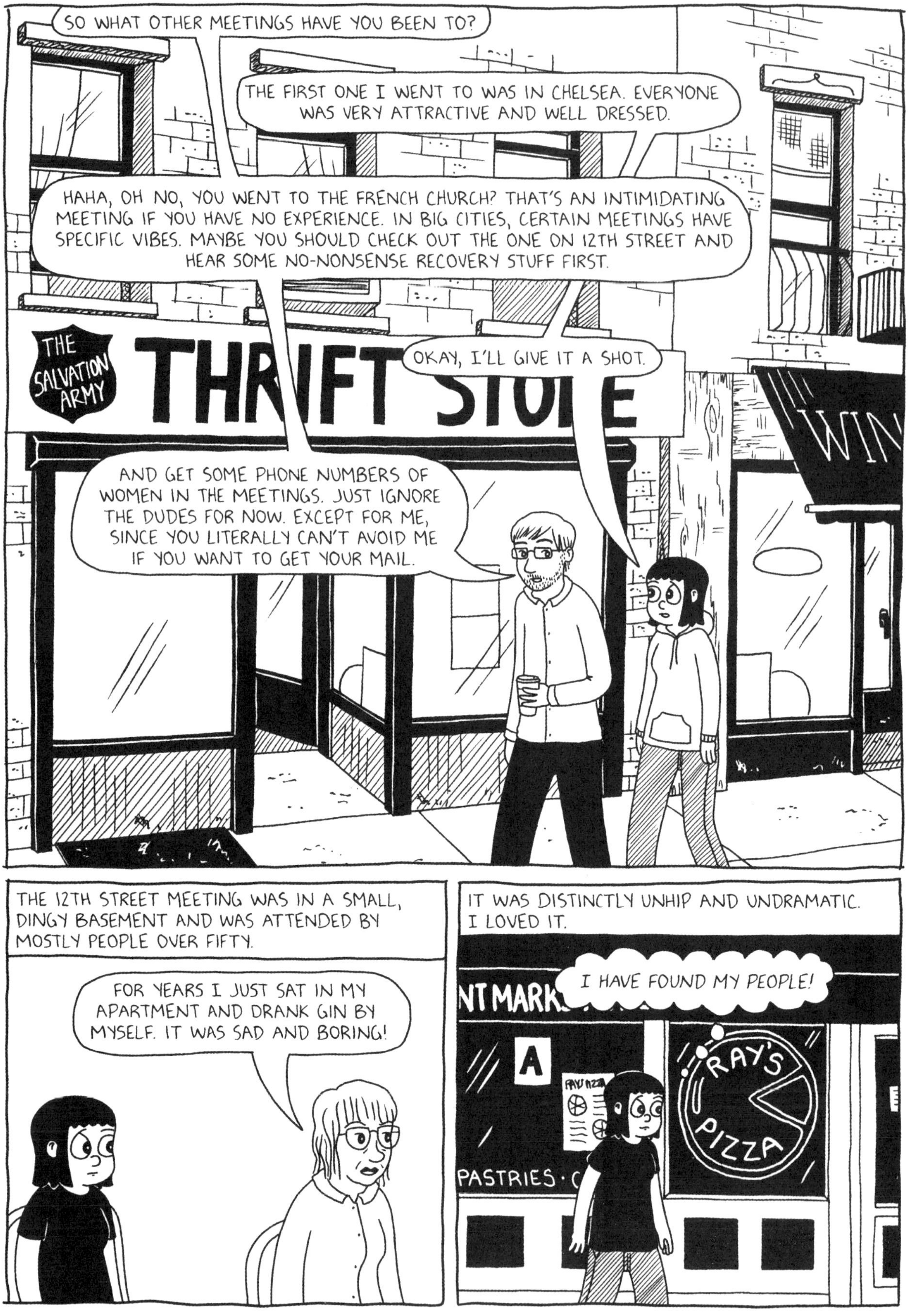
SO WHAT OTHER MEETINGS HAVE YOU BEEN TO?
THE FIRST ONE I WENT TO WAS IN CHELSEA. EVERYONE WAS VERY ATTRACTIVE AND WELL DRESSED.
HAHA, OH NO, YOU WENT TO THE FRENCH CHURCH? THAT'S AN INTIMIDATING MEETING IF YOU HAVE NO EXPERIENCE. IN BIG CITIES, CERTAIN MEETINGS HAVE SPECIFIC VIBES. MAYBE YOU SHOULD CHECK OUT THE ONE ON 12TH STREET AND HEAR SOME NO-NONSENSE RECOVERY STUFF FIRST.
THE SALVATION ARMY
THRIFT STORE
OKAY, I'LL GIVE IT A SHOT.
AND GET SOME PHONE NUMBERS OF WOMEN IN THE MEETINGS. JUST IGNORE THE DUDES FOR NOW. EXCEPT FOR ME, SINCE YOU LITERALLY CAN'T AVOID ME IF YOU WANT TO GET YOUR MAIL.
THE 12TH STREET MEETING WAS IN A SMALL, DINGY BASEMENT AND WAS ATTENDED BY MOSTLY PEOPLE OVER FIFTY.
FOR YEARS I JUST SAT IN MY APARTMENT AND DRANK GIN BY MYSELF. IT WAS SAD AND BORING!
IT WAS DISTINCTLY UNHIP AND UNDRAMATIC. I LOVED IT.
I HAVE FOUND MY PEOPLE!
RAY'S PIZZA
PASTRIES

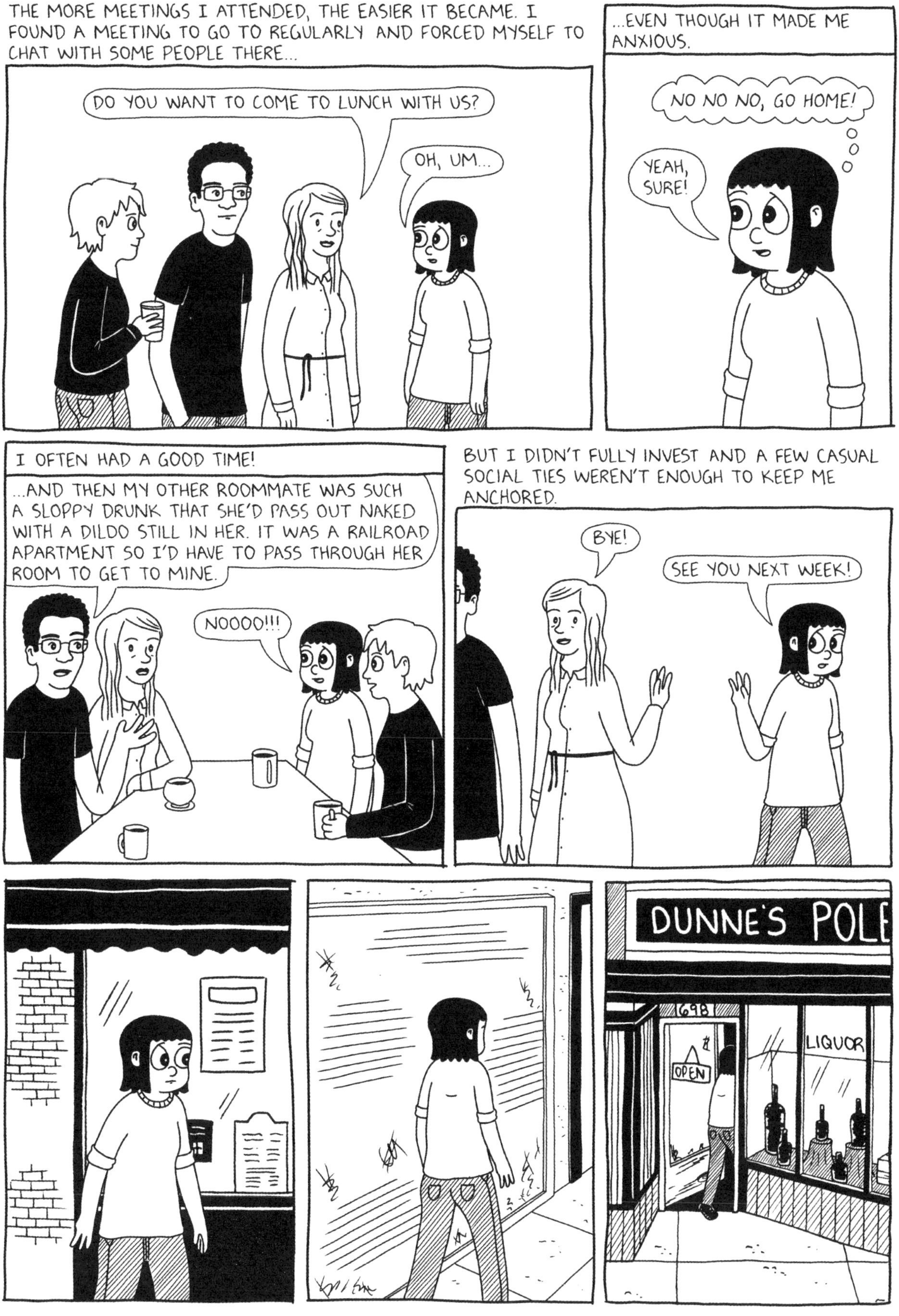
THE MORE MEETINGS I ATTENDED, THE EASIER IT BECAME. I FOUND A MEETING TO GO TO REGULARLY AND FORCED MYSELF TO CHAT WITH SOME PEOPLE THERE...
DO YOU WANT TO COME TO LUNCH WITH US?
OH, UM...
...EVEN THOUGH IT MADE ME ANXIOUS.
NO NO NO, GO HOME!
YEAH, SURE!
I OFTEN HAD A GOOD TIME!
...AND THEN MY OTHER ROOMMATE WAS SUCH A SLOPPY DRUNK THAT SHE'D PASS OUT NAKED WITH A DILDO STILL IN HER. IT WAS A RAILROAD APARTMENT SO I'D HAVE TO PASS THROUGH HER ROOM TO GET TO MINE.
NOOOO!!!
BUT I DIDN'T FULLY INVEST AND A FEW CASUAL SOCIAL TIES WEREN'T ENOUGH TO KEEP ME ANCHORED.
BYE!
SEE YOU NEXT WEEK!
DUNNE'S POLE
698
OPEN
LIQUOR

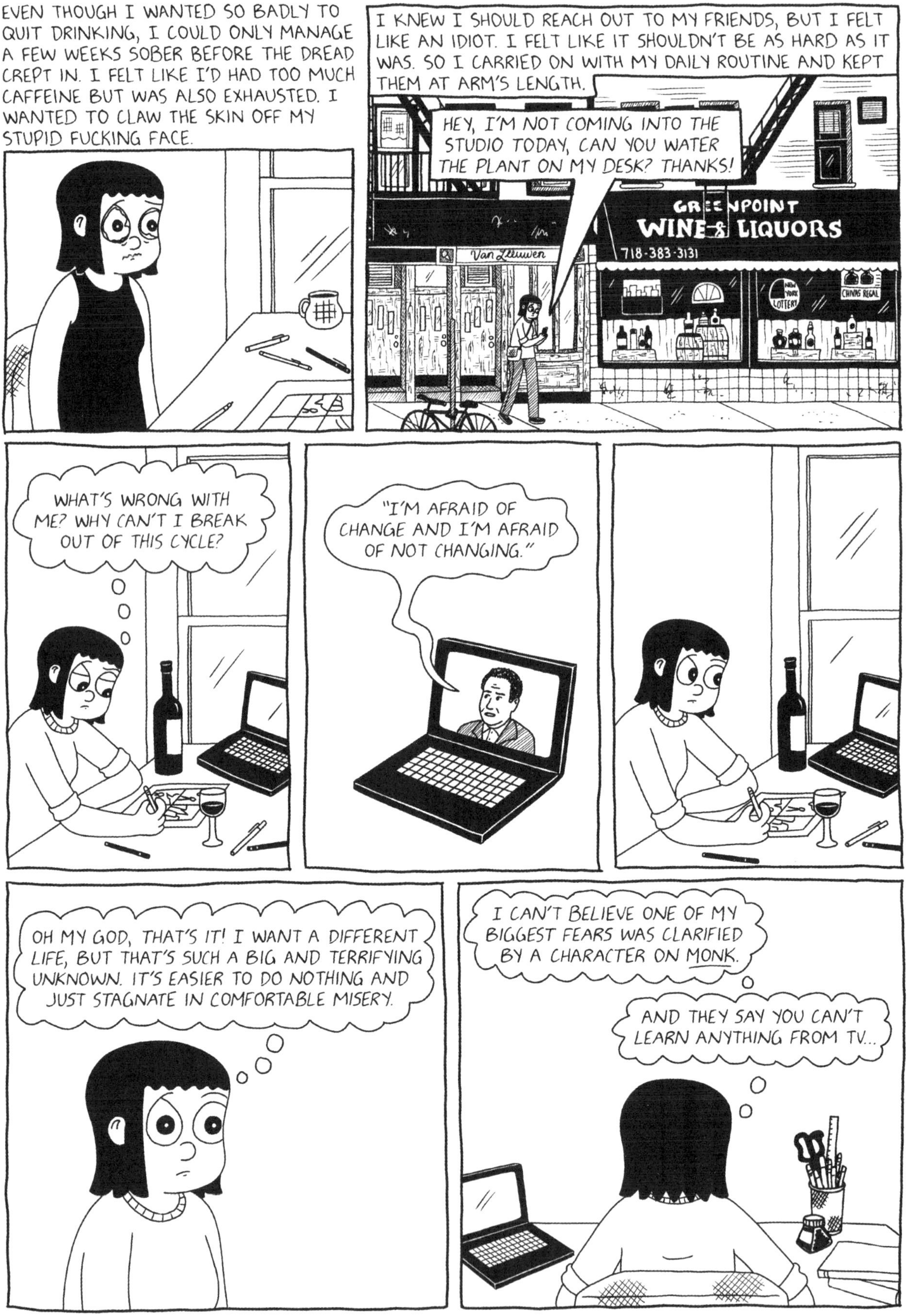
EVEN THOUGH I WANTED SO BADLY TO QUIT DRINKING, I COULD ONLY MANAGE A FEW WEEKS SOBER BEFORE THE DREAD CREPT IN. I FELT LIKE I'D HAD TOO MUCH CAFFEINE BUT WAS ALSO EXHAUSTED. I WANTED TO CLAW THE SKIN OFF MY STUPID FUCKING FACE.
I KNEW I SHOULD REACH OUT TO MY FRIENDS, BUT I FELT LIKE AN IDIOT. I FELT LIKE IT SHOULDN'T BE AS HARD AS IT WAS. SO I CARRIED ON WITH MY DAILY ROUTINE AND KEPT THEM AT ARM'S LENGTH.
HEY, I'M NOT COMING INTO THE STUDIO TODAY, CAN YOU WATER THE PLANT ON MY DESK? THANKS!
GREENPOINT
WINE & LIQUORS
718-383-3131
Van Leeuwen
NEW YORK LOTTERY
CHIVAS REGAL
WHAT'S WRONG WITH ME? WHY CAN'T I BREAK OUT OF THIS CYCLE?
"I'M AFRAID OF CHANGE AND I'M AFRAID OF NOT CHANGING."
OH MY GOD, THAT'S IT! I WANT A DIFFERENT LIFE, BUT THAT'S SUCH A BIG AND TERRIFYING UNKNOWN. IT'S EASIER TO DO NOTHING AND JUST STAGNATE IN COMFORTABLE MISERY.
I CAN'T BELIEVE ONE OF MY BIGGEST FEARS WAS CLARIFIED BY A CHARACTER ON MONK.
AND THEY SAY YOU CAN'T LEARN ANYTHING FROM TV...

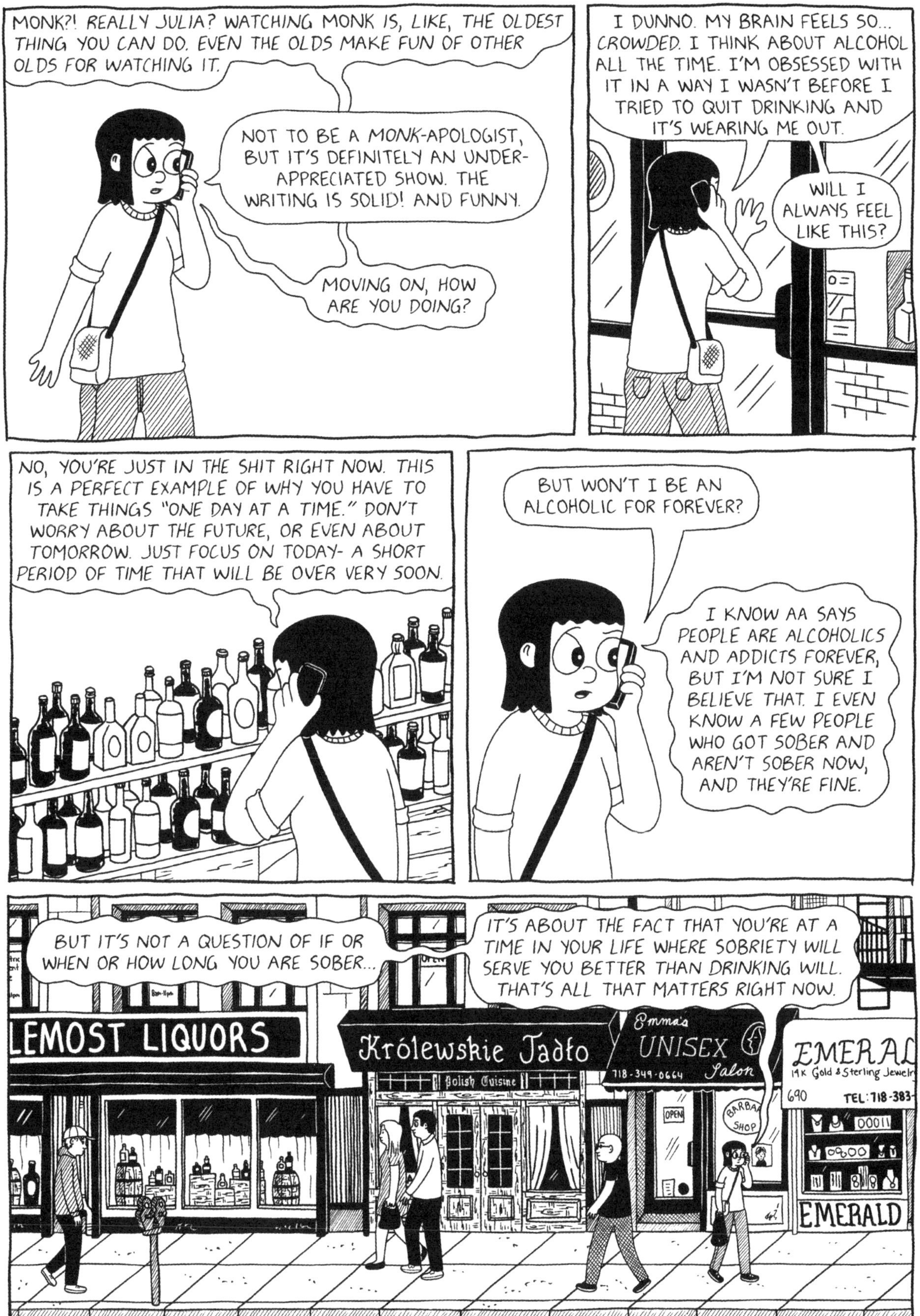
MONK?! REALLY JULIA? WATCHING MONK IS, LIKE, THE OLDEST THING YOU CAN DO. EVEN THE OLDS MAKE FUN OF OTHER OLDS FOR WATCHING IT.
NOT TO BE A MONK-APOLOGIST, BUT IT'S DEFINITELY AN UNDER-APPRECIATED SHOW. THE WRITING IS SOLID! AND FUNNY.
MOVING ON, HOW ARE YOU DOING?
I DUNNO. MY BRAIN FEELS SO... CROWDED. I THINK ABOUT ALCOHOL ALL THE TIME. I'M OBSESSED WITH IT IN A WAY I WASN'T BEFORE I TRIED TO QUIT DRINKING AND IT'S WEARING ME OUT.
WILL I ALWAYS FEEL LIKE THIS?
NO, YOU'RE JUST IN THE SHIT RIGHT NOW. THIS IS A PERFECT EXAMPLE OF WHY YOU HAVE TO TAKE THINGS "ONE DAY AT A TIME." DON'T WORRY ABOUT THE FUTURE, OR EVEN ABOUT TOMORROW. JUST FOCUS ON TODAY- A SHORT PERIOD OF TIME THAT WILL BE OVER VERY SOON.
BUT WON'T I BE AN ALCOHOLIC FOR FOREVER?
I KNOW AA SAYS PEOPLE ARE ALCOHOLICS AND ADDICTS FOREVER, BUT I'M NOT SURE I BELIEVE THAT. I EVEN KNOW A FEW PEOPLE WHO GOT SOBER AND AREN'T SOBER NOW, AND THEY'RE FINE.
BUT IT'S NOT A QUESTION OF IF OR WHEN OR HOW LONG YOU ARE SOBER...
IT'S ABOUT THE FACT THAT YOU'RE AT A TIME IN YOUR LIFE WHERE SOBRIETY WILL SERVE YOU BETTER THAN DRINKING WILL. THAT'S ALL THAT MATTERS RIGHT NOW.
LEMOST LIQUORS
Królewskie Jadło
Polish Cuisine
Emma's UNISEX Salon
718-349-0664
EMERAL
14K Gold & Sterling Jewelr
690
TEL: 718-383-
OPEN
BARBAR SHOP
EMERALD

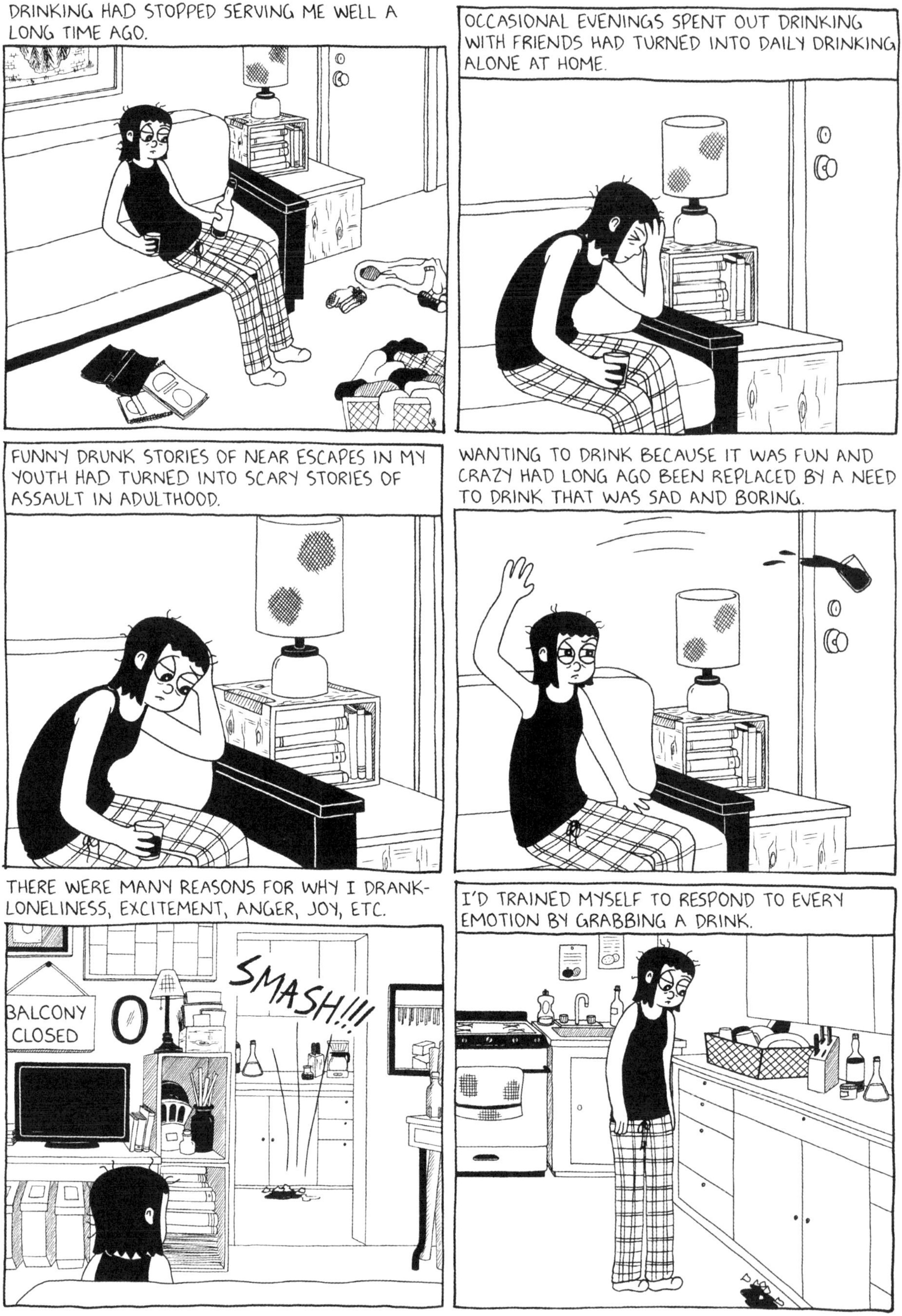
DRINKING HAD STOPPED SERVING ME WELL A LONG TIME AGO.
OCCASIONAL EVENINGS SPENT OUT DRINKING WITH FRIENDS HAD TURNED INTO DAILY DRINKING ALONE AT HOME.
FUNNY DRUNK STORIES OF NEAR ESCAPES IN MY YOUTH HAD TURNED INTO SCARY STORIES OF ASSAULT IN ADULTHOOD.
WANTING TO DRINK BECAUSE IT WAS FUN AND CRAZY HAD LONG AGO BEEN REPLACED BY A NEED TO DRINK THAT WAS SAD AND BORING.
THERE WERE MANY REASONS FOR WHY I DRANK- LONELINESS, EXCITEMENT, ANGER, JOY, ETC.
BALCONY CLOSED
SMASH!!!!
I'D TRAINED MYSELF TO RESPOND TO EVERY EMOTION BY GRABBING A DRINK.

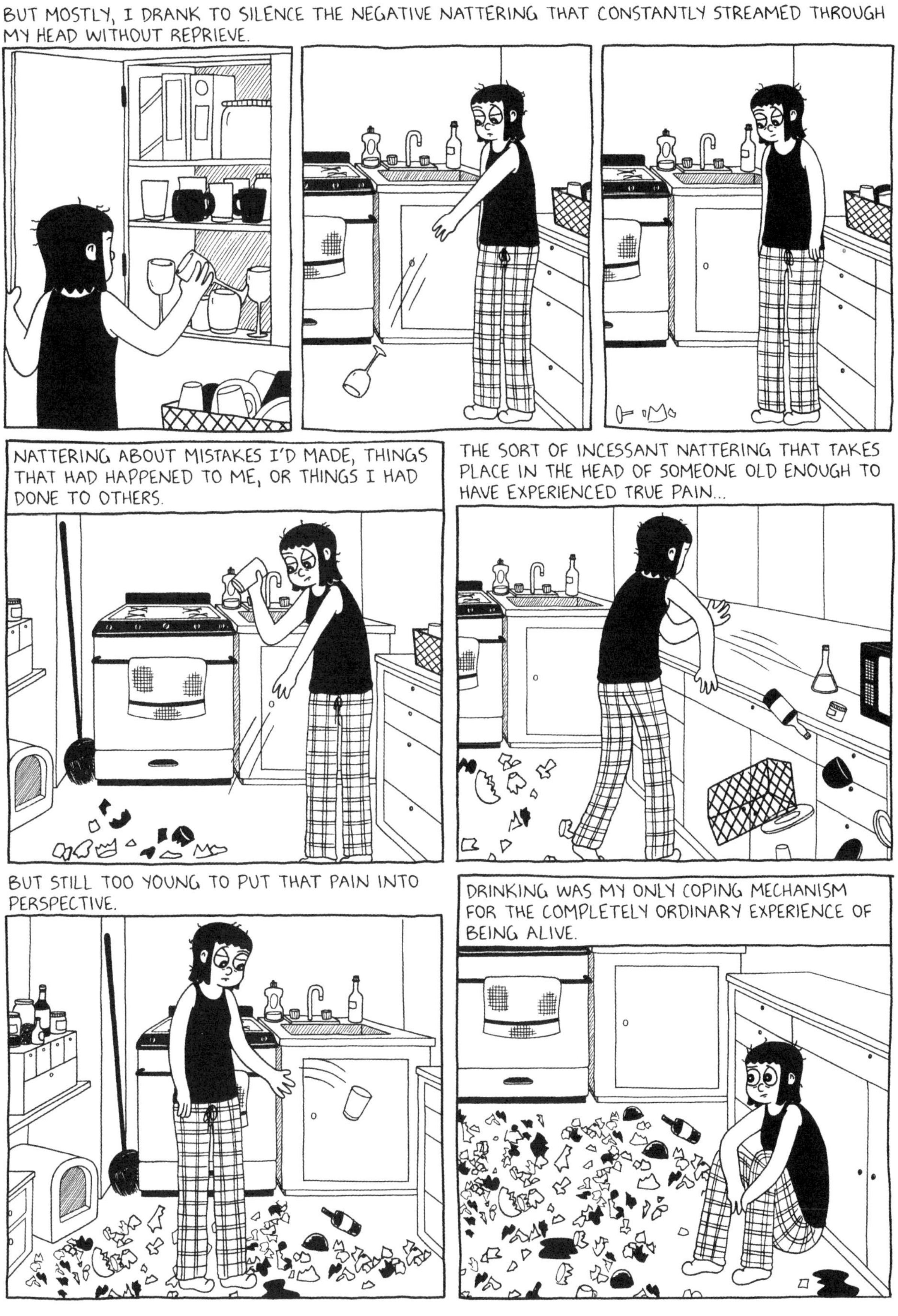
BUT MOSTLY, I DRANK TO SILENCE THE NEGATIVE NATTERING THAT CONSTANTLY STREAMED THROUGH MY HEAD WITHOUT REPRIEVE.
NATTERING ABOUT MISTAKES I'D MADE, THINGS THAT HAD HAPPENED TO ME, OR THINGS I HAD DONE TO OTHERS.
THE SORT OF INCESSANT NATTERING THAT TAKES PLACE IN THE HEAD OF SOMEONE OLD ENOUGH TO HAVE EXPERIENCED TRUE PAIN...
BUT STILL TOO YOUNG TO PUT THAT PAIN INTO PERSPECTIVE.
DRINKING WAS MY ONLY COPING MECHANISM FOR THE COMPLETELY ORDINARY EXPERIENCE OF BEING ALIVE.

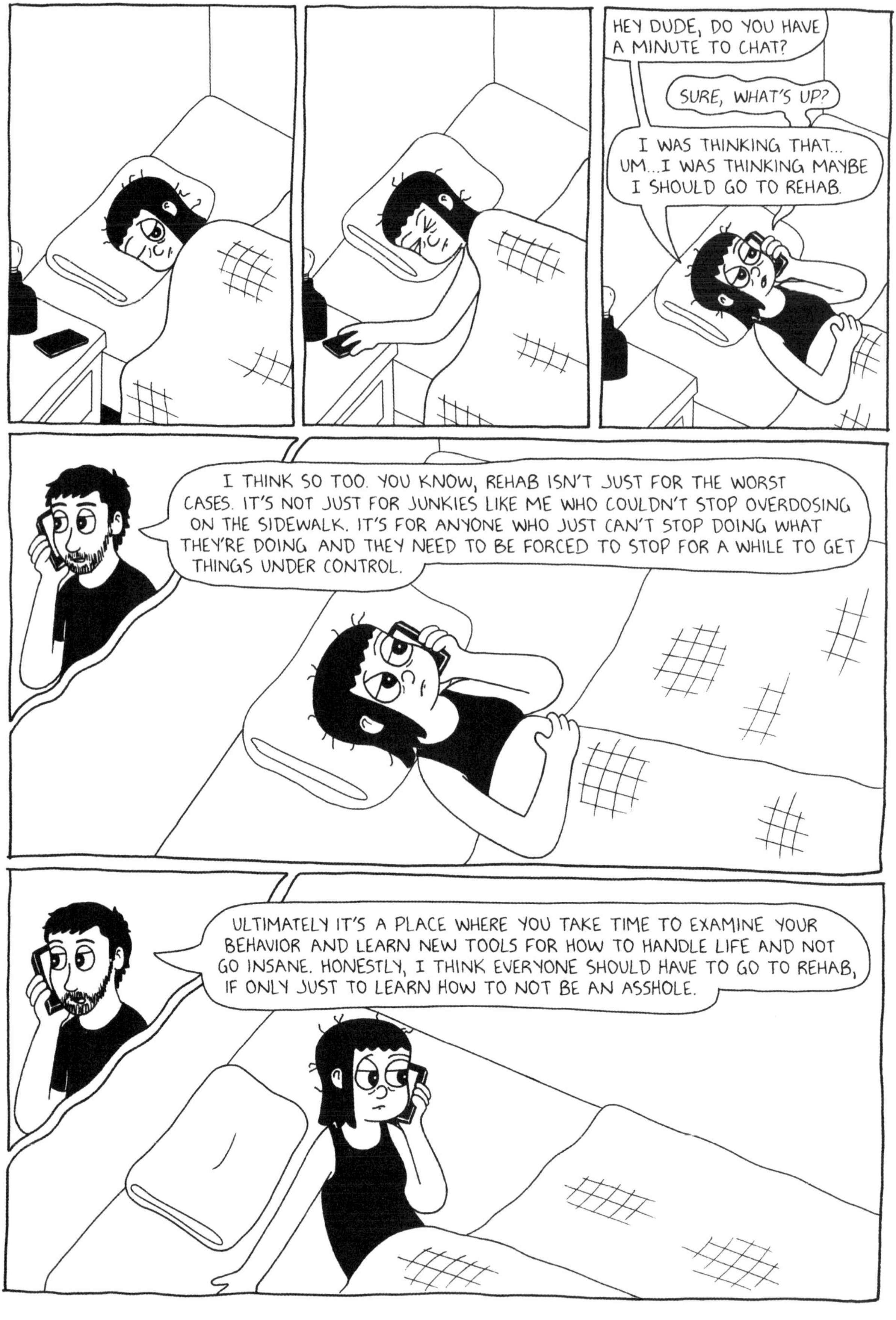
HEY DUDE, DO YOU HAVE A MINUTE TO CHAT?
SURE, WHAT'S UP?
I WAS THINKING THAT... UM...I WAS THINKING MAYBE I SHOULD GO TO REHAB.
I THINK SO TOO. YOU KNOW, REHAB ISN'T JUST FOR THE WORST CASES. IT'S NOT JUST FOR JUNKIES LIKE ME WHO COULDN'T STOP OVERDOSING ON THE SIDEWALK. IT'S FOR ANYONE WHO JUST CAN'T STOP DOING WHAT THEY'RE DOING AND THEY NEED TO BE FORCED TO STOP FOR A WHILE TO GET THINGS UNDER CONTROL.
ULTIMATELY IT'S A PLACE WHERE YOU TAKE TIME TO EXAMINE YOUR BEHAVIOR AND LEARN NEW TOOLS FOR HOW TO HANDLE LIFE AND NOT GO INSANE. HONESTLY, I THINK EVERYONE SHOULD HAVE TO GO TO REHAB, IF ONLY JUST TO LEARN HOW TO NOT BE AN ASSHOLE.

I ASKED AROUND AND FOUND A SMALL REHAB FACILITY IN CONNECTICUT WITH A 21-DAY PROGRAM I COULD (BARELY) AFFORD. I WAS TERRIFIED OF LEAVING, TERRIFIED OF STAYING, AND TERRIFIED THAT I HAD SPENT ALL MY MONEY ON SOMETHING SO UNCERTAIN. I FELT KIND OF RIDICULOUS SINCE I WASN'T THE SPECTACULAR MESS I ASSUMED MOST PEOPLE WERE BEFORE COMMITTING TO SOMETHING AS EXPENSIVE AS REHAB. I COULDN'T SHAKE THE IDEA THAT I SHOULD BE DRAGGED THERE KICKING AND SCREAMING, STRAIGHT FROM THE HOSPITAL OR JAIL, SINCE THAT'S WHAT ALWAYS HAPPENED IN BOOKS AND MOVIES. TO CALMLY DRIVE THERE WITH A FRIEND CLASHED WITH ALL THE REHAB STEREOTYPES I KNEW. BUT I ALSO KNEW I HAD TO DO SOMETHING, BECAUSE WHAT I WAS DOING WASN'T WORKING.

THE DAY BEFORE I LEFT WAS UNEVENTFUL. I TURNED OFF MY VOICE MAIL AND TURNED ON EMAIL AUTO-REPLY. I DROPPED OFF THE CAT AT TOM'S. I SHOPPED, I PACKED, I EVEN DID THE LAUNDRY.

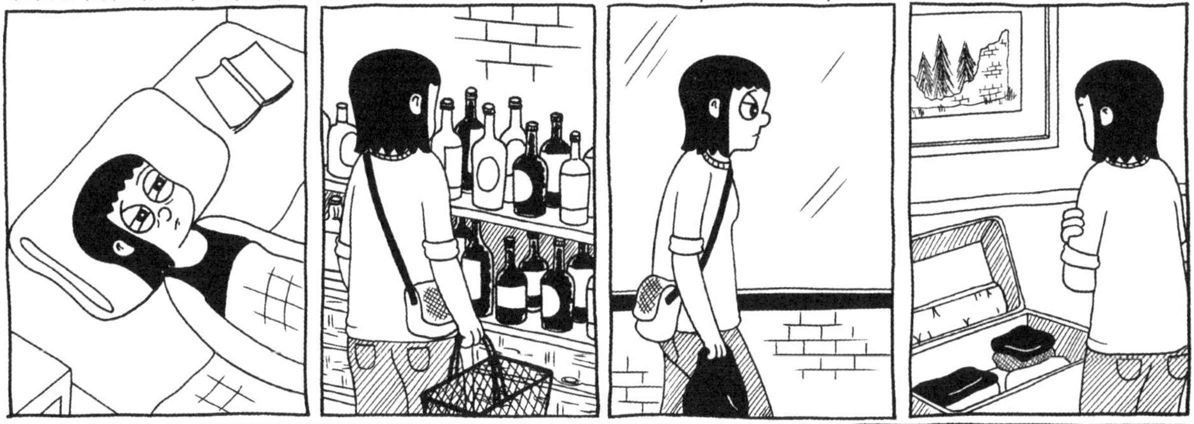

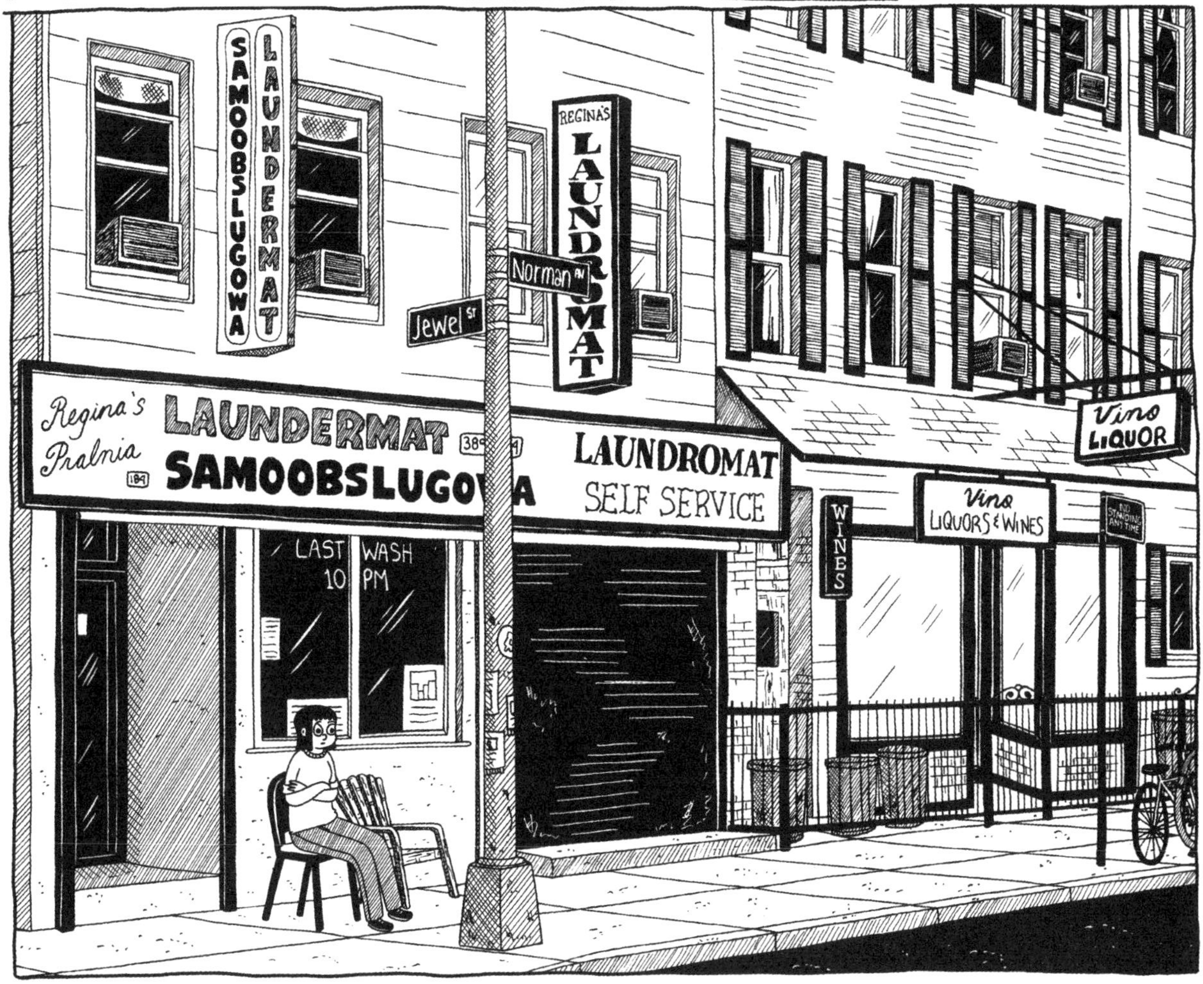
SAMOOBSLUGOWA
LAUNDERMAT
REGINA'S LAUNDROMAT
Norman AV
Jewel ST
Regina's Pralnia
LAUNDERMAT
LAUNDROMAT
SELF SERVICE
LAST WASH 10 PM
WINES
Vino LIQUOR
Vino LIQUORS & WINES
NO STANDING ANY TIME

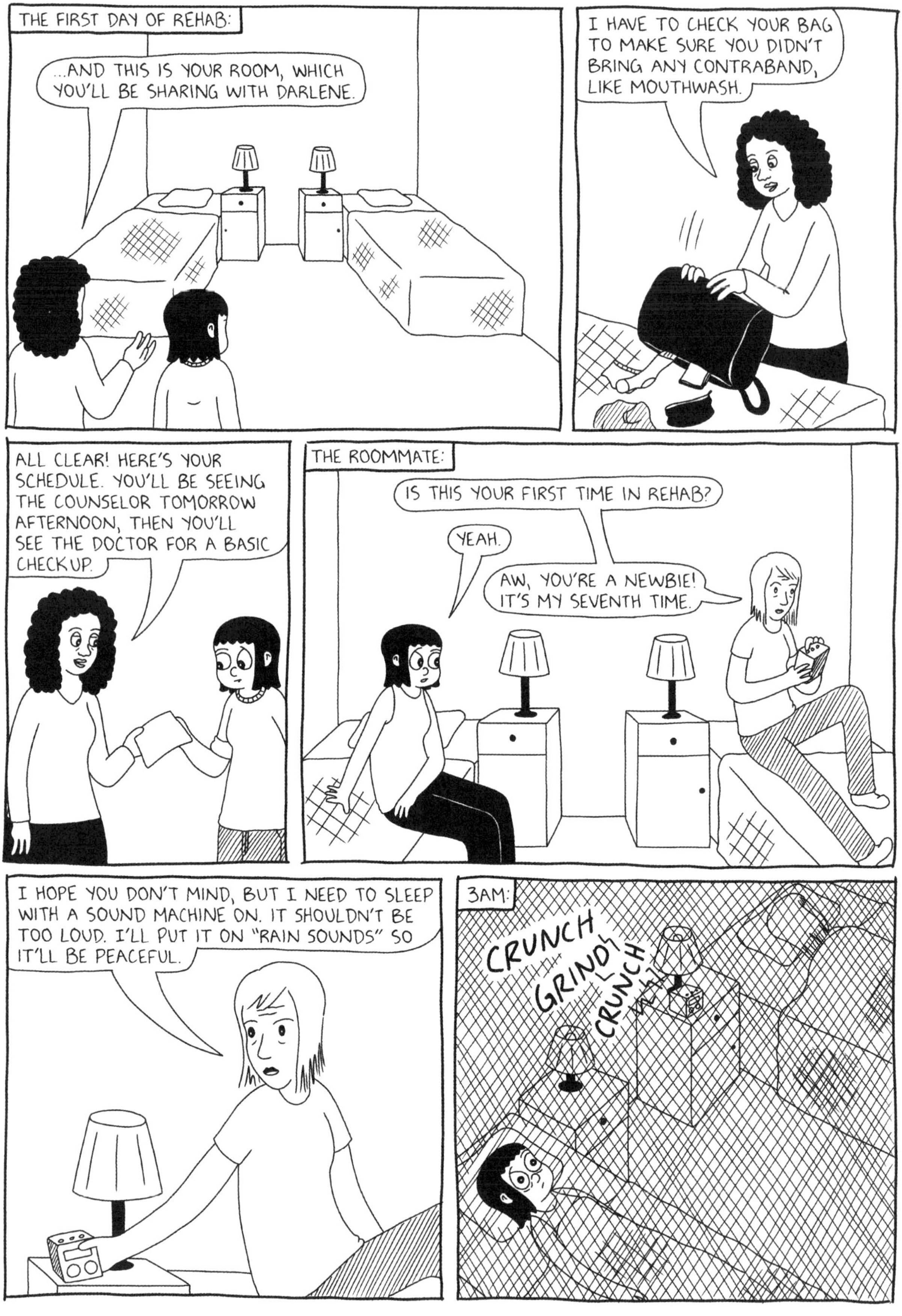
THE FIRST DAY OF REHAB:
...AND THIS IS YOUR ROOM, WHICH YOU'LL BE SHARING WITH DARLENE.
I HAVE TO CHECK YOUR BAG TO MAKE SURE YOU DIDN'T BRING ANY CONTRABAND, LIKE MOUTHWASH.
ALL CLEAR! HERE'S YOUR SCHEDULE. YOU'LL BE SEEING THE COUNSELOR TOMORROW AFTERNOON, THEN YOU'LL SEE THE DOCTOR FOR A BASIC CHECKUP.
THE ROOMMATE:
IS THIS YOUR FIRST TIME IN REHAB?
YEAH.
AW, YOU'RE A NEWBIE! IT'S MY SEVENTH TIME.
I HOPE YOU DON'T MIND, BUT I NEED TO SLEEP WITH A SOUND MACHINE ON. IT SHOULDN'T BE TOO LOUD. I'LL PUT IT ON "RAIN SOUNDS" SO IT'LL BE PEACEFUL.
3AM:
CRUNCH
GRIND
CRUNCH

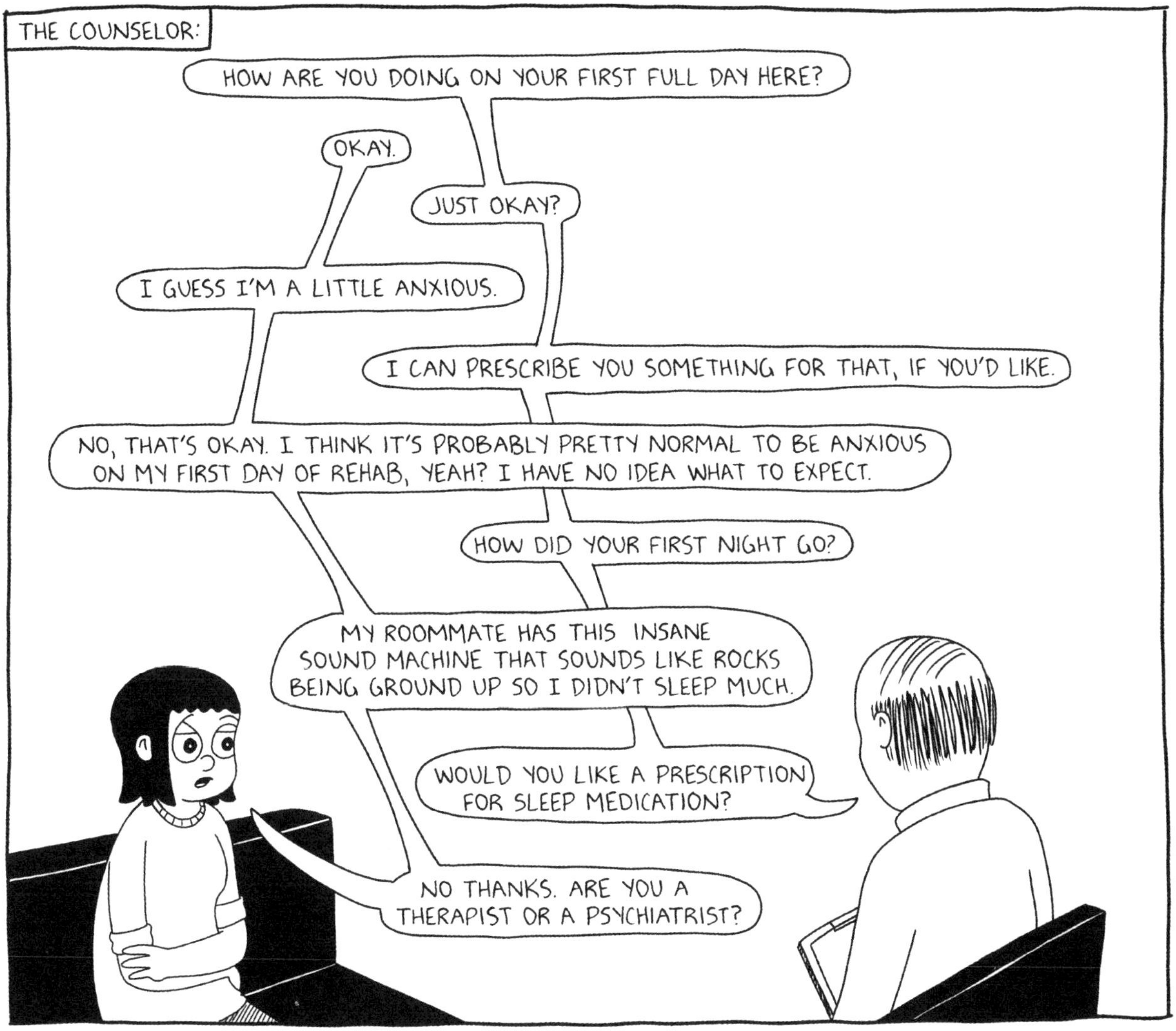
THE COUNSELOR:
HOW ARE YOU DOING ON YOUR FIRST FULL DAY HERE?
OKAY.
JUST OKAY?
I GUESS I'M A LITTLE ANXIOUS.
I CAN PRESCRIBE YOU SOMETHING FOR THAT, IF YOU'D LIKE.
NO, THAT'S OKAY. I THINK IT'S PROBABLY PRETTY NORMAL TO BE ANXIOUS ON MY FIRST DAY OF REHAB, YEAH? I HAVE NO IDEA WHAT TO EXPECT.
HOW DID YOUR FIRST NIGHT GO?
MY ROOMMATE HAS THIS INSANE SOUND MACHINE THAT SOUNDS LIKE ROCKS BEING GROUND UP SO I DIDN'T SLEEP MUCH.
WOULD YOU LIKE A PRESCRIPTION FOR SLEEP MEDICATION?
NO THANKS. ARE YOU A THERAPIST OR A PSYCHIATRIST?

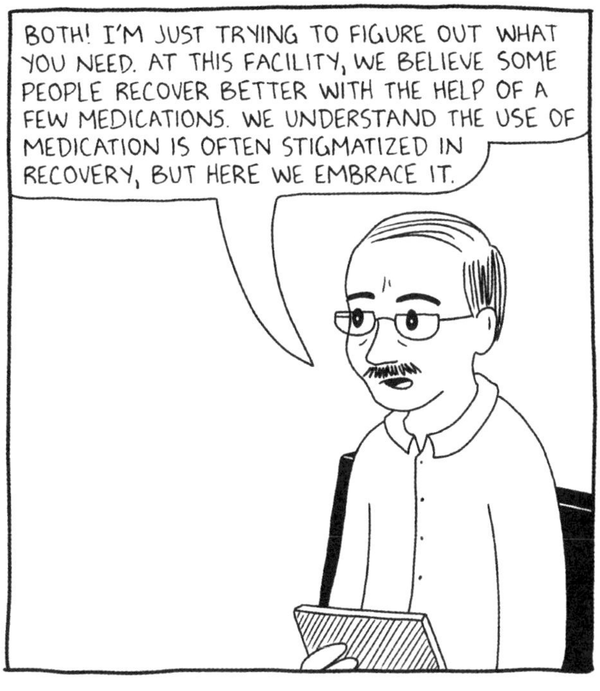
BOTH! I'M JUST TRYING TO FIGURE OUT WHAT YOU NEED. AT THIS FACILITY, WE BELIEVE SOME PEOPLE RECOVER BETTER WITH THE HELP OF A FEW MEDICATIONS. WE UNDERSTAND THE USE OF MEDICATION IS OFTEN STIGMATIZED IN RECOVERY, BUT HERE WE EMBRACE IT.

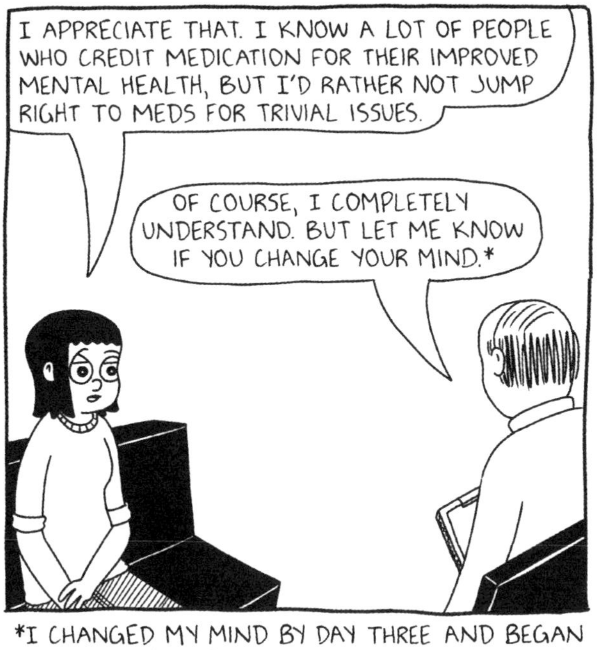
I APPRECIATE THAT. I KNOW A LOT OF PEOPLE WHO CREDIT MEDICATION FOR THEIR IMPROVED MENTAL HEALTH, BUT I'D RATHER NOT JUMP RIGHT TO MEDS FOR TRIVIAL ISSUES.
OF COURSE, I COMPLETELY UNDERSTAND. BUT LET ME KNOW IF YOU CHANGE YOUR MIND.*

*I CHANGED MY MIND BY DAY THREE AND BEGAN TAKING SLEEP MEDICATION. IT DEFINITELY HELPED.

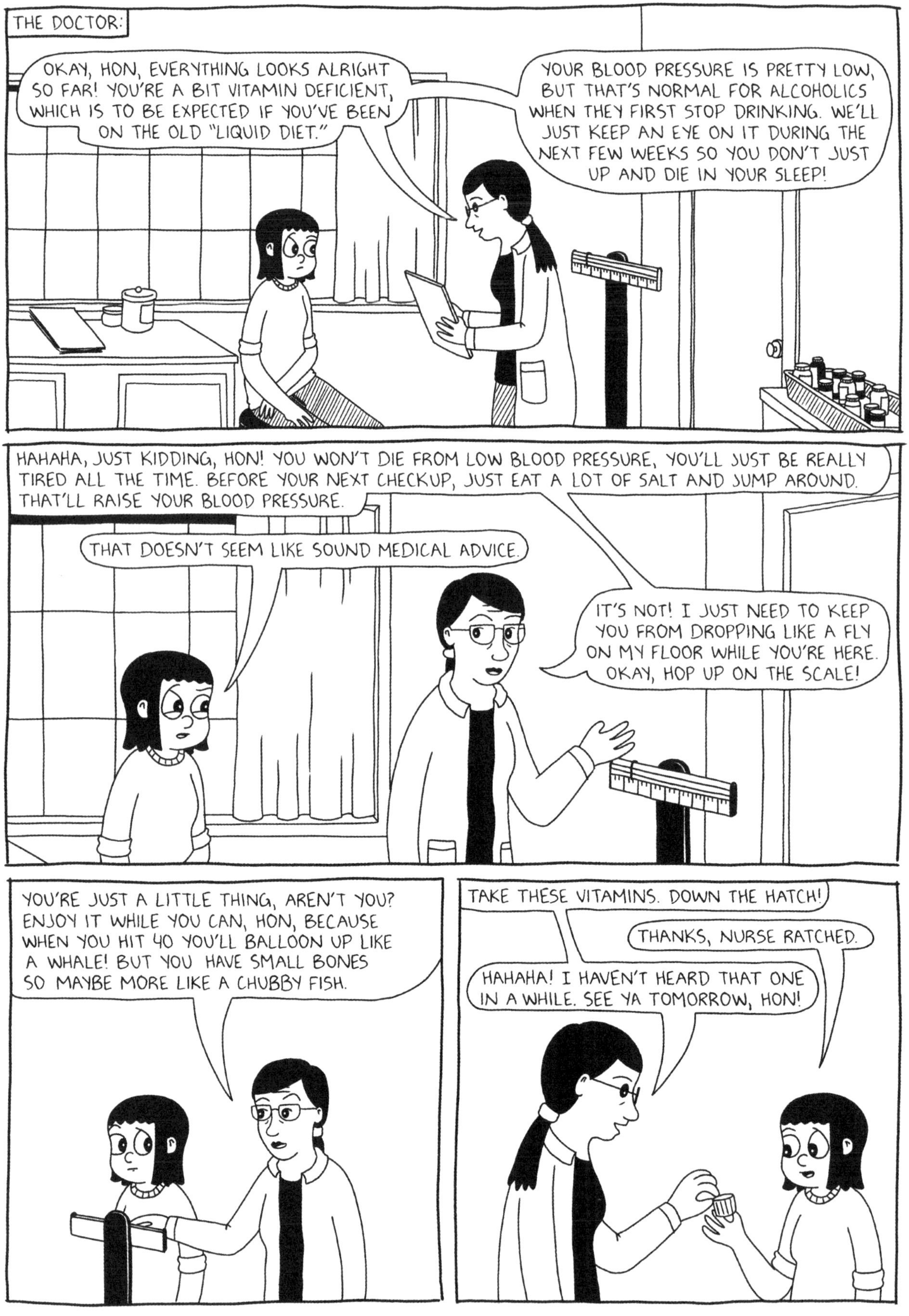
THE DOCTOR:
OKAY, HON, EVERYTHING LOOKS ALRIGHT SO FAR! YOU'RE A BIT VITAMIN DEFICIENT, WHICH IS TO BE EXPECTED IF YOU'VE BEEN ON THE OLD "LIQUID DIET."
YOUR BLOOD PRESSURE IS PRETTY LOW, BUT THAT'S NORMAL FOR ALCOHOLICS WHEN THEY FIRST STOP DRINKING. WE'LL JUST KEEP AN EYE ON IT DURING THE NEXT FEW WEEKS SO YOU DON'T JUST UP AND DIE IN YOUR SLEEP!
HAHAHA, JUST KIDDING, HON! YOU WON'T DIE FROM LOW BLOOD PRESSURE, YOU'LL JUST BE REALLY TIRED ALL THE TIME. BEFORE YOUR NEXT CHECKUP, JUST EAT A LOT OF SALT AND JUMP AROUND. THAT'LL RAISE YOUR BLOOD PRESSURE.
THAT DOESN'T SEEM LIKE SOUND MEDICAL ADVICE.
IT'S NOT! I JUST NEED TO KEEP YOU FROM DROPPING LIKE A FLY ON MY FLOOR WHILE YOU'RE HERE. OKAY, HOP UP ON THE SCALE!
YOU'RE JUST A LITTLE THING, AREN'T YOU? ENJOY IT WHILE YOU CAN, HON, BECAUSE WHEN YOU HIT 40 YOU'LL BALLOON UP LIKE A WHALE! BUT YOU HAVE SMALL BONES SO MAYBE MORE LIKE A CHUBBY FISH.
TAKE THESE VITAMINS. DOWN THE HATCH!
THANKS, NURSE RATCHED.
HAHAHA! I HAVEN'T HEARD THAT ONE IN A WHILE. SEE YA TOMORROW, HON!

I WAS GIVEN A NOTEBOOK OF WORKSHEETS TO DO DURING "FREE TIME." THEY WERE DESIGNED TO HELP EXAMINE ADDICTION HISTORY AND SELF-DESTRUCTIVE BEHAVIORIAL PATTERNS.

THIS IS THE SHITTIEST HOMEWORK EVER.

NO ONE WILL KNOW IF I JUST DON'T DO IT, SO INSTEAD I'M GONNA WRITE NOTES TO MY FRIENDS, JUST LIKE IN GRADE SCHOOL!

Dear **PIZZA ISLAND**,

HELLO, LOVELY LADIES, I MISS YOU ALREADY SOMETHING TERRIBLE. ON THE DAY I ARRIVED HERE, IT RAINED AND A BUNCH OF PEOPLE HAD THE SHITS FROM SOME BAD BURGERS. ON THE SECOND DAY, I CRIED ON MY BED AND THEN TOOK A THREE-HOUR NAP, TWO THINGS I HAVEN'T DONE IN SUCCESSION SINCE I WAS A BABY, SO THAT WAS WEIRD.

GIMMIE MAH WHISKEY!

HERE'S A FUN FACT: PRETTY MUCH EVERYONE'S ON MEDS, SINCE WE'RE ALL OUT OF OUR MINDS, BUT THEY'RE INTENSELY REGULATED, SO WE HAVE TO WAIT TILL "MED TIME" AND THEN LINE UP OUTSIDE THE NURSE'S OFFICE TO TAKE THEM ONE BY ONE UNDER SUPERVISION.

THEY GIVE THEM TO YOU IN A LITTLE CUP LIKE SO→ 🗑 AND MAKE SURE YOU DON'T STASH THEM UNDER YOUR TONGUE.

GOOD JOB, MISS WERTZ

Sound Familiar? →

HEY CHIEF

MY BEST FRIEND SO FAR IS AN OLDER LADY NAMED MARY WHO IS PRETTY MUCH ME IN THE FUTURE. WE WALK AROUND THE PERIMETER AND TALK ABOUT SCRABBLE AND RED WINE. I HAVEN'T TAKEN A SHIT IN 3 DAYS.

XOXO

Julia

My Dearest Pizza Island,

HEY PALS! HERE ARE SOME RULES OF REHAB:

① DO NOT FRATERNIZE. IF YOU TALK TO THE MEN, THEY WILL GET BONERS AND THEN THEY'LL WANT TO DRINK AND EVERYONE WILL GET PREGNANT.

ITEMS OF SEXUALITY BANNED:

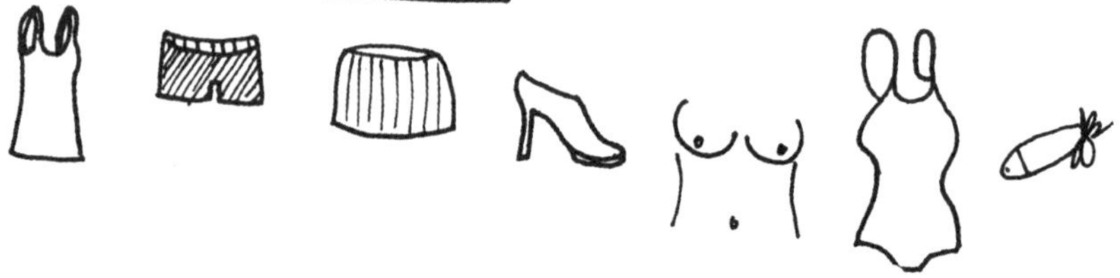

② DO NOT GO BEYOND THE COMPOUND MARKERS. IF YOU DO, YOU WILL DIE?

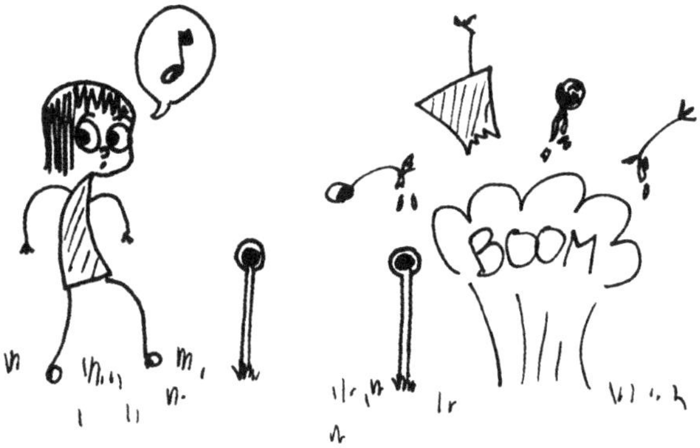
BOOM

③ TRY TO AVOID GRATUITOUS SWEARS.

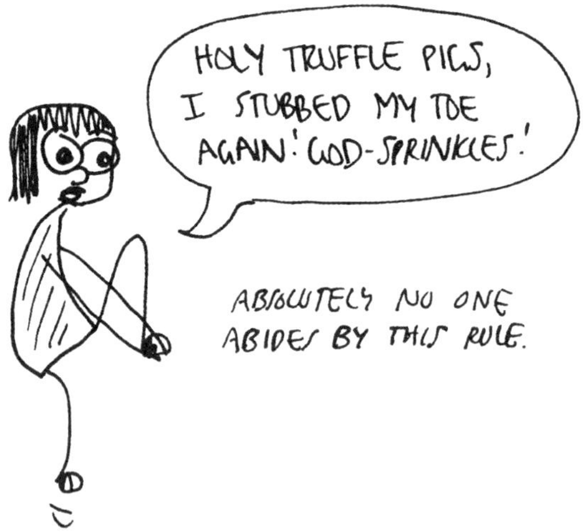
HOLY TRUFFLE PIGS, I STUBBED MY TOE AGAIN! GOD-SPRINKLES!

ABSOLUTELY NO ONE ABIDES BY THIS RULE.

4. DO NOT DRINK ANYTHING IN THE DORMS BUT THE PROVIDED WATER. IF YOU DO, YOU'LL GET WRITTEN UP. NO ONE IS REALLY SURE WHAT THAT MEANS.

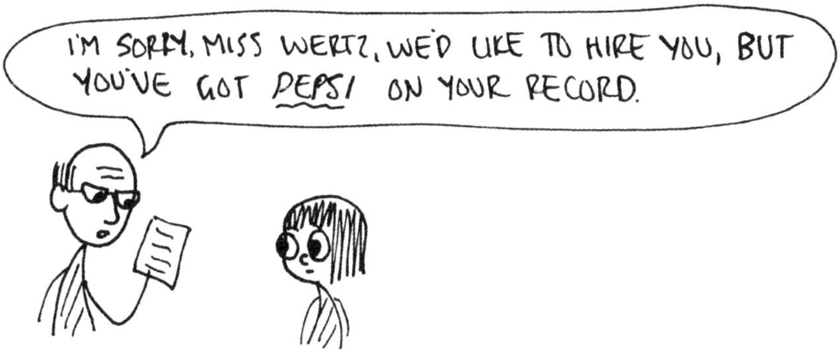
I'M SORRY, MISS WERTZ, WE'D LIKE TO HIRE YOU, BUT YOU'VE GOT PEPSI ON YOUR RECORD.

5. DURING CO-ED, "OFF COMPOUND" EXCURSIONS FOR OUTSIDE AA MEETINGS, TERRIBLE SING-ALONGS AND SEMI-SECRET FRATERNIZING IS WHOLEHEARTEDLY ENCOURAGED.

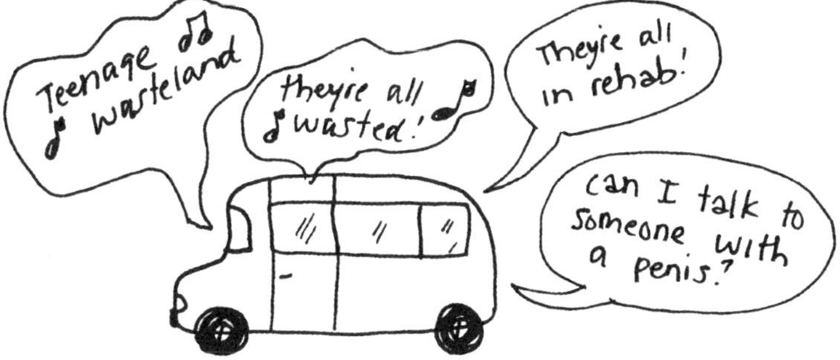
Teenage wasteland
theyre all wasted!
Theyre all in rehab!
can I talk to someone with a penis?

MORE TO COME! MISS Y'ALL! ♥ JULIA

PS - A NOTE ON "CHAPEL" — WHEN WE GATHER FOR 10 MINUTES OF "INSPIRATIONAL MUSIC". (CHEESY, BUT YOU KNOW I LOVE IT) THE OTHER DAY WE LISTENED TO BARBRA STREISAND SING A SONG FROM WEST SIDE STORY BECAUSE THE SPEAKER THAT DAY WAS AN AWESOME OLD MAN WHO USED TO DANCE ON BROADWAY. HE SAID, "ALL THE MEN [IN REHAB] NEED TO LIGHTEN UP," SO HE PLAYED THE "GAYEST SONG" HE COULD THINK OF.

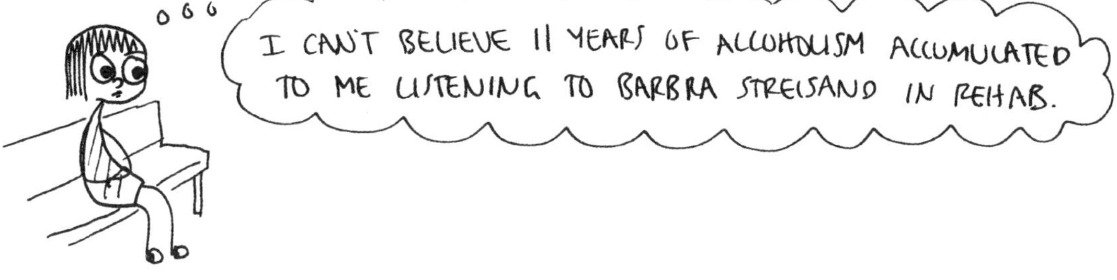
I CAN'T BELIEVE 11 YEARS OF ALCOHOLISM ACCUMULATED TO ME LISTENING TO BARBRA STREISAND IN REHAB.

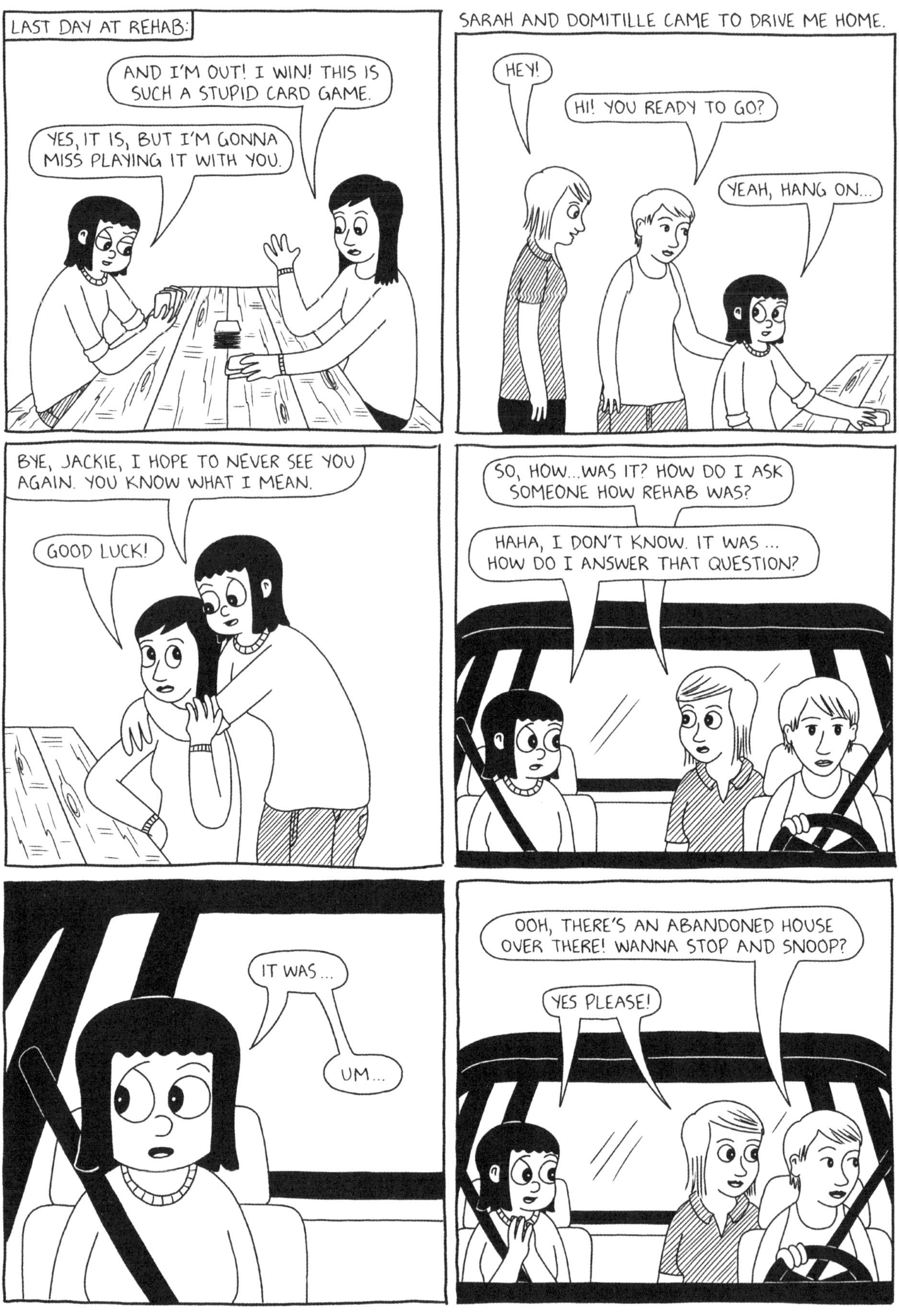
LAST DAY AT REHAB:
AND I'M OUT! I WIN! THIS IS SUCH A STUPID CARD GAME.
YES, IT IS, BUT I'M GONNA MISS PLAYING IT WITH YOU.
SARAH AND DOMITILLE CAME TO DRIVE ME HOME.
HEY!
HI! YOU READY TO GO?
YEAH, HANG ON...
BYE, JACKIE, I HOPE TO NEVER SEE YOU AGAIN. YOU KNOW WHAT I MEAN.
GOOD LUCK!
SO, HOW...WAS IT? HOW DO I ASK SOMEONE HOW REHAB WAS?
HAHA, I DON'T KNOW. IT WAS ... HOW DO I ANSWER THAT QUESTION?
IT WAS...
UM...
OOH, THERE'S AN ABANDONED HOUSE OVER THERE! WANNA STOP AND SNOOP?
YES PLEASE!

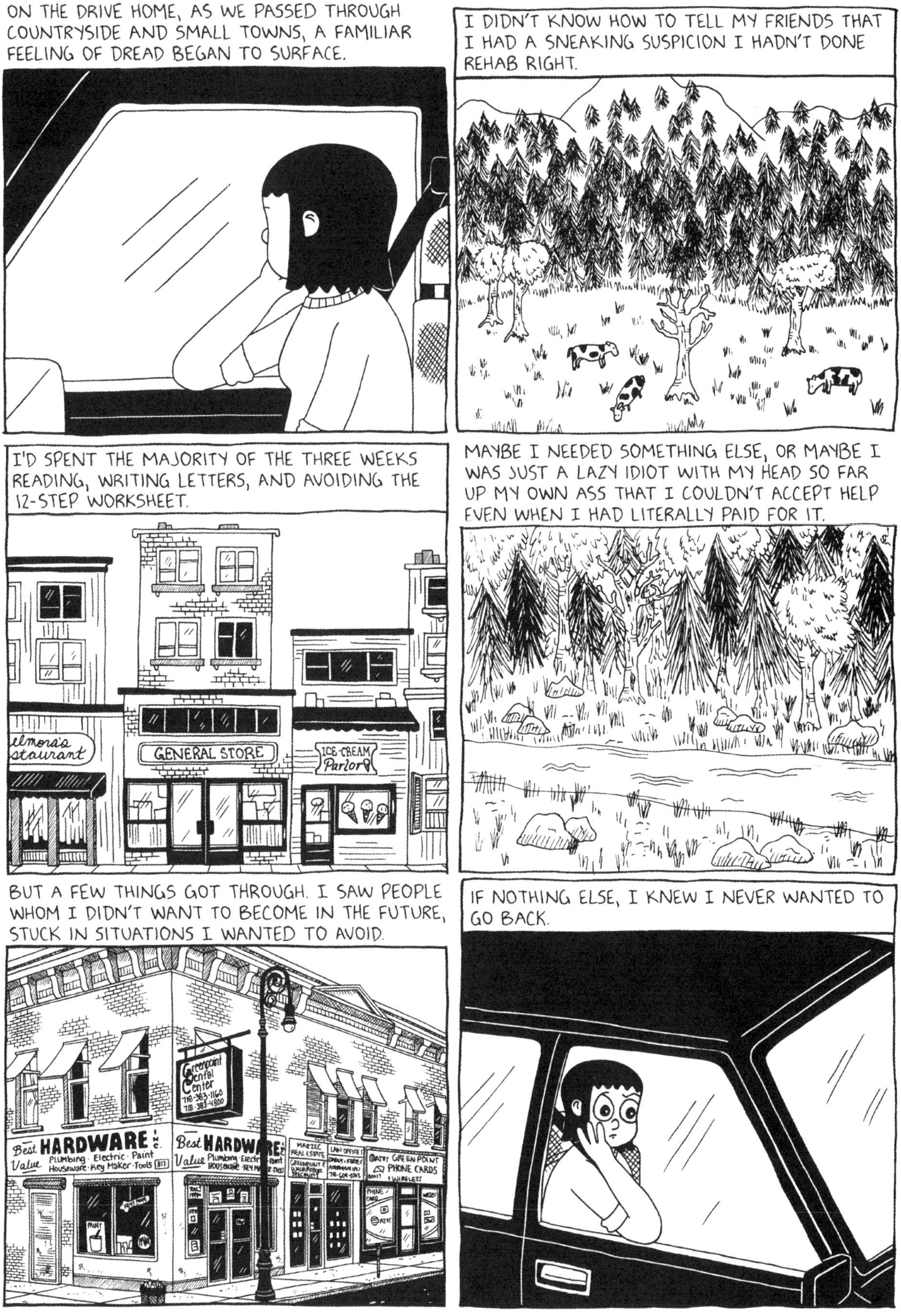
ON THE DRIVE HOME, AS WE PASSED THROUGH COUNTRYSIDE AND SMALL TOWNS, A FAMILIAR FEELING OF DREAD BEGAN TO SURFACE.
I DIDN'T KNOW HOW TO TELL MY FRIENDS THAT I HAD A SNEAKING SUSPICION I HADN'T DONE REHAB RIGHT.
I'D SPENT THE MAJORITY OF THE THREE WEEKS READING, WRITING LETTERS, AND AVOIDING THE 12-STEP WORKSHEET.
elmora's staurant
GENERAL STORE
ICE-CREAM Parlor
MAYBE I NEEDED SOMETHING ELSE, OR MAYBE I WAS JUST A LAZY IDIOT WITH MY HEAD SO FAR UP MY OWN ASS THAT I COULDN'T ACCEPT HELP EVEN WHEN I HAD LITERALLY PAID FOR IT.
BUT A FEW THINGS GOT THROUGH. I SAW PEOPLE WHOM I DIDN'T WANT TO BECOME IN THE FUTURE, STUCK IN SITUATIONS I WANTED TO AVOID.
Greenpoint Dental Center 718-383-1160 718-383-4800
Best Value HARDWARE INC. Plumbing · Electric · Paint Houseware · Key Maker · Tools
GREEN POINT PHONE CARDS
IF NOTHING ELSE, I KNEW I NEVER WANTED TO GO BACK.

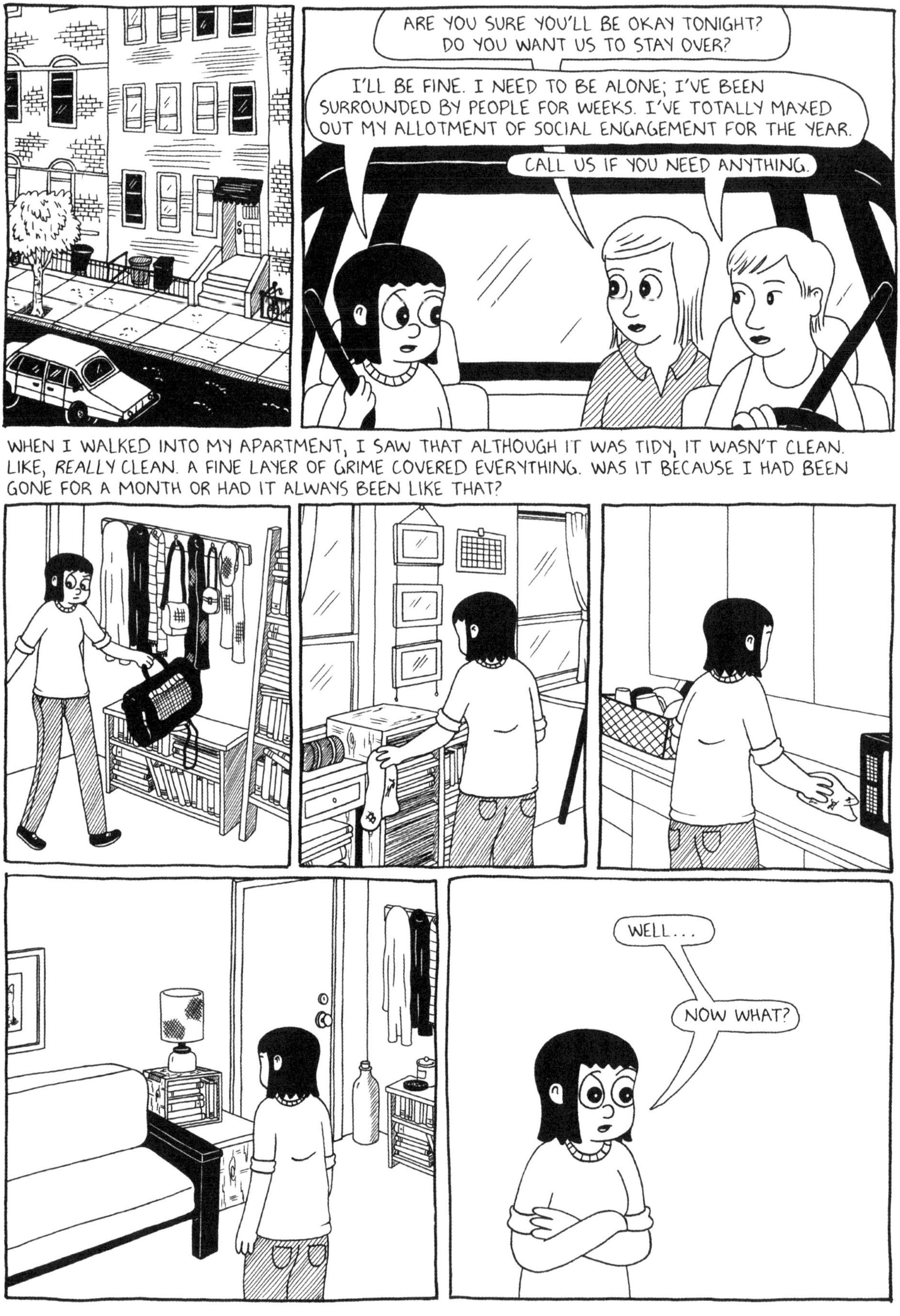
ARE YOU SURE YOU'LL BE OKAY TONIGHT? DO YOU WANT US TO STAY OVER?
I'LL BE FINE. I NEED TO BE ALONE; I'VE BEEN SURROUNDED BY PEOPLE FOR WEEKS. I'VE TOTALLY MAXED OUT MY ALLOTMENT OF SOCIAL ENGAGEMENT FOR THE YEAR.
CALL US IF YOU NEED ANYTHING.
WHEN I WALKED INTO MY APARTMENT, I SAW THAT ALTHOUGH IT WAS TIDY, IT WASN'T CLEAN. LIKE, *REALLY* CLEAN. A FINE LAYER OF GRIME COVERED EVERYTHING. WAS IT BECAUSE I HAD BEEN GONE FOR A MONTH OR HAD IT ALWAYS BEEN LIKE THAT?
WELL...
NOW WHAT?

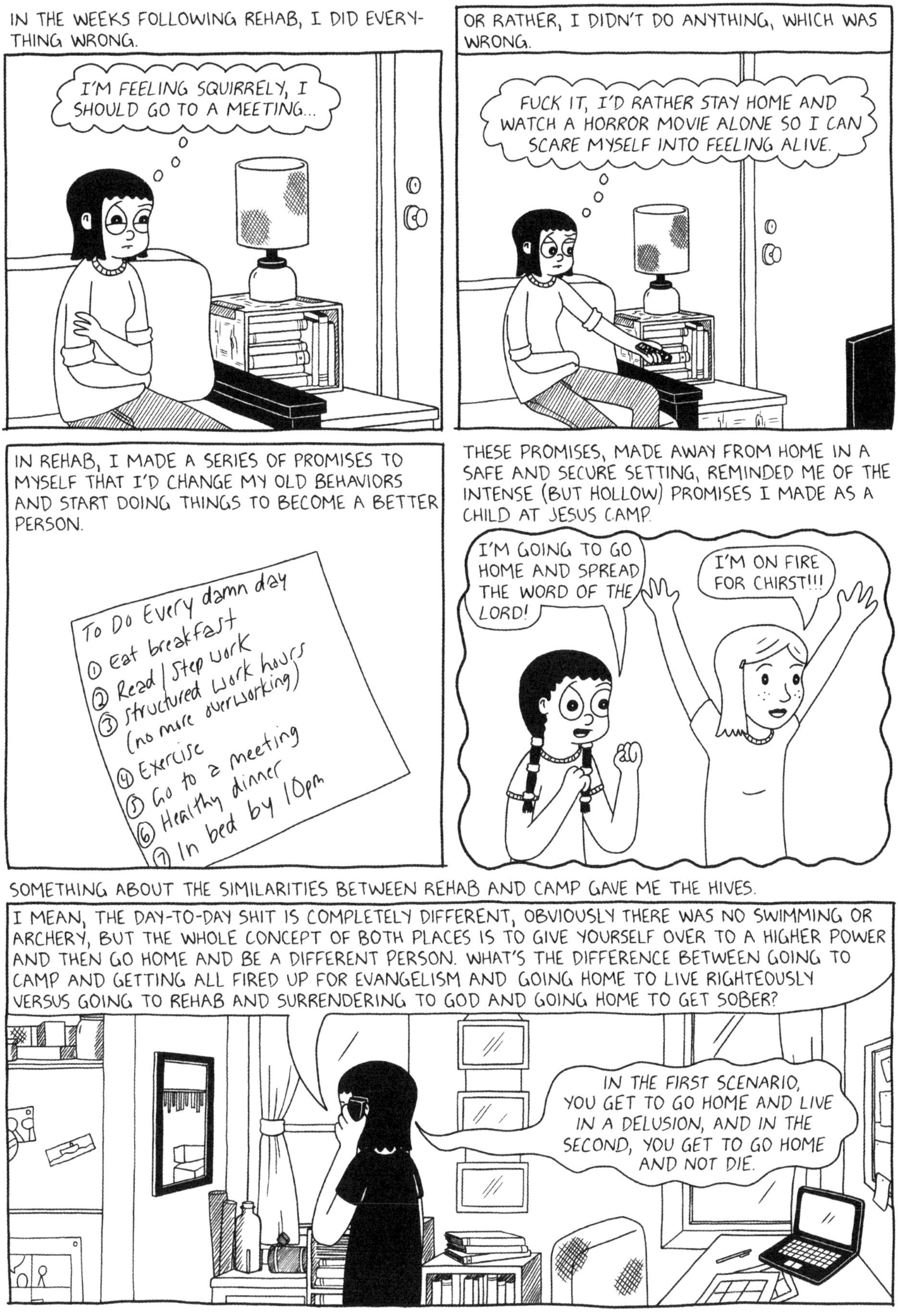
IN THE WEEKS FOLLOWING REHAB, I DID EVERYTHING WRONG.
I'M FEELING SQUIRRELY, I SHOULD GO TO A MEETING...
OR RATHER, I DIDN'T DO ANYTHING, WHICH WAS WRONG.
FUCK IT, I'D RATHER STAY HOME AND WATCH A HORROR MOVIE ALONE SO I CAN SCARE MYSELF INTO FEELING ALIVE.
IN REHAB, I MADE A SERIES OF PROMISES TO MYSELF THAT I'D CHANGE MY OLD BEHAVIORS AND START DOING THINGS TO BECOME A BETTER PERSON.
To Do Every damn day
1 Eat breakfast
2 Read | Step work
3 structured work hours (no more overworking)
4 Exercise
5 Go to a meeting
6 Healthy dinner
7 In bed by 10pm
THESE PROMISES, MADE AWAY FROM HOME IN A SAFE AND SECURE SETTING, REMINDED ME OF THE INTENSE (BUT HOLLOW) PROMISES I MADE AS A CHILD AT JESUS CAMP.
I'M GOING TO GO HOME AND SPREAD THE WORD OF THE LORD!
I'M ON FIRE FOR CHIRST!!!
SOMETHING ABOUT THE SIMILARITIES BETWEEN REHAB AND CAMP GAVE ME THE HIVES.
I MEAN, THE DAY-TO-DAY SHIT IS COMPLETELY DIFFERENT, OBVIOUSLY THERE WAS NO SWIMMING OR ARCHERY, BUT THE WHOLE CONCEPT OF BOTH PLACES IS TO GIVE YOURSELF OVER TO A HIGHER POWER AND THEN GO HOME AND BE A DIFFERENT PERSON. WHAT'S THE DIFFERENCE BETWEEN GOING TO CAMP AND GETTING ALL FIRED UP FOR EVANGELISM AND GOING HOME TO LIVE RIGHTEOUSLY VERSUS GOING TO REHAB AND SURRENDERING TO GOD AND GOING HOME TO GET SOBER?
IN THE FIRST SCENARIO, YOU GET TO GO HOME AND LIVE IN A DELUSION, AND IN THE SECOND, YOU GET TO GO HOME AND NOT DIE.

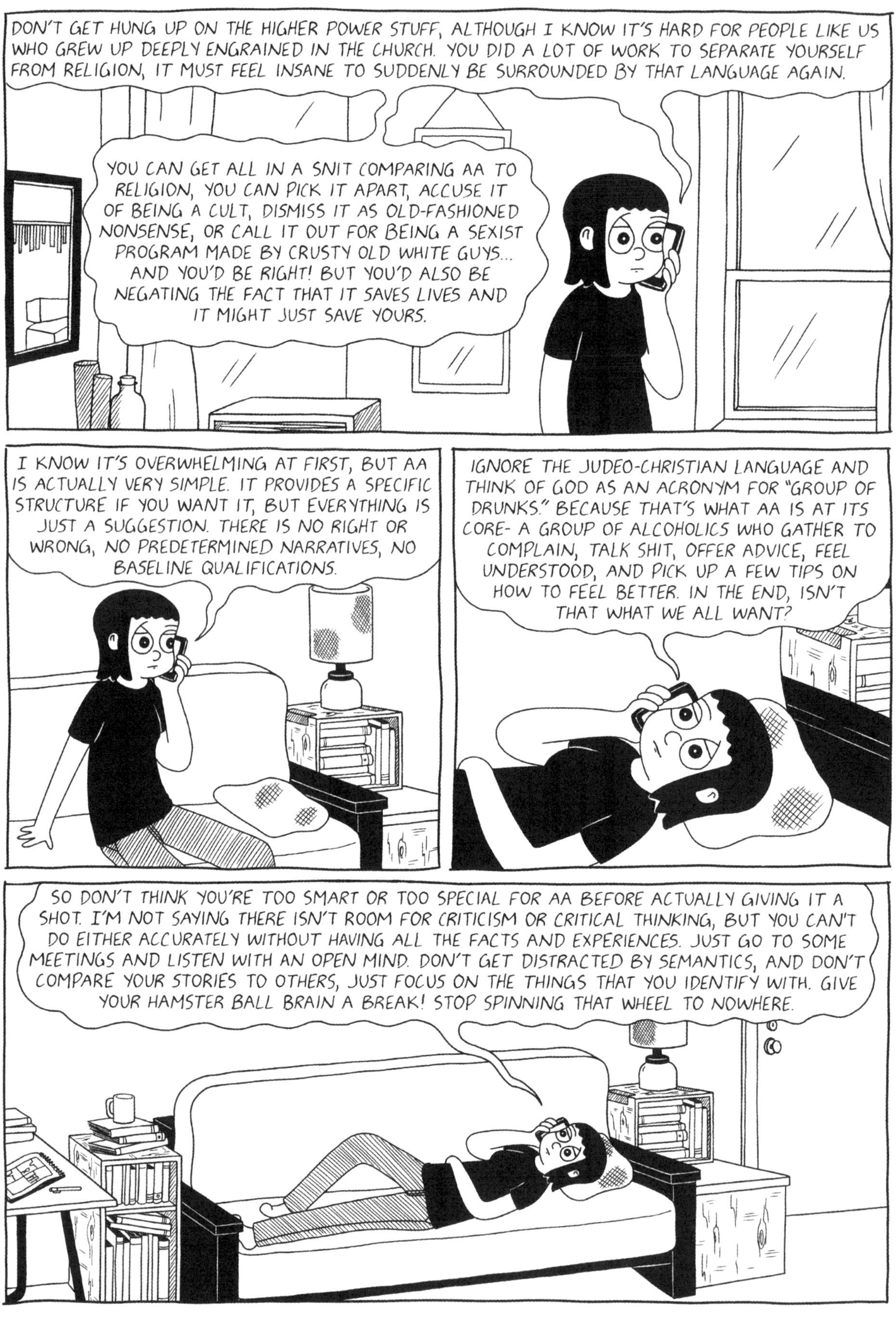
DON'T GET HUNG UP ON THE HIGHER POWER STUFF, ALTHOUGH I KNOW IT'S HARD FOR PEOPLE LIKE US WHO GREW UP DEEPLY ENGRAINED IN THE CHURCH. YOU DID A LOT OF WORK TO SEPARATE YOURSELF FROM RELIGION, IT MUST FEEL INSANE TO SUDDENLY BE SURROUNDED BY THAT LANGUAGE AGAIN.
YOU CAN GET ALL IN A SNIT COMPARING AA TO RELIGION, YOU CAN PICK IT APART, ACCUSE IT OF BEING A CULT, DISMISS IT AS OLD-FASHIONED NONSENSE, OR CALL IT OUT FOR BEING A SEXIST PROGRAM MADE BY CRUSTY OLD WHITE GUYS... AND YOU'D BE RIGHT! BUT YOU'D ALSO BE NEGATING THE FACT THAT IT SAVES LIVES AND IT MIGHT JUST SAVE YOURS.
I KNOW IT'S OVERWHELMING AT FIRST, BUT AA IS ACTUALLY VERY SIMPLE. IT PROVIDES A SPECIFIC STRUCTURE IF YOU WANT IT, BUT EVERYTHING IS JUST A SUGGESTION. THERE IS NO RIGHT OR WRONG, NO PREDETERMINED NARRATIVES, NO BASELINE QUALIFICATIONS.
IGNORE THE JUDEO-CHRISTIAN LANGUAGE AND THINK OF GOD AS AN ACRONYM FOR "GROUP OF DRUNKS." BECAUSE THAT'S WHAT AA IS AT ITS CORE- A GROUP OF ALCOHOLICS WHO GATHER TO COMPLAIN, TALK SHIT, OFFER ADVICE, FEEL UNDERSTOOD, AND PICK UP A FEW TIPS ON HOW TO FEEL BETTER. IN THE END, ISN'T THAT WHAT WE ALL WANT?
SO DON'T THINK YOU'RE TOO SMART OR TOO SPECIAL FOR AA BEFORE ACTUALLY GIVING IT A SHOT. I'M NOT SAYING THERE ISN'T ROOM FOR CRITICISM OR CRITICAL THINKING, BUT YOU CAN'T DO EITHER ACCURATELY WITHOUT HAVING ALL THE FACTS AND EXPERIENCES. JUST GO TO SOME MEETINGS AND LISTEN WITH AN OPEN MIND. DON'T GET DISTRACTED BY SEMANTICS, AND DON'T COMPARE YOUR STORIES TO OTHERS, JUST FOCUS ON THE THINGS THAT YOU IDENTIFY WITH. GIVE YOUR HAMSTER BALL BRAIN A BREAK! STOP SPINNING THAT WHEEL TO NOWHERE.

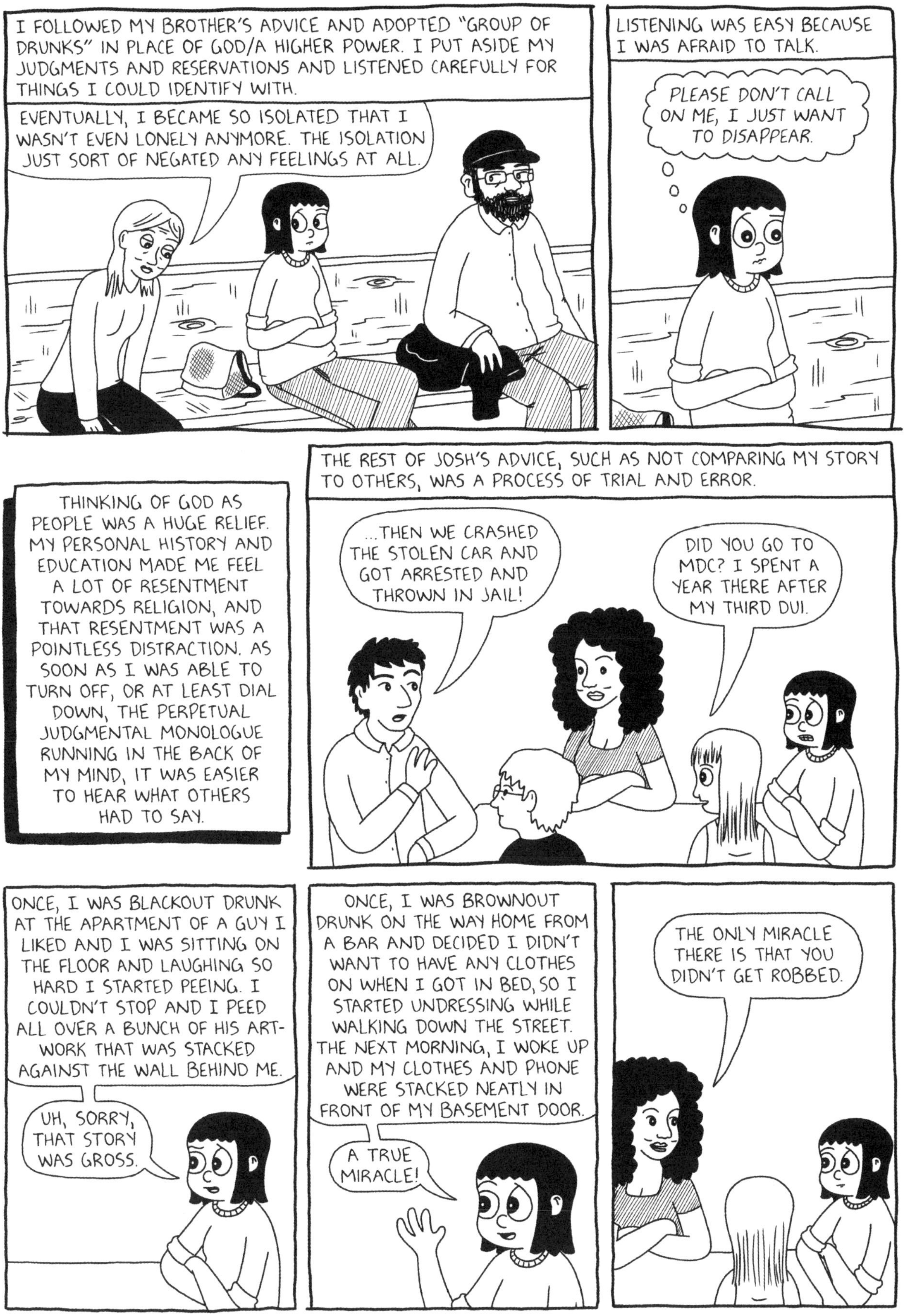

I FOLLOWED MY BROTHER'S ADVICE AND ADOPTED "GROUP OF DRUNKS" IN PLACE OF GOD/A HIGHER POWER. I PUT ASIDE MY JUDGMENTS AND RESERVATIONS AND LISTENED CAREFULLY FOR THINGS I COULD IDENTIFY WITH.
EVENTUALLY, I BECAME SO ISOLATED THAT I WASN'T EVEN LONELY ANYMORE. THE ISOLATION JUST SORT OF NEGATED ANY FEELINGS AT ALL.
LISTENING WAS EASY BECAUSE I WAS AFRAID TO TALK.
PLEASE DON'T CALL ON ME, I JUST WANT TO DISAPPEAR.
THINKING OF GOD AS PEOPLE WAS A HUGE RELIEF. MY PERSONAL HISTORY AND EDUCATION MADE ME FEEL A LOT OF RESENTMENT TOWARDS RELIGION, AND THAT RESENTMENT WAS A POINTLESS DISTRACTION. AS SOON AS I WAS ABLE TO TURN OFF, OR AT LEAST DIAL DOWN, THE PERPETUAL JUDGMENTAL MONOLOGUE RUNNING IN THE BACK OF MY MIND, IT WAS EASIER TO HEAR WHAT OTHERS HAD TO SAY.
THE REST OF JOSH'S ADVICE, SUCH AS NOT COMPARING MY STORY TO OTHERS, WAS A PROCESS OF TRIAL AND ERROR.
...THEN WE CRASHED THE STOLEN CAR AND GOT ARRESTED AND THROWN IN JAIL!
DID YOU GO TO MDC? I SPENT A YEAR THERE AFTER MY THIRD DUI.
ONCE, I WAS BLACKOUT DRUNK AT THE APARTMENT OF A GUY I LIKED AND I WAS SITTING ON THE FLOOR AND LAUGHING SO HARD I STARTED PEEING. I COULDN'T STOP AND I PEED ALL OVER A BUNCH OF HIS ART-WORK THAT WAS STACKED AGAINST THE WALL BEHIND ME.
UH, SORRY, THAT STORY WAS GROSS.
ONCE, I WAS BROWNOUT DRUNK ON THE WAY HOME FROM A BAR AND DECIDED I DIDN'T WANT TO HAVE ANY CLOTHES ON WHEN I GOT IN BED, SO I STARTED UNDRESSING WHILE WALKING DOWN THE STREET. THE NEXT MORNING, I WOKE UP AND MY CLOTHES AND PHONE WERE STACKED NEATLY IN FRONT OF MY BASEMENT DOOR.
A TRUE MIRACLE!
THE ONLY MIRACLE THERE IS THAT YOU DIDN'T GET ROBBED.

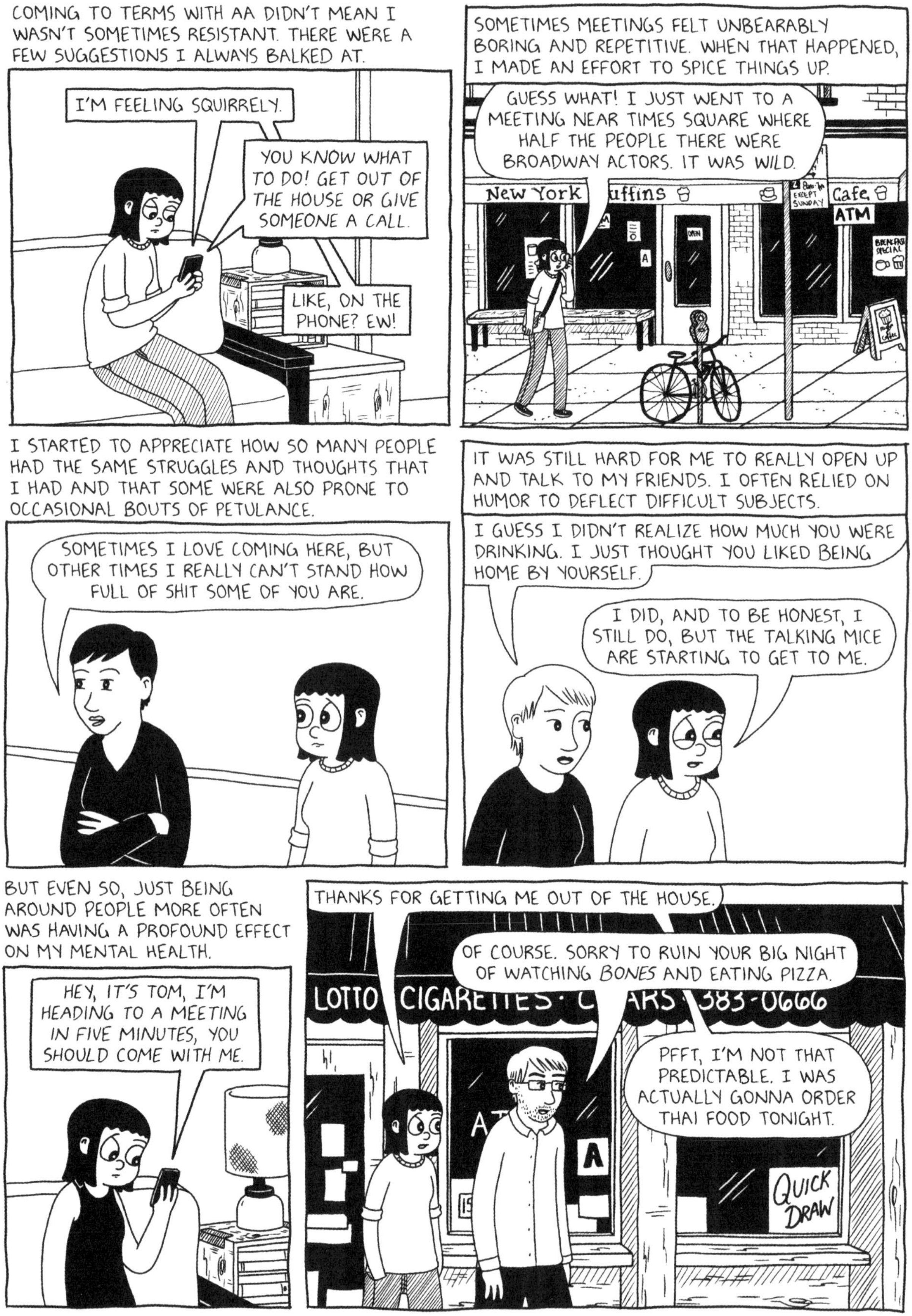
COMING TO TERMS WITH AA DIDN'T MEAN I WASN'T SOMETIMES RESISTANT. THERE WERE A FEW SUGGESTIONS I ALWAYS BALKED AT.
I'M FEELING SQUIRRELY.
YOU KNOW WHAT TO DO! GET OUT OF THE HOUSE OR GIVE SOMEONE A CALL.
LIKE, ON THE PHONE? EW!
SOMETIMES MEETINGS FELT UNBEARABLY BORING AND REPETITIVE. WHEN THAT HAPPENED, I MADE AN EFFORT TO SPICE THINGS UP.
GUESS WHAT! I JUST WENT TO A MEETING NEAR TIMES SQUARE WHERE HALF THE PEOPLE THERE WERE BROADWAY ACTORS. IT WAS WILD.
New York uffins
Cafe
ATM
I STARTED TO APPRECIATE HOW SO MANY PEOPLE HAD THE SAME STRUGGLES AND THOUGHTS THAT I HAD AND THAT SOME WERE ALSO PRONE TO OCCASIONAL BOUTS OF PETULANCE.
SOMETIMES I LOVE COMING HERE, BUT OTHER TIMES I REALLY CAN'T STAND HOW FULL OF SHIT SOME OF YOU ARE.
IT WAS STILL HARD FOR ME TO REALLY OPEN UP AND TALK TO MY FRIENDS. I OFTEN RELIED ON HUMOR TO DEFLECT DIFFICULT SUBJECTS.
I GUESS I DIDN'T REALIZE HOW MUCH YOU WERE DRINKING. I JUST THOUGHT YOU LIKED BEING HOME BY YOURSELF.
I DID, AND TO BE HONEST, I STILL DO, BUT THE TALKING MICE ARE STARTING TO GET TO ME.
BUT EVEN SO, JUST BEING AROUND PEOPLE MORE OFTEN WAS HAVING A PROFOUND EFFECT ON MY MENTAL HEALTH.
HEY, IT'S TOM, I'M HEADING TO A MEETING IN FIVE MINUTES, YOU SHOULD COME WITH ME.
THANKS FOR GETTING ME OUT OF THE HOUSE.
OF COURSE. SORRY TO RUIN YOUR BIG NIGHT OF WATCHING *BONES* AND EATING PIZZA.
PFFT, I'M NOT THAT PREDICTABLE. I WAS ACTUALLY GONNA ORDER THAI FOOD TONIGHT.
LOTTO CIGARETTES
QUICK DRAW

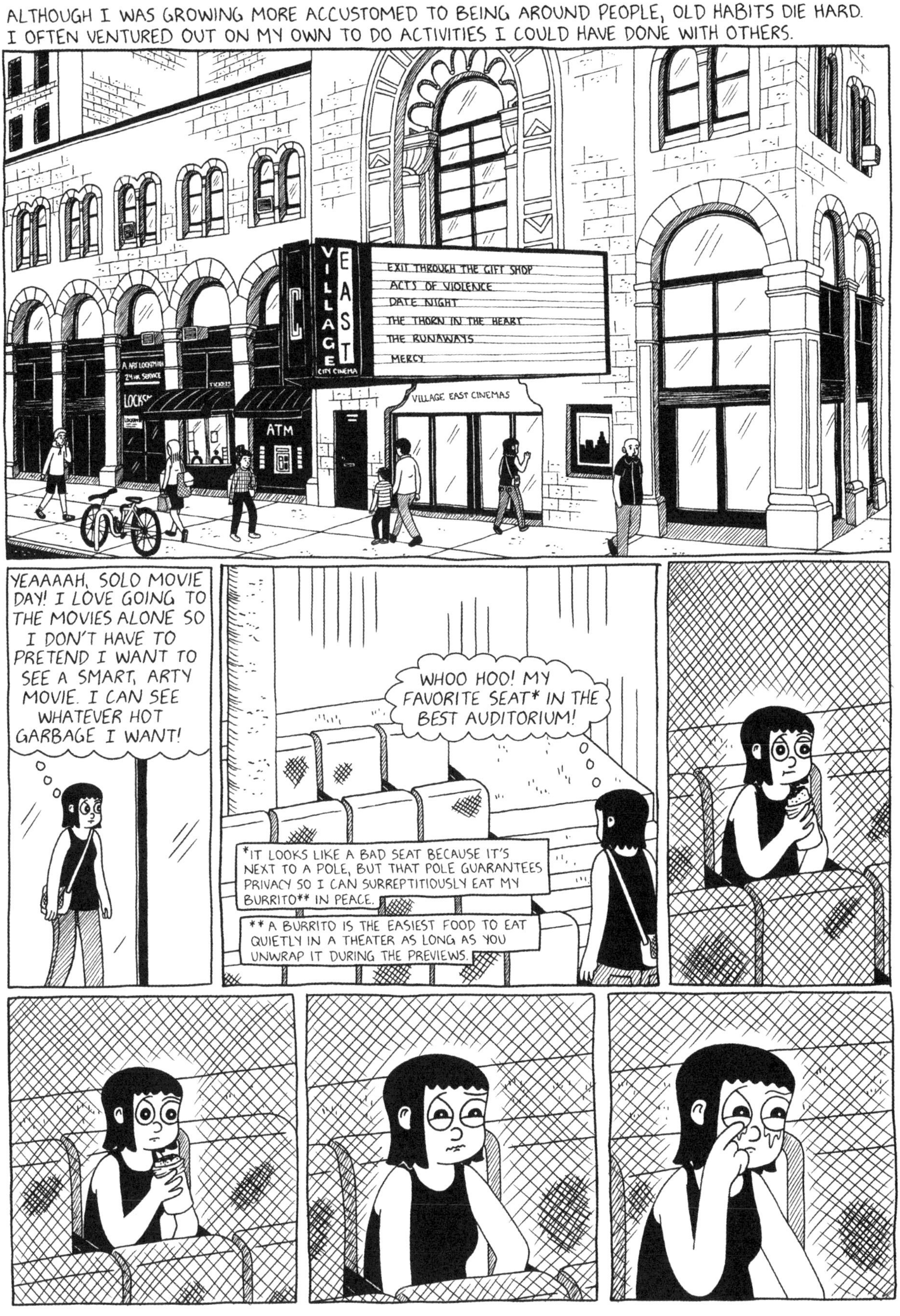
ALTHOUGH I WAS GROWING MORE ACCUSTOMED TO BEING AROUND PEOPLE, OLD HABITS DIE HARD. I OFTEN VENTURED OUT ON MY OWN TO DO ACTIVITIES I COULD HAVE DONE WITH OTHERS.
VILLAGE EAST
CITY CINEMA
EXIT THROUGH THE GIFT SHOP
ACTS OF VIOLENCE
DATE NIGHT
THE THORN IN THE HEART
THE RUNAWAYS
MERCY
VILLAGE EAST CINEMAS
ATM
TICKETS
YEAAAAH, SOLO MOVIE DAY! I LOVE GOING TO THE MOVIES ALONE SO I DON'T HAVE TO PRETEND I WANT TO SEE A SMART, ARTY MOVIE. I CAN SEE WHATEVER HOT GARBAGE I WANT!
WHOO HOO! MY FAVORITE SEAT* IN THE BEST AUDITORIUM!
*IT LOOKS LIKE A BAD SEAT BECAUSE IT'S NEXT TO A POLE, BUT THAT POLE GUARANTEES PRIVACY SO I CAN SURREPTITIOUSLY EAT MY BURRITO** IN PEACE.
**A BURRITO IS THE EASIEST FOOD TO EAT QUIETLY IN A THEATER AS LONG AS YOU UNWRAP IT DURING THE PREVIEWS.

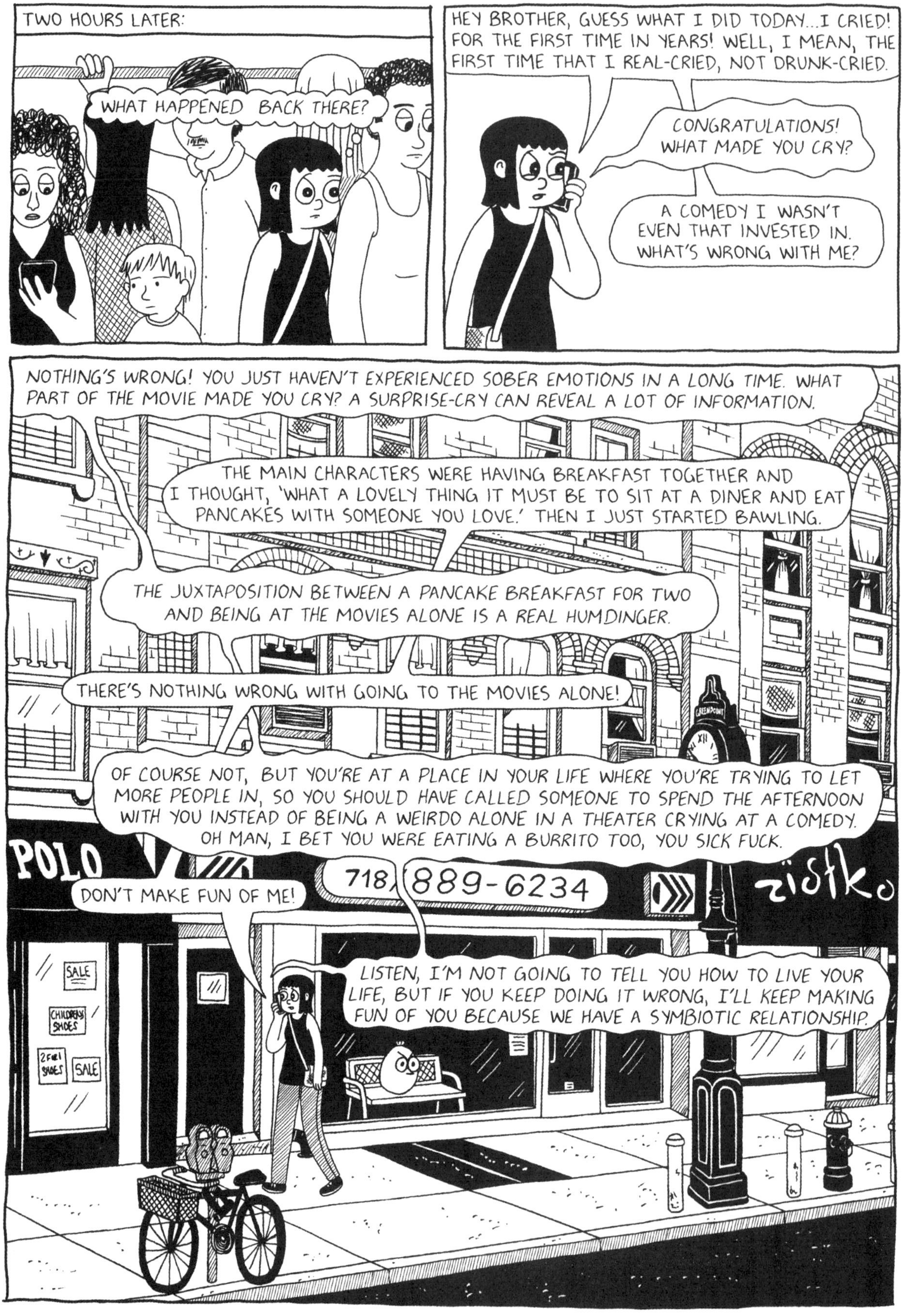
TWO HOURS LATER:
WHAT HAPPENED BACK THERE?
HEY BROTHER, GUESS WHAT I DID TODAY...I CRIED! FOR THE FIRST TIME IN YEARS! WELL, I MEAN, THE FIRST TIME THAT I REAL-CRIED, NOT DRUNK-CRIED.
CONGRATULATIONS! WHAT MADE YOU CRY?
A COMEDY I WASN'T EVEN THAT INVESTED IN. WHAT'S WRONG WITH ME?
NOTHING'S WRONG! YOU JUST HAVEN'T EXPERIENCED SOBER EMOTIONS IN A LONG TIME. WHAT PART OF THE MOVIE MADE YOU CRY? A SURPRISE-CRY CAN REVEAL A LOT OF INFORMATION.
THE MAIN CHARACTERS WERE HAVING BREAKFAST TOGETHER AND I THOUGHT, 'WHAT A LOVELY THING IT MUST BE TO SIT AT A DINER AND EAT PANCAKES WITH SOMEONE YOU LOVE.' THEN I JUST STARTED BAWLING.
THE JUXTAPOSITION BETWEEN A PANCAKE BREAKFAST FOR TWO AND BEING AT THE MOVIES ALONE IS A REAL HUMDINGER.
THERE'S NOTHING WRONG WITH GOING TO THE MOVIES ALONE!
OF COURSE NOT, BUT YOU'RE AT A PLACE IN YOUR LIFE WHERE YOU'RE TRYING TO LET MORE PEOPLE IN, SO YOU SHOULD HAVE CALLED SOMEONE TO SPEND THE AFTERNOON WITH YOU INSTEAD OF BEING A WEIRDO ALONE IN A THEATER CRYING AT A COMEDY. OH MAN, I BET YOU WERE EATING A BURRITO TOO, YOU SICK FUCK.
POLO
718 889-6234
DON'T MAKE FUN OF ME!
LISTEN, I'M NOT GOING TO TELL YOU HOW TO LIVE YOUR LIFE, BUT IF YOU KEEP DOING IT WRONG, I'LL KEEP MAKING FUN OF YOU BECAUSE WE HAVE A SYMBIOTIC RELATIONSHIP.
SALE
CHILDREN'S SHOES
2 FOR 1 SHOES
SALE

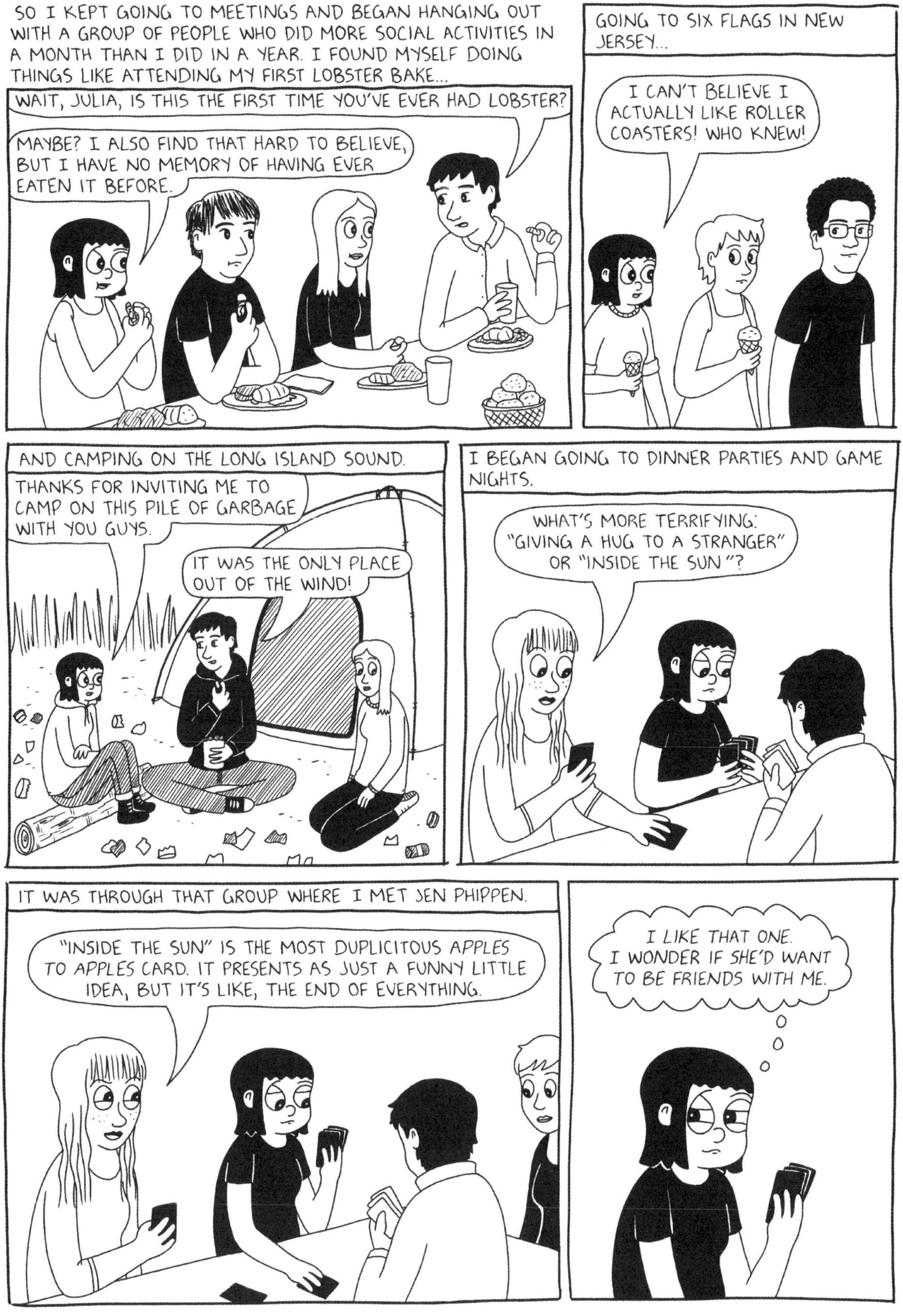
SO I KEPT GOING TO MEETINGS AND BEGAN HANGING OUT WITH A GROUP OF PEOPLE WHO DID MORE SOCIAL ACTIVITIES IN A MONTH THAN I DID IN A YEAR. I FOUND MYSELF DOING THINGS LIKE ATTENDING MY FIRST LOBSTER BAKE...
WAIT, JULIA, IS THIS THE FIRST TIME YOU'VE EVER HAD LOBSTER?
MAYBE? I ALSO FIND THAT HARD TO BELIEVE, BUT I HAVE NO MEMORY OF HAVING EVER EATEN IT BEFORE.
GOING TO SIX FLAGS IN NEW JERSEY...
I CAN'T BELIEVE I ACTUALLY LIKE ROLLER COASTERS! WHO KNEW!
AND CAMPING ON THE LONG ISLAND SOUND.
THANKS FOR INVITING ME TO CAMP ON THIS PILE OF GARBAGE WITH YOU GUYS.
IT WAS THE ONLY PLACE OUT OF THE WIND!
I BEGAN GOING TO DINNER PARTIES AND GAME NIGHTS.
WHAT'S MORE TERRIFYING: "GIVING A HUG TO A STRANGER" OR "INSIDE THE SUN"?
IT WAS THROUGH THAT GROUP WHERE I MET JEN PHIPPEN.
"INSIDE THE SUN" IS THE MOST DUPLICITOUS APPLES TO APPLES CARD. IT PRESENTS AS JUST A FUNNY LITTLE IDEA, BUT IT'S LIKE, THE END OF EVERYTHING.
I LIKE THAT ONE. I WONDER IF SHE'D WANT TO BE FRIENDS WITH ME.

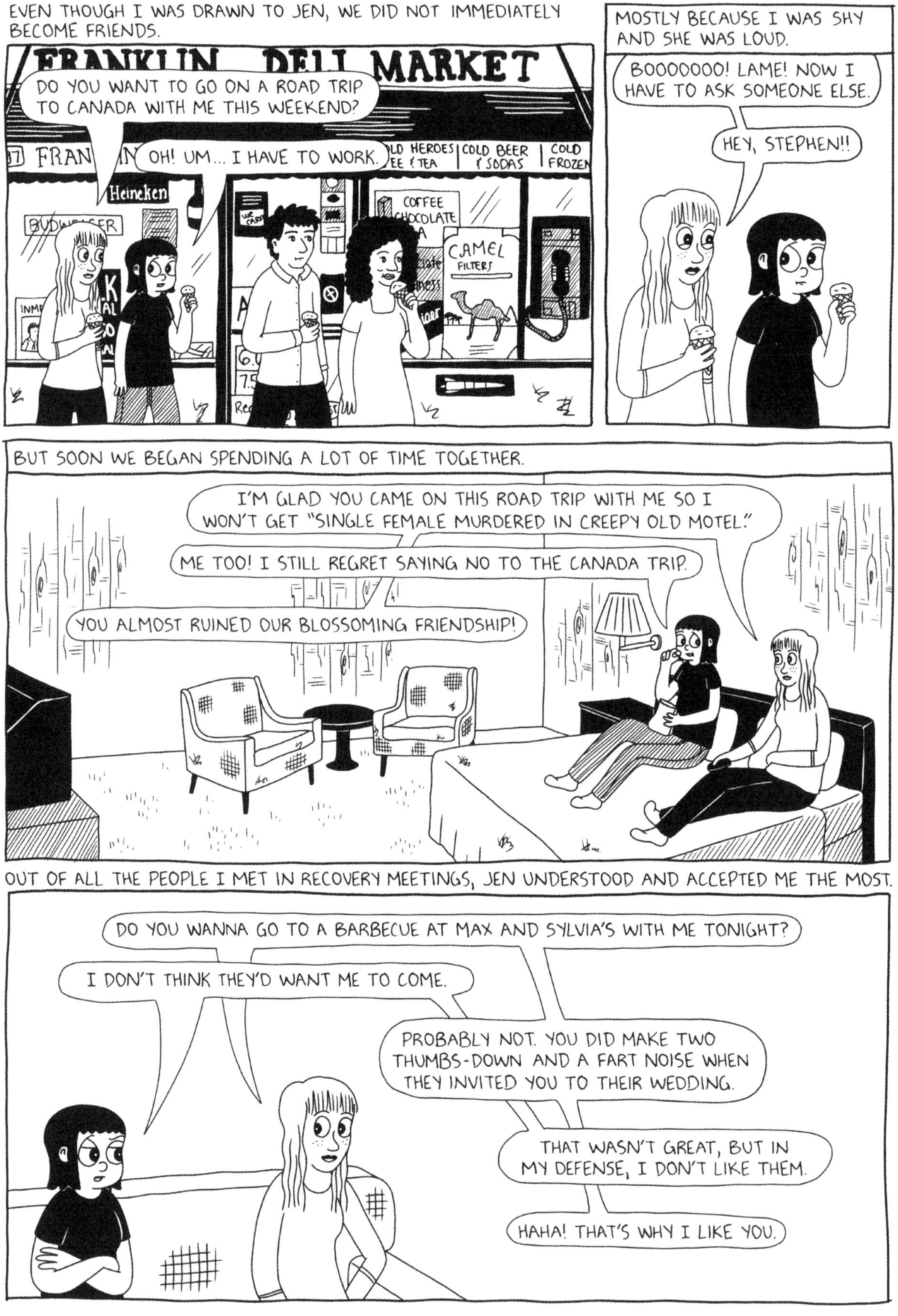
EVEN THOUGH I WAS DRAWN TO JEN, WE DID NOT IMMEDIATELY BECOME FRIENDS.
FRANKLIN DELI MARKET
DO YOU WANT TO GO ON A ROAD TRIP TO CANADA WITH ME THIS WEEKEND?
OH! UM... I HAVE TO WORK.
COLD BEER & SODAS
Heineken
CAMEL FILTERS
MOSTLY BECAUSE I WAS SHY AND SHE WAS LOUD.
BOOOOOOO! LAME! NOW I HAVE TO ASK SOMEONE ELSE.
HEY, STEPHEN!!
BUT SOON WE BEGAN SPENDING A LOT OF TIME TOGETHER.
I'M GLAD YOU CAME ON THIS ROAD TRIP WITH ME SO I WON'T GET "SINGLE FEMALE MURDERED IN CREEPY OLD MOTEL."
ME TOO! I STILL REGRET SAYING NO TO THE CANADA TRIP.
YOU ALMOST RUINED OUR BLOSSOMING FRIENDSHIP!
OUT OF ALL THE PEOPLE I MET IN RECOVERY MEETINGS, JEN UNDERSTOOD AND ACCEPTED ME THE MOST.
DO YOU WANNA GO TO A BARBECUE AT MAX AND SYLVIA'S WITH ME TONIGHT?
I DON'T THINK THEY'D WANT ME TO COME.
PROBABLY NOT. YOU DID MAKE TWO THUMBS-DOWN AND A FART NOISE WHEN THEY INVITED YOU TO THEIR WEDDING.
THAT WASN'T GREAT, BUT IN MY DEFENSE, I DON'T LIKE THEM.
HAHA! THAT'S WHY I LIKE YOU.

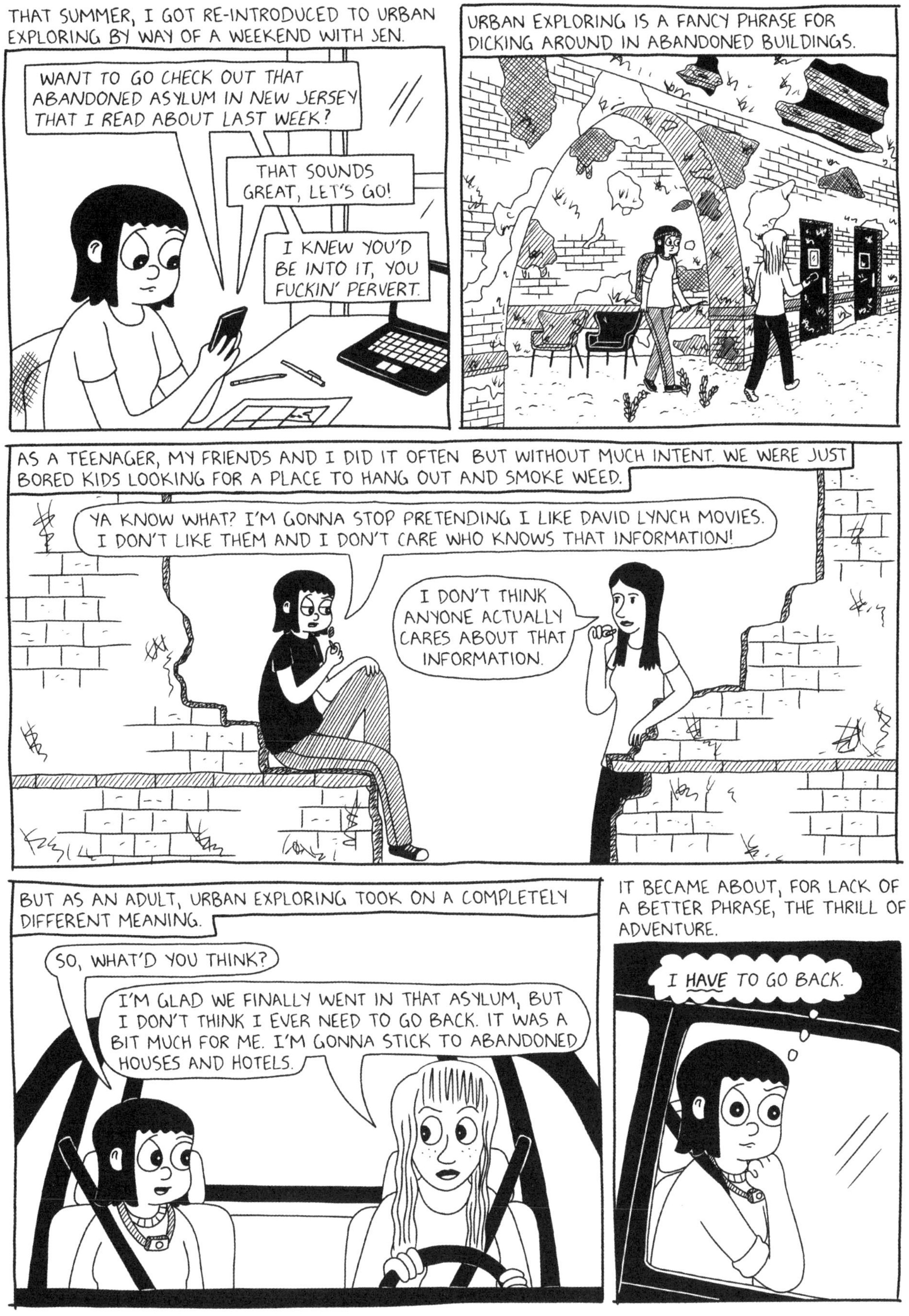
THAT SUMMER, I GOT RE-INTRODUCED TO URBAN EXPLORING BY WAY OF A WEEKEND WITH JEN.
WANT TO GO CHECK OUT THAT ABANDONED ASYLUM IN NEW JERSEY THAT I READ ABOUT LAST WEEK?
THAT SOUNDS GREAT, LET'S GO!
I KNEW YOU'D BE INTO IT, YOU FUCKIN' PERVERT.
URBAN EXPLORING IS A FANCY PHRASE FOR DICKING AROUND IN ABANDONED BUILDINGS.
AS A TEENAGER, MY FRIENDS AND I DID IT OFTEN BUT WITHOUT MUCH INTENT. WE WERE JUST BORED KIDS LOOKING FOR A PLACE TO HANG OUT AND SMOKE WEED.
YA KNOW WHAT? I'M GONNA STOP PRETENDING I LIKE DAVID LYNCH MOVIES. I DON'T LIKE THEM AND I DON'T CARE WHO KNOWS THAT INFORMATION!
I DON'T THINK ANYONE ACTUALLY CARES ABOUT THAT INFORMATION.
BUT AS AN ADULT, URBAN EXPLORING TOOK ON A COMPLETELY DIFFERENT MEANING.
SO, WHAT'D YOU THINK?
I'M GLAD WE FINALLY WENT IN THAT ASYLUM, BUT I DON'T THINK I EVER NEED TO GO BACK. IT WAS A BIT MUCH FOR ME. I'M GONNA STICK TO ABANDONED HOUSES AND HOTELS.
IT BECAME ABOUT, FOR LACK OF A BETTER PHRASE, THE THRILL OF ADVENTURE.
I HAVE TO GO BACK.

AFTER JEN GOT ME BACK INTO EXPLORING, SHE INTRODUCED ME TO SPAS DURING OUR TRAVELS.

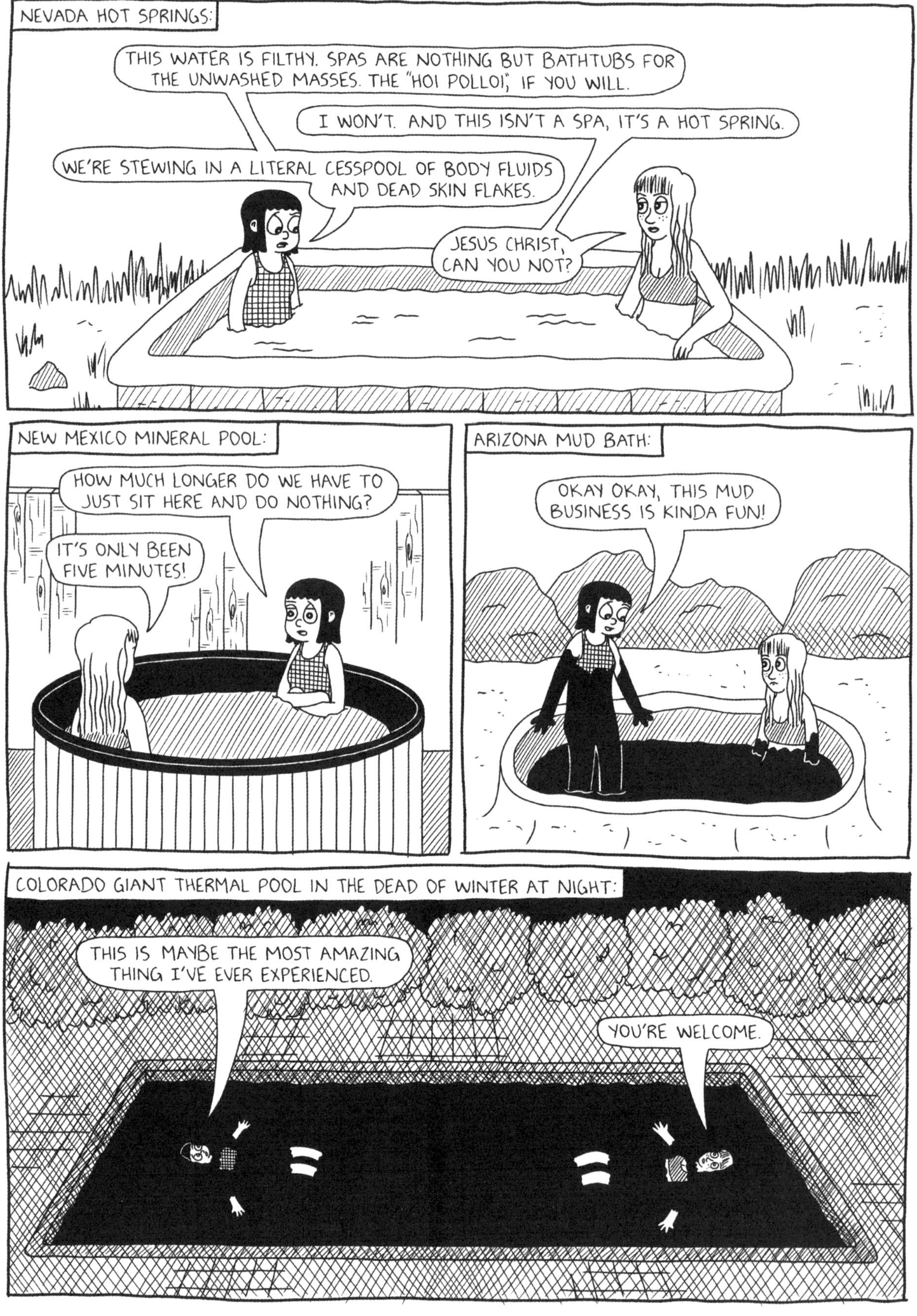
NEVADA HOT SPRINGS:
THIS WATER IS FILTHY. SPAS ARE NOTHING BUT BATHTUBS FOR THE UNWASHED MASSES. THE "HOI POLLOI," IF YOU WILL.
I WON'T. AND THIS ISN'T A SPA, IT'S A HOT SPRING.
WE'RE STEWING IN A LITERAL CESSPOOL OF BODY FLUIDS AND DEAD SKIN FLAKES.
JESUS CHRIST, CAN YOU NOT?
NEW MEXICO MINERAL POOL:
HOW MUCH LONGER DO WE HAVE TO JUST SIT HERE AND DO NOTHING?
IT'S ONLY BEEN FIVE MINUTES!
ARIZONA MUD BATH:
OKAY OKAY, THIS MUD BUSINESS IS KINDA FUN!
COLORADO GIANT THERMAL POOL IN THE DEAD OF WINTER AT NIGHT:
THIS IS MAYBE THE MOST AMAZING THING I'VE EVER EXPERIENCED.
YOU'RE WELCOME.

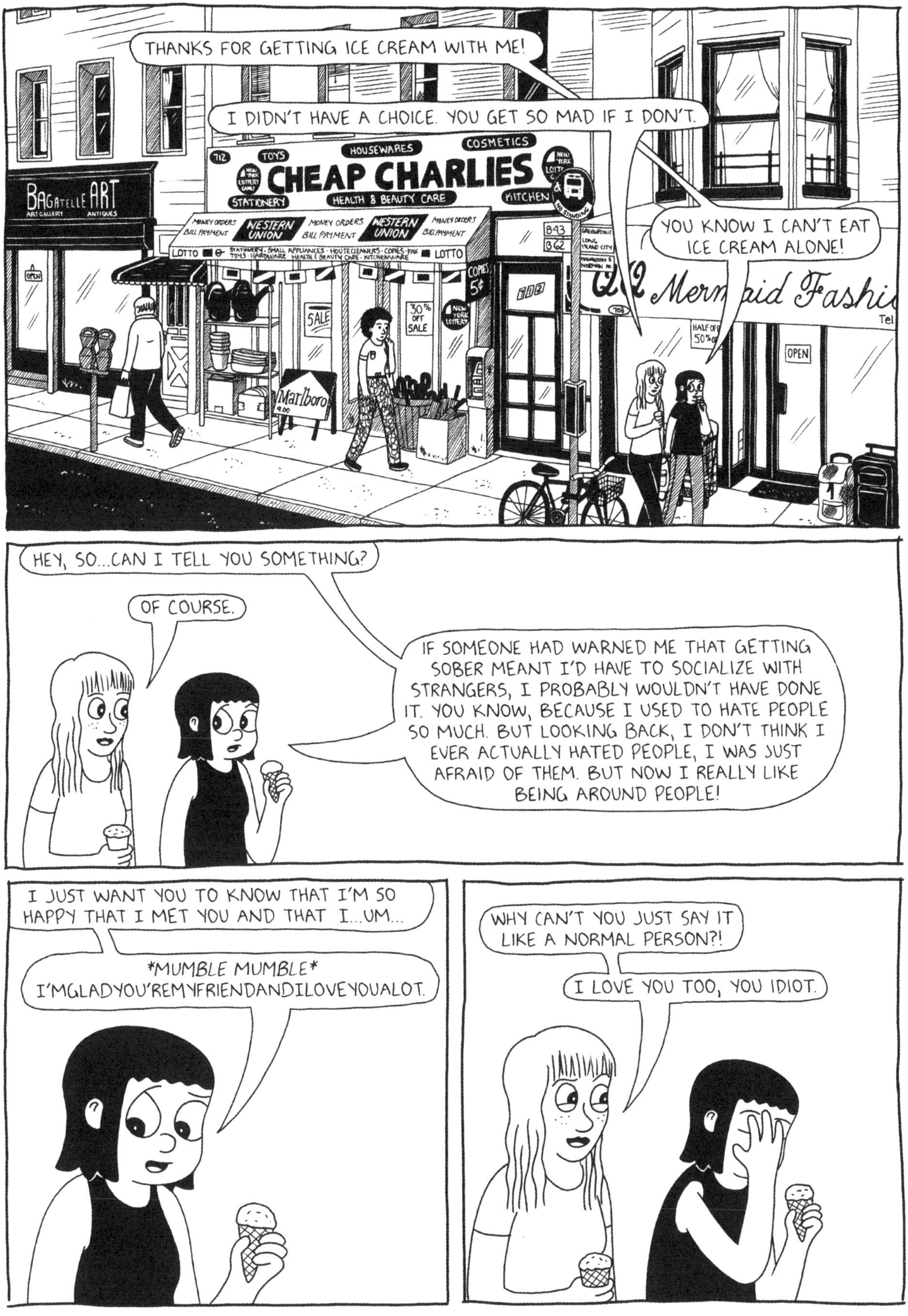
THANKS FOR GETTING ICE CREAM WITH ME!
I DIDN'T HAVE A CHOICE. YOU GET SO MAD IF I DON'T.
YOU KNOW I CAN'T EAT ICE CREAM ALONE!
CHEAP CHARLIES
HOUSEWARES
COSMETICS
TOYS
STATIONERY
HEALTH & BEAUTY CARE
KITCHEN
BAGATELLE ART
WESTERN UNION
MONEY ORDERS
BILL PAYMENT
LOTTO
COPIES 5¢
30% OFF SALE
SALE
OPEN
Marlboro
HEY, SO...CAN I TELL YOU SOMETHING?
OF COURSE.
IF SOMEONE HAD WARNED ME THAT GETTING SOBER MEANT I'D HAVE TO SOCIALIZE WITH STRANGERS, I PROBABLY WOULDN'T HAVE DONE IT. YOU KNOW, BECAUSE I USED TO HATE PEOPLE SO MUCH. BUT LOOKING BACK, I DON'T THINK I EVER ACTUALLY HATED PEOPLE, I WAS JUST AFRAID OF THEM. BUT NOW I REALLY LIKE BEING AROUND PEOPLE!
I JUST WANT YOU TO KNOW THAT I'M SO HAPPY THAT I MET YOU AND THAT I...UM...
MUMBLE MUMBLE I'MGLADYOU'REMYFRIENDANDILOVEYOUALOT.
WHY CAN'T YOU JUST SAY IT LIKE A NORMAL PERSON?!
I LOVE YOU TOO, YOU IDIOT.

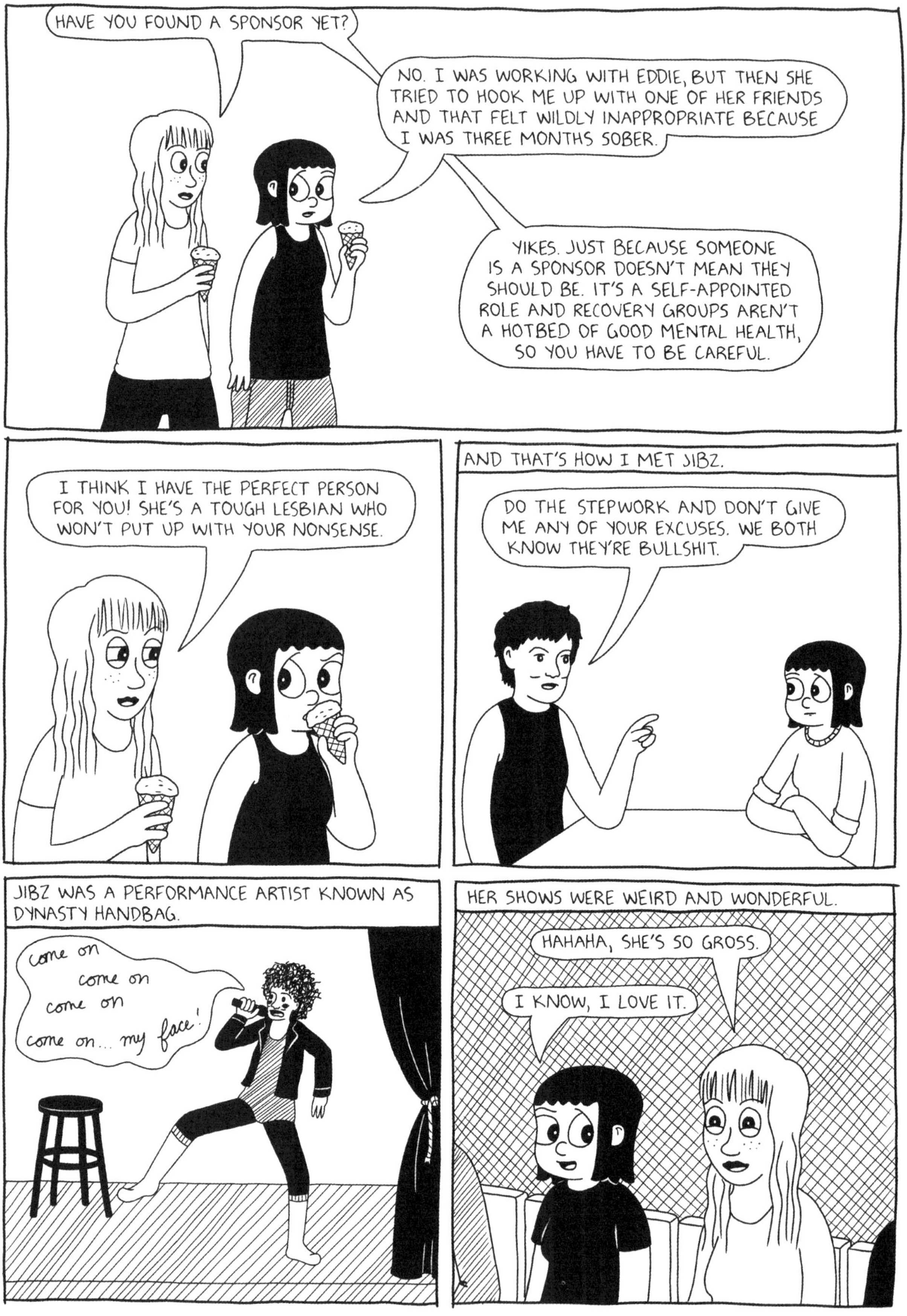
HAVE YOU FOUND A SPONSOR YET?
NO. I WAS WORKING WITH EDDIE, BUT THEN SHE TRIED TO HOOK ME UP WITH ONE OF HER FRIENDS AND THAT FELT WILDLY INAPPROPRIATE BECAUSE I WAS THREE MONTHS SOBER.
YIKES. JUST BECAUSE SOMEONE IS A SPONSOR DOESN'T MEAN THEY SHOULD BE. IT'S A SELF-APPOINTED ROLE AND RECOVERY GROUPS AREN'T A HOTBED OF GOOD MENTAL HEALTH, SO YOU HAVE TO BE CAREFUL.
I THINK I HAVE THE PERFECT PERSON FOR YOU! SHE'S A TOUGH LESBIAN WHO WON'T PUT UP WITH YOUR NONSENSE.
AND THAT'S HOW I MET JIBZ.
DO THE STEPWORK AND DON'T GIVE ME ANY OF YOUR EXCUSES. WE BOTH KNOW THEY'RE BULLSHIT.
JIBZ WAS A PERFORMANCE ARTIST KNOWN AS DYNASTY HANDBAG.
come on come on come on come on... my face!
HER SHOWS WERE WEIRD AND WONDERFUL.
HAHAHA, SHE'S SO GROSS.
I KNOW, I LOVE IT.

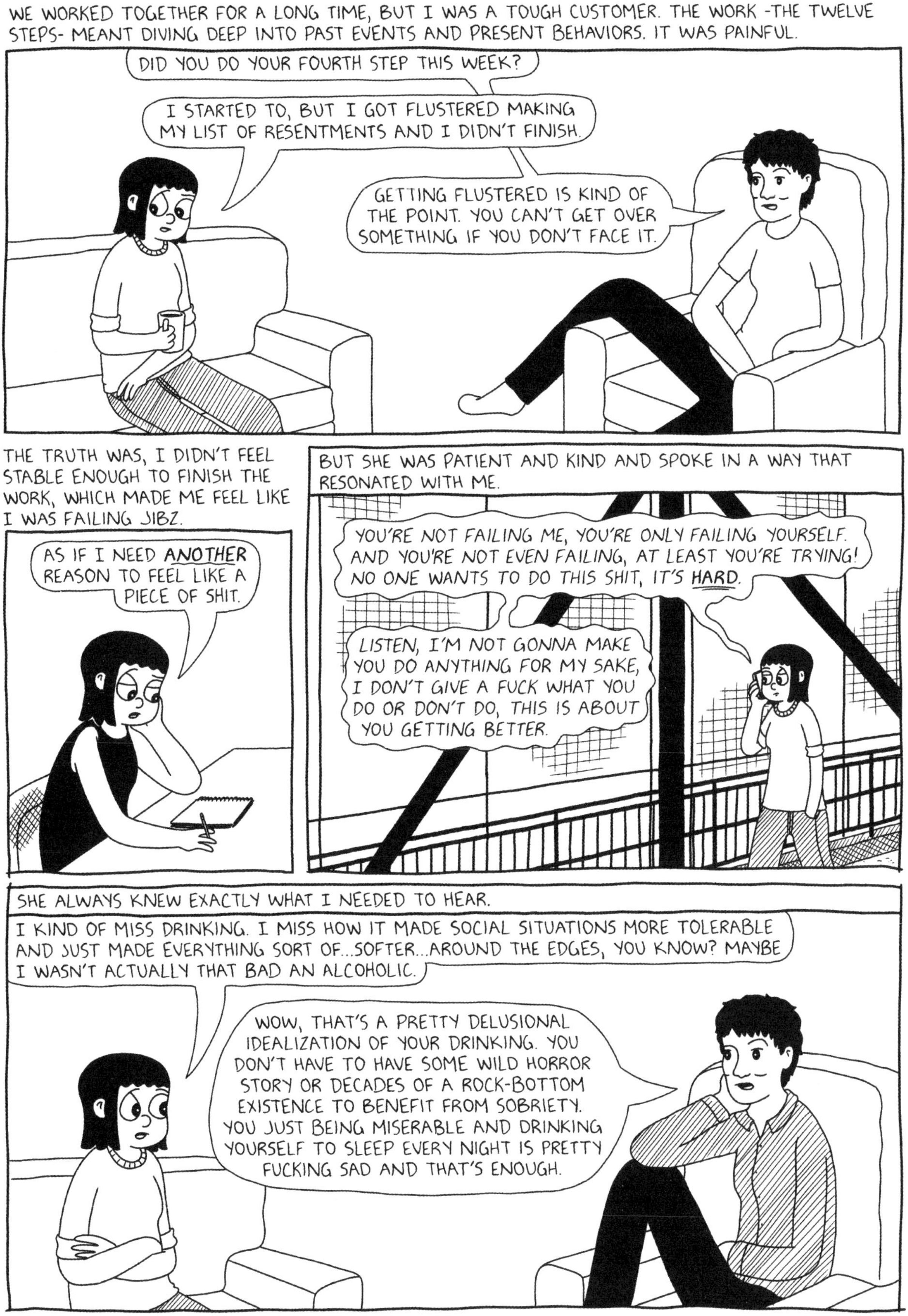
WE WORKED TOGETHER FOR A LONG TIME, BUT I WAS A TOUGH CUSTOMER. THE WORK -THE TWELVE STEPS- MEANT DIVING DEEP INTO PAST EVENTS AND PRESENT BEHAVIORS. IT WAS PAINFUL.
DID YOU DO YOUR FOURTH STEP THIS WEEK?
I STARTED TO, BUT I GOT FLUSTERED MAKING MY LIST OF RESENTMENTS AND I DIDN'T FINISH.
GETTING FLUSTERED IS KIND OF THE POINT. YOU CAN'T GET OVER SOMETHING IF YOU DON'T FACE IT.
THE TRUTH WAS, I DIDN'T FEEL STABLE ENOUGH TO FINISH THE WORK, WHICH MADE ME FEEL LIKE I WAS FAILING JIBZ.
AS IF I NEED ANOTHER REASON TO FEEL LIKE A PIECE OF SHIT.
BUT SHE WAS PATIENT AND KIND AND SPOKE IN A WAY THAT RESONATED WITH ME.
YOU'RE NOT FAILING ME, YOU'RE ONLY FAILING YOURSELF. AND YOU'RE NOT EVEN FAILING, AT LEAST YOU'RE TRYING! NO ONE WANTS TO DO THIS SHIT, IT'S HARD.
LISTEN, I'M NOT GONNA MAKE YOU DO ANYTHING FOR MY SAKE, I DON'T GIVE A FUCK WHAT YOU DO OR DON'T DO, THIS IS ABOUT YOU GETTING BETTER.
SHE ALWAYS KNEW EXACTLY WHAT I NEEDED TO HEAR.
I KIND OF MISS DRINKING. I MISS HOW IT MADE SOCIAL SITUATIONS MORE TOLERABLE AND JUST MADE EVERYTHING SORT OF...SOFTER...AROUND THE EDGES, YOU KNOW? MAYBE I WASN'T ACTUALLY THAT BAD AN ALCOHOLIC.
WOW, THAT'S A PRETTY DELUSIONAL IDEALIZATION OF YOUR DRINKING. YOU DON'T HAVE TO HAVE SOME WILD HORROR STORY OR DECADES OF A ROCK-BOTTOM EXISTENCE TO BENEFIT FROM SOBRIETY. YOU JUST BEING MISERABLE AND DRINKING YOURSELF TO SLEEP EVERY NIGHT IS PRETTY FUCKING SAD AND THAT'S ENOUGH.

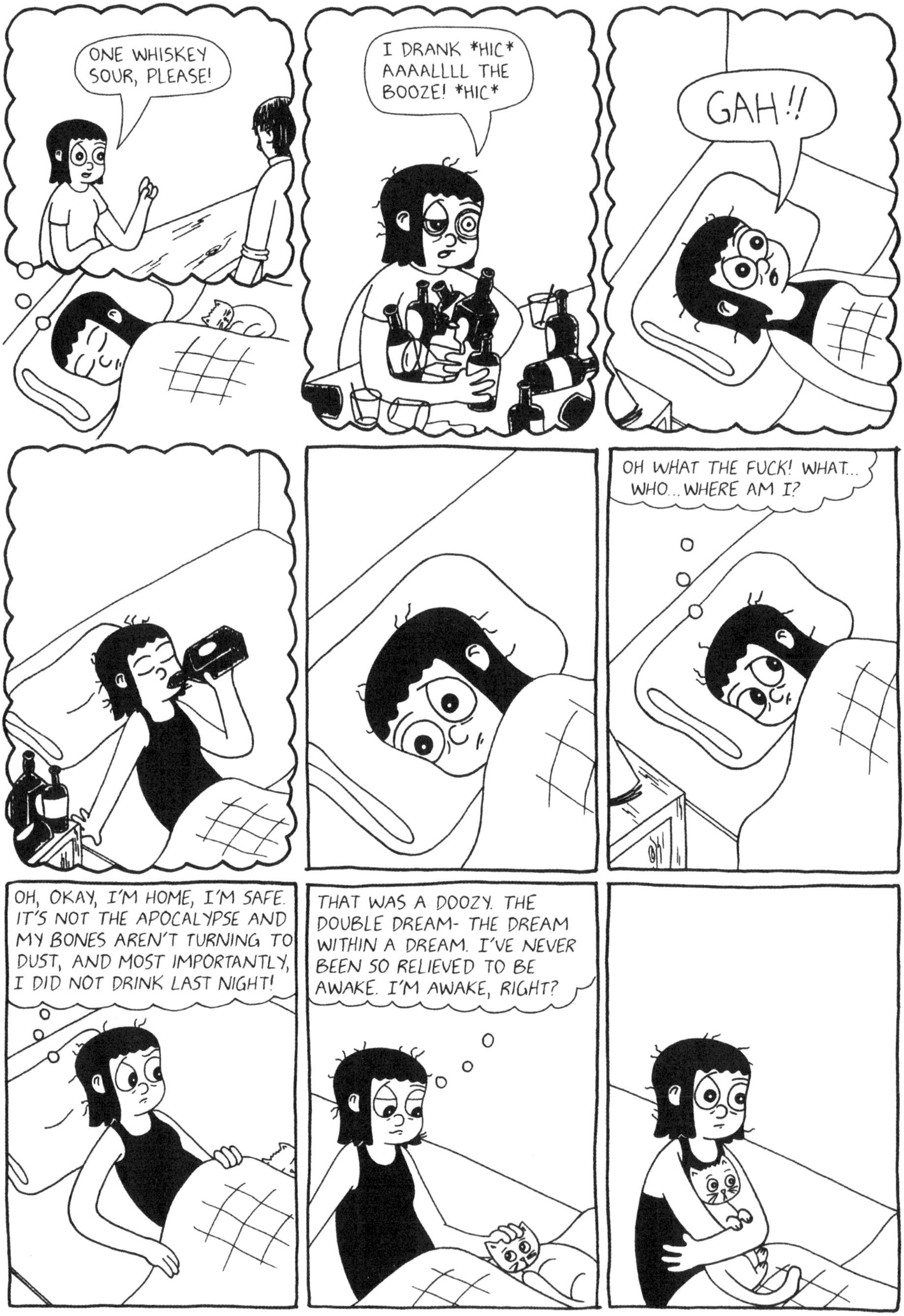

ONE WHISKEY SOUR, PLEASE!
I DRANK *HIC* AAAALLLL THE BOOZE! *HIC*
GAH!!
OH WHAT THE FUCK! WHAT... WHO... WHERE AM I?
OH, OKAY, I'M HOME, I'M SAFE. IT'S NOT THE APOCALYPSE AND MY BONES AREN'T TURNING TO DUST, AND MOST IMPORTANTLY, I DID NOT DRINK LAST NIGHT!
THAT WAS A DOOZY. THE DOUBLE DREAM- THE DREAM WITHIN A DREAM. I'VE NEVER BEEN SO RELIEVED TO BE AWAKE. I'M AWAKE, RIGHT?

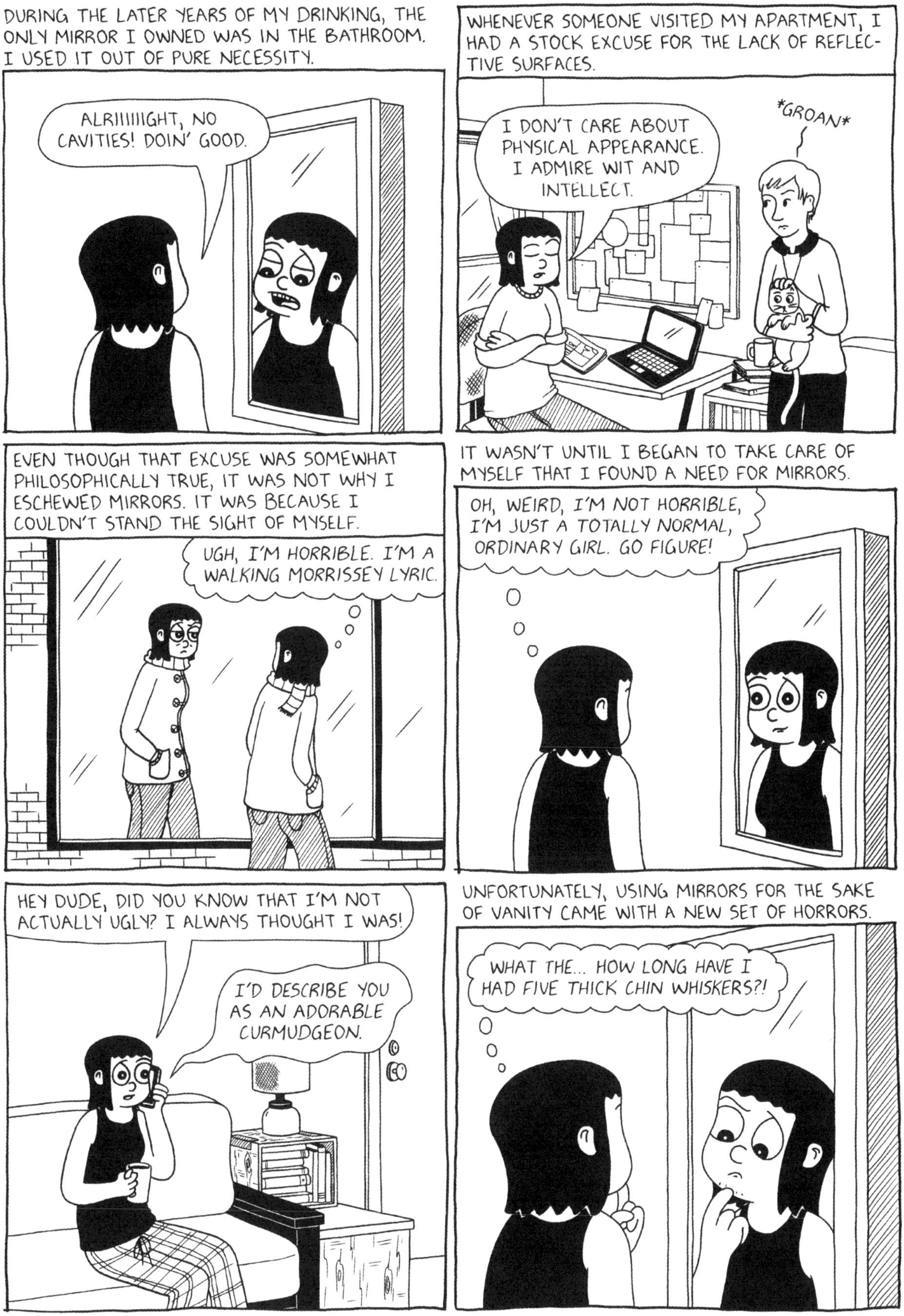
DURING THE LATER YEARS OF MY DRINKING, THE ONLY MIRROR I OWNED WAS IN THE BATHROOM. I USED IT OUT OF PURE NECESSITY.
ALRIIIIIIGHT, NO CAVITIES! DOIN' GOOD.
WHENEVER SOMEONE VISITED MY APARTMENT, I HAD A STOCK EXCUSE FOR THE LACK OF REFLECTIVE SURFACES.
I DON'T CARE ABOUT PHYSICAL APPEARANCE. I ADMIRE WIT AND INTELLECT.
GROAN
EVEN THOUGH THAT EXCUSE WAS SOMEWHAT PHILOSOPHICALLY TRUE, IT WAS NOT WHY I ESCHEWED MIRRORS. IT WAS BECAUSE I COULDN'T STAND THE SIGHT OF MYSELF.
UGH, I'M HORRIBLE. I'M A WALKING MORRISSEY LYRIC.
IT WASN'T UNTIL I BEGAN TO TAKE CARE OF MYSELF THAT I FOUND A NEED FOR MIRRORS.
OH, WEIRD, I'M NOT HORRIBLE, I'M JUST A TOTALLY NORMAL, ORDINARY GIRL. GO FIGURE!
HEY DUDE, DID YOU KNOW THAT I'M NOT ACTUALLY UGLY? I ALWAYS THOUGHT I WAS!
I'D DESCRIBE YOU AS AN ADORABLE CURMUDGEON.
UNFORTUNATELY, USING MIRRORS FOR THE SAKE OF VANITY CAME WITH A NEW SET OF HORRORS.
WHAT THE... HOW LONG HAVE I HAD FIVE THICK CHIN WHISKERS?!

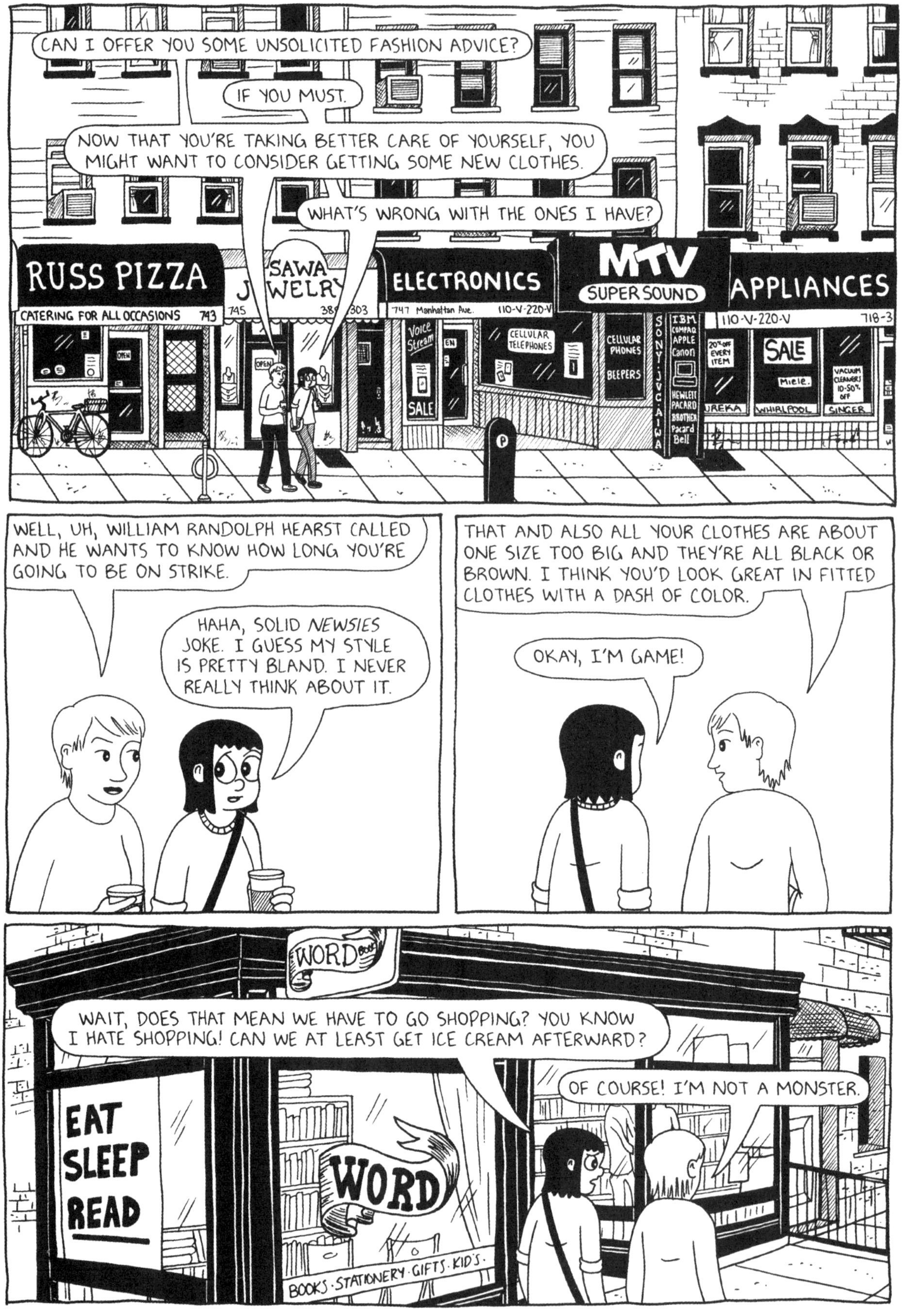
CAN I OFFER YOU SOME UNSOLICITED FASHION ADVICE?
IF YOU MUST.
NOW THAT YOU'RE TAKING BETTER CARE OF YOURSELF, YOU MIGHT WANT TO CONSIDER GETTING SOME NEW CLOTHES.
WHAT'S WRONG WITH THE ONES I HAVE?
RUSS PIZZA
CATERING FOR ALL OCCASIONS 743
ELECTRONICS
747 Manhattan Ave. 110-V-220-V
MTV
SUPER SOUND
APPLIANCES
110-V-220-V
CELLULAR TELEPHONES
CELLULAR PHONES
BEEPERS
SALE
WELL, UH, WILLIAM RANDOLPH HEARST CALLED AND HE WANTS TO KNOW HOW LONG YOU'RE GOING TO BE ON STRIKE.
HAHA, SOLID *NEWSIES* JOKE. I GUESS MY STYLE IS PRETTY BLAND. I NEVER REALLY THINK ABOUT IT.
THAT AND ALSO ALL YOUR CLOTHES ARE ABOUT ONE SIZE TOO BIG AND THEY'RE ALL BLACK OR BROWN. I THINK YOU'D LOOK GREAT IN FITTED CLOTHES WITH A DASH OF COLOR.
OKAY, I'M GAME!
WORD
WAIT, DOES THAT MEAN WE HAVE TO GO SHOPPING? YOU KNOW I HATE SHOPPING! CAN WE AT LEAST GET ICE CREAM AFTERWARD?
OF COURSE! I'M NOT A MONSTER.
EAT SLEEP READ
WORD
BOOKS · STATIONERY · GIFTS · KID'S ·

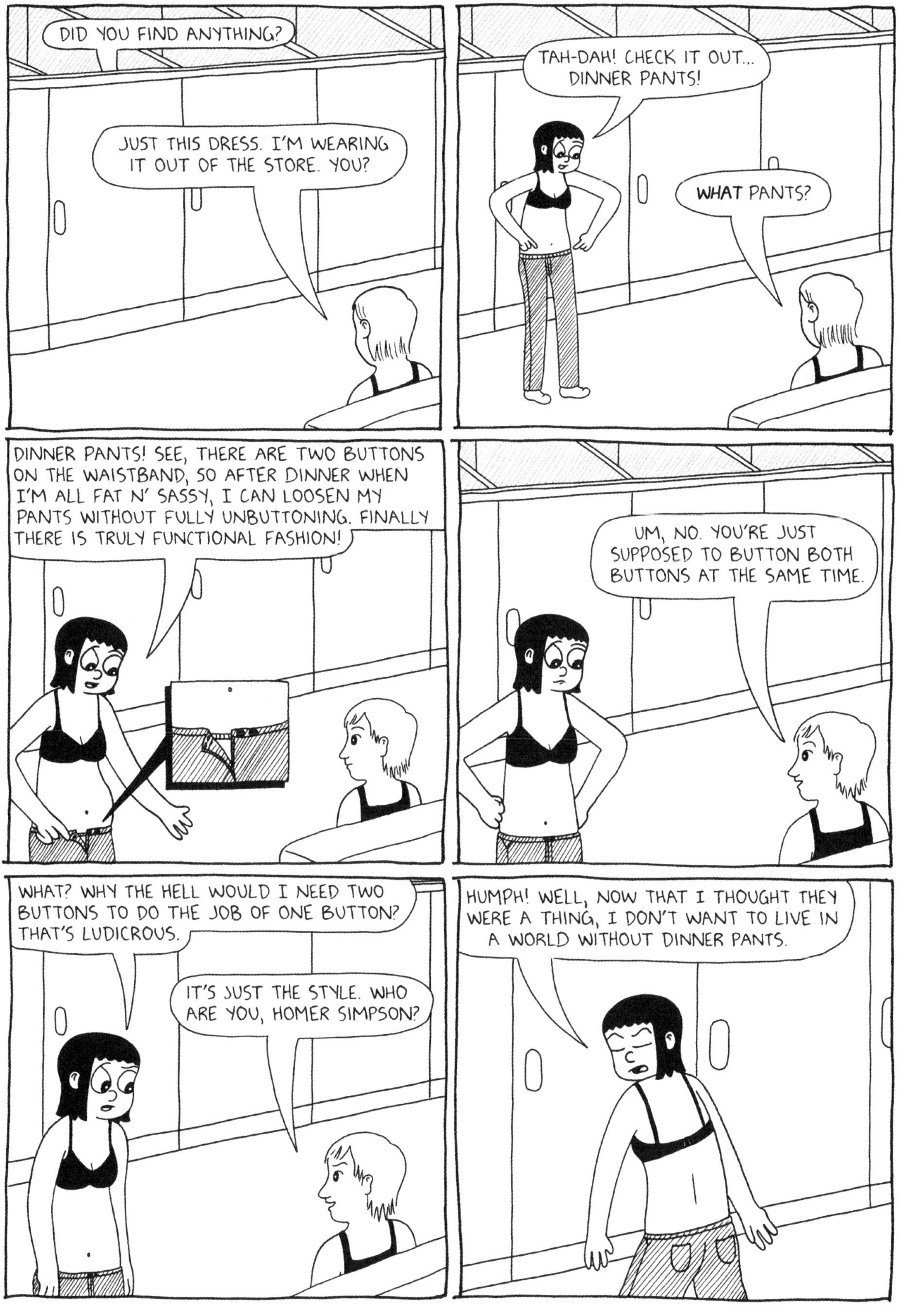
DID YOU FIND ANYTHING?
JUST THIS DRESS. I'M WEARING IT OUT OF THE STORE. YOU?
TAH-DAH! CHECK IT OUT... DINNER PANTS!
WHAT PANTS?
DINNER PANTS! SEE, THERE ARE TWO BUTTONS ON THE WAISTBAND, SO AFTER DINNER WHEN I'M ALL FAT N' SASSY, I CAN LOOSEN MY PANTS WITHOUT FULLY UNBUTTONING. FINALLY THERE IS TRULY FUNCTIONAL FASHION!
UM, NO. YOU'RE JUST SUPPOSED TO BUTTON BOTH BUTTONS AT THE SAME TIME.
WHAT? WHY THE HELL WOULD I NEED TWO BUTTONS TO DO THE JOB OF ONE BUTTON? THAT'S LUDICROUS.
IT'S JUST THE STYLE. WHO ARE YOU, HOMER SIMPSON?
HUMPH! WELL, NOW THAT I THOUGHT THEY WERE A THING, I DON'T WANT TO LIVE IN A WORLD WITHOUT DINNER PANTS.

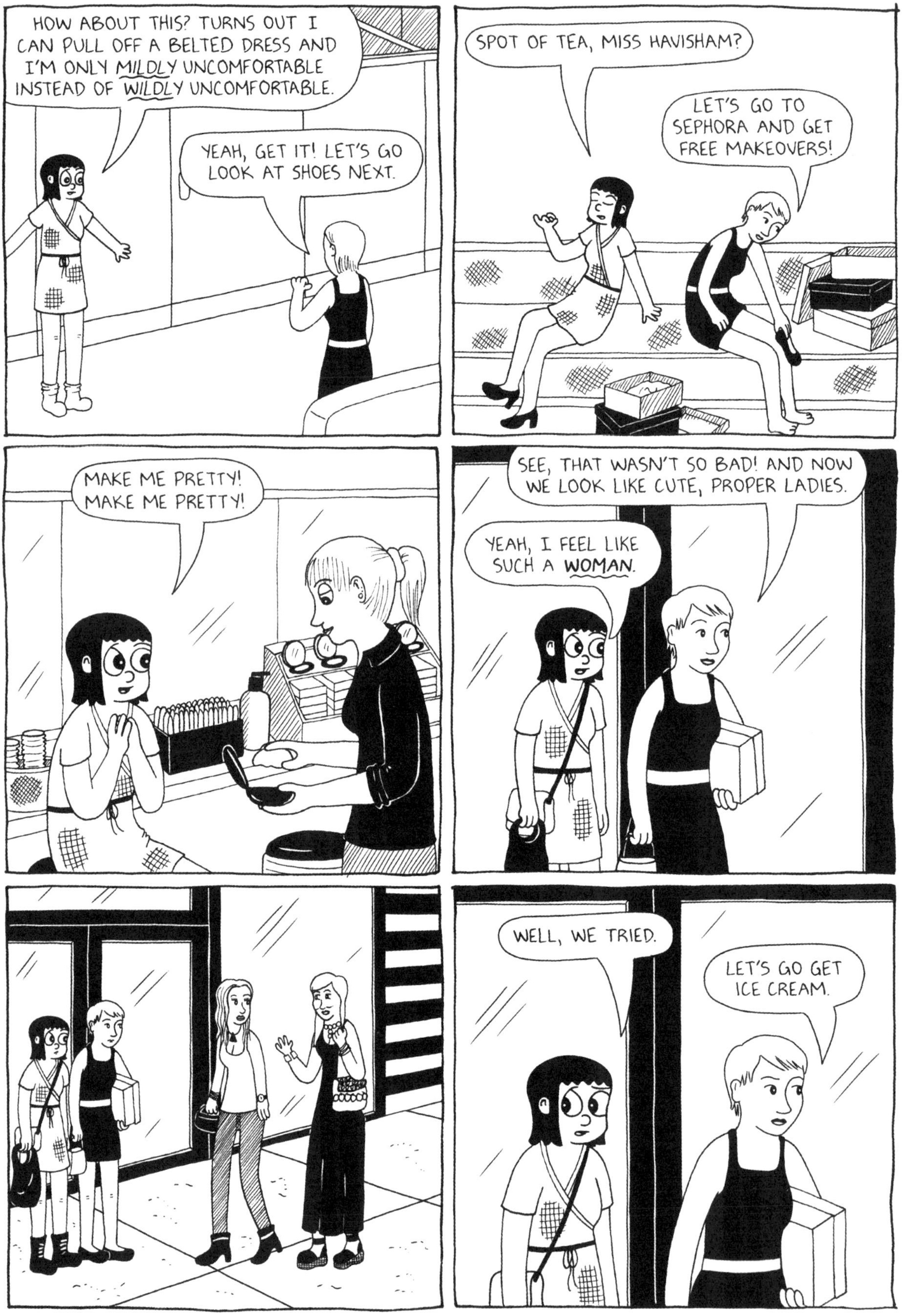
HOW ABOUT THIS? TURNS OUT I CAN PULL OFF A BELTED DRESS AND I'M ONLY MILDLY UNCOMFORTABLE INSTEAD OF WILDLY UNCOMFORTABLE.
YEAH, GET IT! LET'S GO LOOK AT SHOES NEXT.
SPOT OF TEA, MISS HAVISHAM?
LET'S GO TO SEPHORA AND GET FREE MAKEOVERS!
MAKE ME PRETTY! MAKE ME PRETTY!
SEE, THAT WASN'T SO BAD! AND NOW WE LOOK LIKE CUTE, PROPER LADIES.
YEAH, I FEEL LIKE SUCH A WOMAN.
WELL, WE TRIED.
LET'S GO GET ICE CREAM.

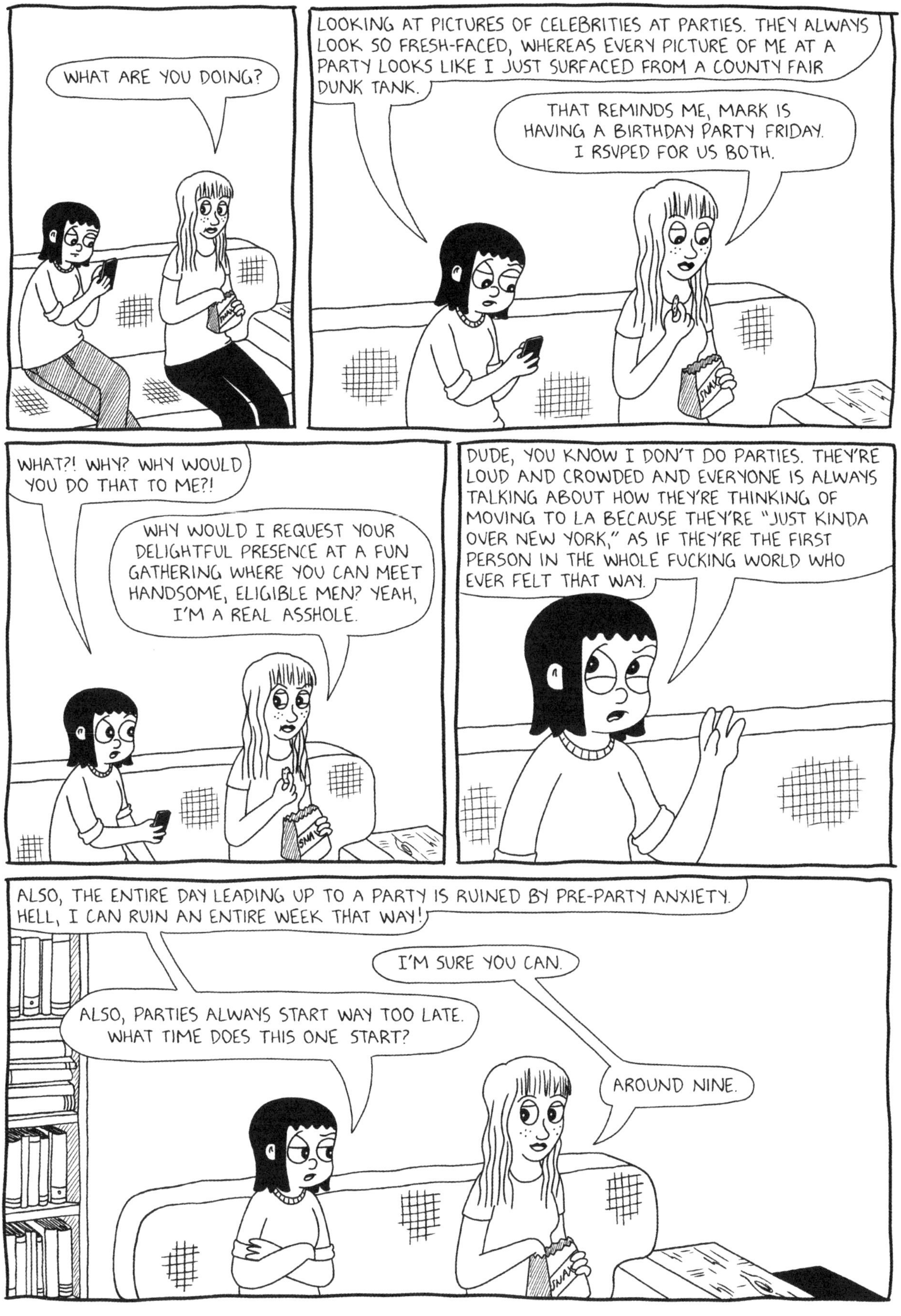
WHAT ARE YOU DOING?
LOOKING AT PICTURES OF CELEBRITIES AT PARTIES. THEY ALWAYS LOOK SO FRESH-FACED, WHEREAS EVERY PICTURE OF ME AT A PARTY LOOKS LIKE I JUST SURFACED FROM A COUNTY FAIR DUNK TANK.
THAT REMINDS ME, MARK IS HAVING A BIRTHDAY PARTY FRIDAY. I RSVPED FOR US BOTH.
WHAT?! WHY? WHY WOULD YOU DO THAT TO ME?!
WHY WOULD I REQUEST YOUR DELIGHTFUL PRESENCE AT A FUN GATHERING WHERE YOU CAN MEET HANDSOME, ELIGIBLE MEN? YEAH, I'M A REAL ASSHOLE.
DUDE, YOU KNOW I DON'T DO PARTIES. THEY'RE LOUD AND CROWDED AND EVERYONE IS ALWAYS TALKING ABOUT HOW THEY'RE THINKING OF MOVING TO LA BECAUSE THEY'RE "JUST KINDA OVER NEW YORK," AS IF THEY'RE THE FIRST PERSON IN THE WHOLE FUCKING WORLD WHO EVER FELT THAT WAY.
ALSO, THE ENTIRE DAY LEADING UP TO A PARTY IS RUINED BY PRE-PARTY ANXIETY. HELL, I CAN RUIN AN ENTIRE WEEK THAT WAY!
I'M SURE YOU CAN.
ALSO, PARTIES ALWAYS START WAY TOO LATE. WHAT TIME DOES THIS ONE START?
AROUND NINE.

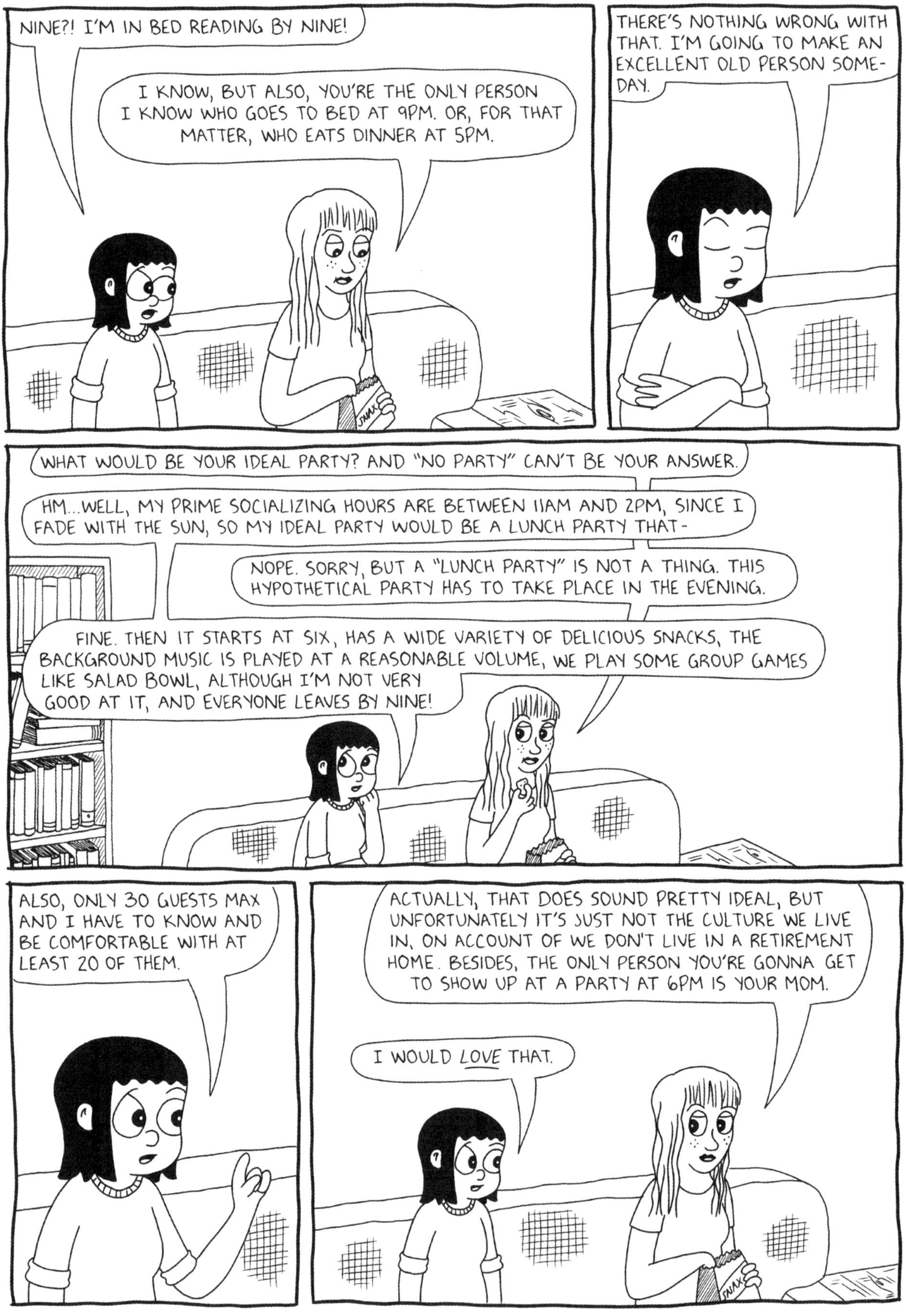
NINE?! I'M IN BED READING BY NINE!
I KNOW, BUT ALSO, YOU'RE THE ONLY PERSON I KNOW WHO GOES TO BED AT 9PM. OR, FOR THAT MATTER, WHO EATS DINNER AT 5PM.
THERE'S NOTHING WRONG WITH THAT. I'M GOING TO MAKE AN EXCELLENT OLD PERSON SOME-DAY.
WHAT WOULD BE YOUR IDEAL PARTY? AND "NO PARTY" CAN'T BE YOUR ANSWER.
HM...WELL, MY PRIME SOCIALIZING HOURS ARE BETWEEN 11AM AND 2PM, SINCE I FADE WITH THE SUN, SO MY IDEAL PARTY WOULD BE A LUNCH PARTY THAT-
NOPE. SORRY, BUT A "LUNCH PARTY" IS NOT A THING. THIS HYPOTHETICAL PARTY HAS TO TAKE PLACE IN THE EVENING.
FINE. THEN IT STARTS AT SIX, HAS A WIDE VARIETY OF DELICIOUS SNACKS, THE BACKGROUND MUSIC IS PLAYED AT A REASONABLE VOLUME, WE PLAY SOME GROUP GAMES LIKE SALAD BOWL, ALTHOUGH I'M NOT VERY GOOD AT IT, AND EVERYONE LEAVES BY NINE!
ALSO, ONLY 30 GUESTS MAX AND I HAVE TO KNOW AND BE COMFORTABLE WITH AT LEAST 20 OF THEM.
ACTUALLY, THAT DOES SOUND PRETTY IDEAL, BUT UNFORTUNATELY IT'S JUST NOT THE CULTURE WE LIVE IN, ON ACCOUNT OF WE DON'T LIVE IN A RETIREMENT HOME. BESIDES, THE ONLY PERSON YOU'RE GONNA GET TO SHOW UP AT A PARTY AT 6PM IS YOUR MOM.
I WOULD LOVE THAT.

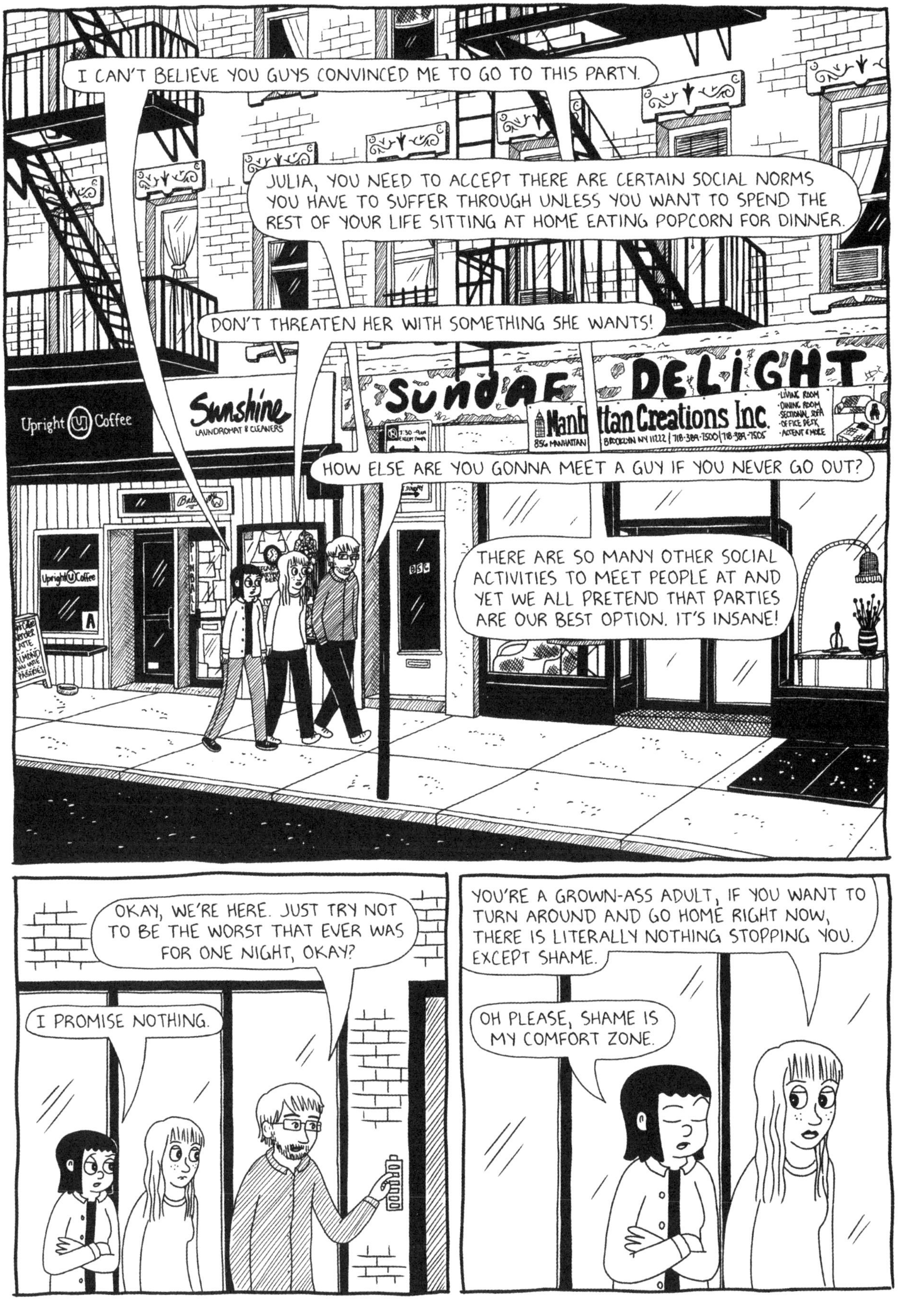
I CAN'T BELIEVE YOU GUYS CONVINCED ME TO GO TO THIS PARTY.
JULIA, YOU NEED TO ACCEPT THERE ARE CERTAIN SOCIAL NORMS YOU HAVE TO SUFFER THROUGH UNLESS YOU WANT TO SPEND THE REST OF YOUR LIFE SITTING AT HOME EATING POPCORN FOR DINNER.
DON'T THREATEN HER WITH SOMETHING SHE WANTS!
Upright Coffee
Sunshine
LAUNDROMAT & CLEANERS
SUNDAE DELIGHT
Manhattan Creations Inc.
HOW ELSE ARE YOU GONNA MEET A GUY IF YOU NEVER GO OUT?
THERE ARE SO MANY OTHER SOCIAL ACTIVITIES TO MEET PEOPLE AT AND YET WE ALL PRETEND THAT PARTIES ARE OUR BEST OPTION. IT'S INSANE!
OKAY, WE'RE HERE. JUST TRY NOT TO BE THE WORST THAT EVER WAS FOR ONE NIGHT, OKAY?
I PROMISE NOTHING.
YOU'RE A GROWN-ASS ADULT, IF YOU WANT TO TURN AROUND AND GO HOME RIGHT NOW, THERE IS LITERALLY NOTHING STOPPING YOU. EXCEPT SHAME.
OH PLEASE, SHAME IS MY COMFORT ZONE.

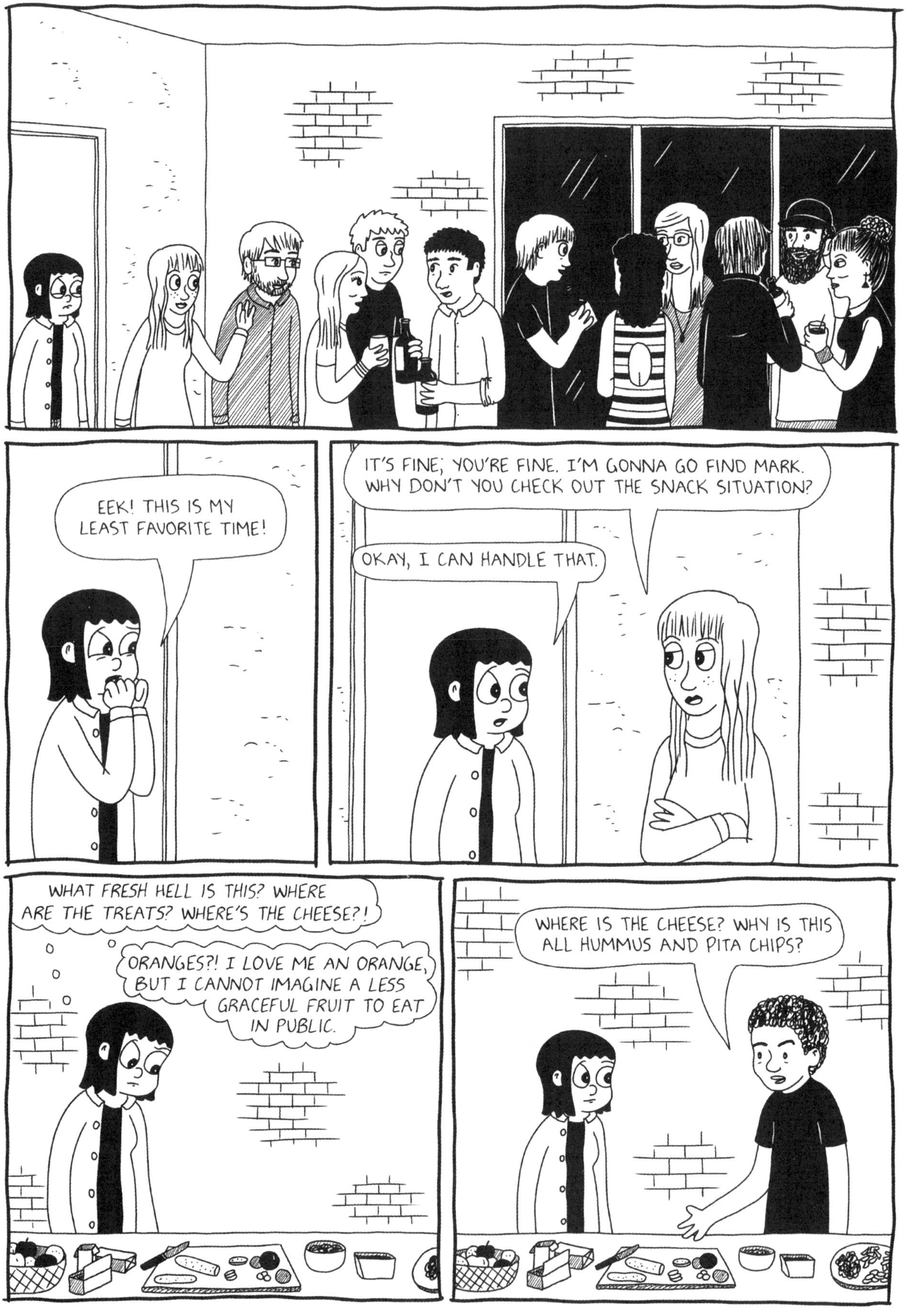
EEK! THIS IS MY LEAST FAVORITE TIME!
IT'S FINE; YOU'RE FINE. I'M GONNA GO FIND MARK. WHY DON'T YOU CHECK OUT THE SNACK SITUATION?
OKAY, I CAN HANDLE THAT.
WHAT FRESH HELL IS THIS? WHERE ARE THE TREATS? WHERE'S THE CHEESE?!
ORANGES?! I LOVE ME AN ORANGE, BUT I CANNOT IMAGINE A LESS GRACEFUL FRUIT TO EAT IN PUBLIC.
WHERE IS THE CHEESE? WHY IS THIS ALL HUMMUS AND PITA CHIPS?

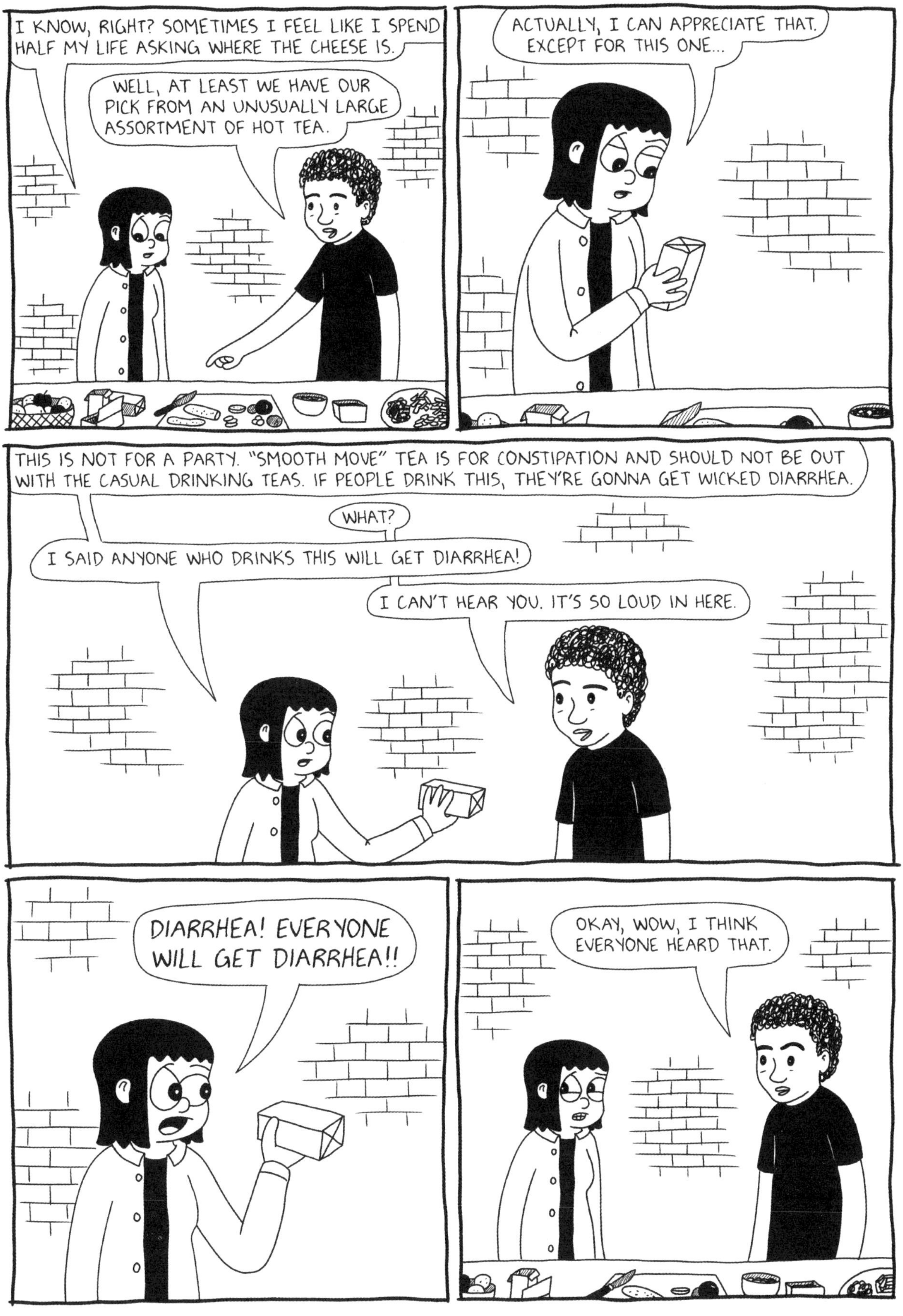
I KNOW, RIGHT? SOMETIMES I FEEL LIKE I SPEND HALF MY LIFE ASKING WHERE THE CHEESE IS.
WELL, AT LEAST WE HAVE OUR PICK FROM AN UNUSUALLY LARGE ASSORTMENT OF HOT TEA.
ACTUALLY, I CAN APPRECIATE THAT. EXCEPT FOR THIS ONE...
THIS IS NOT FOR A PARTY. "SMOOTH MOVE" TEA IS FOR CONSTIPATION AND SHOULD NOT BE OUT WITH THE CASUAL DRINKING TEAS. IF PEOPLE DRINK THIS, THEY'RE GONNA GET WICKED DIARRHEA.
WHAT?
I SAID ANYONE WHO DRINKS THIS WILL GET DIARRHEA!
I CAN'T HEAR YOU. IT'S SO LOUD IN HERE.
DIARRHEA! EVERYONE WILL GET DIARRHEA!!
OKAY, WOW, I THINK EVERYONE HEARD THAT.

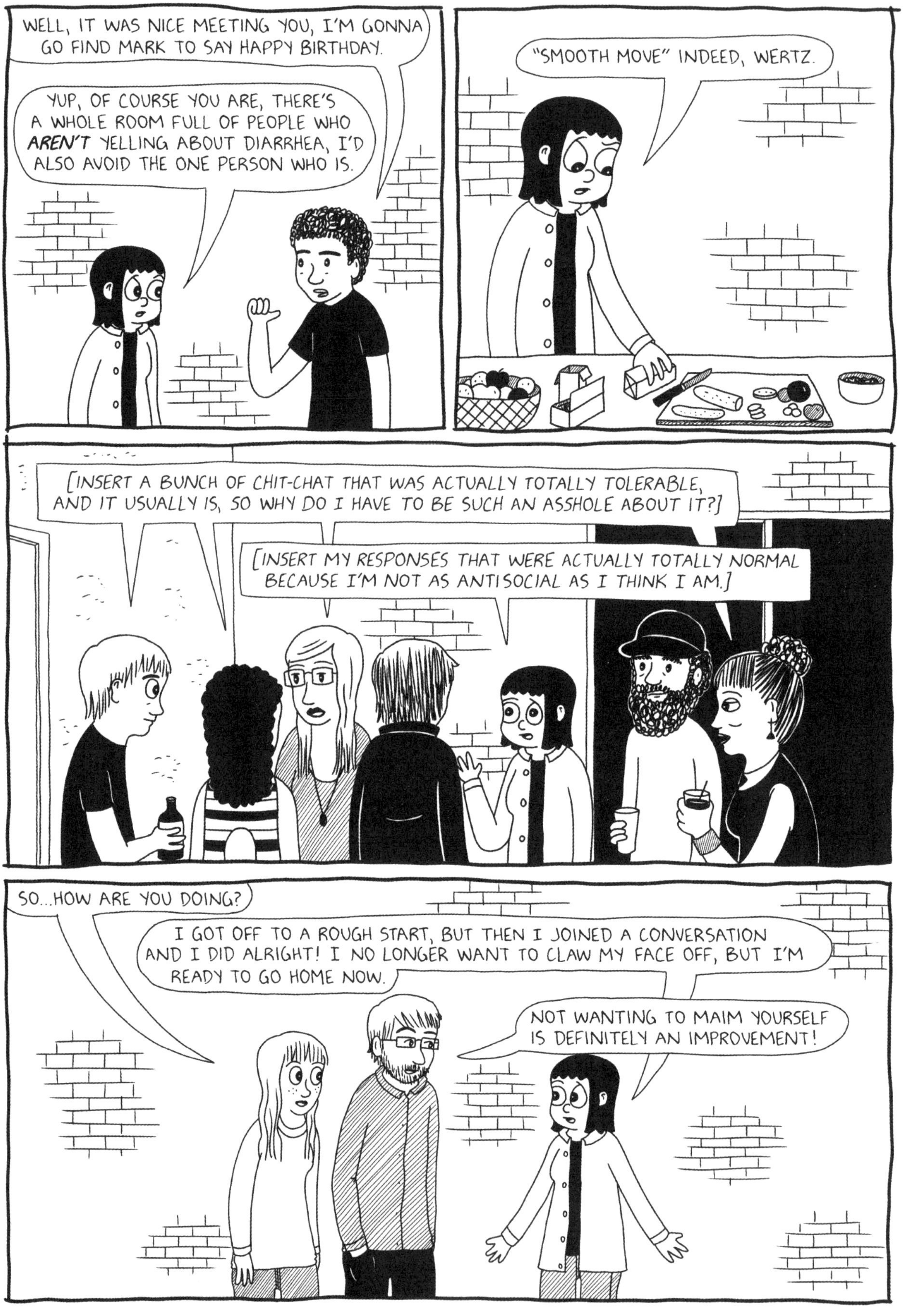
WELL, IT WAS NICE MEETING YOU, I'M GONNA GO FIND MARK TO SAY HAPPY BIRTHDAY.
YUP, OF COURSE YOU ARE, THERE'S A WHOLE ROOM FULL OF PEOPLE WHO **AREN'T** YELLING ABOUT DIARRHEA, I'D ALSO AVOID THE ONE PERSON WHO IS.
"SMOOTH MOVE" INDEED, WERTZ.
[INSERT A BUNCH OF CHIT-CHAT THAT WAS ACTUALLY TOTALLY TOLERABLE, AND IT USUALLY IS, SO WHY DO I HAVE TO BE SUCH AN ASSHOLE ABOUT IT?]
[INSERT MY RESPONSES THAT WERE ACTUALLY TOTALLY NORMAL BECAUSE I'M NOT AS ANTISOCIAL AS I THINK I AM.]
SO...HOW ARE YOU DOING?
I GOT OFF TO A ROUGH START, BUT THEN I JOINED A CONVERSATION AND I DID ALRIGHT! I NO LONGER WANT TO CLAW MY FACE OFF, BUT I'M READY TO GO HOME NOW.
NOT WANTING TO MAIM YOURSELF IS DEFINITELY AN IMPROVEMENT!

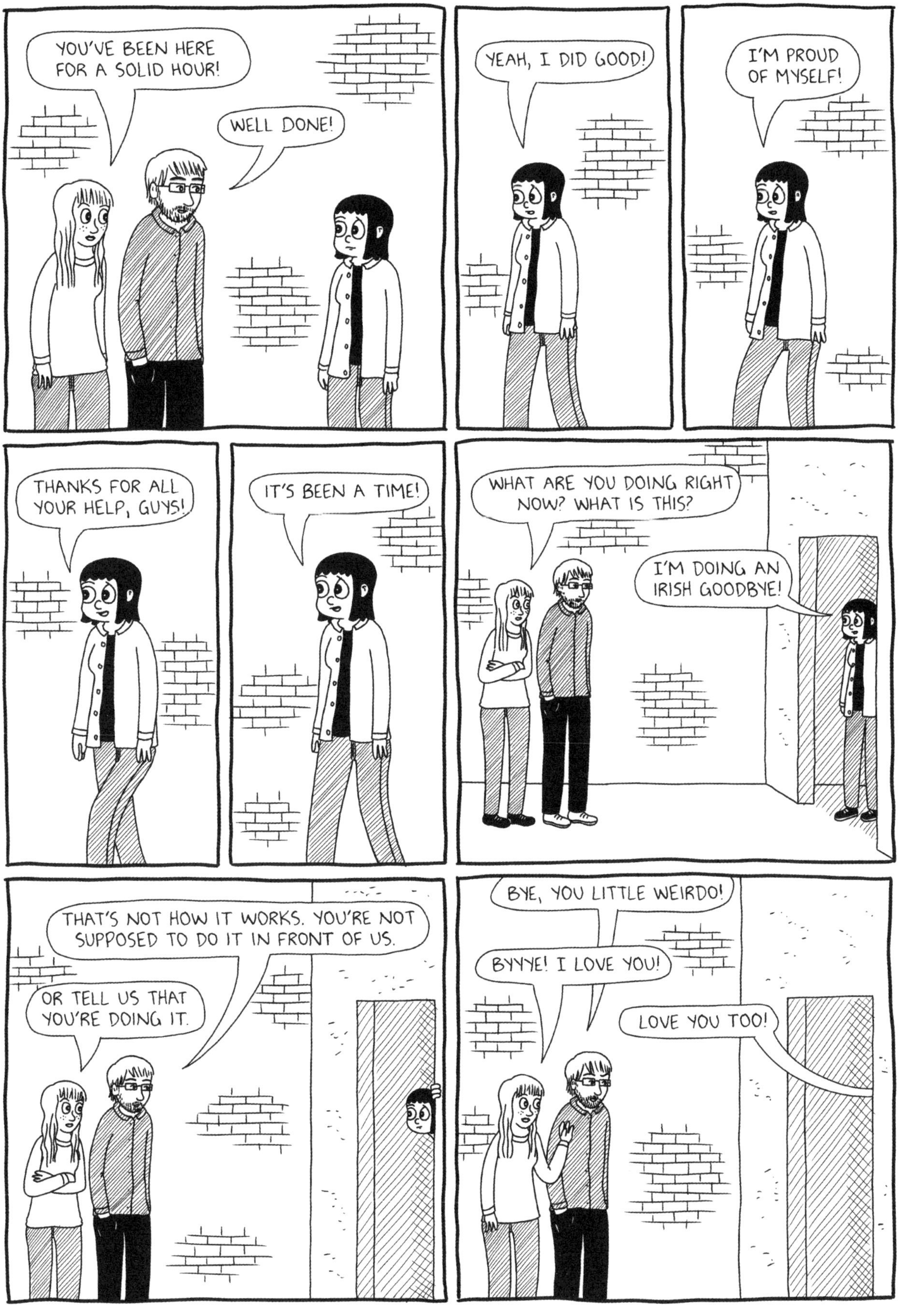
YOU'VE BEEN HERE FOR A SOLID HOUR!
WELL DONE!
YEAH, I DID GOOD!
I'M PROUD OF MYSELF!
THANKS FOR ALL YOUR HELP, GUYS!
IT'S BEEN A TIME!
WHAT ARE YOU DOING RIGHT NOW? WHAT IS THIS?
I'M DOING AN IRISH GOODBYE!
THAT'S NOT HOW IT WORKS. YOU'RE NOT SUPPOSED TO DO IT IN FRONT OF US.
OR TELL US THAT YOU'RE DOING IT.
BYE, YOU LITTLE WEIRDO!
BYYYE! I LOVE YOU!
LOVE YOU TOO!

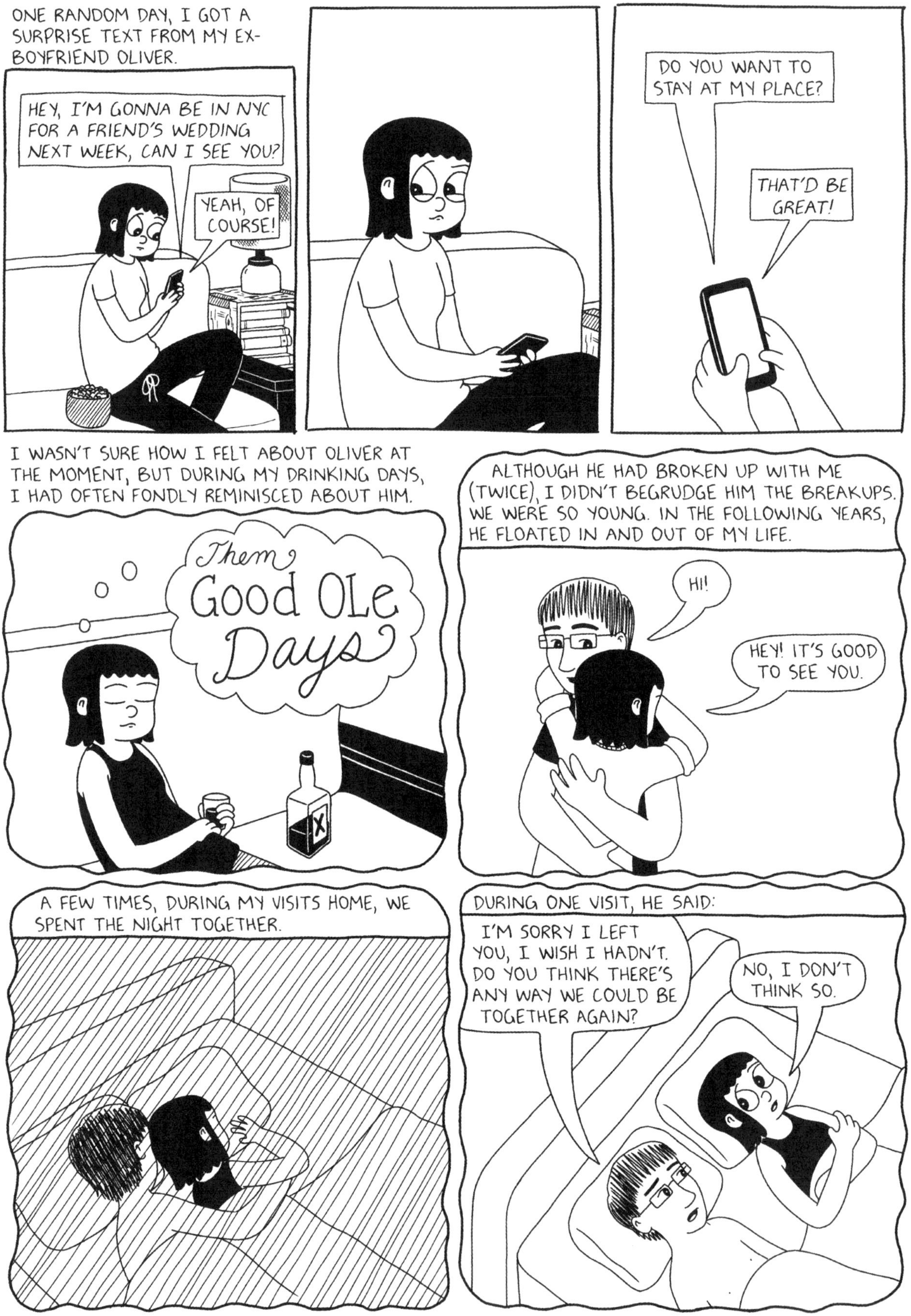
ONE RANDOM DAY, I GOT A SURPRISE TEXT FROM MY EX-BOYFRIEND OLIVER.
HEY, I'M GONNA BE IN NYC FOR A FRIEND'S WEDDING NEXT WEEK, CAN I SEE YOU?
YEAH, OF COURSE!
DO YOU WANT TO STAY AT MY PLACE?
THAT'D BE GREAT!
I WASN'T SURE HOW I FELT ABOUT OLIVER AT THE MOMENT, BUT DURING MY DRINKING DAYS, I HAD OFTEN FONDLY REMINISCED ABOUT HIM.
Them Good OLe Days
ALTHOUGH HE HAD BROKEN UP WITH ME (TWICE), I DIDN'T BEGRUDGE HIM THE BREAKUPS. WE WERE SO YOUNG. IN THE FOLLOWING YEARS, HE FLOATED IN AND OUT OF MY LIFE.
HI!
HEY! IT'S GOOD TO SEE YOU.
A FEW TIMES, DURING MY VISITS HOME, WE SPENT THE NIGHT TOGETHER.
DURING ONE VISIT, HE SAID:
I'M SORRY I LEFT YOU, I WISH I HADN'T. DO YOU THINK THERE'S ANY WAY WE COULD BE TOGETHER AGAIN?
NO, I DON'T THINK SO.

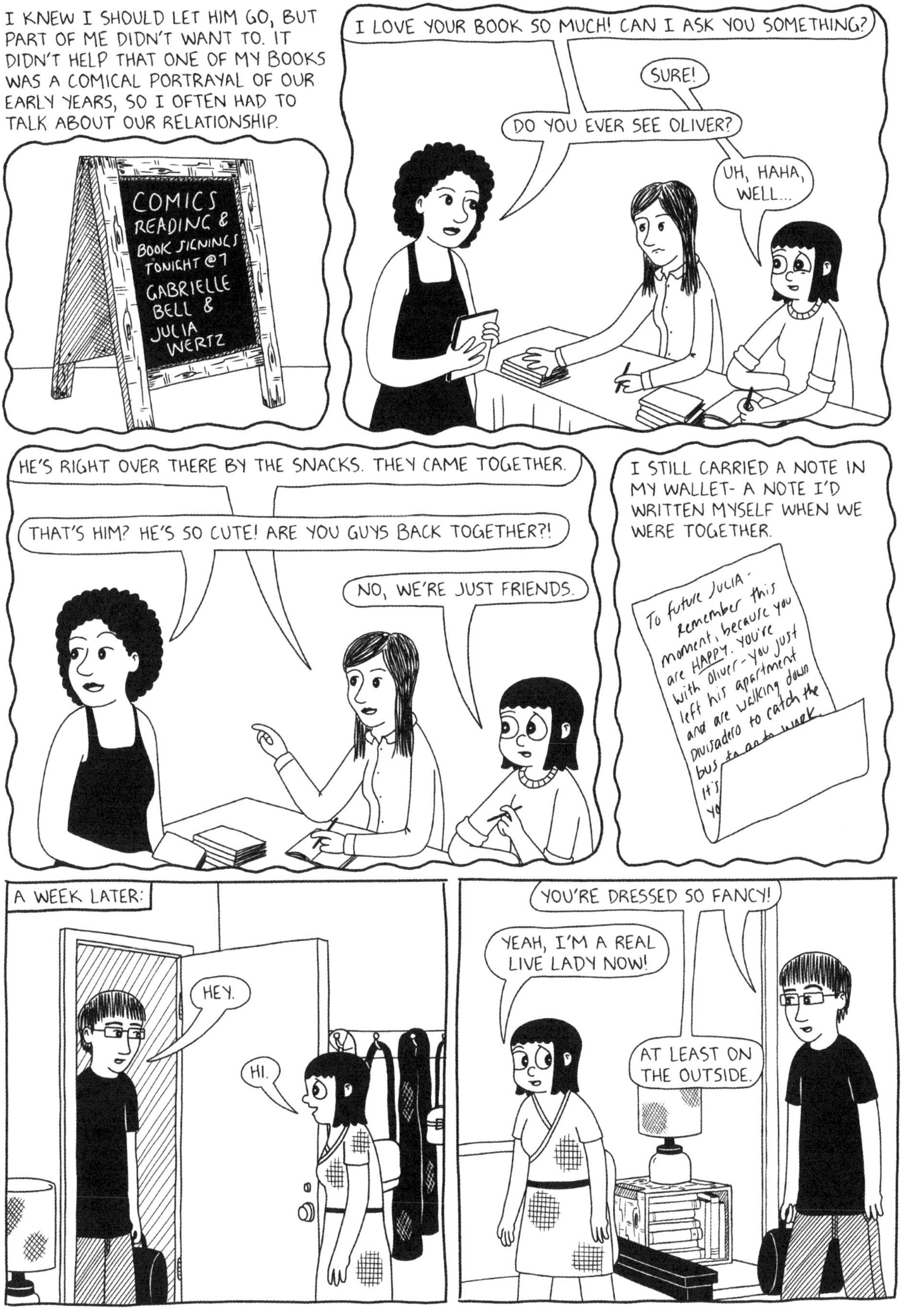
I KNEW I SHOULD LET HIM GO, BUT PART OF ME DIDN'T WANT TO. IT DIDN'T HELP THAT ONE OF MY BOOKS WAS A COMICAL PORTRAYAL OF OUR EARLY YEARS, SO I OFTEN HAD TO TALK ABOUT OUR RELATIONSHIP.
COMICS READING & BOOK SIGNINGS TONIGHT @7 GABRIELLE BELL & JULIA WERTZ
I LOVE YOUR BOOK SO MUCH! CAN I ASK YOU SOMETHING?
SURE!
DO YOU EVER SEE OLIVER?
UH, HAHA, WELL...
HE'S RIGHT OVER THERE BY THE SNACKS. THEY CAME TOGETHER.
THAT'S HIM? HE'S SO CUTE! ARE YOU GUYS BACK TOGETHER?!
NO, WE'RE JUST FRIENDS.
I STILL CARRIED A NOTE IN MY WALLET- A NOTE I'D WRITTEN MYSELF WHEN WE WERE TOGETHER.
To future Julia - Remember this moment, because you are HAPPY. You're with Oliver - you just left his apartment and are walking down Divisadero to catch the bus
A WEEK LATER:
HEY.
HI.
YOU'RE DRESSED SO FANCY!
YEAH, I'M A REAL LIVE LADY NOW!
AT LEAST ON THE OUTSIDE.

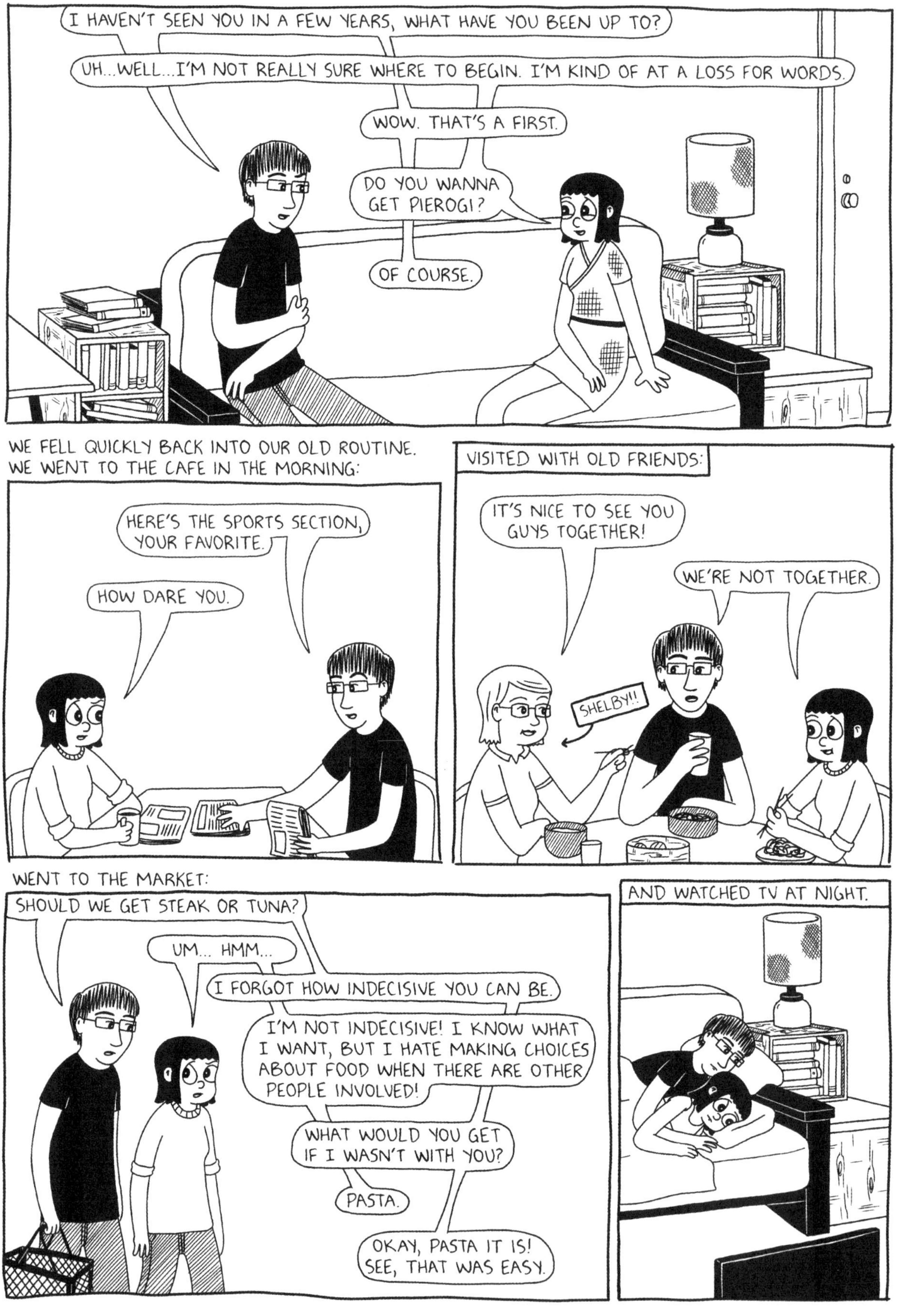
I HAVEN'T SEEN YOU IN A FEW YEARS, WHAT HAVE YOU BEEN UP TO?
UH...WELL...I'M NOT REALLY SURE WHERE TO BEGIN. I'M KIND OF AT A LOSS FOR WORDS.
WOW. THAT'S A FIRST.
DO YOU WANNA GET PIEROGI?
OF COURSE.
WE FELL QUICKLY BACK INTO OUR OLD ROUTINE. WE WENT TO THE CAFE IN THE MORNING:
HERE'S THE SPORTS SECTION, YOUR FAVORITE.
HOW DARE YOU.
VISITED WITH OLD FRIENDS:
IT'S NICE TO SEE YOU GUYS TOGETHER!
WE'RE NOT TOGETHER.
SHELBY!!
WENT TO THE MARKET:
SHOULD WE GET STEAK OR TUNA?
UM... HMM...
I FORGOT HOW INDECISIVE YOU CAN BE.
I'M NOT INDECISIVE! I KNOW WHAT I WANT, BUT I HATE MAKING CHOICES ABOUT FOOD WHEN THERE ARE OTHER PEOPLE INVOLVED!
WHAT WOULD YOU GET IF I WASN'T WITH YOU?
PASTA.
OKAY, PASTA IT IS! SEE, THAT WAS EASY.
AND WATCHED TV AT NIGHT.

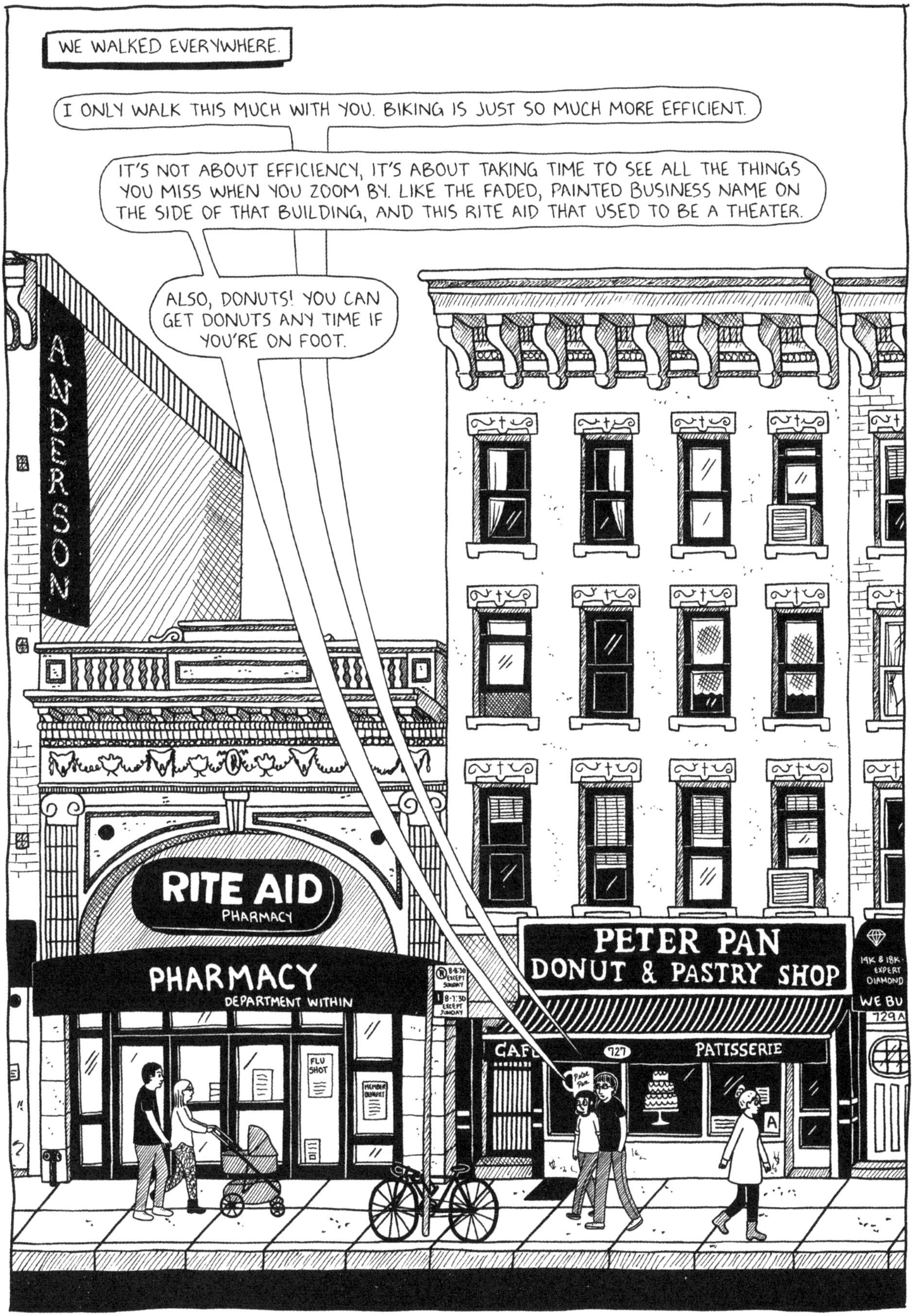
WE WALKED EVERYWHERE.
I ONLY WALK THIS MUCH WITH YOU. BIKING IS JUST SO MUCH MORE EFFICIENT.
IT'S NOT ABOUT EFFICIENCY, IT'S ABOUT TAKING TIME TO SEE ALL THE THINGS YOU MISS WHEN YOU ZOOM BY. LIKE THE FADED, PAINTED BUSINESS NAME ON THE SIDE OF THAT BUILDING, AND THIS RITE AID THAT USED TO BE A THEATER.
ALSO, DONUTS! YOU CAN GET DONUTS ANY TIME IF YOU'RE ON FOOT.
ANDERSON
RITE AID
PHARMACY
PHARMACY
DEPARTMENT WITHIN
FLU SHOT
PETER PAN
DONUT & PASTRY SHOP
727
PATISSERIE

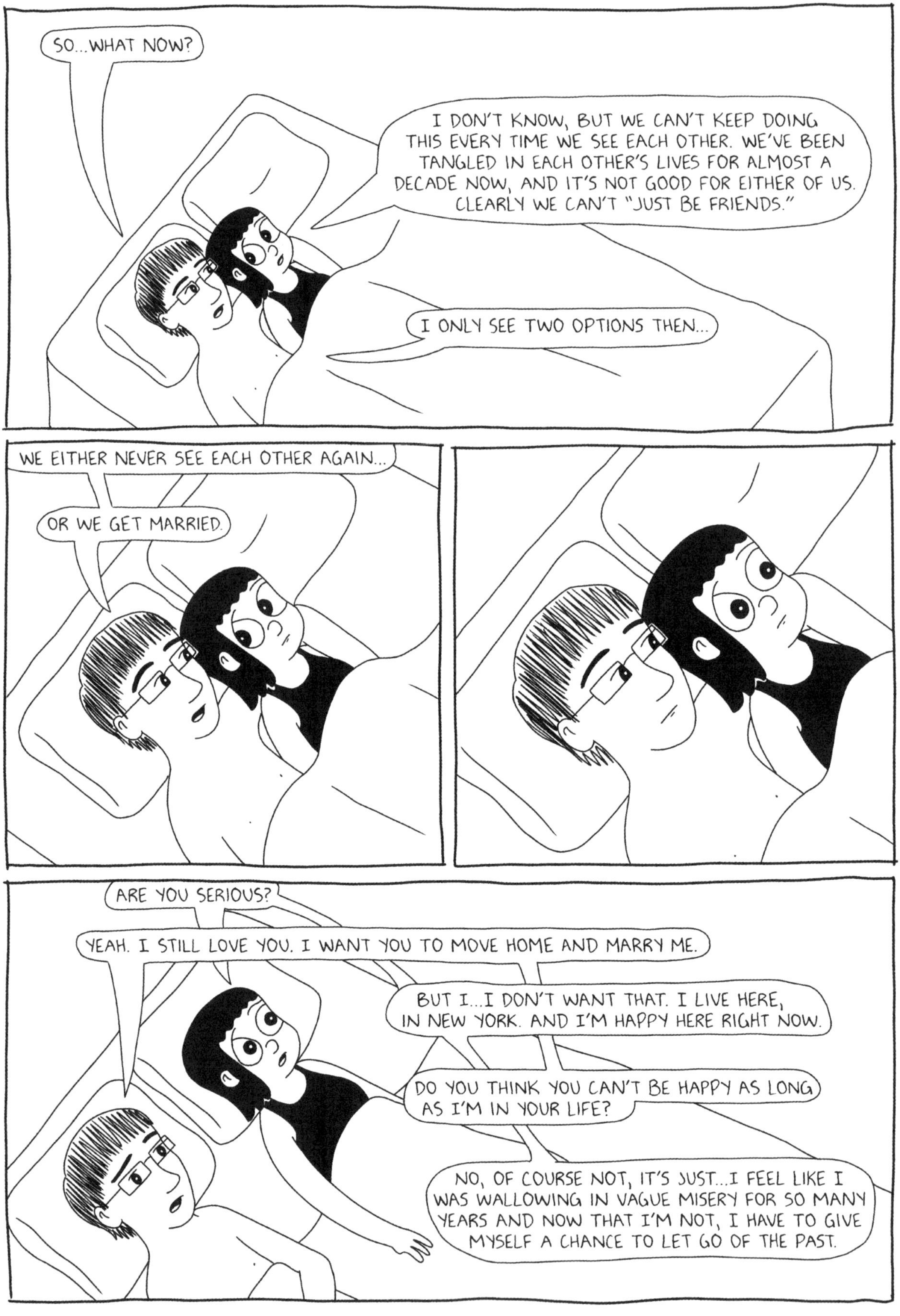
SO... WHAT NOW?
I DON'T KNOW, BUT WE CAN'T KEEP DOING THIS EVERY TIME WE SEE EACH OTHER. WE'VE BEEN TANGLED IN EACH OTHER'S LIVES FOR ALMOST A DECADE NOW, AND IT'S NOT GOOD FOR EITHER OF US. CLEARLY WE CAN'T "JUST BE FRIENDS."
I ONLY SEE TWO OPTIONS THEN...
WE EITHER NEVER SEE EACH OTHER AGAIN...
OR WE GET MARRIED.
ARE YOU SERIOUS?
YEAH. I STILL LOVE YOU. I WANT YOU TO MOVE HOME AND MARRY ME.
BUT I...I DON'T WANT THAT. I LIVE HERE, IN NEW YORK. AND I'M HAPPY HERE RIGHT NOW.
DO YOU THINK YOU CAN'T BE HAPPY AS LONG AS I'M IN YOUR LIFE?
NO, OF COURSE NOT, IT'S JUST...I FEEL LIKE I WAS WALLOWING IN VAGUE MISERY FOR SO MANY YEARS AND NOW THAT I'M NOT, I HAVE TO GIVE MYSELF A CHANCE TO LET GO OF THE PAST.

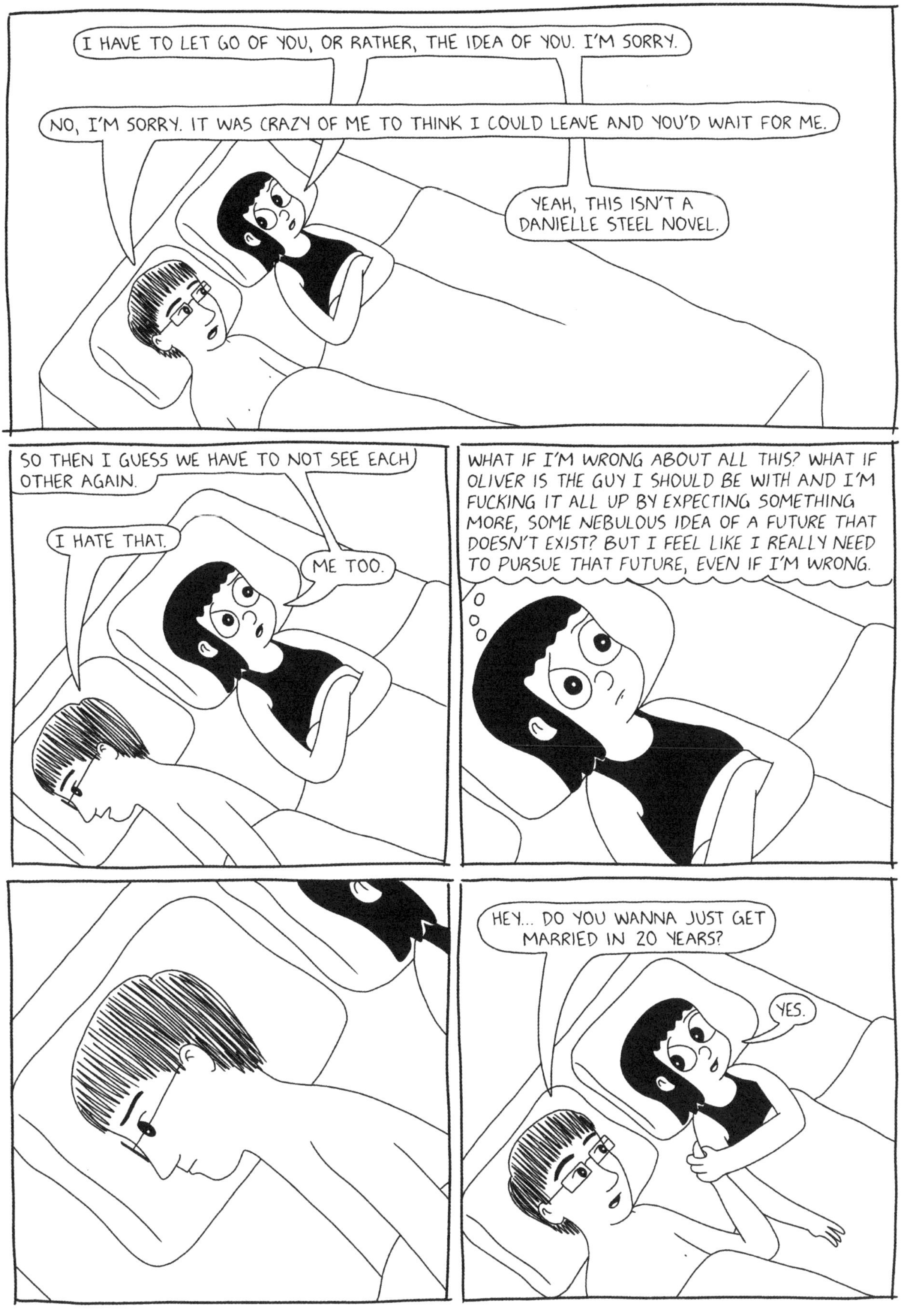
I HAVE TO LET GO OF YOU, OR RATHER, THE IDEA OF YOU. I'M SORRY.
NO, I'M SORRY. IT WAS CRAZY OF ME TO THINK I COULD LEAVE AND YOU'D WAIT FOR ME.
YEAH, THIS ISN'T A DANIELLE STEEL NOVEL.
SO THEN I GUESS WE HAVE TO NOT SEE EACH OTHER AGAIN.
I HATE THAT.
ME TOO.
WHAT IF I'M WRONG ABOUT ALL THIS? WHAT IF OLIVER IS THE GUY I SHOULD BE WITH AND I'M FUCKING IT ALL UP BY EXPECTING SOMETHING MORE, SOME NEBULOUS IDEA OF A FUTURE THAT DOESN'T EXIST? BUT I FEEL LIKE I REALLY NEED TO PURSUE THAT FUTURE, EVEN IF I'M WRONG.
HEY... DO YOU WANNA JUST GET MARRIED IN 20 YEARS?
YES.

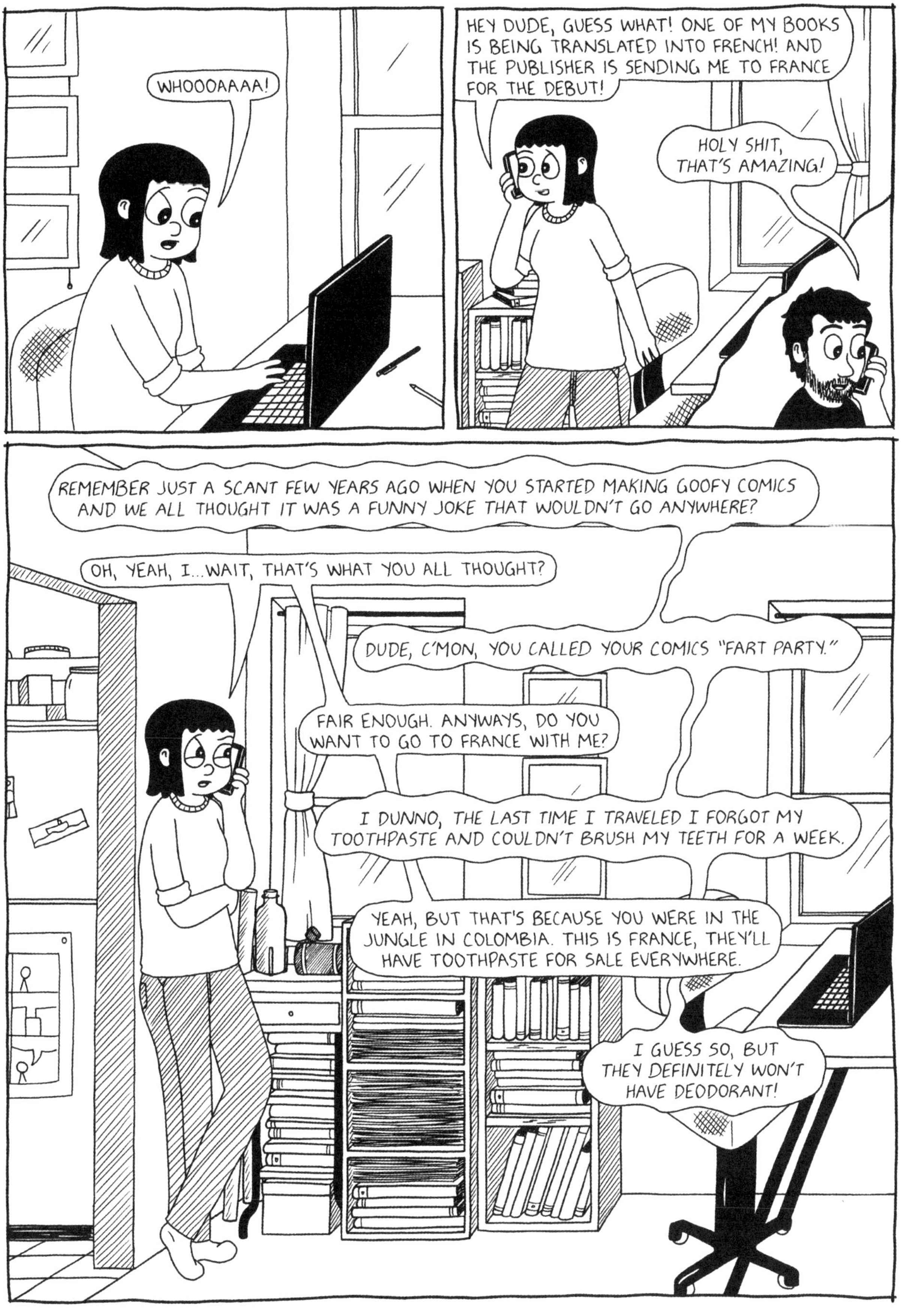
WHOOOAAAA!
HEY DUDE, GUESS WHAT! ONE OF MY BOOKS IS BEING TRANSLATED INTO FRENCH! AND THE PUBLISHER IS SENDING ME TO FRANCE FOR THE DEBUT!
HOLY SHIT, THAT'S AMAZING!
REMEMBER JUST A SCANT FEW YEARS AGO WHEN YOU STARTED MAKING GOOFY COMICS AND WE ALL THOUGHT IT WAS A FUNNY JOKE THAT WOULDN'T GO ANYWHERE?
OH, YEAH, I...WAIT, THAT'S WHAT YOU ALL THOUGHT?
DUDE, C'MON, YOU CALLED YOUR COMICS "FART PARTY."
FAIR ENOUGH. ANYWAYS, DO YOU WANT TO GO TO FRANCE WITH ME?
I DUNNO, THE LAST TIME I TRAVELED I FORGOT MY TOOTHPASTE AND COULDN'T BRUSH MY TEETH FOR A WEEK.
YEAH, BUT THAT'S BECAUSE YOU WERE IN THE JUNGLE IN COLOMBIA. THIS IS FRANCE, THEY'LL HAVE TOOTHPASTE FOR SALE EVERYWHERE.
I GUESS SO, BUT THEY DEFINITELY WON'T HAVE DEODORANT!

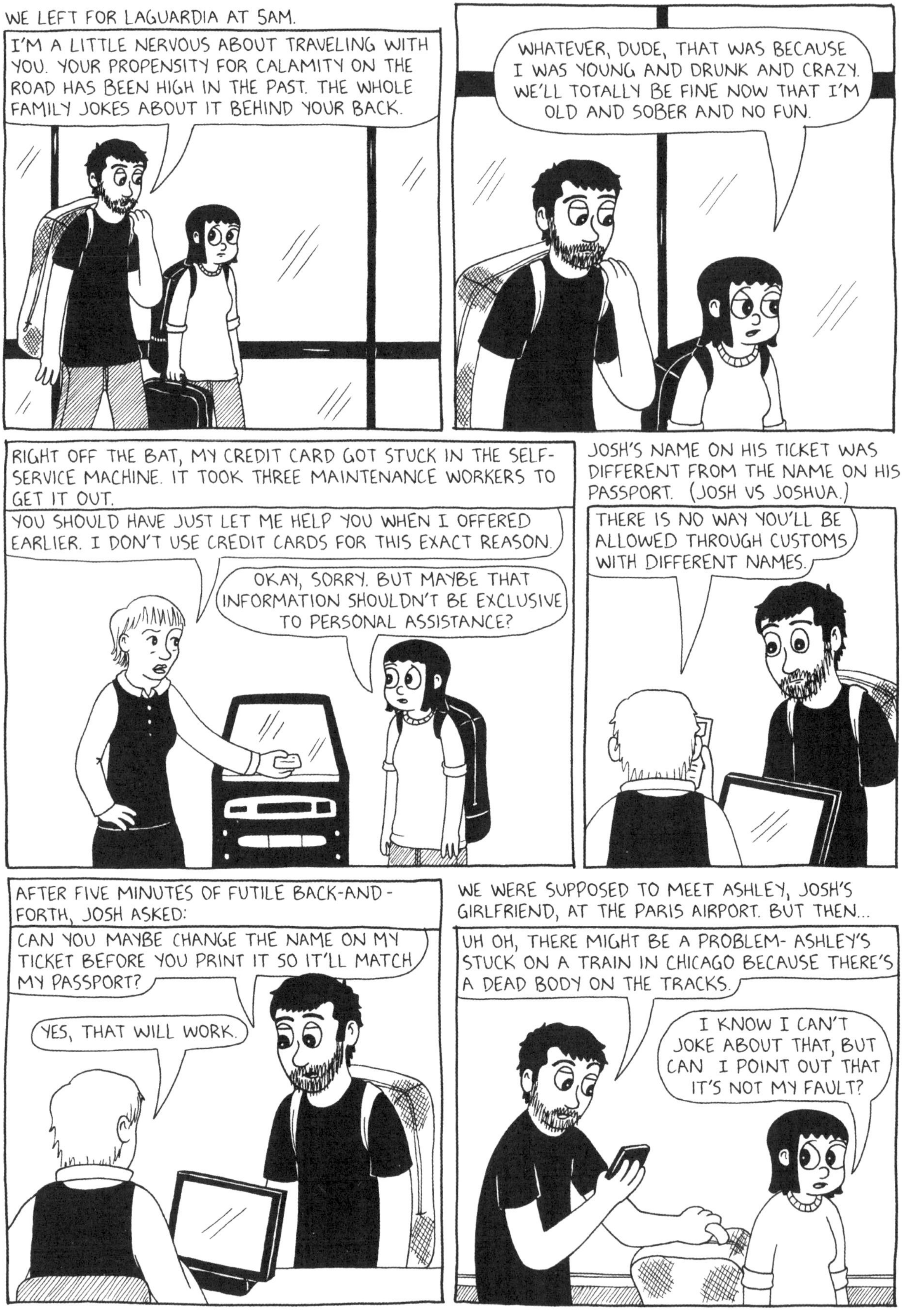

WE LEFT FOR LAGUARDIA AT 5AM.
I'M A LITTLE NERVOUS ABOUT TRAVELING WITH YOU. YOUR PROPENSITY FOR CALAMITY ON THE ROAD HAS BEEN HIGH IN THE PAST. THE WHOLE FAMILY JOKES ABOUT IT BEHIND YOUR BACK.
WHATEVER, DUDE, THAT WAS BECAUSE I WAS YOUNG AND DRUNK AND CRAZY. WE'LL TOTALLY BE FINE NOW THAT I'M OLD AND SOBER AND NO FUN.
RIGHT OFF THE BAT, MY CREDIT CARD GOT STUCK IN THE SELF-SERVICE MACHINE. IT TOOK THREE MAINTENANCE WORKERS TO GET IT OUT.
YOU SHOULD HAVE JUST LET ME HELP YOU WHEN I OFFERED EARLIER. I DON'T USE CREDIT CARDS FOR THIS EXACT REASON.
OKAY, SORRY. BUT MAYBE THAT INFORMATION SHOULDN'T BE EXCLUSIVE TO PERSONAL ASSISTANCE?
JOSH'S NAME ON HIS TICKET WAS DIFFERENT FROM THE NAME ON HIS PASSPORT. (JOSH VS JOSHUA.)
THERE IS NO WAY YOU'LL BE ALLOWED THROUGH CUSTOMS WITH DIFFERENT NAMES.
AFTER FIVE MINUTES OF FUTILE BACK-AND-FORTH, JOSH ASKED:
CAN YOU MAYBE CHANGE THE NAME ON MY TICKET BEFORE YOU PRINT IT SO IT'LL MATCH MY PASSPORT?
YES, THAT WILL WORK.
WE WERE SUPPOSED TO MEET ASHLEY, JOSH'S GIRLFRIEND, AT THE PARIS AIRPORT. BUT THEN...
UH OH, THERE MIGHT BE A PROBLEM- ASHLEY'S STUCK ON A TRAIN IN CHICAGO BECAUSE THERE'S A DEAD BODY ON THE TRACKS.
I KNOW I CAN'T JOKE ABOUT THAT, BUT CAN I POINT OUT THAT IT'S NOT MY FAULT?

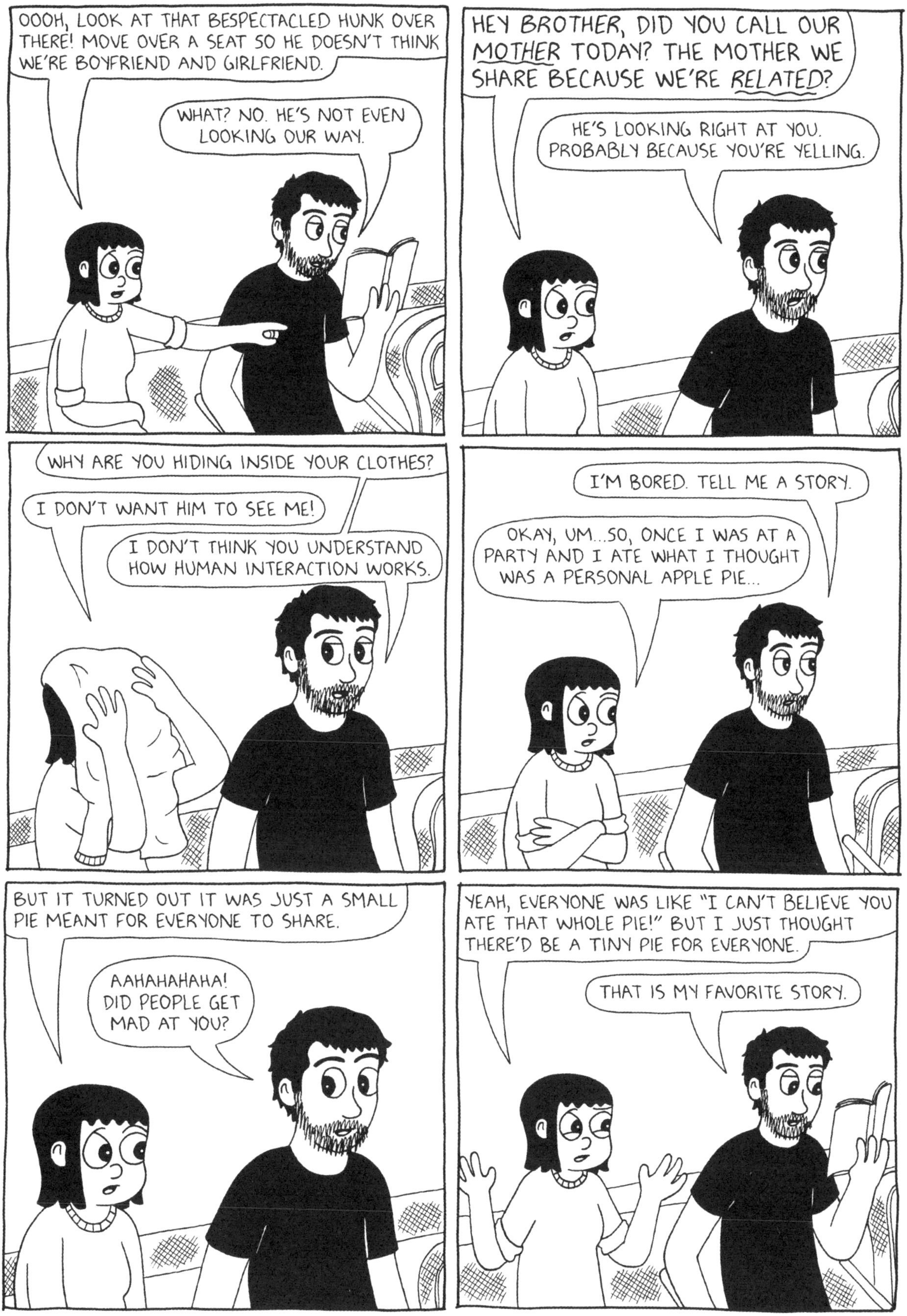
OOOH, LOOK AT THAT BESPECTACLED HUNK OVER THERE! MOVE OVER A SEAT SO HE DOESN'T THINK WE'RE BOYFRIEND AND GIRLFRIEND.
WHAT? NO. HE'S NOT EVEN LOOKING OUR WAY.
HEY BROTHER, DID YOU CALL OUR MOTHER TODAY? THE MOTHER WE SHARE BECAUSE WE'RE RELATED?
HE'S LOOKING RIGHT AT YOU. PROBABLY BECAUSE YOU'RE YELLING.
WHY ARE YOU HIDING INSIDE YOUR CLOTHES?
I DON'T WANT HIM TO SEE ME!
I DON'T THINK YOU UNDERSTAND HOW HUMAN INTERACTION WORKS.
I'M BORED. TELL ME A STORY.
OKAY, UM...SO, ONCE I WAS AT A PARTY AND I ATE WHAT I THOUGHT WAS A PERSONAL APPLE PIE...
BUT IT TURNED OUT IT WAS JUST A SMALL PIE MEANT FOR EVERYONE TO SHARE.
AAHAHAHAHA! DID PEOPLE GET MAD AT YOU?
YEAH, EVERYONE WAS LIKE "I CAN'T BELIEVE YOU ATE THAT WHOLE PIE!" BUT I JUST THOUGHT THERE'D BE A TINY PIE FOR EVERYONE.
THAT IS MY FAVORITE STORY.

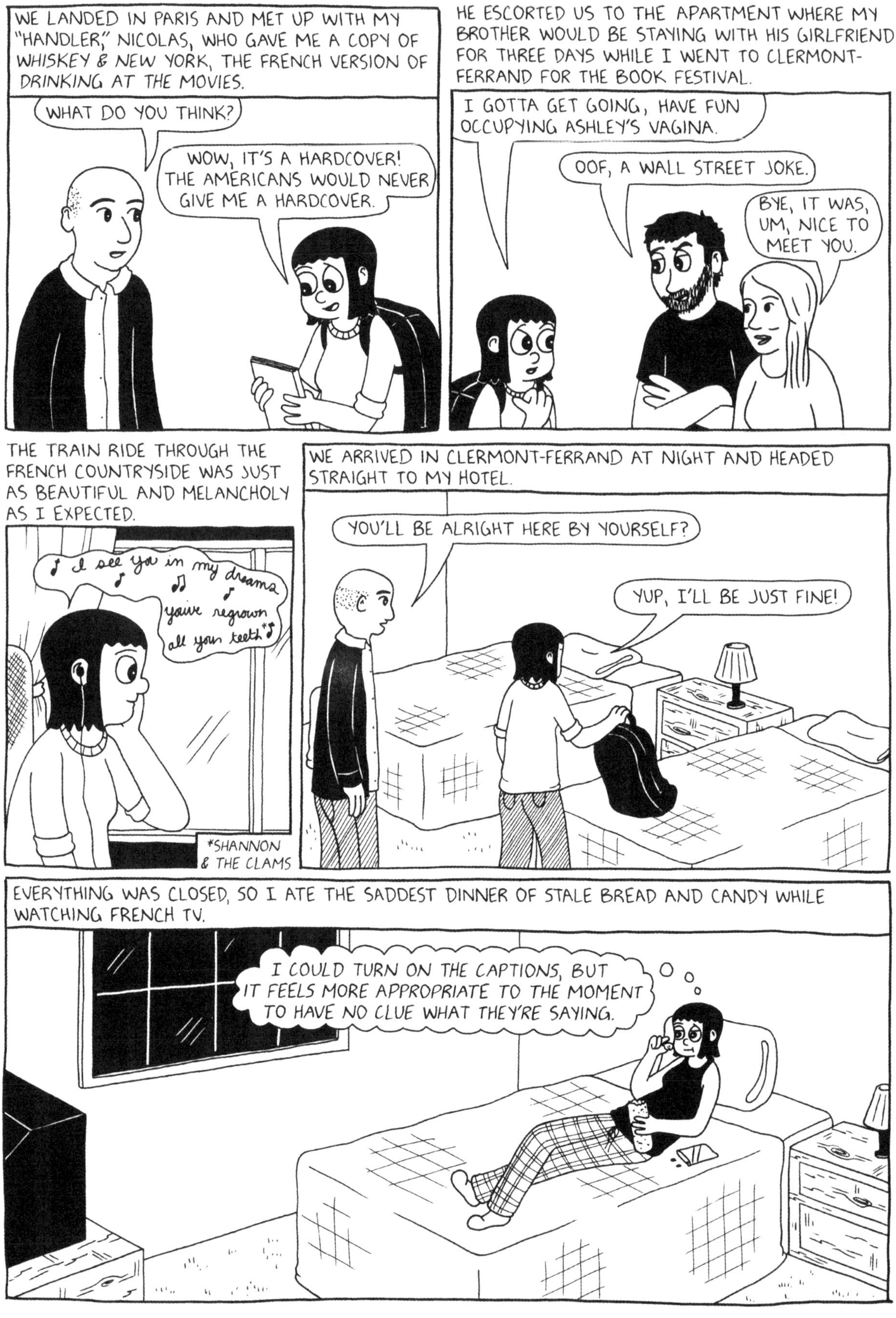
WE LANDED IN PARIS AND MET UP WITH MY "HANDLER," NICOLAS, WHO GAVE ME A COPY OF WHISKEY & NEW YORK, THE FRENCH VERSION OF DRINKING AT THE MOVIES.
WHAT DO YOU THINK?
WOW, IT'S A HARDCOVER! THE AMERICANS WOULD NEVER GIVE ME A HARDCOVER.
HE ESCORTED US TO THE APARTMENT WHERE MY BROTHER WOULD BE STAYING WITH HIS GIRLFRIEND FOR THREE DAYS WHILE I WENT TO CLERMONT-FERRAND FOR THE BOOK FESTIVAL.
I GOTTA GET GOING, HAVE FUN OCCUPYING ASHLEY'S VAGINA.
OOF, A WALL STREET JOKE.
BYE, IT WAS, UM, NICE TO MEET YOU.
THE TRAIN RIDE THROUGH THE FRENCH COUNTRYSIDE WAS JUST AS BEAUTIFUL AND MELANCHOLY AS I EXPECTED.
I see you in my dreams you've regrown all your teeth*
*SHANNON & THE CLAMS
WE ARRIVED IN CLERMONT-FERRAND AT NIGHT AND HEADED STRAIGHT TO MY HOTEL.
YOU'LL BE ALRIGHT HERE BY YOURSELF?
YUP, I'LL BE JUST FINE!
EVERYTHING WAS CLOSED, SO I ATE THE SADDEST DINNER OF STALE BREAD AND CANDY WHILE WATCHING FRENCH TV.
I COULD TURN ON THE CAPTIONS, BUT IT FEELS MORE APPROPRIATE TO THE MOMENT TO HAVE NO CLUE WHAT THEY'RE SAYING.

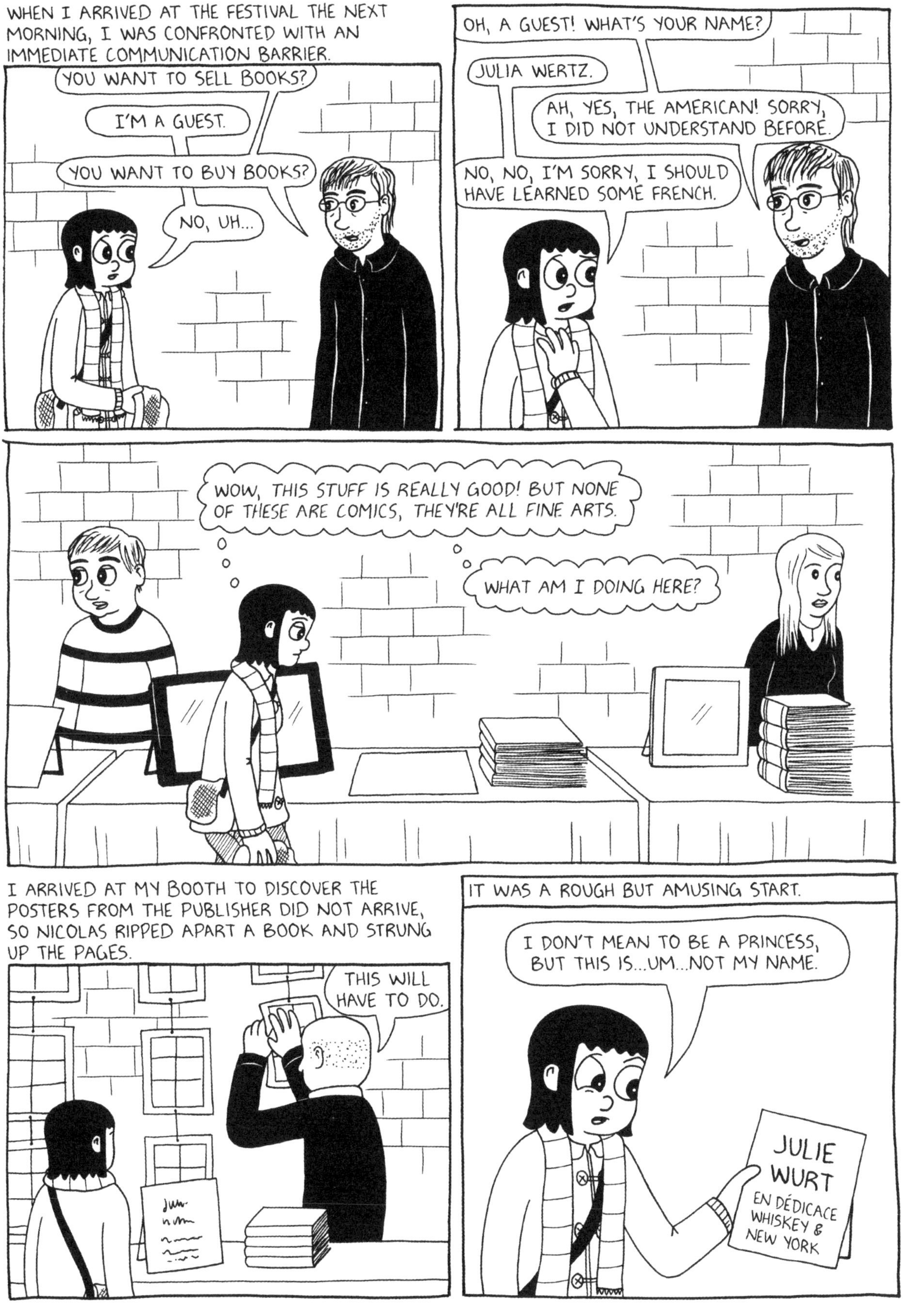
WHEN I ARRIVED AT THE FESTIVAL THE NEXT MORNING, I WAS CONFRONTED WITH AN IMMEDIATE COMMUNICATION BARRIER.
YOU WANT TO SELL BOOKS?
I'M A GUEST.
YOU WANT TO BUY BOOKS?
NO, UH...
OH, A GUEST! WHAT'S YOUR NAME?
JULIA WERTZ.
AH, YES, THE AMERICAN! SORRY, I DID NOT UNDERSTAND BEFORE.
NO, NO, I'M SORRY, I SHOULD HAVE LEARNED SOME FRENCH.
WOW, THIS STUFF IS REALLY GOOD! BUT NONE OF THESE ARE COMICS, THEY'RE ALL FINE ARTS.
WHAT AM I DOING HERE?
I ARRIVED AT MY BOOTH TO DISCOVER THE POSTERS FROM THE PUBLISHER DID NOT ARRIVE, SO NICOLAS RIPPED APART A BOOK AND STRUNG UP THE PAGES.
THIS WILL HAVE TO DO.
IT WAS A ROUGH BUT AMUSING START.
I DON'T MEAN TO BE A PRINCESS, BUT THIS IS...UM...NOT MY NAME.
JULIE WURT
EN DÉDICACE
WHISKEY &
NEW YORK

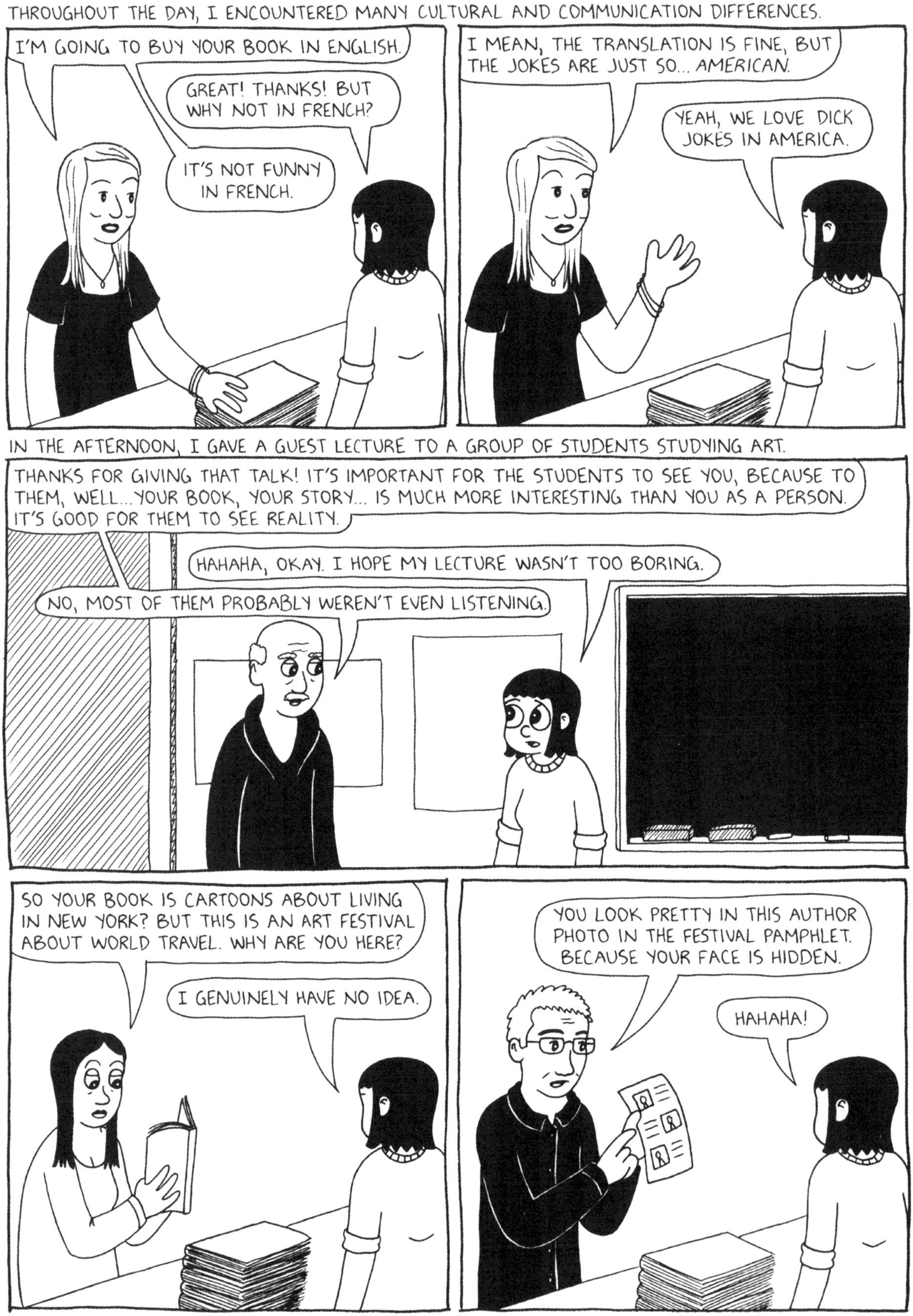
THROUGHOUT THE DAY, I ENCOUNTERED MANY CULTURAL AND COMMUNICATION DIFFERENCES.
I'M GOING TO BUY YOUR BOOK IN ENGLISH.
GREAT! THANKS! BUT WHY NOT IN FRENCH?
IT'S NOT FUNNY IN FRENCH.
I MEAN, THE TRANSLATION IS FINE, BUT THE JOKES ARE JUST SO... AMERICAN.
YEAH, WE LOVE DICK JOKES IN AMERICA.
IN THE AFTERNOON, I GAVE A GUEST LECTURE TO A GROUP OF STUDENTS STUDYING ART.
THANKS FOR GIVING THAT TALK! IT'S IMPORTANT FOR THE STUDENTS TO SEE YOU, BECAUSE TO THEM, WELL... YOUR BOOK, YOUR STORY... IS MUCH MORE INTERESTING THAN YOU AS A PERSON. IT'S GOOD FOR THEM TO SEE REALITY.
HAHAHA, OKAY. I HOPE MY LECTURE WASN'T TOO BORING.
NO, MOST OF THEM PROBABLY WEREN'T EVEN LISTENING.
SO YOUR BOOK IS CARTOONS ABOUT LIVING IN NEW YORK? BUT THIS IS AN ART FESTIVAL ABOUT WORLD TRAVEL. WHY ARE YOU HERE?
I GENUINELY HAVE NO IDEA.
YOU LOOK PRETTY IN THIS AUTHOR PHOTO IN THE FESTIVAL PAMPHLET. BECAUSE YOUR FACE IS HIDDEN.
HAHAHA!

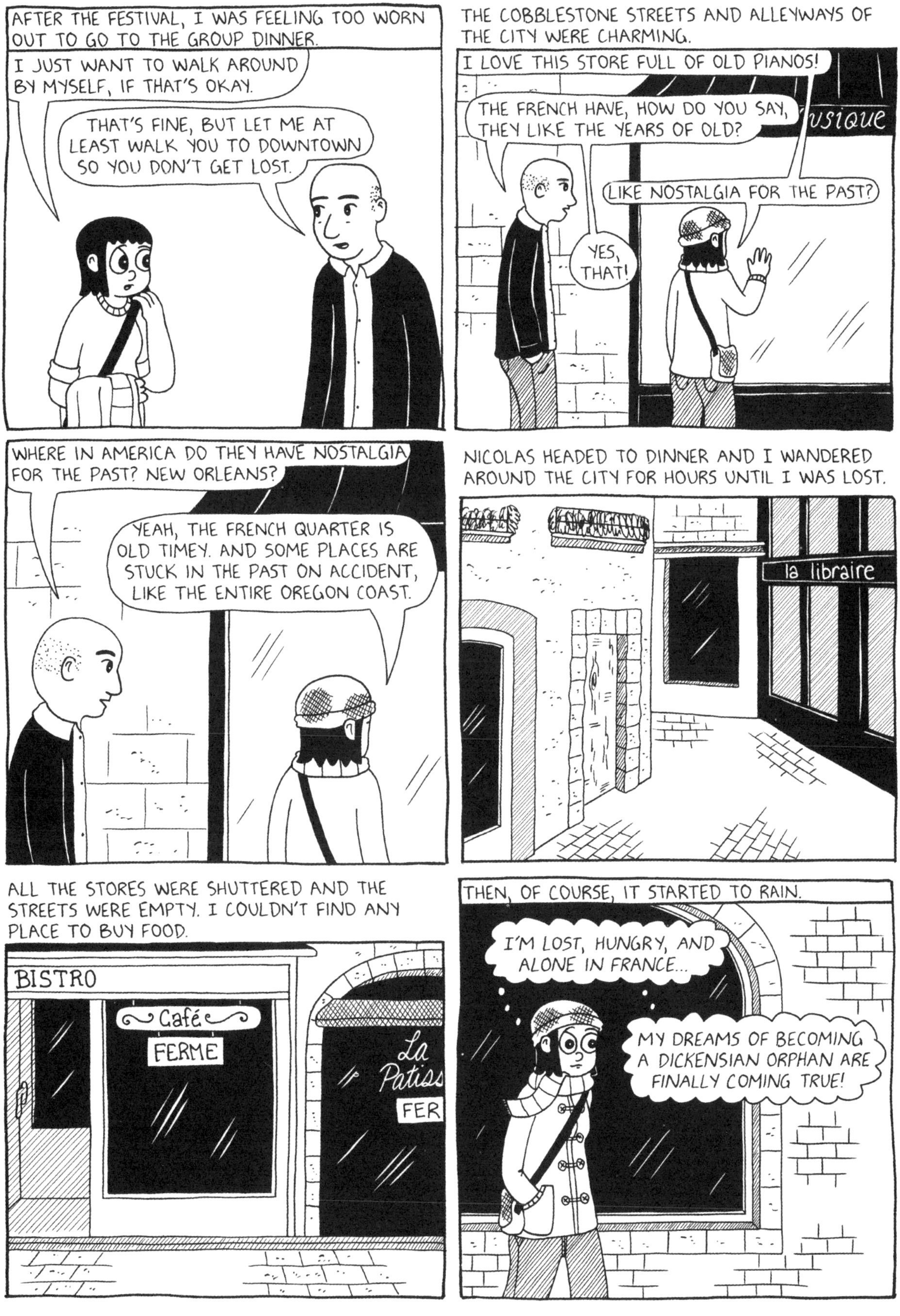
AFTER THE FESTIVAL, I WAS FEELING TOO WORN OUT TO GO TO THE GROUP DINNER.
I JUST WANT TO WALK AROUND BY MYSELF, IF THAT'S OKAY.
THAT'S FINE, BUT LET ME AT LEAST WALK YOU TO DOWNTOWN SO YOU DON'T GET LOST.
THE COBBLESTONE STREETS AND ALLEYWAYS OF THE CITY WERE CHARMING.
I LOVE THIS STORE FULL OF OLD PIANOS!
THE FRENCH HAVE, HOW DO YOU SAY, THEY LIKE THE YEARS OF OLD?
usique
LIKE NOSTALGIA FOR THE PAST?
YES, THAT!
WHERE IN AMERICA DO THEY HAVE NOSTALGIA FOR THE PAST? NEW ORLEANS?
YEAH, THE FRENCH QUARTER IS OLD TIMEY. AND SOME PLACES ARE STUCK IN THE PAST ON ACCIDENT, LIKE THE ENTIRE OREGON COAST.
NICOLAS HEADED TO DINNER AND I WANDERED AROUND THE CITY FOR HOURS UNTIL I WAS LOST.
la libraire
ALL THE STORES WERE SHUTTERED AND THE STREETS WERE EMPTY. I COULDN'T FIND ANY PLACE TO BUY FOOD.
BISTRO
Café
FERME
La Patiss
FER
THEN, OF COURSE, IT STARTED TO RAIN.
I'M LOST, HUNGRY, AND ALONE IN FRANCE...
MY DREAMS OF BECOMING A DICKENSIAN ORPHAN ARE FINALLY COMING TRUE!

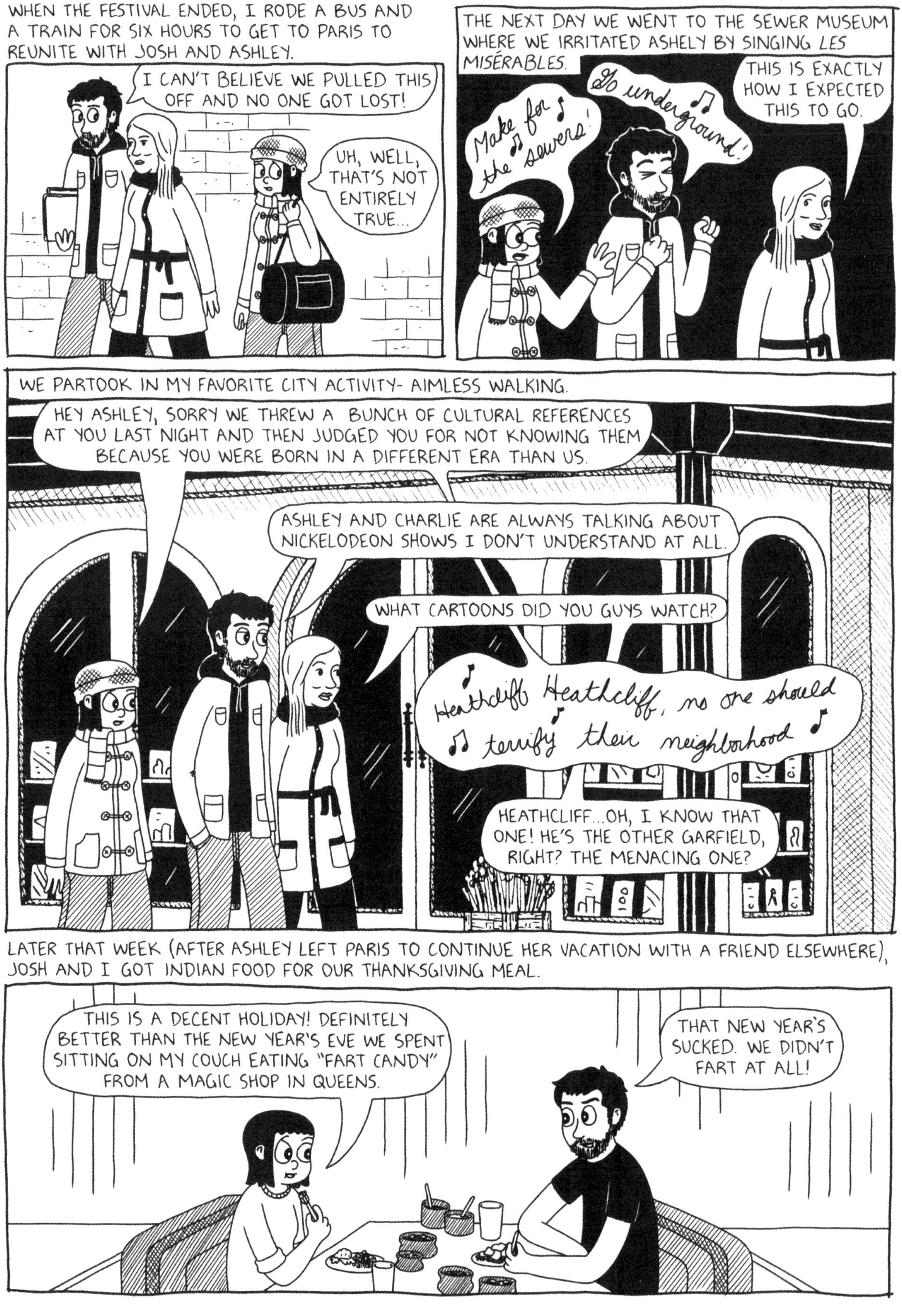
WHEN THE FESTIVAL ENDED, I RODE A BUS AND A TRAIN FOR SIX HOURS TO GET TO PARIS TO REUNITE WITH JOSH AND ASHLEY.
I CAN'T BELIEVE WE PULLED THIS OFF AND NO ONE GOT LOST!
UH, WELL, THAT'S NOT ENTIRELY TRUE...
THE NEXT DAY WE WENT TO THE SEWER MUSEUM WHERE WE IRRITATED ASHELY BY SINGING *LES MISÉRABLES*.
Make for the sewers!
Go underground!
THIS IS EXACTLY HOW I EXPECTED THIS TO GO.
WE PARTOOK IN MY FAVORITE CITY ACTIVITY- AIMLESS WALKING.
HEY ASHLEY, SORRY WE THREW A BUNCH OF CULTURAL REFERENCES AT YOU LAST NIGHT AND THEN JUDGED YOU FOR NOT KNOWING THEM BECAUSE YOU WERE BORN IN A DIFFERENT ERA THAN US.
ASHLEY AND CHARLIE ARE ALWAYS TALKING ABOUT NICKELODEON SHOWS I DON'T UNDERSTAND AT ALL.
WHAT CARTOONS DID YOU GUYS WATCH?
Heathcliff Heathcliff, no one should terrify their neighborhood
HEATHCLIFF...OH, I KNOW THAT ONE! HE'S THE OTHER GARFIELD, RIGHT? THE MENACING ONE?
LATER THAT WEEK (AFTER ASHLEY LEFT PARIS TO CONTINUE HER VACATION WITH A FRIEND ELSEWHERE), JOSH AND I GOT INDIAN FOOD FOR OUR THANKSGIVING MEAL.
THIS IS A DECENT HOLIDAY! DEFINITELY BETTER THAN THE NEW YEAR'S EVE WE SPENT SITTING ON MY COUCH EATING "FART CANDY" FROM A MAGIC SHOP IN QUEENS.
THAT NEW YEAR'S SUCKED. WE DIDN'T FART AT ALL!

ARRIVING HOME FROM FRANCE

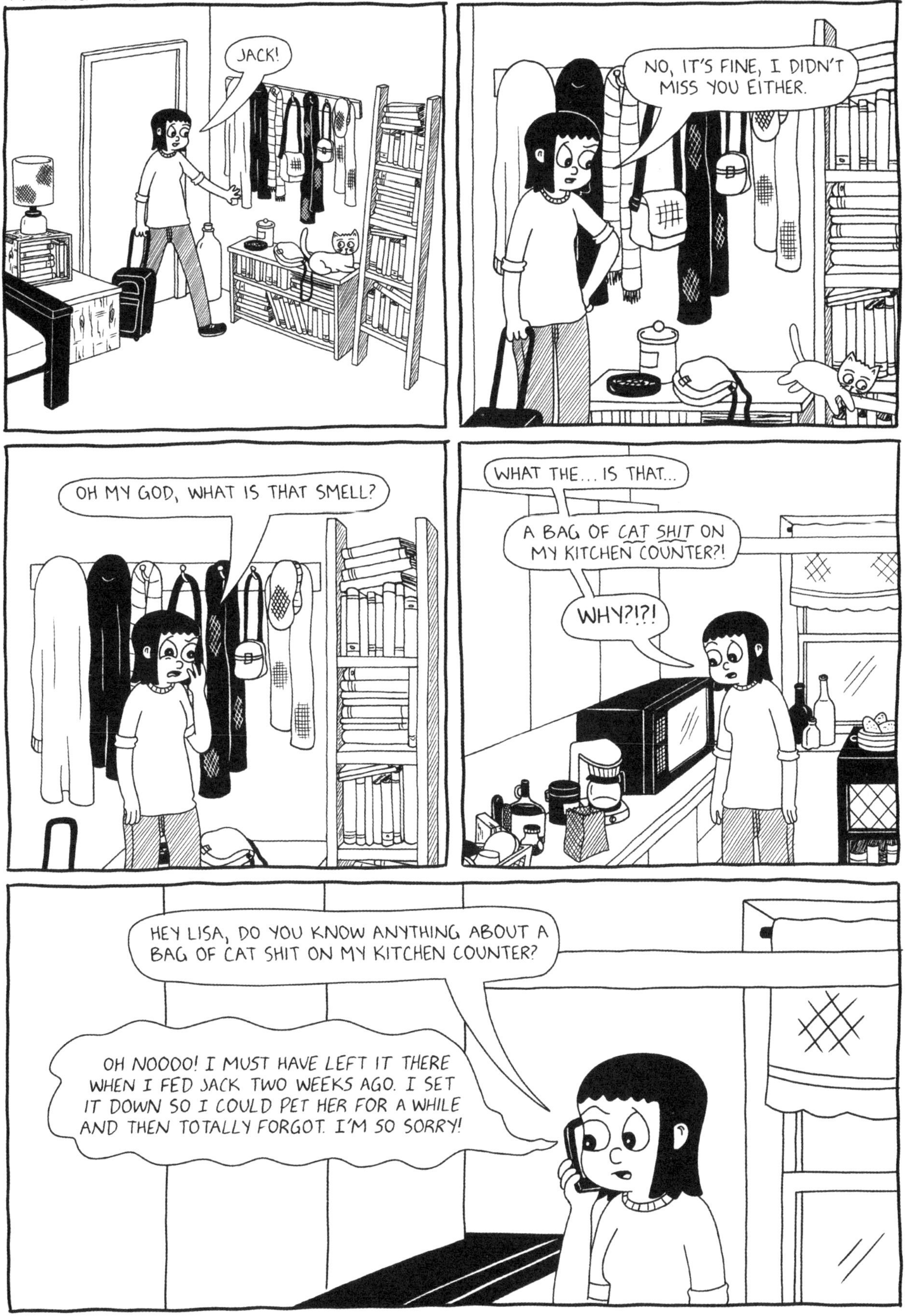
JACK!
NO, IT'S FINE, I DIDN'T MISS YOU EITHER.
OH MY GOD, WHAT IS THAT SMELL?
WHAT THE... IS THAT...
A BAG OF CAT SHIT ON MY KITCHEN COUNTER?!
WHY?!?!
HEY LISA, DO YOU KNOW ANYTHING ABOUT A BAG OF CAT SHIT ON MY KITCHEN COUNTER?
OH NOOOO! I MUST HAVE LEFT IT THERE WHEN I FED JACK TWO WEEKS AGO. I SET IT DOWN SO I COULD PET HER FOR A WHILE AND THEN TOTALLY FORGOT. I'M SO SORRY!

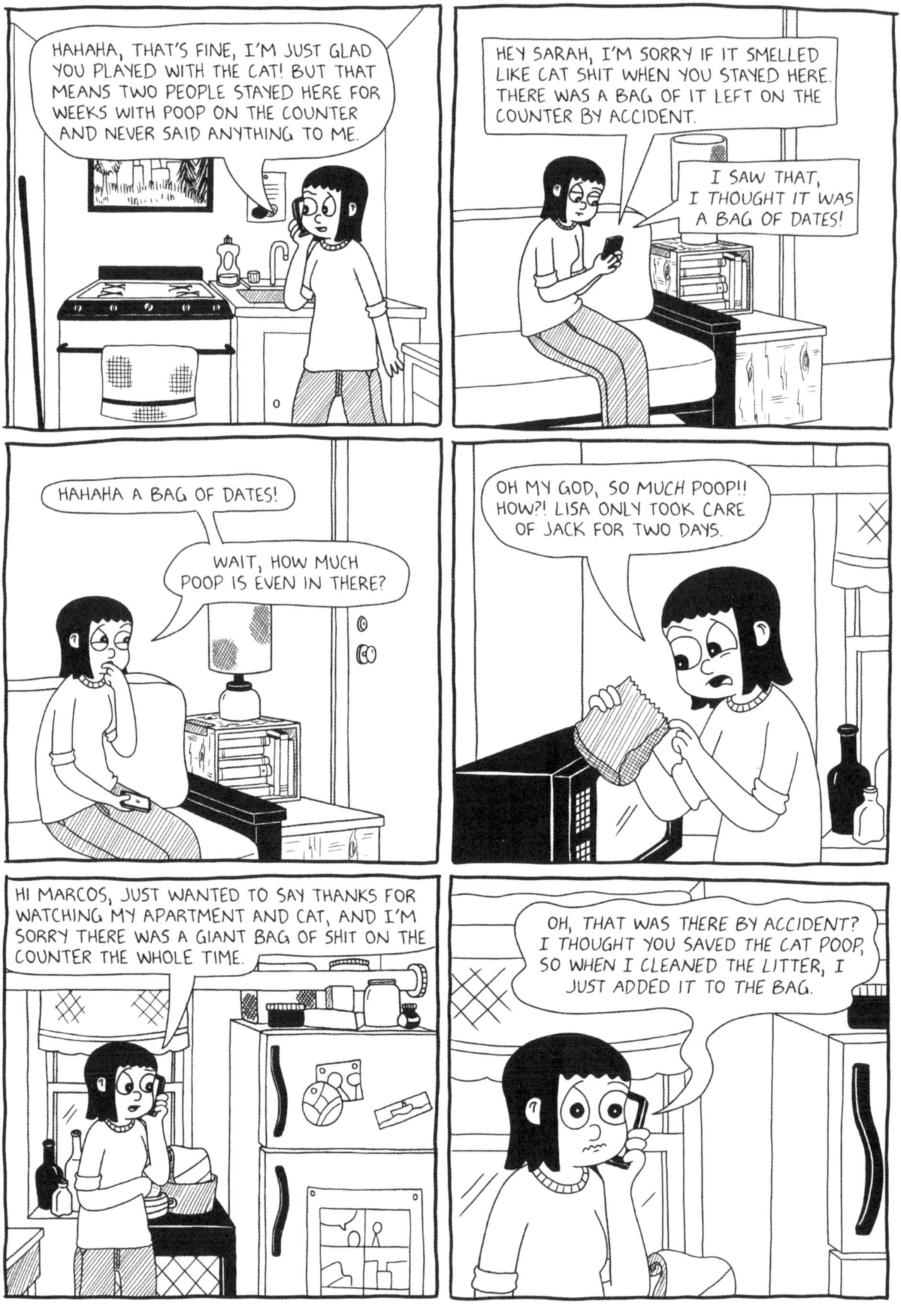
HAHAHA, THAT'S FINE, I'M JUST GLAD YOU PLAYED WITH THE CAT! BUT THAT MEANS TWO PEOPLE STAYED HERE FOR WEEKS WITH POOP ON THE COUNTER AND NEVER SAID ANYTHING TO ME.
HEY SARAH, I'M SORRY IF IT SMELLED LIKE CAT SHIT WHEN YOU STAYED HERE. THERE WAS A BAG OF IT LEFT ON THE COUNTER BY ACCIDENT.
I SAW THAT, I THOUGHT IT WAS A BAG OF DATES!
HAHAHA A BAG OF DATES!
WAIT, HOW MUCH POOP IS EVEN IN THERE?
OH MY GOD, SO MUCH POOP!! HOW?! LISA ONLY TOOK CARE OF JACK FOR TWO DAYS.
HI MARCOS, JUST WANTED TO SAY THANKS FOR WATCHING MY APARTMENT AND CAT, AND I'M SORRY THERE WAS A GIANT BAG OF SHIT ON THE COUNTER THE WHOLE TIME.
OH, THAT WAS THERE BY ACCIDENT? I THOUGHT YOU SAVED THE CAT POOP, SO WHEN I CLEANED THE LITTER, I JUST ADDED IT TO THE BAG.

IT RAINED A LOT THAT WINTER. I HUNKERED DOWN IN MY APARTMENT AND LOST MYSELF IN WORK AND READING. I WASN'T DRINKING, BUT I ALSO WASN'T DOING THE THINGS I NEEDED TO DO.

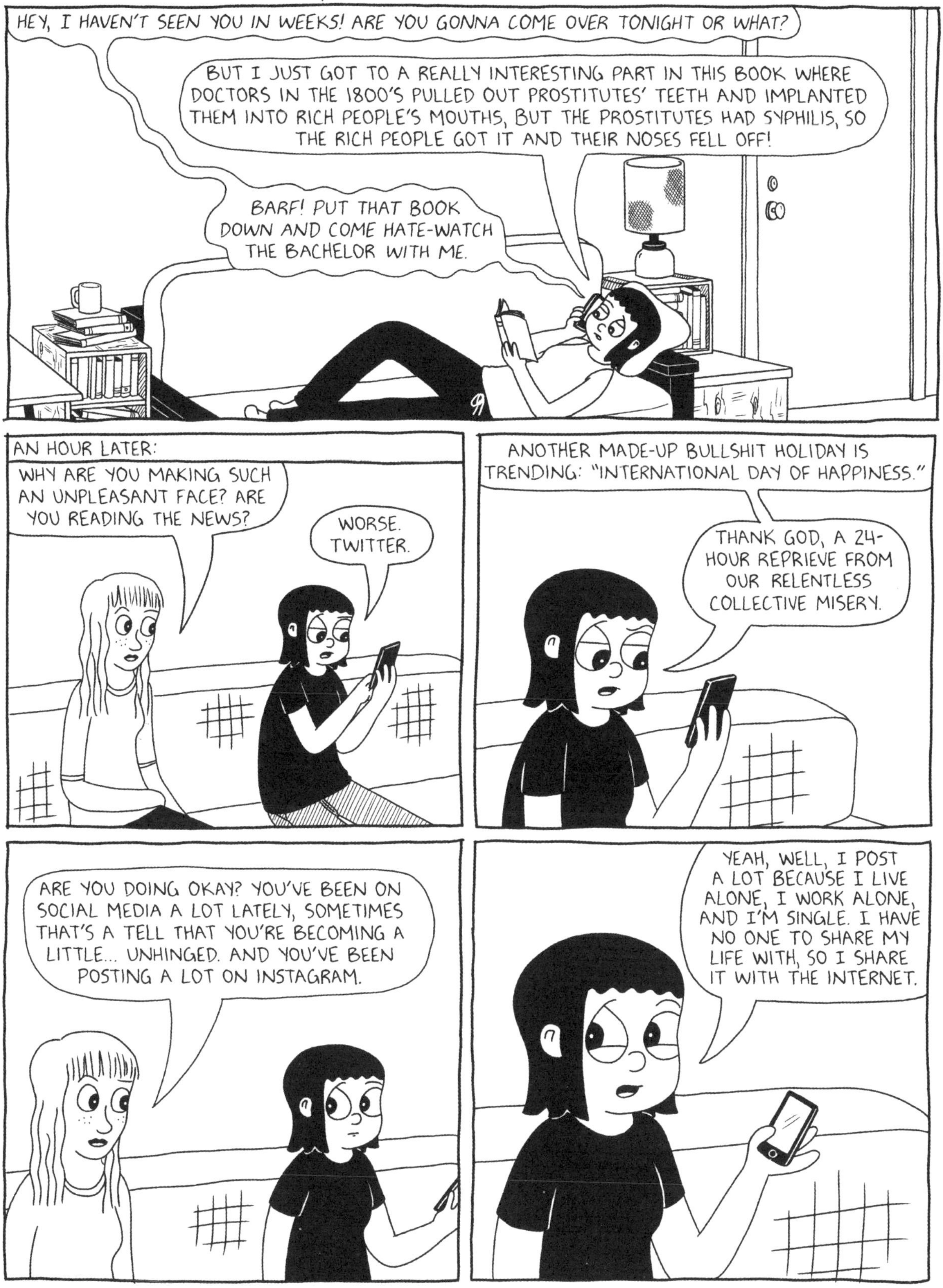

HEY, I HAVEN'T SEEN YOU IN WEEKS! ARE YOU GONNA COME OVER TONIGHT OR WHAT?
BUT I JUST GOT TO A REALLY INTERESTING PART IN THIS BOOK WHERE DOCTORS IN THE 1800'S PULLED OUT PROSTITUTES' TEETH AND IMPLANTED THEM INTO RICH PEOPLE'S MOUTHS, BUT THE PROSTITUTES HAD SYPHILIS, SO THE RICH PEOPLE GOT IT AND THEIR NOSES FELL OFF!
BARF! PUT THAT BOOK DOWN AND COME HATE-WATCH THE BACHELOR WITH ME.
AN HOUR LATER:
WHY ARE YOU MAKING SUCH AN UNPLEASANT FACE? ARE YOU READING THE NEWS?
WORSE. TWITTER.
ANOTHER MADE-UP BULLSHIT HOLIDAY IS TRENDING: "INTERNATIONAL DAY OF HAPPINESS."
THANK GOD, A 24-HOUR REPRIEVE FROM OUR RELENTLESS COLLECTIVE MISERY.
ARE YOU DOING OKAY? YOU'VE BEEN ON SOCIAL MEDIA A LOT LATELY, SOMETIMES THAT'S A TELL THAT YOU'RE BECOMING A LITTLE... UNHINGED. AND YOU'VE BEEN POSTING A LOT ON INSTAGRAM.
YEAH, WELL, I POST A LOT BECAUSE I LIVE ALONE, I WORK ALONE, AND I'M SINGLE. I HAVE NO ONE TO SHARE MY LIFE WITH, SO I SHARE IT WITH THE INTERNET.

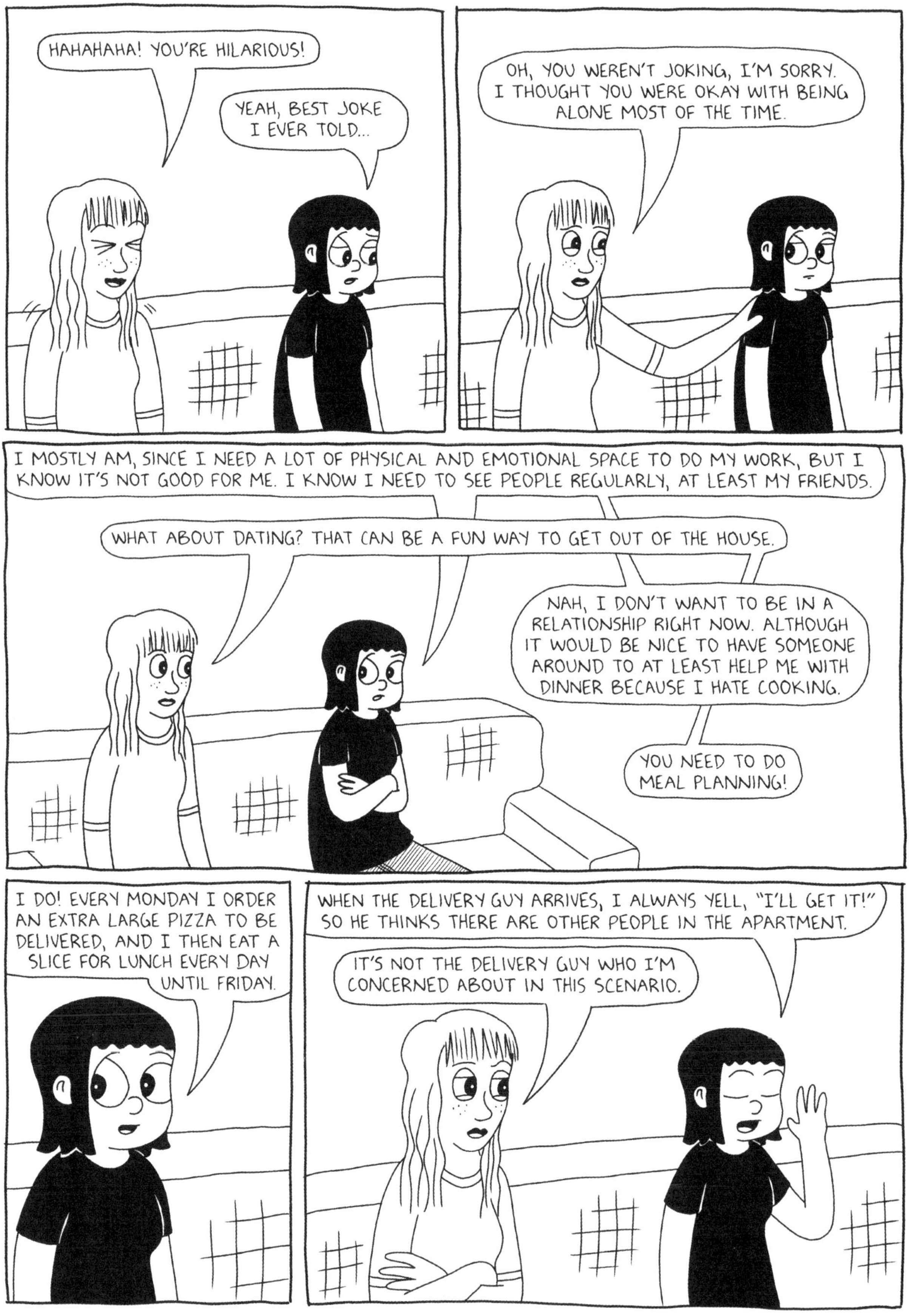
HAHAHAHA! YOU'RE HILARIOUS!
YEAH, BEST JOKE I EVER TOLD...
OH, YOU WEREN'T JOKING, I'M SORRY. I THOUGHT YOU WERE OKAY WITH BEING ALONE MOST OF THE TIME.
I MOSTLY AM, SINCE I NEED A LOT OF PHYSICAL AND EMOTIONAL SPACE TO DO MY WORK, BUT I KNOW IT'S NOT GOOD FOR ME. I KNOW I NEED TO SEE PEOPLE REGULARLY, AT LEAST MY FRIENDS.
WHAT ABOUT DATING? THAT CAN BE A FUN WAY TO GET OUT OF THE HOUSE.
NAH, I DON'T WANT TO BE IN A RELATIONSHIP RIGHT NOW. ALTHOUGH IT WOULD BE NICE TO HAVE SOMEONE AROUND TO AT LEAST HELP ME WITH DINNER BECAUSE I HATE COOKING.
YOU NEED TO DO MEAL PLANNING!
I DO! EVERY MONDAY I ORDER AN EXTRA LARGE PIZZA TO BE DELIVERED, AND I THEN EAT A SLICE FOR LUNCH EVERY DAY UNTIL FRIDAY.
WHEN THE DELIVERY GUY ARRIVES, I ALWAYS YELL, "I'LL GET IT!" SO HE THINKS THERE ARE OTHER PEOPLE IN THE APARTMENT.
IT'S NOT THE DELIVERY GUY WHO I'M CONCERNED ABOUT IN THIS SCENARIO.

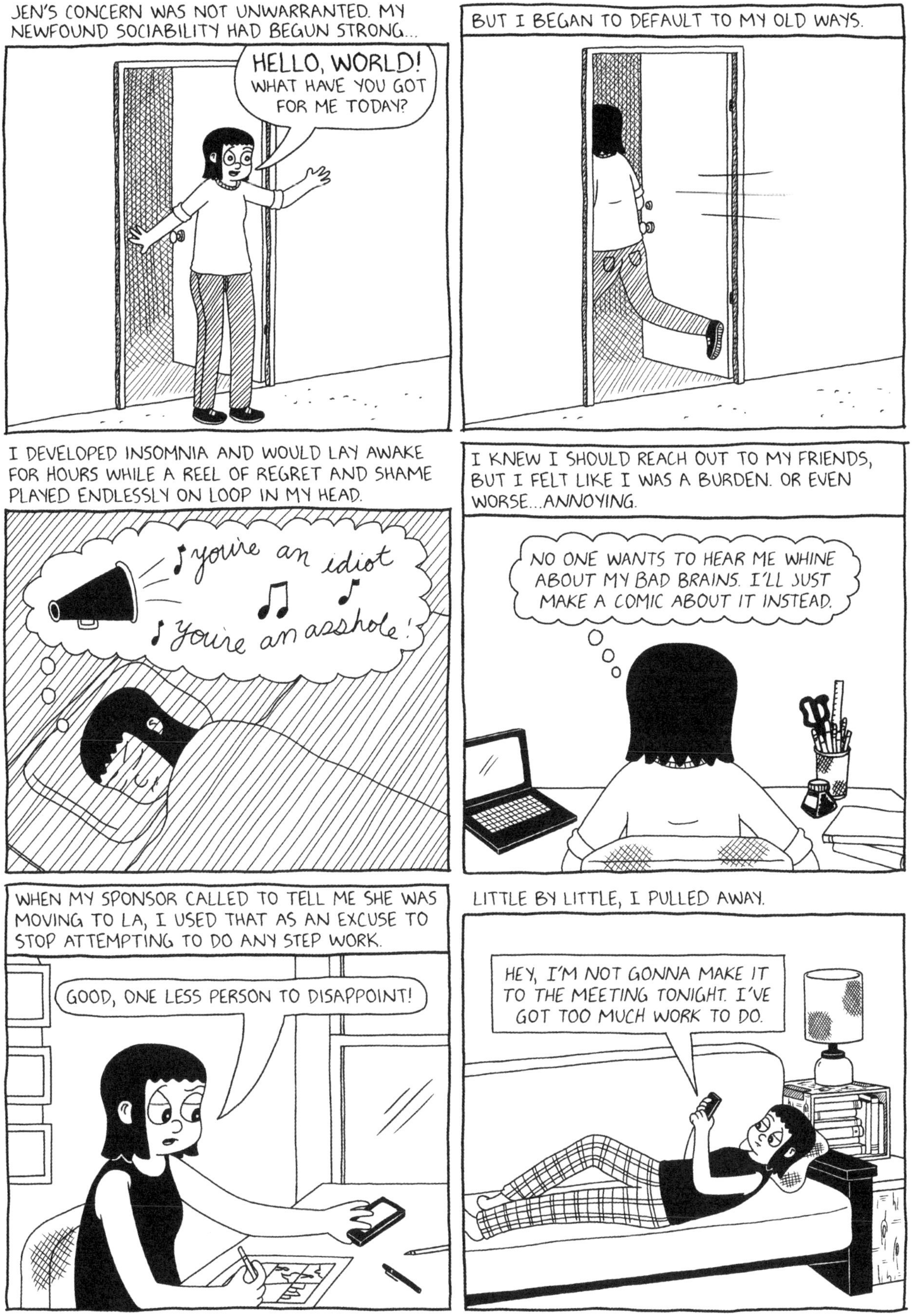
JEN'S CONCERN WAS NOT UNWARRANTED. MY NEWFOUND SOCIABILITY HAD BEGUN STRONG...
HELLO, WORLD! WHAT HAVE YOU GOT FOR ME TODAY?
BUT I BEGAN TO DEFAULT TO MY OLD WAYS.
I DEVELOPED INSOMNIA AND WOULD LAY AWAKE FOR HOURS WHILE A REEL OF REGRET AND SHAME PLAYED ENDLESSLY ON LOOP IN MY HEAD.
you're an idiot
You're an asshole!
I KNEW I SHOULD REACH OUT TO MY FRIENDS, BUT I FELT LIKE I WAS A BURDEN. OR EVEN WORSE...ANNOYING.
NO ONE WANTS TO HEAR ME WHINE ABOUT MY BAD BRAINS. I'LL JUST MAKE A COMIC ABOUT IT INSTEAD.
WHEN MY SPONSOR CALLED TO TELL ME SHE WAS MOVING TO LA, I USED THAT AS AN EXCUSE TO STOP ATTEMPTING TO DO ANY STEP WORK.
GOOD, ONE LESS PERSON TO DISAPPOINT!
LITTLE BY LITTLE, I PULLED AWAY.
HEY, I'M NOT GONNA MAKE IT TO THE MEETING TONIGHT. I'VE GOT TOO MUCH WORK TO DO.

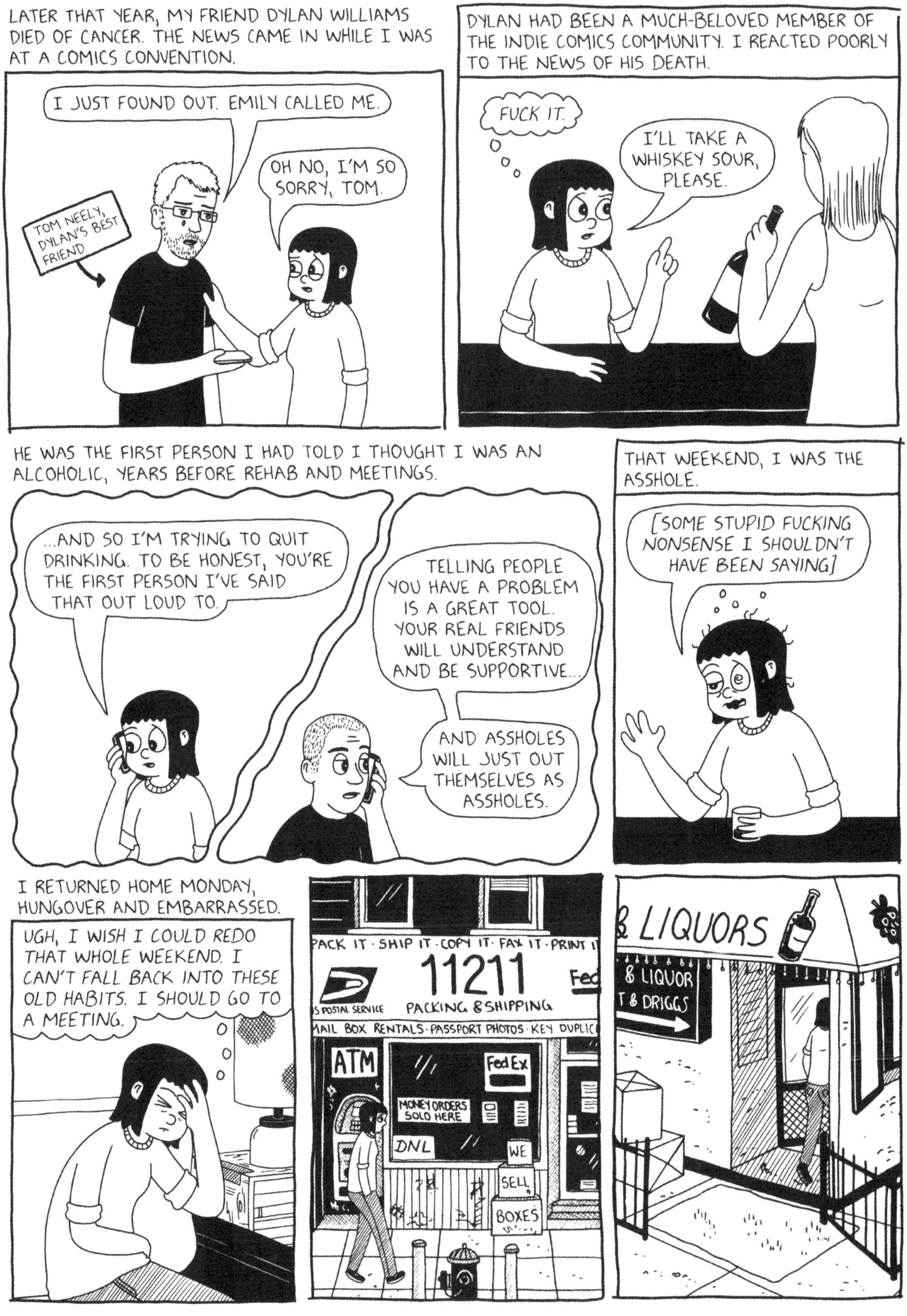
LATER THAT YEAR, MY FRIEND DYLAN WILLIAMS DIED OF CANCER. THE NEWS CAME IN WHILE I WAS AT A COMICS CONVENTION.
I JUST FOUND OUT. EMILY CALLED ME.
OH NO, I'M SO SORRY, TOM.
TOM NEELY, DYLAN'S BEST FRIEND
DYLAN HAD BEEN A MUCH-BELOVED MEMBER OF THE INDIE COMICS COMMUNITY. I REACTED POORLY TO THE NEWS OF HIS DEATH.
FUCK IT.
I'LL TAKE A WHISKEY SOUR, PLEASE.
HE WAS THE FIRST PERSON I HAD TOLD I THOUGHT I WAS AN ALCOHOLIC, YEARS BEFORE REHAB AND MEETINGS.
...AND SO I'M TRYING TO QUIT DRINKING. TO BE HONEST, YOU'RE THE FIRST PERSON I'VE SAID THAT OUT LOUD TO.
TELLING PEOPLE YOU HAVE A PROBLEM IS A GREAT TOOL. YOUR REAL FRIENDS WILL UNDERSTAND AND BE SUPPORTIVE...
AND ASSHOLES WILL JUST OUT THEMSELVES AS ASSHOLES.
THAT WEEKEND, I WAS THE ASSHOLE.
[SOME STUPID FUCKING NONSENSE I SHOULDN'T HAVE BEEN SAYING]
I RETURNED HOME MONDAY, HUNGOVER AND EMBARRASSED.
UGH, I WISH I COULD REDO THAT WHOLE WEEKEND. I CAN'T FALL BACK INTO THESE OLD HABITS. I SHOULD GO TO A MEETING.
PACK IT · SHIP IT · COPY IT · FAX IT · PRINT IT
11211
PACKING & SHIPPING
S POSTAL SERVICE
MAIL BOX RENTALS · PASSPORT PHOTOS · KEY DUPLIC
ATM
FedEx
MONEY ORDERS SOLD HERE
DNL
WE SELL BOXES
& LIQUORS
& LIQUOR
T & DRIGGS

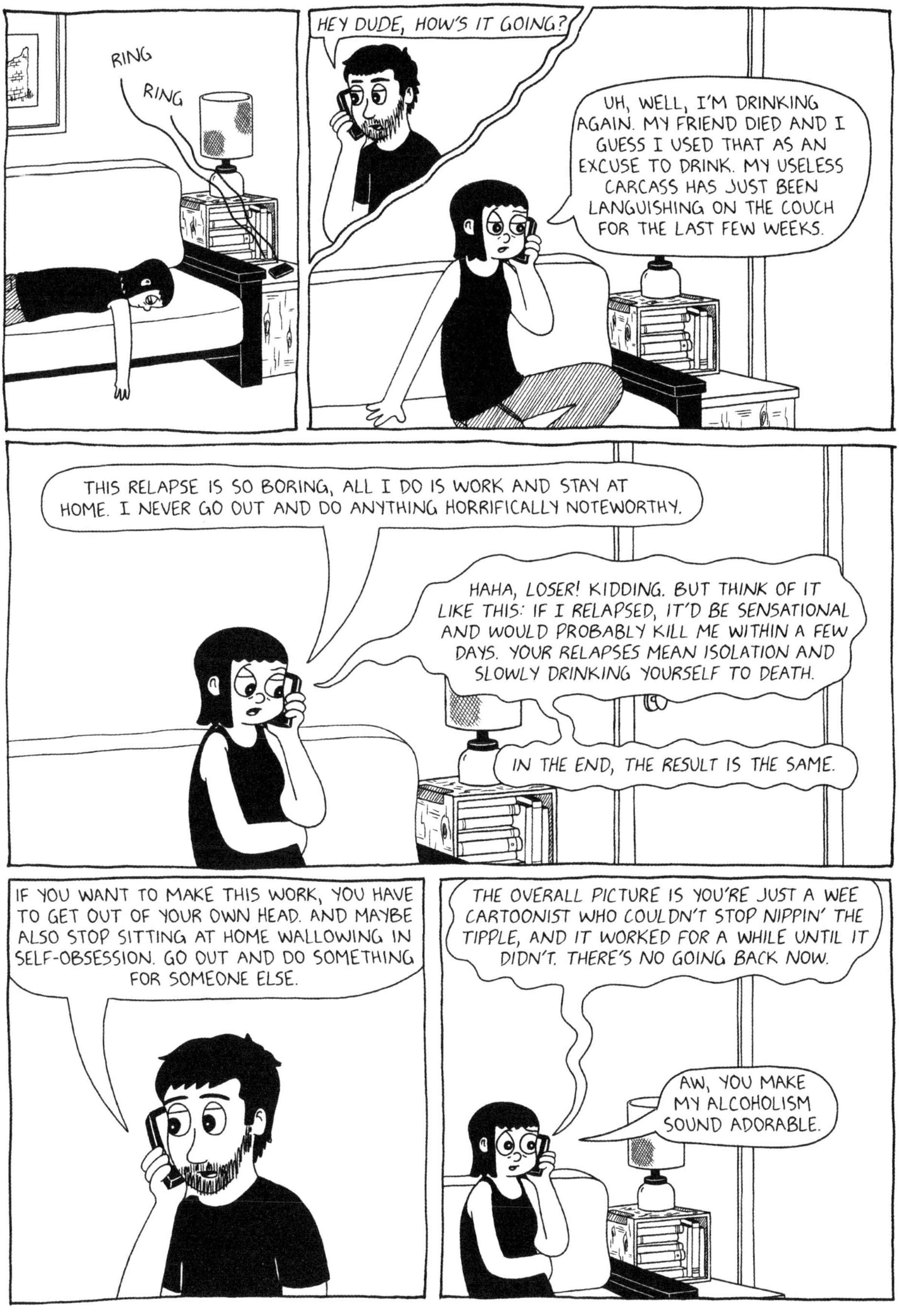
RING
RING
HEY DUDE, HOW'S IT GOING?
UH, WELL, I'M DRINKING AGAIN. MY FRIEND DIED AND I GUESS I USED THAT AS AN EXCUSE TO DRINK. MY USELESS CARCASS HAS JUST BEEN LANGUISHING ON THE COUCH FOR THE LAST FEW WEEKS.
THIS RELAPSE IS SO BORING, ALL I DO IS WORK AND STAY AT HOME. I NEVER GO OUT AND DO ANYTHING HORRIFICALLY NOTEWORTHY.
HAHA, LOSER! KIDDING. BUT THINK OF IT LIKE THIS: IF I RELAPSED, IT'D BE SENSATIONAL AND WOULD PROBABLY KILL ME WITHIN A FEW DAYS. YOUR RELAPSES MEAN ISOLATION AND SLOWLY DRINKING YOURSELF TO DEATH.
IN THE END, THE RESULT IS THE SAME.
IF YOU WANT TO MAKE THIS WORK, YOU HAVE TO GET OUT OF YOUR OWN HEAD. AND MAYBE ALSO STOP SITTING AT HOME WALLOWING IN SELF-OBSESSION. GO OUT AND DO SOMETHING FOR SOMEONE ELSE.
THE OVERALL PICTURE IS YOU'RE JUST A WEE CARTOONIST WHO COULDN'T STOP NIPPIN' THE TIPPLE, AND IT WORKED FOR A WHILE UNTIL IT DIDN'T. THERE'S NO GOING BACK NOW.
AW, YOU MAKE MY ALCOHOLISM SOUND ADORABLE.

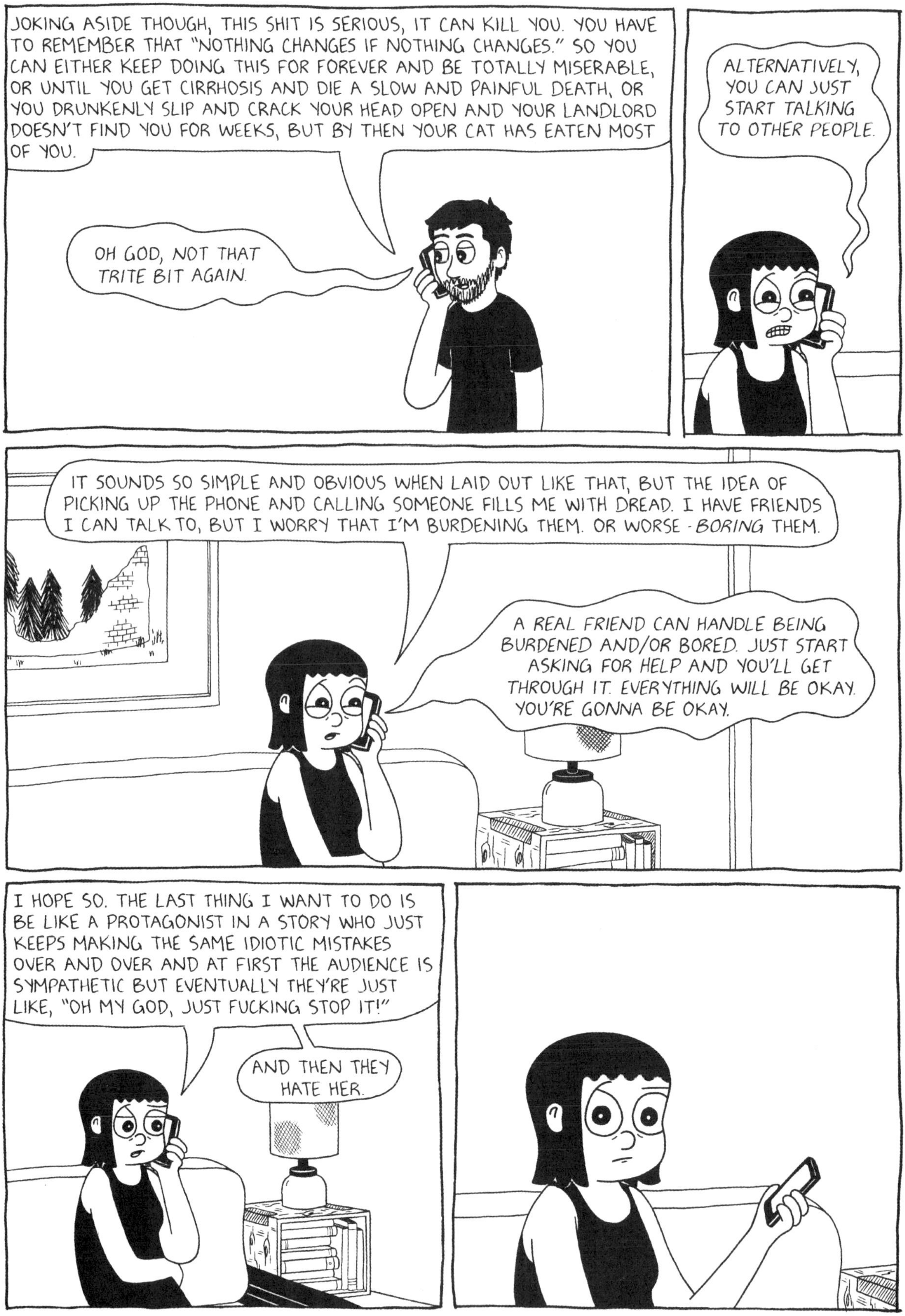
JOKING ASIDE THOUGH, THIS SHIT IS SERIOUS, IT CAN KILL YOU. YOU HAVE TO REMEMBER THAT "NOTHING CHANGES IF NOTHING CHANGES." SO YOU CAN EITHER KEEP DOING THIS FOR FOREVER AND BE TOTALLY MISERABLE, OR UNTIL YOU GET CIRRHOSIS AND DIE A SLOW AND PAINFUL DEATH, OR YOU DRUNKENLY SLIP AND CRACK YOUR HEAD OPEN AND YOUR LANDLORD DOESN'T FIND YOU FOR WEEKS, BUT BY THEN YOUR CAT HAS EATEN MOST OF YOU.
OH GOD, NOT THAT *TRITE BIT* AGAIN.
ALTERNATIVELY, YOU CAN JUST START TALKING TO *OTHER PEOPLE*.
IT SOUNDS SO SIMPLE AND OBVIOUS WHEN LAID OUT LIKE THAT, BUT THE IDEA OF PICKING UP THE PHONE AND CALLING SOMEONE FILLS ME WITH DREAD. I HAVE FRIENDS I CAN TALK TO, BUT I WORRY THAT I'M BURDENING THEM. OR WORSE - *BORING* THEM.
A *REAL* FRIEND CAN HANDLE BEING BURDENED AND/OR BORED. JUST START ASKING FOR HELP AND YOU'LL GET THROUGH IT. EVERYTHING WILL BE OKAY. YOU'RE GONNA BE OKAY.
I HOPE SO. THE LAST THING I WANT TO DO IS BE LIKE A PROTAGONIST IN A STORY WHO JUST KEEPS MAKING THE SAME IDIOTIC MISTAKES OVER AND OVER AND AT FIRST THE AUDIENCE IS SYMPATHETIC BUT EVENTUALLY THEY'RE JUST LIKE, "OH MY GOD, JUST FUCKING STOP IT!"
AND THEN THEY HATE HER.

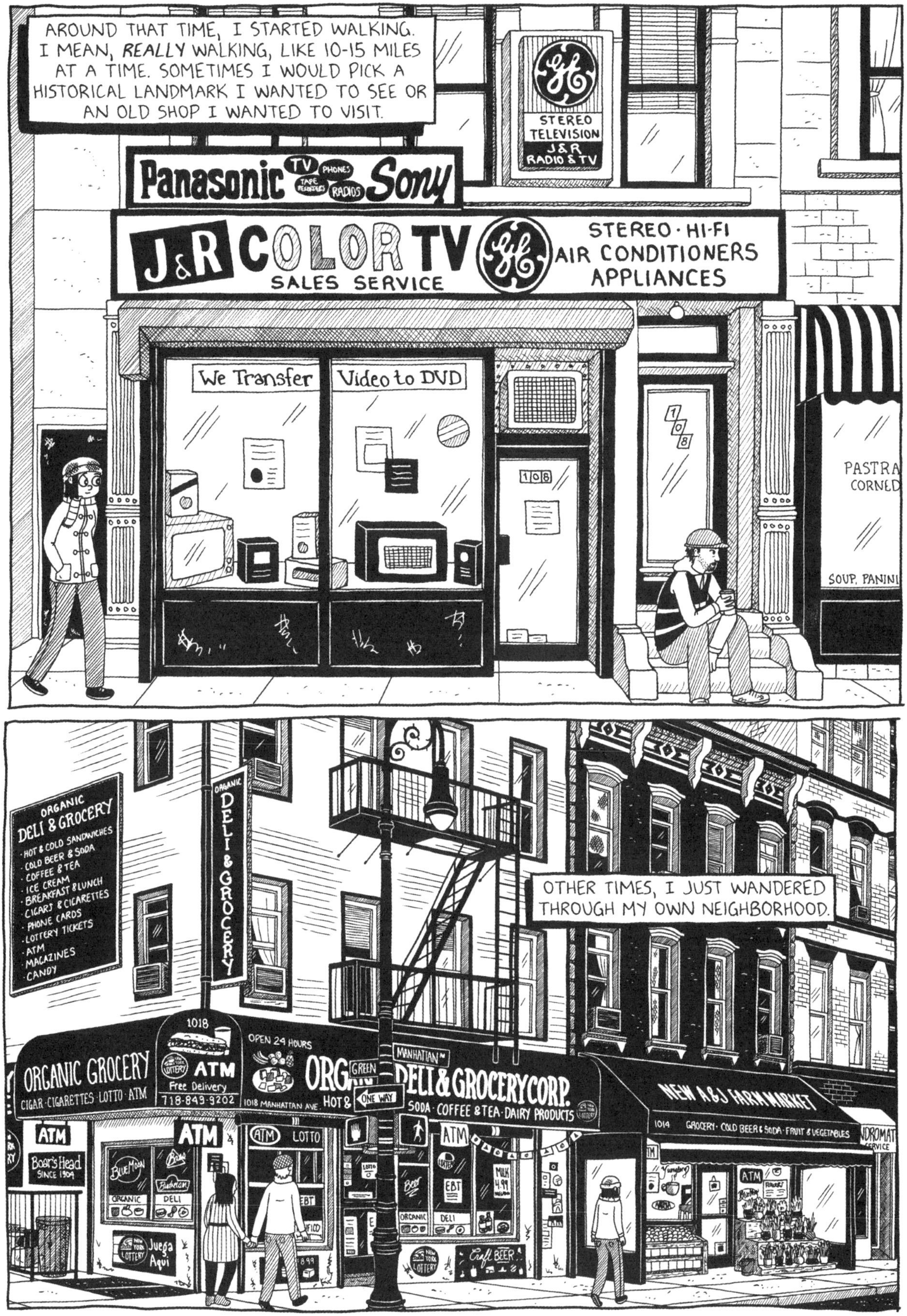
AROUND THAT TIME, I STARTED WALKING. I MEAN, *REALLY* WALKING, LIKE 10-15 MILES AT A TIME. SOMETIMES I WOULD PICK A HISTORICAL LANDMARK I WANTED TO SEE OR AN OLD SHOP I WANTED TO VISIT.
STEREO TELEVISION J&R RADIO & TV
Panasonic TV PHONES RADIOS Sony
J&R COLOR TV SALES SERVICE
STEREO · HI-FI AIR CONDITIONERS APPLIANCES
We Transfer Video to DVD
108
PASTRA CORNED
SOUP, PANINI
OTHER TIMES, I JUST WANDERED THROUGH MY OWN NEIGHBORHOOD.
ORGANIC DELI & GROCERY
· HOT & COLD SANDWICHES
· COLD BEER & SODA
· COFFEE & TEA
· ICE CREAM
· BREAKFAST & LUNCH
· CIGARS & CIGARETTES
· PHONE CARDS
· LOTTERY TICKETS
· ATM
· MAGAZINES
· CANDY
ORGANIC DELI & GROCERY
1018
ORGANIC GROCERY
CIGAR · CIGARETTES · LOTTO · ATM
ATM
Free Delivery
718-849-9202
OPEN 24 HOURS
1018 MANHATTAN AVE.
MANHATTAN AV
ONE WAY
DELI & GROCERY CORP.
SODA · COFFEE & TEA · DAIRY PRODUCTS
NEW A&J FARM MARKET
1014 GROCERY · COLD BEER & SODA · FRUIT & VEGETABLES
Boar's Head SINCE 1904
ATM
LOTTO
Juega Aqui
EBT
MILK 4.99
Craft BEER

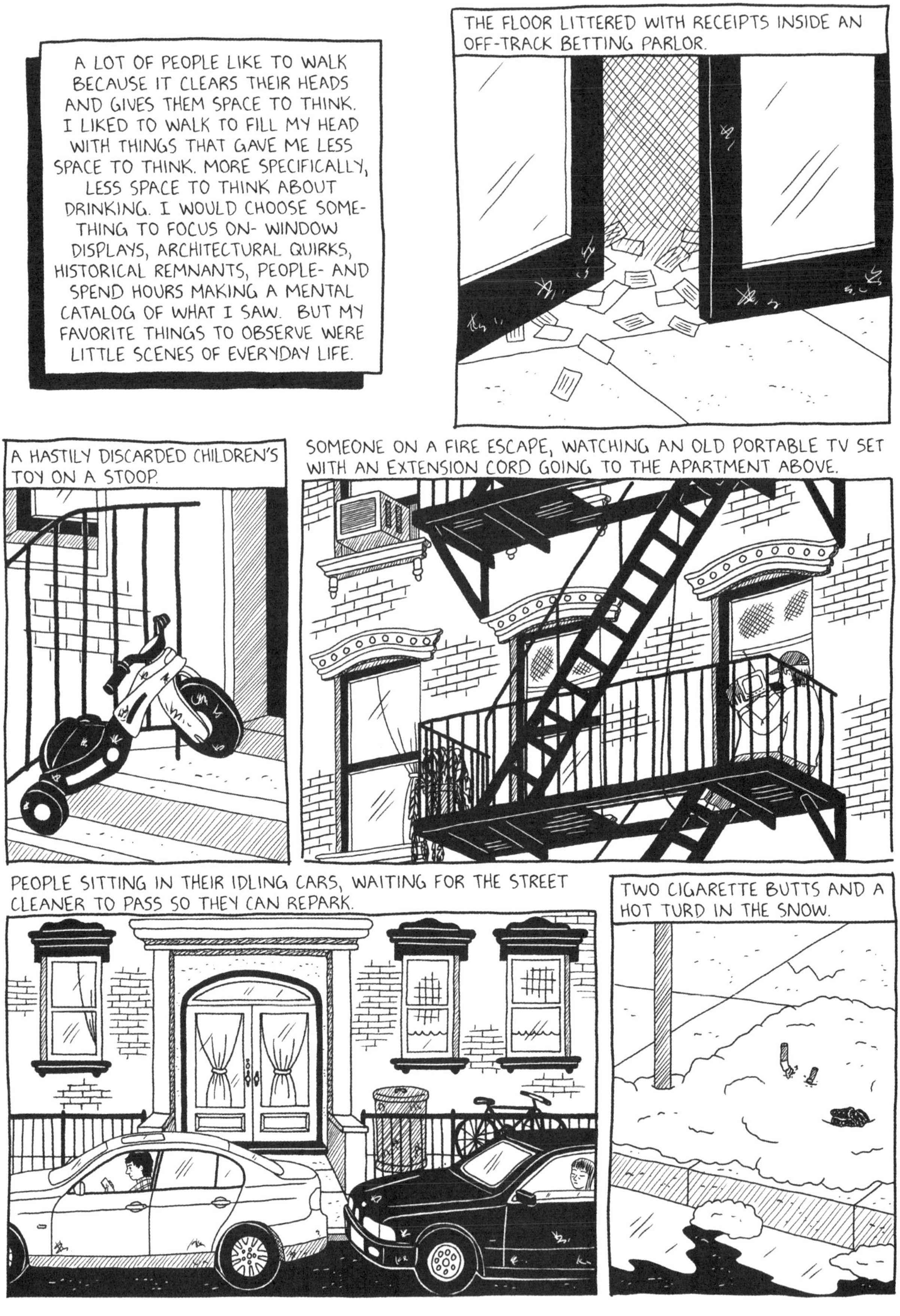
A LOT OF PEOPLE LIKE TO WALK BECAUSE IT CLEARS THEIR HEADS AND GIVES THEM SPACE TO THINK. I LIKED TO WALK TO FILL MY HEAD WITH THINGS THAT GAVE ME LESS SPACE TO THINK. MORE SPECIFICALLY, LESS SPACE TO THINK ABOUT DRINKING. I WOULD CHOOSE SOMETHING TO FOCUS ON- WINDOW DISPLAYS, ARCHITECTURAL QUIRKS, HISTORICAL REMNANTS, PEOPLE- AND SPEND HOURS MAKING A MENTAL CATALOG OF WHAT I SAW. BUT MY FAVORITE THINGS TO OBSERVE WERE LITTLE SCENES OF EVERYDAY LIFE.
THE FLOOR LITTERED WITH RECEIPTS INSIDE AN OFF-TRACK BETTING PARLOR.
A HASTILY DISCARDED CHILDREN'S TOY ON A STOOP.
SOMEONE ON A FIRE ESCAPE, WATCHING AN OLD PORTABLE TV SET WITH AN EXTENSION CORD GOING TO THE APARTMENT ABOVE.
PEOPLE SITTING IN THEIR IDLING CARS, WAITING FOR THE STREET CLEANER TO PASS SO THEY CAN REPARK.
TWO CIGARETTE BUTTS AND A HOT TURD IN THE SNOW.

I TOOK JOSH'S ADVICE ABOUT DOING SOMETHING FOR OTHERS AND I STARTED VOLUNTEERING WITH A WOMAN I MET AT A MEETING. ON SATURDAYS, WE MET AT 6AM TO MAKE PEANUT BUTTER AND JELLY SANDWICHES THAT WE PASSED OUT TO THE HOMELESS IN THE NEIGHBORHOOD.

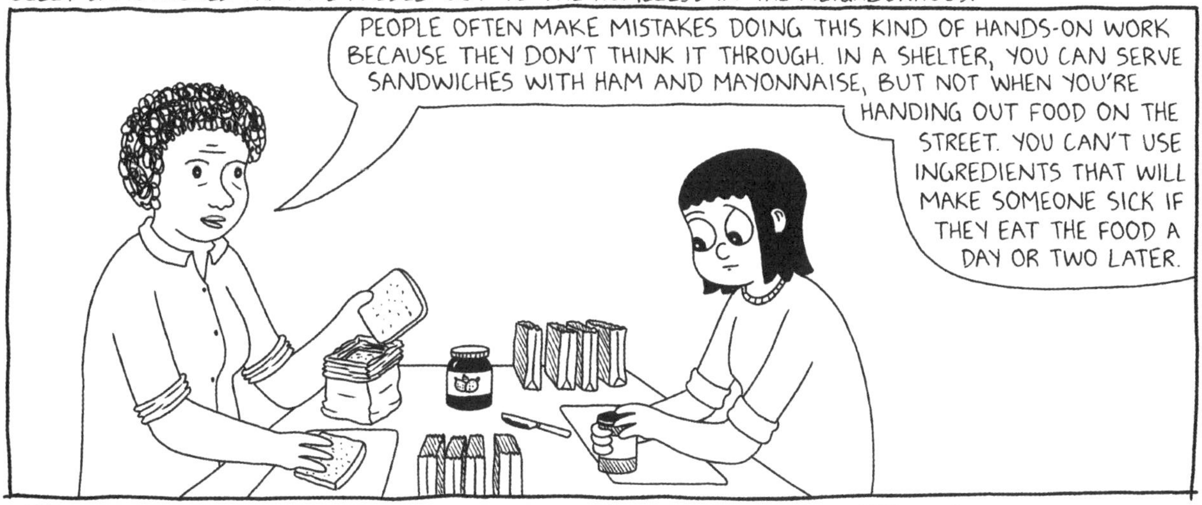
PEOPLE OFTEN MAKE MISTAKES DOING THIS KIND OF HANDS-ON WORK BECAUSE THEY DON'T THINK IT THROUGH. IN A SHELTER, YOU CAN SERVE SANDWICHES WITH HAM AND MAYONNAISE, BUT NOT WHEN YOU'RE HANDING OUT FOOD ON THE STREET. YOU CAN'T USE INGREDIENTS THAT WILL MAKE SOMEONE SICK IF THEY EAT THE FOOD A DAY OR TWO LATER.

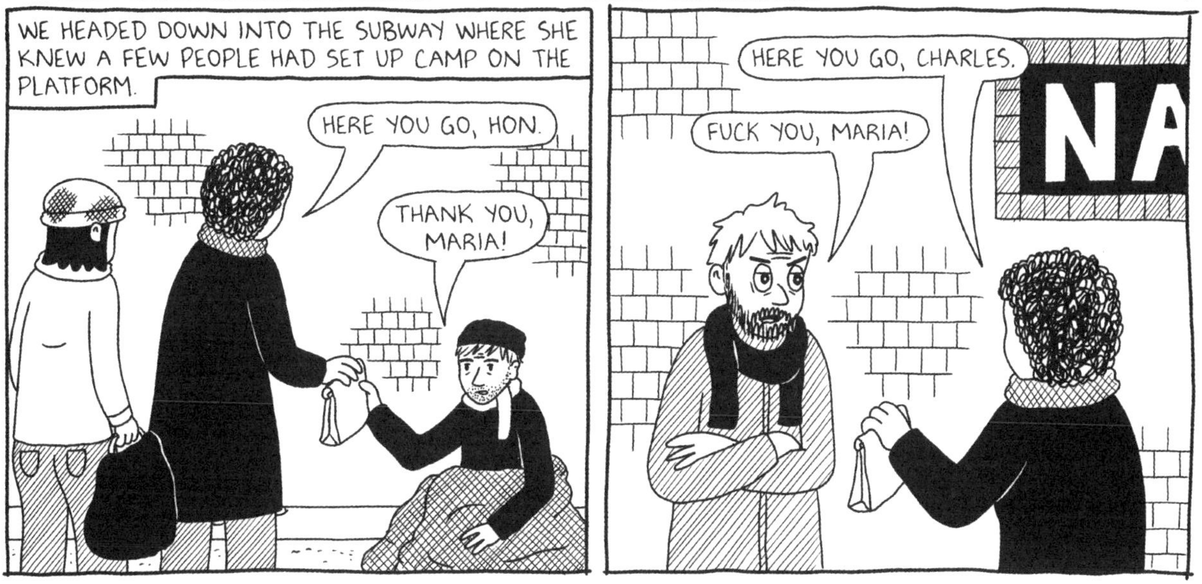
WE HEADED DOWN INTO THE SUBWAY WHERE SHE KNEW A FEW PEOPLE HAD SET UP CAMP ON THE PLATFORM.
HERE YOU GO, HON.
THANK YOU, MARIA!
HERE YOU GO, CHARLES.
FUCK YOU, MARIA!
NA

I ONLY HELPED MARIA ON SATURDAYS, BUT SHE MADE AND HANDED OUT FOOD EVERY SINGLE DAY.

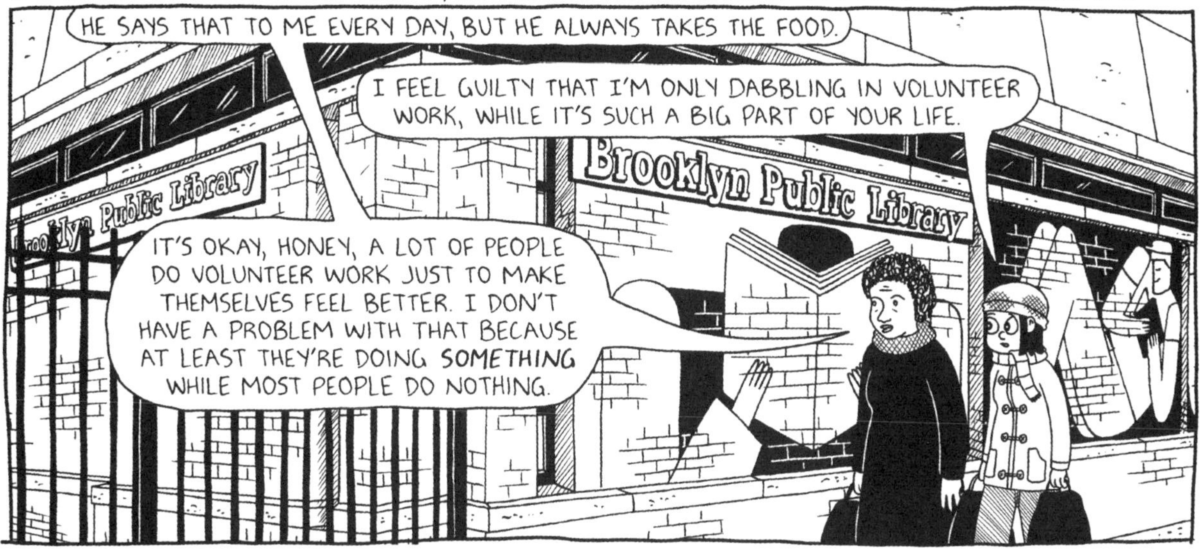
HE SAYS THAT TO ME EVERY DAY, BUT HE ALWAYS TAKES THE FOOD.
I FEEL GUILTY THAT I'M ONLY DABBLING IN VOLUNTEER WORK, WHILE IT'S SUCH A BIG PART OF YOUR LIFE.
Brooklyn Public Library
Brooklyn Public Library
IT'S OKAY, HONEY, A LOT OF PEOPLE DO VOLUNTEER WORK JUST TO MAKE THEMSELVES FEEL BETTER. I DON'T HAVE A PROBLEM WITH THAT BECAUSE AT LEAST THEY'RE DOING **SOMETHING** WHILE MOST PEOPLE DO NOTHING.

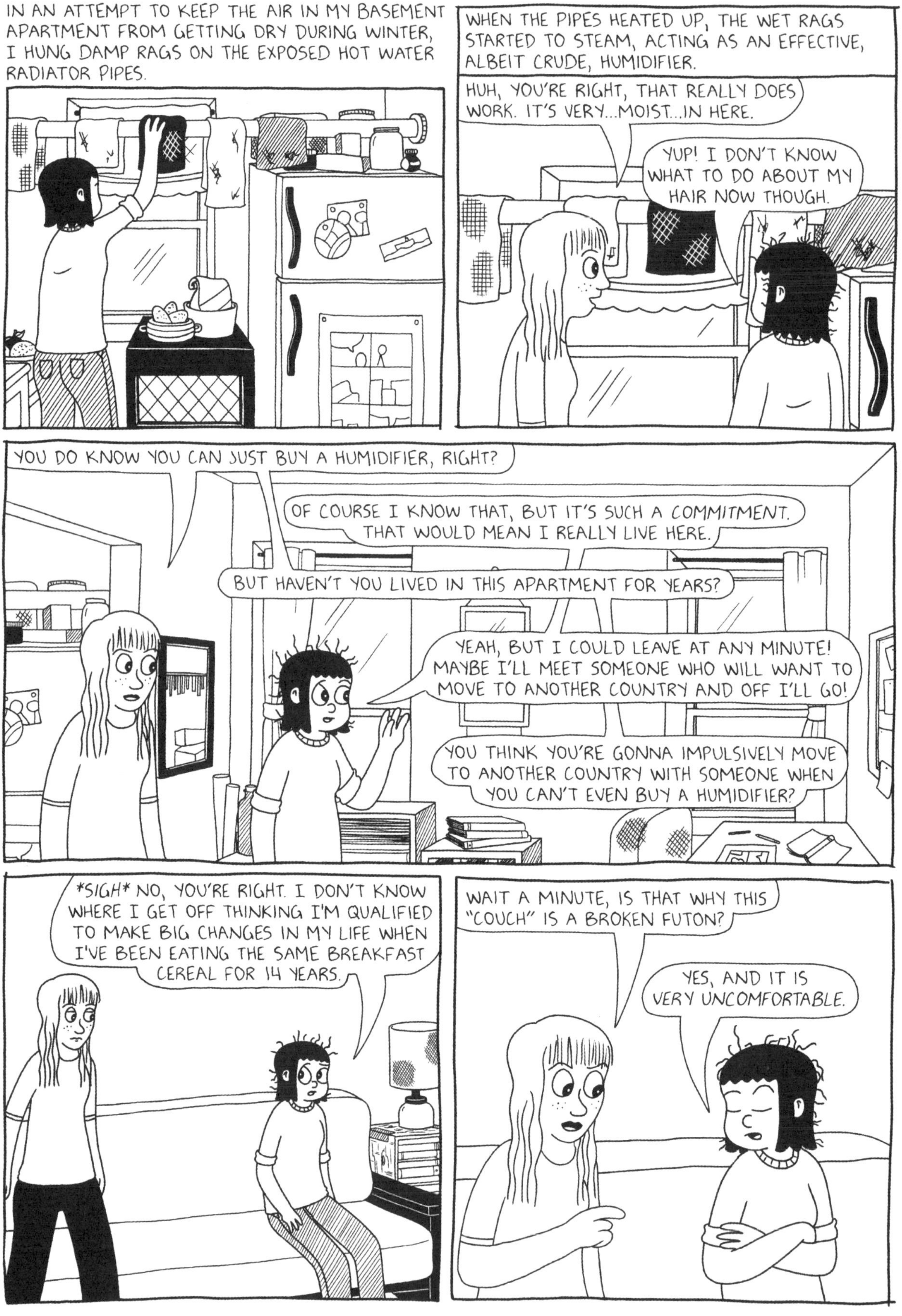

IN AN ATTEMPT TO KEEP THE AIR IN MY BASEMENT APARTMENT FROM GETTING DRY DURING WINTER, I HUNG DAMP RAGS ON THE EXPOSED HOT WATER RADIATOR PIPES.
WHEN THE PIPES HEATED UP, THE WET RAGS STARTED TO STEAM, ACTING AS AN EFFECTIVE, ALBEIT CRUDE, HUMIDIFIER.
HUH, YOU'RE RIGHT, THAT REALLY DOES WORK. IT'S VERY...MOIST...IN HERE.
YUP! I DON'T KNOW WHAT TO DO ABOUT MY HAIR NOW THOUGH.
YOU DO KNOW YOU CAN JUST BUY A HUMIDIFIER, RIGHT?
OF COURSE I KNOW THAT, BUT IT'S SUCH A COMMITMENT. THAT WOULD MEAN I REALLY LIVE HERE.
BUT HAVEN'T YOU LIVED IN THIS APARTMENT FOR YEARS?
YEAH, BUT I COULD LEAVE AT ANY MINUTE! MAYBE I'LL MEET SOMEONE WHO WILL WANT TO MOVE TO ANOTHER COUNTRY AND OFF I'LL GO!
YOU THINK YOU'RE GONNA IMPULSIVELY MOVE TO ANOTHER COUNTRY WITH SOMEONE WHEN YOU CAN'T EVEN BUY A HUMIDIFIER?
SIGH NO, YOU'RE RIGHT. I DON'T KNOW WHERE I GET OFF THINKING I'M QUALIFIED TO MAKE BIG CHANGES IN MY LIFE WHEN I'VE BEEN EATING THE SAME BREAKFAST CEREAL FOR 14 YEARS.
WAIT A MINUTE, IS THAT WHY THIS "COUCH" IS A BROKEN FUTON?
YES, AND IT IS VERY UNCOMFORTABLE.

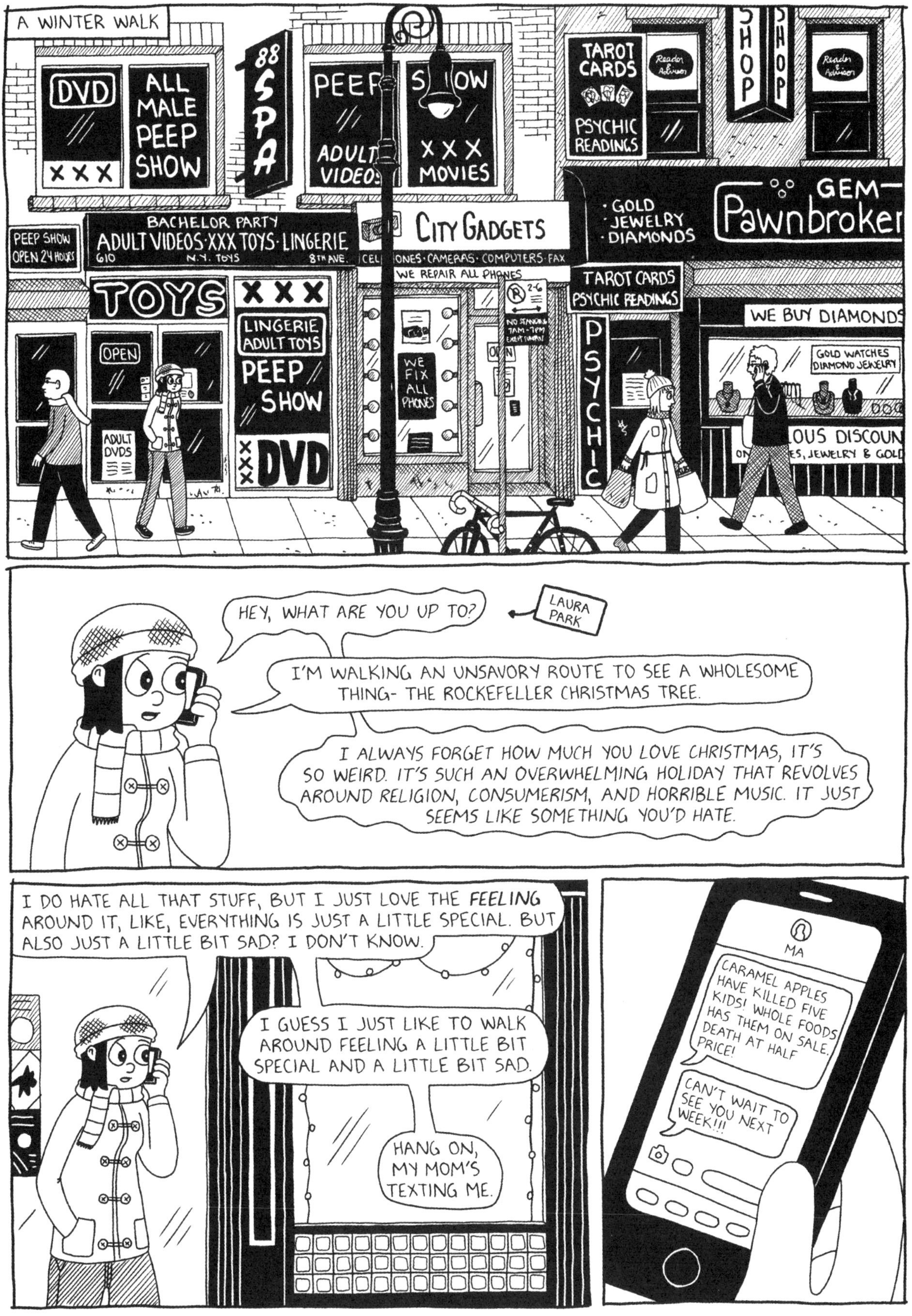
A WINTER WALK
DVD
XXX
ALL MALE PEEP SHOW
88 SPA
PEEP SHOW
ADULT VIDEOS
XXX MOVIES
TAROT CARDS
PSYCHIC READINGS
Reader & Advisor
SHOP
SHOP
Reader & Advisor
PEEP SHOW OPEN 24 HOURS
BACHELOR PARTY
ADULT VIDEOS·XXX TOYS·LINGERIE
610 N.Y. TOYS 8TH AVE.
CITY GADGETS
CELLPHONES·CAMERAS·COMPUTERS·FAX
WE REPAIR ALL PHONES
·GOLD ·JEWELRY ·DIAMONDS
GEM-Pawnbroker
TOYS
XXX
LINGERIE ADULT TOYS
PEEP SHOW
XXX DVD
OPEN
ADULT DVDS
WE FIX ALL PHONES
OPEN
NO STANDING 7AM-7PM
TAROT CARDS PSYCHIC READINGS
PSYCHIC
WE BUY DIAMONDS
GOLD WATCHES DIAMOND JEWELRY
HEY, WHAT ARE YOU UP TO?
LAURA PARK
I'M WALKING AN UNSAVORY ROUTE TO SEE A WHOLESOME THING- THE ROCKEFELLER CHRISTMAS TREE.
I ALWAYS FORGET HOW MUCH YOU LOVE CHRISTMAS, IT'S SO WEIRD. IT'S SUCH AN OVERWHELMING HOLIDAY THAT REVOLVES AROUND RELIGION, CONSUMERISM, AND HORRIBLE MUSIC. IT JUST SEEMS LIKE SOMETHING YOU'D HATE.
I DO HATE ALL THAT STUFF, BUT I JUST LOVE THE **FEELING** AROUND IT, LIKE, EVERYTHING IS JUST A LITTLE SPECIAL. BUT ALSO JUST A LITTLE BIT SAD? I DON'T KNOW.
I GUESS I JUST LIKE TO WALK AROUND FEELING A LITTLE BIT SPECIAL AND A LITTLE BIT SAD.
HANG ON, MY MOM'S TEXTING ME.
MA
CARAMEL APPLES HAVE KILLED FIVE KIDS! WHOLE FOODS HAS THEM ON SALE. DEATH AT HALF PRICE!
CAN'T WAIT TO SEE YOU NEXT WEEK!!!

AFTER SPENDING THE LAST TWO CHRISTMASES ALONE IN MY APARTMENT, I WAS HAPPY TO BE FLYING HOME TO CALIFORNIA TO SEE MY FAMILY. SO HAPPY THAT I DIDN'T CARE THAT IT TOOK 21 HOURS, THERE WERE THREE CONNECTING FLIGHTS, AND I WAS IN THE LAST ROW WITH SEATS THAT DON'T RECLINE.

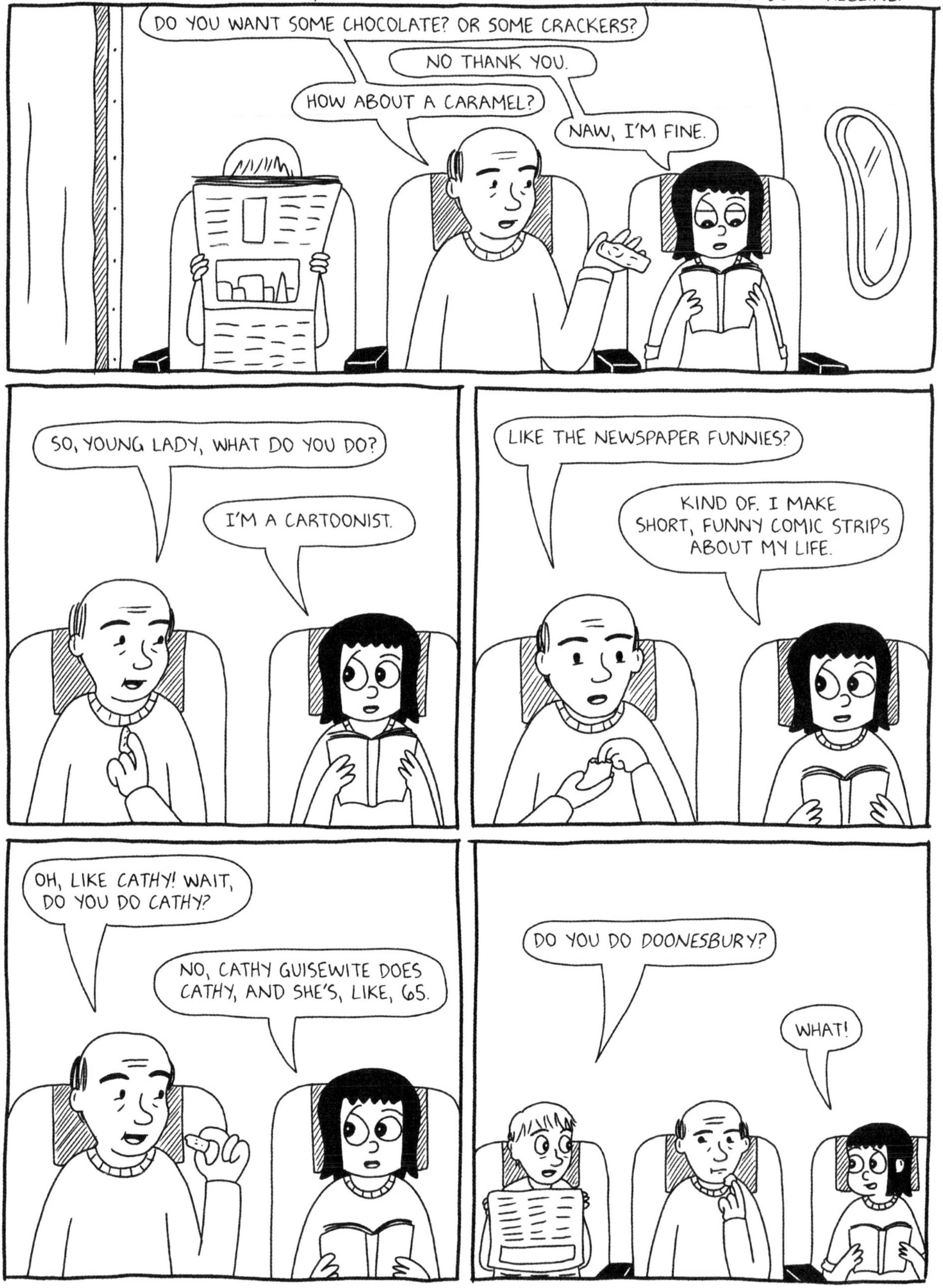
DO YOU WANT SOME CHOCOLATE? OR SOME CRACKERS?
NO THANK YOU.
HOW ABOUT A CARAMEL?
NAW, I'M FINE.
SO, YOUNG LADY, WHAT DO YOU DO?
I'M A CARTOONIST.
LIKE THE NEWSPAPER FUNNIES?
KIND OF. I MAKE SHORT, FUNNY COMIC STRIPS ABOUT MY LIFE.
OH, LIKE CATHY! WAIT, DO YOU DO CATHY?
NO, CATHY GUISEWITE DOES CATHY, AND SHE'S, LIKE, 65.
DO YOU DO DOONESBURY?
WHAT!

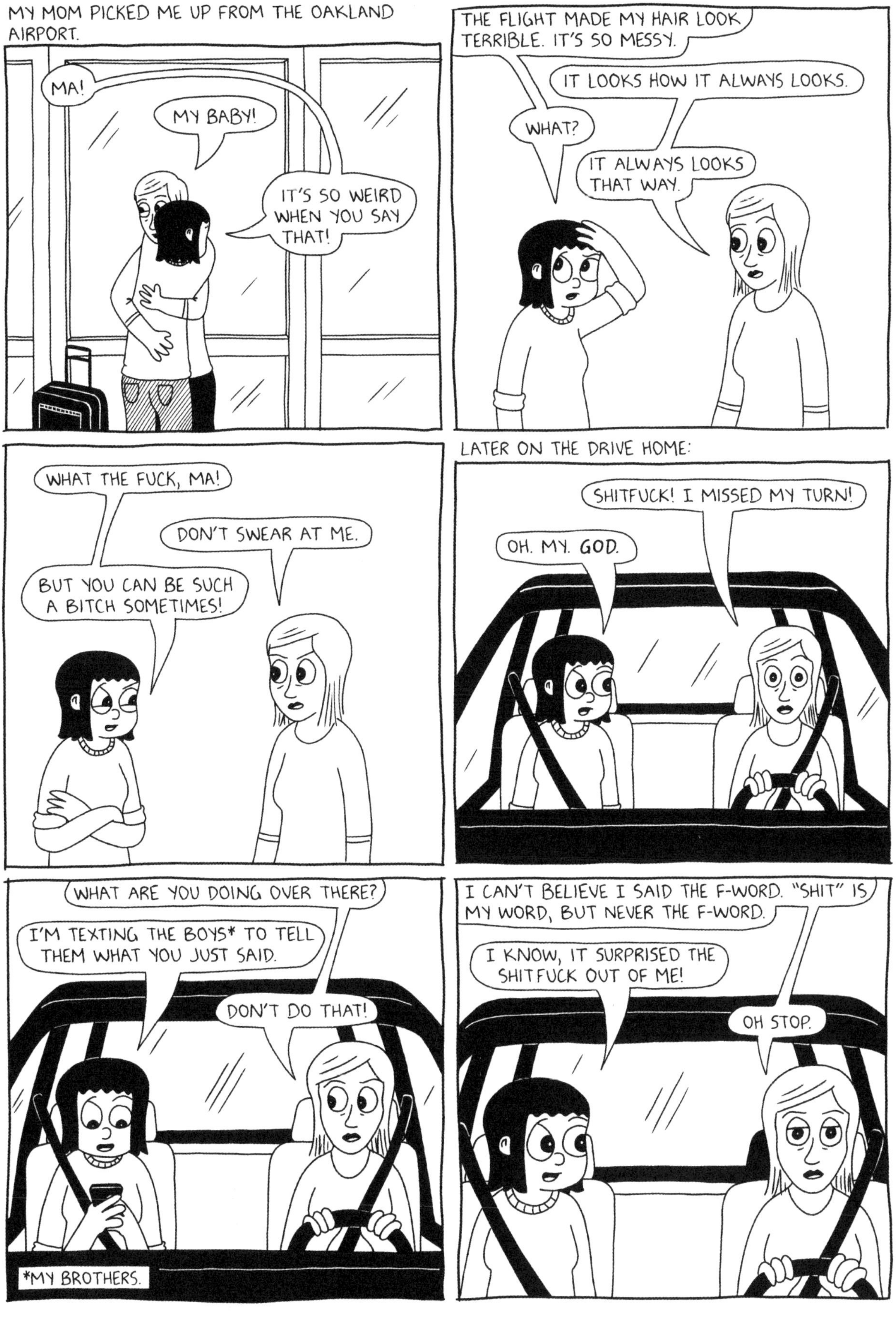
MY MOM PICKED ME UP FROM THE OAKLAND AIRPORT.
MA!
MY BABY!
IT'S SO WEIRD WHEN YOU SAY THAT!
THE FLIGHT MADE MY HAIR LOOK TERRIBLE. IT'S SO MESSY.
IT LOOKS HOW IT ALWAYS LOOKS.
WHAT?
IT ALWAYS LOOKS THAT WAY.
WHAT THE FUCK, MA!
DON'T SWEAR AT ME.
BUT YOU CAN BE SUCH A BITCH SOMETIMES!
LATER ON THE DRIVE HOME:
SHITFUCK! I MISSED MY TURN!
OH. MY. GOD.
WHAT ARE YOU DOING OVER THERE?
I'M TEXTING THE BOYS* TO TELL THEM WHAT YOU JUST SAID.
DON'T DO THAT!
*MY BROTHERS.
I CAN'T BELIEVE I SAID THE F-WORD. "SHIT" IS MY WORD, BUT NEVER THE F-WORD.
I KNOW, IT SURPRISED THE SHITFUCK OUT OF ME!
OH STOP.

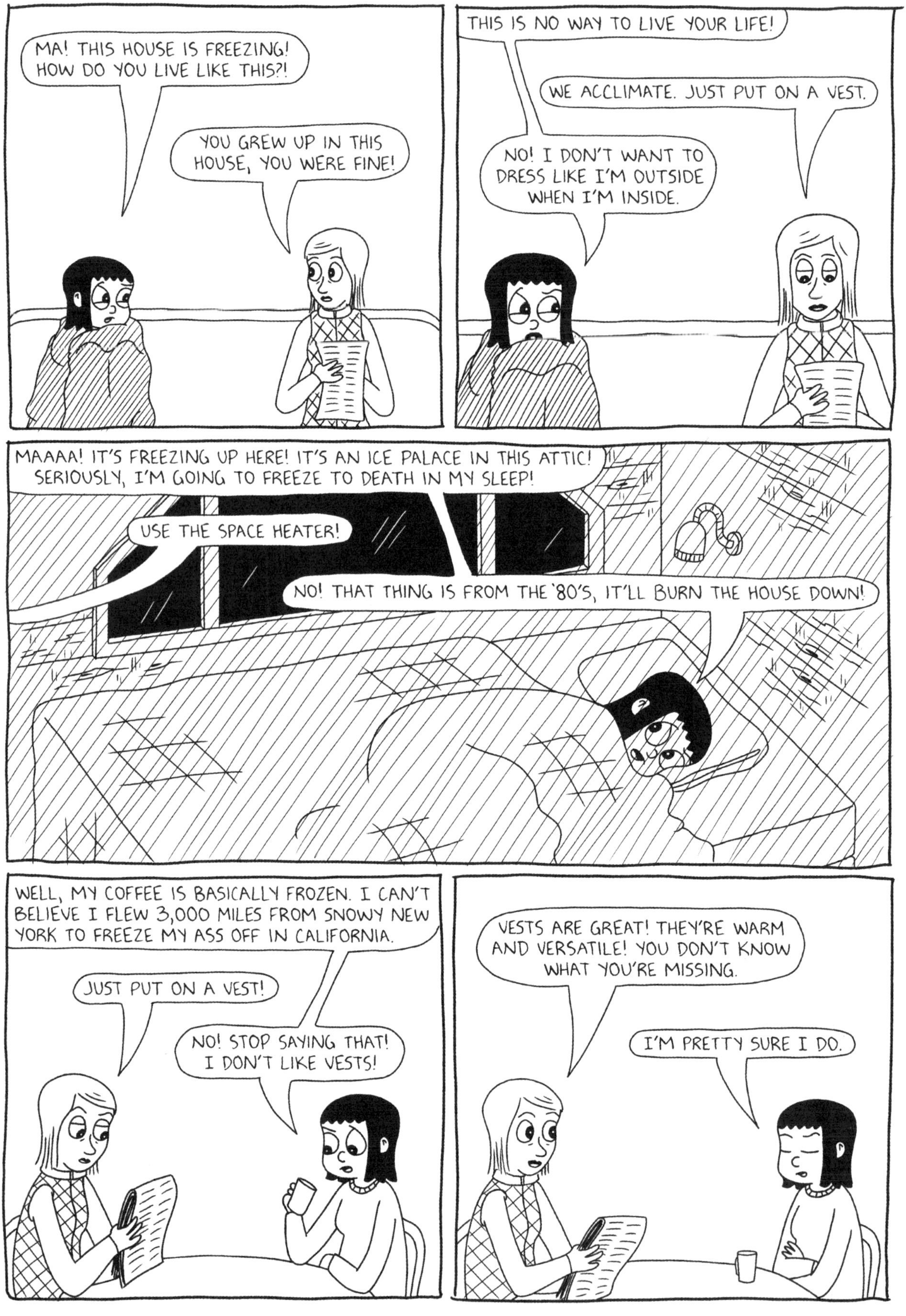
MA! THIS HOUSE IS FREEZING! HOW DO YOU LIVE LIKE THIS?!
YOU GREW UP IN THIS HOUSE, YOU WERE FINE!
THIS IS NO WAY TO LIVE YOUR LIFE!
WE ACCLIMATE. JUST PUT ON A VEST.
NO! I DON'T WANT TO DRESS LIKE I'M OUTSIDE WHEN I'M INSIDE.
MAAAA! IT'S FREEZING UP HERE! IT'S AN ICE PALACE IN THIS ATTIC! SERIOUSLY, I'M GOING TO FREEZE TO DEATH IN MY SLEEP!
USE THE SPACE HEATER!
NO! THAT THING IS FROM THE '80'S, IT'LL BURN THE HOUSE DOWN!
WELL, MY COFFEE IS BASICALLY FROZEN. I CAN'T BELIEVE I FLEW 3,000 MILES FROM SNOWY NEW YORK TO FREEZE MY ASS OFF IN CALIFORNIA.
JUST PUT ON A VEST!
NO! STOP SAYING THAT! I DON'T LIKE VESTS!
VESTS ARE GREAT! THEY'RE WARM AND VERSATILE! YOU DON'T KNOW WHAT YOU'RE MISSING.
I'M PRETTY SURE I DO.

ON CHRISTMAS EVE DAY, MY BROTHERS AND I WENT TO BODEGA BAY AND STROLLED THE DUNES.

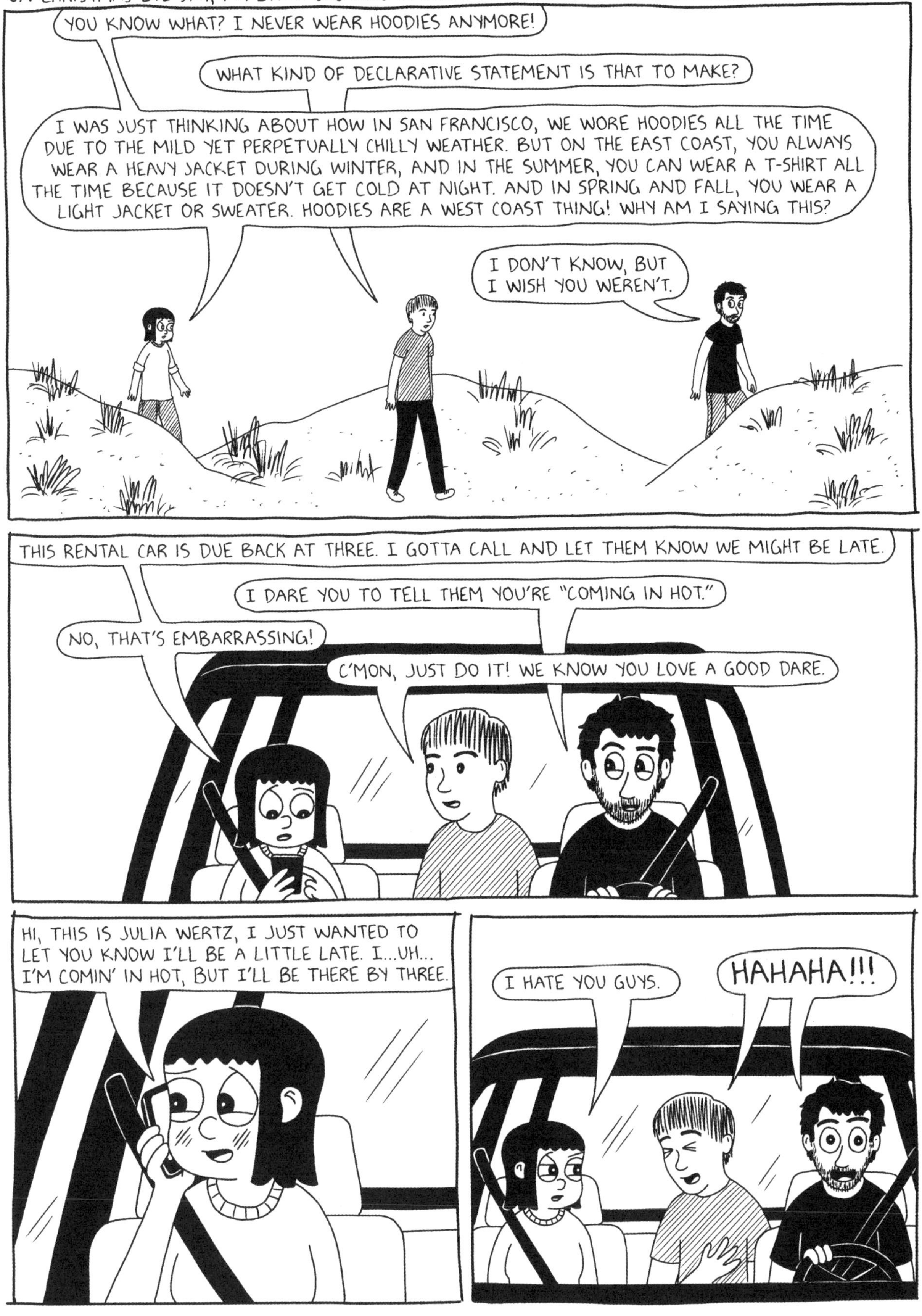
YOU KNOW WHAT? I NEVER WEAR HOODIES ANYMORE!
WHAT KIND OF DECLARATIVE STATEMENT IS THAT TO MAKE?
I WAS JUST THINKING ABOUT HOW IN SAN FRANCISCO, WE WORE HOODIES ALL THE TIME DUE TO THE MILD YET PERPETUALLY CHILLY WEATHER. BUT ON THE EAST COAST, YOU ALWAYS WEAR A HEAVY JACKET DURING WINTER, AND IN THE SUMMER, YOU CAN WEAR A T-SHIRT ALL THE TIME BECAUSE IT DOESN'T GET COLD AT NIGHT. AND IN SPRING AND FALL, YOU WEAR A LIGHT JACKET OR SWEATER. HOODIES ARE A WEST COAST THING! WHY AM I SAYING THIS?
I DON'T KNOW, BUT I WISH YOU WEREN'T.
THIS RENTAL CAR IS DUE BACK AT THREE. I GOTTA CALL AND LET THEM KNOW WE MIGHT BE LATE.
I DARE YOU TO TELL THEM YOU'RE "COMING IN HOT."
NO, THAT'S EMBARRASSING!
C'MON, JUST DO IT! WE KNOW YOU LOVE A GOOD DARE.
HI, THIS IS JULIA WERTZ, I JUST WANTED TO LET YOU KNOW I'LL BE A LITTLE LATE. I...UH... I'M COMIN' IN HOT, BUT I'LL BE THERE BY THREE.
I HATE YOU GUYS.
HAHAHA!!!

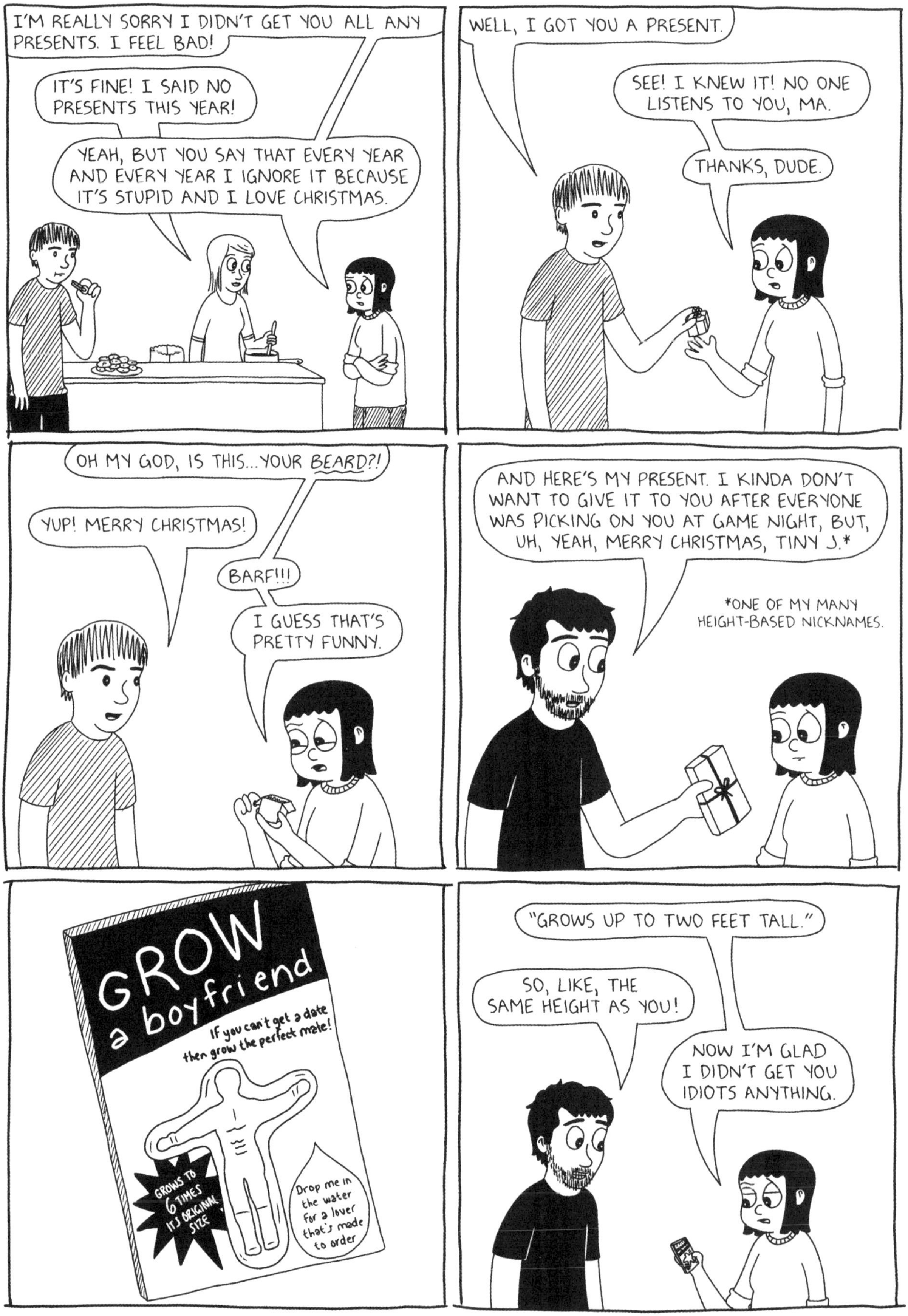
I'M REALLY SORRY I DIDN'T GET YOU ALL ANY PRESENTS. I FEEL BAD!
IT'S FINE! I SAID NO PRESENTS THIS YEAR!
YEAH, BUT YOU SAY THAT EVERY YEAR AND EVERY YEAR I IGNORE IT BECAUSE IT'S STUPID AND I LOVE CHRISTMAS.
WELL, I GOT YOU A PRESENT.
SEE! I KNEW IT! NO ONE LISTENS TO YOU, MA.
THANKS, DUDE.
OH MY GOD, IS THIS...YOUR BEARD?!
YUP! MERRY CHRISTMAS!
BARF!!!
I GUESS THAT'S PRETTY FUNNY.
AND HERE'S MY PRESENT. I KINDA DON'T WANT TO GIVE IT TO YOU AFTER EVERYONE WAS PICKING ON YOU AT GAME NIGHT, BUT, UH, YEAH, MERRY CHRISTMAS, TINY J.*
*ONE OF MY MANY HEIGHT-BASED NICKNAMES.
GROW a boyfriend
If you can't get a date then grow the perfect mate!
GROWS TO 6 TIMES ITS ORIGINAL SIZE
Drop me in the water for a lover that's made to order
"GROWS UP TO TWO FEET TALL."
SO, LIKE, THE SAME HEIGHT AS YOU!
NOW I'M GLAD I DIDN'T GET YOU IDIOTS ANYTHING.

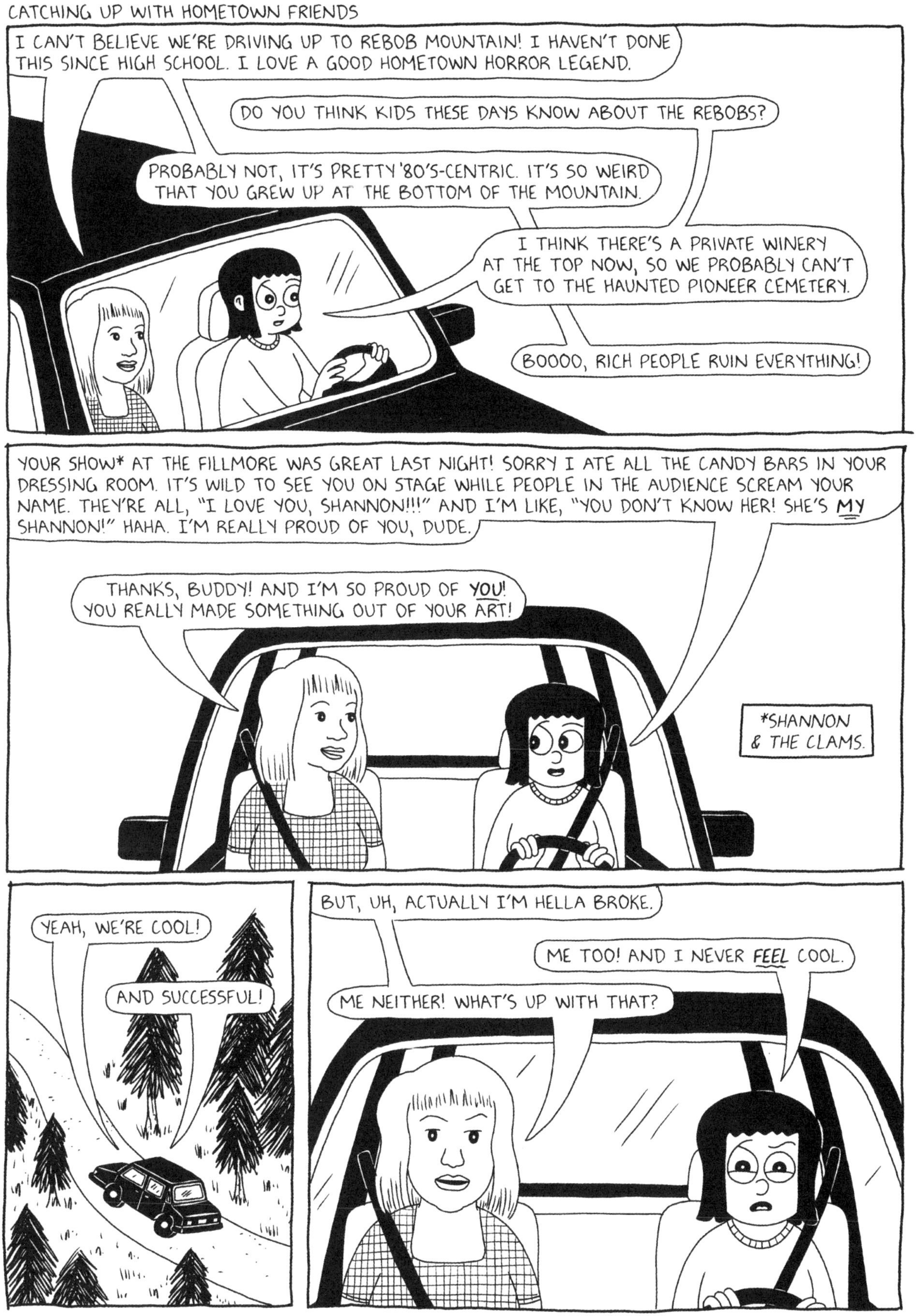
CATCHING UP WITH HOMETOWN FRIENDS
I CAN'T BELIEVE WE'RE DRIVING UP TO REBOB MOUNTAIN! I HAVEN'T DONE THIS SINCE HIGH SCHOOL. I LOVE A GOOD HOMETOWN HORROR LEGEND.
DO YOU THINK KIDS THESE DAYS KNOW ABOUT THE REBOBS?
PROBABLY NOT, IT'S PRETTY '80'S-CENTRIC. IT'S SO WEIRD THAT YOU GREW UP AT THE BOTTOM OF THE MOUNTAIN.
I THINK THERE'S A PRIVATE WINERY AT THE TOP NOW, SO WE PROBABLY CAN'T GET TO THE HAUNTED PIONEER CEMETERY.
BOOOO, RICH PEOPLE RUIN EVERYTHING!
YOUR SHOW* AT THE FILLMORE WAS GREAT LAST NIGHT! SORRY I ATE ALL THE CANDY BARS IN YOUR DRESSING ROOM. IT'S WILD TO SEE YOU ON STAGE WHILE PEOPLE IN THE AUDIENCE SCREAM YOUR NAME. THEY'RE ALL, "I LOVE YOU, SHANNON!!!" AND I'M LIKE, "YOU DON'T KNOW HER! SHE'S MY SHANNON!" HAHA. I'M REALLY PROUD OF YOU, DUDE.
THANKS, BUDDY! AND I'M SO PROUD OF YOU! YOU REALLY MADE SOMETHING OUT OF YOUR ART!
*SHANNON & THE CLAMS.
YEAH, WE'RE COOL!
AND SUCCESSFUL!
BUT, UH, ACTUALLY I'M HELLA BROKE.
ME TOO! AND I NEVER FEEL COOL.
ME NEITHER! WHAT'S UP WITH THAT?

MAKING CHRISTMAS COOKIES WITH MA

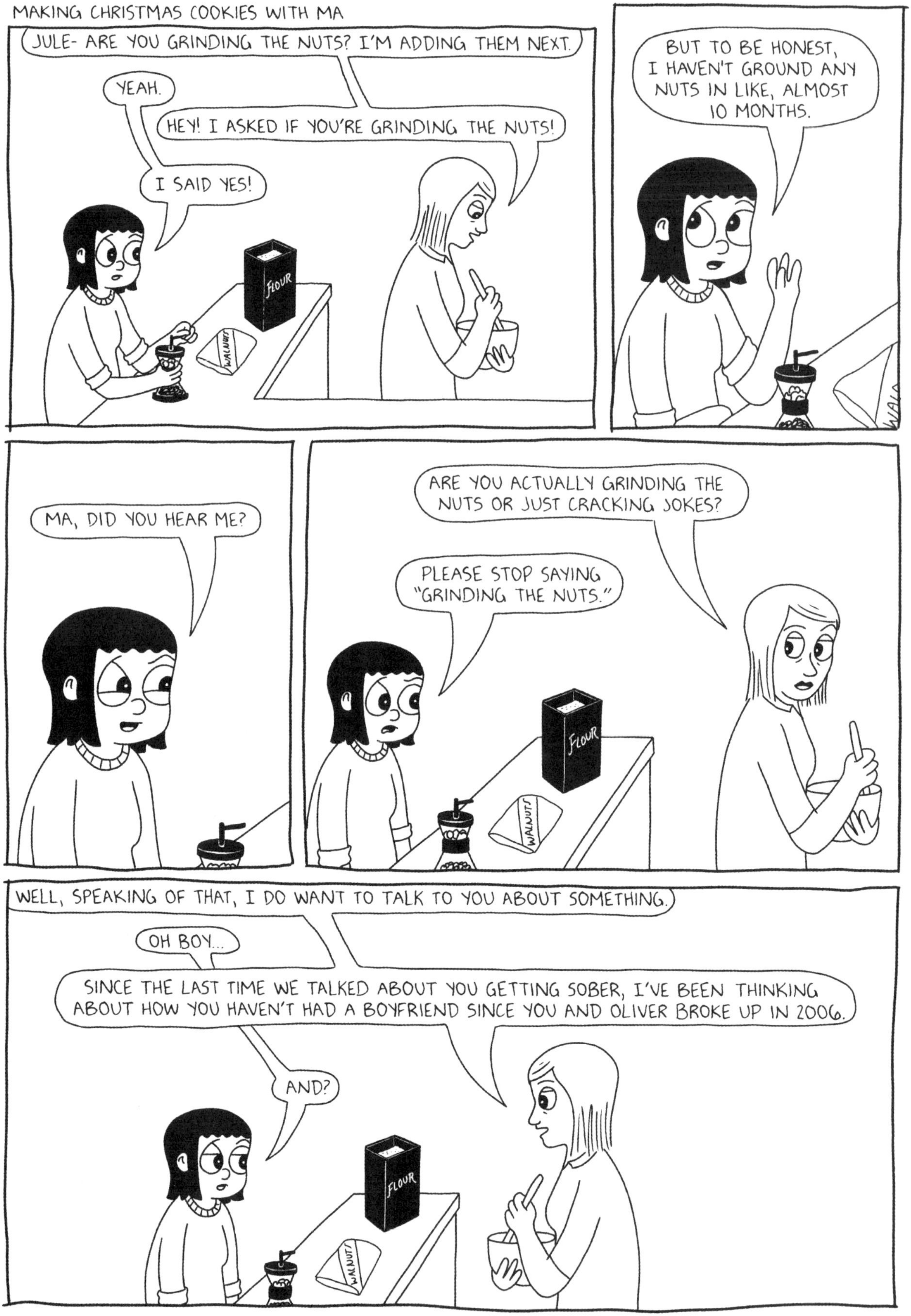
JULE- ARE YOU GRINDING THE NUTS? I'M ADDING THEM NEXT.
YEAH.
HEY! I ASKED IF YOU'RE GRINDING THE NUTS!
I SAID YES!
FLOUR
WALNUTS
BUT TO BE HONEST, I HAVEN'T GROUND ANY NUTS IN LIKE, ALMOST 10 MONTHS.
MA, DID YOU HEAR ME?
ARE YOU ACTUALLY GRINDING THE NUTS OR JUST CRACKING JOKES?
PLEASE STOP SAYING "GRINDING THE NUTS."
FLOUR
WALNUTS
WELL, SPEAKING OF THAT, I DO WANT TO TALK TO YOU ABOUT SOMETHING.
OH BOY...
SINCE THE LAST TIME WE TALKED ABOUT YOU GETTING SOBER, I'VE BEEN THINKING ABOUT HOW YOU HAVEN'T HAD A BOYFRIEND SINCE YOU AND OLIVER BROKE UP IN 2006.
AND?
FLOUR
WALNUTS

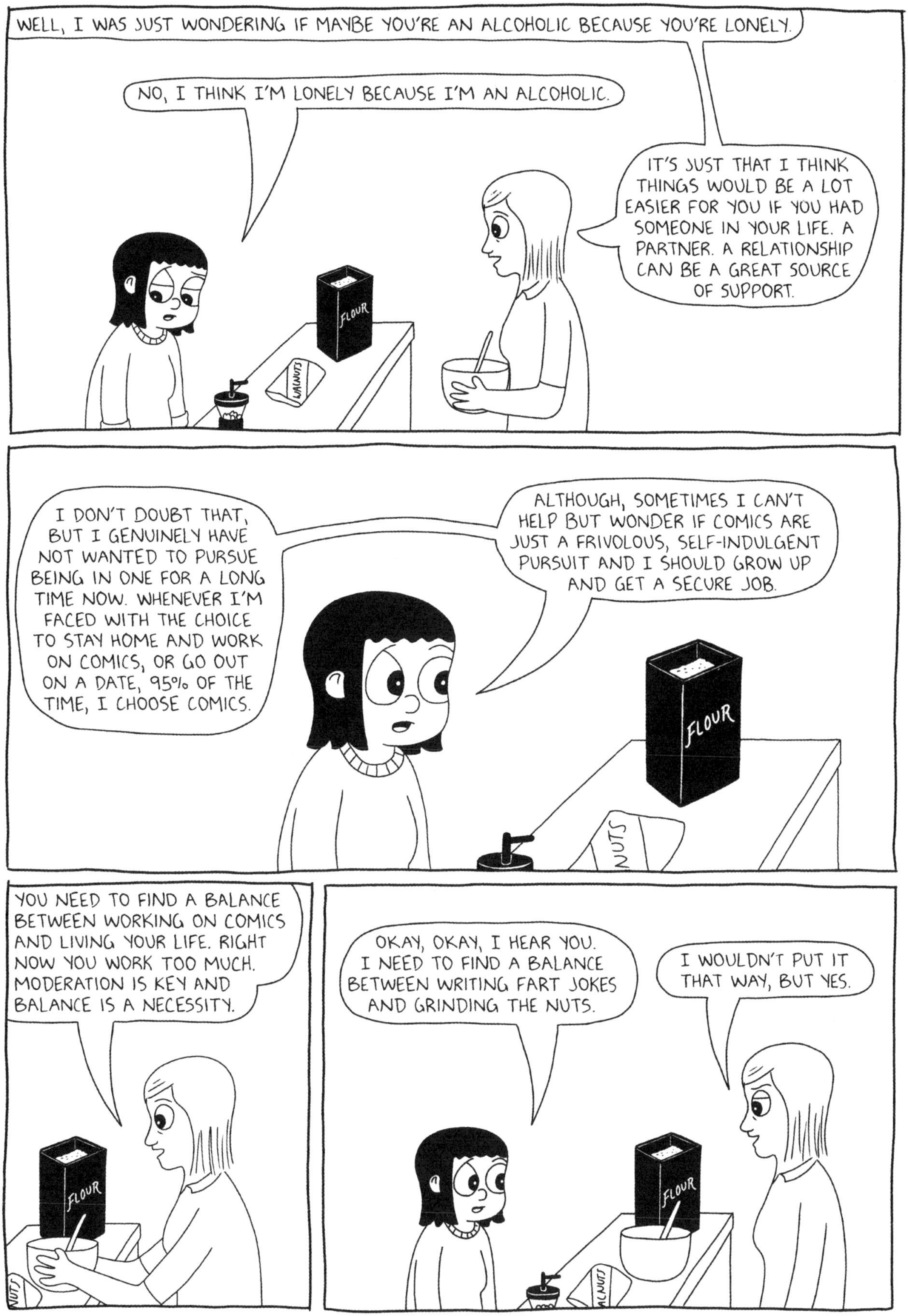
WELL, I WAS JUST WONDERING IF MAYBE YOU'RE AN ALCOHOLIC BECAUSE YOU'RE LONELY.
NO, I THINK I'M LONELY BECAUSE I'M AN ALCOHOLIC.
IT'S JUST THAT I THINK THINGS WOULD BE A LOT EASIER FOR YOU IF YOU HAD SOMEONE IN YOUR LIFE. A PARTNER. A RELATIONSHIP CAN BE A GREAT SOURCE OF SUPPORT.
FLOUR
WALNUTS
I DON'T DOUBT THAT, BUT I GENUINELY HAVE NOT WANTED TO PURSUE BEING IN ONE FOR A LONG TIME NOW. WHENEVER I'M FACED WITH THE CHOICE TO STAY HOME AND WORK ON COMICS, OR GO OUT ON A DATE, 95% OF THE TIME, I CHOOSE COMICS.
ALTHOUGH, SOMETIMES I CAN'T HELP BUT WONDER IF COMICS ARE JUST A FRIVOLOUS, SELF-INDULGENT PURSUIT AND I SHOULD GROW UP AND GET A SECURE JOB.
FLOUR
NUTS
YOU NEED TO FIND A BALANCE BETWEEN WORKING ON COMICS AND LIVING YOUR LIFE. RIGHT NOW YOU WORK TOO MUCH. MODERATION IS KEY AND BALANCE IS A NECESSITY.
FLOUR
OKAY, OKAY, I HEAR YOU. I NEED TO FIND A BALANCE BETWEEN WRITING FART JOKES AND GRINDING THE NUTS.
I WOULDN'T PUT IT THAT WAY, BUT YES.
FLOUR

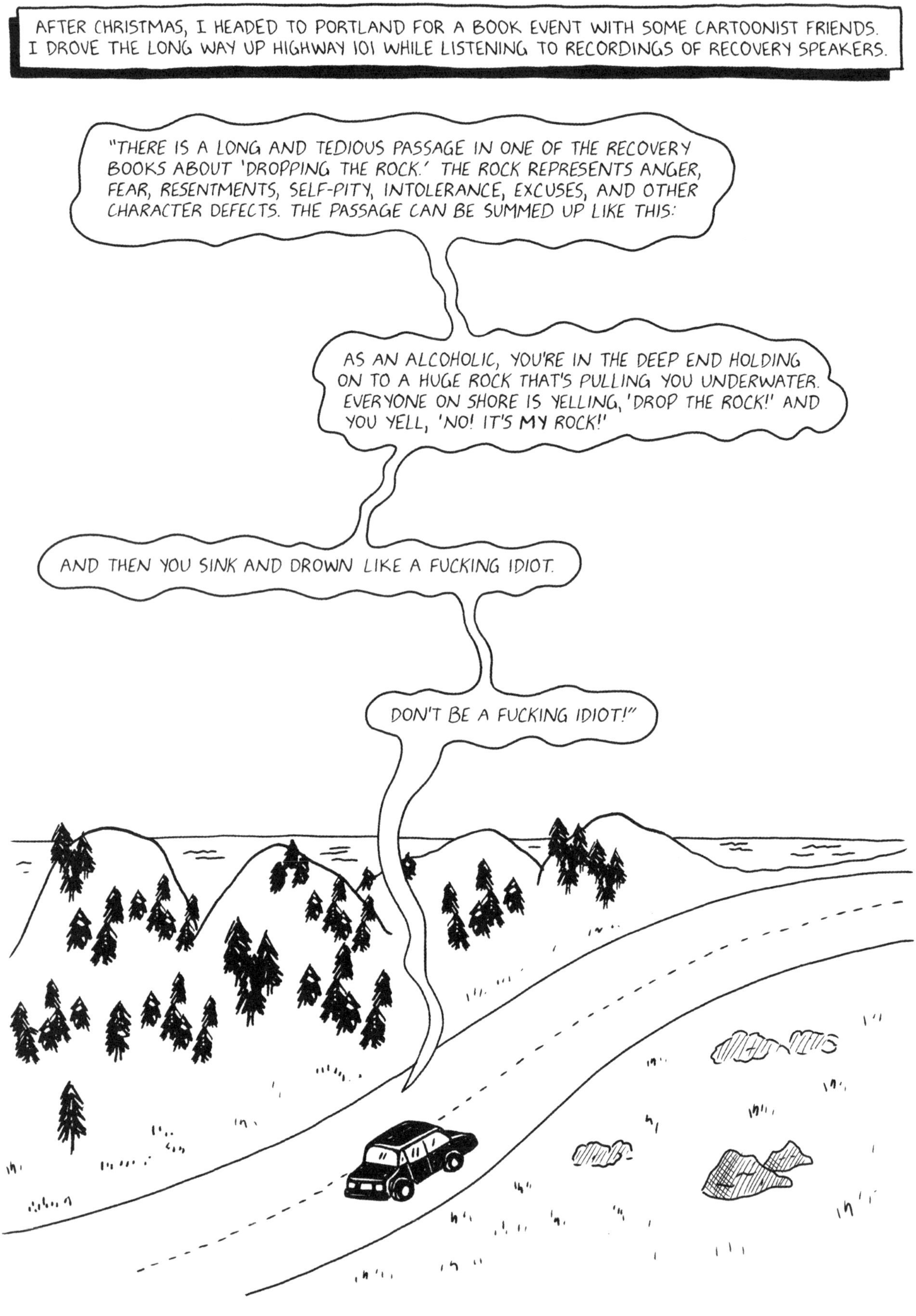
AFTER CHRISTMAS, I HEADED TO PORTLAND FOR A BOOK EVENT WITH SOME CARTOONIST FRIENDS. I DROVE THE LONG WAY UP HIGHWAY 101 WHILE LISTENING TO RECORDINGS OF RECOVERY SPEAKERS.
"THERE IS A LONG AND TEDIOUS PASSAGE IN ONE OF THE RECOVERY BOOKS ABOUT 'DROPPING THE ROCK.' THE ROCK REPRESENTS ANGER, FEAR, RESENTMENTS, SELF-PITY, INTOLERANCE, EXCUSES, AND OTHER CHARACTER DEFECTS. THE PASSAGE CAN BE SUMMED UP LIKE THIS:
AS AN ALCOHOLIC, YOU'RE IN THE DEEP END HOLDING ON TO A HUGE ROCK THAT'S PULLING YOU UNDERWATER. EVERYONE ON SHORE IS YELLING, 'DROP THE ROCK!' AND YOU YELL, 'NO! IT'S **MY** ROCK!'
AND THEN YOU SINK AND DROWN LIKE A FUCKING IDIOT.
DON'T BE A FUCKING IDIOT!"

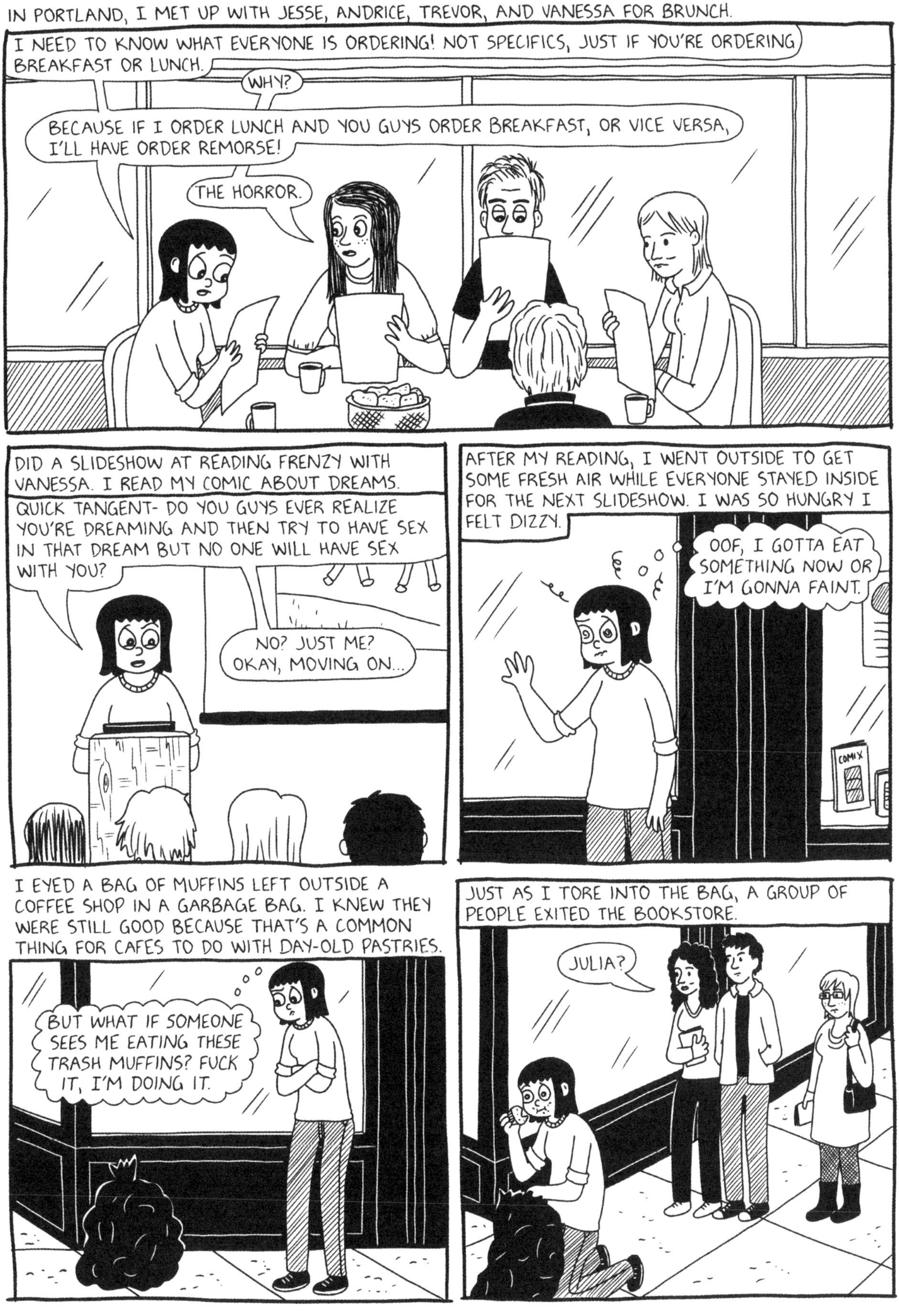

IN PORTLAND, I MET UP WITH JESSE, ANDRICE, TREVOR, AND VANESSA FOR BRUNCH.
I NEED TO KNOW WHAT EVERYONE IS ORDERING! NOT SPECIFICS, JUST IF YOU'RE ORDERING BREAKFAST OR LUNCH.
WHY?
BECAUSE IF I ORDER LUNCH AND YOU GUYS ORDER BREAKFAST, OR VICE VERSA, I'LL HAVE ORDER REMORSE!
THE HORROR.
DID A SLIDESHOW AT READING FRENZY WITH VANESSA. I READ MY COMIC ABOUT DREAMS.
QUICK TANGENT- DO YOU GUYS EVER REALIZE YOU'RE DREAMING AND THEN TRY TO HAVE SEX IN THAT DREAM BUT NO ONE WILL HAVE SEX WITH YOU?
NO? JUST ME? OKAY, MOVING ON...
AFTER MY READING, I WENT OUTSIDE TO GET SOME FRESH AIR WHILE EVERYONE STAYED INSIDE FOR THE NEXT SLIDESHOW. I WAS SO HUNGRY I FELT DIZZY.
OOF, I GOTTA EAT SOMETHING NOW OR I'M GONNA FAINT.
COMIX
I EYED A BAG OF MUFFINS LEFT OUTSIDE A COFFEE SHOP IN A GARBAGE BAG. I KNEW THEY WERE STILL GOOD BECAUSE THAT'S A COMMON THING FOR CAFES TO DO WITH DAY-OLD PASTRIES.
BUT WHAT IF SOMEONE SEES ME EATING THESE TRASH MUFFINS? FUCK IT, I'M DOING IT.
JUST AS I TORE INTO THE BAG, A GROUP OF PEOPLE EXITED THE BOOKSTORE.
JULIA?

THE NEXT DAY AT JESSE AND ANDRICE'S HOUSE

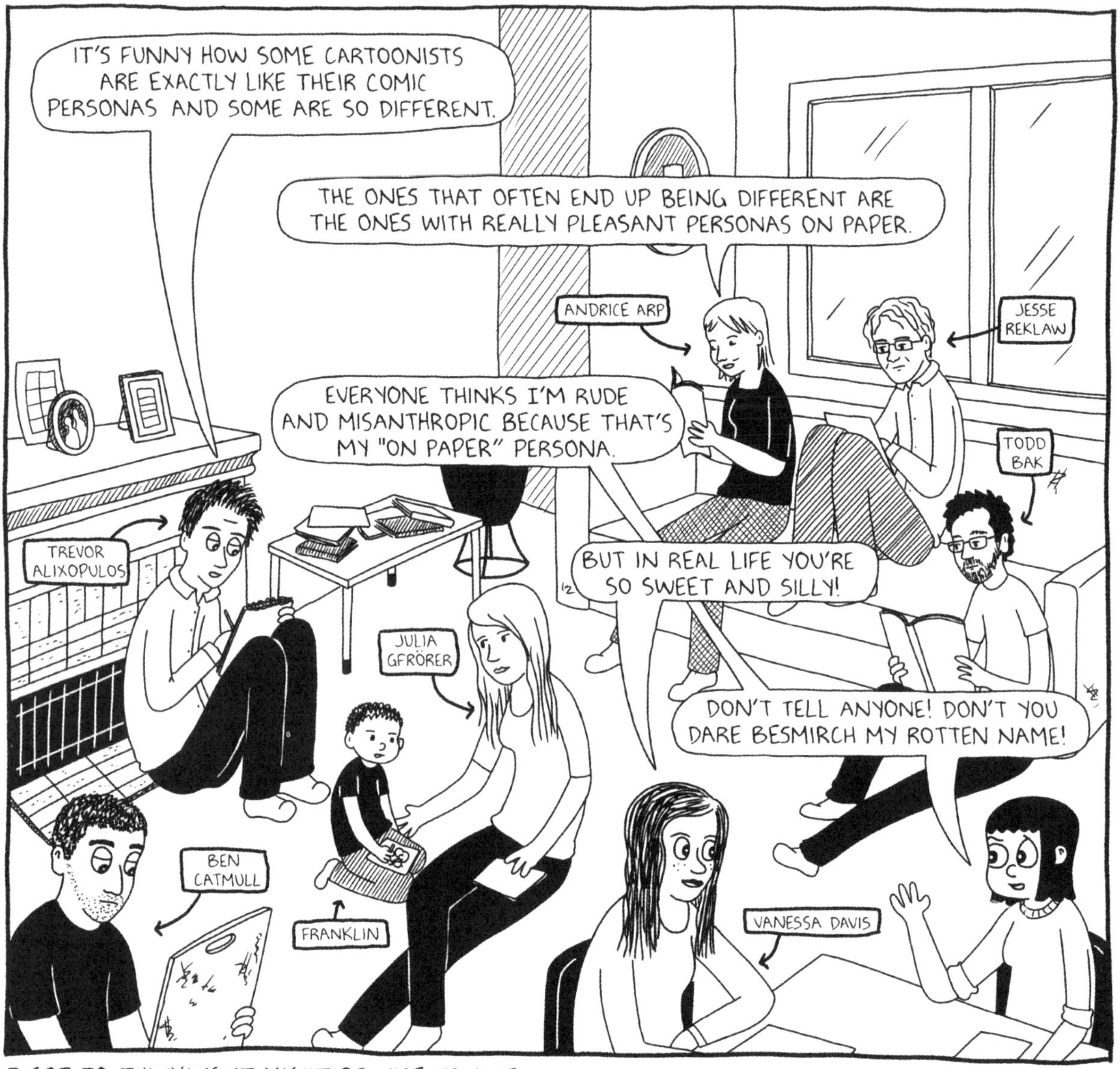

IT'S FUNNY HOW SOME CARTOONISTS ARE EXACTLY LIKE THEIR COMIC PERSONAS AND SOME ARE SO DIFFERENT.
THE ONES THAT OFTEN END UP BEING DIFFERENT ARE THE ONES WITH REALLY PLEASANT PERSONAS ON PAPER.
ANDRICE ARP
JESSE REKLAW
EVERYONE THINKS I'M RUDE AND MISANTHROPIC BECAUSE THAT'S MY "ON PAPER" PERSONA.
TODD BAK
TREVOR ALIXOPULOS
BUT IN REAL LIFE YOU'RE SO SWEET AND SILLY!
JULIA GFRÖRER
DON'T TELL ANYONE! DON'T YOU DARE BESMIRCH MY ROTTEN NAME!
BEN CATMULL
FRANKLIN
VANESSA DAVIS

I GOT TO THINKING IT MIGHT BE NICE TO LIVE IN PORTLAND, TO LIVE IN A SMALLER CITY WHERE I COULD BE A DIFFERENT PERSON. I STILL THOUGHT THAT BY CHANGING THE SCENERY, I COULD CHANGE MYSELF.

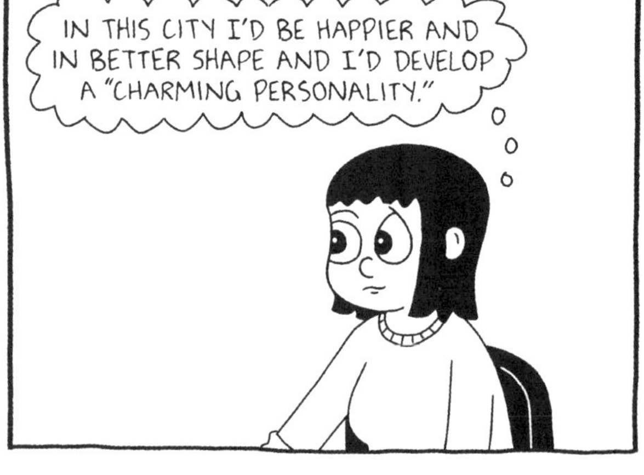

IN THIS CITY I'D BE HAPPIER AND IN BETTER SHAPE AND I'D DEVELOP A "CHARMING PERSONALITY."

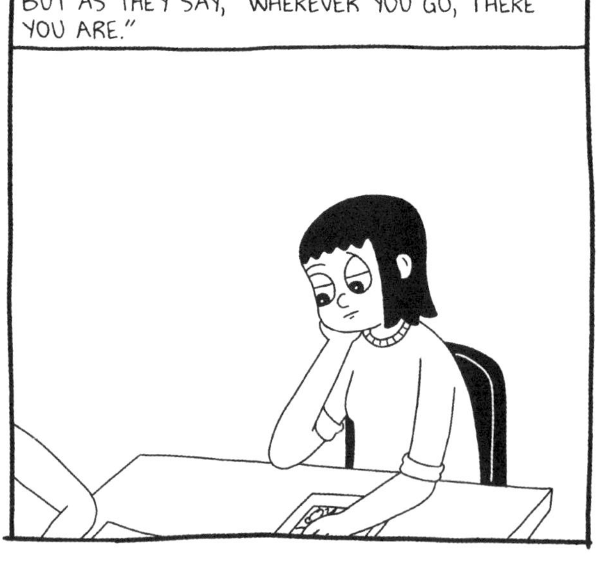

BUT AS THEY SAY, "WHEREVER YOU GO, THERE YOU ARE."

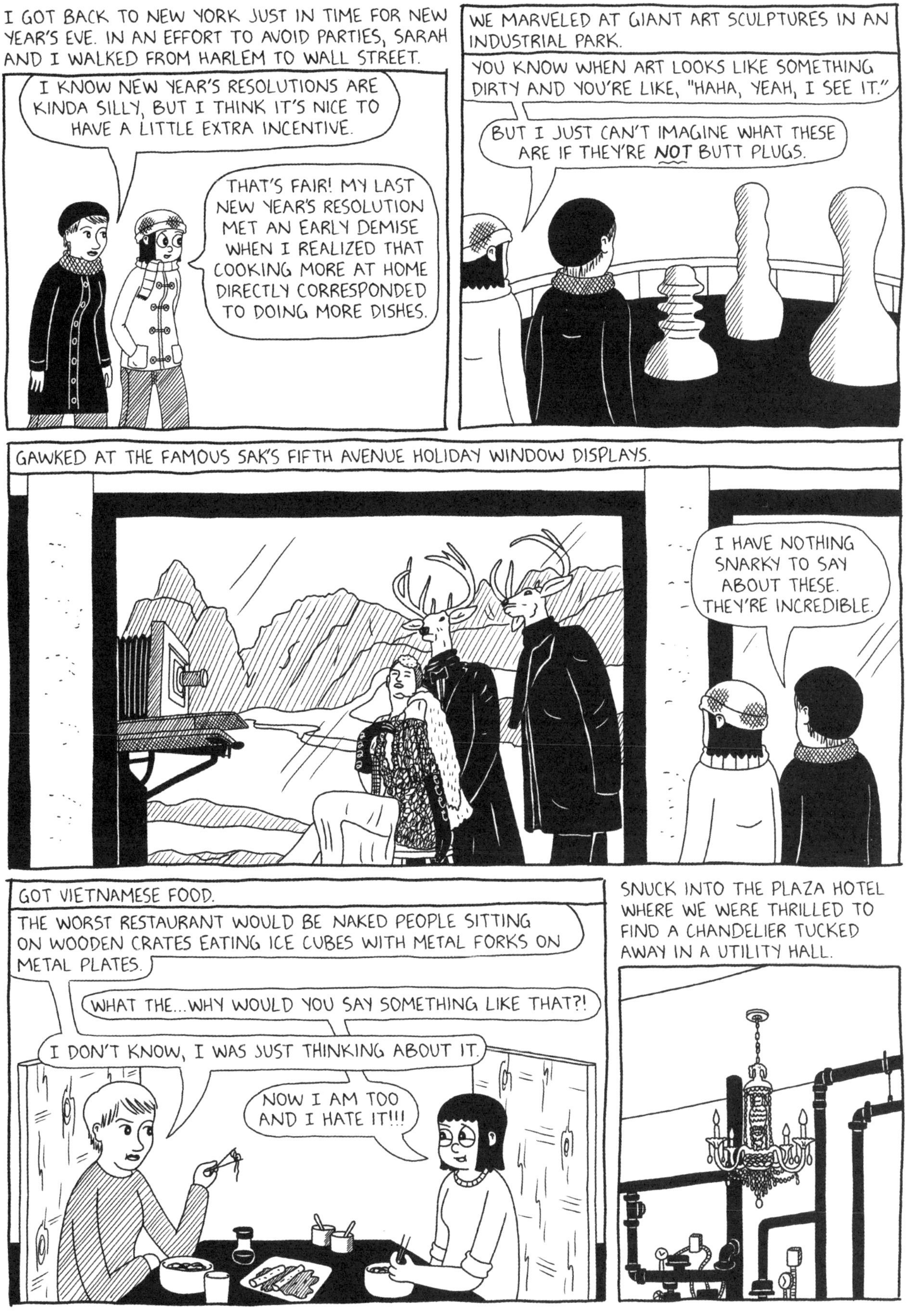
I GOT BACK TO NEW YORK JUST IN TIME FOR NEW YEAR'S EVE. IN AN EFFORT TO AVOID PARTIES, SARAH AND I WALKED FROM HARLEM TO WALL STREET.
I KNOW NEW YEAR'S RESOLUTIONS ARE KINDA SILLY, BUT I THINK IT'S NICE TO HAVE A LITTLE EXTRA INCENTIVE.
THAT'S FAIR! MY LAST NEW YEAR'S RESOLUTION MET AN EARLY DEMISE WHEN I REALIZED THAT COOKING MORE AT HOME DIRECTLY CORRESPONDED TO DOING MORE DISHES.
WE MARVELED AT GIANT ART SCULPTURES IN AN INDUSTRIAL PARK.
YOU KNOW WHEN ART LOOKS LIKE SOMETHING DIRTY AND YOU'RE LIKE, "HAHA, YEAH, I SEE IT."
BUT I JUST CAN'T IMAGINE WHAT THESE ARE IF THEY'RE NOT BUTT PLUGS.
GAWKED AT THE FAMOUS SAK'S FIFTH AVENUE HOLIDAY WINDOW DISPLAYS.
I HAVE NOTHING SNARKY TO SAY ABOUT THESE. THEY'RE INCREDIBLE.
GOT VIETNAMESE FOOD.
THE WORST RESTAURANT WOULD BE NAKED PEOPLE SITTING ON WOODEN CRATES EATING ICE CUBES WITH METAL FORKS ON METAL PLATES.
WHAT THE...WHY WOULD YOU SAY SOMETHING LIKE THAT?!
I DON'T KNOW, I WAS JUST THINKING ABOUT IT.
NOW I AM TOO AND I HATE IT!!!
SNUCK INTO THE PLAZA HOTEL WHERE WE WERE THRILLED TO FIND A CHANDELIER TUCKED AWAY IN A UTILITY HALL.

WE WANDERED THROUGH AN UNUSUALLY EMPTY MIDTOWN.

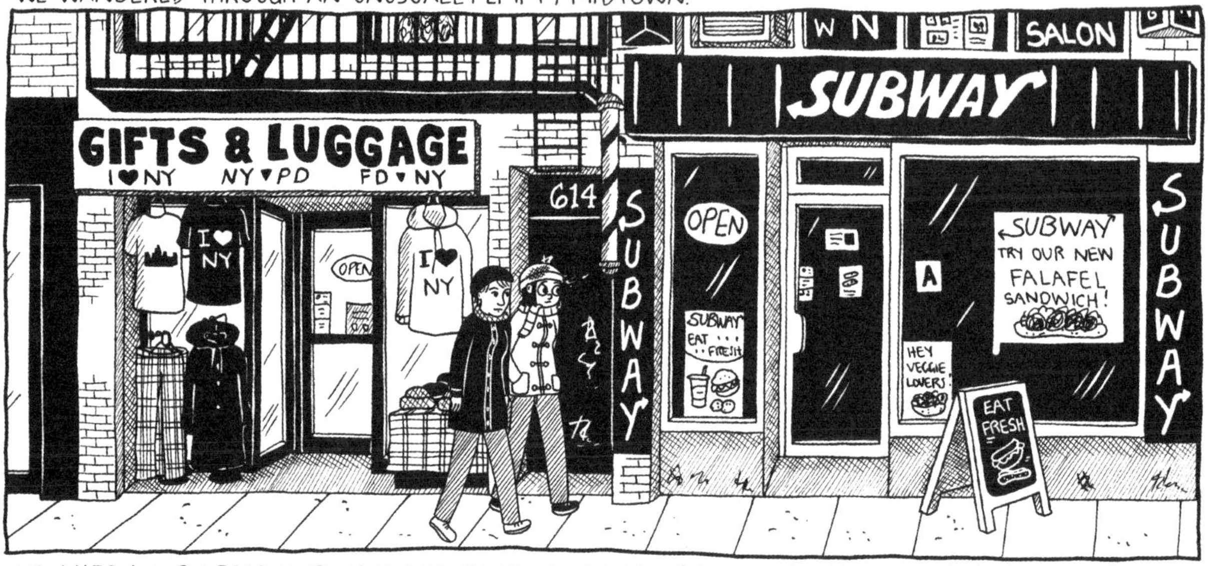
SALON
SUBWAY
GIFTS & LUGGAGE
I♥NY NY♥PD FD♥NY
614
SUBWAY
OPEN
I♥NY
OPEN
SUBWAY EAT FRESH
HEY VEGGIE LOVERS!
A
SUBWAY TRY OUR NEW FALAFEL SANDWICH!
EAT FRESH
SUBWAY

AT 11:45PM, WE APPROACHED ZUCCOTTI PARK WHERE OCCUPY WALL STREET PROTESTORS HAD ERECTED A BARRICADE USING METAL POLICE FENCING.

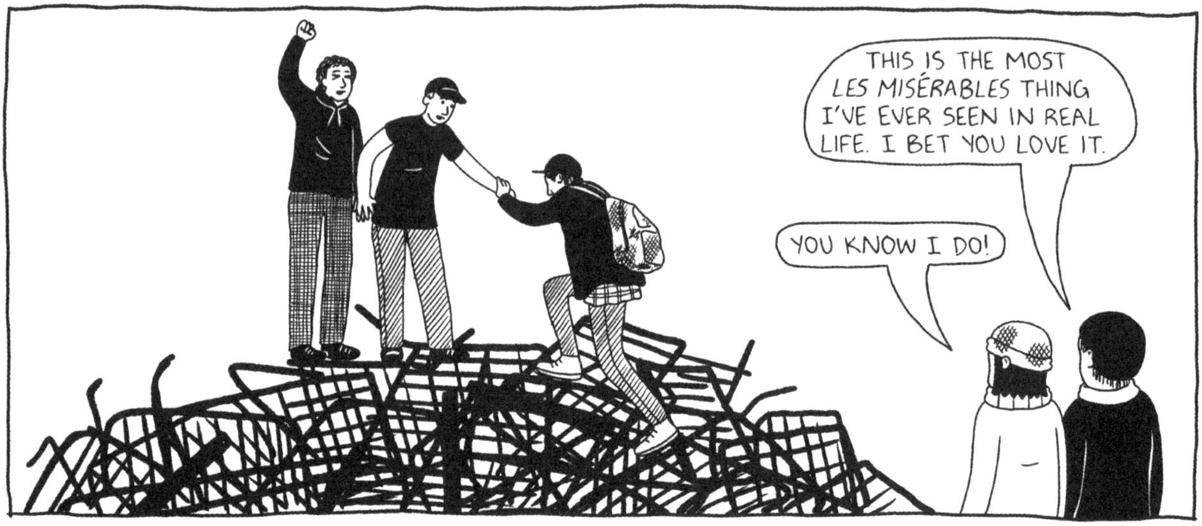
THIS IS THE MOST *LES MISÉRABLES* THING I'VE EVER SEEN IN REAL LIFE. I BET YOU LOVE IT.
YOU KNOW I DO!

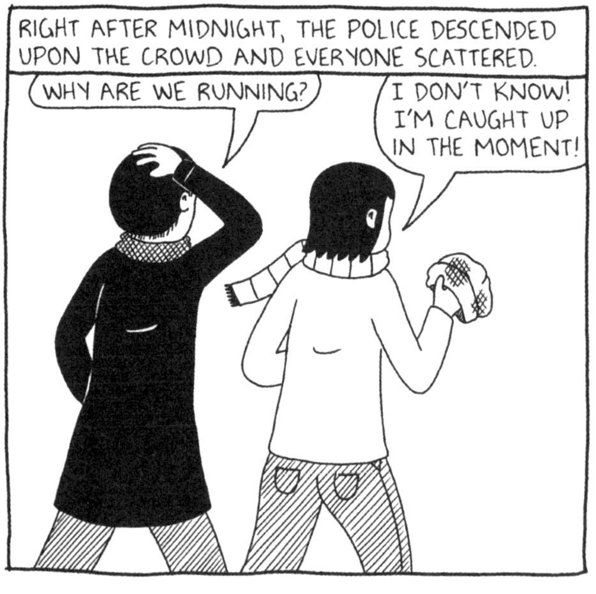
RIGHT AFTER MIDNIGHT, THE POLICE DESCENDED UPON THE CROWD AND EVERYONE SCATTERED.
WHY ARE WE RUNNING?
I DON'T KNOW! I'M CAUGHT UP IN THE MOMENT!

WE RODE THE SUBWAY HOME.

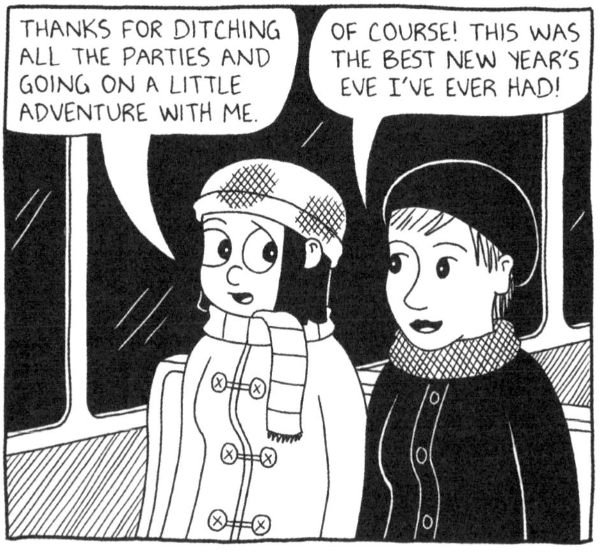
THANKS FOR DITCHING ALL THE PARTIES AND GOING ON A LITTLE ADVENTURE WITH ME.
OF COURSE! THIS WAS THE BEST NEW YEAR'S EVE I'VE EVER HAD!

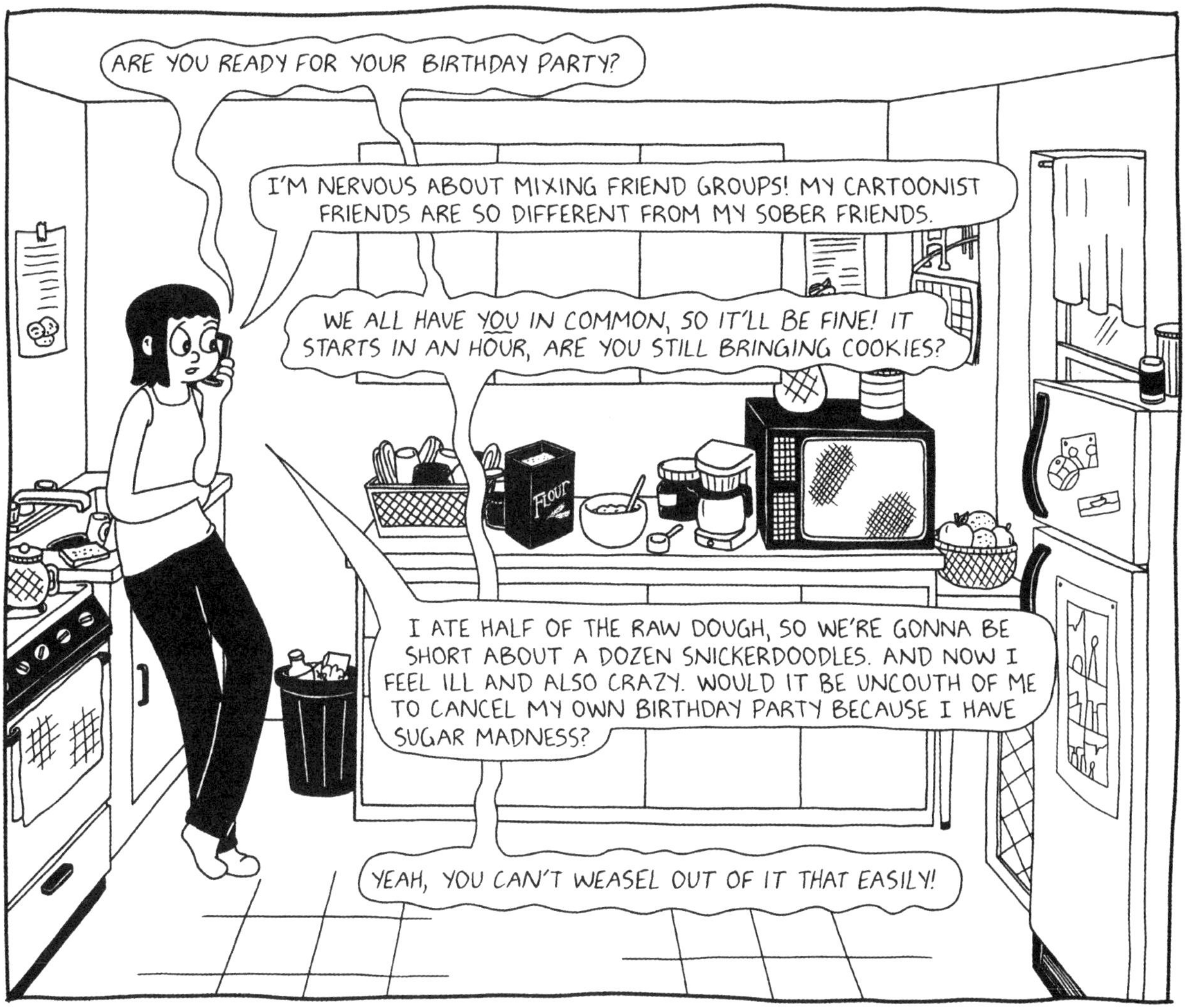
ARE YOU READY FOR YOUR BIRTHDAY PARTY?
I'M NERVOUS ABOUT MIXING FRIEND GROUPS! MY CARTOONIST FRIENDS ARE SO DIFFERENT FROM MY SOBER FRIENDS.
WE ALL HAVE YOU IN COMMON, SO IT'LL BE FINE! IT STARTS IN AN HOUR, ARE YOU STILL BRINGING COOKIES?
FLOUR
I ATE HALF OF THE RAW DOUGH, SO WE'RE GONNA BE SHORT ABOUT A DOZEN SNICKERDOODLES. AND NOW I FEEL ILL AND ALSO CRAZY. WOULD IT BE UNCOUTH OF ME TO CANCEL MY OWN BIRTHDAY PARTY BECAUSE I HAVE SUGAR MADNESS?
YEAH, YOU CAN'T WEASEL OUT OF IT THAT EASILY!

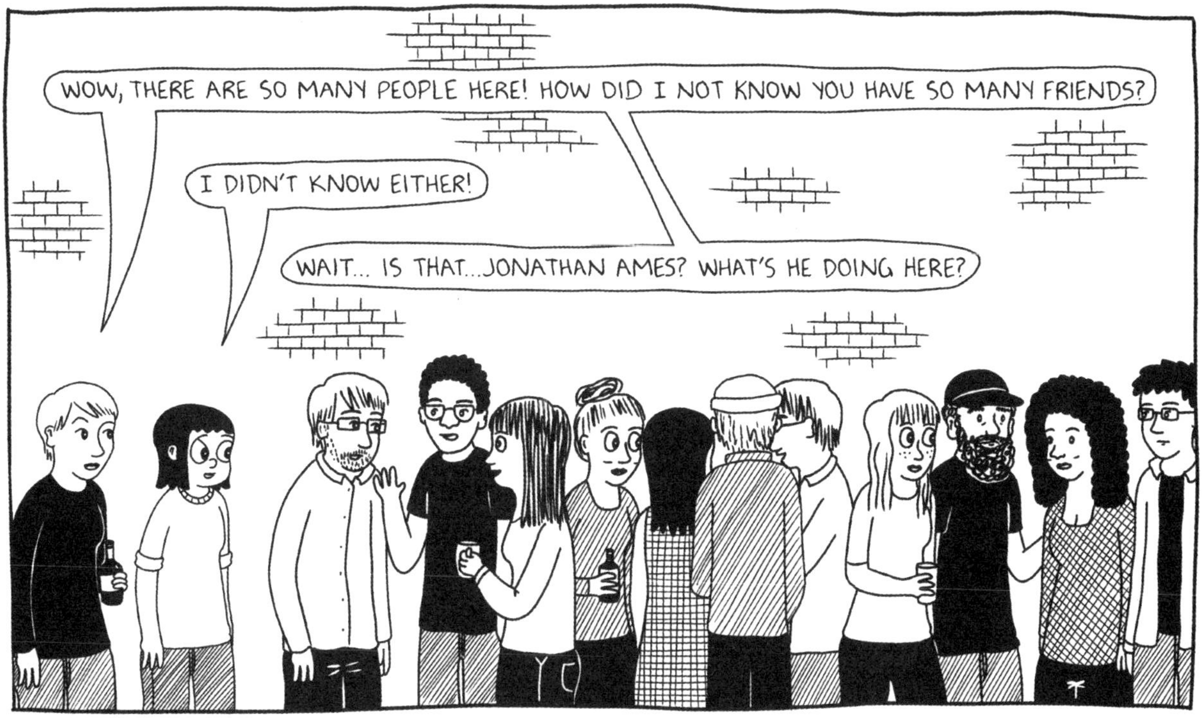
WOW, THERE ARE SO MANY PEOPLE HERE! HOW DID I NOT KNOW YOU HAVE SO MANY FRIENDS?
I DIDN'T KNOW EITHER!
WAIT... IS THAT...JONATHAN AMES? WHAT'S HE DOING HERE?

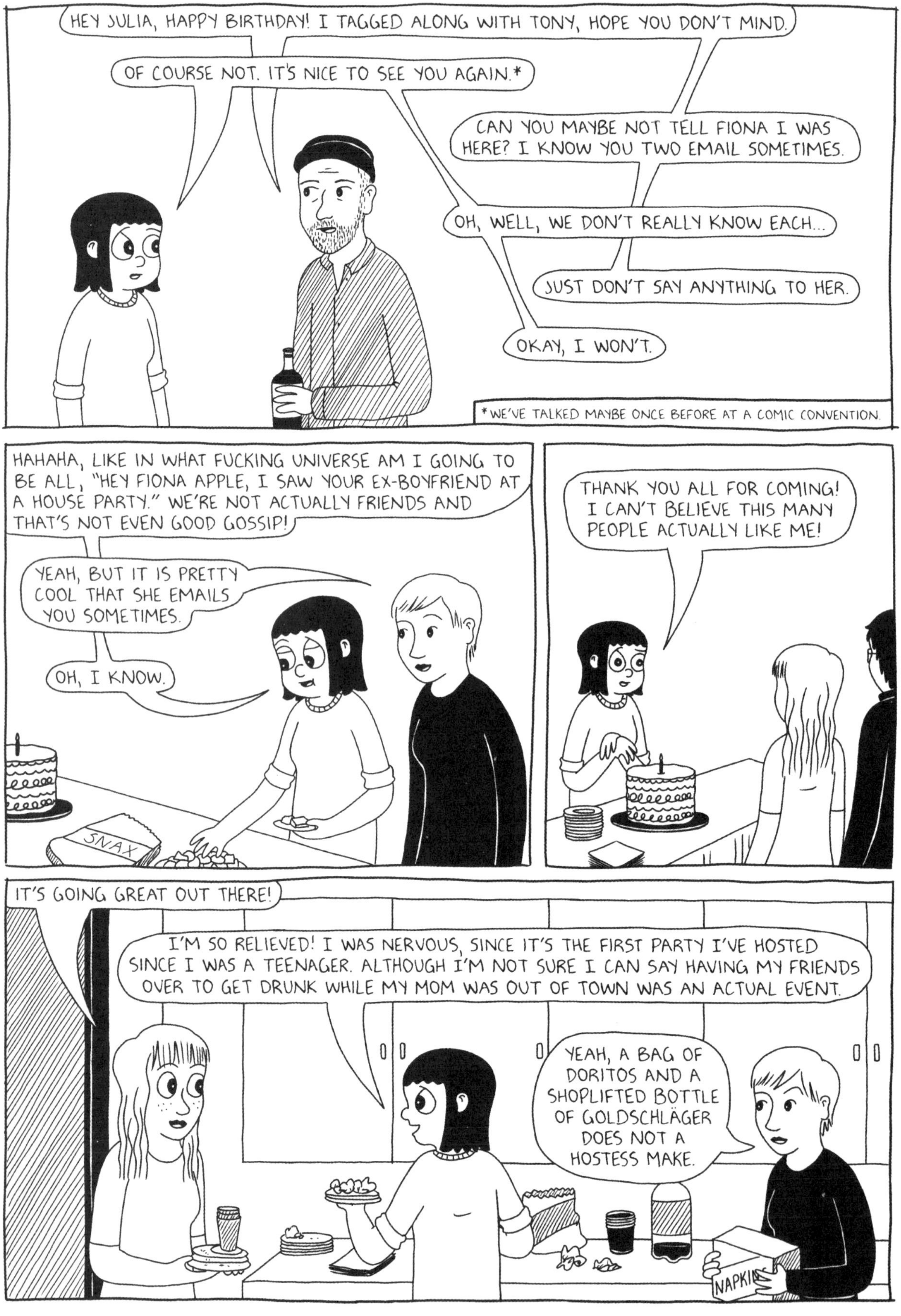
HEY JULIA, HAPPY BIRTHDAY! I TAGGED ALONG WITH TONY, HOPE YOU DON'T MIND.
OF COURSE NOT. IT'S NICE TO SEE YOU AGAIN.*
CAN YOU MAYBE NOT TELL FIONA I WAS HERE? I KNOW YOU TWO EMAIL SOMETIMES.
OH, WELL, WE DON'T REALLY KNOW EACH...
JUST DON'T SAY ANYTHING TO HER.
OKAY, I WON'T.
* WE'VE TALKED MAYBE ONCE BEFORE AT A COMIC CONVENTION.
HAHAHA, LIKE IN WHAT FUCKING UNIVERSE AM I GOING TO BE ALL, "HEY FIONA APPLE, I SAW YOUR EX-BOYFRIEND AT A HOUSE PARTY." WE'RE NOT ACTUALLY FRIENDS AND THAT'S NOT EVEN GOOD GOSSIP!
YEAH, BUT IT IS PRETTY COOL THAT SHE EMAILS YOU SOMETIMES.
OH, I KNOW.
SNAX
THANK YOU ALL FOR COMING! I CAN'T BELIEVE THIS MANY PEOPLE ACTUALLY LIKE ME!
IT'S GOING GREAT OUT THERE!
I'M SO RELIEVED! I WAS NERVOUS, SINCE IT'S THE FIRST PARTY I'VE HOSTED SINCE I WAS A TEENAGER. ALTHOUGH I'M NOT SURE I CAN SAY HAVING MY FRIENDS OVER TO GET DRUNK WHILE MY MOM WAS OUT OF TOWN WAS AN ACTUAL EVENT.
YEAH, A BAG OF DORITOS AND A SHOPLIFTED BOTTLE OF GOLDSCHLÄGER DOES NOT A HOSTESS MAKE.
NAPKI

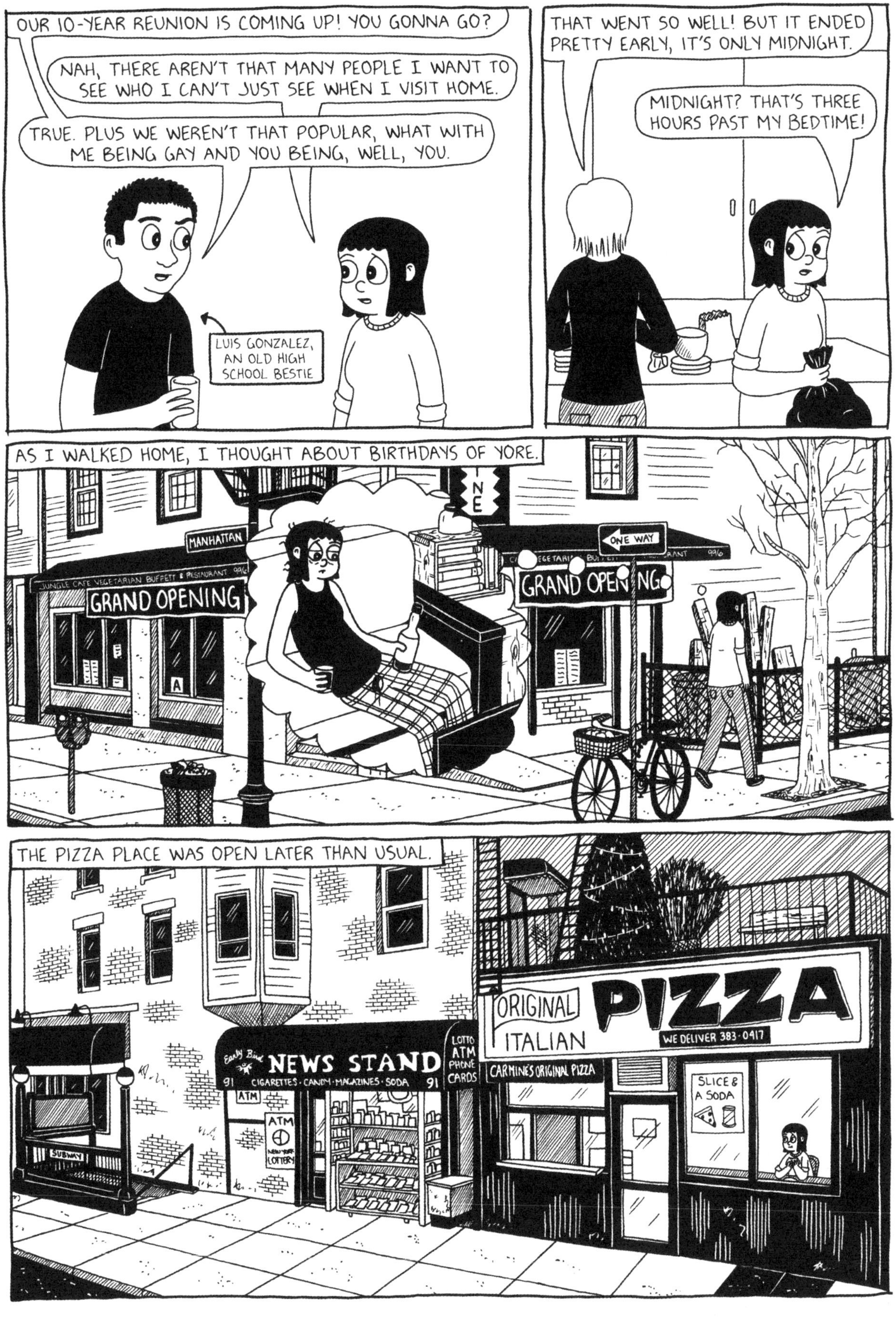
OUR 10-YEAR REUNION IS COMING UP! YOU GONNA GO?
NAH, THERE AREN'T THAT MANY PEOPLE I WANT TO SEE WHO I CAN'T JUST SEE WHEN I VISIT HOME.
TRUE. PLUS WE WEREN'T THAT POPULAR, WHAT WITH ME BEING GAY AND YOU BEING, WELL, YOU.
LUIS GONZALEZ, AN OLD HIGH SCHOOL BESTIE
THAT WENT SO WELL! BUT IT ENDED PRETTY EARLY, IT'S ONLY MIDNIGHT.
MIDNIGHT? THAT'S THREE HOURS PAST MY BEDTIME!
AS I WALKED HOME, I THOUGHT ABOUT BIRTHDAYS OF YORE.
MANHATTAN
JUNGLE CAFE VEGETARIAN BUFFETT & RESTAURANT 996
GRAND OPENING
ONE WAY
GRAND OPENING
THE PIZZA PLACE WAS OPEN LATER THAN USUAL.
Early Bird NEWS STAND
91 CIGARETTES · CANDY · MAGAZINES · SODA 91
LOTTO ATM PHONE CARDS
ATM
SUBWAY
ORIGINAL ITALIAN PIZZA
WE DELIVER 383-0417
CARMINE'S ORIGINAL PIZZA
SLICE & A SODA

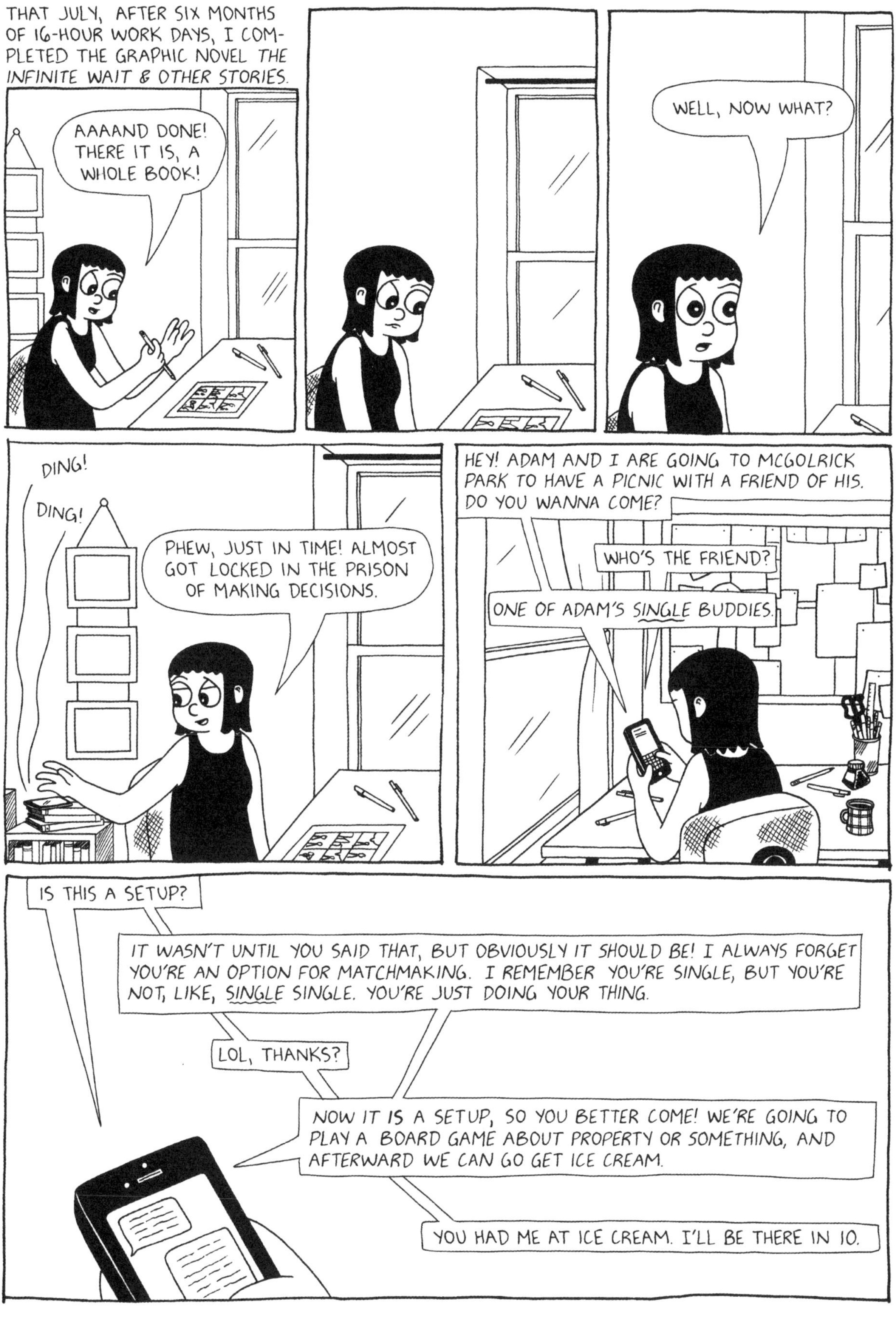
THAT JULY, AFTER SIX MONTHS OF 16-HOUR WORK DAYS, I COMPLETED THE GRAPHIC NOVEL *THE INFINITE WAIT & OTHER STORIES*.
AAAAND DONE! THERE IT IS, A WHOLE BOOK!
WELL, NOW WHAT?
DING!
DING!
PHEW, JUST IN TIME! ALMOST GOT LOCKED IN THE PRISON OF MAKING DECISIONS.
HEY! ADAM AND I ARE GOING TO MCGOLRICK PARK TO HAVE A PICNIC WITH A FRIEND OF HIS. DO YOU WANNA COME?
WHO'S THE FRIEND?
ONE OF ADAM'S SINGLE BUDDIES.
IS THIS A SETUP?
IT WASN'T UNTIL YOU SAID THAT, BUT OBVIOUSLY IT SHOULD BE! I ALWAYS FORGET YOU'RE AN OPTION FOR MATCHMAKING. I REMEMBER YOU'RE SINGLE, BUT YOU'RE NOT, LIKE, SINGLE SINGLE. YOU'RE JUST DOING YOUR THING.
LOL, THANKS?
NOW IT IS A SETUP, SO YOU BETTER COME! WE'RE GOING TO PLAY A BOARD GAME ABOUT PROPERTY OR SOMETHING, AND AFTERWARD WE CAN GO GET ICE CREAM.
YOU HAD ME AT ICE CREAM. I'LL BE THERE IN 10.

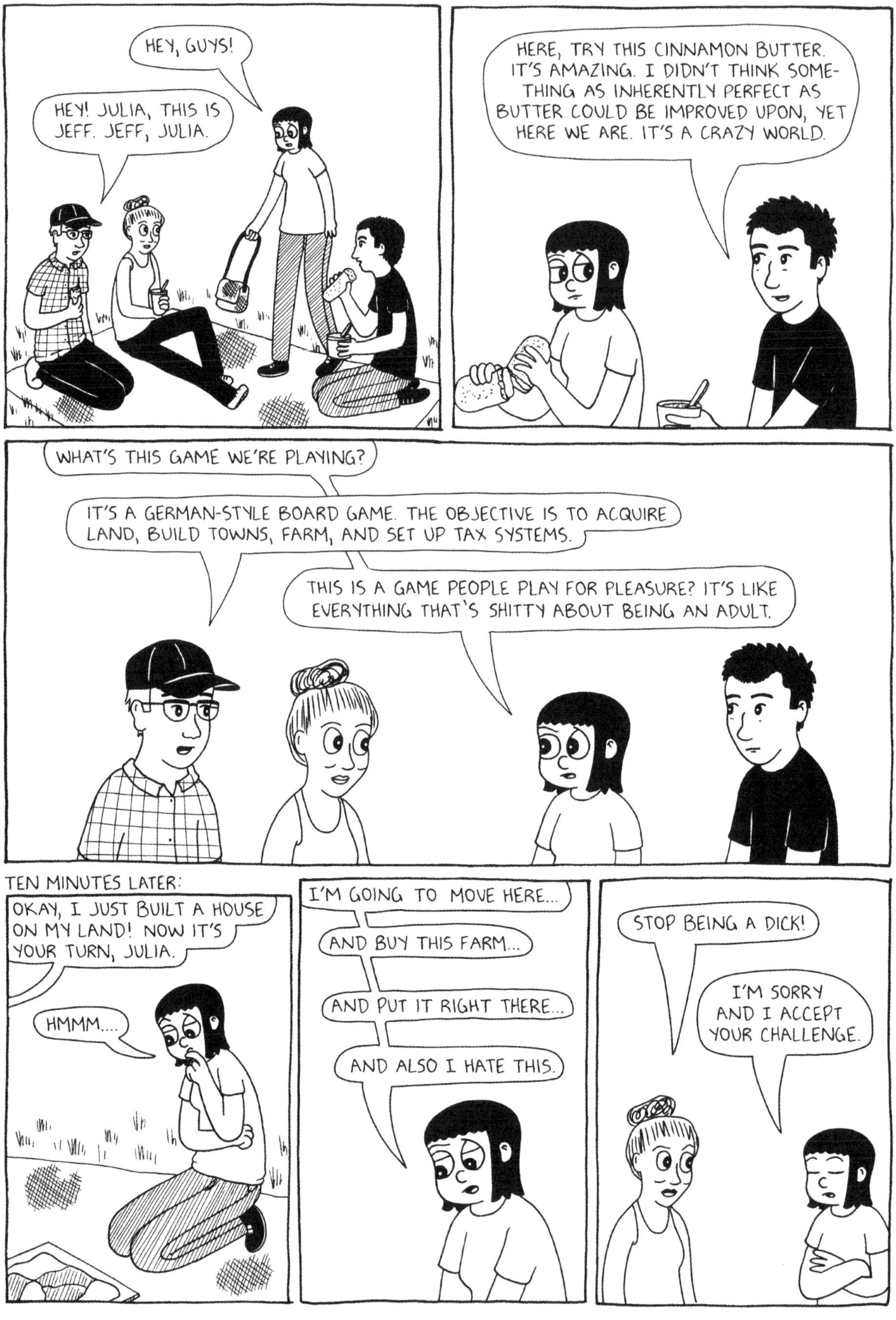
HEY, GUYS!
HEY! JULIA, THIS IS JEFF. JEFF, JULIA.
HERE, TRY THIS CINNAMON BUTTER. IT'S AMAZING. I DIDN'T THINK SOMETHING AS INHERENTLY PERFECT AS BUTTER COULD BE IMPROVED UPON, YET HERE WE ARE. IT'S A CRAZY WORLD.
WHAT'S THIS GAME WE'RE PLAYING?
IT'S A GERMAN-STYLE BOARD GAME. THE OBJECTIVE IS TO ACQUIRE LAND, BUILD TOWNS, FARM, AND SET UP TAX SYSTEMS.
THIS IS A GAME PEOPLE PLAY FOR PLEASURE? IT'S LIKE EVERYTHING THAT'S SHITTY ABOUT BEING AN ADULT.
TEN MINUTES LATER:
OKAY, I JUST BUILT A HOUSE ON MY LAND! NOW IT'S YOUR TURN, JULIA.
HMMM....
I'M GOING TO MOVE HERE...
AND BUY THIS FARM...
AND PUT IT RIGHT THERE...
AND ALSO I HATE THIS.
STOP BEING A DICK!
I'M SORRY AND I ACCEPT YOUR CHALLENGE.

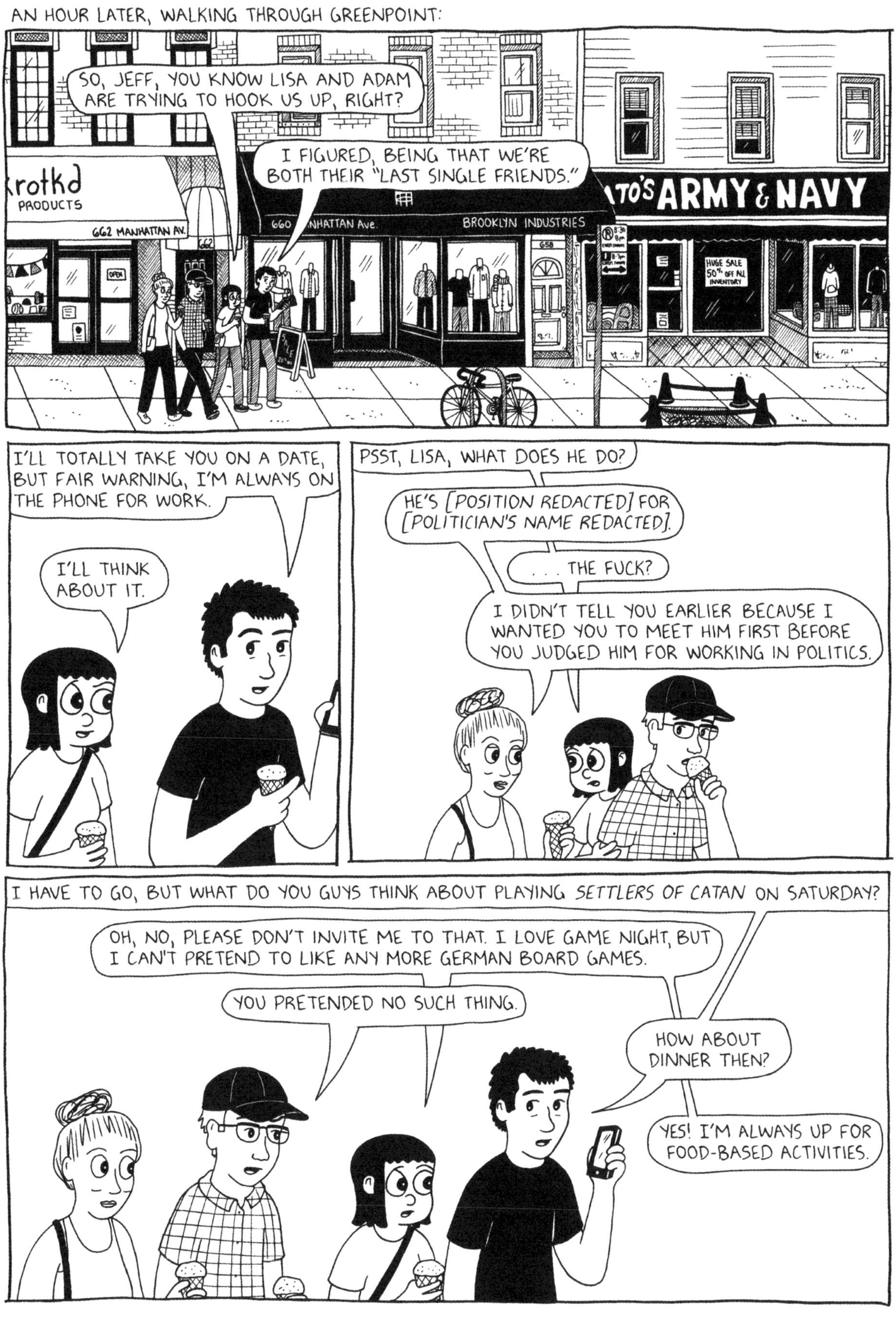
AN HOUR LATER, WALKING THROUGH GREENPOINT:
SO, JEFF, YOU KNOW LISA AND ADAM ARE TRYING TO HOOK US UP, RIGHT?
I FIGURED, BEING THAT WE'RE BOTH THEIR "LAST SINGLE FRIENDS."
krotkd PRODUCTS
662 MANHATTAN AV.
BROOKLYN INDUSTRIES
ARMY & NAVY
HUGE SALE 50% OFF ALL INVENTORY
I'LL TOTALLY TAKE YOU ON A DATE, BUT FAIR WARNING, I'M ALWAYS ON THE PHONE FOR WORK.
I'LL THINK ABOUT IT.
PSST, LISA, WHAT DOES HE DO?
HE'S [POSITION REDACTED] FOR [POLITICIAN'S NAME REDACTED].
. . . THE FUCK?
I DIDN'T TELL YOU EARLIER BECAUSE I WANTED YOU TO MEET HIM FIRST BEFORE YOU JUDGED HIM FOR WORKING IN POLITICS.
I HAVE TO GO, BUT WHAT DO YOU GUYS THINK ABOUT PLAYING SETTLERS OF CATAN ON SATURDAY?
OH, NO, PLEASE DON'T INVITE ME TO THAT. I LOVE GAME NIGHT, BUT I CAN'T PRETEND TO LIKE ANY MORE GERMAN BOARD GAMES.
YOU PRETENDED NO SUCH THING.
HOW ABOUT DINNER THEN?
YES! I'M ALWAYS UP FOR FOOD-BASED ACTIVITIES.

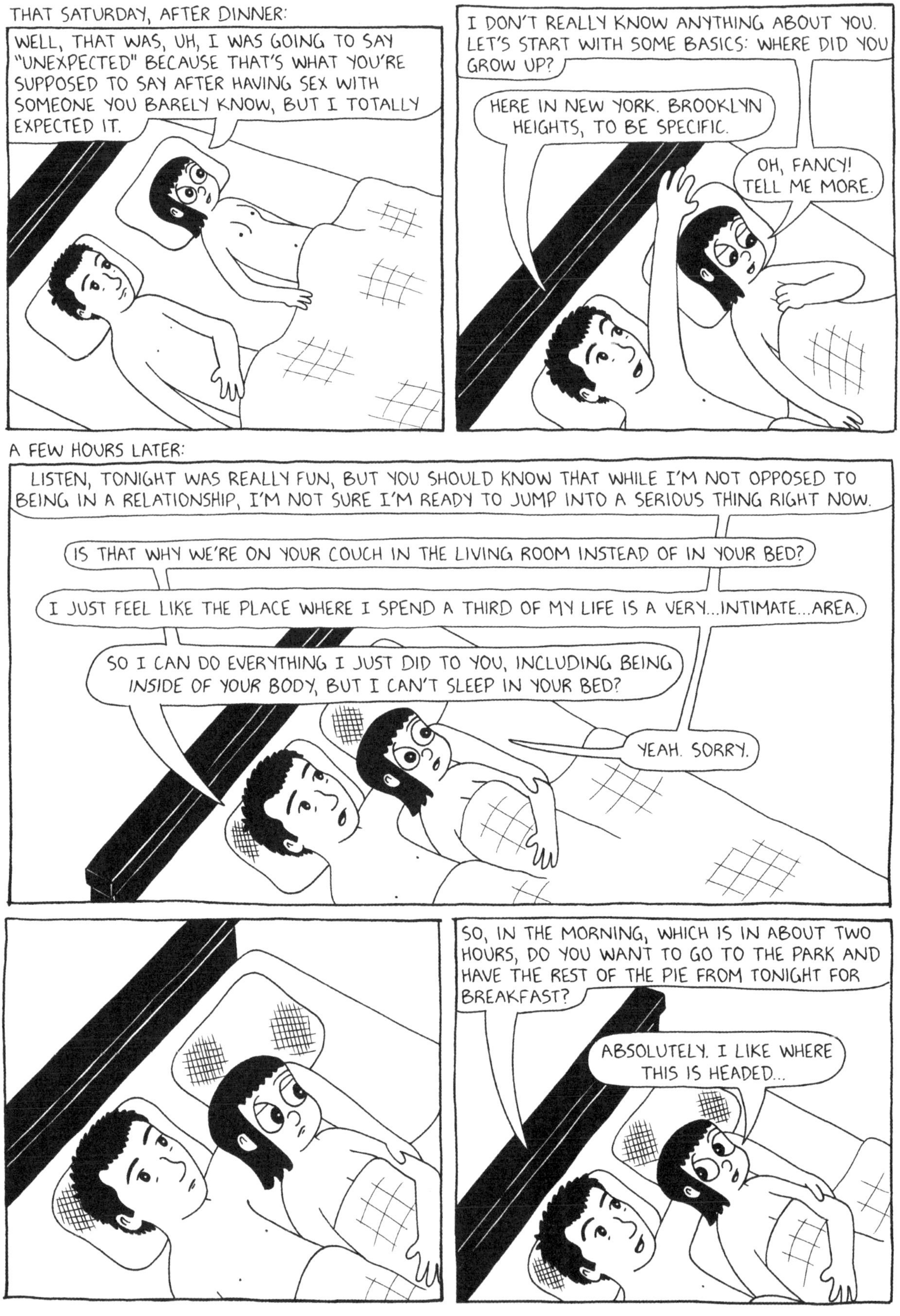
THAT SATURDAY, AFTER DINNER:
WELL, THAT WAS, UH, I WAS GOING TO SAY "UNEXPECTED" BECAUSE THAT'S WHAT YOU'RE SUPPOSED TO SAY AFTER HAVING SEX WITH SOMEONE YOU BARELY KNOW, BUT I TOTALLY EXPECTED IT.
I DON'T REALLY KNOW ANYTHING ABOUT YOU. LET'S START WITH SOME BASICS: WHERE DID YOU GROW UP?
HERE IN NEW YORK. BROOKLYN HEIGHTS, TO BE SPECIFIC.
OH, FANCY! TELL ME MORE.
A FEW HOURS LATER:
LISTEN, TONIGHT WAS REALLY FUN, BUT YOU SHOULD KNOW THAT WHILE I'M NOT OPPOSED TO BEING IN A RELATIONSHIP, I'M NOT SURE I'M READY TO JUMP INTO A SERIOUS THING RIGHT NOW.
IS THAT WHY WE'RE ON YOUR COUCH IN THE LIVING ROOM INSTEAD OF IN YOUR BED?
I JUST FEEL LIKE THE PLACE WHERE I SPEND A THIRD OF MY LIFE IS A VERY...INTIMATE...AREA.
SO I CAN DO EVERYTHING I JUST DID TO YOU, INCLUDING BEING INSIDE OF YOUR BODY, BUT I CAN'T SLEEP IN YOUR BED?
YEAH. SORRY.
SO, IN THE MORNING, WHICH IS IN ABOUT TWO HOURS, DO YOU WANT TO GO TO THE PARK AND HAVE THE REST OF THE PIE FROM TONIGHT FOR BREAKFAST?
ABSOLUTELY. I LIKE WHERE THIS IS HEADED...

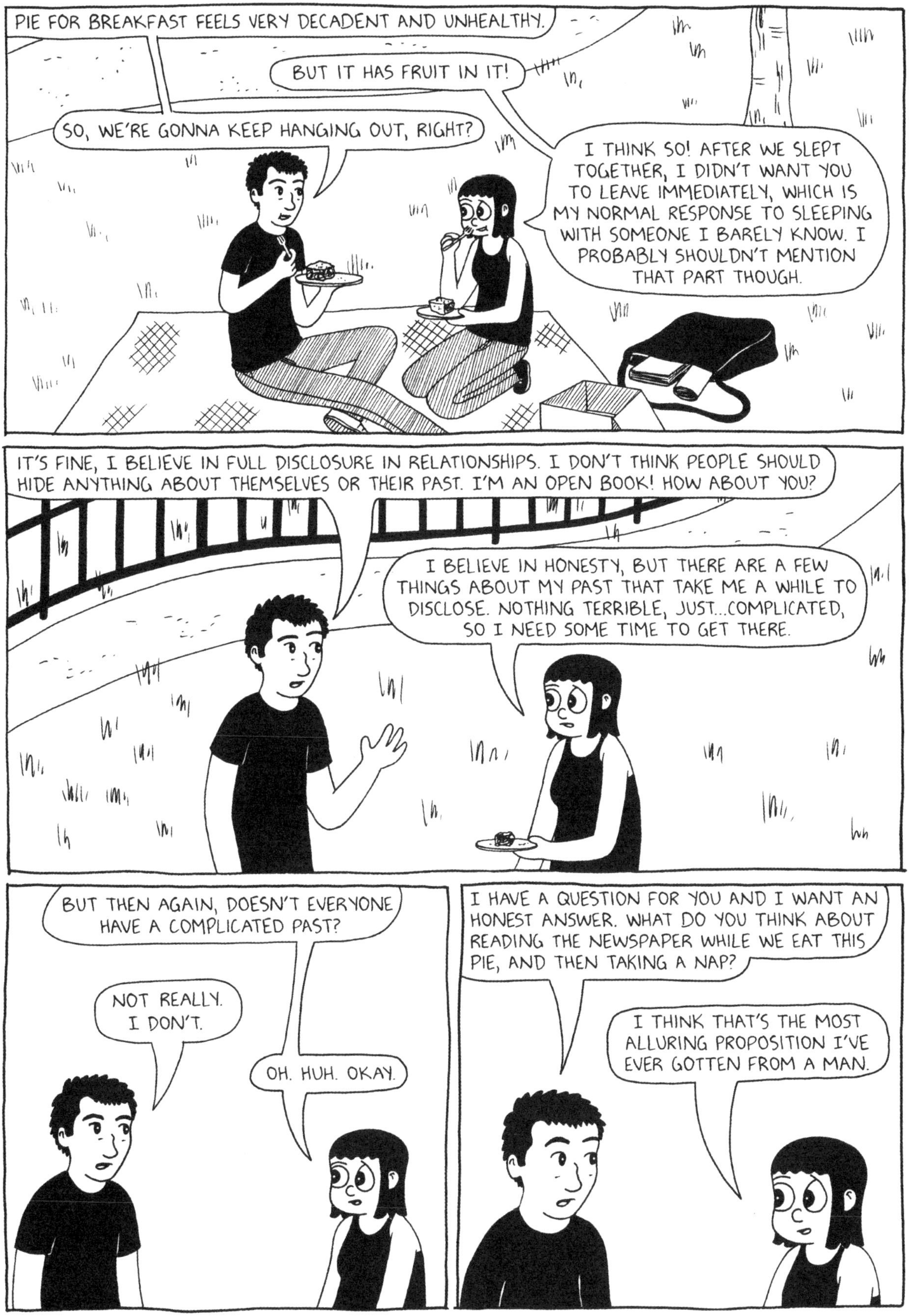
PIE FOR BREAKFAST FEELS VERY DECADENT AND UNHEALTHY.
BUT IT HAS FRUIT IN IT!
SO, WE'RE GONNA KEEP HANGING OUT, RIGHT?
I THINK SO! AFTER WE SLEPT TOGETHER, I DIDN'T WANT YOU TO LEAVE IMMEDIATELY, WHICH IS MY NORMAL RESPONSE TO SLEEPING WITH SOMEONE I BARELY KNOW. I PROBABLY SHOULDN'T MENTION THAT PART THOUGH.
IT'S FINE, I BELIEVE IN FULL DISCLOSURE IN RELATIONSHIPS. I DON'T THINK PEOPLE SHOULD HIDE ANYTHING ABOUT THEMSELVES OR THEIR PAST. I'M AN OPEN BOOK! HOW ABOUT YOU?
I BELIEVE IN HONESTY, BUT THERE ARE A FEW THINGS ABOUT MY PAST THAT TAKE ME A WHILE TO DISCLOSE. NOTHING TERRIBLE, JUST...COMPLICATED, SO I NEED SOME TIME TO GET THERE.
BUT THEN AGAIN, DOESN'T EVERYONE HAVE A COMPLICATED PAST?
NOT REALLY. I DON'T.
OH. HUH. OKAY.
I HAVE A QUESTION FOR YOU AND I WANT AN HONEST ANSWER. WHAT DO YOU THINK ABOUT READING THE NEWSPAPER WHILE WE EAT THIS PIE, AND THEN TAKING A NAP?
I THINK THAT'S THE MOST ALLURING PROPOSITION I'VE EVER GOTTEN FROM A MAN.

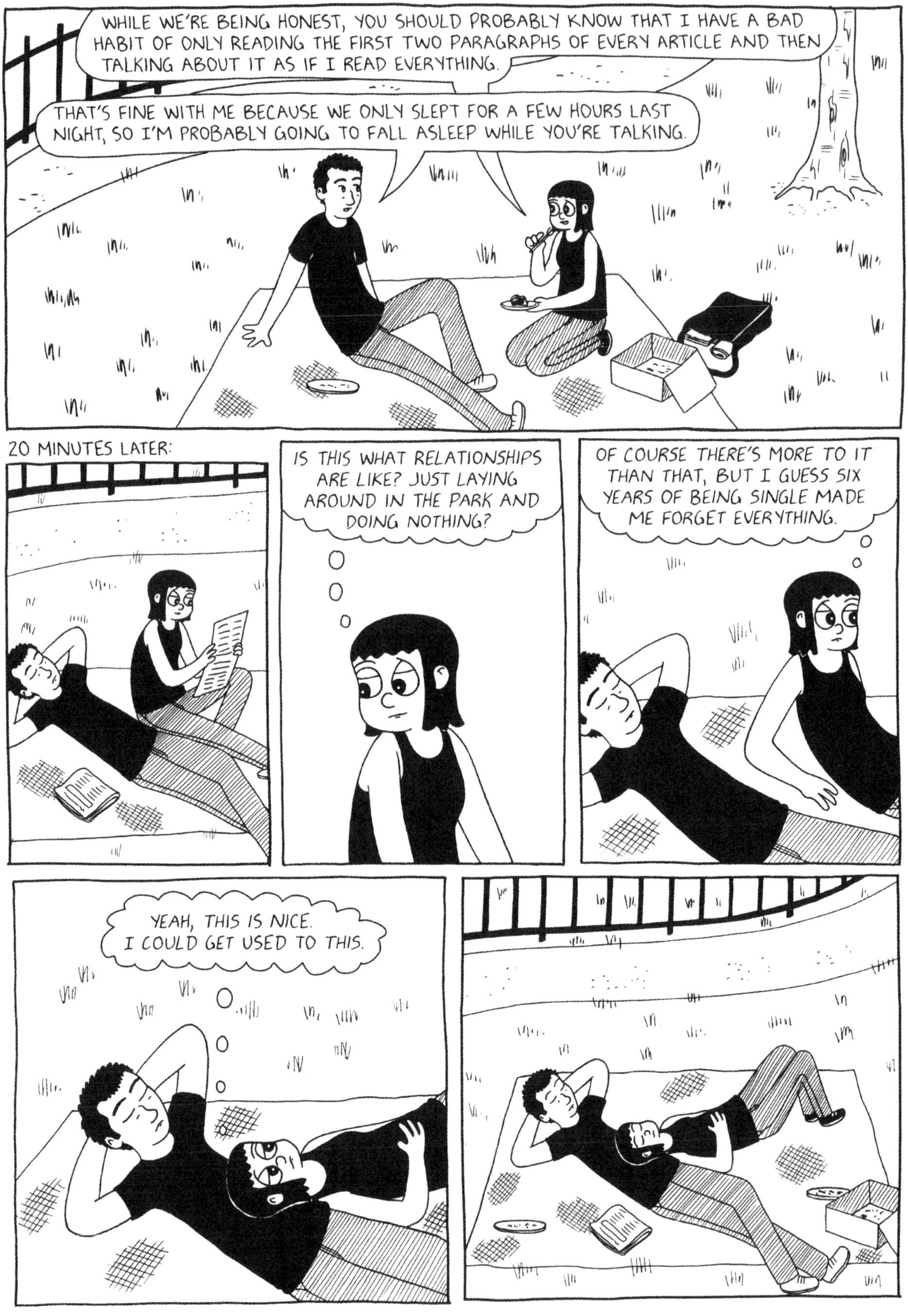
WHILE WE'RE BEING HONEST, YOU SHOULD PROBABLY KNOW THAT I HAVE A BAD HABIT OF ONLY READING THE FIRST TWO PARAGRAPHS OF EVERY ARTICLE AND THEN TALKING ABOUT IT AS IF I READ EVERYTHING.
THAT'S FINE WITH ME BECAUSE WE ONLY SLEPT FOR A FEW HOURS LAST NIGHT, SO I'M PROBABLY GOING TO FALL ASLEEP WHILE YOU'RE TALKING.
20 MINUTES LATER:
IS THIS WHAT RELATIONSHIPS ARE LIKE? JUST LAYING AROUND IN THE PARK AND DOING NOTHING?
OF COURSE THERE'S MORE TO IT THAN THAT, BUT I GUESS SIX YEARS OF BEING SINGLE MADE ME FORGET EVERYTHING.
YEAH, THIS IS NICE. I COULD GET USED TO THIS.

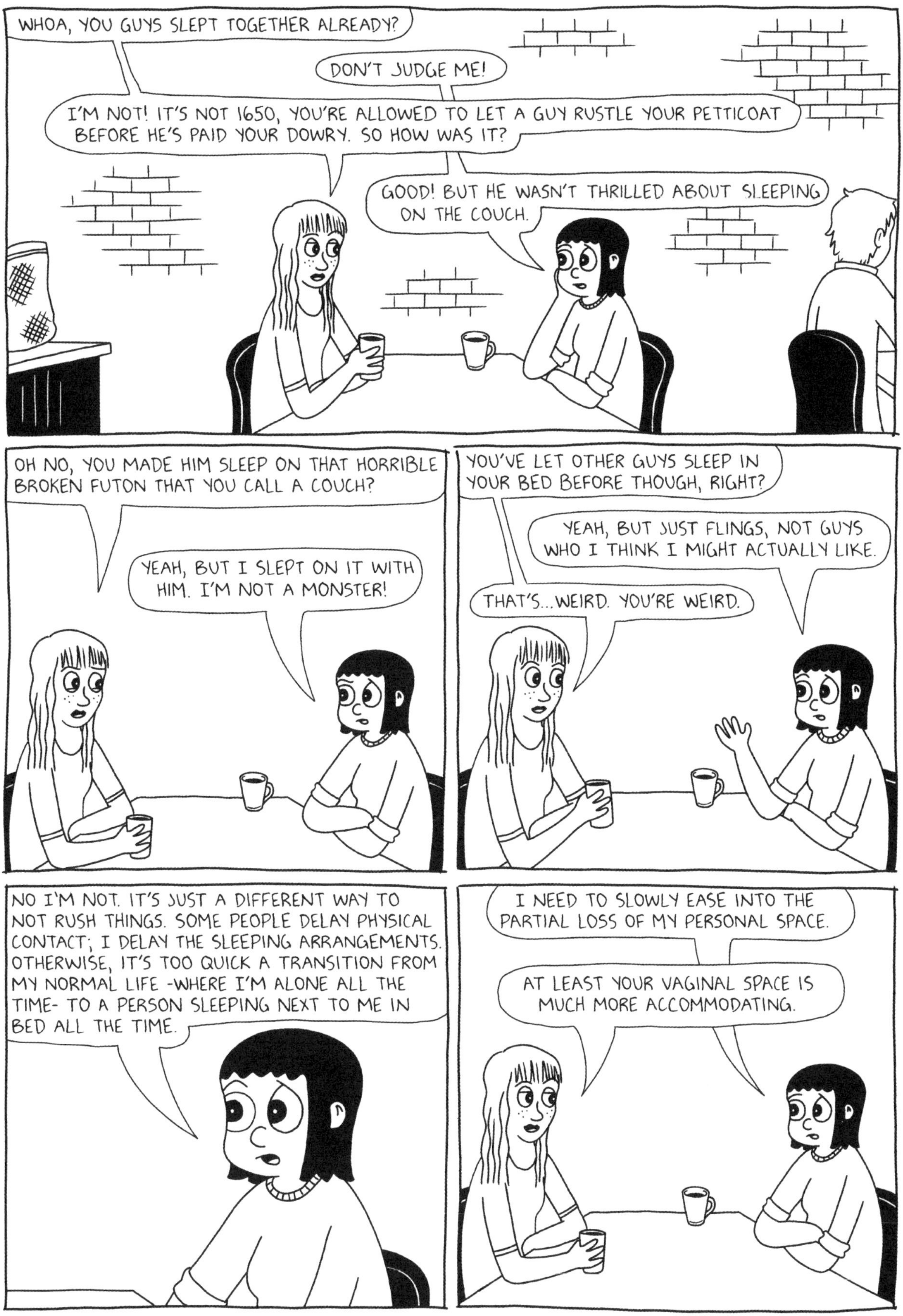
WHOA, YOU GUYS SLEPT TOGETHER ALREADY?
DON'T JUDGE ME!
I'M NOT! IT'S NOT 1650, YOU'RE ALLOWED TO LET A GUY RUSTLE YOUR PETTICOAT BEFORE HE'S PAID YOUR DOWRY. SO HOW WAS IT?
GOOD! BUT HE WASN'T THRILLED ABOUT SLEEPING ON THE COUCH.
OH NO, YOU MADE HIM SLEEP ON THAT HORRIBLE BROKEN FUTON THAT YOU CALL A COUCH?
YEAH, BUT I SLEPT ON IT WITH HIM. I'M NOT A MONSTER!
YOU'VE LET OTHER GUYS SLEEP IN YOUR BED BEFORE THOUGH, RIGHT?
YEAH, BUT JUST FLINGS, NOT GUYS WHO I THINK I MIGHT ACTUALLY LIKE.
THAT'S...WEIRD. YOU'RE WEIRD.
NO I'M NOT. IT'S JUST A DIFFERENT WAY TO NOT RUSH THINGS. SOME PEOPLE DELAY PHYSICAL CONTACT; I DELAY THE SLEEPING ARRANGEMENTS. OTHERWISE, IT'S TOO QUICK A TRANSITION FROM MY NORMAL LIFE -WHERE I'M ALONE ALL THE TIME- TO A PERSON SLEEPING NEXT TO ME IN BED ALL THE TIME.
I NEED TO SLOWLY EASE INTO THE PARTIAL LOSS OF MY PERSONAL SPACE.
AT LEAST YOUR VAGINAL SPACE IS MUCH MORE ACCOMMODATING.

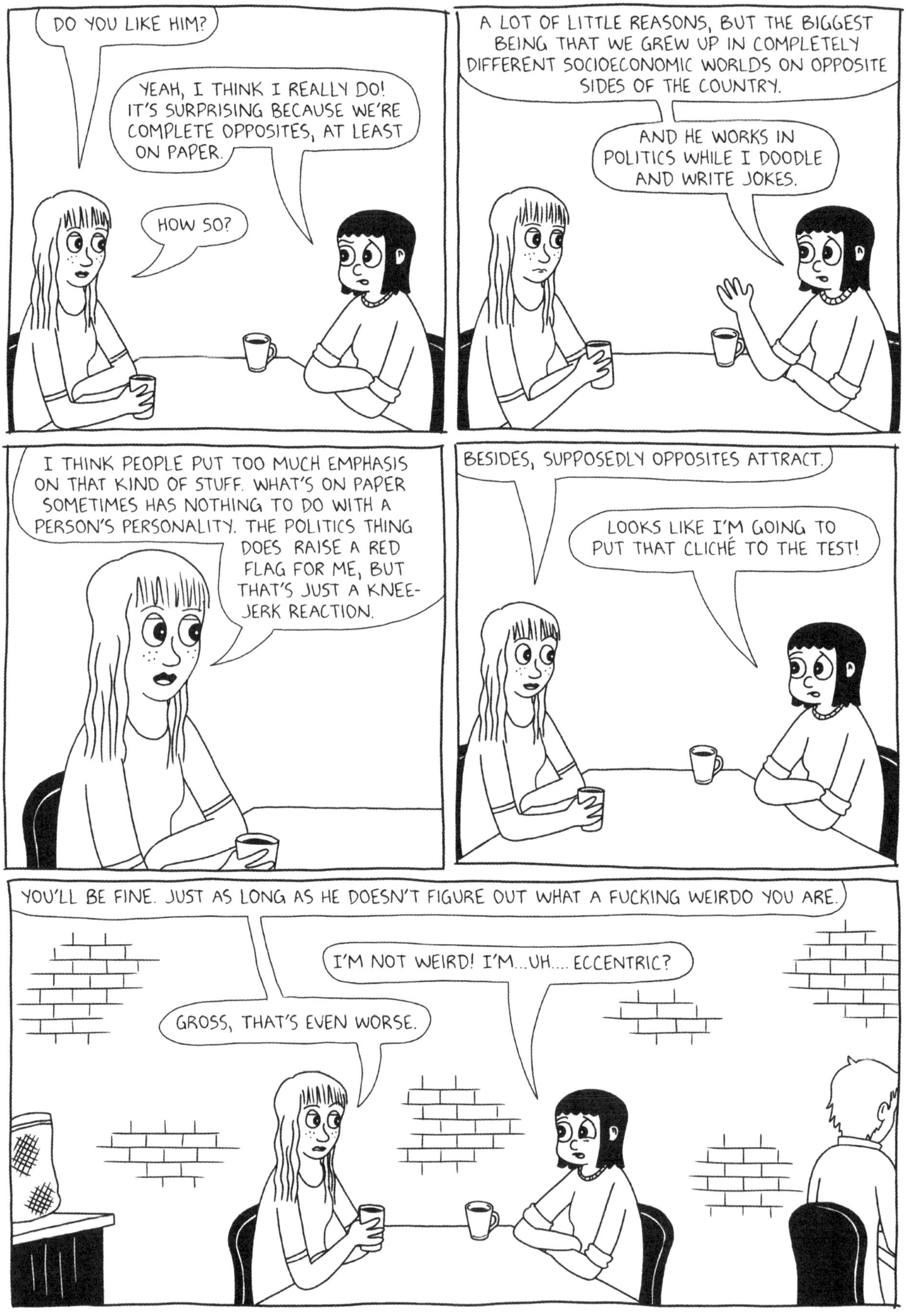
DO YOU LIKE HIM?
YEAH, I THINK I REALLY DO! IT'S SURPRISING BECAUSE WE'RE COMPLETE OPPOSITES, AT LEAST ON PAPER.
HOW SO?
A LOT OF LITTLE REASONS, BUT THE BIGGEST BEING THAT WE GREW UP IN COMPLETELY DIFFERENT SOCIOECONOMIC WORLDS ON OPPOSITE SIDES OF THE COUNTRY.
AND HE WORKS IN POLITICS WHILE I DOODLE AND WRITE JOKES.
I THINK PEOPLE PUT TOO MUCH EMPHASIS ON THAT KIND OF STUFF. WHAT'S ON PAPER SOMETIMES HAS NOTHING TO DO WITH A PERSON'S PERSONALITY. THE POLITICS THING DOES RAISE A RED FLAG FOR ME, BUT THAT'S JUST A KNEE-JERK REACTION.
BESIDES, SUPPOSEDLY OPPOSITES ATTRACT.
LOOKS LIKE I'M GOING TO PUT THAT CLICHÉ TO THE TEST!
YOU'LL BE FINE. JUST AS LONG AS HE DOESN'T FIGURE OUT WHAT A FUCKING WEIRDO YOU ARE.
I'M NOT WEIRD! I'M...UH.... ECCENTRIC?
GROSS, THAT'S EVEN WORSE.

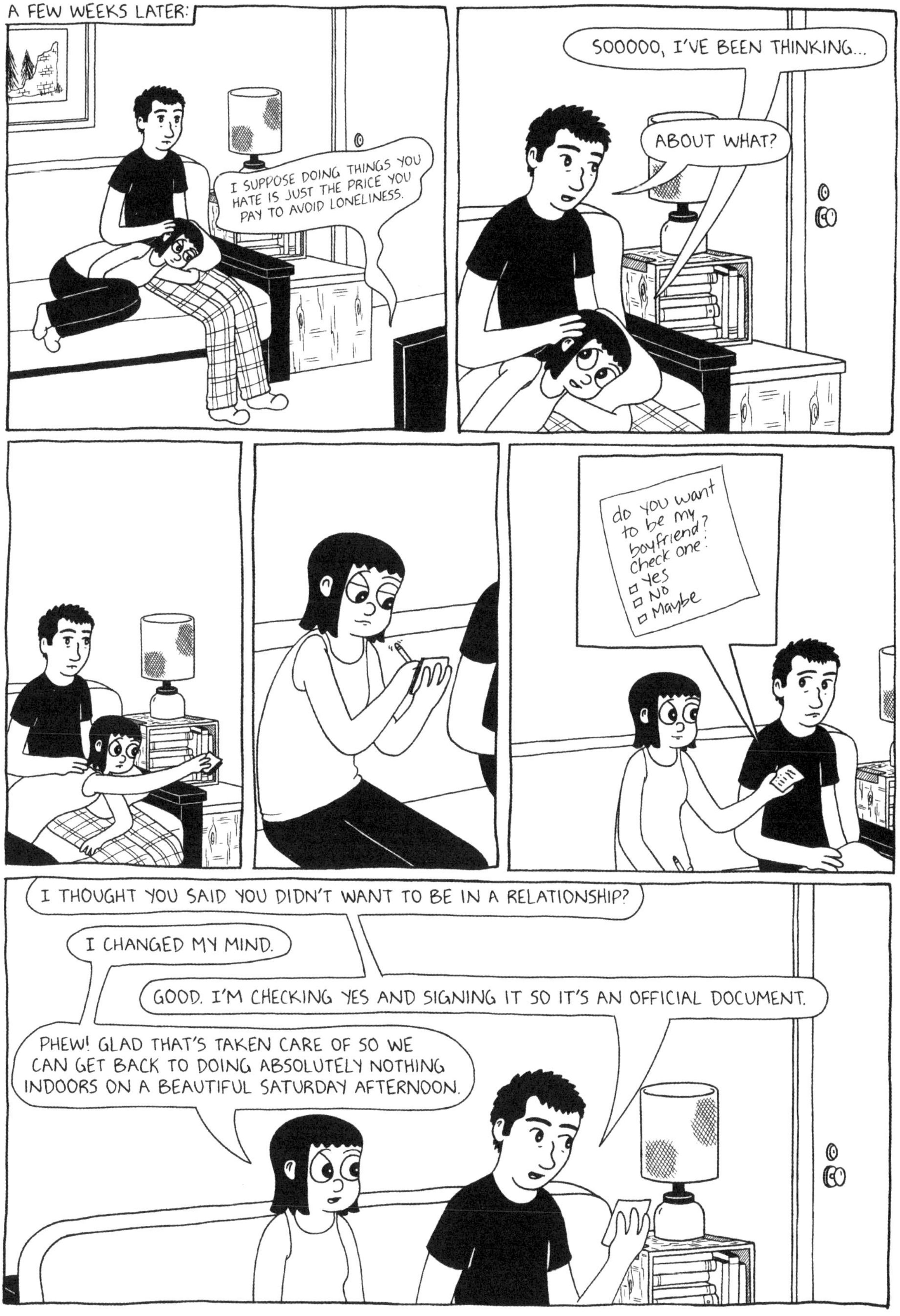
A FEW WEEKS LATER:
I SUPPOSE DOING THINGS YOU HATE IS JUST THE PRICE YOU PAY TO AVOID LONELINESS.
SOOOOO, I'VE BEEN THINKING...
ABOUT WHAT?
do you want to be my boyfriend? Check one:
Yes
No
Maybe
I THOUGHT YOU SAID YOU DIDN'T WANT TO BE IN A RELATIONSHIP?
I CHANGED MY MIND.
GOOD. I'M CHECKING YES AND SIGNING IT SO IT'S AN OFFICIAL DOCUMENT.
PHEW! GLAD THAT'S TAKEN CARE OF SO WE CAN GET BACK TO DOING ABSOLUTELY NOTHING INDOORS ON A BEAUTIFUL SATURDAY AFTERNOON.

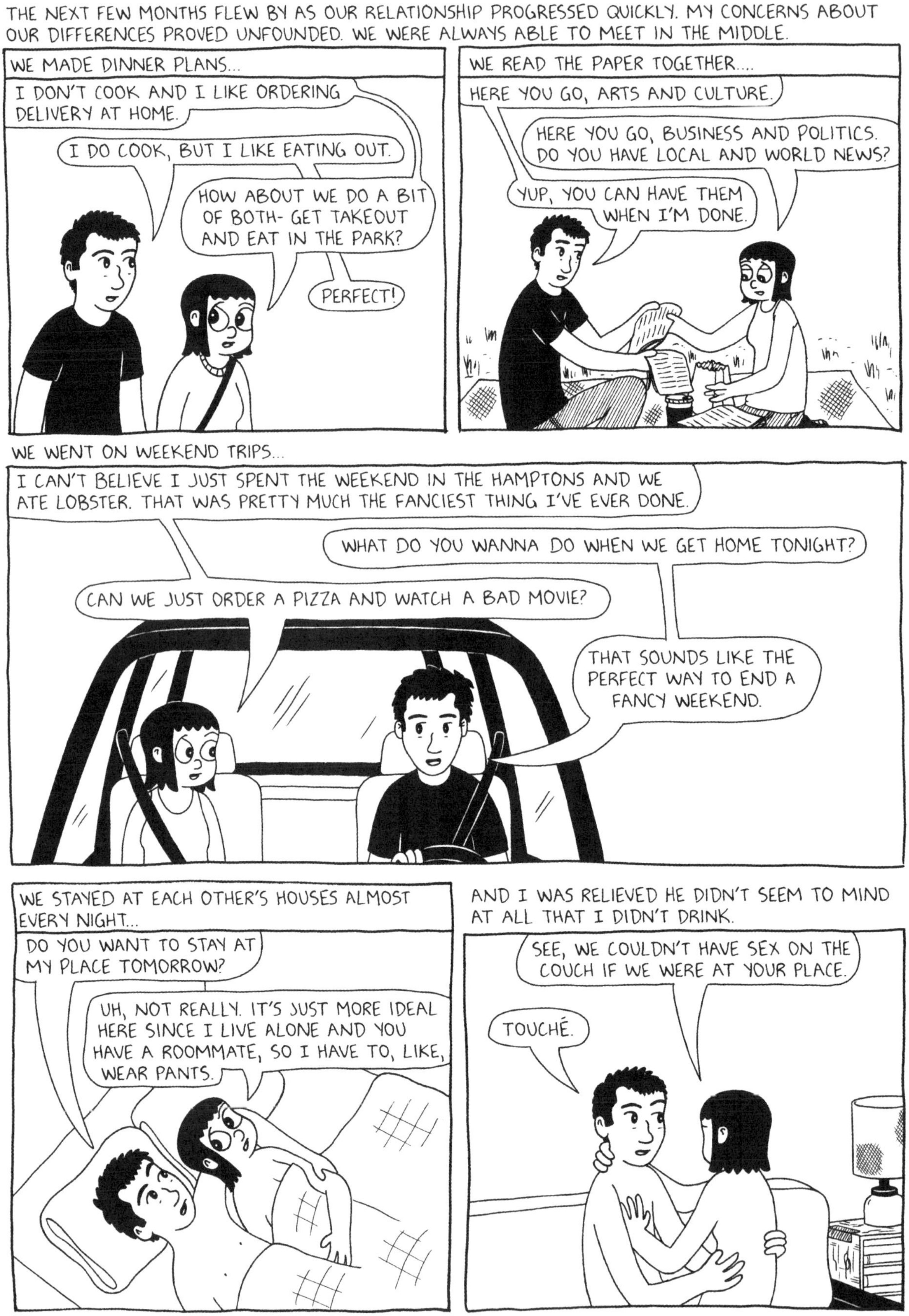
THE NEXT FEW MONTHS FLEW BY AS OUR RELATIONSHIP PROGRESSED QUICKLY. MY CONCERNS ABOUT OUR DIFFERENCES PROVED UNFOUNDED. WE WERE ALWAYS ABLE TO MEET IN THE MIDDLE.
WE MADE DINNER PLANS...
I DON'T COOK AND I LIKE ORDERING DELIVERY AT HOME.
I DO COOK, BUT I LIKE EATING OUT.
HOW ABOUT WE DO A BIT OF BOTH- GET TAKEOUT AND EAT IN THE PARK?
PERFECT!
WE READ THE PAPER TOGETHER....
HERE YOU GO, ARTS AND CULTURE.
HERE YOU GO, BUSINESS AND POLITICS. DO YOU HAVE LOCAL AND WORLD NEWS?
YUP, YOU CAN HAVE THEM WHEN I'M DONE.
WE WENT ON WEEKEND TRIPS...
I CAN'T BELIEVE I JUST SPENT THE WEEKEND IN THE HAMPTONS AND WE ATE LOBSTER. THAT WAS PRETTY MUCH THE FANCIEST THING I'VE EVER DONE.
WHAT DO YOU WANNA DO WHEN WE GET HOME TONIGHT?
CAN WE JUST ORDER A PIZZA AND WATCH A BAD MOVIE?
THAT SOUNDS LIKE THE PERFECT WAY TO END A FANCY WEEKEND.
WE STAYED AT EACH OTHER'S HOUSES ALMOST EVERY NIGHT...
DO YOU WANT TO STAY AT MY PLACE TOMORROW?
UH, NOT REALLY. IT'S JUST MORE IDEAL HERE SINCE I LIVE ALONE AND YOU HAVE A ROOMMATE, SO I HAVE TO, LIKE, WEAR PANTS.
AND I WAS RELIEVED HE DIDN'T SEEM TO MIND AT ALL THAT I DIDN'T DRINK.
SEE, WE COULDN'T HAVE SEX ON THE COUCH IF WE WERE AT YOUR PLACE.
TOUCHÉ.

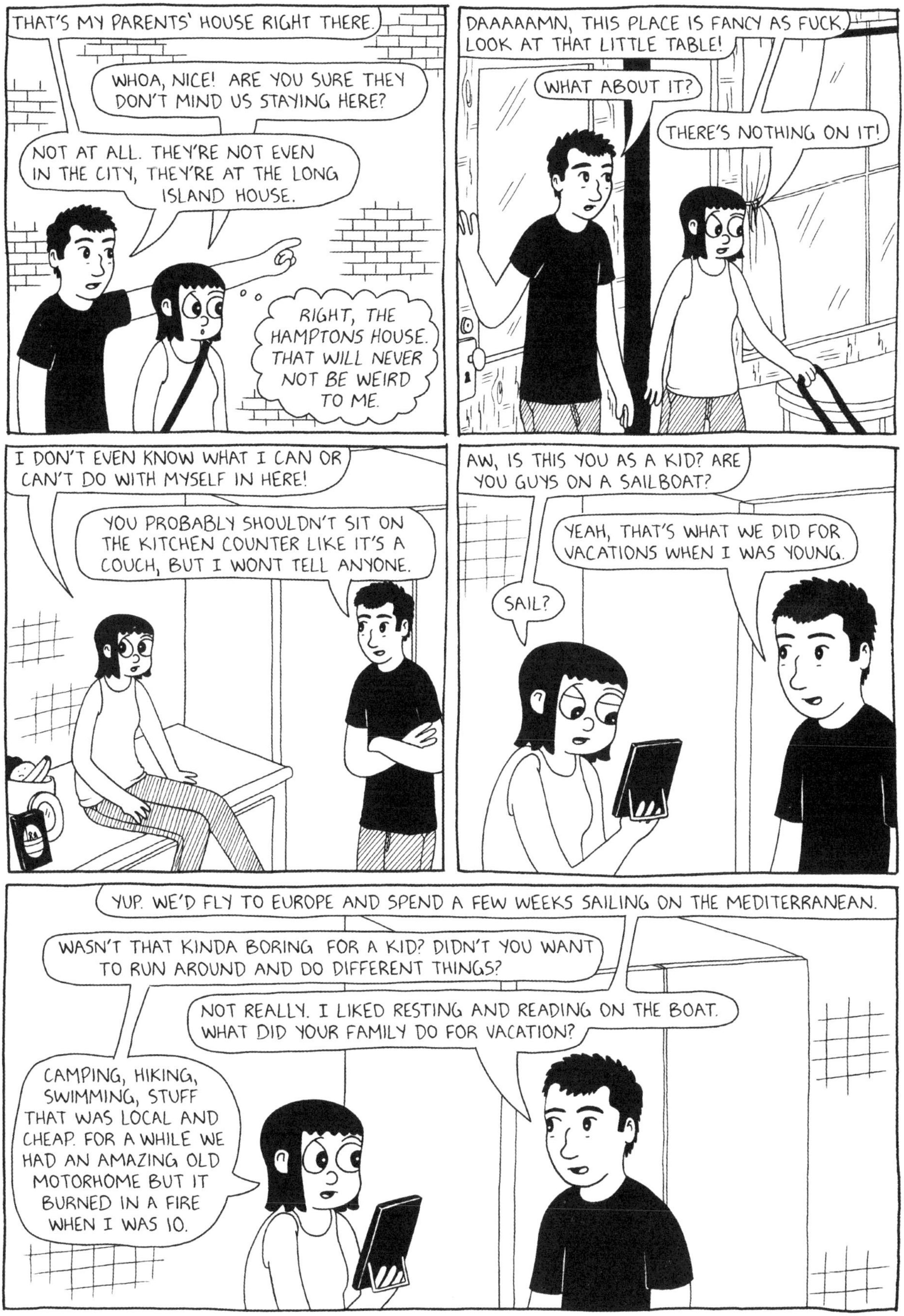
THAT'S MY PARENTS' HOUSE RIGHT THERE.
WHOA, NICE! ARE YOU SURE THEY DON'T MIND US STAYING HERE?
NOT AT ALL. THEY'RE NOT EVEN IN THE CITY, THEY'RE AT THE LONG ISLAND HOUSE.
RIGHT, THE HAMPTONS HOUSE. THAT WILL NEVER NOT BE WEIRD TO ME.
DAAAAAMN, THIS PLACE IS FANCY AS FUCK. LOOK AT THAT LITTLE TABLE!
WHAT ABOUT IT?
THERE'S NOTHING ON IT!
I DON'T EVEN KNOW WHAT I CAN OR CAN'T DO WITH MYSELF IN HERE!
YOU PROBABLY SHOULDN'T SIT ON THE KITCHEN COUNTER LIKE IT'S A COUCH, BUT I WONT TELL ANYONE.
AW, IS THIS YOU AS A KID? ARE YOU GUYS ON A SAILBOAT?
YEAH, THAT'S WHAT WE DID FOR VACATIONS WHEN I WAS YOUNG.
SAIL?
YUP. WE'D FLY TO EUROPE AND SPEND A FEW WEEKS SAILING ON THE MEDITERRANEAN.
WASN'T THAT KINDA BORING FOR A KID? DIDN'T YOU WANT TO RUN AROUND AND DO DIFFERENT THINGS?
NOT REALLY. I LIKED RESTING AND READING ON THE BOAT. WHAT DID YOUR FAMILY DO FOR VACATION?
CAMPING, HIKING, SWIMMING, STUFF THAT WAS LOCAL AND CHEAP. FOR A WHILE WE HAD AN AMAZING OLD MOTORHOME BUT IT BURNED IN A FIRE WHEN I WAS 10.

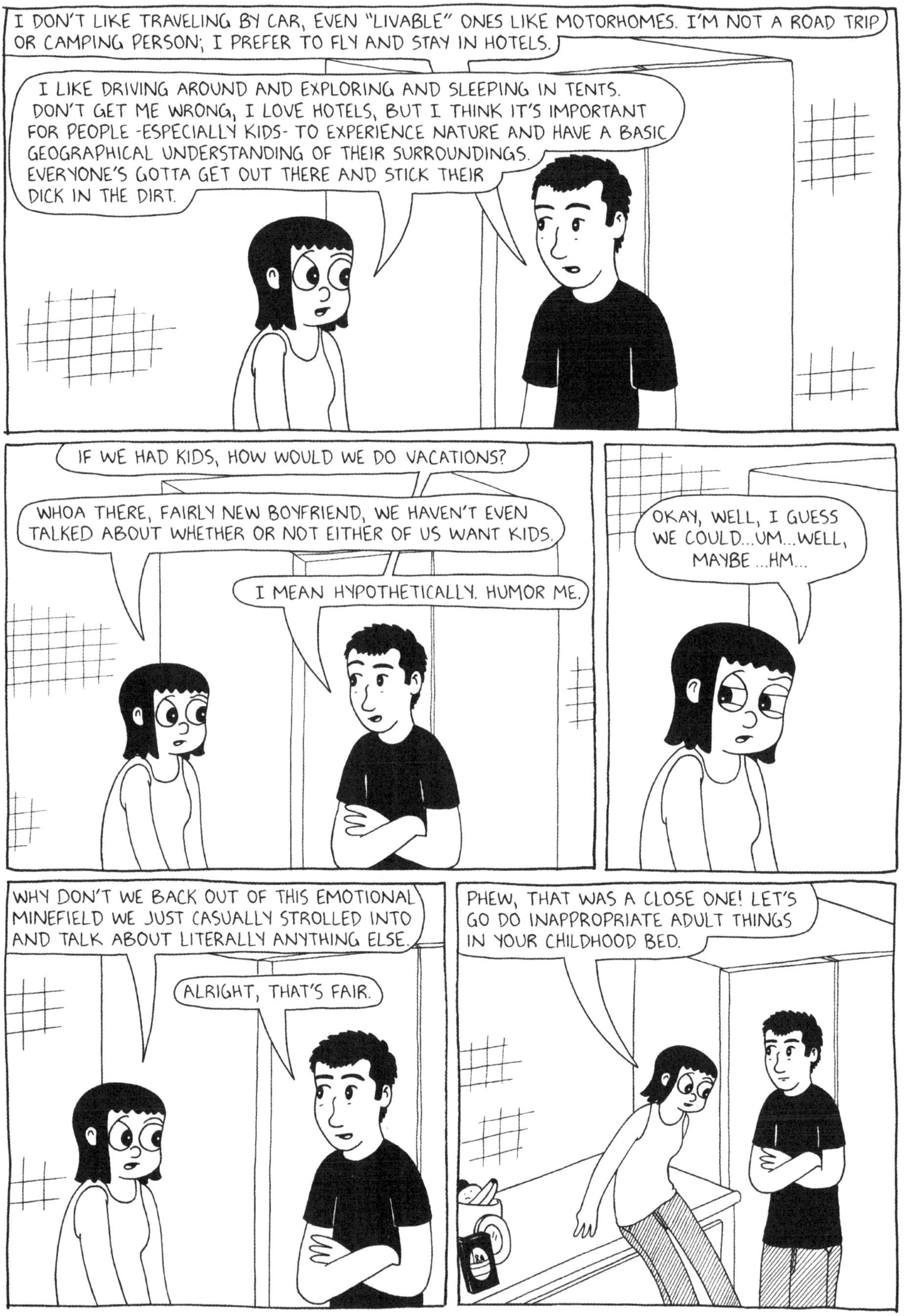
I DON'T LIKE TRAVELING BY CAR, EVEN "LIVABLE" ONES LIKE MOTORHOMES. I'M NOT A ROAD TRIP OR CAMPING PERSON; I PREFER TO FLY AND STAY IN HOTELS.
I LIKE DRIVING AROUND AND EXPLORING AND SLEEPING IN TENTS. DON'T GET ME WRONG, I LOVE HOTELS, BUT I THINK IT'S IMPORTANT FOR PEOPLE -ESPECIALLY KIDS- TO EXPERIENCE NATURE AND HAVE A BASIC GEOGRAPHICAL UNDERSTANDING OF THEIR SURROUNDINGS. EVERYONE'S GOTTA GET OUT THERE AND STICK THEIR DICK IN THE DIRT.
IF WE HAD KIDS, HOW WOULD WE DO VACATIONS?
WHOA THERE, FAIRLY NEW BOYFRIEND, WE HAVEN'T EVEN TALKED ABOUT WHETHER OR NOT EITHER OF US WANT KIDS.
I MEAN HYPOTHETICALLY. HUMOR ME.
OKAY, WELL, I GUESS WE COULD...UM...WELL, MAYBE ...HM...
WHY DON'T WE BACK OUT OF THIS EMOTIONAL MINEFIELD WE JUST CASUALLY STROLLED INTO AND TALK ABOUT LITERALLY ANYTHING ELSE.
ALRIGHT, THAT'S FAIR.
PHEW, THAT WAS A CLOSE ONE! LET'S GO DO INAPPROPRIATE ADULT THINGS IN YOUR CHILDHOOD BED.

THE THRILL OF A NEW AND FAST-MOVING RELATIONSHIP WAS EXHILARATING BUT DISTRACTING. WHEN I WAS SINGLE, MY FOCUS WAS ON WORK AND RECOVERY. BUT WHEN MY FOCUS SHIFTED TO THE RELATIONSHIP, THOSE THINGS BEGAN TO FALTER.

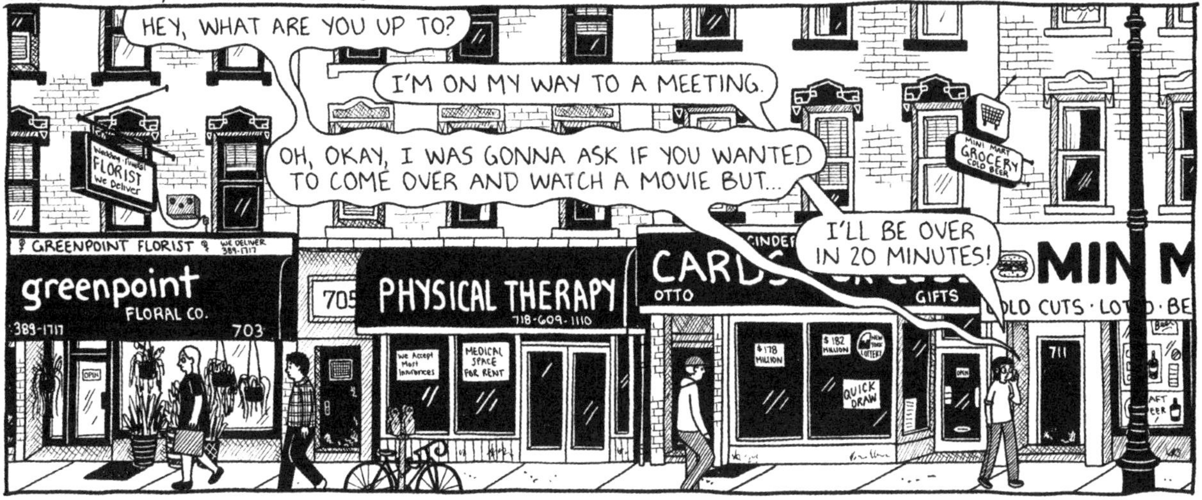

HEY, WHAT ARE YOU UP TO?
I'M ON MY WAY TO A MEETING.
OH, OKAY, I WAS GONNA ASK IF YOU WANTED TO COME OVER AND WATCH A MOVIE BUT...
I'LL BE OVER IN 20 MINUTES!
GREENPOINT FLORIST
greenpoint FLORAL CO.
PHYSICAL THERAPY
718-609-1110
MEDICAL SPACE FOR RENT
QUICK DRAW
GIFTS
MINI MART GROCERY COLD BEER

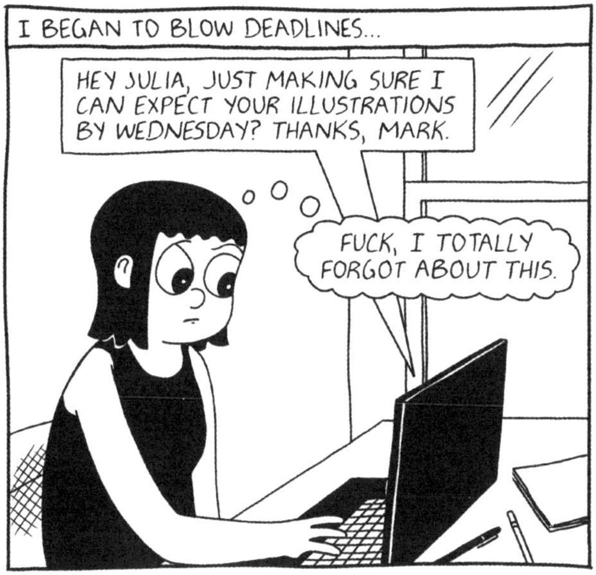

I BEGAN TO BLOW DEADLINES...
HEY JULIA, JUST MAKING SURE I CAN EXPECT YOUR ILLUSTRATIONS BY WEDNESDAY? THANKS, MARK.
FUCK, I TOTALLY FORGOT ABOUT THIS.

AND WHEN I STUMBLED ACROSS A BOTTLE OF PAINKILLERS IN A BATHROOM AT A HOUSE PARTY, I BARELY HESITATED BEFORE POCKETING A FEW.

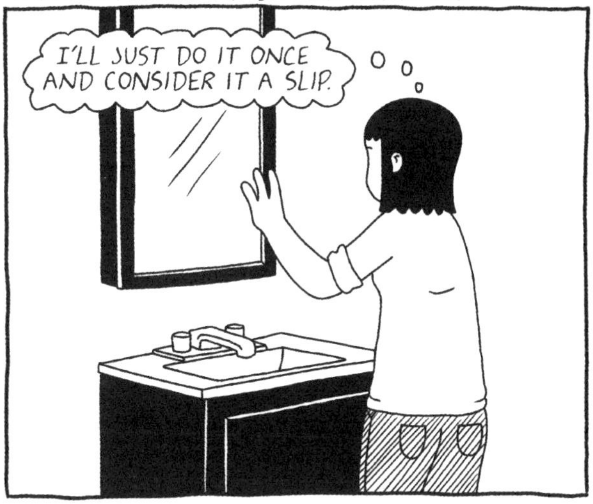

I'LL JUST DO IT ONCE AND CONSIDER IT A SLIP.

THAT "SLIP" REMINDED ME THAT I GOT A LOT OF WORK DONE WHEN I WAS HIGH ON PAINKILLERS.

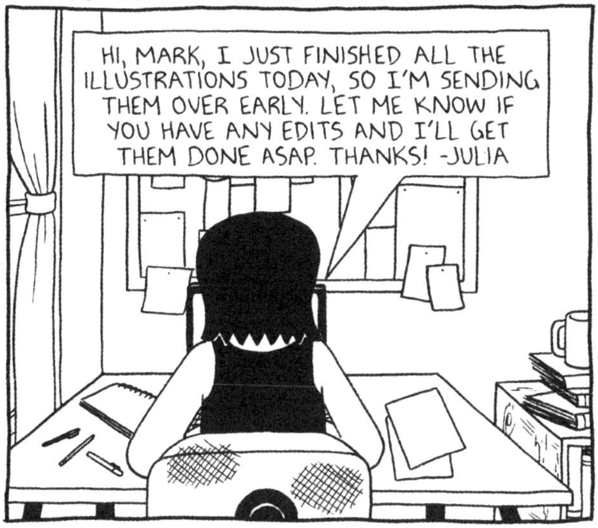

HI, MARK, I JUST FINISHED ALL THE ILLUSTRATIONS TODAY, SO I'M SENDING THEM OVER EARLY. LET ME KNOW IF YOU HAVE ANY EDITS AND I'LL GET THEM DONE ASAP. THANKS! -JULIA

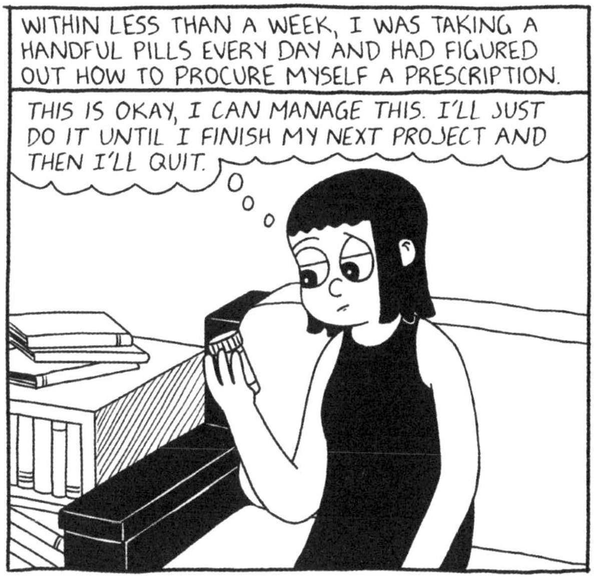

WITHIN LESS THAN A WEEK, I WAS TAKING A HANDFUL PILLS EVERY DAY AND HAD FIGURED OUT HOW TO PROCURE MYSELF A PRESCRIPTION.
THIS IS OKAY, I CAN MANAGE THIS. I'LL JUST DO IT UNTIL I FINISH MY NEXT PROJECT AND THEN I'LL QUIT.

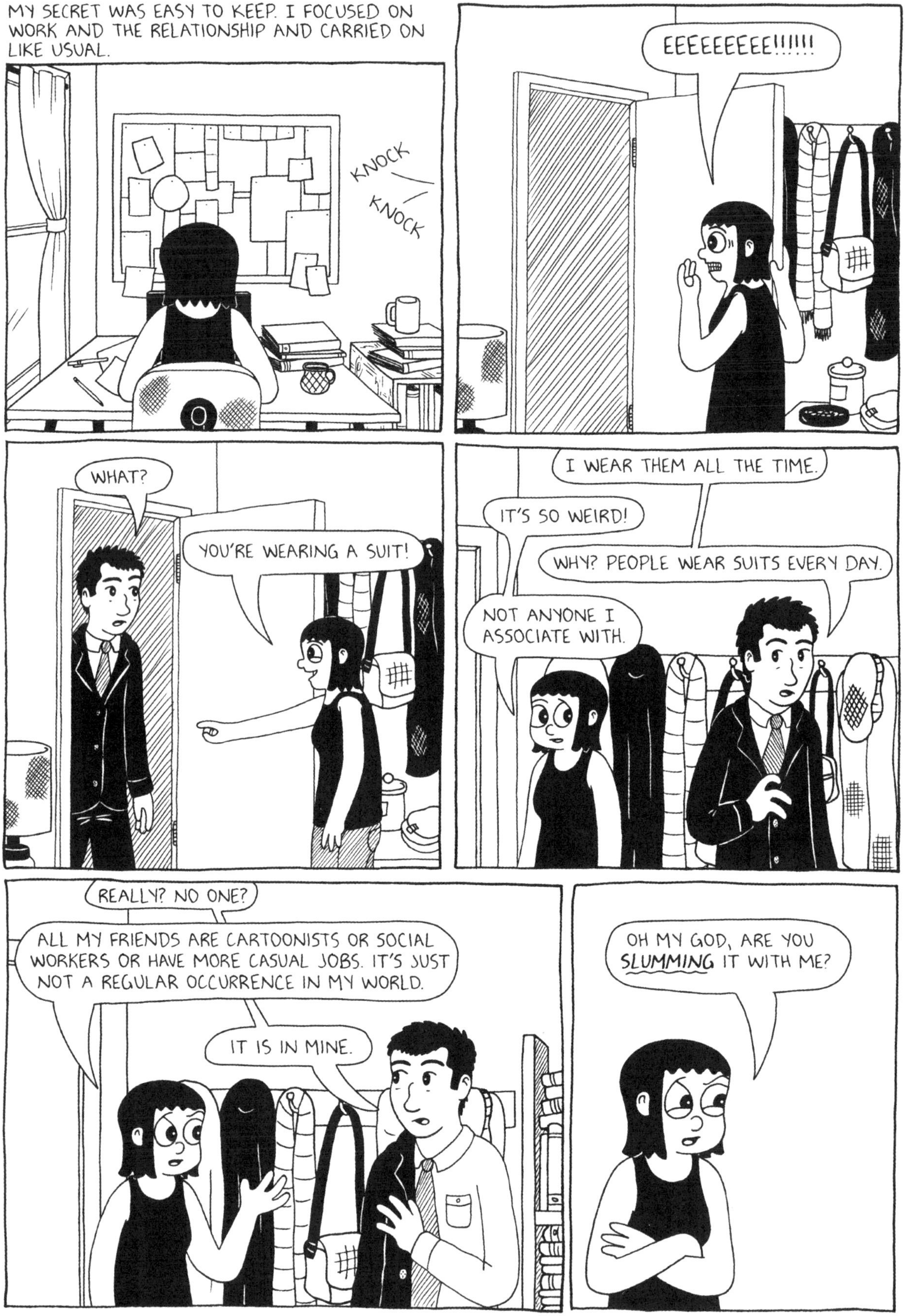

MY SECRET WAS EASY TO KEEP. I FOCUSED ON WORK AND THE RELATIONSHIP AND CARRIED ON LIKE USUAL.
KNOCK KNOCK
EEEEEEEEE!!!!!!
WHAT?
YOU'RE WEARING A SUIT!
I WEAR THEM ALL THE TIME.
IT'S SO WEIRD!
WHY? PEOPLE WEAR SUITS EVERY DAY.
NOT ANYONE I ASSOCIATE WITH.
REALLY? NO ONE?
ALL MY FRIENDS ARE CARTOONISTS OR SOCIAL WORKERS OR HAVE MORE CASUAL JOBS. IT'S JUST NOT A REGULAR OCCURRENCE IN MY WORLD.
IT IS IN MINE.
OH MY GOD, ARE YOU SLUMMING IT WITH ME?

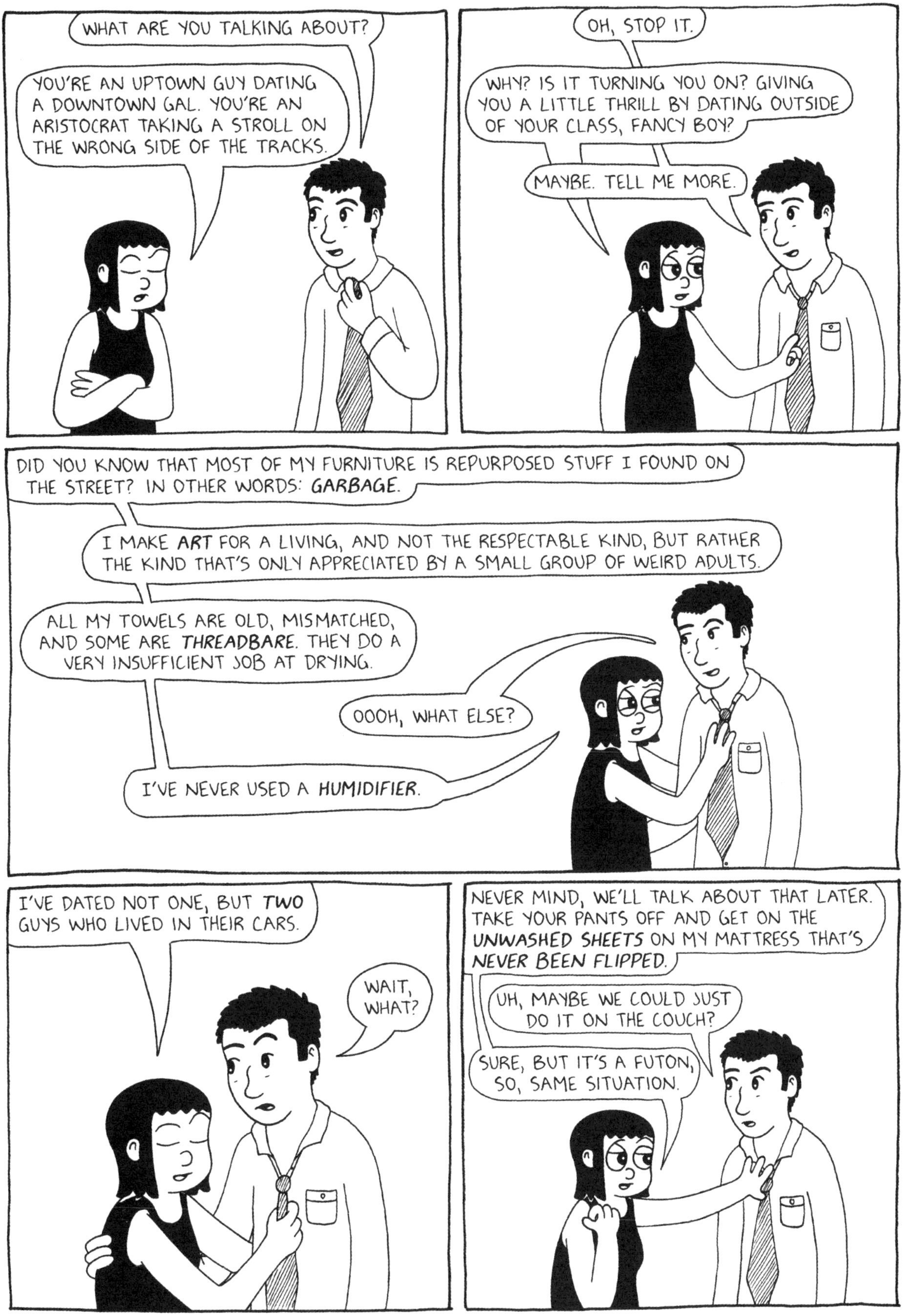
WHAT ARE YOU TALKING ABOUT?
YOU'RE AN UPTOWN GUY DATING A DOWNTOWN GAL. YOU'RE AN ARISTOCRAT TAKING A STROLL ON THE WRONG SIDE OF THE TRACKS.
OH, STOP IT.
WHY? IS IT TURNING YOU ON? GIVING YOU A LITTLE THRILL BY DATING OUTSIDE OF YOUR CLASS, FANCY BOY?
MAYBE. TELL ME MORE.
DID YOU KNOW THAT MOST OF MY FURNITURE IS REPURPOSED STUFF I FOUND ON THE STREET? IN OTHER WORDS: **GARBAGE**.
I MAKE **ART** FOR A LIVING, AND NOT THE RESPECTABLE KIND, BUT RATHER THE KIND THAT'S ONLY APPRECIATED BY A SMALL GROUP OF WEIRD ADULTS.
ALL MY TOWELS ARE OLD, MISMATCHED, AND SOME ARE ***THREADBARE***. THEY DO A VERY INSUFFICIENT JOB AT DRYING.
OOOH, WHAT ELSE?
I'VE NEVER USED A **HUMIDIFIER**.
I'VE DATED NOT ONE, BUT ***TWO*** GUYS WHO LIVED IN THEIR CARS.
WAIT, WHAT?
NEVER MIND, WE'LL TALK ABOUT THAT LATER. TAKE YOUR PANTS OFF AND GET ON THE ***UNWASHED SHEETS*** ON MY MATTRESS THAT'S ***NEVER BEEN FLIPPED***.
UH, MAYBE WE COULD JUST DO IT ON THE COUCH?
SURE, BUT IT'S A FUTON, SO, SAME SITUATION.

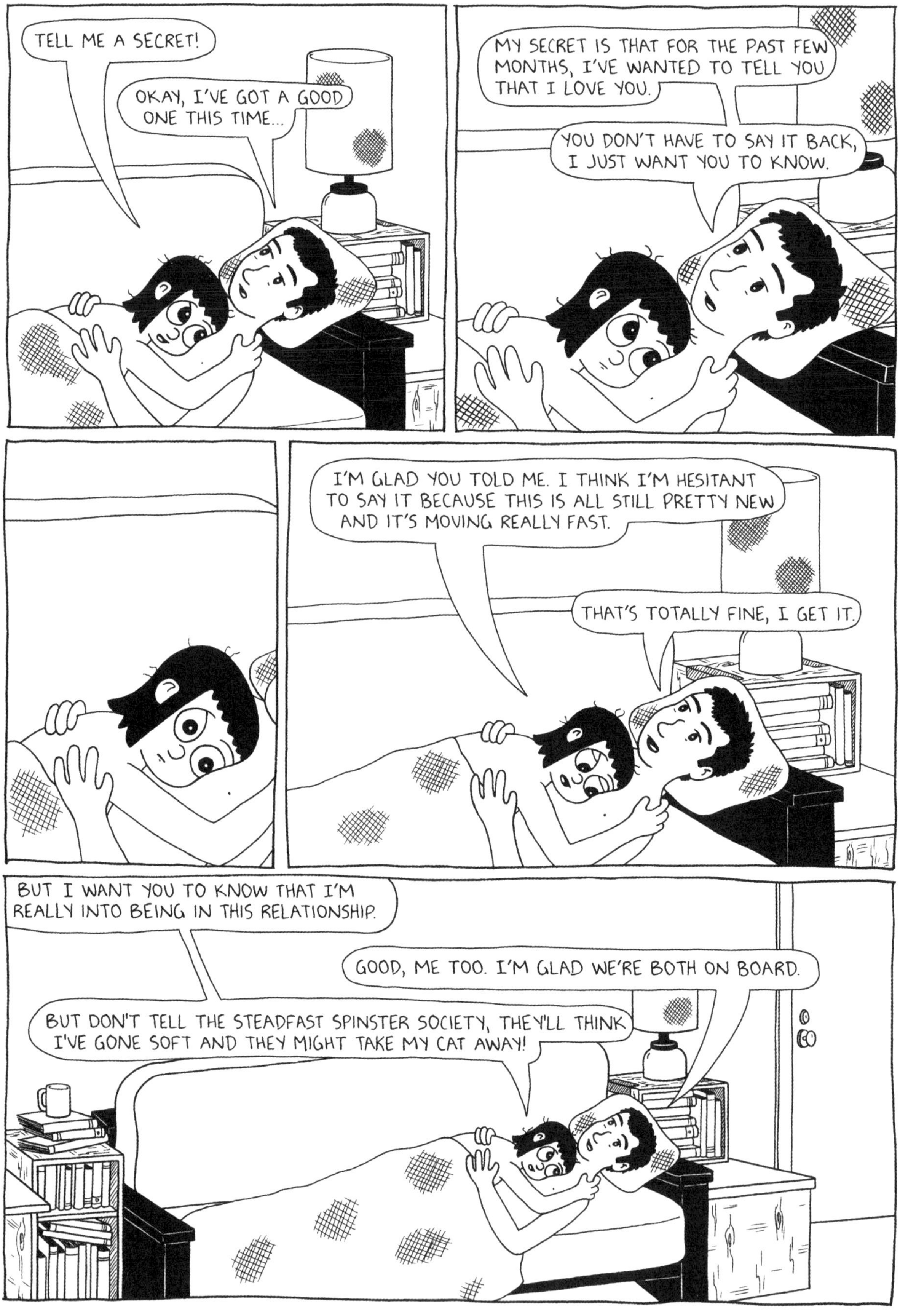
TELL ME A SECRET!
OKAY, I'VE GOT A GOOD ONE THIS TIME...
MY SECRET IS THAT FOR THE PAST FEW MONTHS, I'VE WANTED TO TELL YOU THAT I LOVE YOU.
YOU DON'T HAVE TO SAY IT BACK, I JUST WANT YOU TO KNOW.
I'M GLAD YOU TOLD ME. I THINK I'M HESITANT TO SAY IT BECAUSE THIS IS ALL STILL PRETTY NEW AND IT'S MOVING REALLY FAST.
THAT'S TOTALLY FINE, I GET IT.
BUT I WANT YOU TO KNOW THAT I'M REALLY INTO BEING IN THIS RELATIONSHIP.
GOOD, ME TOO. I'M GLAD WE'RE BOTH ON BOARD.
BUT DON'T TELL THE STEADFAST SPINSTER SOCIETY, THEY'LL THINK I'VE GONE SOFT AND THEY MIGHT TAKE MY CAT AWAY!

DRIVING HOME FROM A WEEKEND TRIP WITH JEN:

...AND THEN HE WANTED TO GO TO A PLACE THAT SERVES KOMBUCHA LIKE HOW A BAR SERVES BEER.

I LIKE KOMBUCHA, BUT THERE ARE FEWER WORDS THAT MAKE ME LESS HORNY THAN "KOMBUCHA ON TAP."

GOT A TEXT FROM A FRIEND IN BROOKLYN.

HEADS UP, THERE'S A HURRICANE WARNING IN THE CITY. I THINK YOUR BASEMENT IS IN A FLOOD ZONE.

IS THIS A REAL THING I NEED TO WORRY ABOUT?

UNFORTUNATELY, I THINK SO.

WE PULLED OVER TO GET COFFEE AND CHECK THE NEWS, WHICH NEITHER OF US HAD BEEN PAYING ATTENTION TO ALL WEEK.

OH SHIT, THERE'S A HUGE HURRICANE HEADED STRAIGHT FOR NEW YORK CITY! WHAT ARE WE SUPPOSED TO DO? HOW DO WE PREPARE?

I DON'T KNOW, I'M FROM COLORADO!

AND I'M FROM CALIFORNIA! WE DO EARTHQUAKES, NOT ALL HELL BREAKING LOOSE FROM THE SKY!

WE DROVE QUICKLY BACK TO THE CITY AND BEGAN PREPARATIONS.

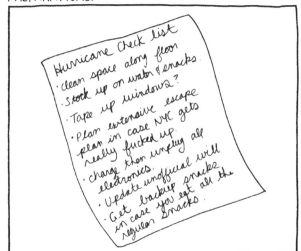
Hurricane Check list
· clean space along floor.
· Stock up on water & snacks.
· Tape up windows?
· Plan extensive escape plan in case NYC gets really fucked up.
· charge then unplug all electronics.
· Update unofficial will
· Get backup snacks in case you eat all the regular snacks.

I WAS UP ALL NIGHT.

IF MY STUDIO FLOODS, I THINK I MIGHT JUST LEAVE MY ARTWORK BEHIND TO GET RUINED? IT WOULD BE SUCH A BUMMER THAT I'D PROBABLY WANT TO QUIT COMICS AND DO SOMETHING TOTALLY DIFFERENT. AND THAT'S...EXCITING?

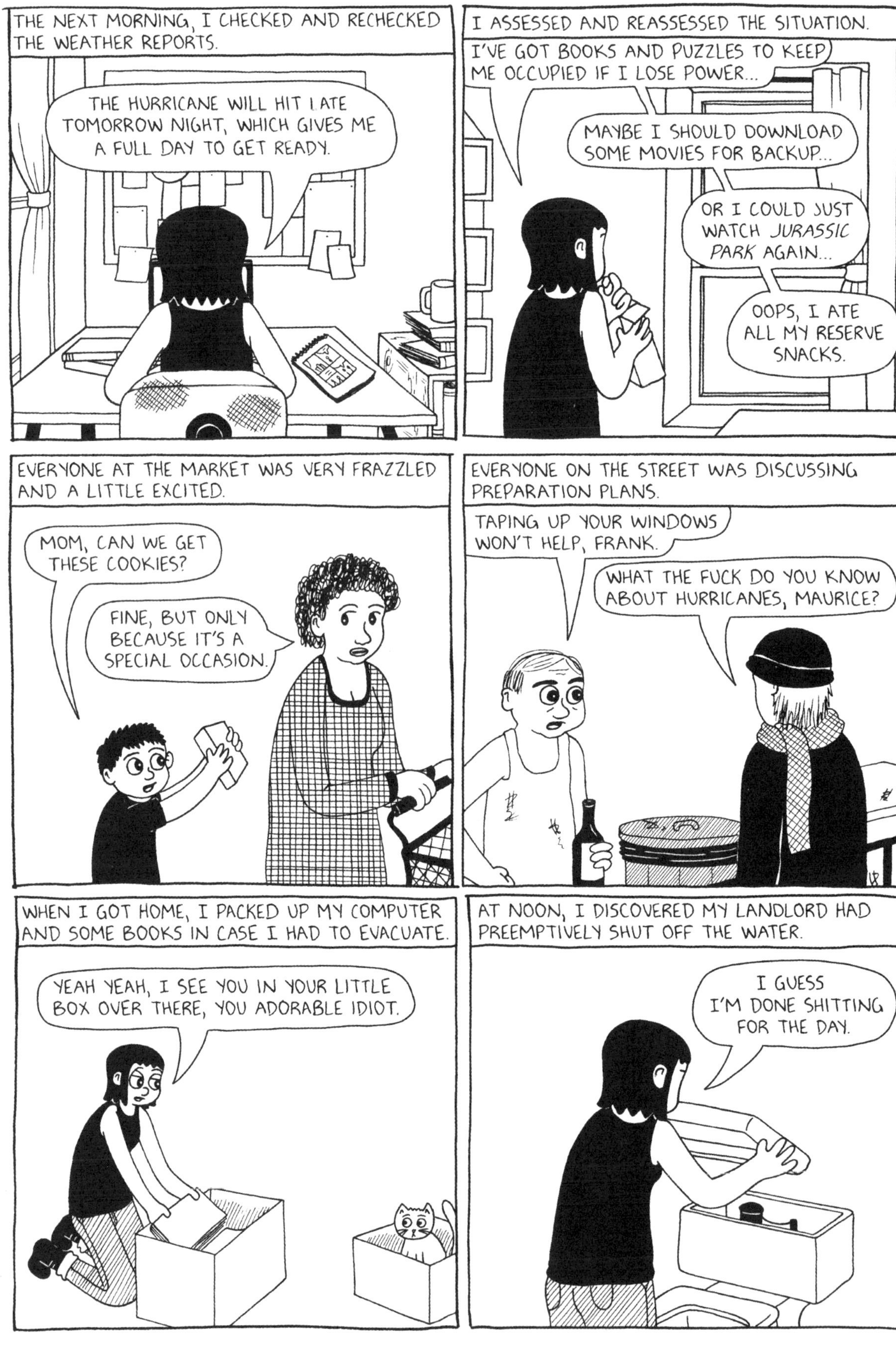

THE NEXT MORNING, I CHECKED AND RECHECKED THE WEATHER REPORTS.
THE HURRICANE WILL HIT LATE TOMORROW NIGHT, WHICH GIVES ME A FULL DAY TO GET READY.
I ASSESSED AND REASSESSED THE SITUATION.
I'VE GOT BOOKS AND PUZZLES TO KEEP ME OCCUPIED IF I LOSE POWER...
MAYBE I SHOULD DOWNLOAD SOME MOVIES FOR BACKUP...
OR I COULD JUST WATCH *JURASSIC PARK* AGAIN...
OOPS, I ATE ALL MY RESERVE SNACKS.
EVERYONE AT THE MARKET WAS VERY FRAZZLED AND A LITTLE EXCITED.
MOM, CAN WE GET THESE COOKIES?
FINE, BUT ONLY BECAUSE IT'S A SPECIAL OCCASION.
EVERYONE ON THE STREET WAS DISCUSSING PREPARATION PLANS.
TAPING UP YOUR WINDOWS WON'T HELP, FRANK.
WHAT THE FUCK DO YOU KNOW ABOUT HURRICANES, MAURICE?
WHEN I GOT HOME, I PACKED UP MY COMPUTER AND SOME BOOKS IN CASE I HAD TO EVACUATE.
YEAH YEAH, I SEE YOU IN YOUR LITTLE BOX OVER THERE, YOU ADORABLE IDIOT.
AT NOON, I DISCOVERED MY LANDLORD HAD PREEMPTIVELY SHUT OFF THE WATER.
I GUESS I'M DONE SHITTING FOR THE DAY.

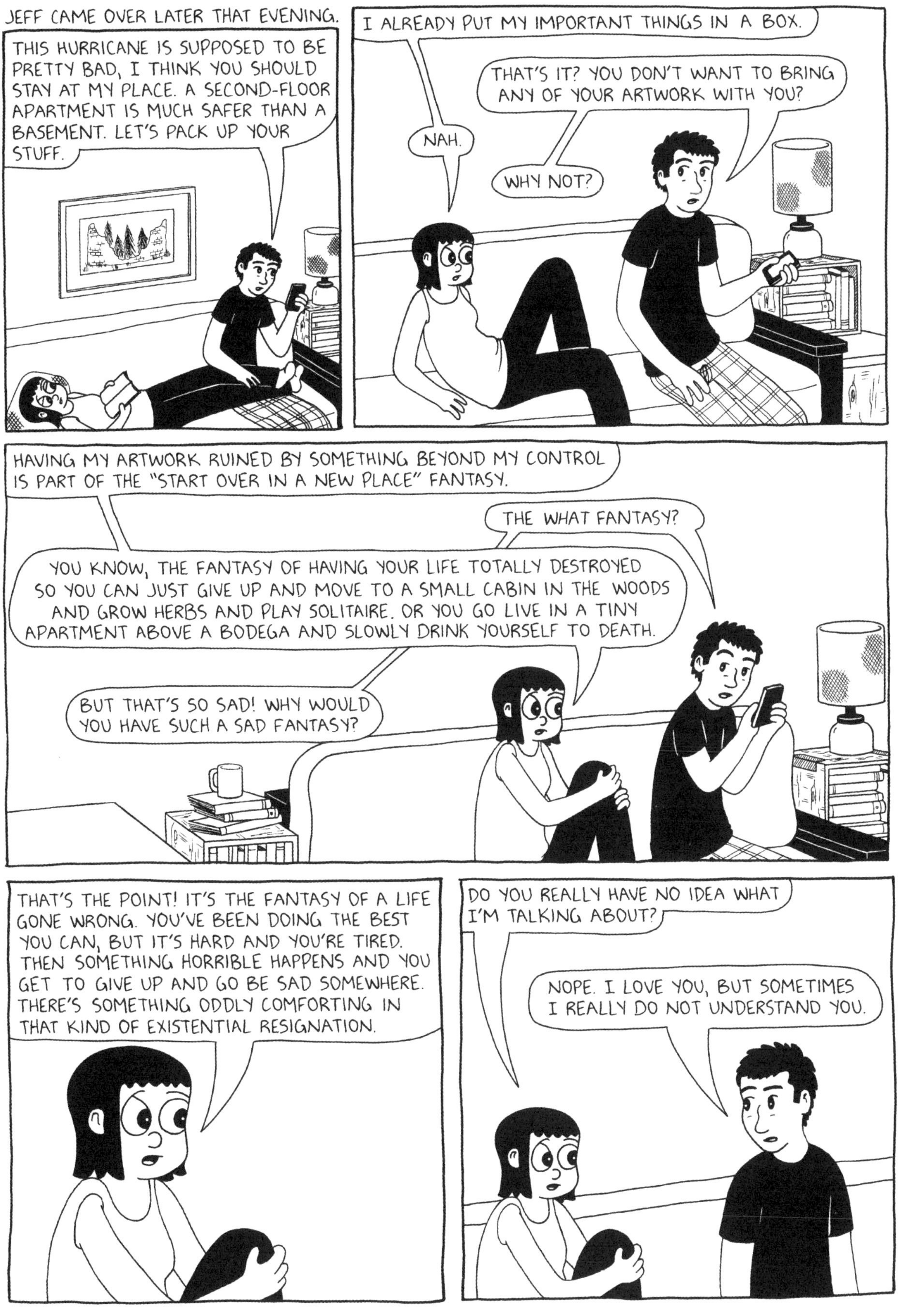
JEFF CAME OVER LATER THAT EVENING.
THIS HURRICANE IS SUPPOSED TO BE PRETTY BAD, I THINK YOU SHOULD STAY AT MY PLACE. A SECOND-FLOOR APARTMENT IS MUCH SAFER THAN A BASEMENT. LET'S PACK UP YOUR STUFF.
I ALREADY PUT MY IMPORTANT THINGS IN A BOX.
THAT'S IT? YOU DON'T WANT TO BRING ANY OF YOUR ARTWORK WITH YOU?
NAH.
WHY NOT?
HAVING MY ARTWORK RUINED BY SOMETHING BEYOND MY CONTROL IS PART OF THE "START OVER IN A NEW PLACE" FANTASY.
THE WHAT FANTASY?
YOU KNOW, THE FANTASY OF HAVING YOUR LIFE TOTALLY DESTROYED SO YOU CAN JUST GIVE UP AND MOVE TO A SMALL CABIN IN THE WOODS AND GROW HERBS AND PLAY SOLITAIRE. OR YOU GO LIVE IN A TINY APARTMENT ABOVE A BODEGA AND SLOWLY DRINK YOURSELF TO DEATH.
BUT THAT'S SO SAD! WHY WOULD YOU HAVE SUCH A SAD FANTASY?
THAT'S THE POINT! IT'S THE FANTASY OF A LIFE GONE WRONG. YOU'VE BEEN DOING THE BEST YOU CAN, BUT IT'S HARD AND YOU'RE TIRED. THEN SOMETHING HORRIBLE HAPPENS AND YOU GET TO GIVE UP AND GO BE SAD SOMEWHERE. THERE'S SOMETHING ODDLY COMFORTING IN THAT KIND OF EXISTENTIAL RESIGNATION.
DO YOU REALLY HAVE NO IDEA WHAT I'M TALKING ABOUT?
NOPE. I LOVE YOU, BUT SOMETIMES I REALLY DO NOT UNDERSTAND YOU.

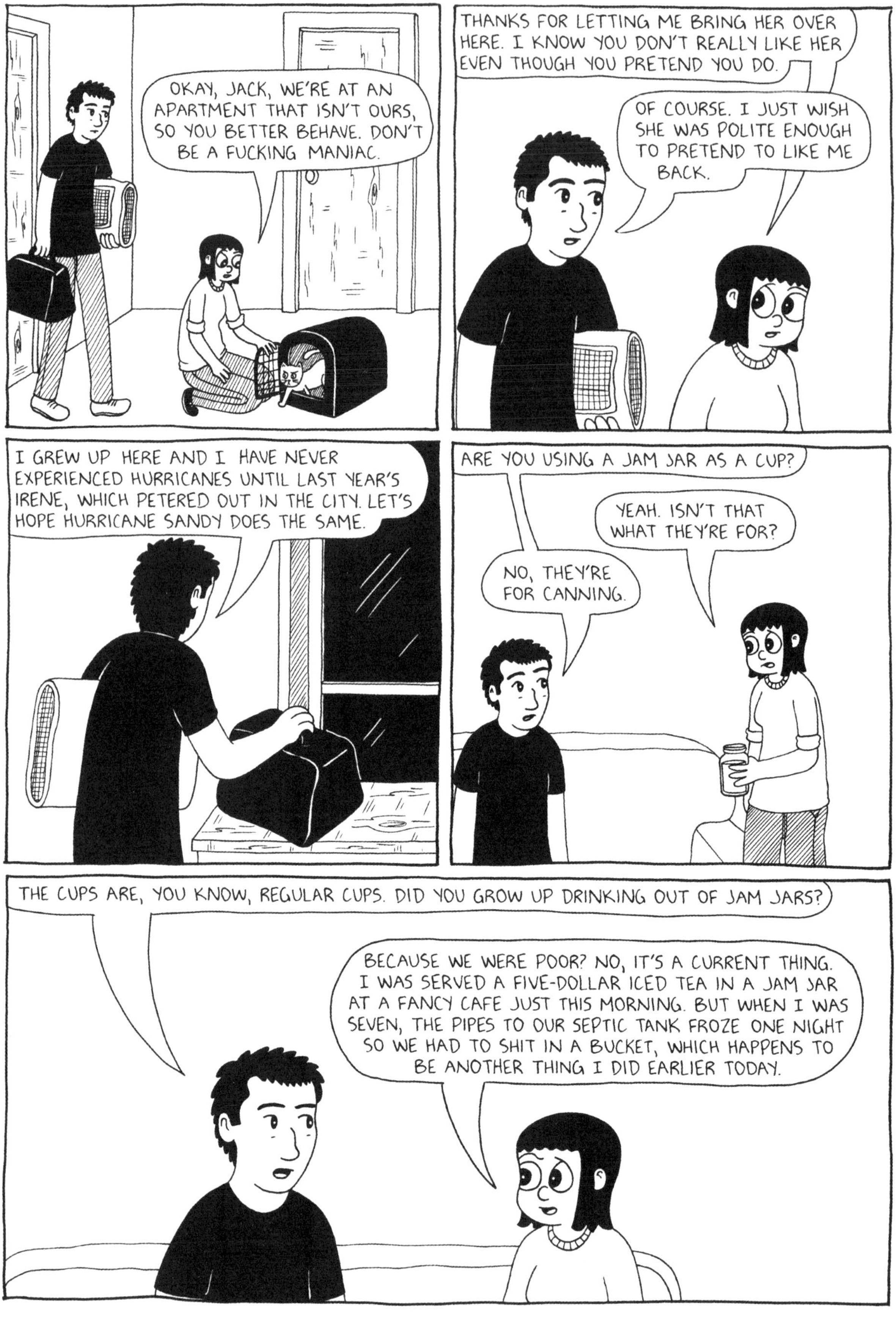
OKAY, JACK, WE'RE AT AN APARTMENT THAT ISN'T OURS, SO YOU BETTER BEHAVE. DON'T BE A FUCKING MANIAC.
THANKS FOR LETTING ME BRING HER OVER HERE. I KNOW YOU DON'T REALLY LIKE HER EVEN THOUGH YOU PRETEND YOU DO.
OF COURSE. I JUST WISH SHE WAS POLITE ENOUGH TO PRETEND TO LIKE ME BACK.
I GREW UP HERE AND I HAVE NEVER EXPERIENCED HURRICANES UNTIL LAST YEAR'S IRENE, WHICH PETERED OUT IN THE CITY. LET'S HOPE HURRICANE SANDY DOES THE SAME.
ARE YOU USING A JAM JAR AS A CUP?
YEAH. ISN'T THAT WHAT THEY'RE FOR?
NO, THEY'RE FOR CANNING.
THE CUPS ARE, YOU KNOW, REGULAR CUPS. DID YOU GROW UP DRINKING OUT OF JAM JARS?
BECAUSE WE WERE POOR? NO, IT'S A CURRENT THING. I WAS SERVED A FIVE-DOLLAR ICED TEA IN A JAM JAR AT A FANCY CAFE JUST THIS MORNING. BUT WHEN I WAS SEVEN, THE PIPES TO OUR SEPTIC TANK FROZE ONE NIGHT SO WE HAD TO SHIT IN A BUCKET, WHICH HAPPENS TO BE ANOTHER THING I DID EARLIER TODAY.

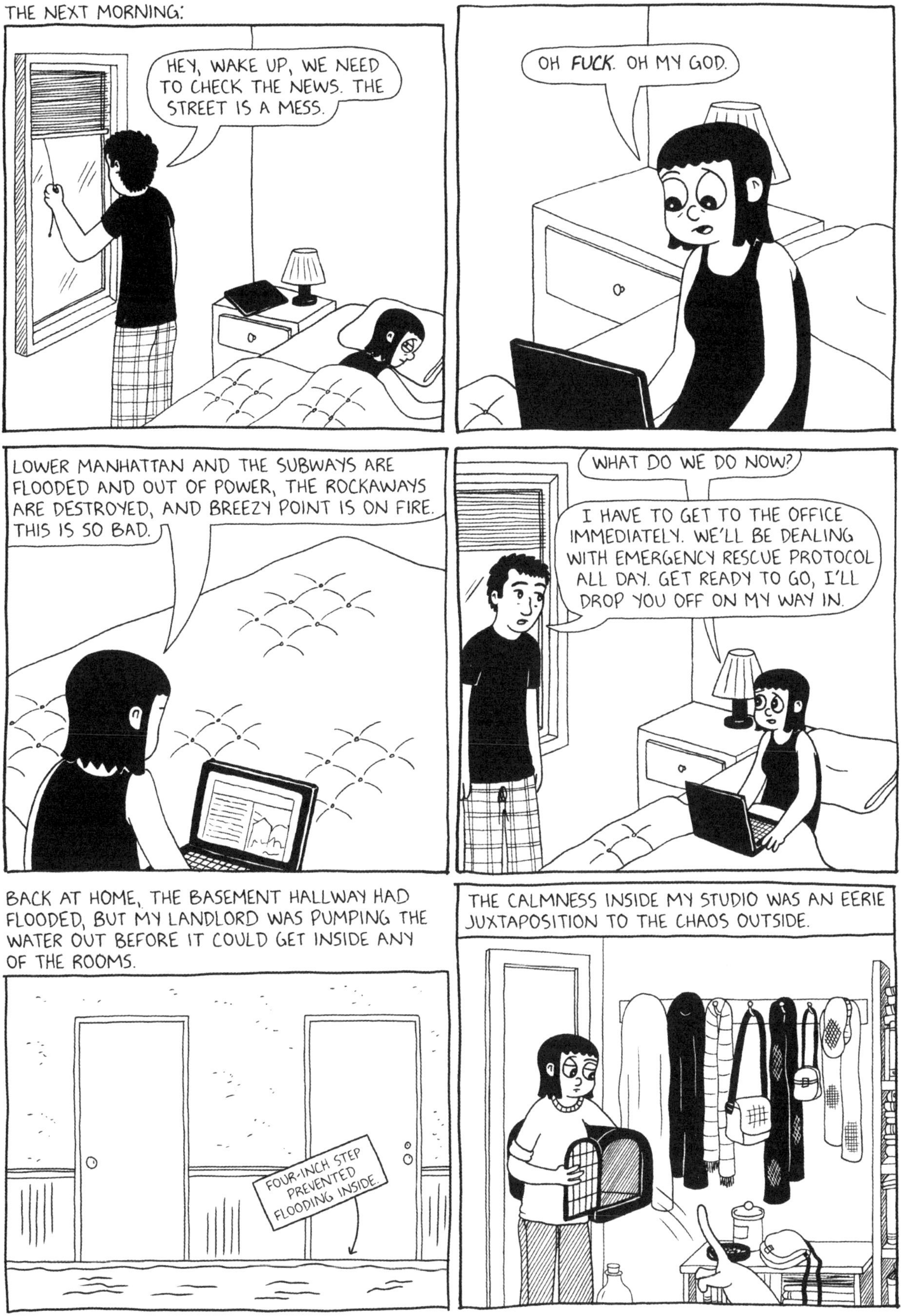
THE NEXT MORNING:
HEY, WAKE UP, WE NEED TO CHECK THE NEWS. THE STREET IS A MESS.
OH FUCK. OH MY GOD.
LOWER MANHATTAN AND THE SUBWAYS ARE FLOODED AND OUT OF POWER, THE ROCKAWAYS ARE DESTROYED, AND BREEZY POINT IS ON FIRE. THIS IS SO BAD.
WHAT DO WE DO NOW?
I HAVE TO GET TO THE OFFICE IMMEDIATELY. WE'LL BE DEALING WITH EMERGENCY RESCUE PROTOCOL ALL DAY. GET READY TO GO, I'LL DROP YOU OFF ON MY WAY IN.
BACK AT HOME, THE BASEMENT HALLWAY HAD FLOODED, BUT MY LANDLORD WAS PUMPING THE WATER OUT BEFORE IT COULD GET INSIDE ANY OF THE ROOMS.
FOUR-INCH STEP PREVENTED FLOODING INSIDE.
THE CALMNESS INSIDE MY STUDIO WAS AN EERIE JUXTAPOSITION TO THE CHAOS OUTSIDE.

I READ THE NEWS OBSESSIVELY OVER THE COURSE OF THE DAY. THE CITY WAS DECLARED AN OFFICIAL STATE OF EMERGENCY. THE STREETS WERE DARK, THE SHELTERS WERE OVERCROWDED, AND PEOPLE WERE GETTING IN FIGHTS AT GAS STATIONS. NO ONE HAD BEEN FULLY PREPARED FOR THE MAGNITUDE OF THE STORM.

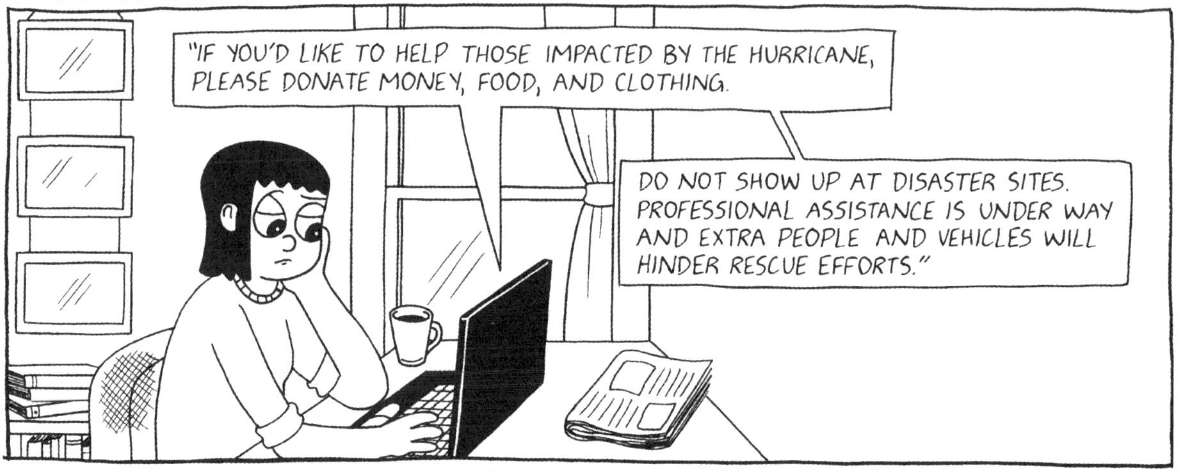
"IF YOU'D LIKE TO HELP THOSE IMPACTED BY THE HURRICANE, PLEASE DONATE MONEY, FOOD, AND CLOTHING.
DO NOT SHOW UP AT DISASTER SITES. PROFESSIONAL ASSISTANCE IS UNDER WAY AND EXTRA PEOPLE AND VEHICLES WILL HINDER RESCUE EFFORTS."

I GAVE SOME MONEY TO A LOCAL HURRICANE RELIEF CHARITY AND DONATED A BOX OF OLD CLOTHES AT A NEIGHBORHOOD CHURCH, BUT THE GESTURES FELT FUTILE.

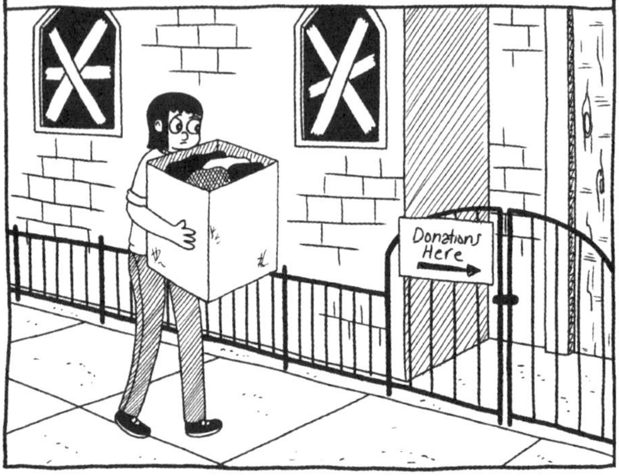
Donations Here

MY ACTIONS WERE JUST A FEEBLE ATTEMPT TO ASSUAGE MY GUILT OVER NOT BEING ABLE TO PHYSICALLY HELP. ALL I COULD DO WAS STARE AT MY COMPUTER, SCROLL THROUGH SOCIAL MEDIA, AND WATCH FOR UPDATES.

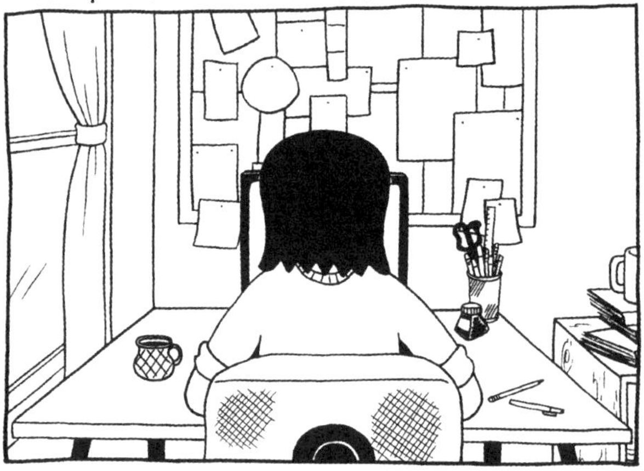

UNABLE TO FULLY GRASP THE ENORMITY OF A WHOLE CITY IN CRISIS, I TURNED MY ATTENTION TO A MORE TANGIBLE PERSONAL CRISIS.

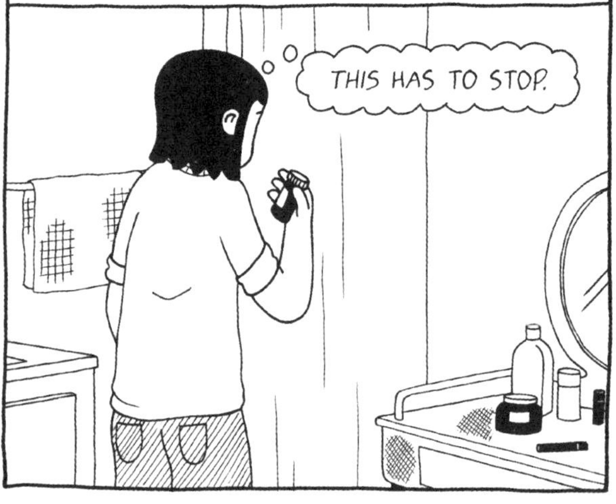
THIS HAS TO STOP.

I HAD BEEN WAITING FOR SOMETHING BIG AND OUTSIDE OF MY CONTROL TO FORCE ME TO QUIT, BUT WHEN THAT FAILED TO HAPPEN, I KNEW I HAD TO DO IT ON MY OWN.

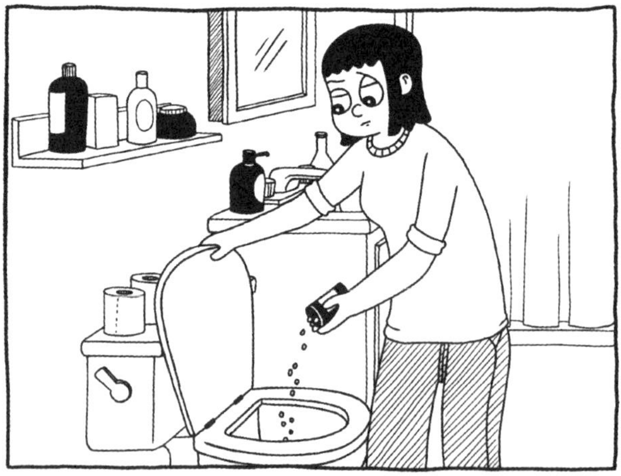

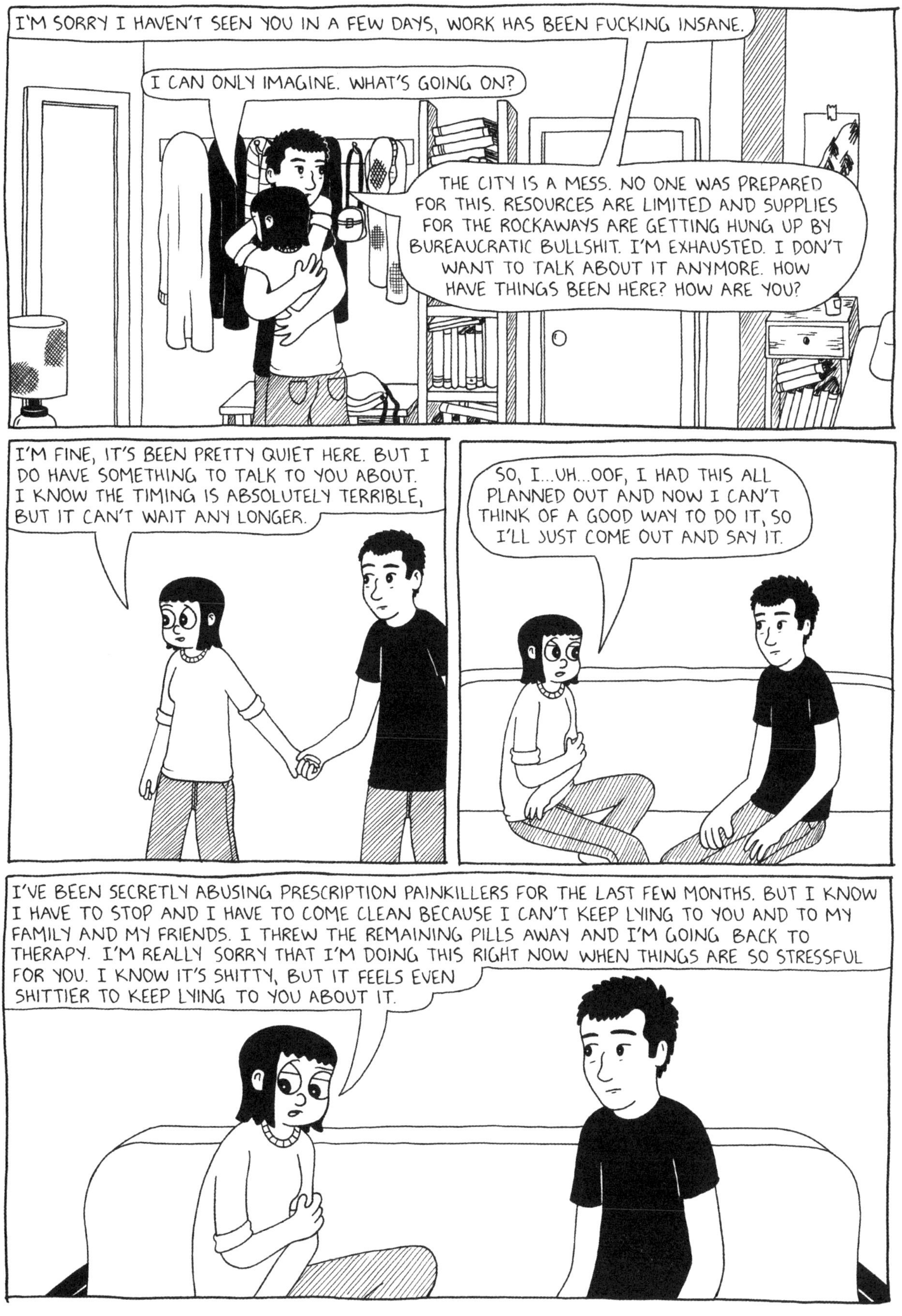
I'M SORRY I HAVEN'T SEEN YOU IN A FEW DAYS, WORK HAS BEEN FUCKING INSANE.
I CAN ONLY IMAGINE. WHAT'S GOING ON?
THE CITY IS A MESS. NO ONE WAS PREPARED FOR THIS. RESOURCES ARE LIMITED AND SUPPLIES FOR THE ROCKAWAYS ARE GETTING HUNG UP BY BUREAUCRATIC BULLSHIT. I'M EXHAUSTED. I DON'T WANT TO TALK ABOUT IT ANYMORE. HOW HAVE THINGS BEEN HERE? HOW ARE YOU?
I'M FINE, IT'S BEEN PRETTY QUIET HERE. BUT I DO HAVE SOMETHING TO TALK TO YOU ABOUT. I KNOW THE TIMING IS ABSOLUTELY TERRIBLE, BUT IT CAN'T WAIT ANY LONGER.
SO, I...UH...OOF, I HAD THIS ALL PLANNED OUT AND NOW I CAN'T THINK OF A GOOD WAY TO DO IT, SO I'LL JUST COME OUT AND SAY IT.
I'VE BEEN SECRETLY ABUSING PRESCRIPTION PAINKILLERS FOR THE LAST FEW MONTHS. BUT I KNOW I HAVE TO STOP AND I HAVE TO COME CLEAN BECAUSE I CAN'T KEEP LYING TO YOU AND TO MY FAMILY AND MY FRIENDS. I THREW THE REMAINING PILLS AWAY AND I'M GOING BACK TO THERAPY. I'M REALLY SORRY THAT I'M DOING THIS RIGHT NOW WHEN THINGS ARE SO STRESSFUL FOR YOU. I KNOW IT'S SHITTY, BUT IT FEELS EVEN SHITTIER TO KEEP LYING TO YOU ABOUT IT.

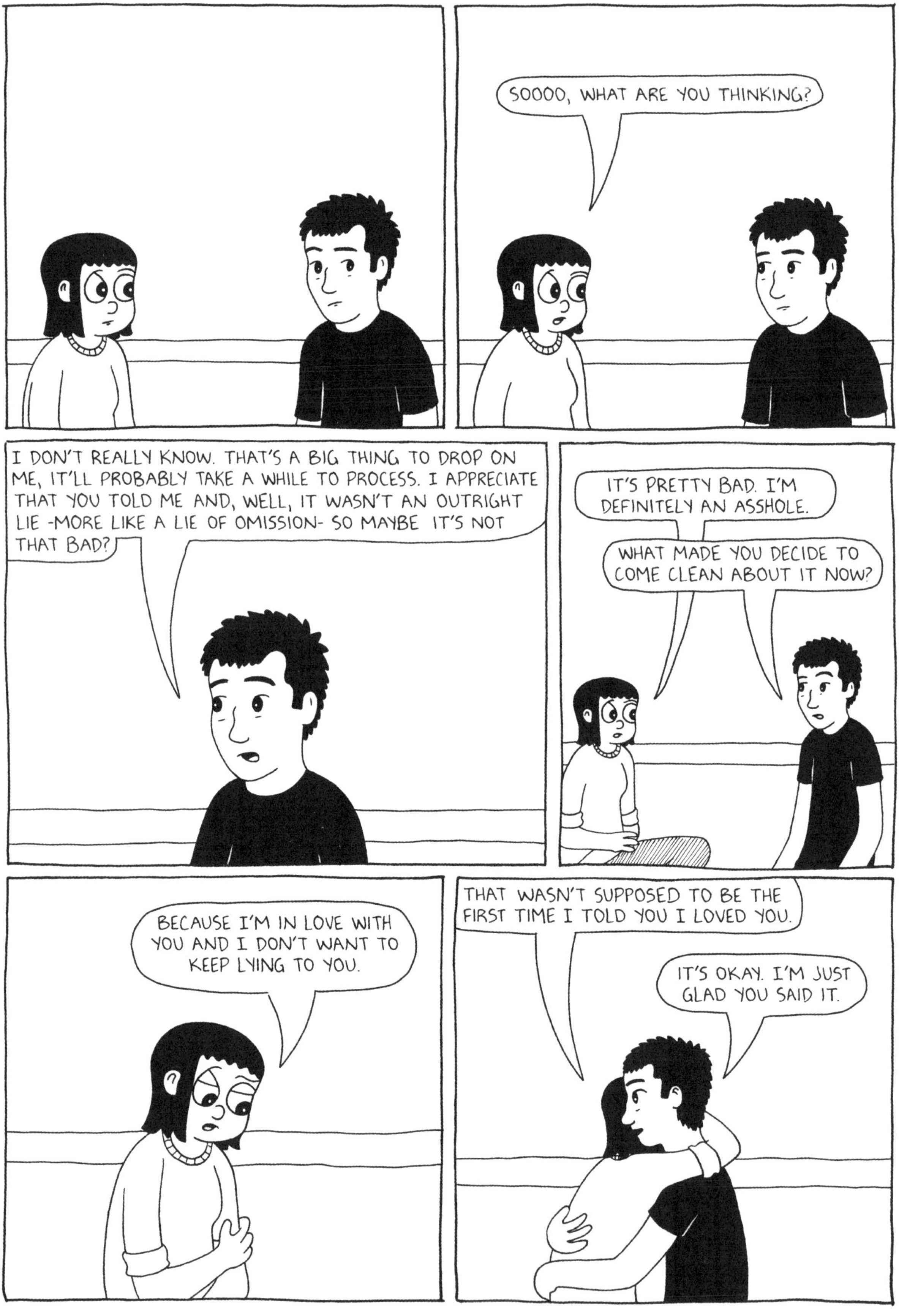
SOOOO, WHAT ARE YOU THINKING?
I DON'T REALLY KNOW. THAT'S A BIG THING TO DROP ON ME, IT'LL PROBABLY TAKE A WHILE TO PROCESS. I APPRECIATE THAT YOU TOLD ME AND, WELL, IT WASN'T AN OUTRIGHT LIE -MORE LIKE A LIE OF OMISSION- SO MAYBE IT'S NOT THAT BAD?
IT'S PRETTY BAD. I'M DEFINITELY AN ASSHOLE.
WHAT MADE YOU DECIDE TO COME CLEAN ABOUT IT NOW?
BECAUSE I'M IN LOVE WITH YOU AND I DON'T WANT TO KEEP LYING TO YOU.
THAT WASN'T SUPPOSED TO BE THE FIRST TIME I TOLD YOU I LOVED YOU.
IT'S OKAY. I'M JUST GLAD YOU SAID IT.

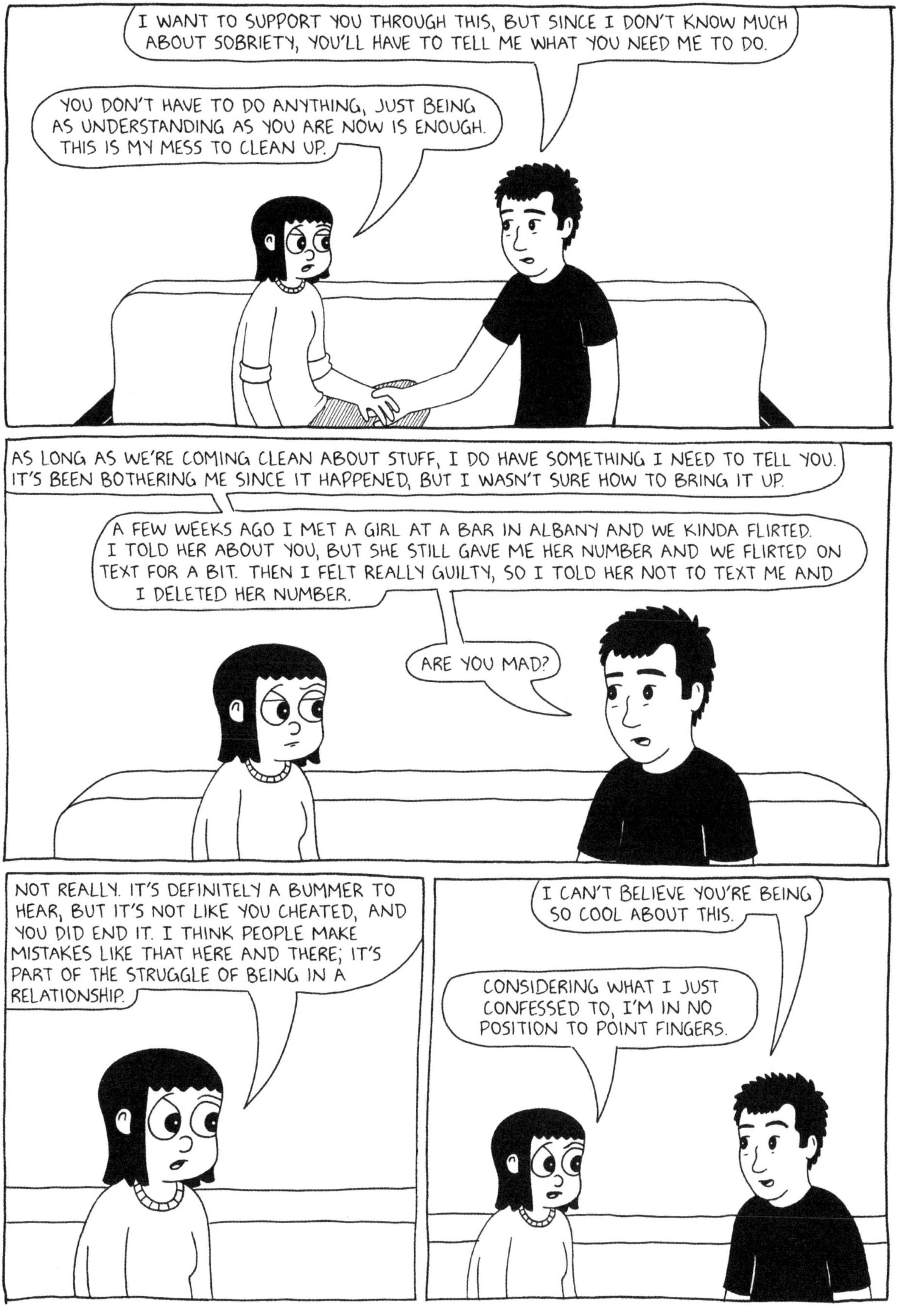
I WANT TO SUPPORT YOU THROUGH THIS, BUT SINCE I DON'T KNOW MUCH ABOUT SOBRIETY, YOU'LL HAVE TO TELL ME WHAT YOU NEED ME TO DO.
YOU DON'T HAVE TO DO ANYTHING, JUST BEING AS UNDERSTANDING AS YOU ARE NOW IS ENOUGH. THIS IS MY MESS TO CLEAN UP.
AS LONG AS WE'RE COMING CLEAN ABOUT STUFF, I DO HAVE SOMETHING I NEED TO TELL YOU. IT'S BEEN BOTHERING ME SINCE IT HAPPENED, BUT I WASN'T SURE HOW TO BRING IT UP.
A FEW WEEKS AGO I MET A GIRL AT A BAR IN ALBANY AND WE KINDA FLIRTED. I TOLD HER ABOUT YOU, BUT SHE STILL GAVE ME HER NUMBER AND WE FLIRTED ON TEXT FOR A BIT. THEN I FELT REALLY GUILTY, SO I TOLD HER NOT TO TEXT ME AND I DELETED HER NUMBER.
ARE YOU MAD?
NOT REALLY. IT'S DEFINITELY A BUMMER TO HEAR, BUT IT'S NOT LIKE YOU CHEATED, AND YOU DID END IT. I THINK PEOPLE MAKE MISTAKES LIKE THAT HERE AND THERE; IT'S PART OF THE STRUGGLE OF BEING IN A RELATIONSHIP.
I CAN'T BELIEVE YOU'RE BEING SO COOL ABOUT THIS.
CONSIDERING WHAT I JUST CONFESSED TO, I'M IN NO POSITION TO POINT FINGERS.

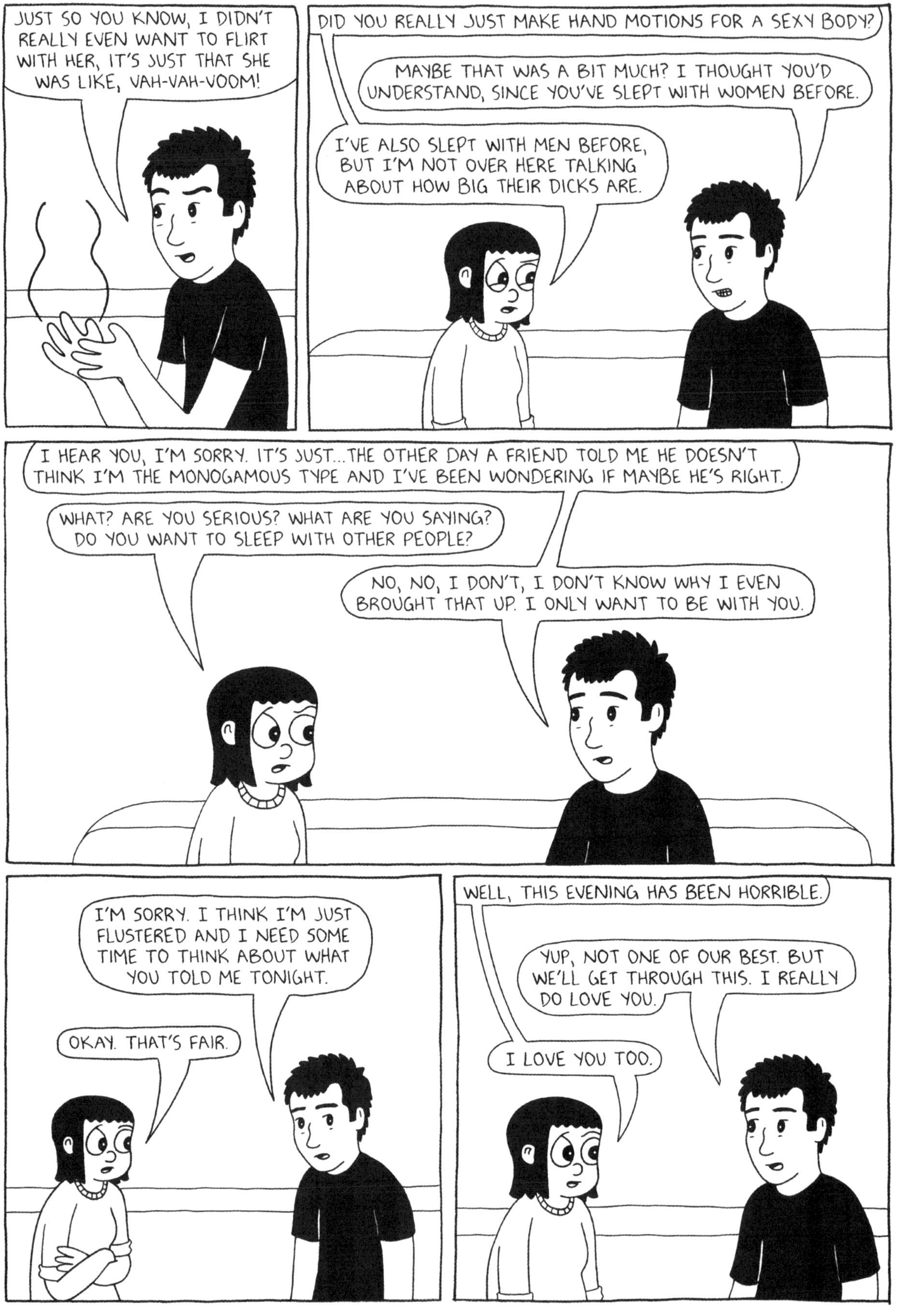
JUST SO YOU KNOW, I DIDN'T REALLY EVEN WANT TO FLIRT WITH HER, IT'S JUST THAT SHE WAS LIKE, VAH-VAH-VOOM!
DID YOU REALLY JUST MAKE HAND MOTIONS FOR A SEXY BODY?
MAYBE THAT WAS A BIT MUCH? I THOUGHT YOU'D UNDERSTAND, SINCE YOU'VE SLEPT WITH WOMEN BEFORE.
I'VE ALSO SLEPT WITH MEN BEFORE, BUT I'M NOT OVER HERE TALKING ABOUT HOW BIG THEIR DICKS ARE.
I HEAR YOU, I'M SORRY. IT'S JUST...THE OTHER DAY A FRIEND TOLD ME HE DOESN'T THINK I'M THE MONOGAMOUS TYPE AND I'VE BEEN WONDERING IF MAYBE HE'S RIGHT.
WHAT? ARE YOU SERIOUS? WHAT ARE YOU SAYING? DO YOU WANT TO SLEEP WITH OTHER PEOPLE?
NO, NO, I DON'T, I DON'T KNOW WHY I EVEN BROUGHT THAT UP. I ONLY WANT TO BE WITH YOU.
I'M SORRY. I THINK I'M JUST FLUSTERED AND I NEED SOME TIME TO THINK ABOUT WHAT YOU TOLD ME TONIGHT.
OKAY. THAT'S FAIR.
WELL, THIS EVENING HAS BEEN HORRIBLE.
YUP, NOT ONE OF OUR BEST. BUT WE'LL GET THROUGH THIS. I REALLY DO LOVE YOU.
I LOVE YOU TOO.

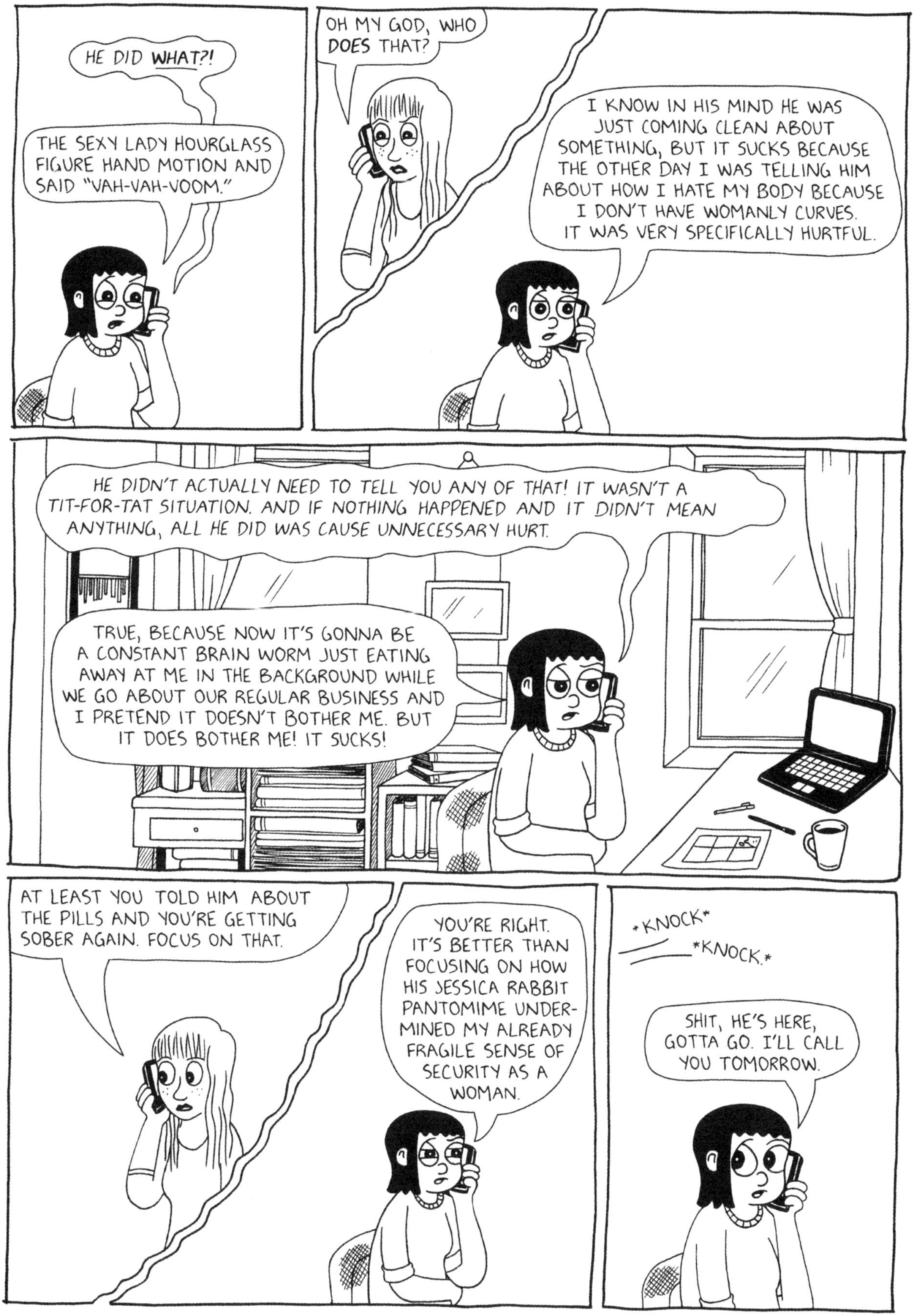
HE DID WHAT?!
THE SEXY LADY HOURGLASS FIGURE HAND MOTION AND SAID "VAH-VAH-VOOM."
OH MY GOD, WHO DOES THAT?
I KNOW IN HIS MIND HE WAS JUST COMING CLEAN ABOUT SOMETHING, BUT IT SUCKS BECAUSE THE OTHER DAY I WAS TELLING HIM ABOUT HOW I HATE MY BODY BECAUSE I DON'T HAVE WOMANLY CURVES. IT WAS VERY SPECIFICALLY HURTFUL.
HE DIDN'T ACTUALLY NEED TO TELL YOU ANY OF THAT! IT WASN'T A TIT-FOR-TAT SITUATION. AND IF NOTHING HAPPENED AND IT DIDN'T MEAN ANYTHING, ALL HE DID WAS CAUSE UNNECESSARY HURT.
TRUE, BECAUSE NOW IT'S GONNA BE A CONSTANT BRAIN WORM JUST EATING AWAY AT ME IN THE BACKGROUND WHILE WE GO ABOUT OUR REGULAR BUSINESS AND I PRETEND IT DOESN'T BOTHER ME. BUT IT DOES BOTHER ME! IT SUCKS!
AT LEAST YOU TOLD HIM ABOUT THE PILLS AND YOU'RE GETTING SOBER AGAIN. FOCUS ON THAT.
YOU'RE RIGHT. IT'S BETTER THAN FOCUSING ON HOW HIS JESSICA RABBIT PANTOMIME UNDERMINED MY ALREADY FRAGILE SENSE OF SECURITY AS A WOMAN.
KNOCK
KNOCK.
SHIT, HE'S HERE, GOTTA GO. I'LL CALL YOU TOMORROW.

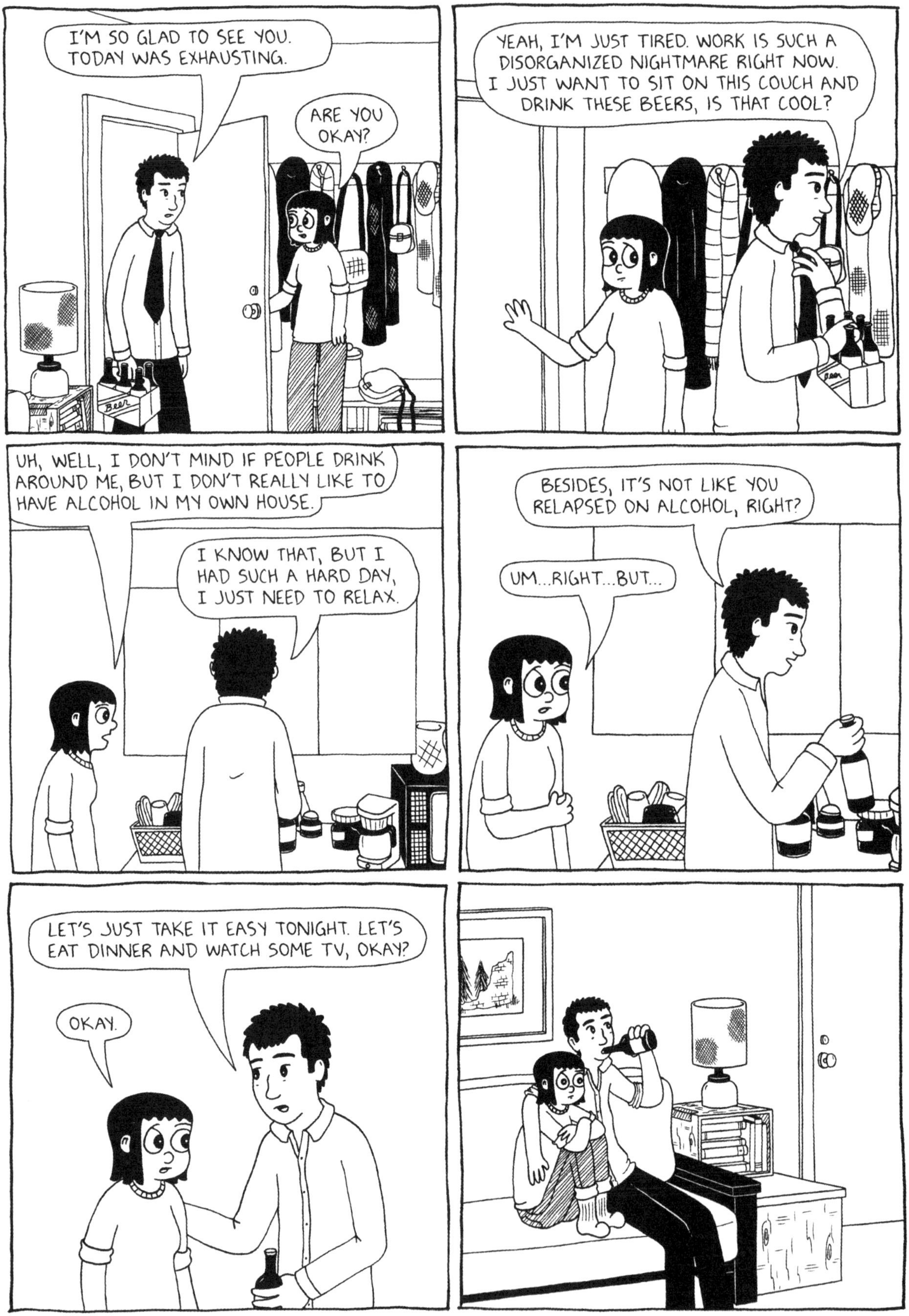
I'M SO GLAD TO SEE YOU. TODAY WAS EXHAUSTING.
ARE YOU OKAY?
YEAH, I'M JUST TIRED. WORK IS SUCH A DISORGANIZED NIGHTMARE RIGHT NOW. I JUST WANT TO SIT ON THIS COUCH AND DRINK THESE BEERS, IS THAT COOL?
UH, WELL, I DON'T MIND IF PEOPLE DRINK AROUND ME, BUT I DON'T REALLY LIKE TO HAVE ALCOHOL IN MY OWN HOUSE.
I KNOW THAT, BUT I HAD SUCH A HARD DAY, I JUST NEED TO RELAX.
BESIDES, IT'S NOT LIKE YOU RELAPSED ON ALCOHOL, RIGHT?
UM...RIGHT...BUT...
LET'S JUST TAKE IT EASY TONIGHT. LET'S EAT DINNER AND WATCH SOME TV, OKAY?
OKAY.

A FEW DAYS LATER, I HAD A BOOK RELEASE PARTY FOR *THE INFINITE WAIT & OTHER STORIES* AT DESERT ISLAND.

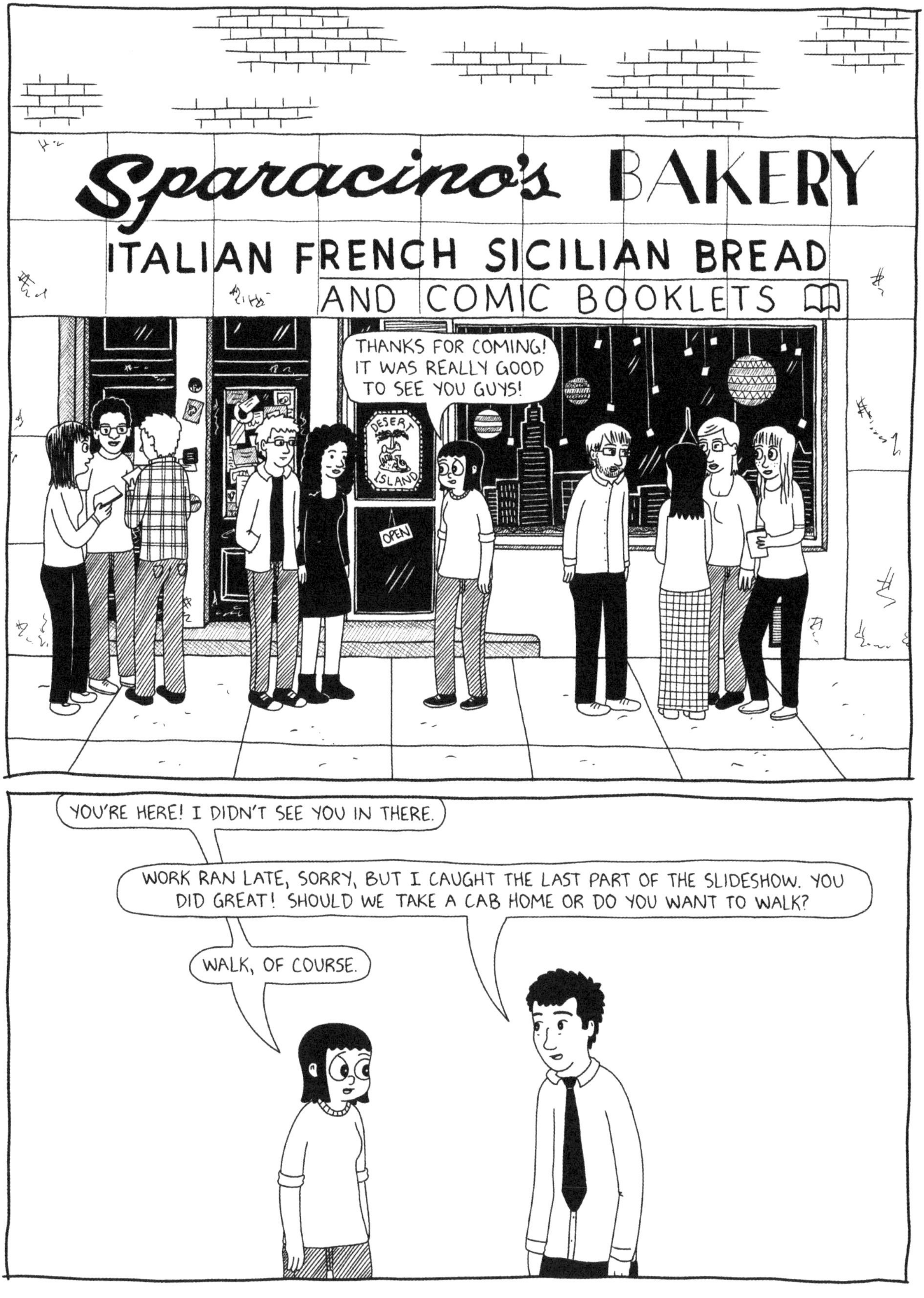
Sparacino's BAKERY
ITALIAN FRENCH SICILIAN BREAD
AND COMIC BOOKLETS
THANKS FOR COMING! IT WAS REALLY GOOD TO SEE YOU GUYS!
DESERT ISLAND
OPEN
YOU'RE HERE! I DIDN'T SEE YOU IN THERE.
WORK RAN LATE, SORRY, BUT I CAUGHT THE LAST PART OF THE SLIDESHOW. YOU DID GREAT! SHOULD WE TAKE A CAB HOME OR DO YOU WANT TO WALK?
WALK, OF COURSE.

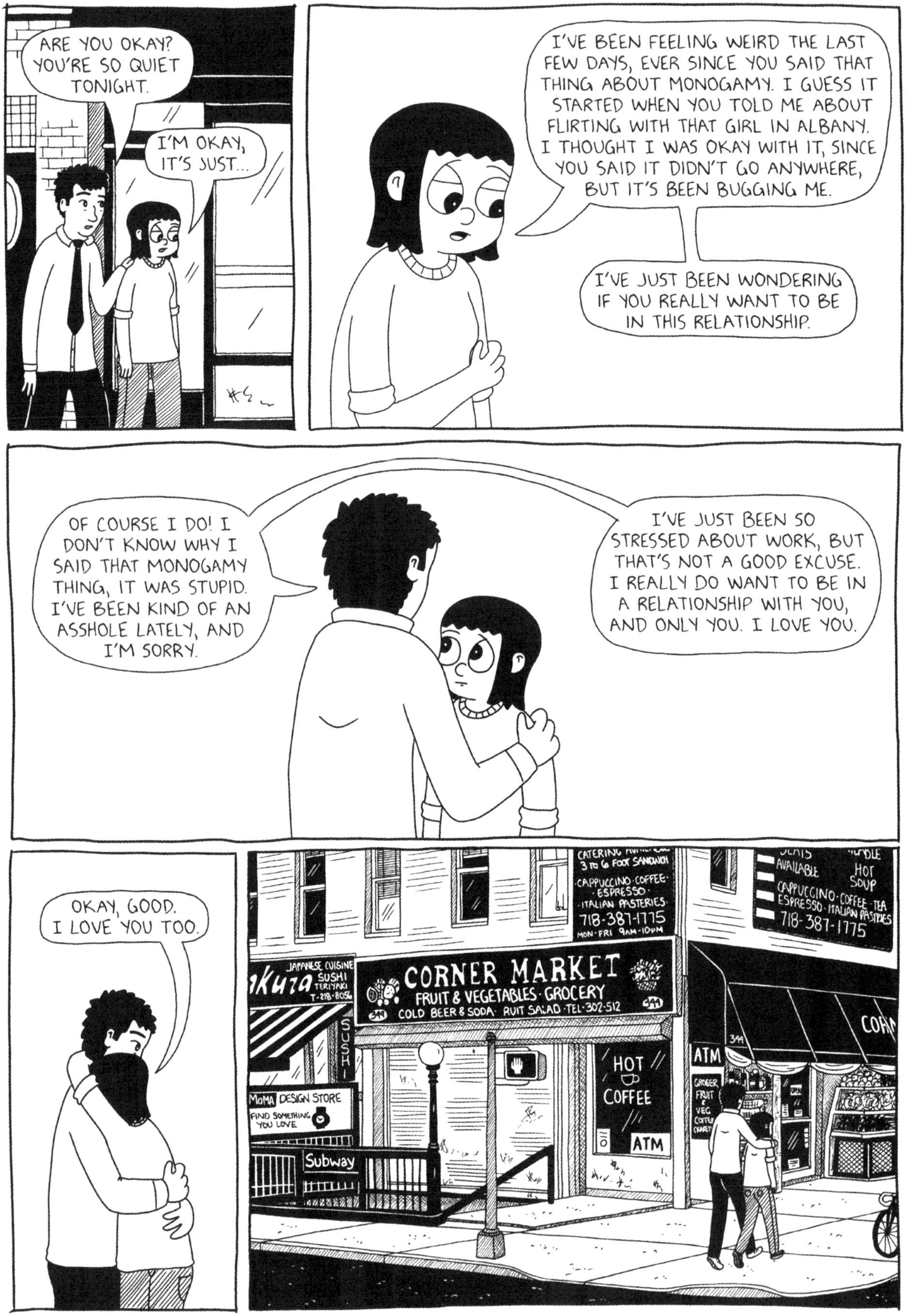
ARE YOU OKAY? YOU'RE SO QUIET TONIGHT.
I'M OKAY, IT'S JUST...
I'VE BEEN FEELING WEIRD THE LAST FEW DAYS, EVER SINCE YOU SAID THAT THING ABOUT MONOGAMY. I GUESS IT STARTED WHEN YOU TOLD ME ABOUT FLIRTING WITH THAT GIRL IN ALBANY. I THOUGHT I WAS OKAY WITH IT, SINCE YOU SAID IT DIDN'T GO ANYWHERE, BUT IT'S BEEN BUGGING ME.
I'VE JUST BEEN WONDERING IF YOU REALLY WANT TO BE IN THIS RELATIONSHIP.
OF COURSE I DO! I DON'T KNOW WHY I SAID THAT MONOGAMY THING, IT WAS STUPID. I'VE BEEN KIND OF AN ASSHOLE LATELY, AND I'M SORRY.
I'VE JUST BEEN SO STRESSED ABOUT WORK, BUT THAT'S NOT A GOOD EXCUSE. I REALLY DO WANT TO BE IN A RELATIONSHIP WITH YOU, AND ONLY YOU. I LOVE YOU.
OKAY, GOOD. I LOVE YOU TOO.
3 TO 6 FOOT SANDWICH
CAPPUCCINO · COFFEE · ESPRESSO · ITALIAN PASTERIES
718-387-1775
MON-FRI 9AM-10PM
AVAILABLE
HOT SOUP
CAPPUCCINO · COFFEE · TEA ESPRESSO · ITALIAN PASTRIES
718-387-1775
JAPANESE CUISINE SUSHI TERIYAKI
CORNER MARKET
FRUIT & VEGETABLES · GROCERY
COLD BEER & SODA · RUIT SALAD · TEL · 302-512
SUSHI
HOT COFFEE
ATM
ATM
MoMA DESIGN STORE
FIND SOMETHING YOU LOVE
Subway

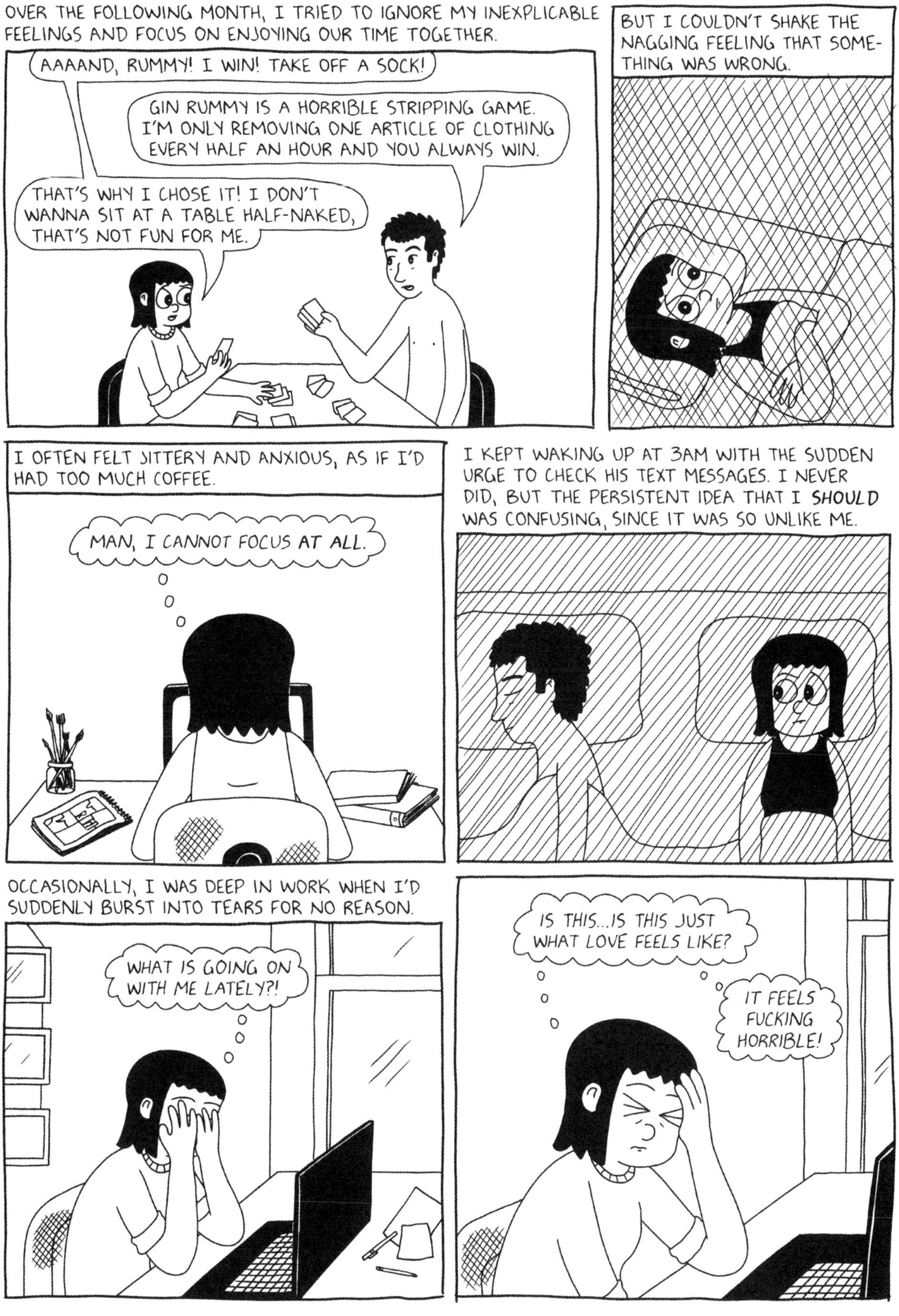
OVER THE FOLLOWING MONTH, I TRIED TO IGNORE MY INEXPLICABLE FEELINGS AND FOCUS ON ENJOYING OUR TIME TOGETHER.
AAAAND, RUMMY! I WIN! TAKE OFF A SOCK!
GIN RUMMY IS A HORRIBLE STRIPPING GAME. I'M ONLY REMOVING ONE ARTICLE OF CLOTHING EVERY HALF AN HOUR AND YOU ALWAYS WIN.
THAT'S WHY I CHOSE IT! I DON'T WANNA SIT AT A TABLE HALF-NAKED, THAT'S NOT FUN FOR ME.
BUT I COULDN'T SHAKE THE NAGGING FEELING THAT SOMETHING WAS WRONG.
I OFTEN FELT JITTERY AND ANXIOUS, AS IF I'D HAD TOO MUCH COFFEE.
MAN, I CANNOT FOCUS AT ALL.
I KEPT WAKING UP AT 3AM WITH THE SUDDEN URGE TO CHECK HIS TEXT MESSAGES. I NEVER DID, BUT THE PERSISTENT IDEA THAT I SHOULD WAS CONFUSING, SINCE IT WAS SO UNLIKE ME.
OCCASIONALLY, I WAS DEEP IN WORK WHEN I'D SUDDENLY BURST INTO TEARS FOR NO REASON.
WHAT IS GOING ON WITH ME LATELY?!
IS THIS...IS THIS JUST WHAT LOVE FEELS LIKE?
IT FEELS FUCKING HORRIBLE!

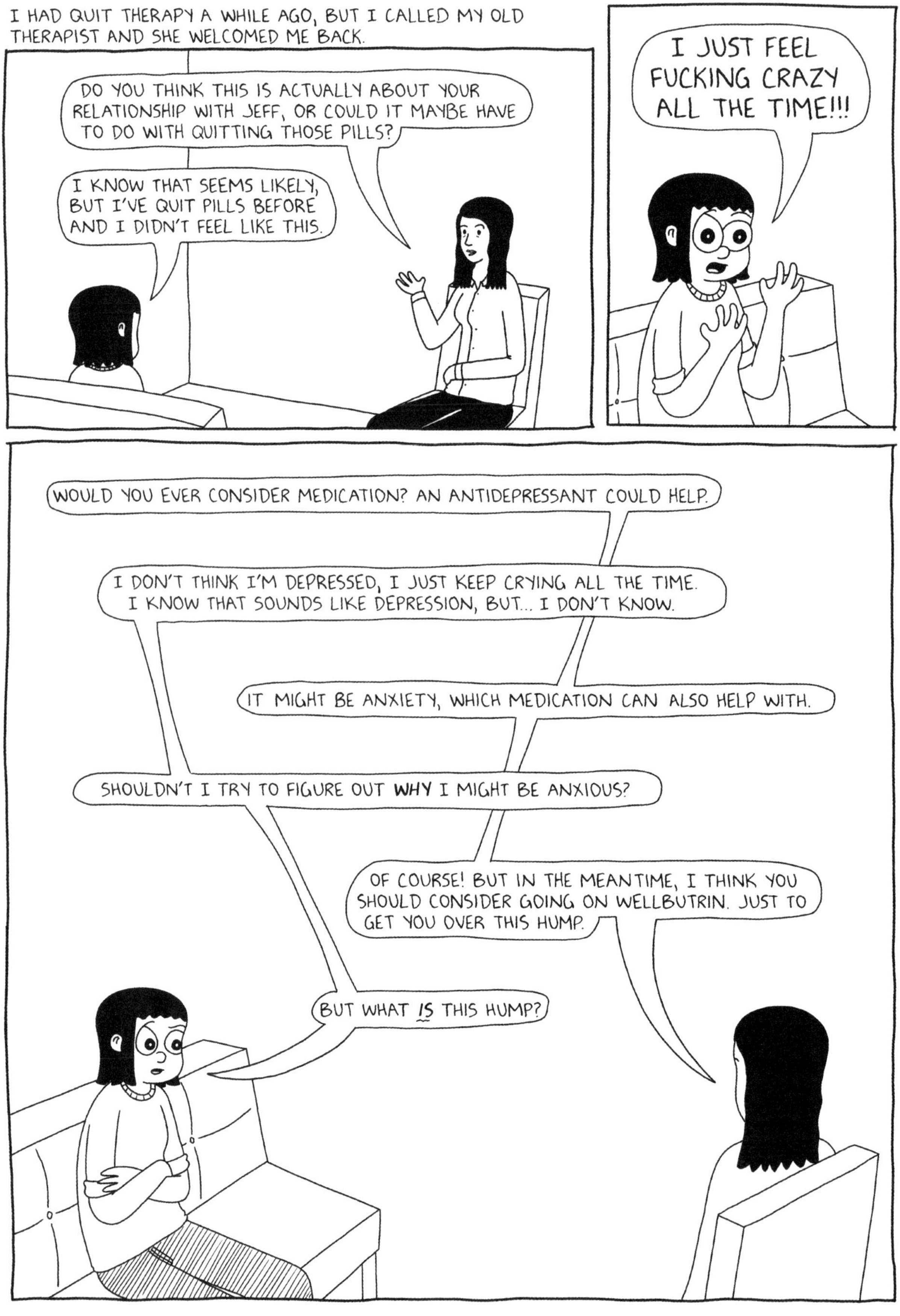
I HAD QUIT THERAPY A WHILE AGO, BUT I CALLED MY OLD THERAPIST AND SHE WELCOMED ME BACK.
DO YOU THINK THIS IS ACTUALLY ABOUT YOUR RELATIONSHIP WITH JEFF, OR COULD IT MAYBE HAVE TO DO WITH QUITTING THOSE PILLS?
I KNOW THAT SEEMS LIKELY, BUT I'VE QUIT PILLS BEFORE AND I DIDN'T FEEL LIKE THIS.
I JUST FEEL FUCKING CRAZY ALL THE TIME!!!
WOULD YOU EVER CONSIDER MEDICATION? AN ANTIDEPRESSANT COULD HELP.
I DON'T THINK I'M DEPRESSED, I JUST KEEP CRYING ALL THE TIME. I KNOW THAT SOUNDS LIKE DEPRESSION, BUT... I DON'T KNOW.
IT MIGHT BE ANXIETY, WHICH MEDICATION CAN ALSO HELP WITH.
SHOULDN'T I TRY TO FIGURE OUT **WHY** I MIGHT BE ANXIOUS?
OF COURSE! BUT IN THE MEANTIME, I THINK YOU SHOULD CONSIDER GOING ON WELLBUTRIN. JUST TO GET YOU OVER THIS HUMP.
BUT WHAT IS THIS HUMP?

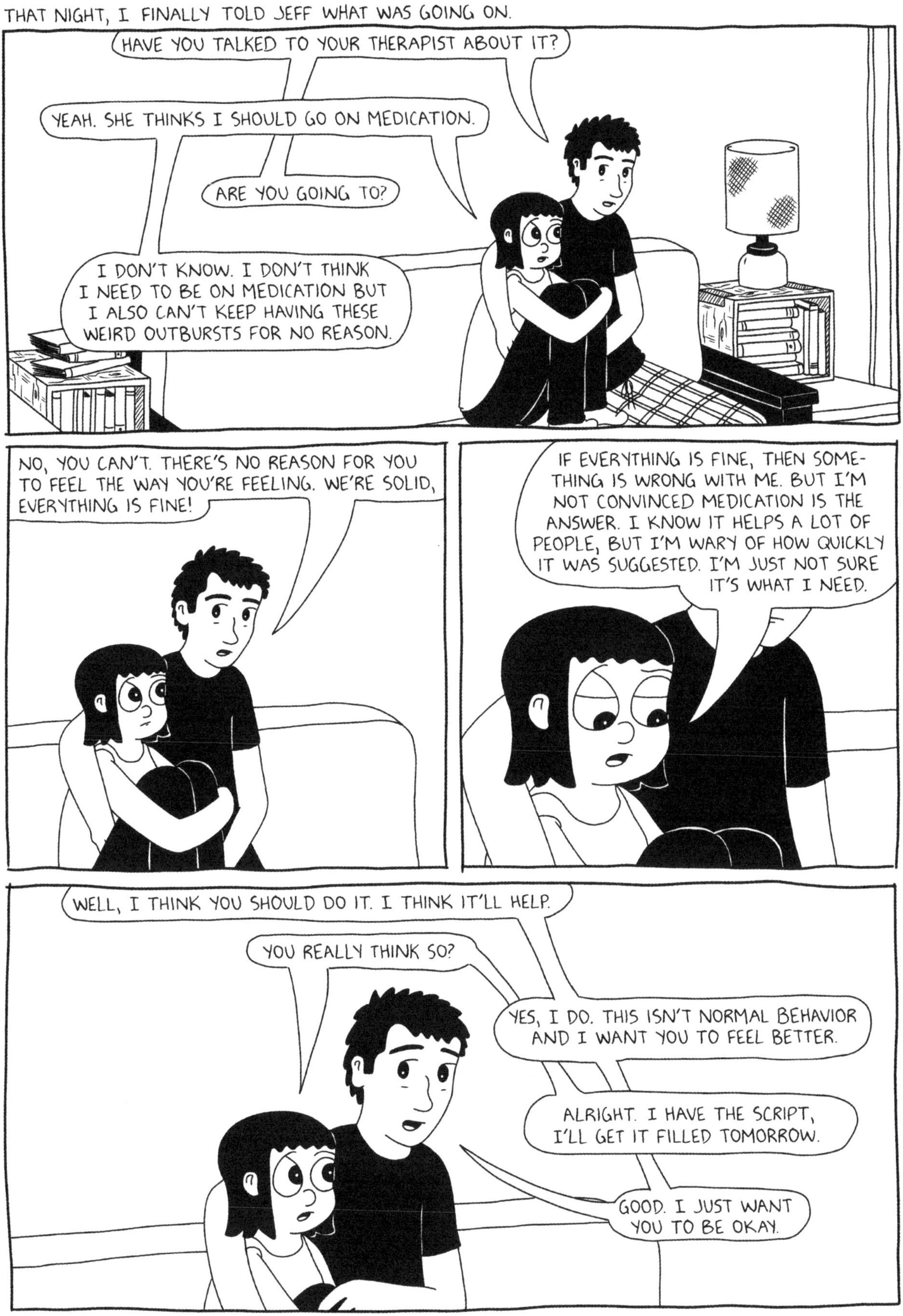
THAT NIGHT, I FINALLY TOLD JEFF WHAT WAS GOING ON.
HAVE YOU TALKED TO YOUR THERAPIST ABOUT IT?
YEAH. SHE THINKS I SHOULD GO ON MEDICATION.
ARE YOU GOING TO?
I DON'T KNOW. I DON'T THINK I NEED TO BE ON MEDICATION BUT I ALSO CAN'T KEEP HAVING THESE WEIRD OUTBURSTS FOR NO REASON.
NO, YOU CAN'T. THERE'S NO REASON FOR YOU TO FEEL THE WAY YOU'RE FEELING. WE'RE SOLID, EVERYTHING IS FINE!
IF EVERYTHING IS FINE, THEN SOMETHING IS WRONG WITH ME. BUT I'M NOT CONVINCED MEDICATION IS THE ANSWER. I KNOW IT HELPS A LOT OF PEOPLE, BUT I'M WARY OF HOW QUICKLY IT WAS SUGGESTED. I'M JUST NOT SURE IT'S WHAT I NEED.
WELL, I THINK YOU SHOULD DO IT. I THINK IT'LL HELP.
YOU REALLY THINK SO?
YES, I DO. THIS ISN'T NORMAL BEHAVIOR AND I WANT YOU TO FEEL BETTER.
ALRIGHT. I HAVE THE SCRIPT, I'LL GET IT FILLED TOMORROW.
GOOD. I JUST WANT YOU TO BE OKAY.

A FEW WEEKS LATER:

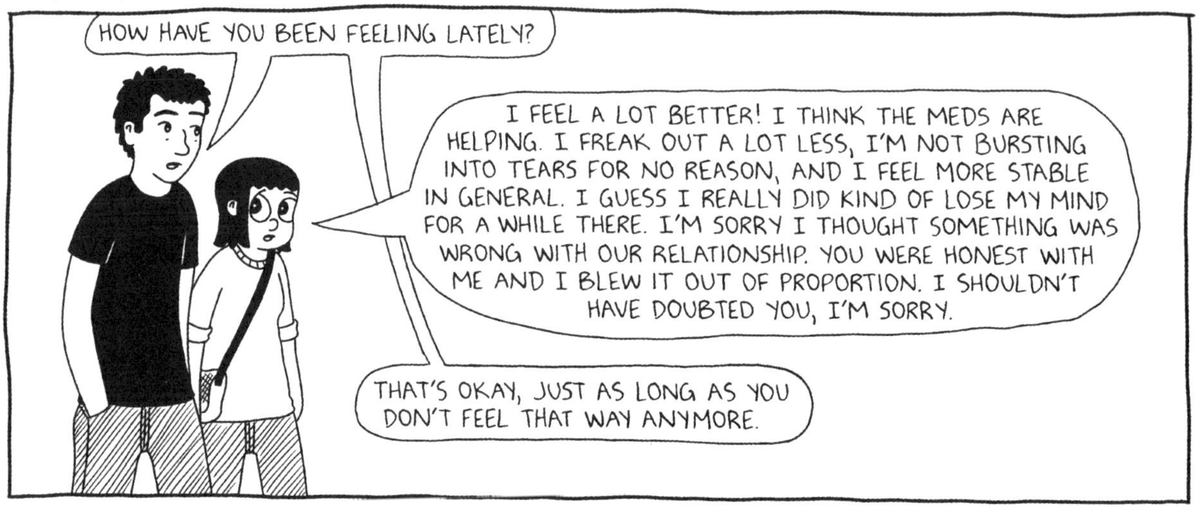

HOW HAVE YOU BEEN FEELING LATELY?
I FEEL A LOT BETTER! I THINK THE MEDS ARE HELPING. I FREAK OUT A LOT LESS, I'M NOT BURSTING INTO TEARS FOR NO REASON, AND I FEEL MORE STABLE IN GENERAL. I GUESS I REALLY DID KIND OF LOSE MY MIND FOR A WHILE THERE. I'M SORRY I THOUGHT SOMETHING WAS WRONG WITH OUR RELATIONSHIP. YOU WERE HONEST WITH ME AND I BLEW IT OUT OF PROPORTION. I SHOULDN'T HAVE DOUBTED YOU, I'M SORRY.
THAT'S OKAY, JUST AS LONG AS YOU DON'T FEEL THAT WAY ANYMORE.

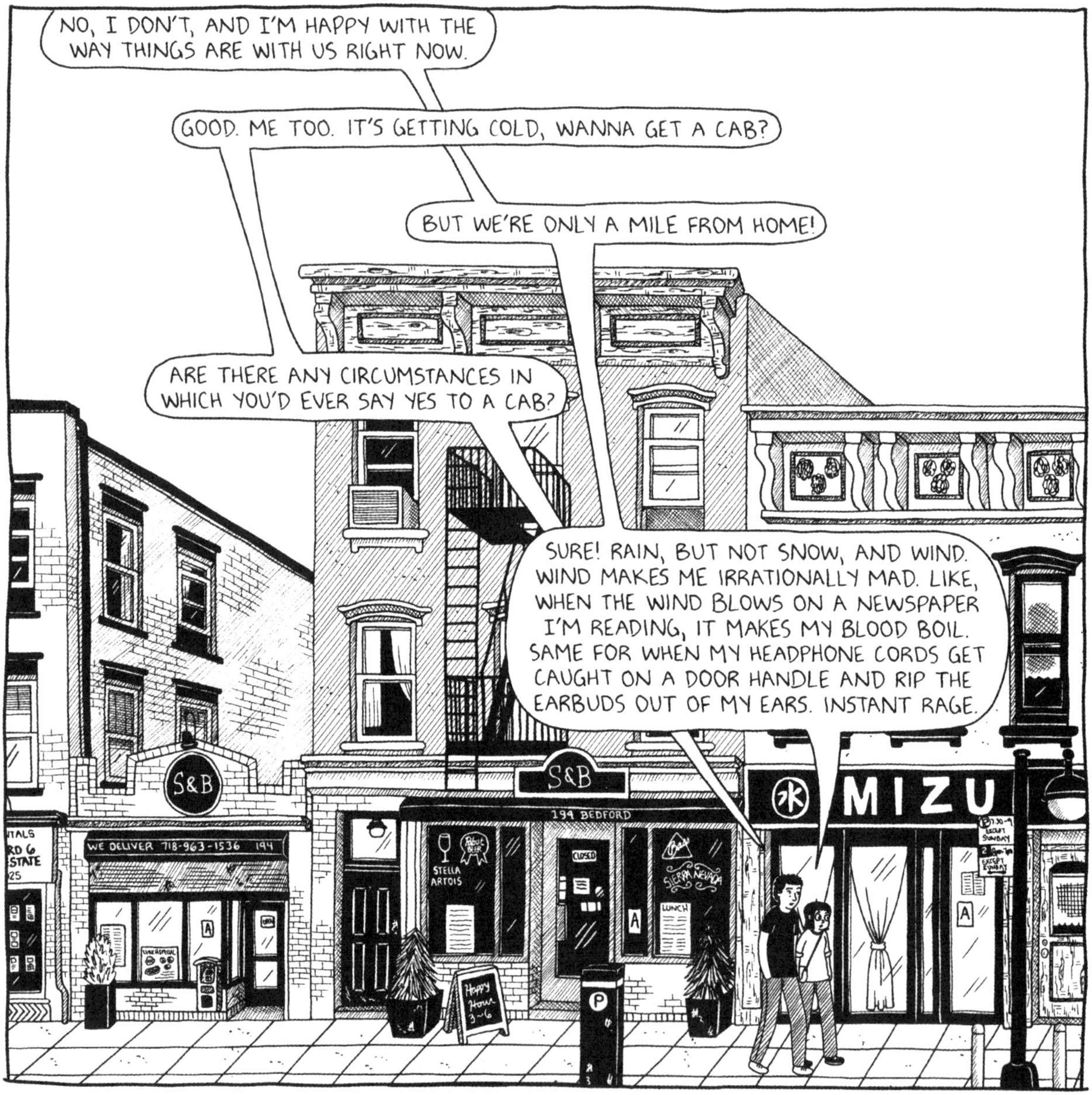

NO, I DON'T, AND I'M HAPPY WITH THE WAY THINGS ARE WITH US RIGHT NOW.
GOOD. ME TOO. IT'S GETTING COLD, WANNA GET A CAB?
BUT WE'RE ONLY A MILE FROM HOME!
ARE THERE ANY CIRCUMSTANCES IN WHICH YOU'D EVER SAY YES TO A CAB?
SURE! RAIN, BUT NOT SNOW, AND WIND. WIND MAKES ME IRRATIONALLY MAD. LIKE, WHEN THE WIND BLOWS ON A NEWSPAPER I'M READING, IT MAKES MY BLOOD BOIL. SAME FOR WHEN MY HEADPHONE CORDS GET CAUGHT ON A DOOR HANDLE AND RIP THE EARBUDS OUT OF MY EARS. INSTANT RAGE.
S&B
WE DELIVER 718-963-1536 194
S&B
194 BEDFORD
STELLA ARTOIS
CLOSED
SIERRA NEVADA
LUNCH
Happy Hour 3~6
MIZU

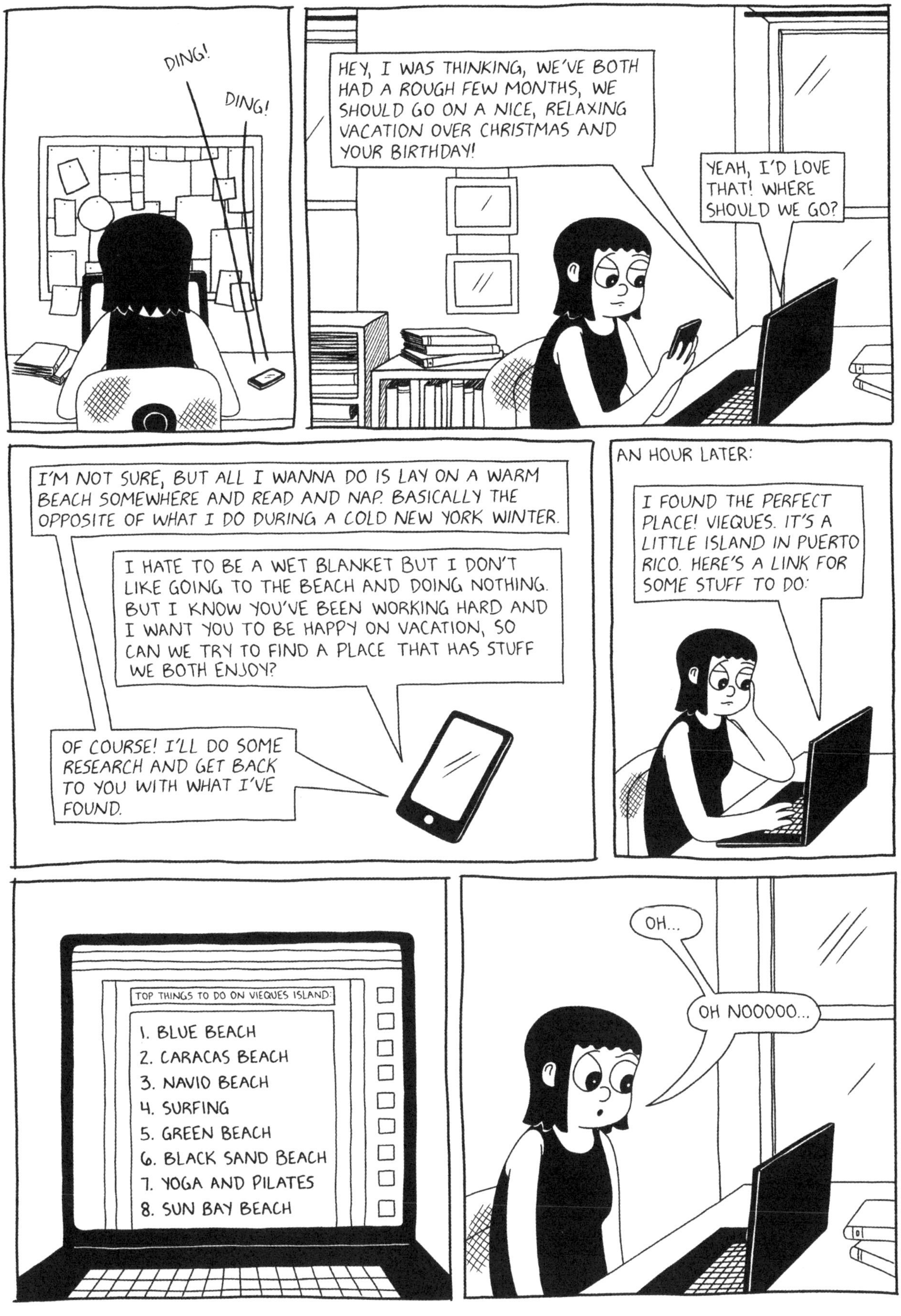
DING!
DING!
HEY, I WAS THINKING, WE'VE BOTH HAD A ROUGH FEW MONTHS, WE SHOULD GO ON A NICE, RELAXING VACATION OVER CHRISTMAS AND YOUR BIRTHDAY!
YEAH, I'D LOVE THAT! WHERE SHOULD WE GO?
I'M NOT SURE, BUT ALL I WANNA DO IS LAY ON A WARM BEACH SOMEWHERE AND READ AND NAP. BASICALLY THE OPPOSITE OF WHAT I DO DURING A COLD NEW YORK WINTER.
I HATE TO BE A WET BLANKET BUT I DON'T LIKE GOING TO THE BEACH AND DOING NOTHING. BUT I KNOW YOU'VE BEEN WORKING HARD AND I WANT YOU TO BE HAPPY ON VACATION, SO CAN WE TRY TO FIND A PLACE THAT HAS STUFF WE BOTH ENJOY?
OF COURSE! I'LL DO SOME RESEARCH AND GET BACK TO YOU WITH WHAT I'VE FOUND.
AN HOUR LATER:
I FOUND THE PERFECT PLACE! VIEQUES. IT'S A LITTLE ISLAND IN PUERTO RICO. HERE'S A LINK FOR SOME STUFF TO DO:
TOP THINGS TO DO ON VIEQUES ISLAND:
1. BLUE BEACH
2. CARACAS BEACH
3. NAVIO BEACH
4. SURFING
5. GREEN BEACH
6. BLACK SAND BEACH
7. YOGA AND PILATES
8. SUN BAY BEACH
OH...
OH NOOOOO...

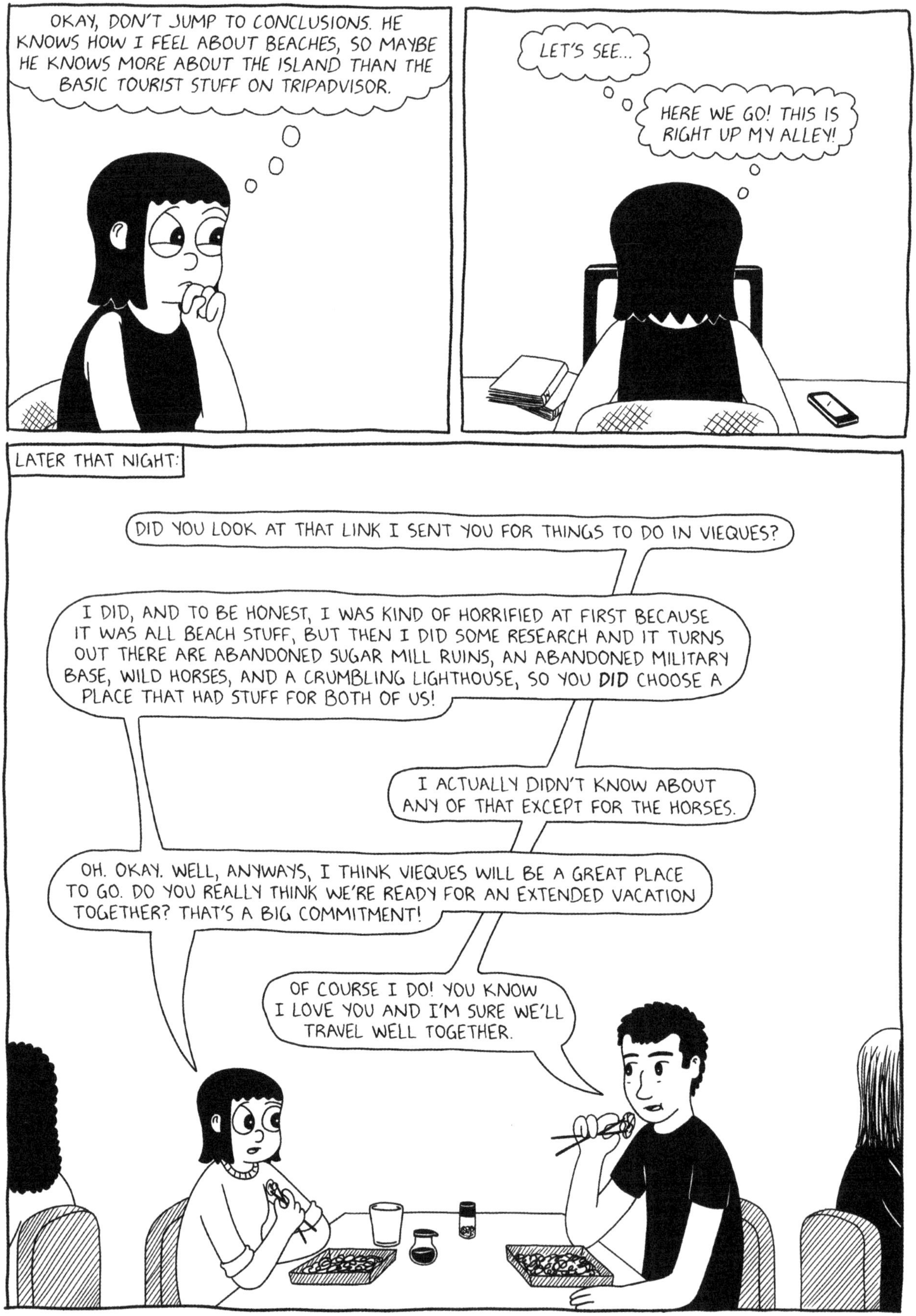
OKAY, DON'T JUMP TO CONCLUSIONS. HE KNOWS HOW I FEEL ABOUT BEACHES, SO MAYBE HE KNOWS MORE ABOUT THE ISLAND THAN THE BASIC TOURIST STUFF ON TRIPADVISOR.
LET'S SEE...
HERE WE GO! THIS IS RIGHT UP MY ALLEY!
LATER THAT NIGHT:
DID YOU LOOK AT THAT LINK I SENT YOU FOR THINGS TO DO IN VIEQUES?
I DID, AND TO BE HONEST, I WAS KIND OF HORRIFIED AT FIRST BECAUSE IT WAS ALL BEACH STUFF, BUT THEN I DID SOME RESEARCH AND IT TURNS OUT THERE ARE ABANDONED SUGAR MILL RUINS, AN ABANDONED MILITARY BASE, WILD HORSES, AND A CRUMBLING LIGHTHOUSE, SO YOU **DID** CHOOSE A PLACE THAT HAD STUFF FOR BOTH OF US!
I ACTUALLY DIDN'T KNOW ABOUT ANY OF THAT EXCEPT FOR THE HORSES.
OH. OKAY. WELL, ANYWAYS, I THINK VIEQUES WILL BE A GREAT PLACE TO GO. DO YOU REALLY THINK WE'RE READY FOR AN EXTENDED VACATION TOGETHER? THAT'S A BIG COMMITMENT!
OF COURSE I DO! YOU KNOW I LOVE YOU AND I'M SURE WE'LL TRAVEL WELL TOGETHER.

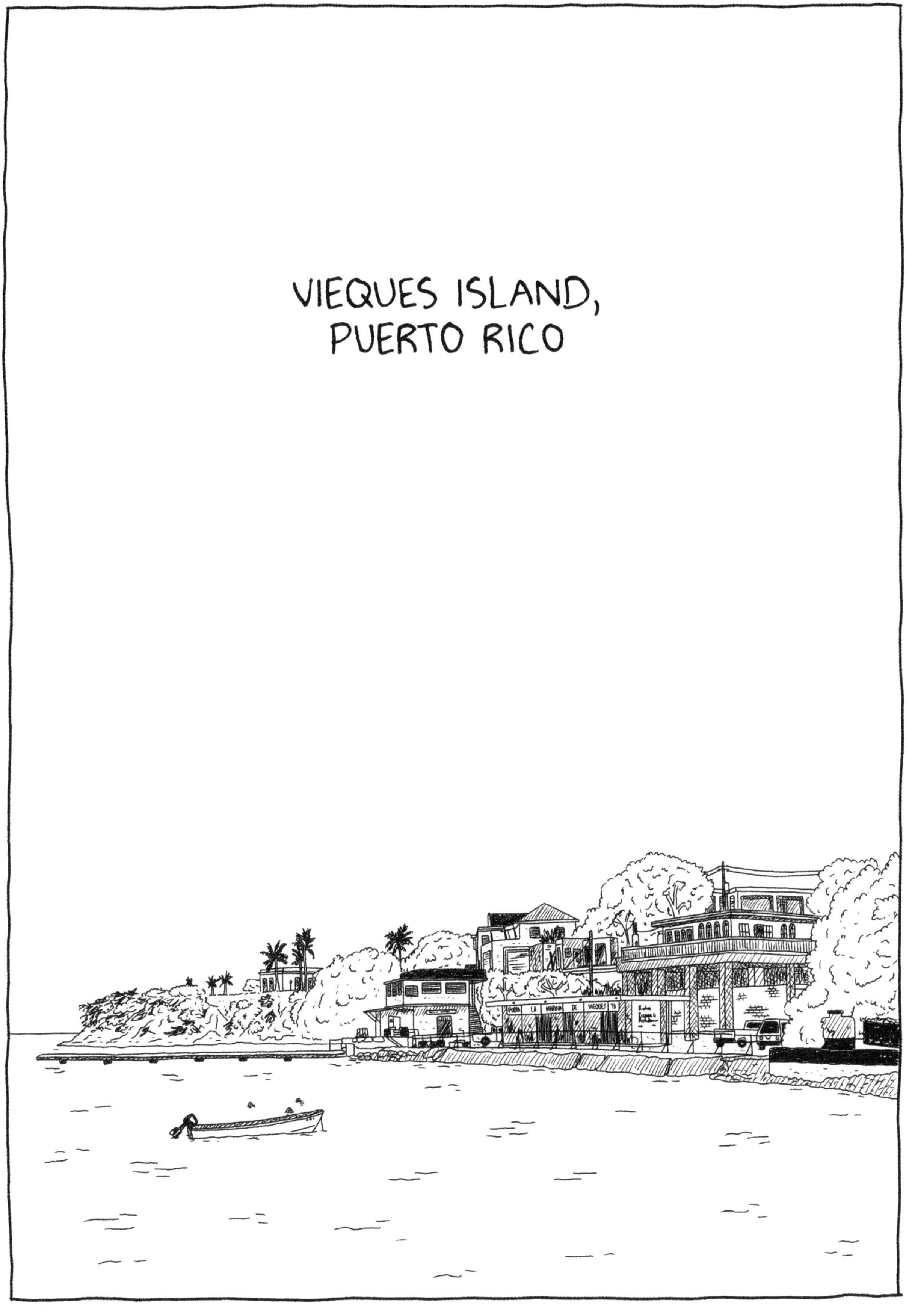
VIEQUES ISLAND,
PUERTO RICO
FUERA LA MARINA DE VIEQUES YA

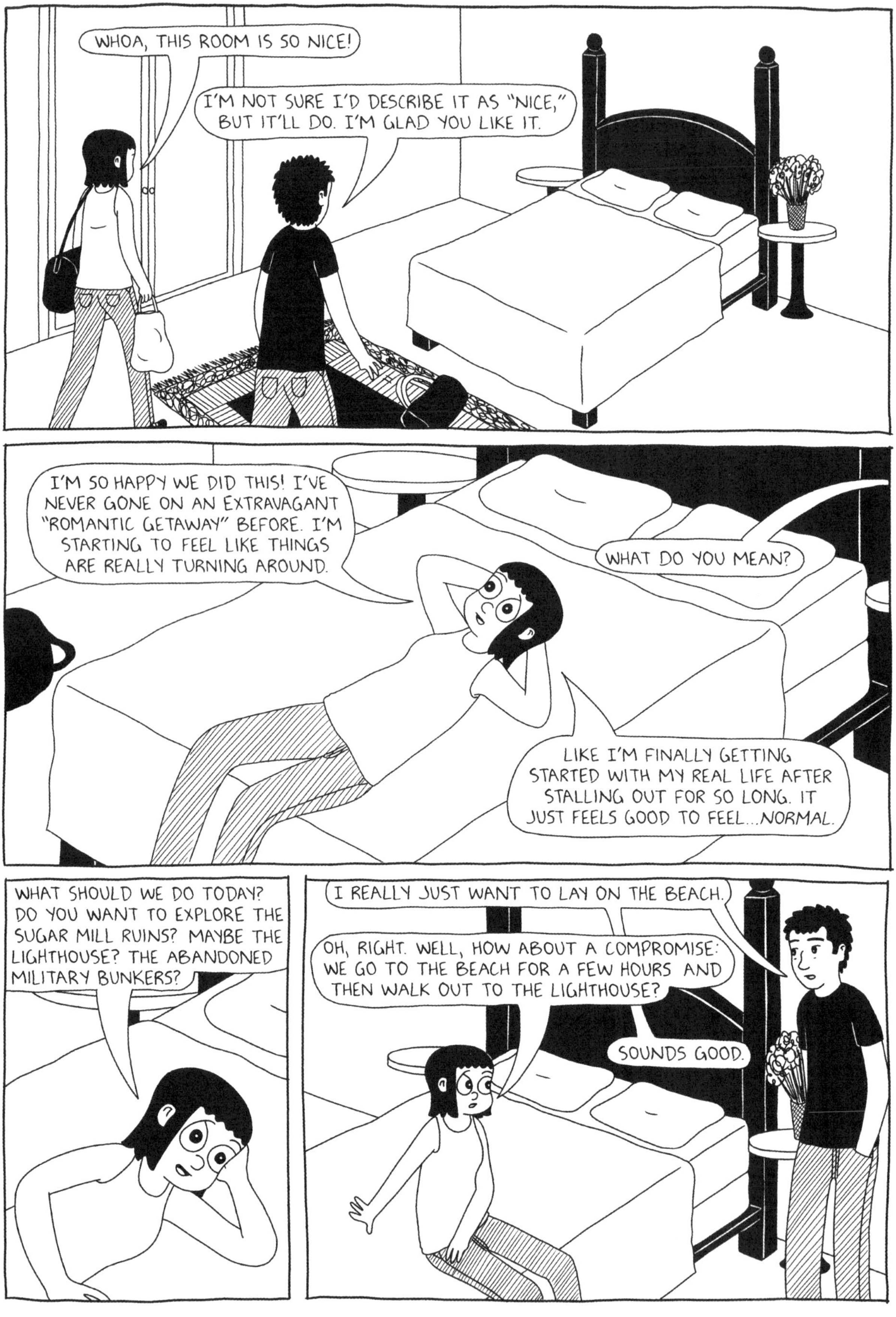
WHOA, THIS ROOM IS SO NICE!
I'M NOT SURE I'D DESCRIBE IT AS "NICE," BUT IT'LL DO. I'M GLAD YOU LIKE IT.
I'M SO HAPPY WE DID THIS! I'VE NEVER GONE ON AN EXTRAVAGANT "ROMANTIC GETAWAY" BEFORE. I'M STARTING TO FEEL LIKE THINGS ARE REALLY TURNING AROUND.
WHAT DO YOU MEAN?
LIKE I'M FINALLY GETTING STARTED WITH MY REAL LIFE AFTER STALLING OUT FOR SO LONG. IT JUST FEELS GOOD TO FEEL...NORMAL.
WHAT SHOULD WE DO TODAY? DO YOU WANT TO EXPLORE THE SUGAR MILL RUINS? MAYBE THE LIGHTHOUSE? THE ABANDONED MILITARY BUNKERS?
I REALLY JUST WANT TO LAY ON THE BEACH.
OH, RIGHT. WELL, HOW ABOUT A COMPROMISE: WE GO TO THE BEACH FOR A FEW HOURS AND THEN WALK OUT TO THE LIGHTHOUSE?
SOUNDS GOOD.

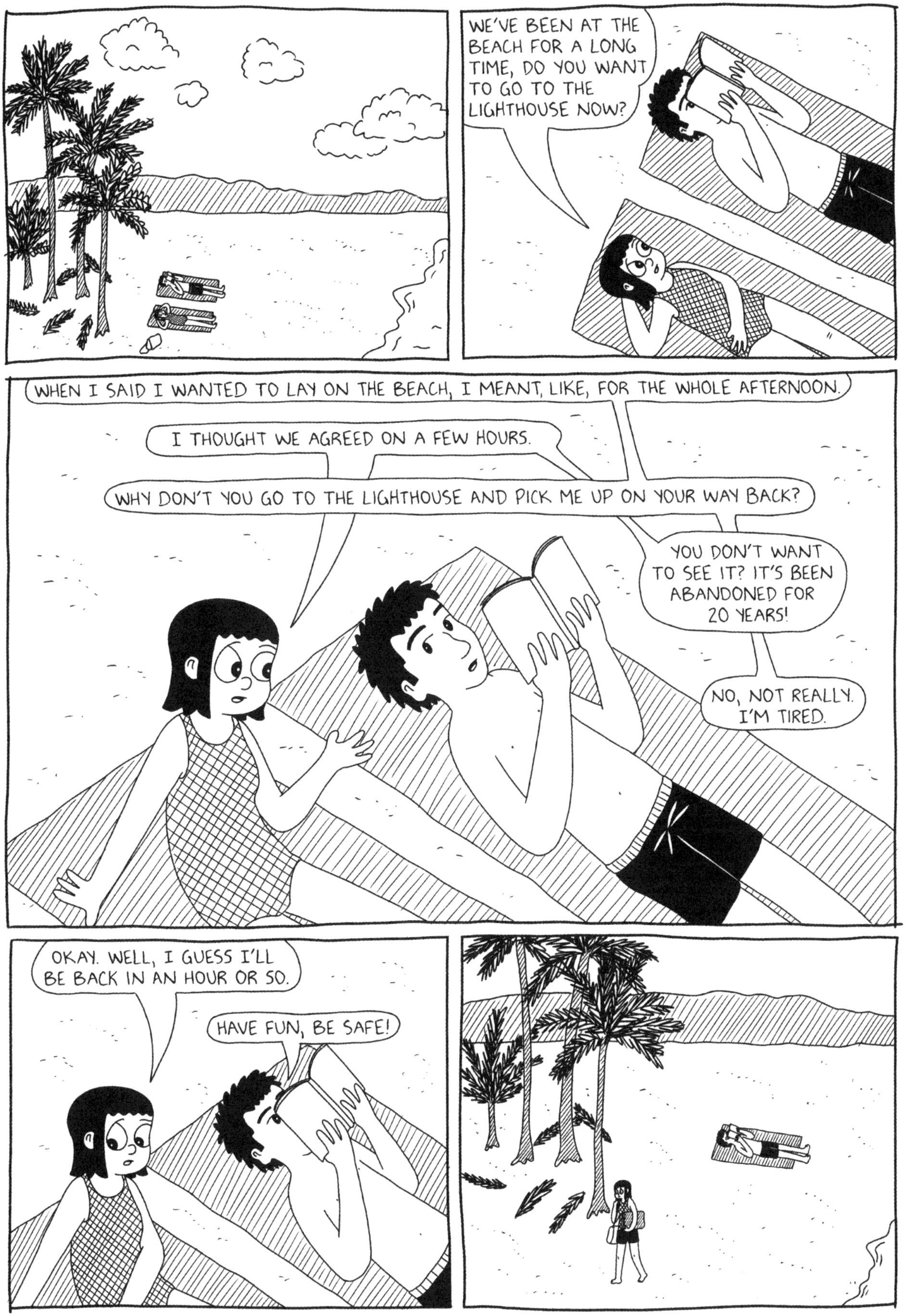
WE'VE BEEN AT THE BEACH FOR A LONG TIME, DO YOU WANT TO GO TO THE LIGHTHOUSE NOW?
WHEN I SAID I WANTED TO LAY ON THE BEACH, I MEANT, LIKE, FOR THE WHOLE AFTERNOON.
I THOUGHT WE AGREED ON A FEW HOURS.
WHY DON'T YOU GO TO THE LIGHTHOUSE AND PICK ME UP ON YOUR WAY BACK?
YOU DON'T WANT TO SEE IT? IT'S BEEN ABANDONED FOR 20 YEARS!
NO, NOT REALLY. I'M TIRED.
OKAY. WELL, I GUESS I'LL BE BACK IN AN HOUR OR SO.
HAVE FUN, BE SAFE!

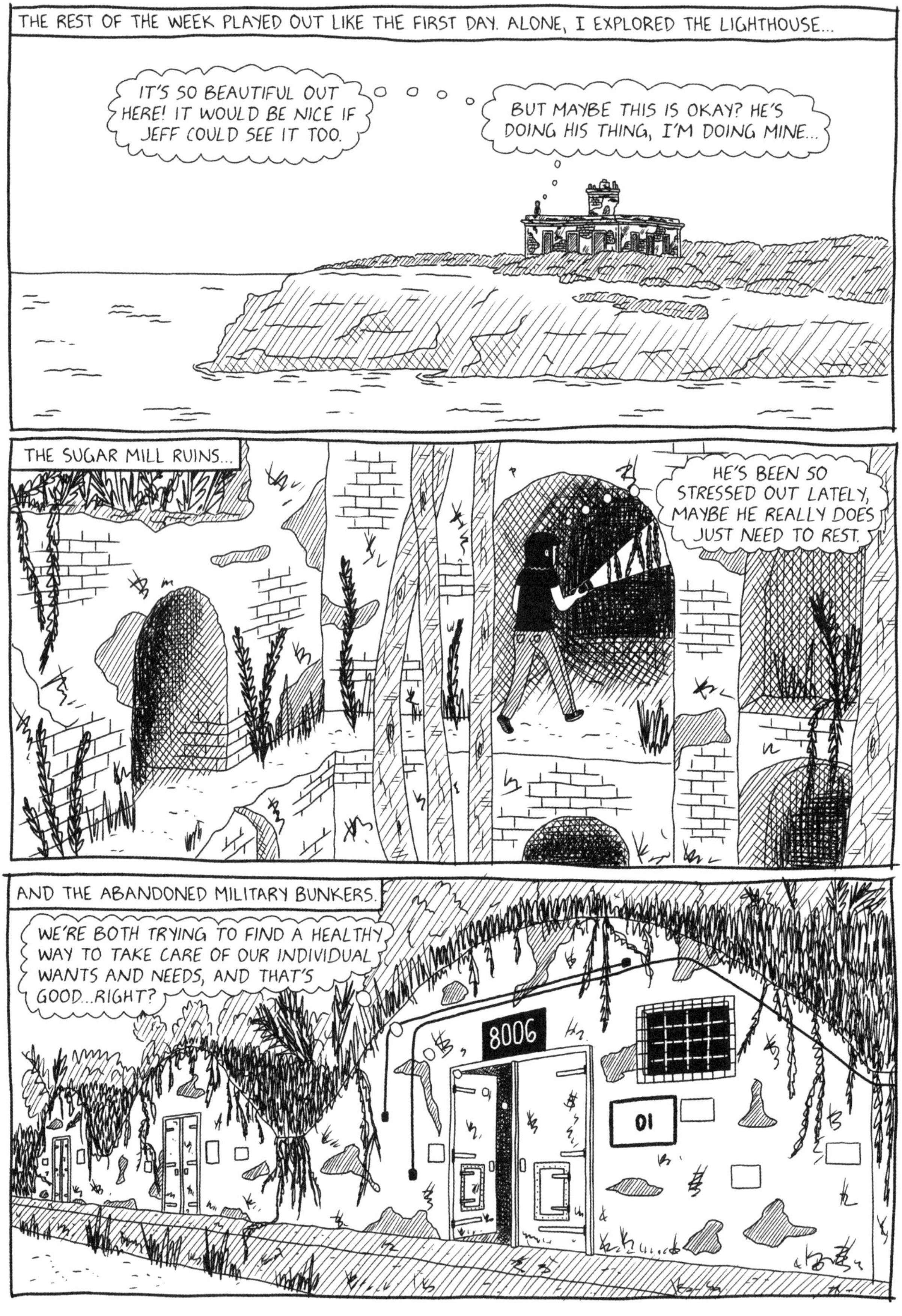
THE REST OF THE WEEK PLAYED OUT LIKE THE FIRST DAY. ALONE, I EXPLORED THE LIGHTHOUSE...
IT'S SO BEAUTIFUL OUT HERE! IT WOULD BE NICE IF JEFF COULD SEE IT TOO.
BUT MAYBE THIS IS OKAY? HE'S DOING HIS THING, I'M DOING MINE...
THE SUGAR MILL RUINS...
HE'S BEEN SO STRESSED OUT LATELY, MAYBE HE REALLY DOES JUST NEED TO REST.
AND THE ABANDONED MILITARY BUNKERS.
WE'RE BOTH TRYING TO FIND A HEALTHY WAY TO TAKE CARE OF OUR INDIVIDUAL WANTS AND NEEDS, AND THAT'S GOOD...RIGHT?
8006
01

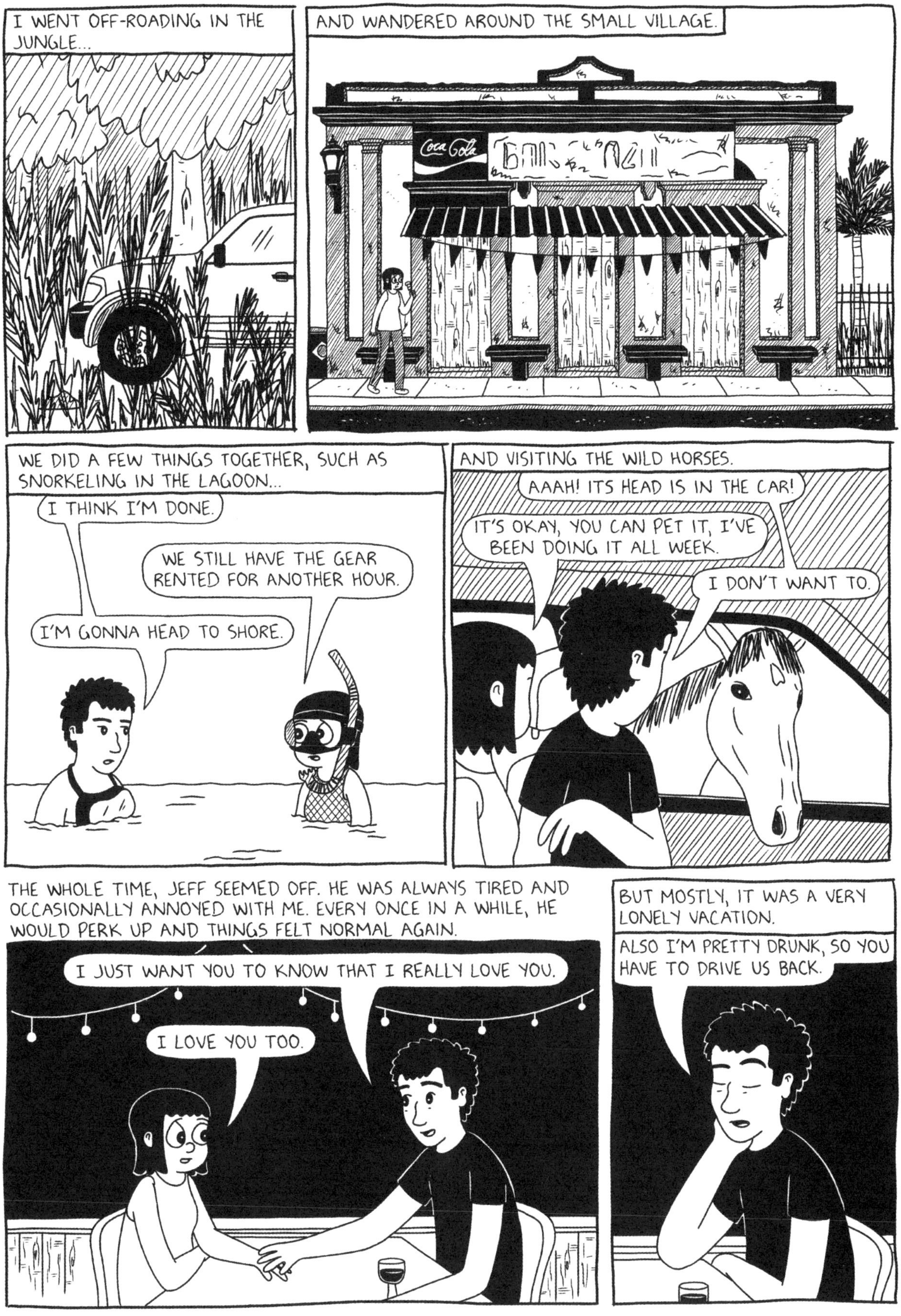
I WENT OFF-ROADING IN THE JUNGLE...
AND WANDERED AROUND THE SMALL VILLAGE.
Coca Cola
WE DID A FEW THINGS TOGETHER, SUCH AS SNORKELING IN THE LAGOON...
I THINK I'M DONE.
WE STILL HAVE THE GEAR RENTED FOR ANOTHER HOUR.
I'M GONNA HEAD TO SHORE.
AND VISITING THE WILD HORSES.
AAAH! ITS HEAD IS IN THE CAR!
IT'S OKAY, YOU CAN PET IT, I'VE BEEN DOING IT ALL WEEK.
I DON'T WANT TO.
THE WHOLE TIME, JEFF SEEMED OFF. HE WAS ALWAYS TIRED AND OCCASIONALLY ANNOYED WITH ME. EVERY ONCE IN A WHILE, HE WOULD PERK UP AND THINGS FELT NORMAL AGAIN.
I JUST WANT YOU TO KNOW THAT I REALLY LOVE YOU.
I LOVE YOU TOO.
BUT MOSTLY, IT WAS A VERY LONELY VACATION.
ALSO I'M PRETTY DRUNK, SO YOU HAVE TO DRIVE US BACK.

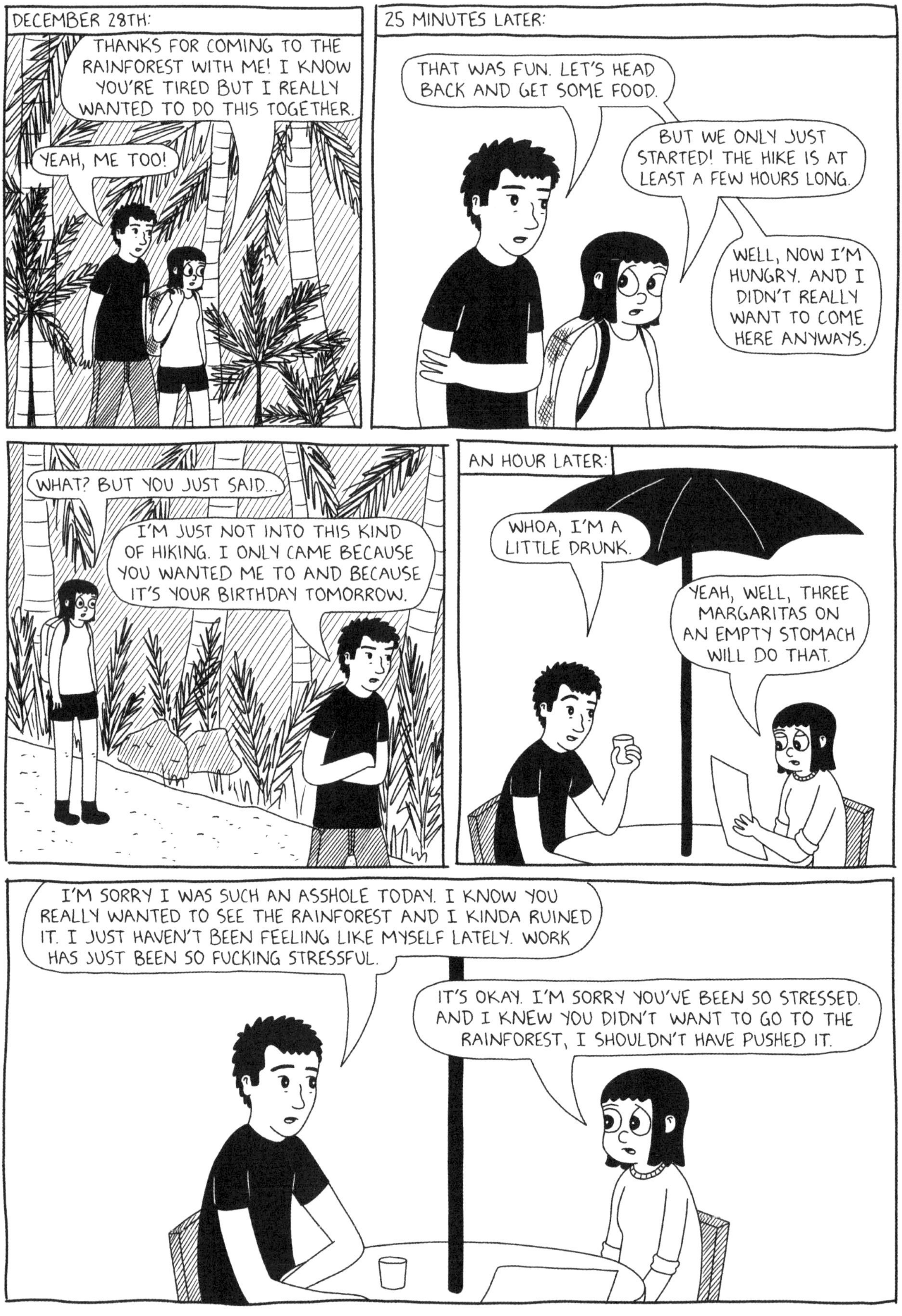
DECEMBER 28TH:
THANKS FOR COMING TO THE RAINFOREST WITH ME! I KNOW YOU'RE TIRED BUT I REALLY WANTED TO DO THIS TOGETHER.
YEAH, ME TOO!
25 MINUTES LATER:
THAT WAS FUN. LET'S HEAD BACK AND GET SOME FOOD.
BUT WE ONLY JUST STARTED! THE HIKE IS AT LEAST A FEW HOURS LONG.
WELL, NOW I'M HUNGRY. AND I DIDN'T REALLY WANT TO COME HERE ANYWAYS.
WHAT? BUT YOU JUST SAID...
I'M JUST NOT INTO THIS KIND OF HIKING. I ONLY CAME BECAUSE YOU WANTED ME TO AND BECAUSE IT'S YOUR BIRTHDAY TOMORROW.
AN HOUR LATER:
WHOA, I'M A LITTLE DRUNK.
YEAH, WELL, THREE MARGARITAS ON AN EMPTY STOMACH WILL DO THAT.
I'M SORRY I WAS SUCH AN ASSHOLE TODAY. I KNOW YOU REALLY WANTED TO SEE THE RAINFOREST AND I KINDA RUINED IT. I JUST HAVEN'T BEEN FEELING LIKE MYSELF LATELY. WORK HAS JUST BEEN SO FUCKING STRESSFUL.
IT'S OKAY. I'M SORRY YOU'VE BEEN SO STRESSED. AND I KNEW YOU DIDN'T WANT TO GO TO THE RAINFOREST, I SHOULDN'T HAVE PUSHED IT.

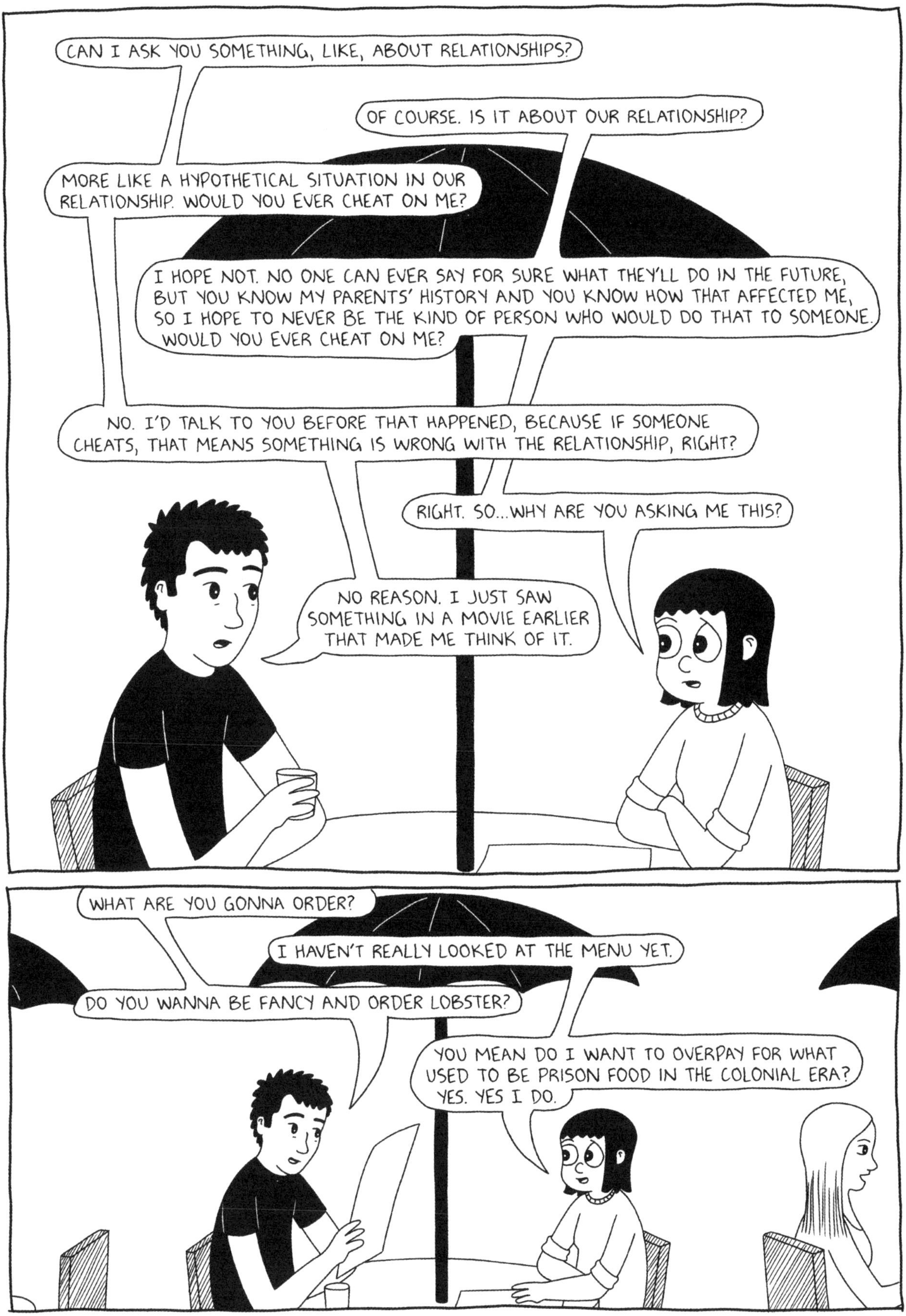
CAN I ASK YOU SOMETHING, LIKE, ABOUT RELATIONSHIPS?
OF COURSE. IS IT ABOUT OUR RELATIONSHIP?
MORE LIKE A HYPOTHETICAL SITUATION IN OUR RELATIONSHIP. WOULD YOU EVER CHEAT ON ME?
I HOPE NOT. NO ONE CAN EVER SAY FOR SURE WHAT THEY'LL DO IN THE FUTURE, BUT YOU KNOW MY PARENTS' HISTORY AND YOU KNOW HOW THAT AFFECTED ME, SO I HOPE TO NEVER BE THE KIND OF PERSON WHO WOULD DO THAT TO SOMEONE. WOULD YOU EVER CHEAT ON ME?
NO. I'D TALK TO YOU BEFORE THAT HAPPENED, BECAUSE IF SOMEONE CHEATS, THAT MEANS SOMETHING IS WRONG WITH THE RELATIONSHIP, RIGHT?
RIGHT. SO...WHY ARE YOU ASKING ME THIS?
NO REASON. I JUST SAW SOMETHING IN A MOVIE EARLIER THAT MADE ME THINK OF IT.
WHAT ARE YOU GONNA ORDER?
I HAVEN'T REALLY LOOKED AT THE MENU YET.
DO YOU WANNA BE FANCY AND ORDER LOBSTER?
YOU MEAN DO I WANT TO OVERPAY FOR WHAT USED TO BE PRISON FOOD IN THE COLONIAL ERA? YES. YES I DO.

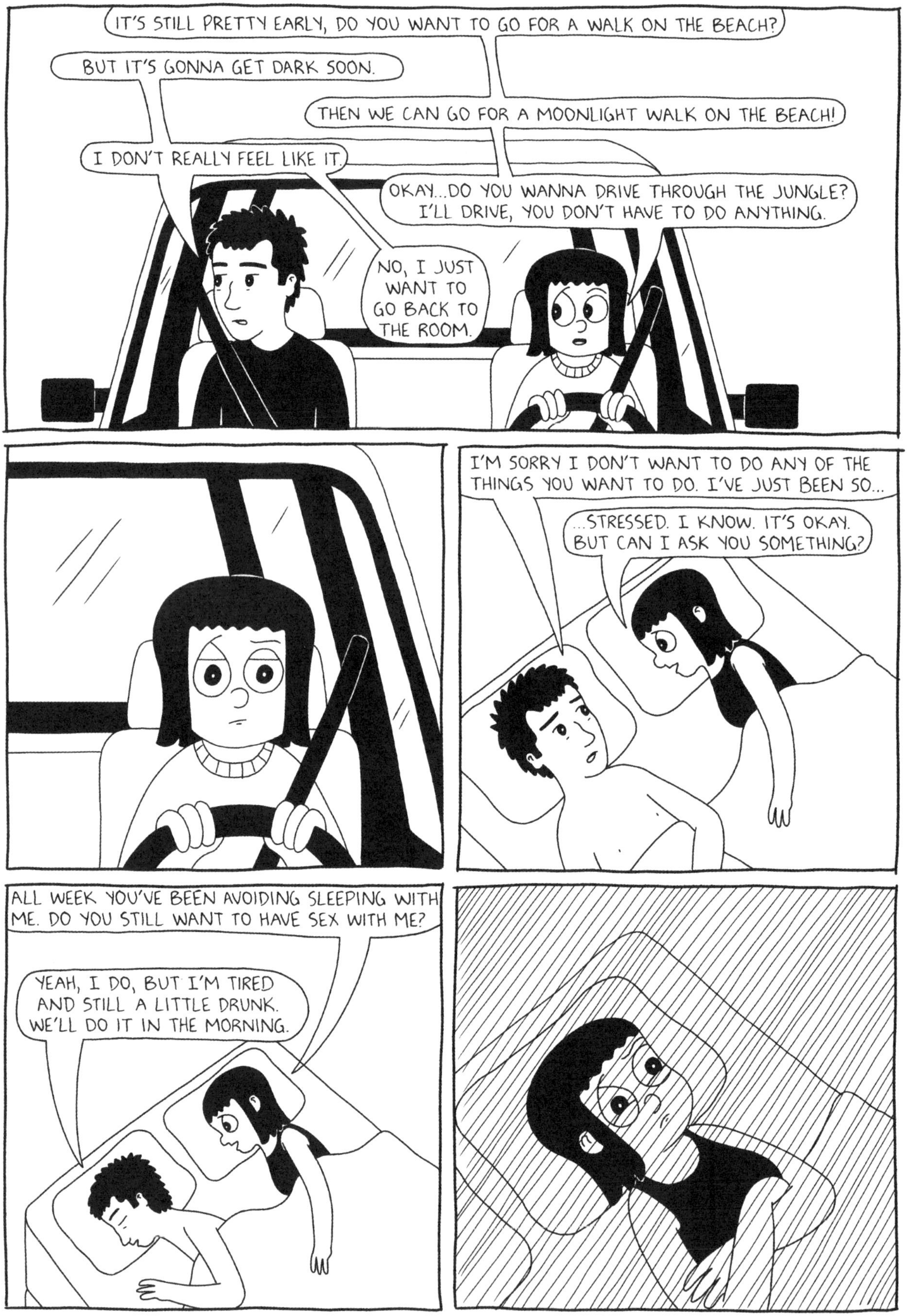
IT'S STILL PRETTY EARLY, DO YOU WANT TO GO FOR A WALK ON THE BEACH?
BUT IT'S GONNA GET DARK SOON.
THEN WE CAN GO FOR A MOONLIGHT WALK ON THE BEACH!
I DON'T REALLY FEEL LIKE IT.
OKAY...DO YOU WANNA DRIVE THROUGH THE JUNGLE? I'LL DRIVE, YOU DON'T HAVE TO DO ANYTHING.
NO, I JUST WANT TO GO BACK TO THE ROOM.
I'M SORRY I DON'T WANT TO DO ANY OF THE THINGS YOU WANT TO DO. I'VE JUST BEEN SO...
...STRESSED. I KNOW. IT'S OKAY. BUT CAN I ASK YOU SOMETHING?
ALL WEEK YOU'VE BEEN AVOIDING SLEEPING WITH ME. DO YOU STILL WANT TO HAVE SEX WITH ME?
YEAH, I DO, BUT I'M TIRED AND STILL A LITTLE DRUNK. WE'LL DO IT IN THE MORNING.

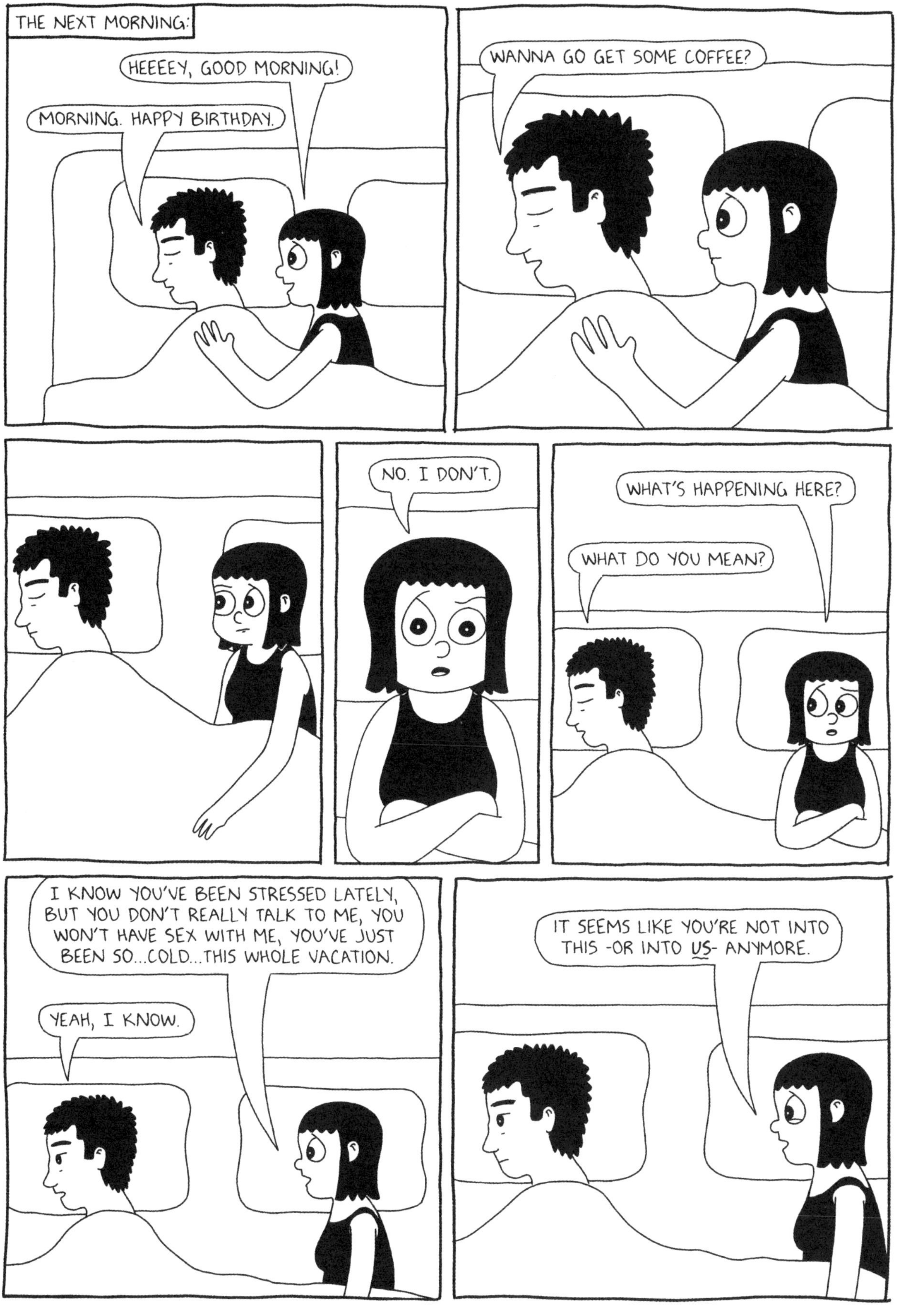
THE NEXT MORNING:
HEEEEY, GOOD MORNING!
MORNING. HAPPY BIRTHDAY.
WANNA GO GET SOME COFFEE?
NO. I DON'T.
WHAT'S HAPPENING HERE?
WHAT DO YOU MEAN?
I KNOW YOU'VE BEEN STRESSED LATELY, BUT YOU DON'T REALLY TALK TO ME, YOU WON'T HAVE SEX WITH ME, YOU'VE JUST BEEN SO...COLD...THIS WHOLE VACATION.
YEAH, I KNOW.
IT SEEMS LIKE YOU'RE NOT INTO THIS -OR INTO US- ANYMORE.

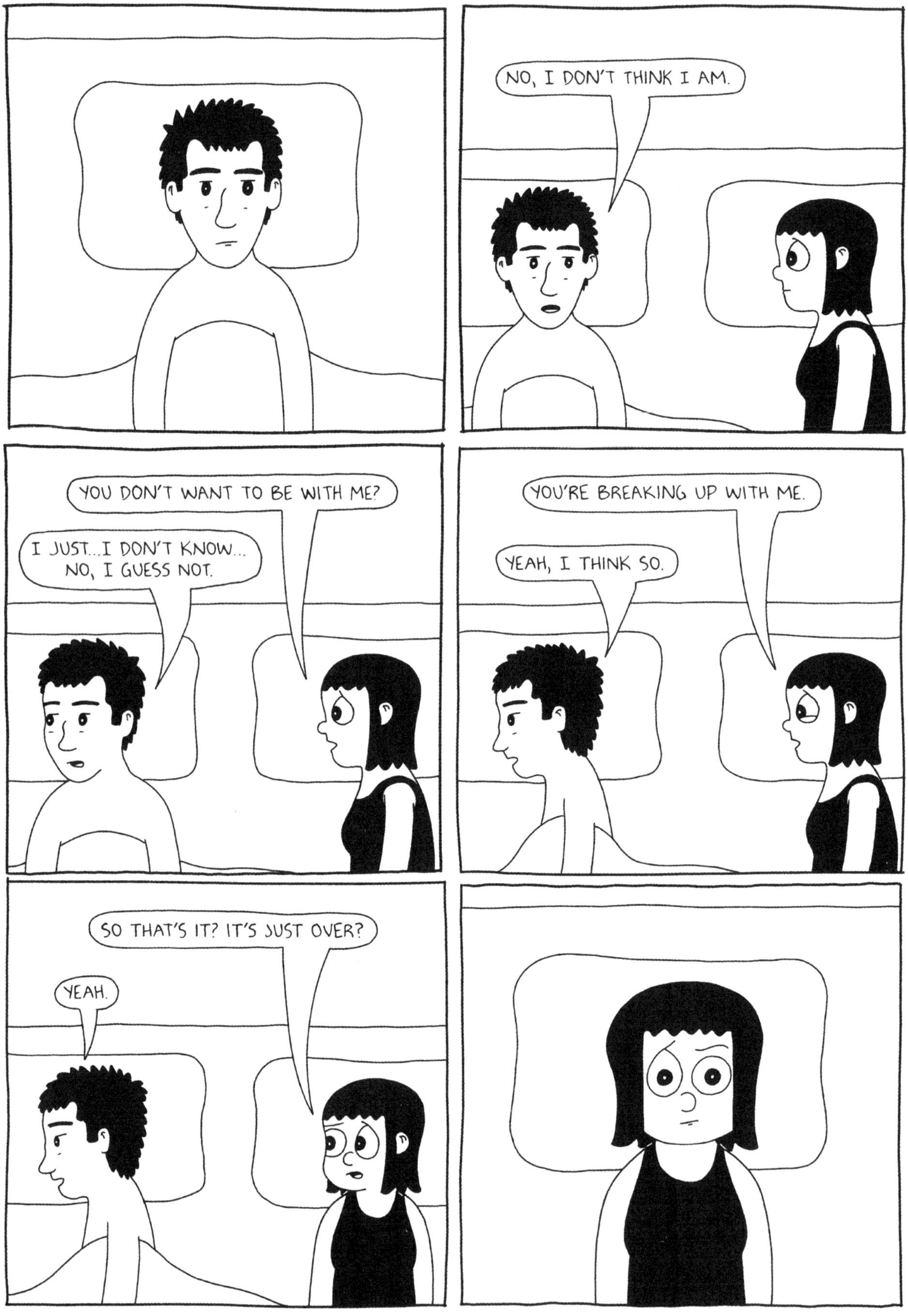
NO, I DON'T THINK I AM.
YOU DON'T WANT TO BE WITH ME?
I JUST...I DON'T KNOW... NO, I GUESS NOT.
YOU'RE BREAKING UP WITH ME.
YEAH, I THINK SO.
SO THAT'S IT? IT'S JUST OVER?
YEAH.

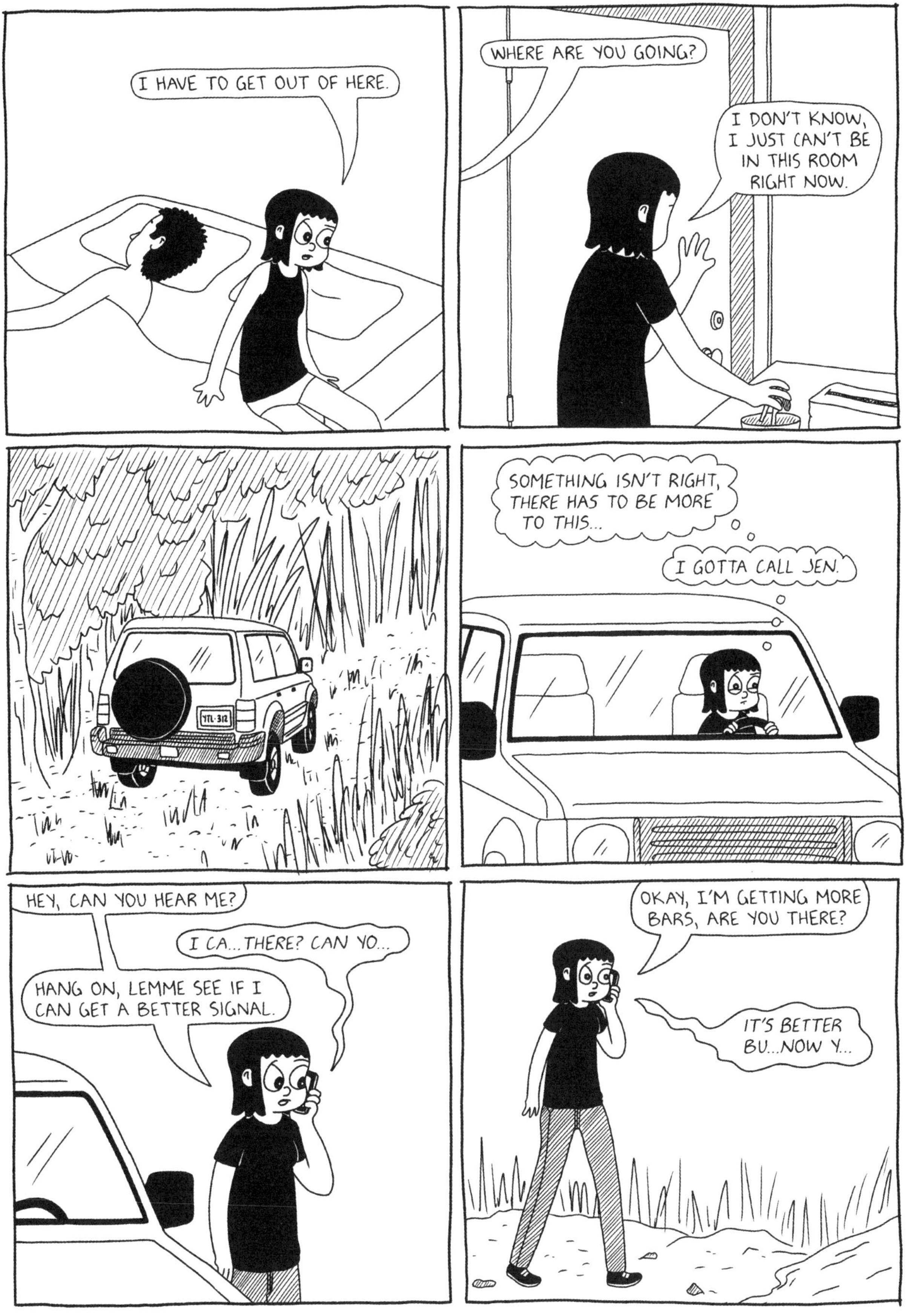
I HAVE TO GET OUT OF HERE.
WHERE ARE YOU GOING?
I DON'T KNOW, I JUST CAN'T BE IN THIS ROOM RIGHT NOW.
SOMETHING ISN'T RIGHT, THERE HAS TO BE MORE TO THIS...
I GOTTA CALL JEN.
HEY, CAN YOU HEAR ME?
I CA... THERE? CAN YO...
HANG ON, LEMME SEE IF I CAN GET A BETTER SIGNAL.
OKAY, I'M GETTING MORE BARS, ARE YOU THERE?
IT'S BETTER BU... NOW Y...

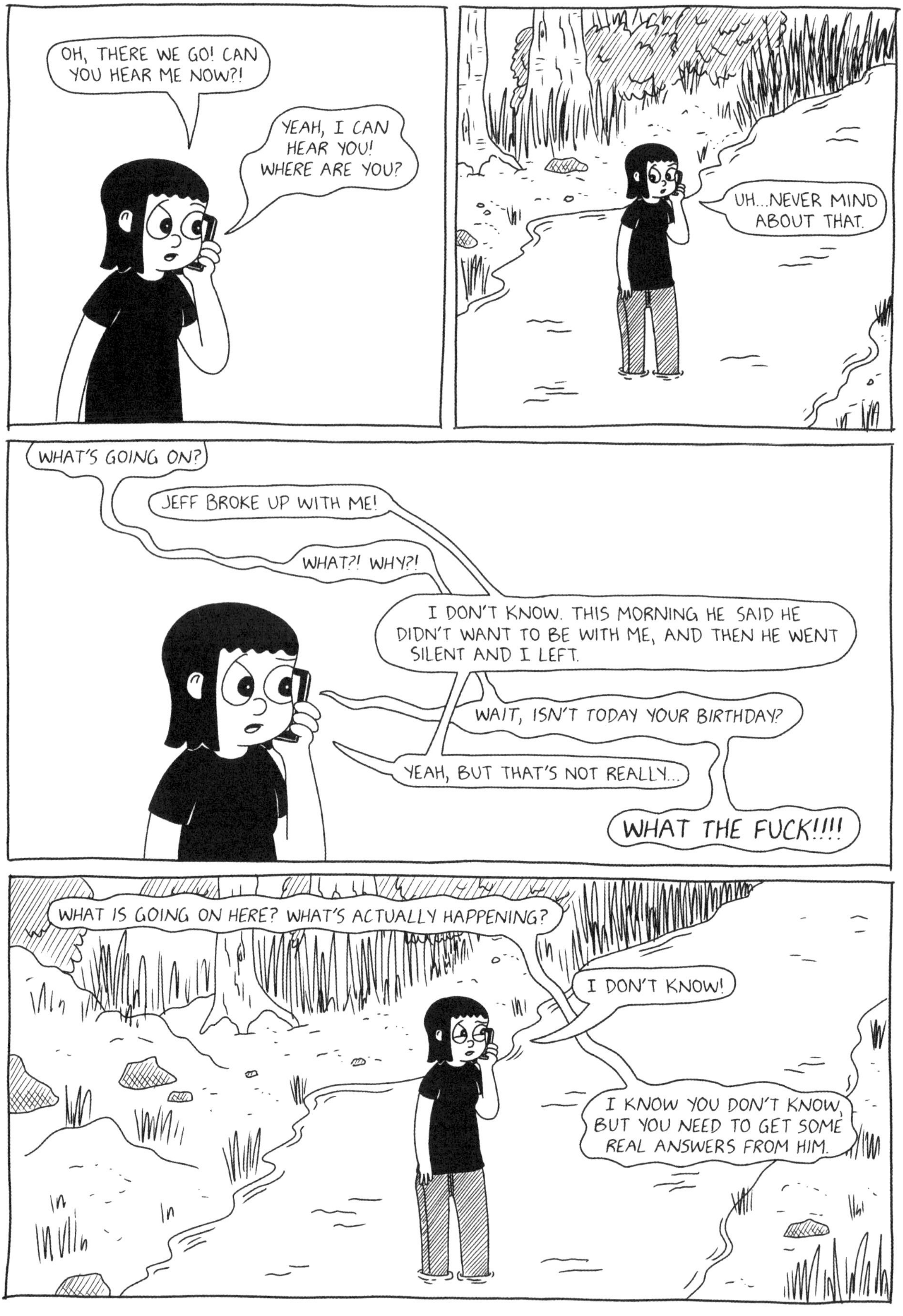
OH, THERE WE GO! CAN YOU HEAR ME NOW?!
YEAH, I CAN HEAR YOU! WHERE ARE YOU?
UH...NEVER MIND ABOUT THAT.
WHAT'S GOING ON?
JEFF BROKE UP WITH ME!
WHAT?! WHY?!
I DON'T KNOW. THIS MORNING HE SAID HE DIDN'T WANT TO BE WITH ME, AND THEN HE WENT SILENT AND I LEFT.
WAIT, ISN'T TODAY YOUR BIRTHDAY?
YEAH, BUT THAT'S NOT REALLY...
WHAT THE FUCK!!!!
WHAT IS GOING ON HERE? WHAT'S ACTUALLY HAPPENING?
I DON'T KNOW!
I KNOW YOU DON'T KNOW, BUT YOU NEED TO GET SOME REAL ANSWERS FROM HIM.

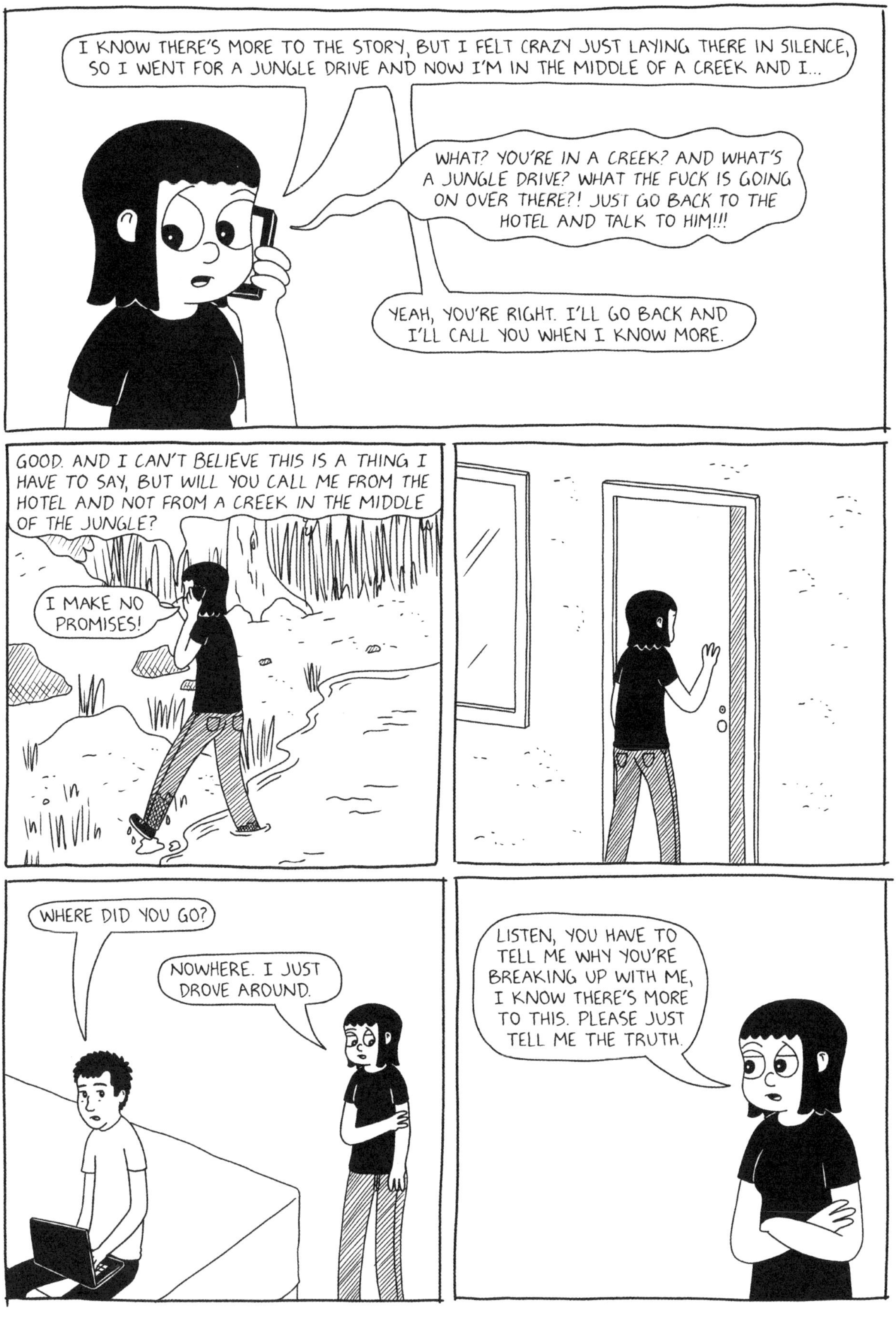
I KNOW THERE'S MORE TO THE STORY, BUT I FELT CRAZY JUST LAYING THERE IN SILENCE, SO I WENT FOR A JUNGLE DRIVE AND NOW I'M IN THE MIDDLE OF A CREEK AND I...
WHAT? YOU'RE IN A CREEK? AND WHAT'S A JUNGLE DRIVE? WHAT THE FUCK IS GOING ON OVER THERE?! JUST GO BACK TO THE HOTEL AND TALK TO HIM!!!
YEAH, YOU'RE RIGHT. I'LL GO BACK AND I'LL CALL YOU WHEN I KNOW MORE.
GOOD. AND I CAN'T BELIEVE THIS IS A THING I HAVE TO SAY, BUT WILL YOU CALL ME FROM THE HOTEL AND NOT FROM A CREEK IN THE MIDDLE OF THE JUNGLE?
I MAKE NO PROMISES!
WHERE DID YOU GO?
NOWHERE. I JUST DROVE AROUND.
LISTEN, YOU HAVE TO TELL ME WHY YOU'RE BREAKING UP WITH ME, I KNOW THERE'S MORE TO THIS. PLEASE JUST TELL ME THE TRUTH.

OVER THE NEXT 15 MINUTES, JEFF LISTED A VARIETY OF REASONS FOR WHY WE WERE INCOMPATIBLE. MY BRAIN, PERHAPS IN AN ATTEMPT TO PROTECT ITSELF, HAS BLURRED THE SPECIFICS OF HIS WORDS, LEAVING ONLY THE MEMORY OF THE ACUTE HORROR ONE FEELS WHEN SOMEONE YOU LOVE TAPS INTO THE INSECURITIES YOU HAVE AS A PERSON AND PARTNER, AND THEN BLAMES THOSE INSECURITIES FOR THE FAILURE OF THE RELATIONSHIP.

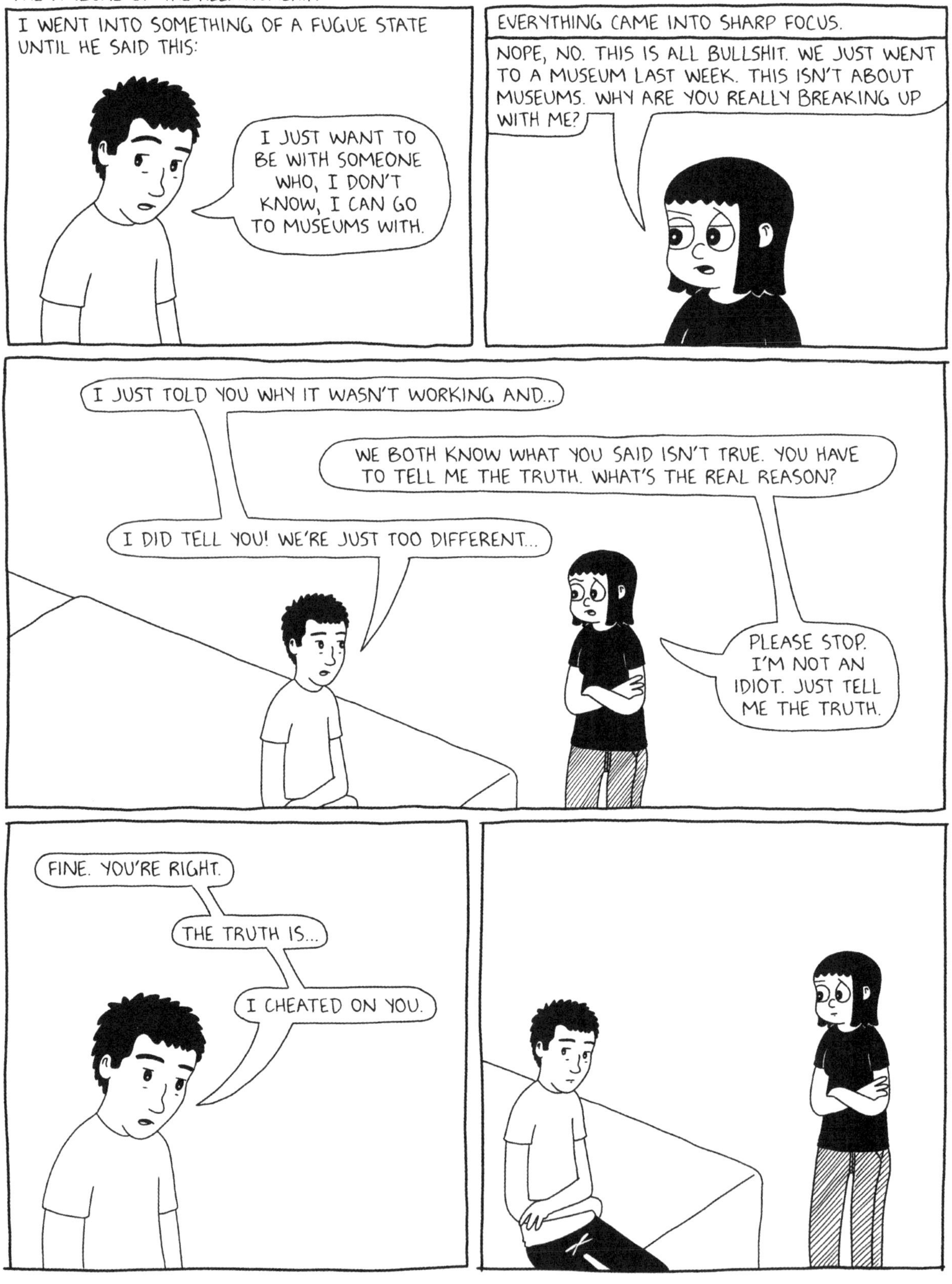
I WENT INTO SOMETHING OF A FUGUE STATE UNTIL HE SAID THIS:
I JUST WANT TO BE WITH SOMEONE WHO, I DON'T KNOW, I CAN GO TO MUSEUMS WITH.
EVERYTHING CAME INTO SHARP FOCUS.
NOPE, NO. THIS IS ALL BULLSHIT. WE JUST WENT TO A MUSEUM LAST WEEK. THIS ISN'T ABOUT MUSEUMS. WHY ARE YOU REALLY BREAKING UP WITH ME?
I JUST TOLD YOU WHY IT WASN'T WORKING AND...
WE BOTH KNOW WHAT YOU SAID ISN'T TRUE. YOU HAVE TO TELL ME THE TRUTH. WHAT'S THE REAL REASON?
I DID TELL YOU! WE'RE JUST TOO DIFFERENT...
PLEASE STOP. I'M NOT AN IDIOT. JUST TELL ME THE TRUTH.
FINE. YOU'RE RIGHT.
THE TRUTH IS...
I CHEATED ON YOU.

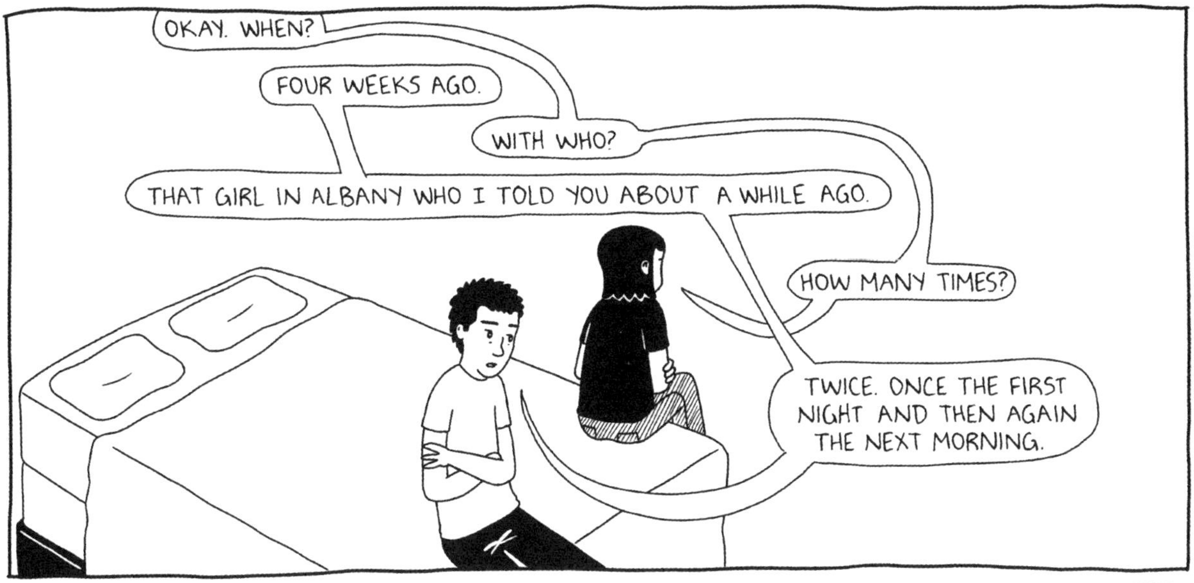
OKAY. WHEN?
FOUR WEEKS AGO.
WITH WHO?
THAT GIRL IN ALBANY WHO I TOLD YOU ABOUT A WHILE AGO.
HOW MANY TIMES?
TWICE. ONCE THE FIRST NIGHT AND THEN AGAIN THE NEXT MORNING.

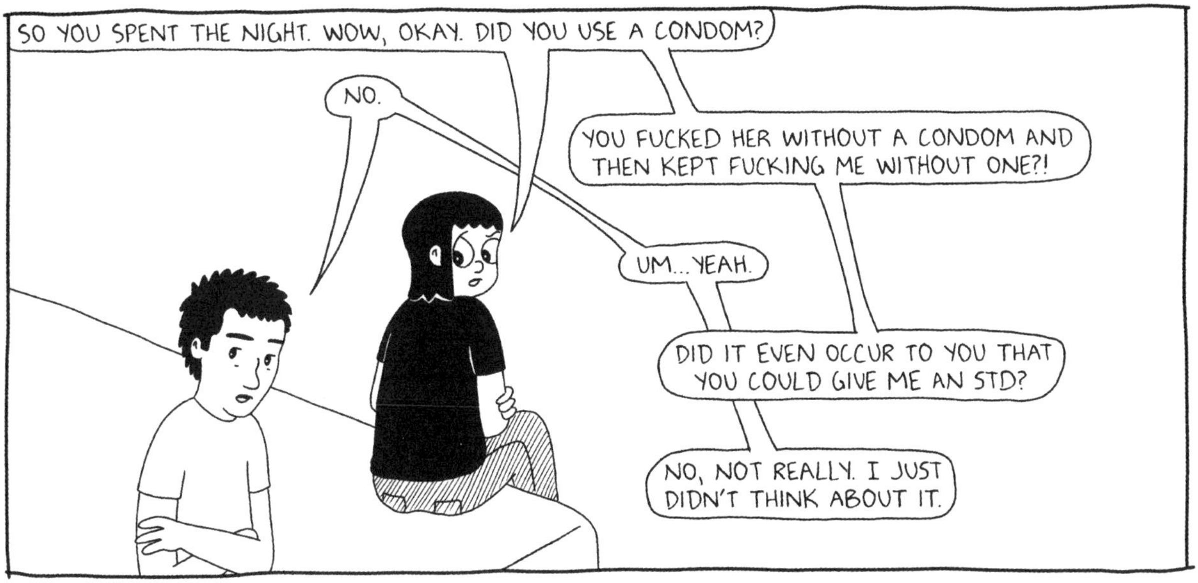
SO YOU SPENT THE NIGHT. WOW, OKAY. DID YOU USE A CONDOM?
NO.
YOU FUCKED HER WITHOUT A CONDOM AND THEN KEPT FUCKING ME WITHOUT ONE?!
UM... YEAH.
DID IT EVEN OCCUR TO YOU THAT YOU COULD GIVE ME AN STD?
NO, NOT REALLY. I JUST DIDN'T THINK ABOUT IT.

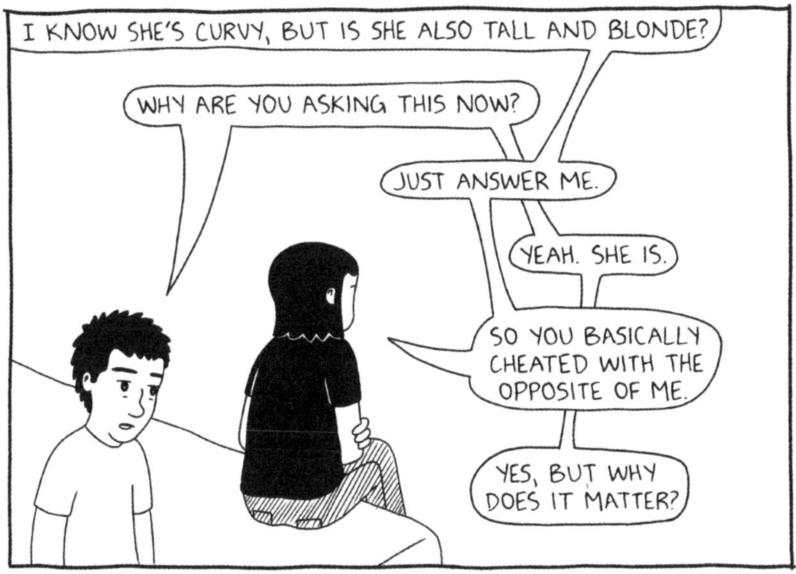
I KNOW SHE'S CURVY, BUT IS SHE ALSO TALL AND BLONDE?
WHY ARE YOU ASKING THIS NOW?
JUST ANSWER ME.
YEAH. SHE IS.
SO YOU BASICALLY CHEATED WITH THE OPPOSITE OF ME.
YES, BUT WHY DOES IT MATTER?

IT DIDN'T MATTER. I WAS JUST POURING SALT ON THE WOUND IN AN ATTEMPT TO SHIFT MY FOCUS AWAY FROM THE REAL QUESTION I WANTED TO ASK.

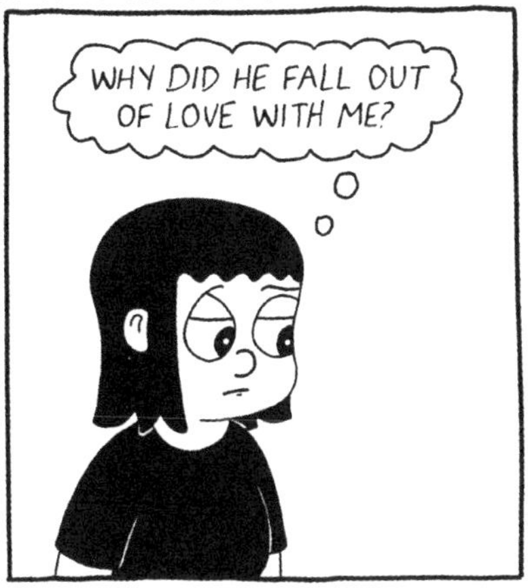
WHY DID HE FALL OUT OF LOVE WITH ME?

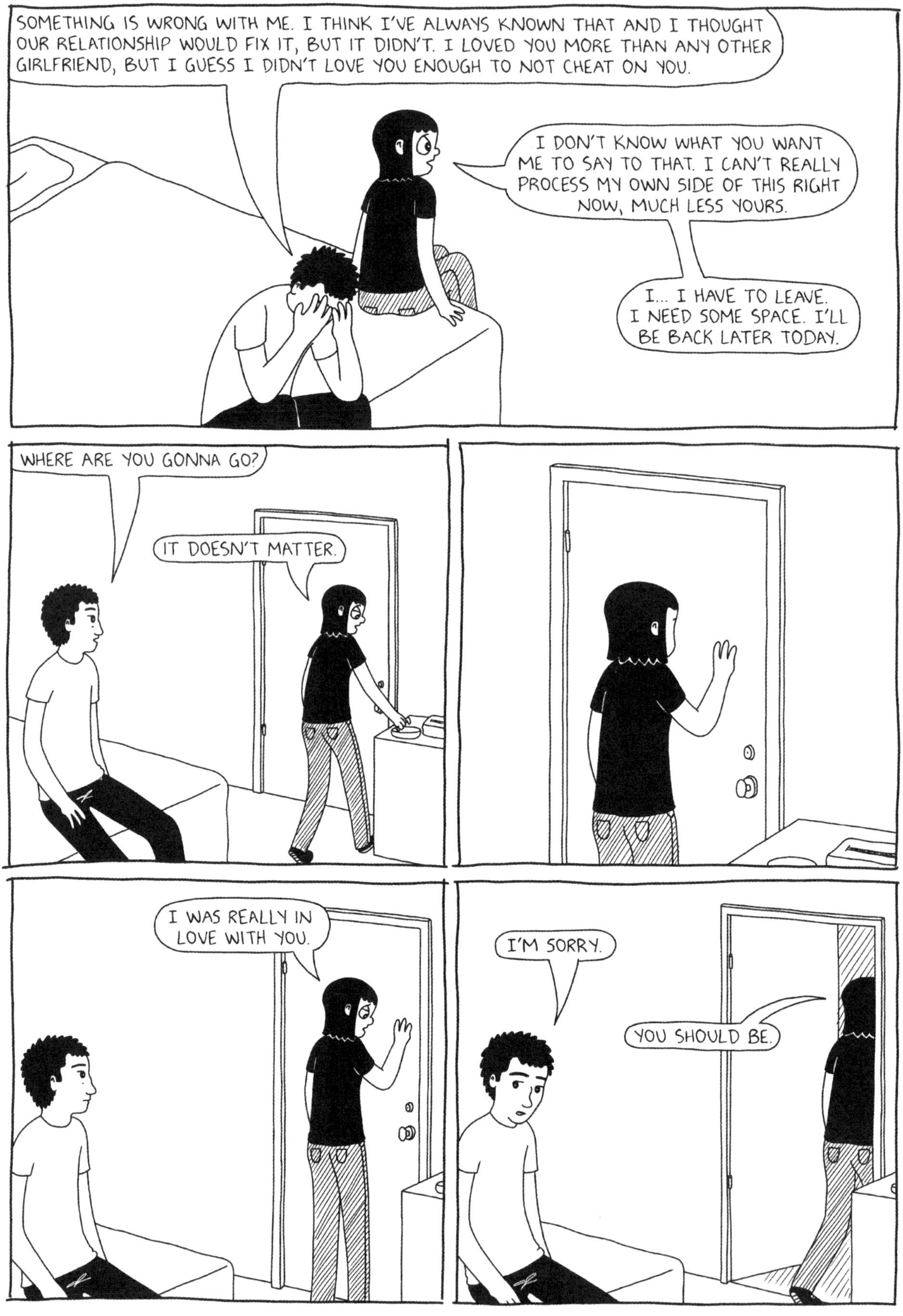
SOMETHING IS WRONG WITH ME. I THINK I'VE ALWAYS KNOWN THAT AND I THOUGHT OUR RELATIONSHIP WOULD FIX IT, BUT IT DIDN'T. I LOVED YOU MORE THAN ANY OTHER GIRLFRIEND, BUT I GUESS I DIDN'T LOVE YOU ENOUGH TO NOT CHEAT ON YOU.
I DON'T KNOW WHAT YOU WANT ME TO SAY TO THAT. I CAN'T REALLY PROCESS MY OWN SIDE OF THIS RIGHT NOW, MUCH LESS YOURS.
I... I HAVE TO LEAVE. I NEED SOME SPACE. I'LL BE BACK LATER TODAY.
WHERE ARE YOU GONNA GO?
IT DOESN'T MATTER.
I WAS REALLY IN LOVE WITH YOU.
I'M SORRY.
YOU SHOULD BE.

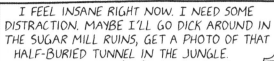
I FEEL INSANE RIGHT NOW. I NEED SOME DISTRACTION. MAYBE I'LL GO DICK AROUND IN THE SUGAR MILL RUINS, GET A PHOTO OF THAT HALF-BURIED TUNNEL IN THE JUNGLE.

THERE IT IS!

IT'S PITCH BLACK IN HERE, I'LL HAVE TO USE THE FLASH.

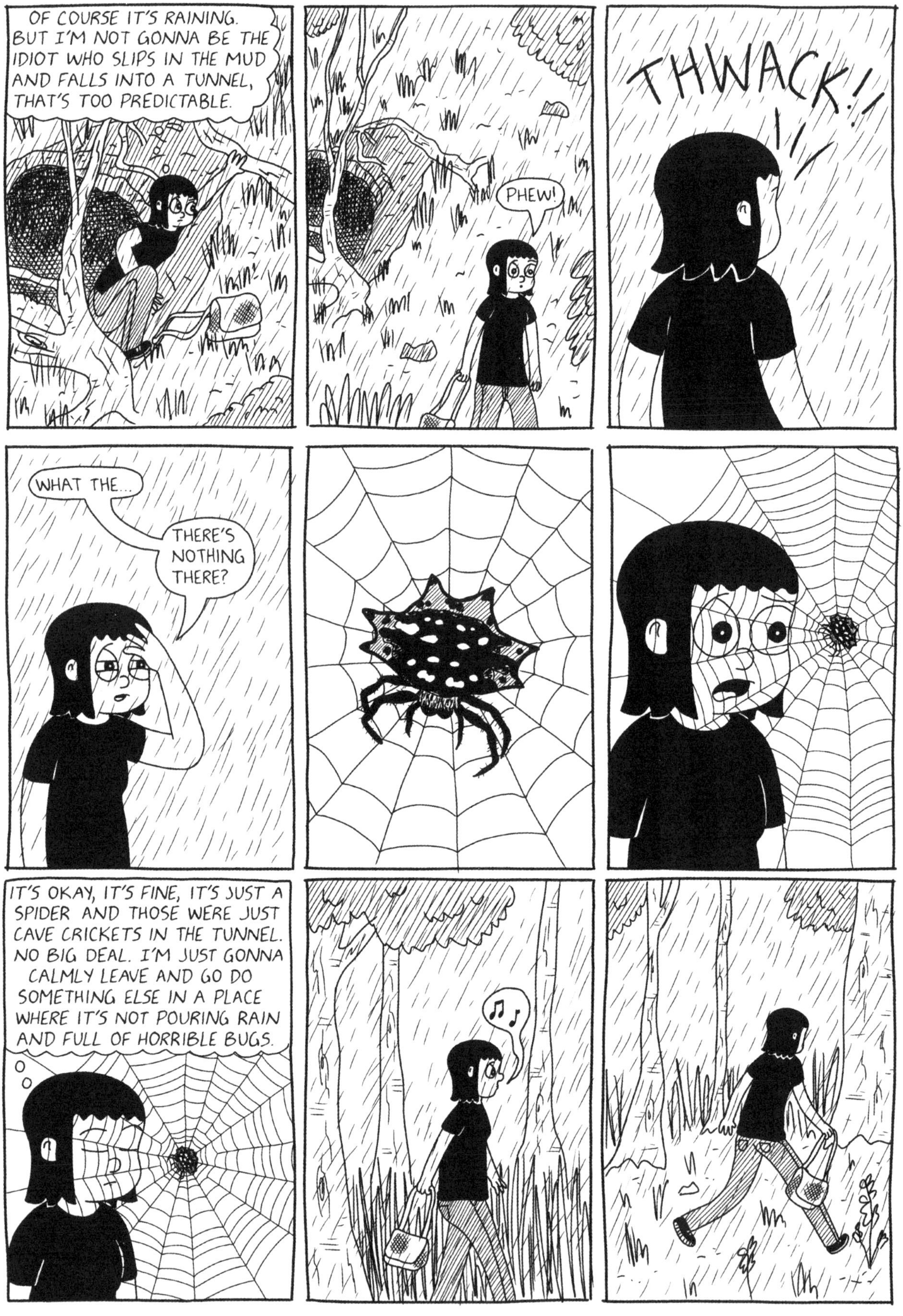
OF COURSE IT'S RAINING. BUT I'M NOT GONNA BE THE IDIOT WHO SLIPS IN THE MUD AND FALLS INTO A TUNNEL, THAT'S TOO PREDICTABLE.
PHEW!
THWACK!!
WHAT THE...
THERE'S NOTHING THERE?
IT'S OKAY, IT'S FINE, IT'S JUST A SPIDER AND THOSE WERE JUST CAVE CRICKETS IN THE TUNNEL. NO BIG DEAL. I'M JUST GONNA CALMLY LEAVE AND GO DO SOMETHING ELSE IN A PLACE WHERE IT'S NOT POURING RAIN AND FULL OF HORRIBLE BUGS.
♫

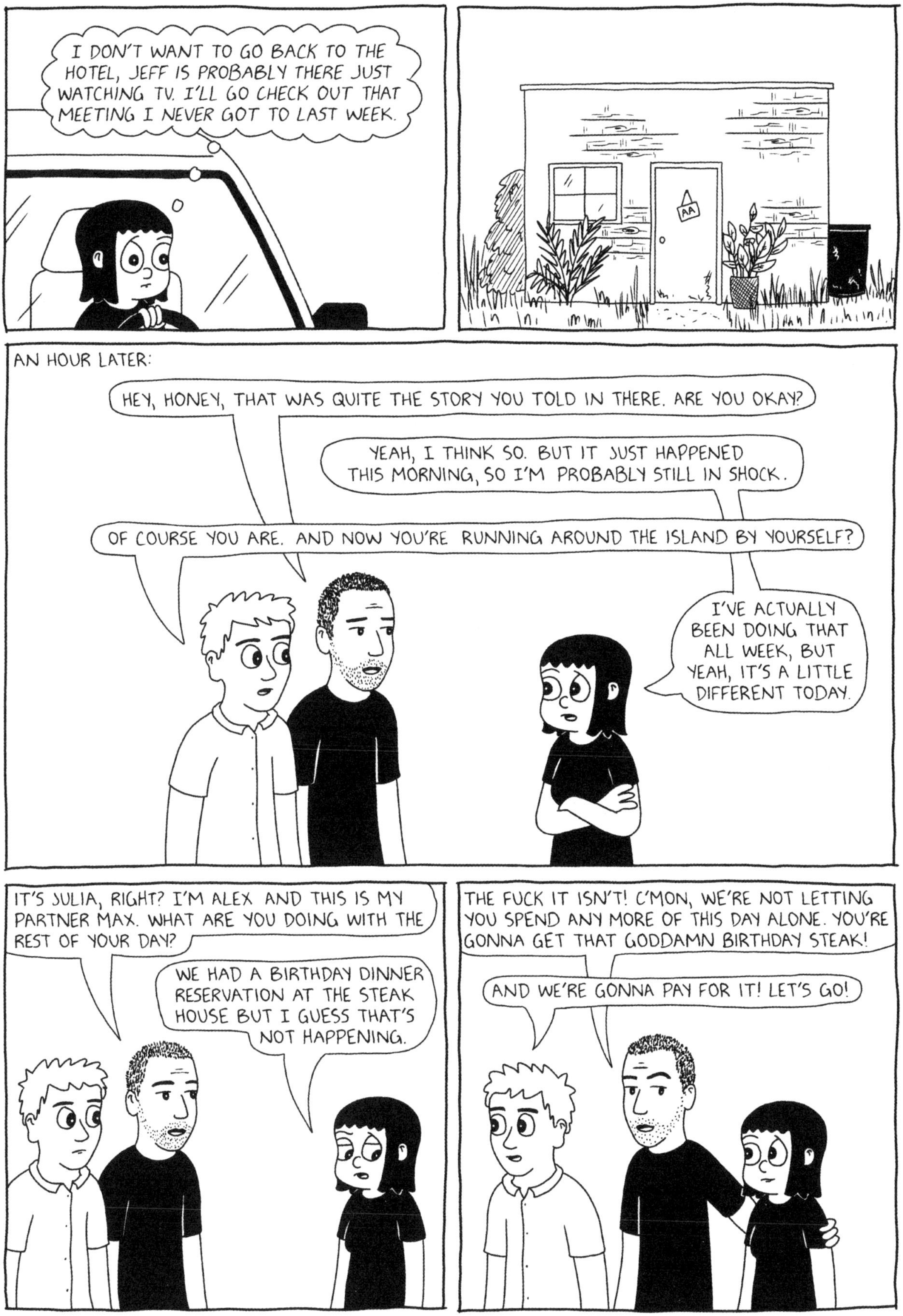
I DON'T WANT TO GO BACK TO THE HOTEL, JEFF IS PROBABLY THERE JUST WATCHING TV. I'LL GO CHECK OUT THAT MEETING I NEVER GOT TO LAST WEEK.
AA
AN HOUR LATER:
HEY, HONEY, THAT WAS QUITE THE STORY YOU TOLD IN THERE. ARE YOU OKAY?
YEAH, I THINK SO. BUT IT JUST HAPPENED THIS MORNING, SO I'M PROBABLY STILL IN SHOCK.
OF COURSE YOU ARE. AND NOW YOU'RE RUNNING AROUND THE ISLAND BY YOURSELF?
I'VE ACTUALLY BEEN DOING THAT ALL WEEK, BUT YEAH, IT'S A LITTLE DIFFERENT TODAY.
IT'S JULIA, RIGHT? I'M ALEX AND THIS IS MY PARTNER MAX. WHAT ARE YOU DOING WITH THE REST OF YOUR DAY?
WE HAD A BIRTHDAY DINNER RESERVATION AT THE STEAK HOUSE BUT I GUESS THAT'S NOT HAPPENING.
THE FUCK IT ISN'T! C'MON, WE'RE NOT LETTING YOU SPEND ANY MORE OF THIS DAY ALONE. YOU'RE GONNA GET THAT GODDAMN BIRTHDAY STEAK!
AND WE'RE GONNA PAY FOR IT! LET'S GO!

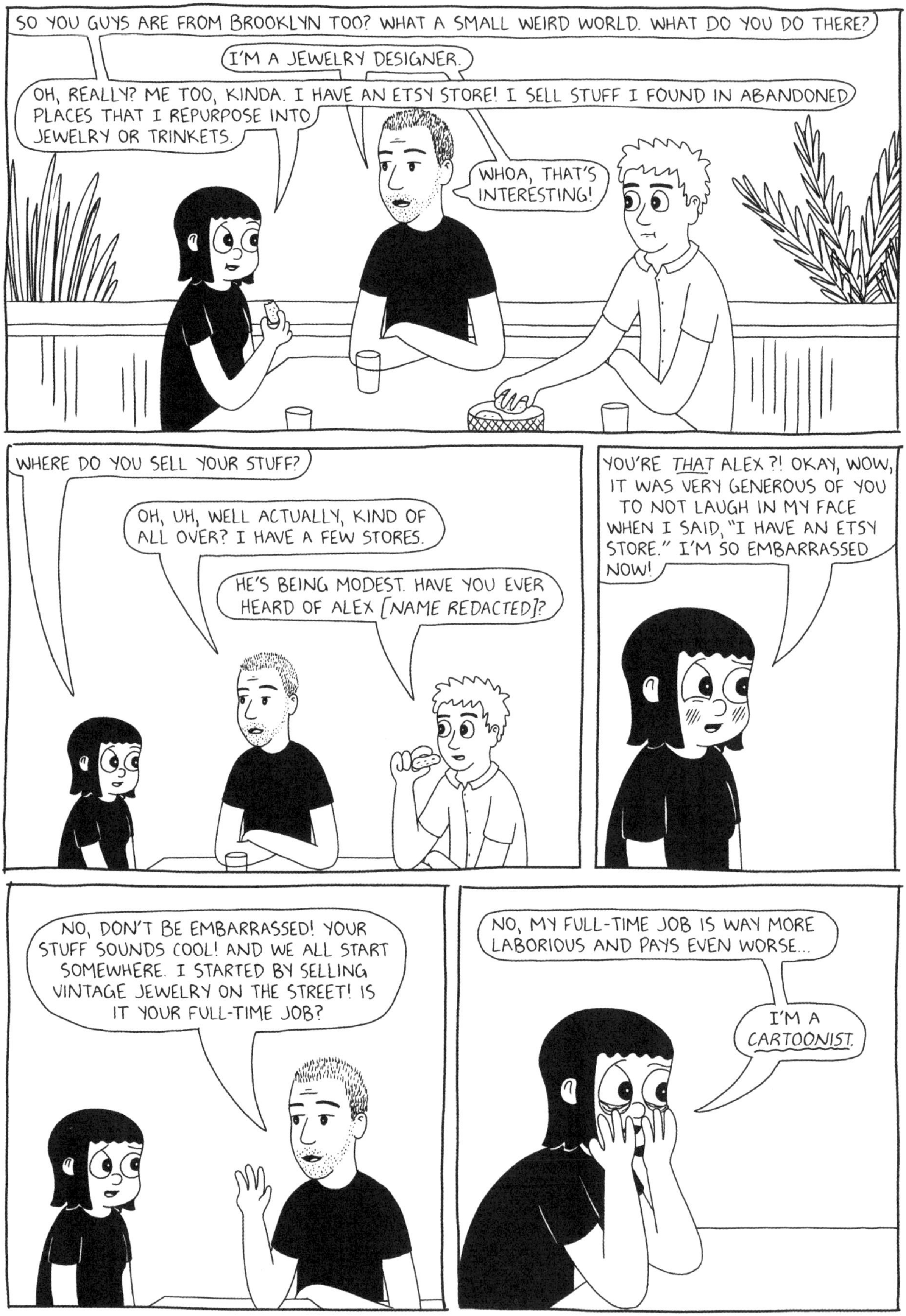
SO YOU GUYS ARE FROM BROOKLYN TOO? WHAT A SMALL WEIRD WORLD. WHAT DO YOU DO THERE?
I'M A JEWELRY DESIGNER.
OH, REALLY? ME TOO, KINDA. I HAVE AN ETSY STORE! I SELL STUFF I FOUND IN ABANDONED PLACES THAT I REPURPOSE INTO JEWELRY OR TRINKETS.
WHOA, THAT'S INTERESTING!
WHERE DO YOU SELL YOUR STUFF?
OH, UH, WELL ACTUALLY, KIND OF ALL OVER? I HAVE A FEW STORES.
HE'S BEING MODEST. HAVE YOU EVER HEARD OF ALEX [NAME REDACTED]?
YOU'RE THAT ALEX?! OKAY, WOW, IT WAS VERY GENEROUS OF YOU TO NOT LAUGH IN MY FACE WHEN I SAID, "I HAVE AN ETSY STORE." I'M SO EMBARRASSED NOW!
NO, DON'T BE EMBARRASSED! YOUR STUFF SOUNDS COOL! AND WE ALL START SOMEWHERE. I STARTED BY SELLING VINTAGE JEWELRY ON THE STREET! IS IT YOUR FULL-TIME JOB?
NO, MY FULL-TIME JOB IS WAY MORE LABORIOUS AND PAYS EVEN WORSE...
I'M A CARTOONIST.

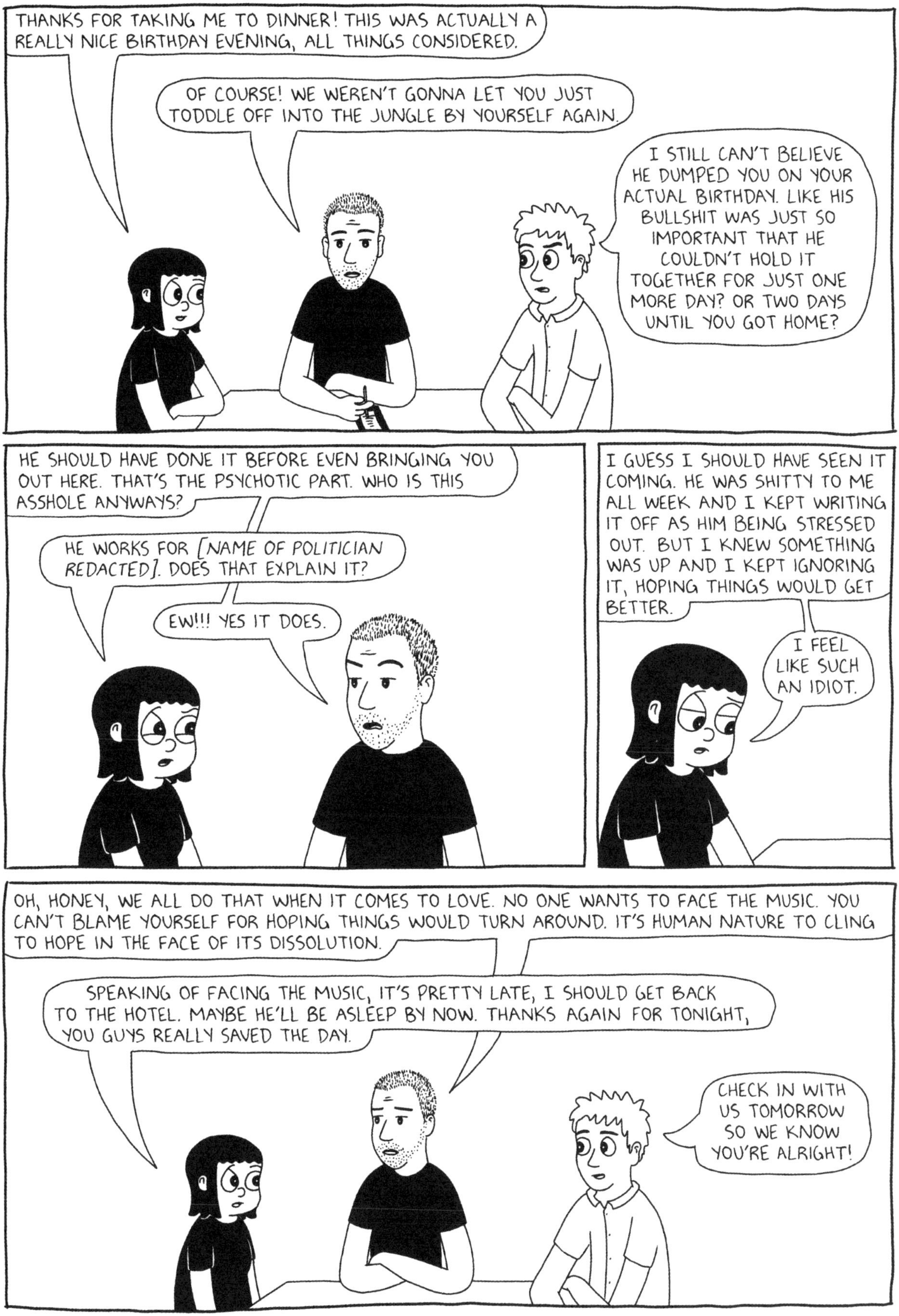
THANKS FOR TAKING ME TO DINNER! THIS WAS ACTUALLY A REALLY NICE BIRTHDAY EVENING, ALL THINGS CONSIDERED.
OF COURSE! WE WEREN'T GONNA LET YOU JUST TODDLE OFF INTO THE JUNGLE BY YOURSELF AGAIN.
I STILL CAN'T BELIEVE HE DUMPED YOU ON YOUR ACTUAL BIRTHDAY. LIKE HIS BULLSHIT WAS JUST SO IMPORTANT THAT HE COULDN'T HOLD IT TOGETHER FOR JUST ONE MORE DAY? OR TWO DAYS UNTIL YOU GOT HOME?
HE SHOULD HAVE DONE IT BEFORE EVEN BRINGING YOU OUT HERE. THAT'S THE PSYCHOTIC PART. WHO IS THIS ASSHOLE ANYWAYS?
HE WORKS FOR [NAME OF POLITICIAN REDACTED]. DOES THAT EXPLAIN IT?
EW!!! YES IT DOES.
I GUESS I SHOULD HAVE SEEN IT COMING. HE WAS SHITTY TO ME ALL WEEK AND I KEPT WRITING IT OFF AS HIM BEING STRESSED OUT. BUT I KNEW SOMETHING WAS UP AND I KEPT IGNORING IT, HOPING THINGS WOULD GET BETTER.
I FEEL LIKE SUCH AN IDIOT.
OH, HONEY, WE ALL DO THAT WHEN IT COMES TO LOVE. NO ONE WANTS TO FACE THE MUSIC. YOU CAN'T BLAME YOURSELF FOR HOPING THINGS WOULD TURN AROUND. IT'S HUMAN NATURE TO CLING TO HOPE IN THE FACE OF ITS DISSOLUTION.
SPEAKING OF FACING THE MUSIC, IT'S PRETTY LATE, I SHOULD GET BACK TO THE HOTEL. MAYBE HE'LL BE ASLEEP BY NOW. THANKS AGAIN FOR TONIGHT, YOU GUYS REALLY SAVED THE DAY.
CHECK IN WITH US TOMORROW SO WE KNOW YOU'RE ALRIGHT!

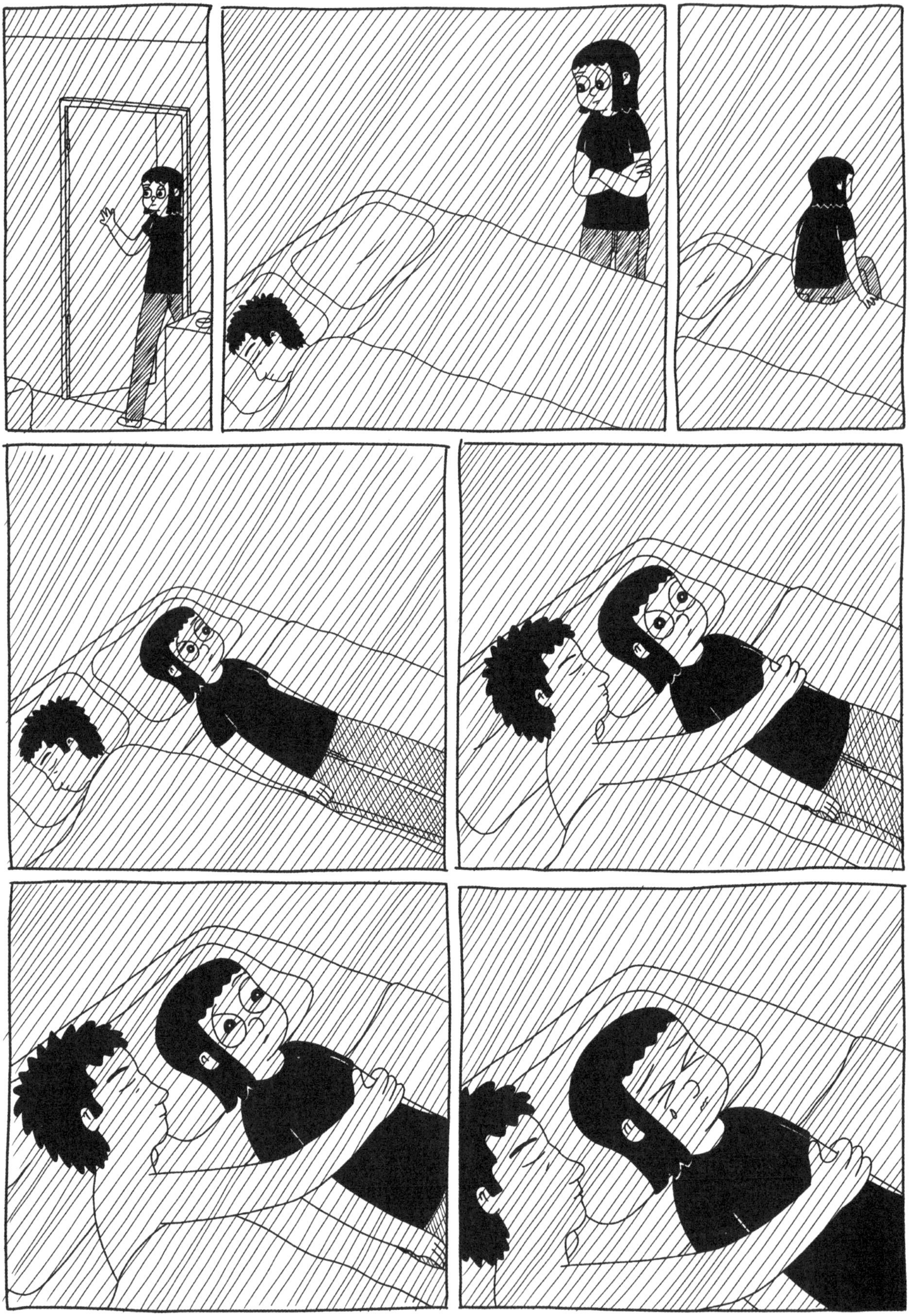

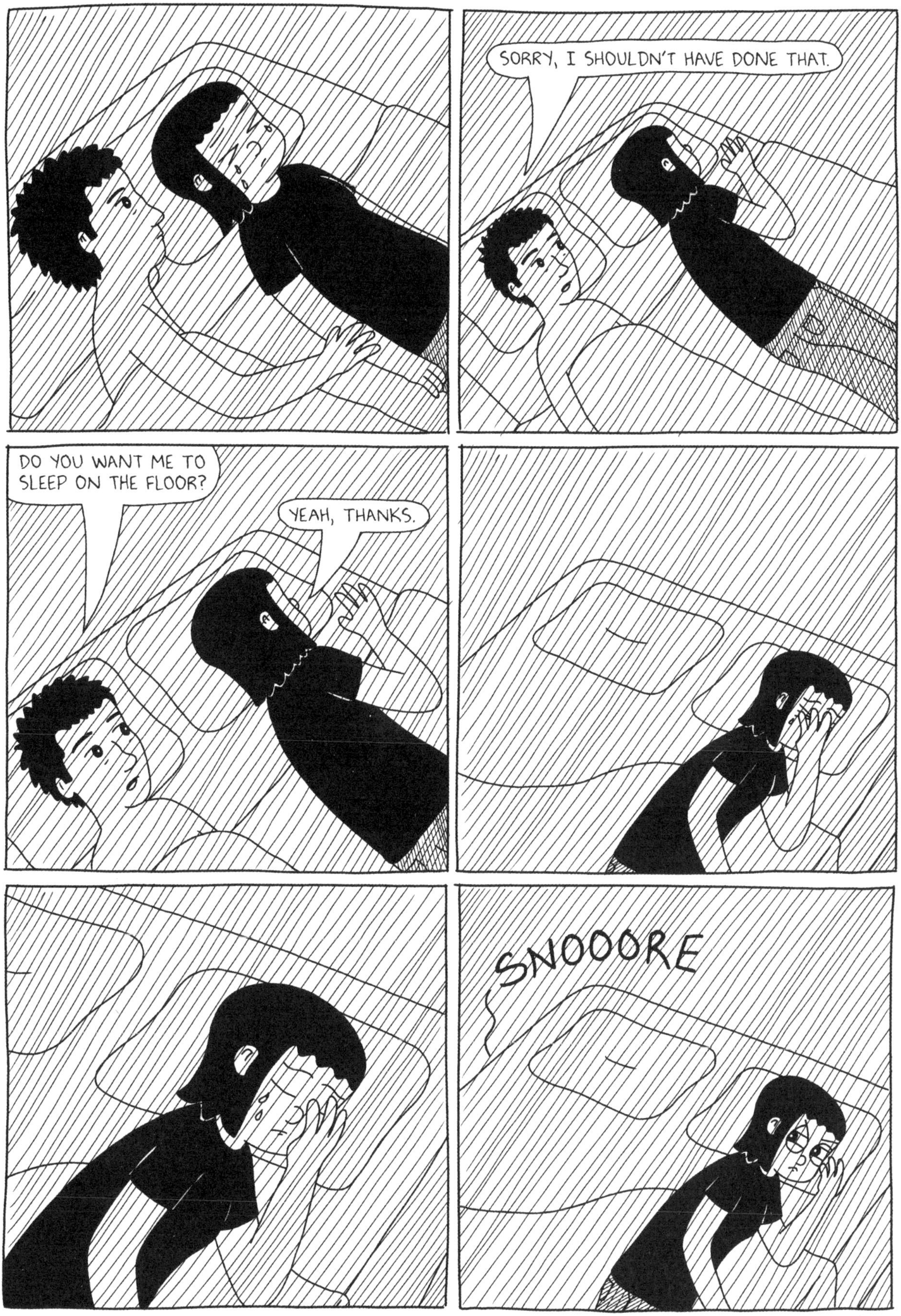
SORRY, I SHOULDN'T HAVE DONE THAT.
DO YOU WANT ME TO SLEEP ON THE FLOOR?
YEAH, THANKS.
SNOOORE

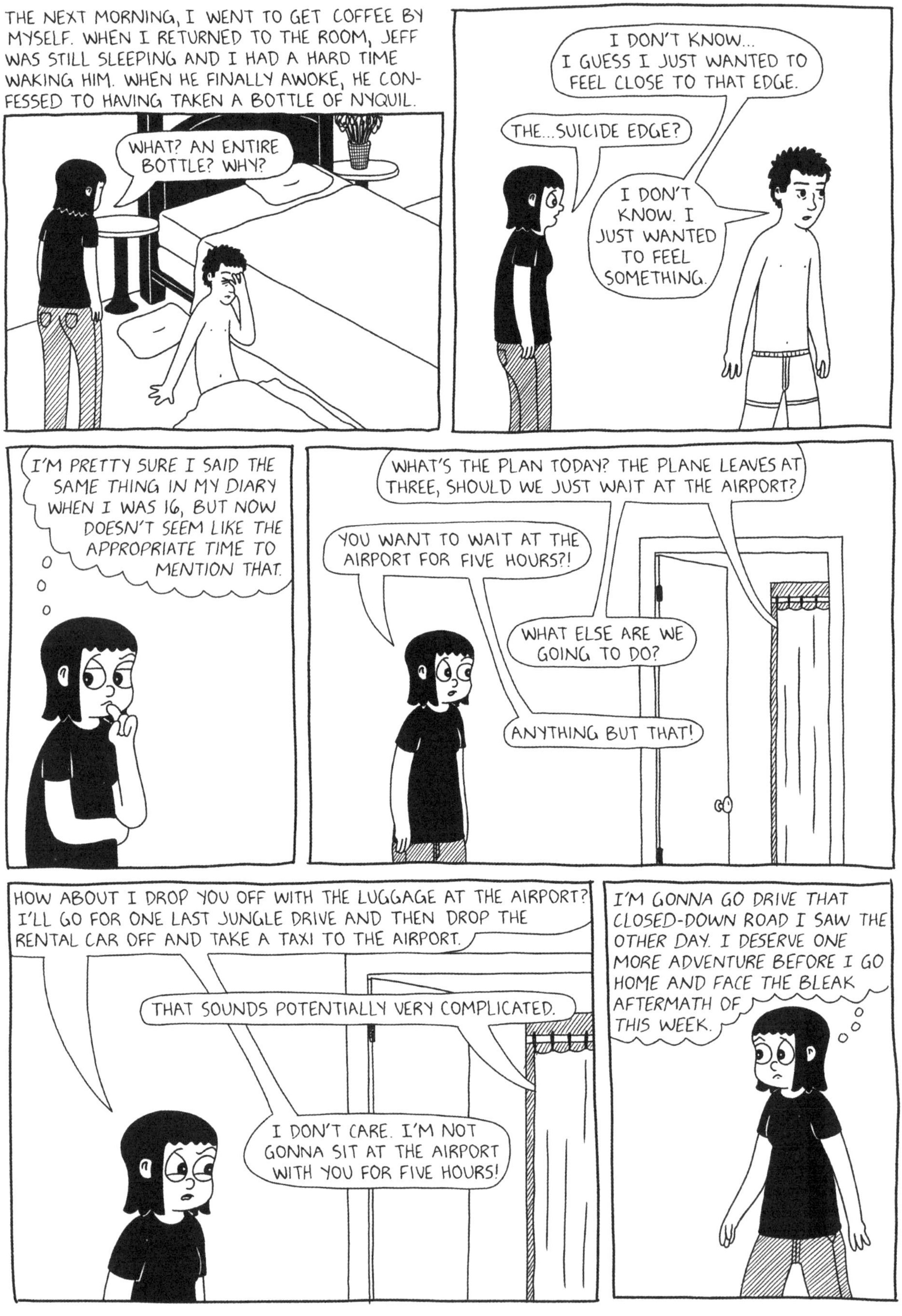
THE NEXT MORNING, I WENT TO GET COFFEE BY MYSELF. WHEN I RETURNED TO THE ROOM, JEFF WAS STILL SLEEPING AND I HAD A HARD TIME WAKING HIM. WHEN HE FINALLY AWOKE, HE CONFESSED TO HAVING TAKEN A BOTTLE OF NYQUIL.
WHAT? AN ENTIRE BOTTLE? WHY?
I DON'T KNOW. I JUST WANTED TO FEEL SOMETHING.
THE...SUICIDE EDGE?
I DON'T KNOW... I GUESS I JUST WANTED TO FEEL CLOSE TO THAT EDGE.
I'M PRETTY SURE I SAID THE SAME THING IN MY DIARY WHEN I WAS 16, BUT NOW DOESN'T SEEM LIKE THE APPROPRIATE TIME TO MENTION THAT.
WHAT'S THE PLAN TODAY? THE PLANE LEAVES AT THREE, SHOULD WE JUST WAIT AT THE AIRPORT?
YOU WANT TO WAIT AT THE AIRPORT FOR FIVE HOURS?!
WHAT ELSE ARE WE GOING TO DO?
ANYTHING BUT THAT!
HOW ABOUT I DROP YOU OFF WITH THE LUGGAGE AT THE AIRPORT? I'LL GO FOR ONE LAST JUNGLE DRIVE AND THEN DROP THE RENTAL CAR OFF AND TAKE A TAXI TO THE AIRPORT.
THAT SOUNDS POTENTIALLY VERY COMPLICATED.
I DON'T CARE. I'M NOT GONNA SIT AT THE AIRPORT WITH YOU FOR FIVE HOURS!
I'M GONNA GO DRIVE THAT CLOSED-DOWN ROAD I SAW THE OTHER DAY. I DESERVE ONE MORE ADVENTURE BEFORE I GO HOME AND FACE THE BLEAK AFTERMATH OF THIS WEEK.

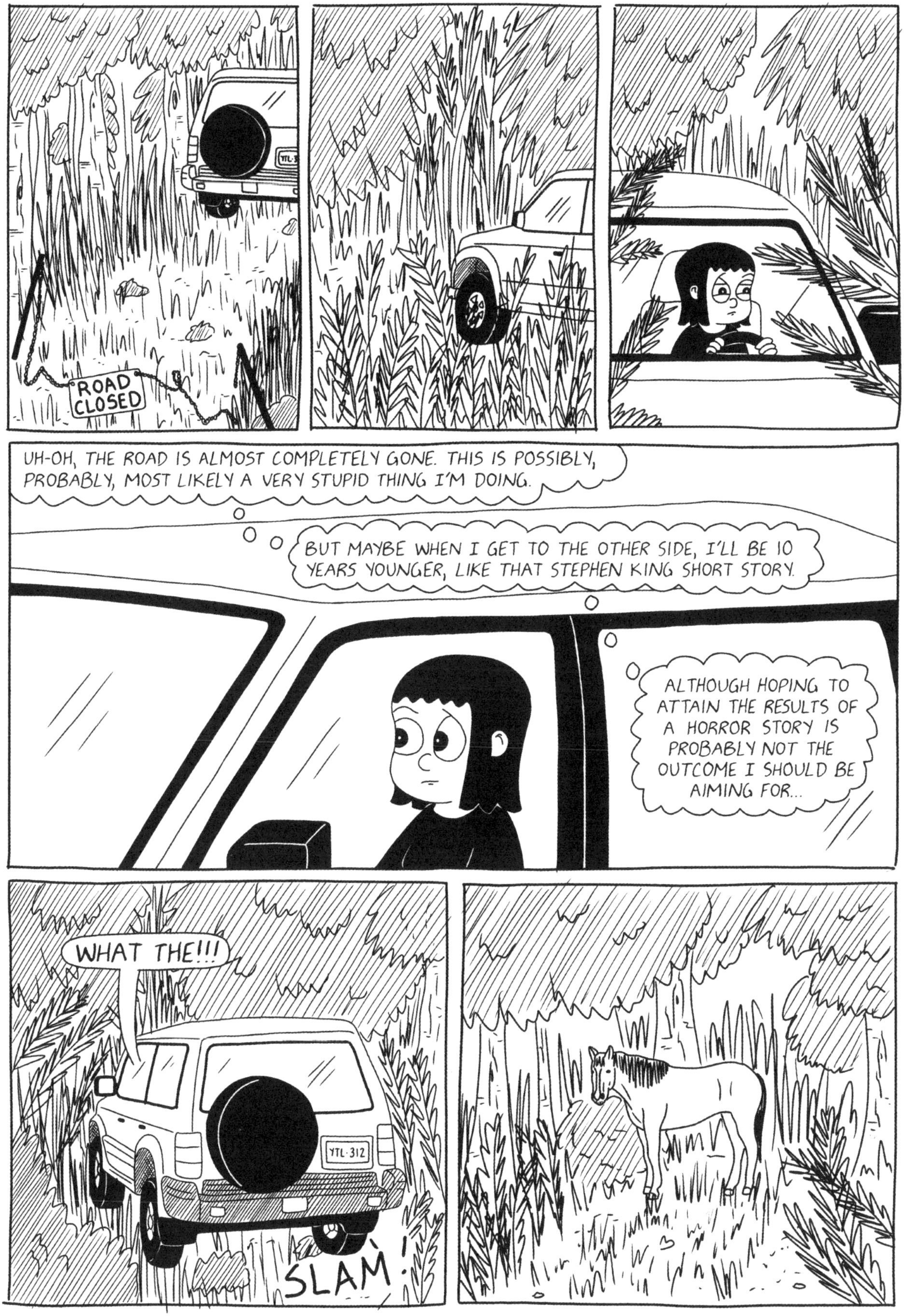
ROAD CLOSED
YTL-3
UH-OH, THE ROAD IS ALMOST COMPLETELY GONE. THIS IS POSSIBLY, PROBABLY, MOST LIKELY A VERY STUPID THING I'M DOING.
BUT MAYBE WHEN I GET TO THE OTHER SIDE, I'LL BE 10 YEARS YOUNGER, LIKE THAT STEPHEN KING SHORT STORY.
ALTHOUGH HOPING TO ATTAIN THE RESULTS OF A HORROR STORY IS PROBABLY NOT THE OUTCOME I SHOULD BE AIMING FOR...
WHAT THE!!!
YTL-312
SLAM!

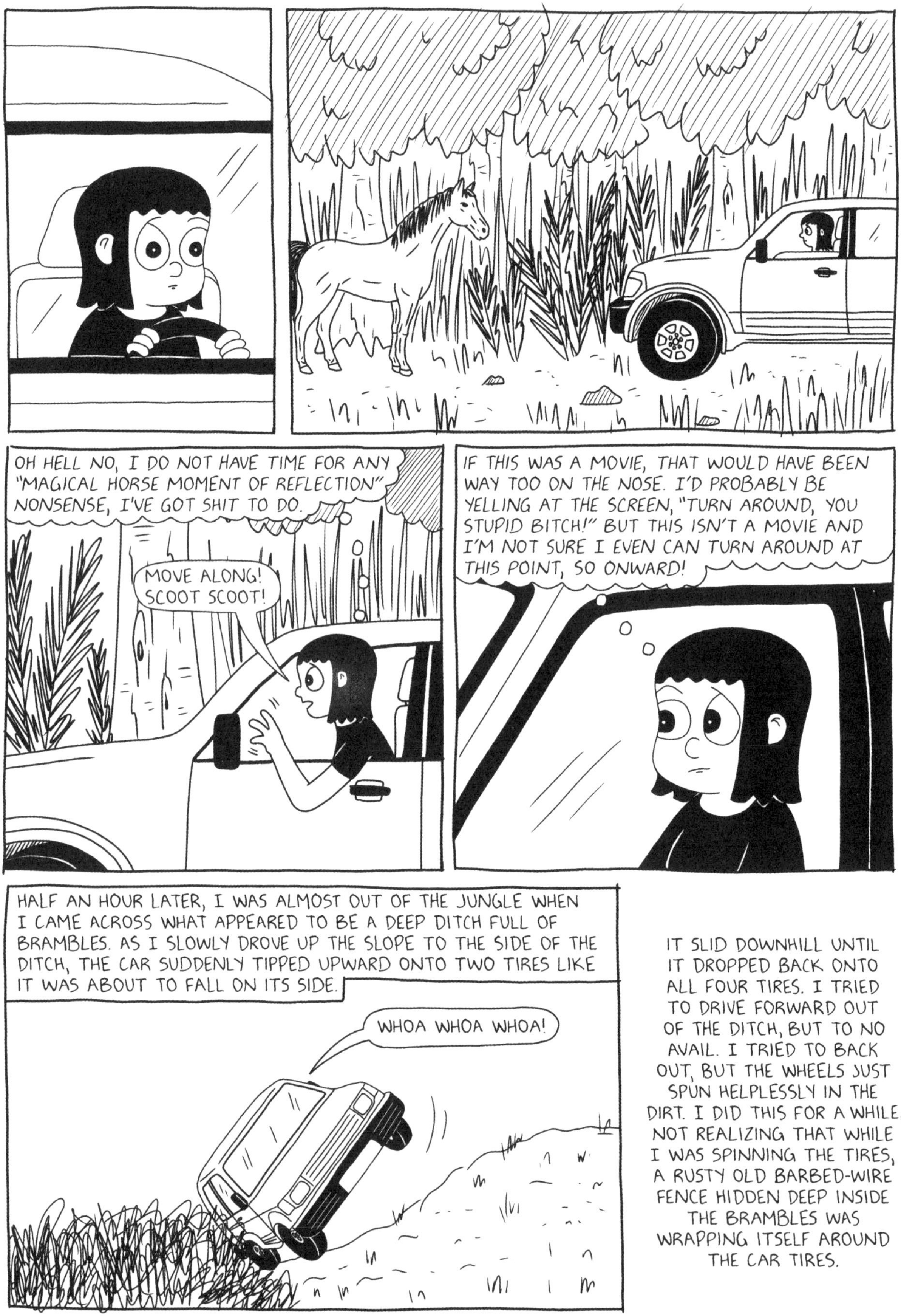

OH HELL NO, I DO NOT HAVE TIME FOR ANY "MAGICAL HORSE MOMENT OF REFLECTION" NONSENSE, I'VE GOT SHIT TO DO.
MOVE ALONG! SCOOT SCOOT!
IF THIS WAS A MOVIE, THAT WOULD HAVE BEEN WAY TOO ON THE NOSE. I'D PROBABLY BE YELLING AT THE SCREEN, "TURN AROUND, YOU STUPID BITCH!" BUT THIS ISN'T A MOVIE AND I'M NOT SURE I EVEN CAN TURN AROUND AT THIS POINT, SO ONWARD!
HALF AN HOUR LATER, I WAS ALMOST OUT OF THE JUNGLE WHEN I CAME ACROSS WHAT APPEARED TO BE A DEEP DITCH FULL OF BRAMBLES. AS I SLOWLY DROVE UP THE SLOPE TO THE SIDE OF THE DITCH, THE CAR SUDDENLY TIPPED UPWARD ONTO TWO TIRES LIKE IT WAS ABOUT TO FALL ON ITS SIDE.
WHOA WHOA WHOA!
IT SLID DOWNHILL UNTIL IT DROPPED BACK ONTO ALL FOUR TIRES. I TRIED TO DRIVE FORWARD OUT OF THE DITCH, BUT TO NO AVAIL. I TRIED TO BACK OUT, BUT THE WHEELS JUST SPUN HELPLESSLY IN THE DIRT. I DID THIS FOR A WHILE, NOT REALIZING THAT WHILE I WAS SPINNING THE TIRES, A RUSTY OLD BARBED-WIRE FENCE HIDDEN DEEP INSIDE THE BRAMBLES WAS WRAPPING ITSELF AROUND THE CAR TIRES.

I HAD NO CELL SERVICE AND THE ONLINE MAP WOULDN'T LOAD.

OH, OF COURSE. OF COURSE.

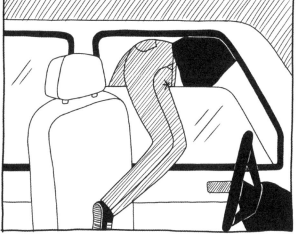

THE CAR DOORS WOULDN'T UNLOCK BUT THANK-FULLY THE WINDOW WAS HALF OPEN.

WHUMP

WHERE... WHERE'S THE REST OF THE ROAD? HOW DO I KNOW WHICH WAY TO WALK OUT OF HERE?

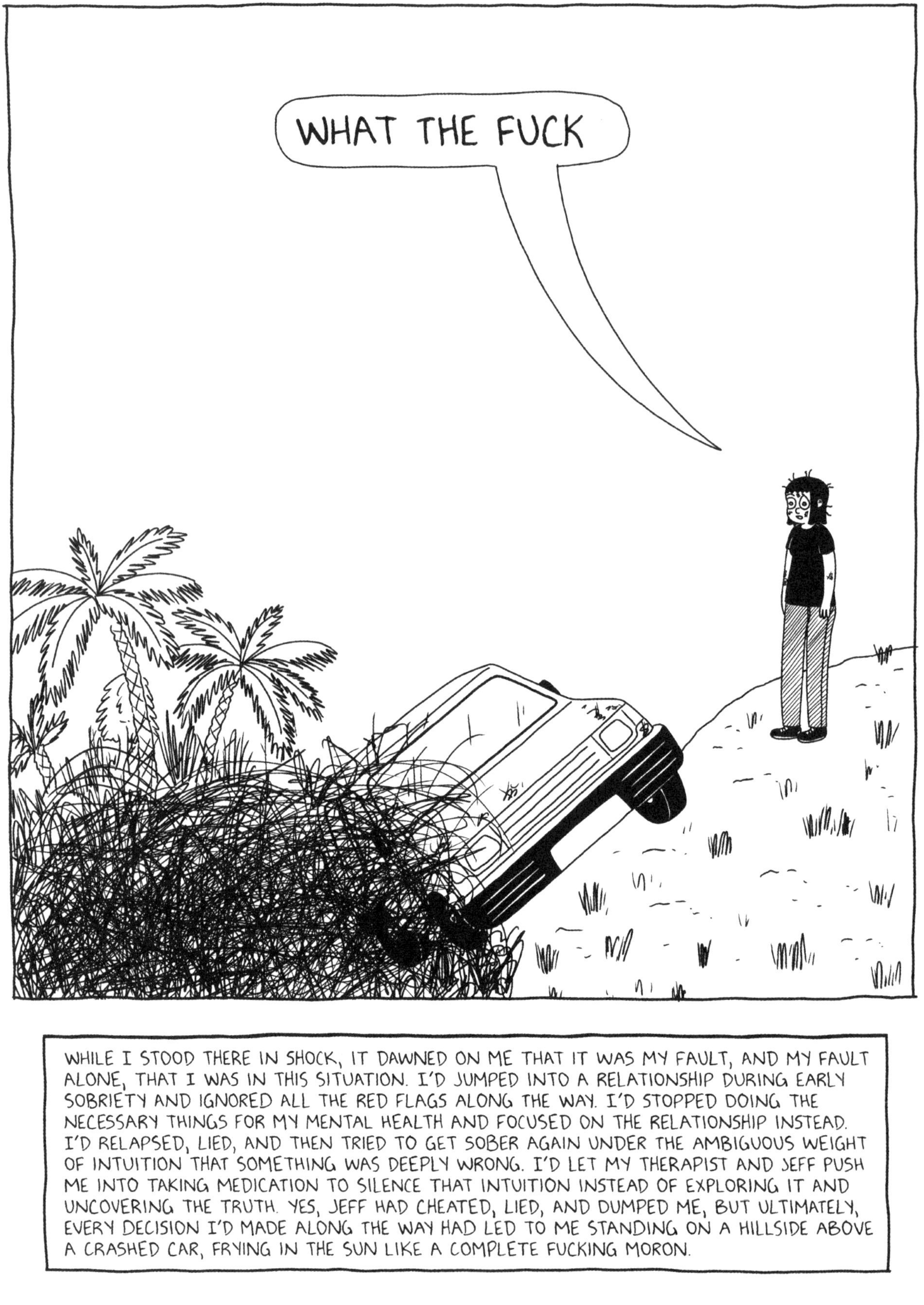
WHAT THE FUCK

WHILE I STOOD THERE IN SHOCK, IT DAWNED ON ME THAT IT WAS MY FAULT, AND MY FAULT ALONE, THAT I WAS IN THIS SITUATION. I'D JUMPED INTO A RELATIONSHIP DURING EARLY SOBRIETY AND IGNORED ALL THE RED FLAGS ALONG THE WAY. I'D STOPPED DOING THE NECESSARY THINGS FOR MY MENTAL HEALTH AND FOCUSED ON THE RELATIONSHIP INSTEAD. I'D RELAPSED, LIED, AND THEN TRIED TO GET SOBER AGAIN UNDER THE AMBIGUOUS WEIGHT OF INTUITION THAT SOMETHING WAS DEEPLY WRONG. I'D LET MY THERAPIST AND JEFF PUSH ME INTO TAKING MEDICATION TO SILENCE THAT INTUITION INSTEAD OF EXPLORING IT AND UNCOVERING THE TRUTH. YES, JEFF HAD CHEATED, LIED, AND DUMPED ME, BUT ULTIMATELY, EVERY DECISION I'D MADE ALONG THE WAY HAD LED TO ME STANDING ON A HILLSIDE ABOVE A CRASHED CAR, FRYING IN THE SUN LIKE A COMPLETE FUCKING MORON.

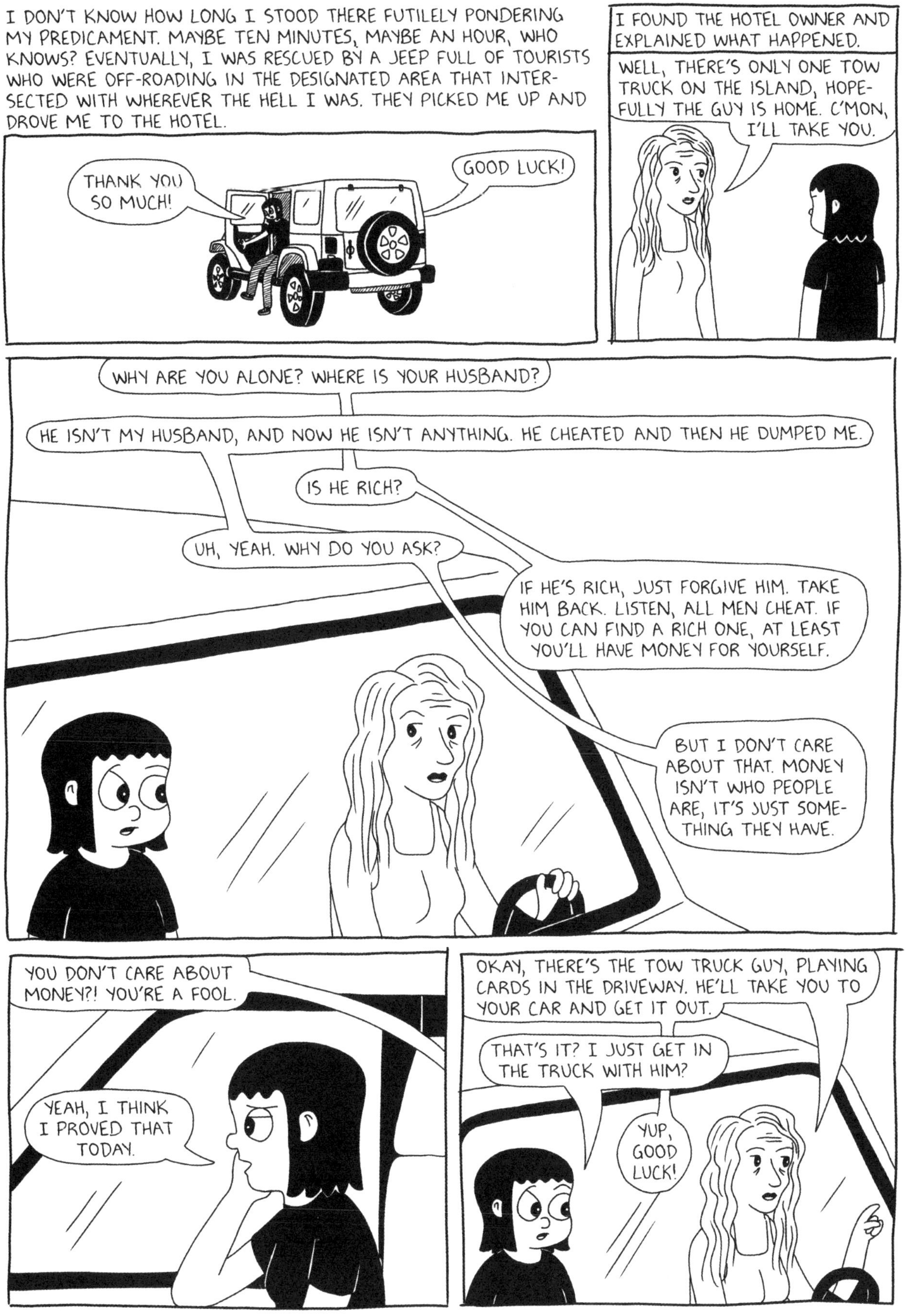
I DON'T KNOW HOW LONG I STOOD THERE FUTILELY PONDERING MY PREDICAMENT. MAYBE TEN MINUTES, MAYBE AN HOUR, WHO KNOWS? EVENTUALLY, I WAS RESCUED BY A JEEP FULL OF TOURISTS WHO WERE OFF-ROADING IN THE DESIGNATED AREA THAT INTERSECTED WITH WHEREVER THE HELL I WAS. THEY PICKED ME UP AND DROVE ME TO THE HOTEL.
THANK YOU SO MUCH!
GOOD LUCK!
I FOUND THE HOTEL OWNER AND EXPLAINED WHAT HAPPENED.
WELL, THERE'S ONLY ONE TOW TRUCK ON THE ISLAND, HOPEFULLY THE GUY IS HOME. C'MON, I'LL TAKE YOU.
WHY ARE YOU ALONE? WHERE IS YOUR HUSBAND?
HE ISN'T MY HUSBAND, AND NOW HE ISN'T ANYTHING. HE CHEATED AND THEN HE DUMPED ME.
IS HE RICH?
UH, YEAH. WHY DO YOU ASK?
IF HE'S RICH, JUST FORGIVE HIM. TAKE HIM BACK. LISTEN, ALL MEN CHEAT. IF YOU CAN FIND A RICH ONE, AT LEAST YOU'LL HAVE MONEY FOR YOURSELF.
BUT I DON'T CARE ABOUT THAT. MONEY ISN'T WHO PEOPLE ARE, IT'S JUST SOMETHING THEY HAVE.
YOU DON'T CARE ABOUT MONEY?! YOU'RE A FOOL.
YEAH, I THINK I PROVED THAT TODAY.
OKAY, THERE'S THE TOW TRUCK GUY, PLAYING CARDS IN THE DRIVEWAY. HE'LL TAKE YOU TO YOUR CAR AND GET IT OUT.
THAT'S IT? I JUST GET IN THE TRUCK WITH HIM?
YUP, GOOD LUCK!

30 MINUTES LATER:

THIS IS PRETTY BAD, BUT NOT AS BAD AS I EXPECTED. THE BARBED WIRE IS MOSTLY WRAPPED AROUND THE WHEEL WELL, NOT THE ACTUAL TIRES.

GRAB SOME GLOVES FROM MY TRUCK AND GIVE ME A HAND.

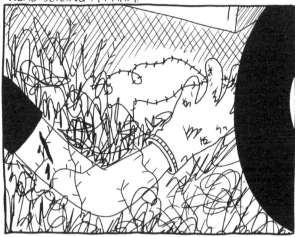

WE GINGERLY UNWRAPPED AND CUT THE BARBED WIRE FROM THE TIRES. I WAS SO AMPED UP THAT I DIDN'T REALIZE THE THICK BRAMBLE THORNS WERE SLICING MY ARM.

WE FREED THE CAR AND TOWED IT BACK TO THE HOTEL. I CALLED A CAB AND WAS AT THE AIRPORT WITHIN AN HOUR.

SORRY I'M SO LATE, BUT AT LEAST I MADE IT!

WHAT THE...???

WHAT?

WHAT HAPPENED TO YOU?!

OH, UH, HAHAHAHA...

HAHA! HAHAHA HAHA!! HAHA HA...

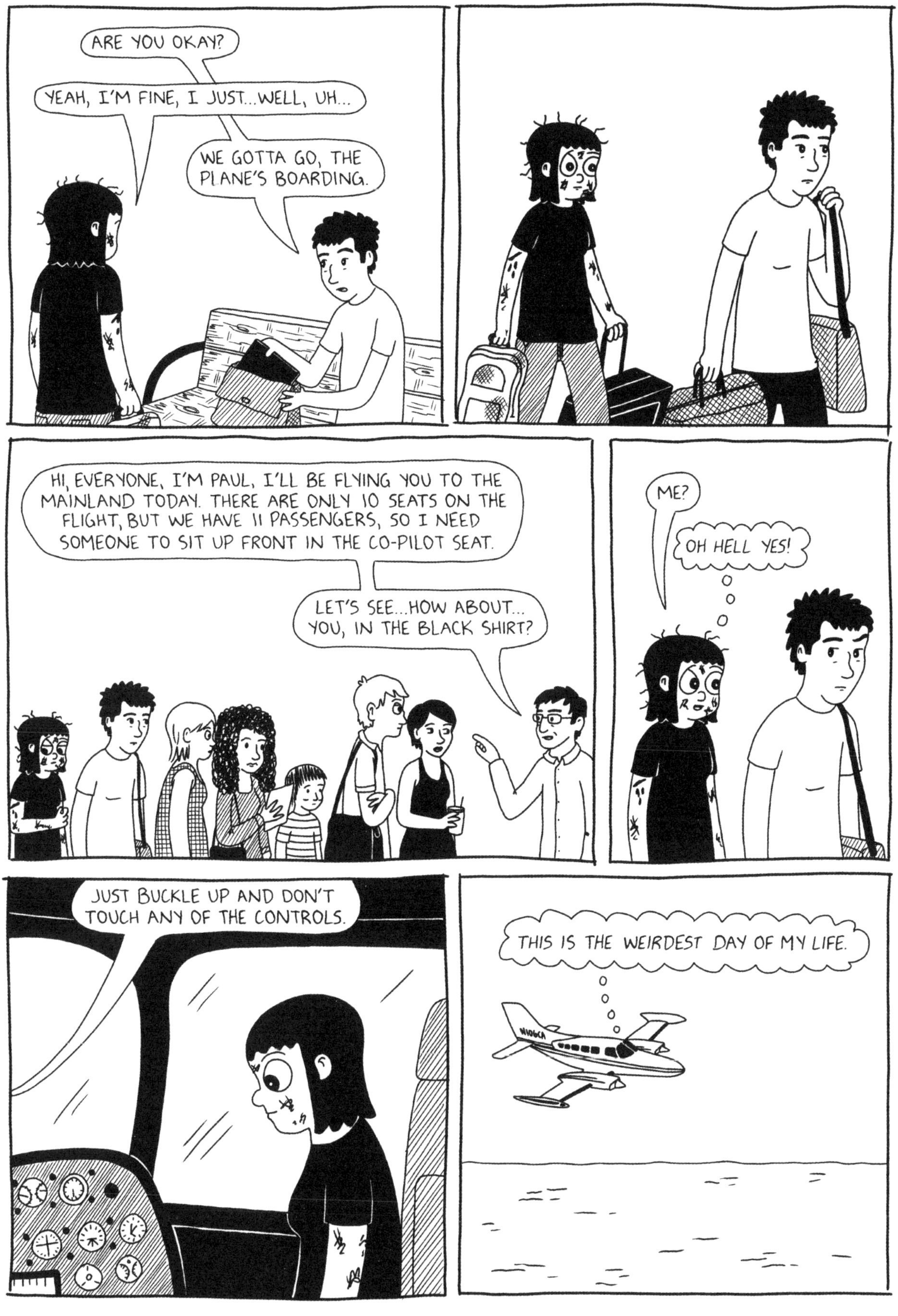
ARE YOU OKAY?
YEAH, I'M FINE, I JUST...WELL, UH...
WE GOTTA GO, THE PLANE'S BOARDING.
HI, EVERYONE, I'M PAUL, I'LL BE FLYING YOU TO THE MAINLAND TODAY. THERE ARE ONLY 10 SEATS ON THE FLIGHT, BUT WE HAVE 11 PASSENGERS, SO I NEED SOMEONE TO SIT UP FRONT IN THE CO-PILOT SEAT.
LET'S SEE...HOW ABOUT... YOU, IN THE BLACK SHIRT?
ME?
OH HELL YES!
JUST BUCKLE UP AND DON'T TOUCH ANY OF THE CONTROLS.
THIS IS THE WEIRDEST DAY OF MY LIFE.

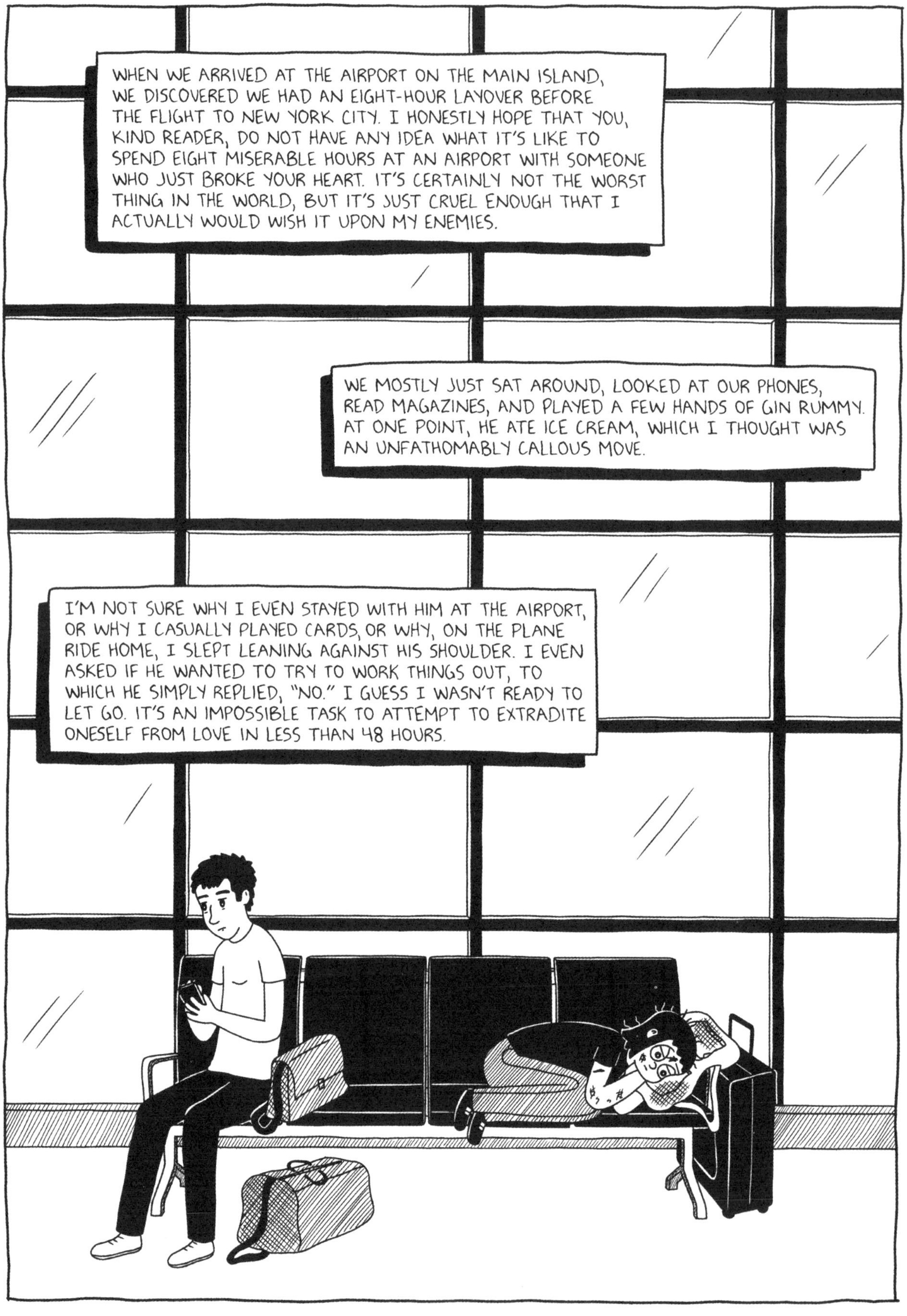
WHEN WE ARRIVED AT THE AIRPORT ON THE MAIN ISLAND, WE DISCOVERED WE HAD AN EIGHT-HOUR LAYOVER BEFORE THE FLIGHT TO NEW YORK CITY. I HONESTLY HOPE THAT YOU, KIND READER, DO NOT HAVE ANY IDEA WHAT IT'S LIKE TO SPEND EIGHT MISERABLE HOURS AT AN AIRPORT WITH SOMEONE WHO JUST BROKE YOUR HEART. IT'S CERTAINLY NOT THE WORST THING IN THE WORLD, BUT IT'S JUST CRUEL ENOUGH THAT I ACTUALLY WOULD WISH IT UPON MY ENEMIES.
WE MOSTLY JUST SAT AROUND, LOOKED AT OUR PHONES, READ MAGAZINES, AND PLAYED A FEW HANDS OF GIN RUMMY. AT ONE POINT, HE ATE ICE CREAM, WHICH I THOUGHT WAS AN UNFATHOMABLY CALLOUS MOVE.
I'M NOT SURE WHY I EVEN STAYED WITH HIM AT THE AIRPORT, OR WHY I CASUALLY PLAYED CARDS, OR WHY, ON THE PLANE RIDE HOME, I SLEPT LEANING AGAINST HIS SHOULDER. I EVEN ASKED IF HE WANTED TO TRY TO WORK THINGS OUT, TO WHICH HE SIMPLY REPLIED, "NO." I GUESS I WASN'T READY TO LET GO. IT'S AN IMPOSSIBLE TASK TO ATTEMPT TO EXTRADITE ONESELF FROM LOVE IN LESS THAN 48 HOURS.

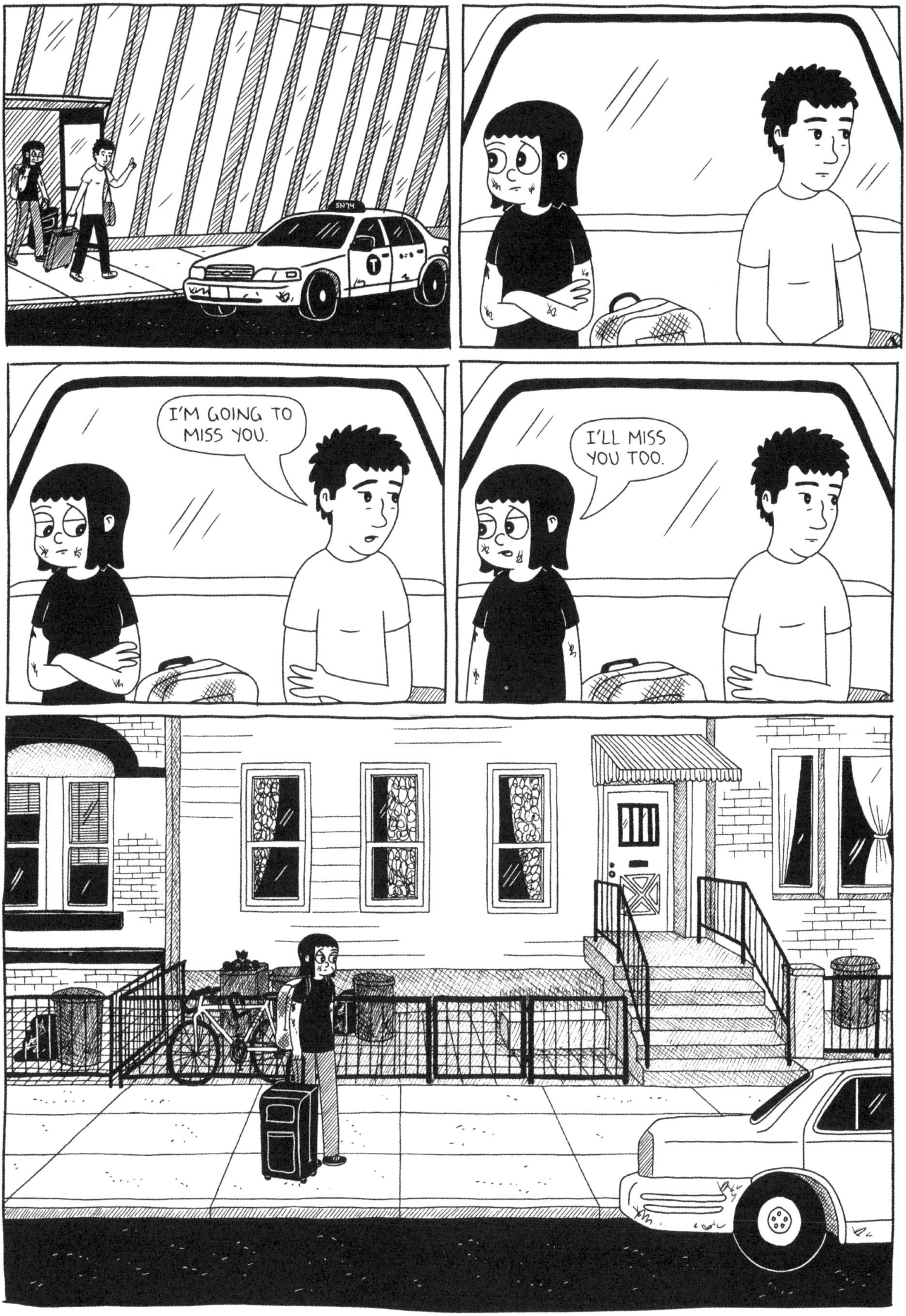
5N74
I'M GOING TO MISS YOU.
I'LL MISS YOU TOO.

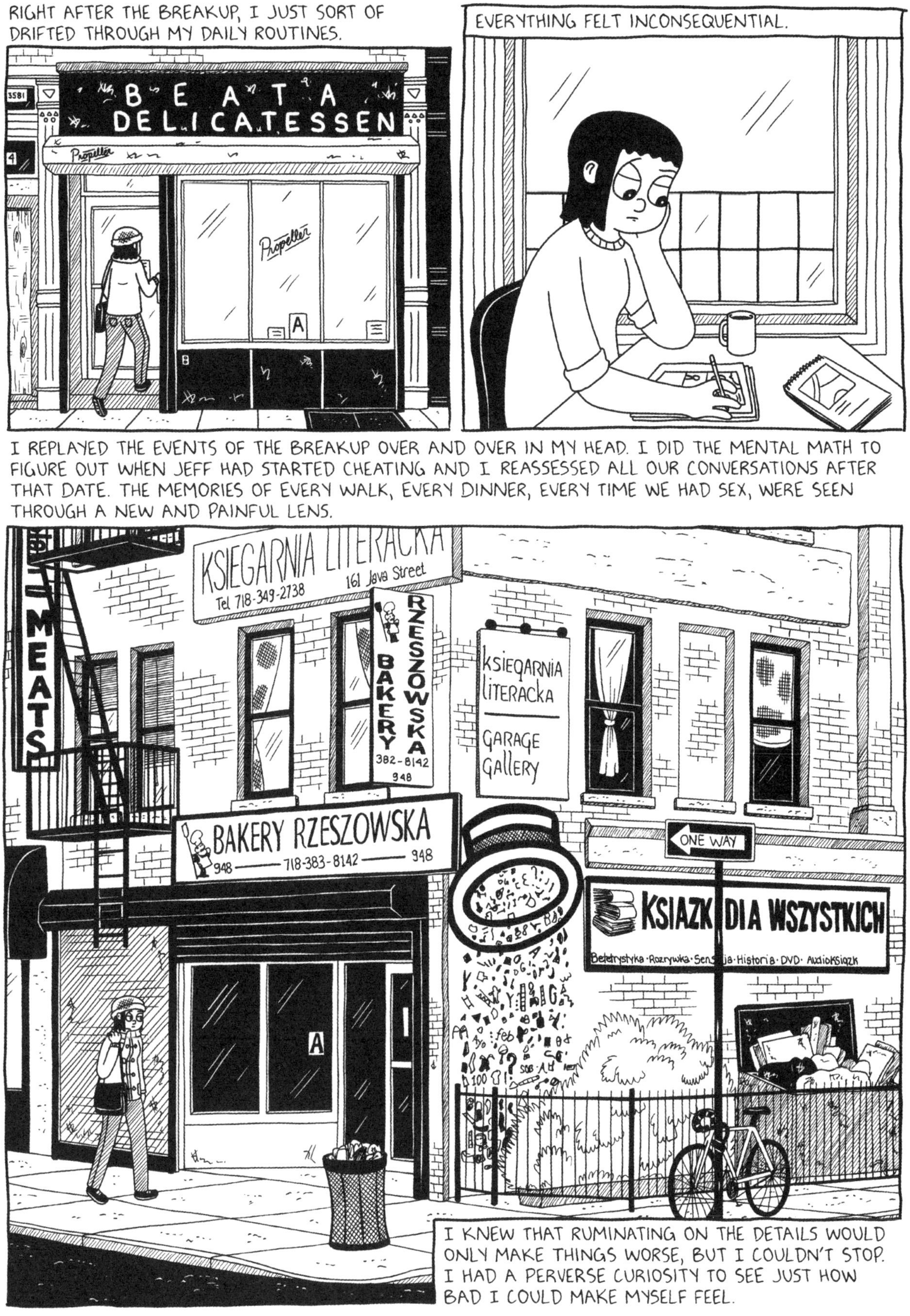
RIGHT AFTER THE BREAKUP, I JUST SORT OF DRIFTED THROUGH MY DAILY ROUTINES.
BEATA DELICATESSEN
Propeller
EVERYTHING FELT INCONSEQUENTIAL.
I REPLAYED THE EVENTS OF THE BREAKUP OVER AND OVER IN MY HEAD. I DID THE MENTAL MATH TO FIGURE OUT WHEN JEFF HAD STARTED CHEATING AND I REASSESSED ALL OUR CONVERSATIONS AFTER THAT DATE. THE MEMORIES OF EVERY WALK, EVERY DINNER, EVERY TIME WE HAD SEX, WERE SEEN THROUGH A NEW AND PAINFUL LENS.
KSIEGARNIA LITERACKA
Tel 718-349-2738
161 Java Street
MEATS
RZESZOWSKA BAKERY 382-8142 948
ksiegarnia literacka
GARAGE GALLERY
BAKERY RZESZOWSKA
948 718-383-8142 948
ONE WAY
KSIAZK DIA WSZYSTKICH
I KNEW THAT RUMINATING ON THE DETAILS WOULD ONLY MAKE THINGS WORSE, BUT I COULDN'T STOP. I HAD A PERVERSE CURIOSITY TO SEE JUST HOW BAD I COULD MAKE MYSELF FEEL.

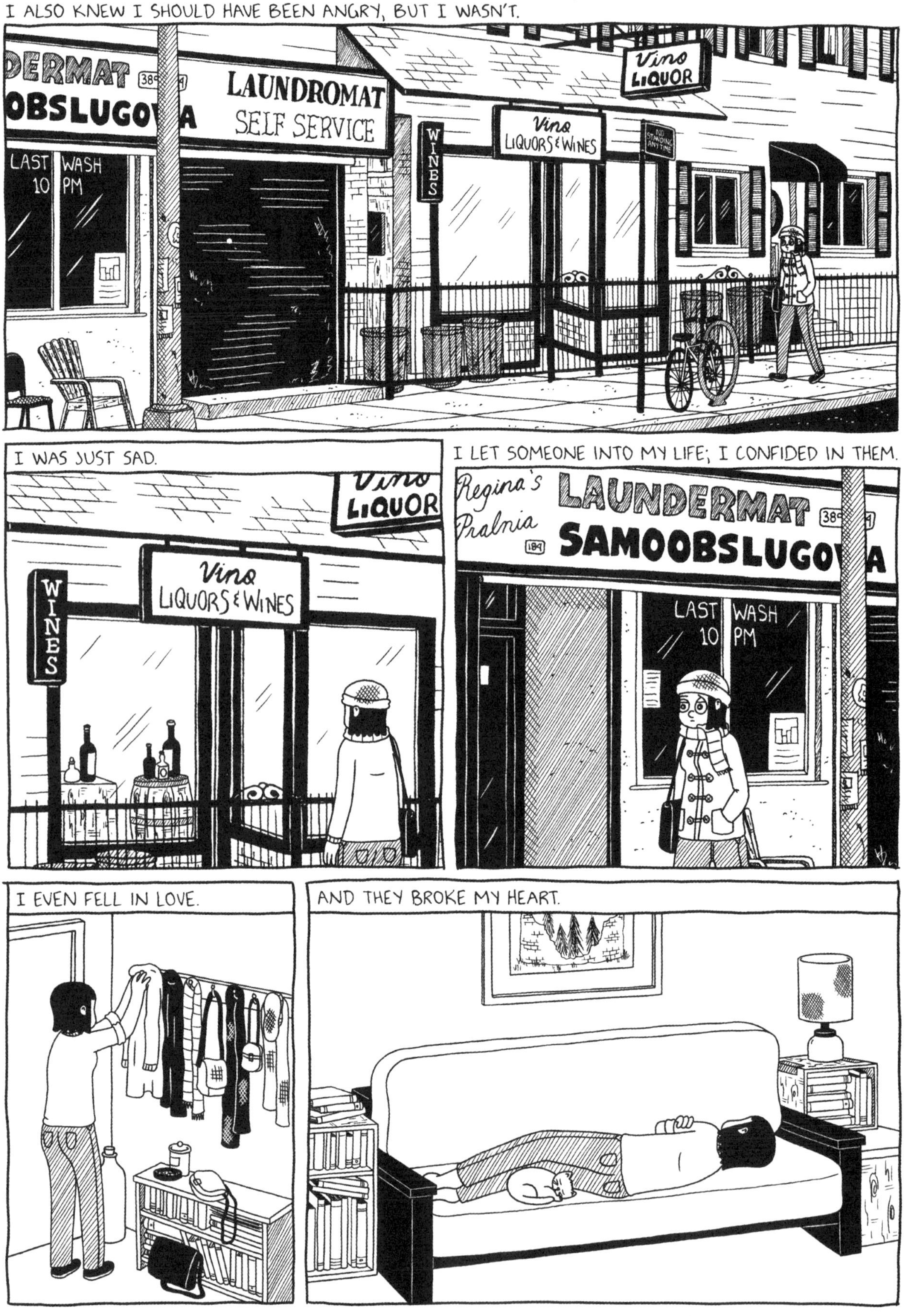
I ALSO KNEW I SHOULD HAVE BEEN ANGRY, BUT I WASN'T.
LAUNDROMAT
SELF SERVICE
LAST WASH
10 PM
Vino
LIQUOR
Vino
LIQUORS & WINES
WINES
I WAS JUST SAD.
I LET SOMEONE INTO MY LIFE; I CONFIDED IN THEM.
Regina's
Pralnia
LAUNDERMAT
SAMOOBSLUGOW A
LAST WASH
10 PM
I EVEN FELL IN LOVE.
AND THEY BROKE MY HEART.

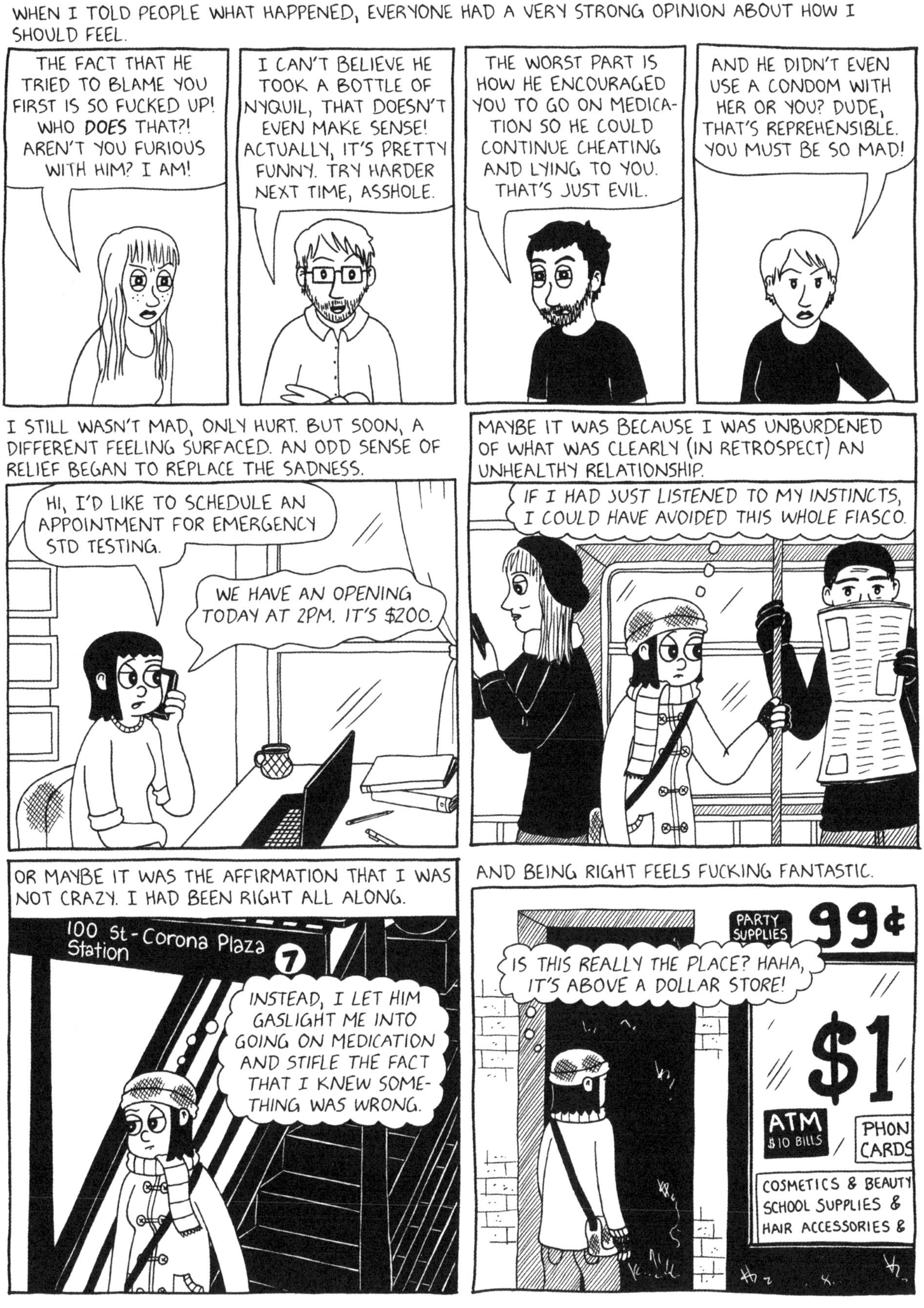
WHEN I TOLD PEOPLE WHAT HAPPENED, EVERYONE HAD A VERY STRONG OPINION ABOUT HOW I SHOULD FEEL.
THE FACT THAT HE TRIED TO BLAME YOU FIRST IS SO FUCKED UP! WHO **DOES** THAT?! AREN'T YOU FURIOUS WITH HIM? I AM!
I CAN'T BELIEVE HE TOOK A BOTTLE OF NYQUIL, THAT DOESN'T EVEN MAKE SENSE! ACTUALLY, IT'S PRETTY FUNNY. TRY HARDER NEXT TIME, ASSHOLE.
THE WORST PART IS HOW HE ENCOURAGED YOU TO GO ON MEDICATION SO HE COULD CONTINUE CHEATING AND LYING TO YOU. THAT'S JUST EVIL.
AND HE DIDN'T EVEN USE A CONDOM WITH HER OR YOU? DUDE, THAT'S REPREHENSIBLE. YOU MUST BE SO MAD!
I STILL WASN'T MAD, ONLY HURT. BUT SOON, A DIFFERENT FEELING SURFACED. AN ODD SENSE OF RELIEF BEGAN TO REPLACE THE SADNESS.
HI, I'D LIKE TO SCHEDULE AN APPOINTMENT FOR EMERGENCY STD TESTING.
WE HAVE AN OPENING TODAY AT 2PM. IT'S $200.
MAYBE IT WAS BECAUSE I WAS UNBURDENED OF WHAT WAS CLEARLY (IN RETROSPECT) AN UNHEALTHY RELATIONSHIP.
IF I HAD JUST LISTENED TO MY INSTINCTS, I COULD HAVE AVOIDED THIS WHOLE FIASCO.
OR MAYBE IT WAS THE AFFIRMATION THAT I WAS NOT CRAZY. I HAD BEEN RIGHT ALL ALONG.
100 St - Corona Plaza Station
7
INSTEAD, I LET HIM GASLIGHT ME INTO GOING ON MEDICATION AND STIFLE THE FACT THAT I KNEW SOMETHING WAS WRONG.
AND BEING RIGHT FEELS FUCKING FANTASTIC.
PARTY SUPPLIES
99¢
IS THIS REALLY THE PLACE? HAHA, IT'S ABOVE A DOLLAR STORE!
$1
ATM $10 BILLS
PHON CARDS
COSMETICS & BEAUTY
SCHOOL SUPPLIES &
HAIR ACCESSORIES &

WHEN I TALKED TO MY MOM ABOUT THE BREAK-UP, SHE TOLD ME TO PREPARE TO FEEL THE CLASSIC "FIVE STAGES OF GRIEF." I'D ALREADY EXPERIENCED DENIAL AND ISOLATION IN PUERTO RICO, WHICH HAD LED TO SOME HALF-HEARTED BARGAINING.

HI, I HAVE A TWO O'CLOCK APPOINTMENT.

WE'RE A BIT BACKED UP, THE WAIT IS ABOUT AN HOUR OR SO.

BUT I WAS UNSURE ABOUT THE OTHER STAGES. DEPRESSION WAS TOO EXTREME. I KNEW IT WAS JUST TEMPORARY SADNESS THAT I FELT.

CELEBZ N' SHIT

IT SEEMED WAY TOO EARLY TO EXPERIENCE THE LAST STAGE: ACCEPTANCE.

HOW DOES THIS WORK?

WE TAKE SOME BLOOD SAMPLES AND YOU GET YOUR RESULTS IN 24 HOURS.

THE ONLY STAGE I HADN'T EXPERIENCED YET WAS ANGER, EVEN THOUGH IT WOULD HAVE BEEN VERY JUSTIFIED.

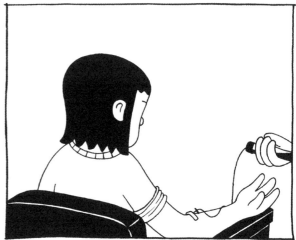

IT'S SO UNFAIR THAT HE GETS TO CHEAT AND DUMP ME AND GO ON WITH HIS LIFE LIKE NOTHING HAPPENED WHILE I HAVE TO SPEND MY SATURDAY AFTERNOON IN AN STD CLINIC WHILE HE'S PROBABLY ON THE COUCH EATING PIE.

HIV

AND THEN IT HIT ME.

THAT *MOTHERFUCKER*!!!!

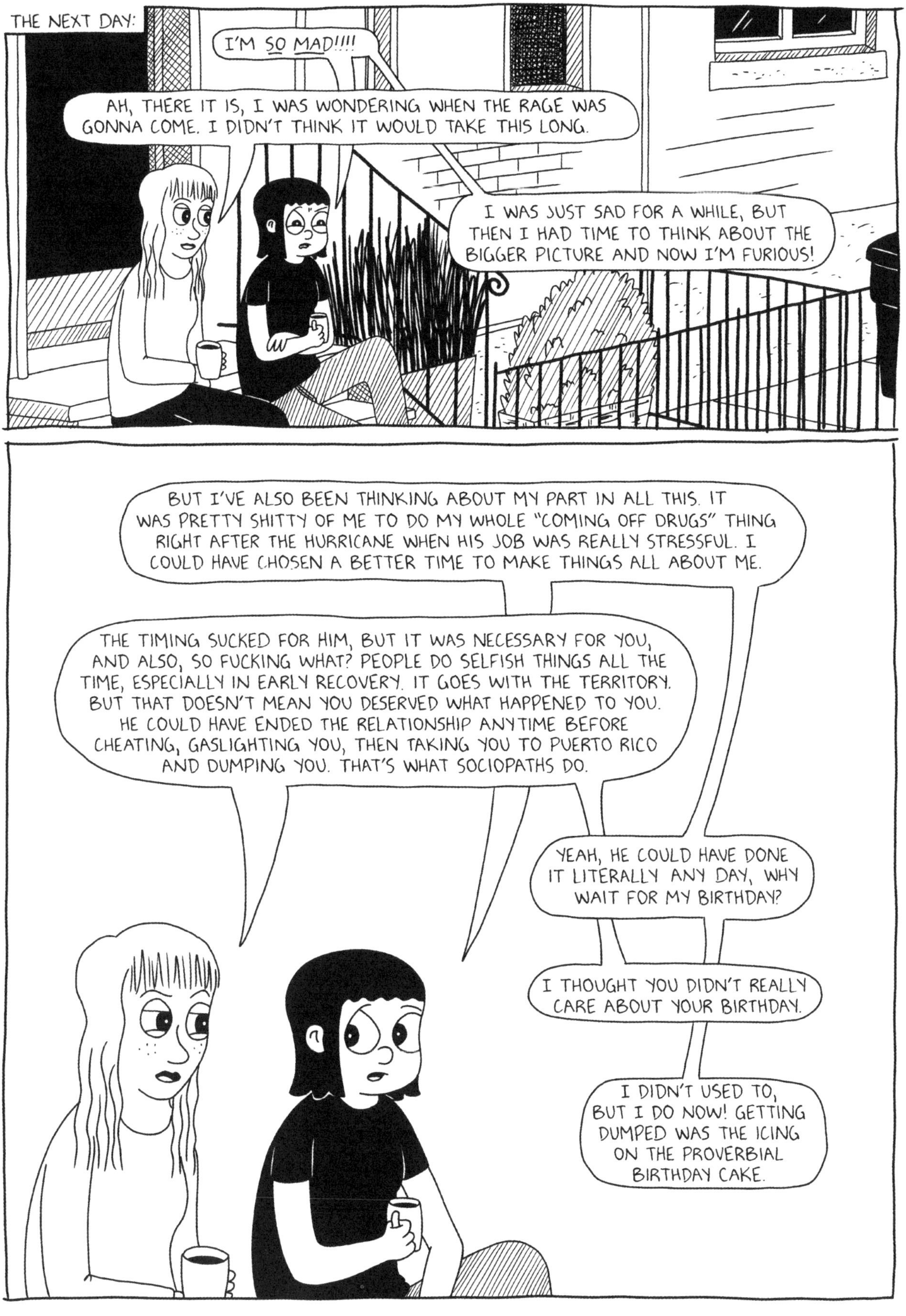
THE NEXT DAY:
I'M SO MAD!!!!
AH, THERE IT IS, I WAS WONDERING WHEN THE RAGE WAS GONNA COME. I DIDN'T THINK IT WOULD TAKE THIS LONG.
I WAS JUST SAD FOR A WHILE, BUT THEN I HAD TIME TO THINK ABOUT THE BIGGER PICTURE AND NOW I'M FURIOUS!
BUT I'VE ALSO BEEN THINKING ABOUT MY PART IN ALL THIS. IT WAS PRETTY SHITTY OF ME TO DO MY WHOLE "COMING OFF DRUGS" THING RIGHT AFTER THE HURRICANE WHEN HIS JOB WAS REALLY STRESSFUL. I COULD HAVE CHOSEN A BETTER TIME TO MAKE THINGS ALL ABOUT ME.
THE TIMING SUCKED FOR HIM, BUT IT WAS NECESSARY FOR YOU, AND ALSO, SO FUCKING WHAT? PEOPLE DO SELFISH THINGS ALL THE TIME, ESPECIALLY IN EARLY RECOVERY. IT GOES WITH THE TERRITORY. BUT THAT DOESN'T MEAN YOU DESERVED WHAT HAPPENED TO YOU. HE COULD HAVE ENDED THE RELATIONSHIP ANYTIME BEFORE CHEATING, GASLIGHTING YOU, THEN TAKING YOU TO PUERTO RICO AND DUMPING YOU. THAT'S WHAT SOCIOPATHS DO.
YEAH, HE COULD HAVE DONE IT LITERALLY ANY DAY, WHY WAIT FOR MY BIRTHDAY?
I THOUGHT YOU DIDN'T REALLY CARE ABOUT YOUR BIRTHDAY.
I DIDN'T USED TO, BUT I DO NOW! GETTING DUMPED WAS THE ICING ON THE PROVERBIAL BIRTHDAY CAKE.

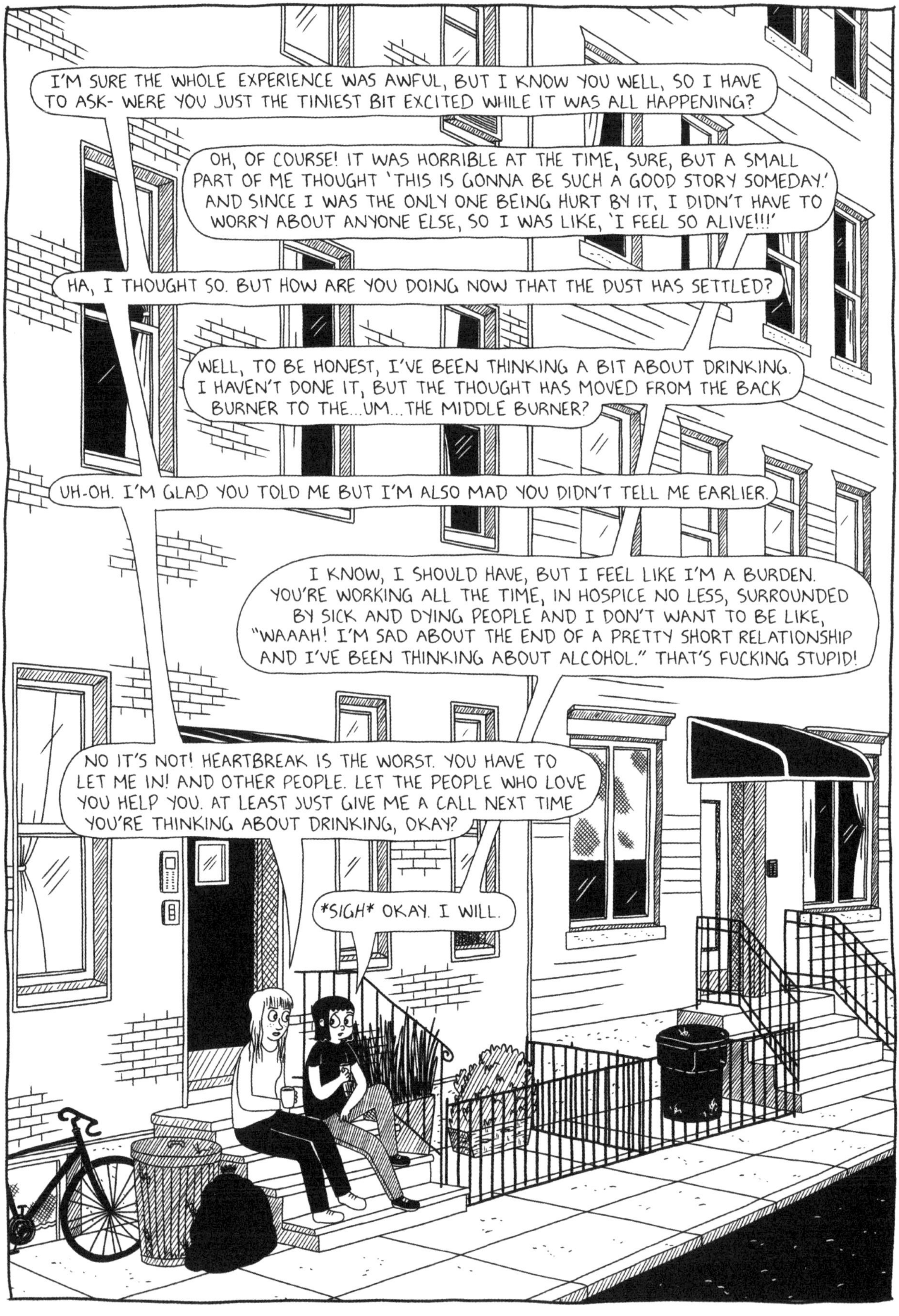
I'M SURE THE WHOLE EXPERIENCE WAS AWFUL, BUT I KNOW YOU WELL, SO I HAVE TO ASK- WERE YOU JUST THE TINIEST BIT EXCITED WHILE IT WAS ALL HAPPENING?
OH, OF COURSE! IT WAS HORRIBLE AT THE TIME, SURE, BUT A SMALL PART OF ME THOUGHT 'THIS IS GONNA BE SUCH A GOOD STORY SOMEDAY.' AND SINCE I WAS THE ONLY ONE BEING HURT BY IT, I DIDN'T HAVE TO WORRY ABOUT ANYONE ELSE, SO I WAS LIKE, 'I FEEL SO ALIVE!!!'
HA, I THOUGHT SO. BUT HOW ARE YOU DOING NOW THAT THE DUST HAS SETTLED?
WELL, TO BE HONEST, I'VE BEEN THINKING A BIT ABOUT DRINKING. I HAVEN'T DONE IT, BUT THE THOUGHT HAS MOVED FROM THE BACK BURNER TO THE...UM...THE MIDDLE BURNER?
UH-OH. I'M GLAD YOU TOLD ME BUT I'M ALSO MAD YOU DIDN'T TELL ME EARLIER.
I KNOW, I SHOULD HAVE, BUT I FEEL LIKE I'M A BURDEN. YOU'RE WORKING ALL THE TIME, IN HOSPICE NO LESS, SURROUNDED BY SICK AND DYING PEOPLE AND I DON'T WANT TO BE LIKE, "WAAAH! I'M SAD ABOUT THE END OF A PRETTY SHORT RELATIONSHIP AND I'VE BEEN THINKING ABOUT ALCOHOL." THAT'S FUCKING STUPID!
NO IT'S NOT! HEARTBREAK IS THE WORST. YOU HAVE TO LET ME IN! AND OTHER PEOPLE. LET THE PEOPLE WHO LOVE YOU HELP YOU. AT LEAST JUST GIVE ME A CALL NEXT TIME YOU'RE THINKING ABOUT DRINKING, OKAY?
SIGH OKAY. I WILL.

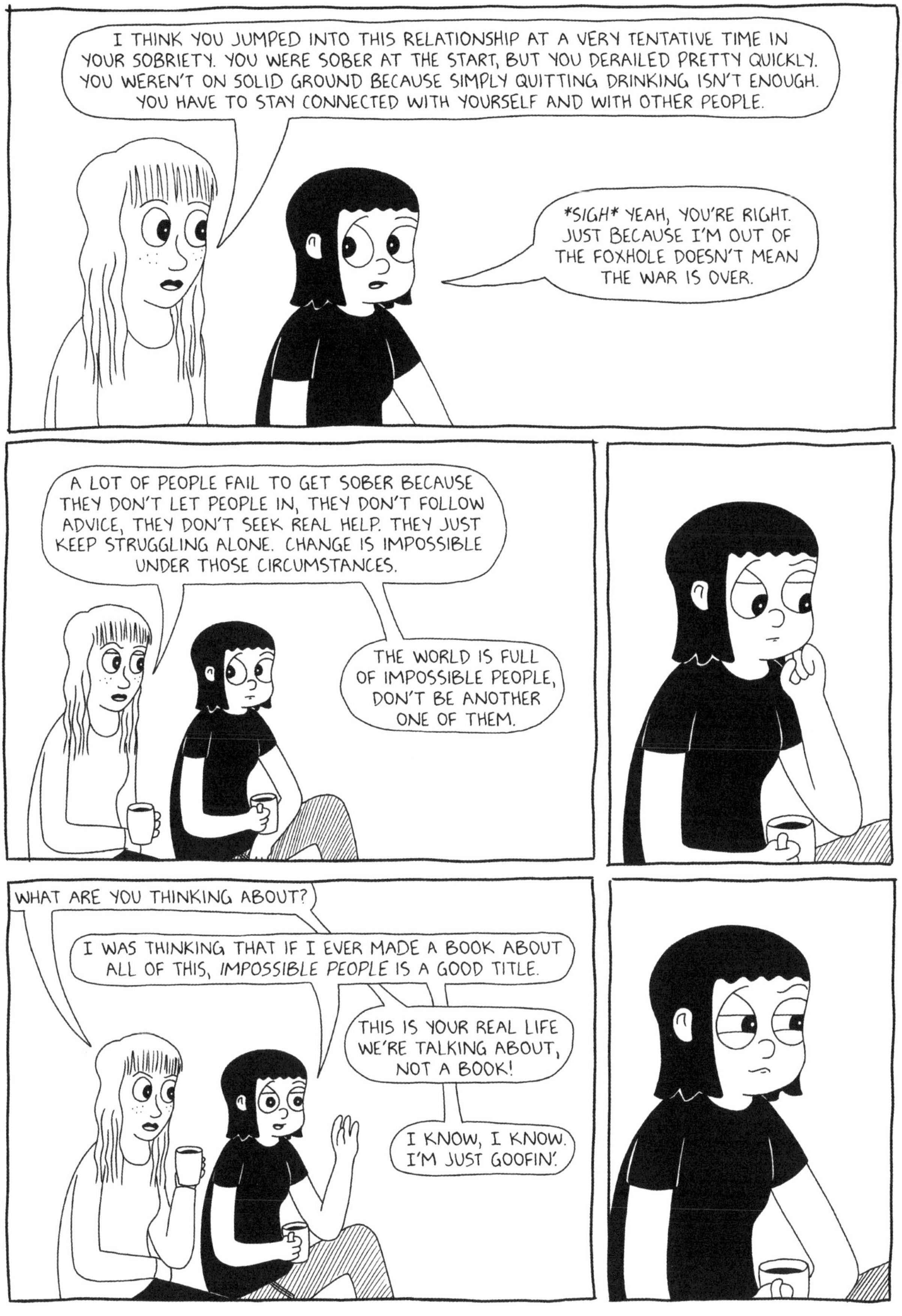
I THINK YOU JUMPED INTO THIS RELATIONSHIP AT A VERY TENTATIVE TIME IN YOUR SOBRIETY. YOU WERE SOBER AT THE START, BUT YOU DERAILED PRETTY QUICKLY. YOU WEREN'T ON SOLID GROUND BECAUSE SIMPLY QUITTING DRINKING ISN'T ENOUGH. YOU HAVE TO STAY CONNECTED WITH YOURSELF AND WITH OTHER PEOPLE.
SIGH YEAH, YOU'RE RIGHT. JUST BECAUSE I'M OUT OF THE FOXHOLE DOESN'T MEAN THE WAR IS OVER.
A LOT OF PEOPLE FAIL TO GET SOBER BECAUSE THEY DON'T LET PEOPLE IN, THEY DON'T FOLLOW ADVICE, THEY DON'T SEEK REAL HELP. THEY JUST KEEP STRUGGLING ALONE. CHANGE IS IMPOSSIBLE UNDER THOSE CIRCUMSTANCES.
THE WORLD IS FULL OF IMPOSSIBLE PEOPLE, DON'T BE ANOTHER ONE OF THEM.
WHAT ARE YOU THINKING ABOUT?
I WAS THINKING THAT IF I EVER MADE A BOOK ABOUT ALL OF THIS, *IMPOSSIBLE PEOPLE* IS A GOOD TITLE.
THIS IS YOUR REAL LIFE WE'RE TALKING ABOUT, NOT A BOOK!
I KNOW, I KNOW. I'M JUST GOOFIN'.

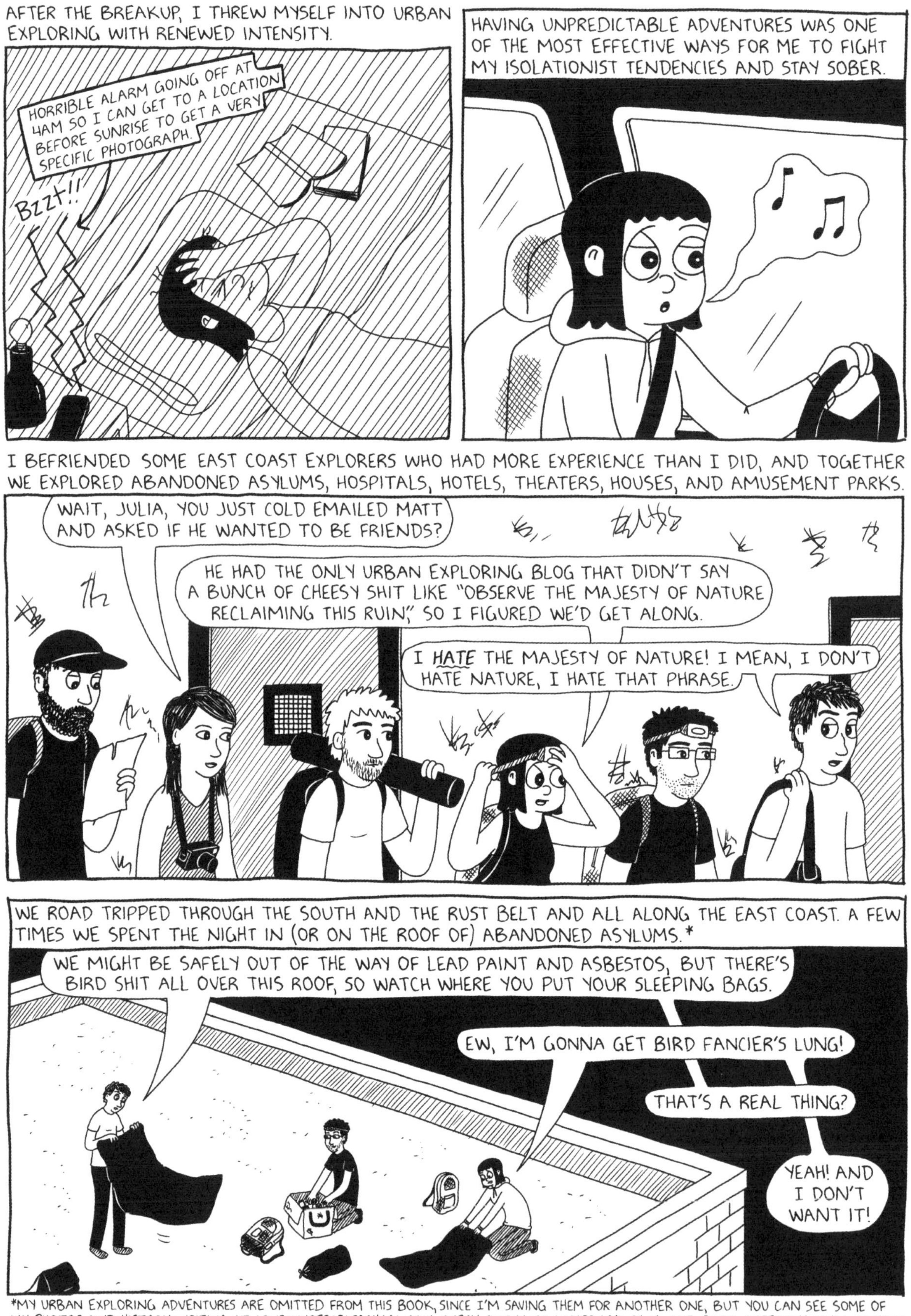
AFTER THE BREAKUP, I THREW MYSELF INTO URBAN EXPLORING WITH RENEWED INTENSITY.
HORRIBLE ALARM GOING OFF AT 4AM SO I CAN GET TO A LOCATION BEFORE SUNRISE TO GET A VERY SPECIFIC PHOTOGRAPH.
Bzzt!!
HAVING UNPREDICTABLE ADVENTURES WAS ONE OF THE MOST EFFECTIVE WAYS FOR ME TO FIGHT MY ISOLATIONIST TENDENCIES AND STAY SOBER.
I BEFRIENDED SOME EAST COAST EXPLORERS WHO HAD MORE EXPERIENCE THAN I DID, AND TOGETHER WE EXPLORED ABANDONED ASYLUMS, HOSPITALS, HOTELS, THEATERS, HOUSES, AND AMUSEMENT PARKS.
WAIT, JULIA, YOU JUST COLD EMAILED MATT AND ASKED IF HE WANTED TO BE FRIENDS?
HE HAD THE ONLY URBAN EXPLORING BLOG THAT DIDN'T SAY A BUNCH OF CHEESY SHIT LIKE "OBSERVE THE MAJESTY OF NATURE RECLAIMING THIS RUIN," SO I FIGURED WE'D GET ALONG.
I HATE THE MAJESTY OF NATURE! I MEAN, I DON'T HATE NATURE, I HATE THAT PHRASE.
WE ROAD TRIPPED THROUGH THE SOUTH AND THE RUST BELT AND ALL ALONG THE EAST COAST. A FEW TIMES WE SPENT THE NIGHT IN (OR ON THE ROOF OF) ABANDONED ASYLUMS.*
WE MIGHT BE SAFELY OUT OF THE WAY OF LEAD PAINT AND ASBESTOS, BUT THERE'S BIRD SHIT ALL OVER THIS ROOF, SO WATCH WHERE YOU PUT YOUR SLEEPING BAGS.
EW, I'M GONNA GET BIRD FANCIER'S LUNG!
THAT'S A REAL THING?
YEAH! AND I DON'T WANT IT!

*MY URBAN EXPLORING ADVENTURES ARE OMITTED FROM THIS BOOK, SINCE I'M SAVING THEM FOR ANOTHER ONE, BUT YOU CAN SEE SOME OF MY PHOTOS AND HISTORY WRITING AT ADVENTUREBIBLESCHOOL.COM. CHECK OUT MATT LAMBROS'S BLOG AND BOOK *AFTER THE FINAL CURTAIN.*

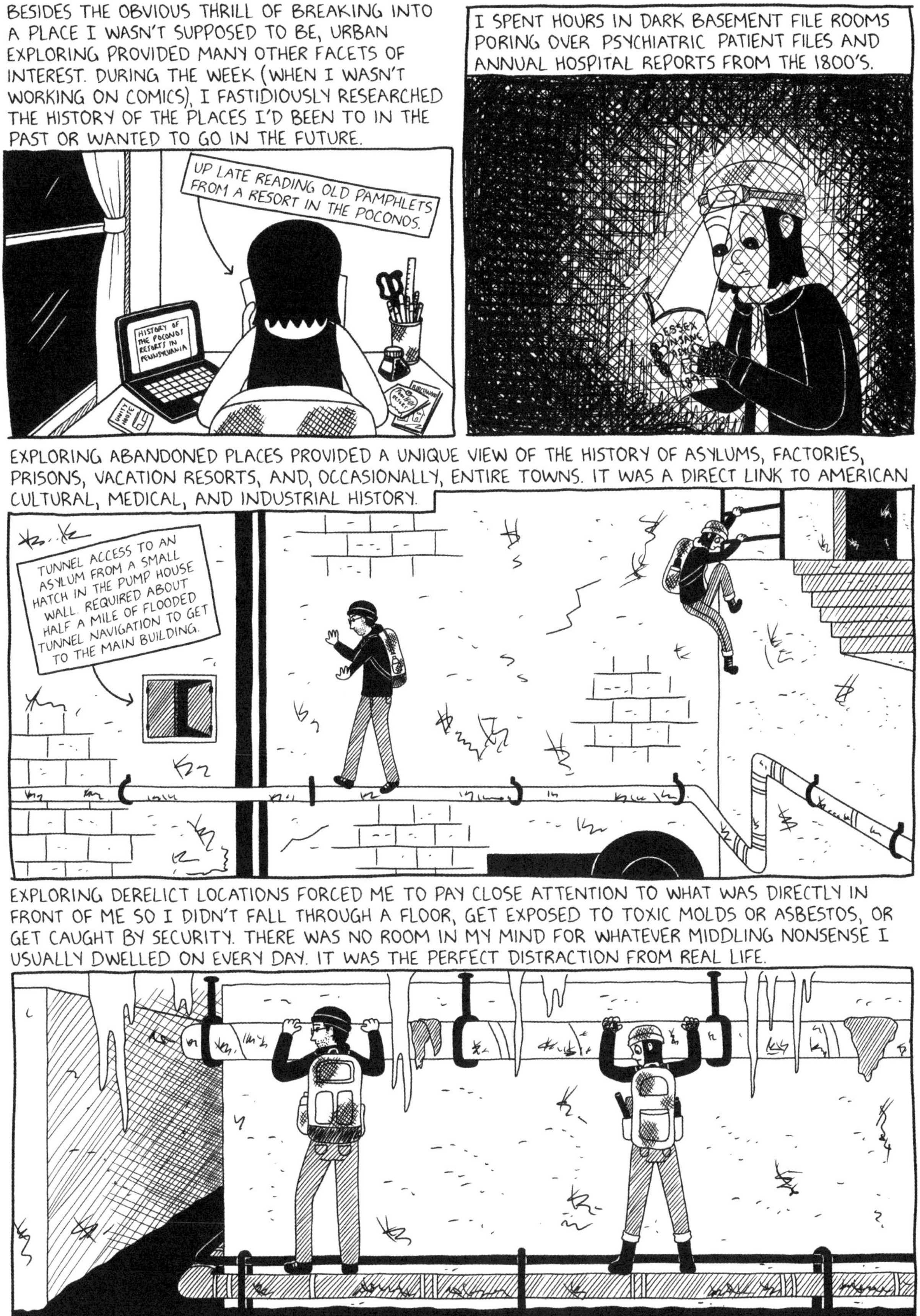
BESIDES THE OBVIOUS THRILL OF BREAKING INTO A PLACE I WASN'T SUPPOSED TO BE, URBAN EXPLORING PROVIDED MANY OTHER FACETS OF INTEREST. DURING THE WEEK (WHEN I WASN'T WORKING ON COMICS), I FASTIDIOUSLY RESEARCHED THE HISTORY OF THE PLACES I'D BEEN TO IN THE PAST OR WANTED TO GO IN THE FUTURE.
UP LATE READING OLD PAMPHLETS FROM A RESORT IN THE POCONOS.
HISTORY OF THE POCONOS RESORTS IN PENNSYLVANIA
UNITY HOUSE
I SPENT HOURS IN DARK BASEMENT FILE ROOMS PORING OVER PSYCHIATRIC PATIENT FILES AND ANNUAL HOSPITAL REPORTS FROM THE 1800'S.
EXPLORING ABANDONED PLACES PROVIDED A UNIQUE VIEW OF THE HISTORY OF ASYLUMS, FACTORIES, PRISONS, VACATION RESORTS, AND, OCCASIONALLY, ENTIRE TOWNS. IT WAS A DIRECT LINK TO AMERICAN CULTURAL, MEDICAL, AND INDUSTRIAL HISTORY.
TUNNEL ACCESS TO AN ASYLUM FROM A SMALL HATCH IN THE PUMP HOUSE WALL. REQUIRED ABOUT HALF A MILE OF FLOODED TUNNEL NAVIGATION TO GET TO THE MAIN BUILDING.
EXPLORING DERELICT LOCATIONS FORCED ME TO PAY CLOSE ATTENTION TO WHAT WAS DIRECTLY IN FRONT OF ME SO I DIDN'T FALL THROUGH A FLOOR, GET EXPOSED TO TOXIC MOLDS OR ASBESTOS, OR GET CAUGHT BY SECURITY. THERE WAS NO ROOM IN MY MIND FOR WHATEVER MIDDLING NONSENSE I USUALLY DWELLED ON EVERY DAY. IT WAS THE PERFECT DISTRACTION FROM REAL LIFE.

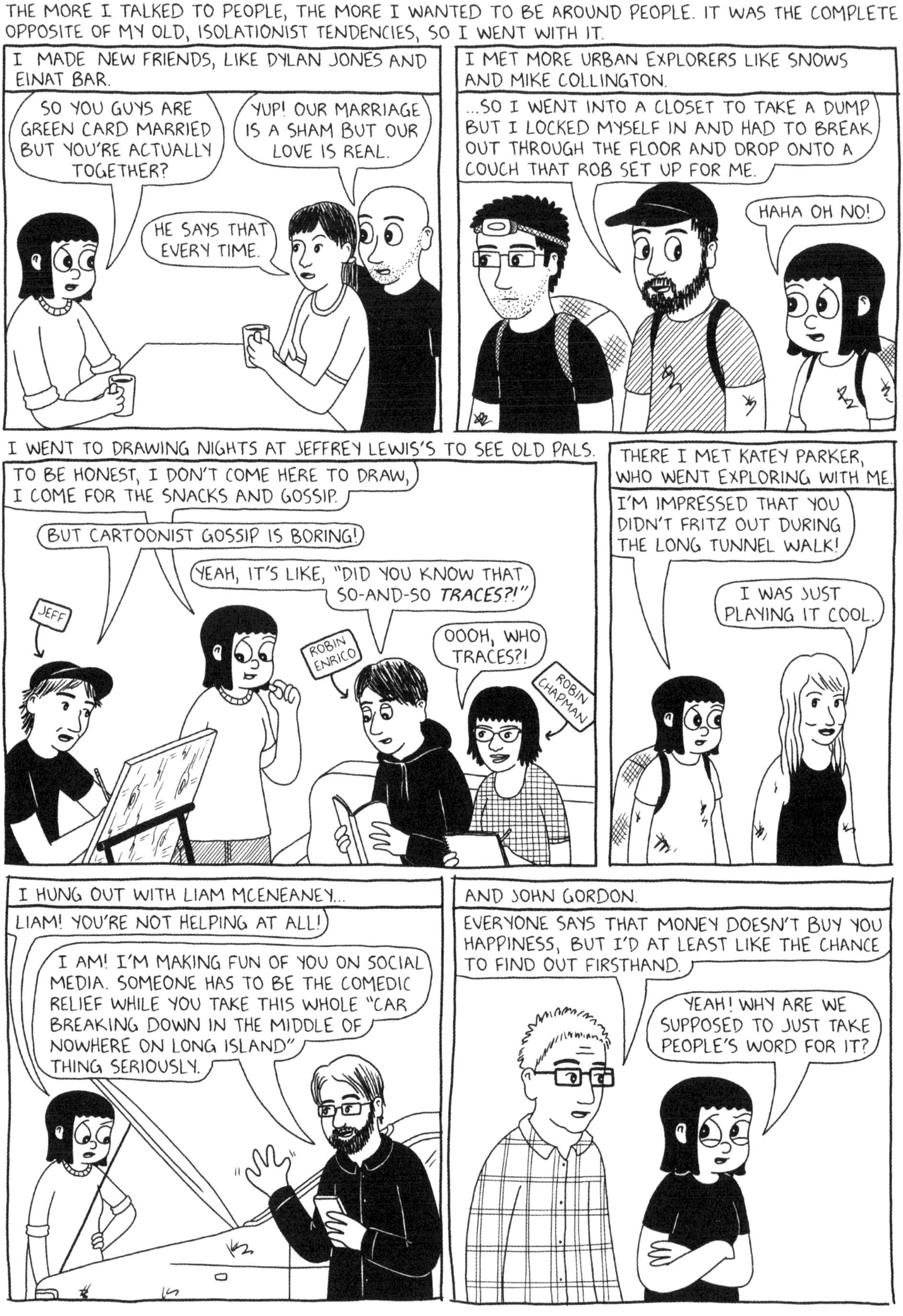
THE MORE I TALKED TO PEOPLE, THE MORE I WANTED TO BE AROUND PEOPLE. IT WAS THE COMPLETE OPPOSITE OF MY OLD, ISOLATIONIST TENDENCIES, SO I WENT WITH IT.
I MADE NEW FRIENDS, LIKE DYLAN JONES AND EINAT BAR.
SO YOU GUYS ARE GREEN CARD MARRIED BUT YOU'RE ACTUALLY TOGETHER?
YUP! OUR MARRIAGE IS A SHAM BUT OUR LOVE IS REAL.
HE SAYS THAT EVERY TIME.
I MET MORE URBAN EXPLORERS LIKE SNOWS AND MIKE COLLINGTON.
...SO I WENT INTO A CLOSET TO TAKE A DUMP BUT I LOCKED MYSELF IN AND HAD TO BREAK OUT THROUGH THE FLOOR AND DROP ONTO A COUCH THAT ROB SET UP FOR ME.
HAHA OH NO!
I WENT TO DRAWING NIGHTS AT JEFFREY LEWIS'S TO SEE OLD PALS.
TO BE HONEST, I DON'T COME HERE TO DRAW, I COME FOR THE SNACKS AND GOSSIP.
BUT CARTOONIST GOSSIP IS BORING!
YEAH, IT'S LIKE, "DID YOU KNOW THAT SO-AND-SO *TRACES?!*"
OOOH, WHO TRACES?!
JEFF
ROBIN ENRICO
ROBIN CHAPMAN
THERE I MET KATEY PARKER, WHO WENT EXPLORING WITH ME.
I'M IMPRESSED THAT YOU DIDN'T FRITZ OUT DURING THE LONG TUNNEL WALK!
I WAS JUST PLAYING IT COOL.
I HUNG OUT WITH LIAM MCENEANEY...
LIAM! YOU'RE NOT HELPING AT ALL!
I AM! I'M MAKING FUN OF YOU ON SOCIAL MEDIA. SOMEONE HAS TO BE THE COMEDIC RELIEF WHILE YOU TAKE THIS WHOLE "CAR BREAKING DOWN IN THE MIDDLE OF NOWHERE ON LONG ISLAND" THING SERIOUSLY.
AND JOHN GORDON.
EVERYONE SAYS THAT MONEY DOESN'T BUY YOU HAPPINESS, BUT I'D AT LEAST LIKE THE CHANCE TO FIND OUT FIRSTHAND.
YEAH! WHY ARE WE SUPPOSED TO JUST TAKE PEOPLE'S WORD FOR IT?

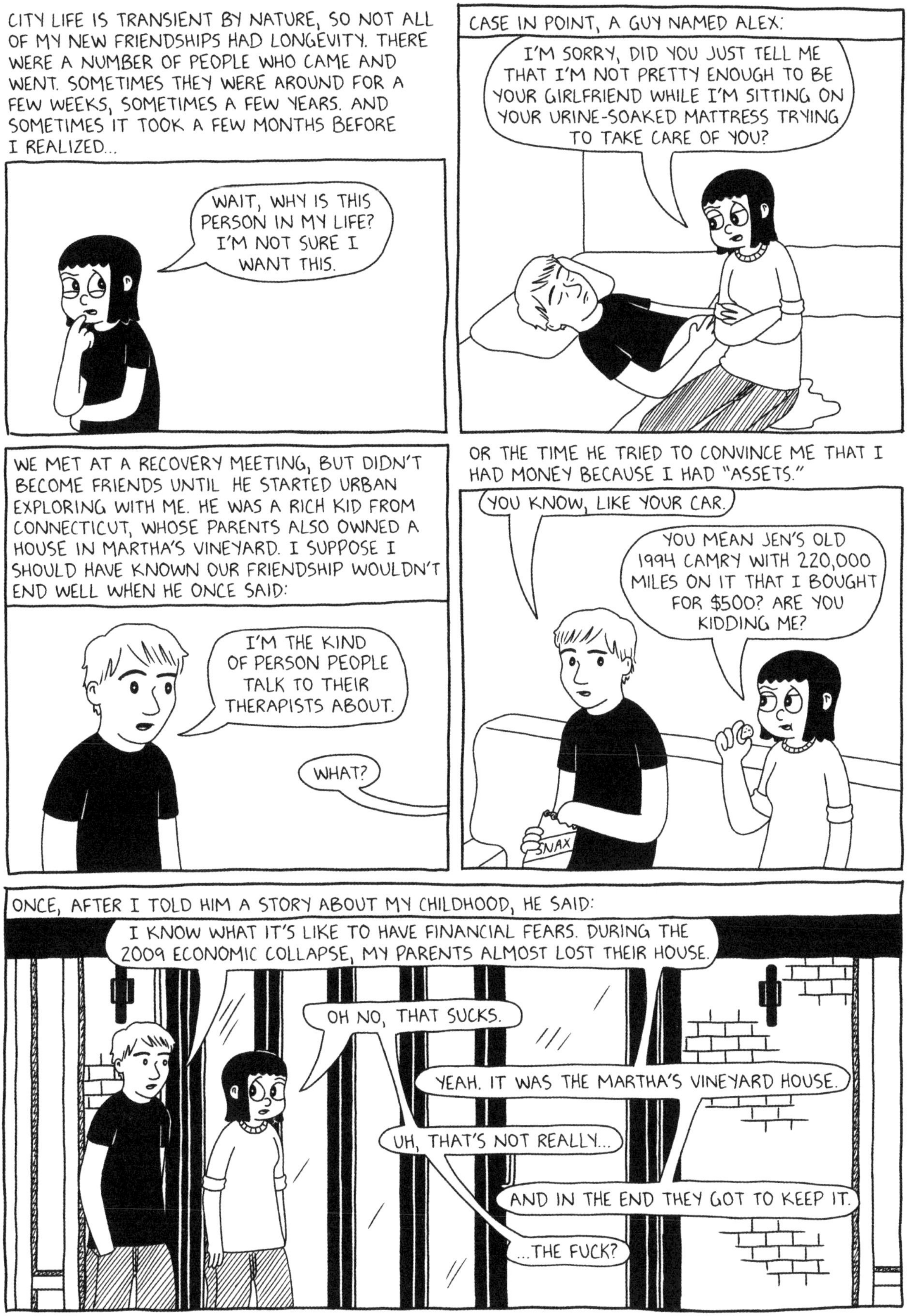
CITY LIFE IS TRANSIENT BY NATURE, SO NOT ALL OF MY NEW FRIENDSHIPS HAD LONGEVITY. THERE WERE A NUMBER OF PEOPLE WHO CAME AND WENT. SOMETIMES THEY WERE AROUND FOR A FEW WEEKS, SOMETIMES A FEW YEARS. AND SOMETIMES IT TOOK A FEW MONTHS BEFORE I REALIZED...
WAIT, WHY IS THIS PERSON IN MY LIFE? I'M NOT SURE I WANT THIS.
CASE IN POINT, A GUY NAMED ALEX:
I'M SORRY, DID YOU JUST TELL ME THAT I'M NOT PRETTY ENOUGH TO BE YOUR GIRLFRIEND WHILE I'M SITTING ON YOUR URINE-SOAKED MATTRESS TRYING TO TAKE CARE OF YOU?
WE MET AT A RECOVERY MEETING, BUT DIDN'T BECOME FRIENDS UNTIL HE STARTED URBAN EXPLORING WITH ME. HE WAS A RICH KID FROM CONNECTICUT, WHOSE PARENTS ALSO OWNED A HOUSE IN MARTHA'S VINEYARD. I SUPPOSE I SHOULD HAVE KNOWN OUR FRIENDSHIP WOULDN'T END WELL WHEN HE ONCE SAID:
I'M THE KIND OF PERSON PEOPLE TALK TO THEIR THERAPISTS ABOUT.
WHAT?
OR THE TIME HE TRIED TO CONVINCE ME THAT I HAD MONEY BECAUSE I HAD "ASSETS."
YOU KNOW, LIKE YOUR CAR.
YOU MEAN JEN'S OLD 1994 CAMRY WITH 220,000 MILES ON IT THAT I BOUGHT FOR $500? ARE YOU KIDDING ME?
SNAX
ONCE, AFTER I TOLD HIM A STORY ABOUT MY CHILDHOOD, HE SAID:
I KNOW WHAT IT'S LIKE TO HAVE FINANCIAL FEARS. DURING THE 2009 ECONOMIC COLLAPSE, MY PARENTS ALMOST LOST THEIR HOUSE.
OH NO, THAT SUCKS.
YEAH. IT WAS THE MARTHA'S VINEYARD HOUSE.
UH, THAT'S NOT REALLY...
AND IN THE END THEY GOT TO KEEP IT.
...THE FUCK?

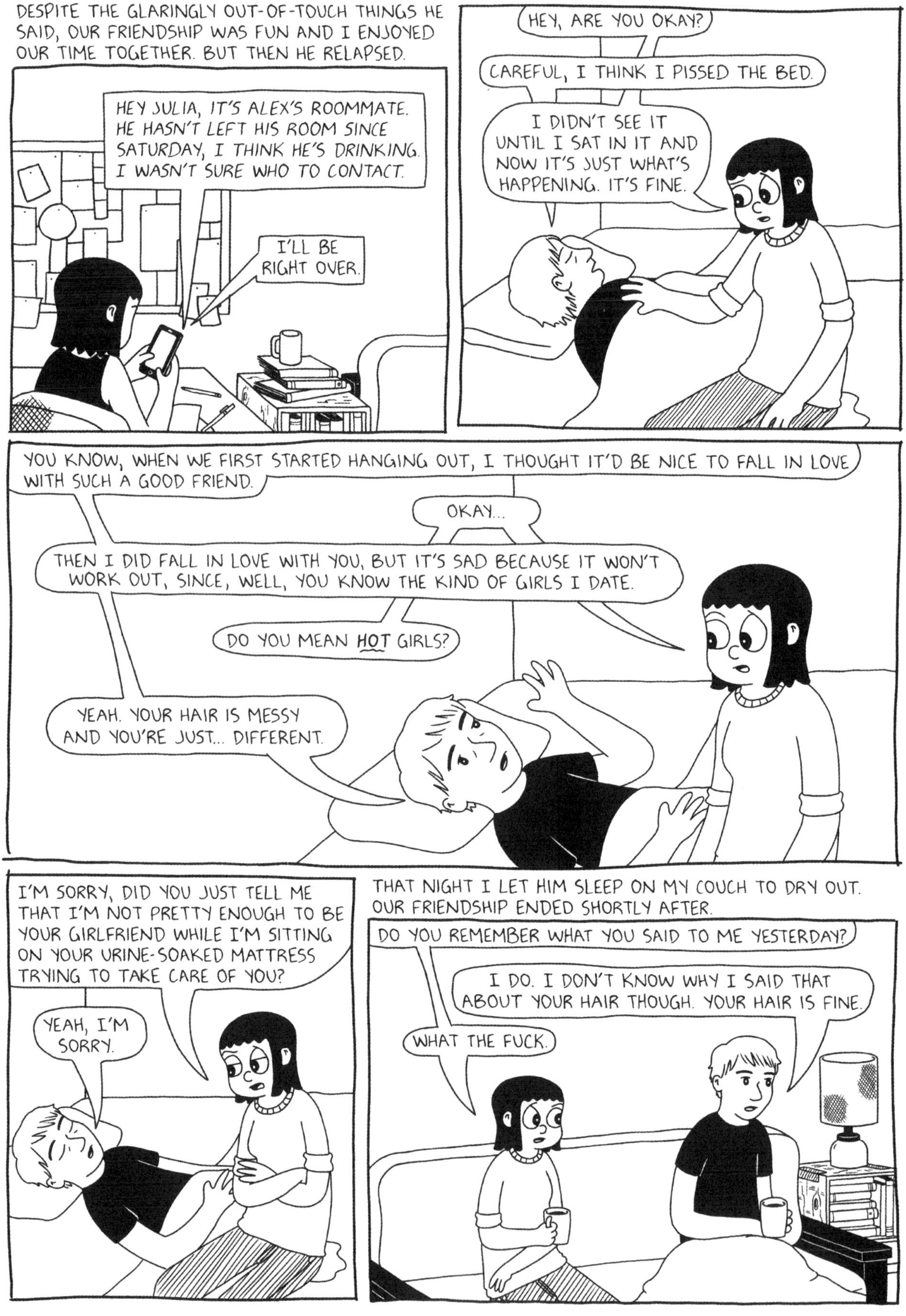
DESPITE THE GLARINGLY OUT-OF-TOUCH THINGS HE SAID, OUR FRIENDSHIP WAS FUN AND I ENJOYED OUR TIME TOGETHER. BUT THEN HE RELAPSED.
HEY JULIA, IT'S ALEX'S ROOMMATE. HE HASN'T LEFT HIS ROOM SINCE SATURDAY, I THINK HE'S DRINKING. I WASN'T SURE WHO TO CONTACT.
I'LL BE RIGHT OVER.
HEY, ARE YOU OKAY?
CAREFUL, I THINK I PISSED THE BED.
I DIDN'T SEE IT UNTIL I SAT IN IT AND NOW IT'S JUST WHAT'S HAPPENING. IT'S FINE.
YOU KNOW, WHEN WE FIRST STARTED HANGING OUT, I THOUGHT IT'D BE NICE TO FALL IN LOVE WITH SUCH A GOOD FRIEND.
OKAY...
THEN I DID FALL IN LOVE WITH YOU, BUT IT'S SAD BECAUSE IT WON'T WORK OUT, SINCE, WELL, YOU KNOW THE KIND OF GIRLS I DATE.
DO YOU MEAN HOT GIRLS?
YEAH. YOUR HAIR IS MESSY AND YOU'RE JUST... DIFFERENT.
I'M SORRY, DID YOU JUST TELL ME THAT I'M NOT PRETTY ENOUGH TO BE YOUR GIRLFRIEND WHILE I'M SITTING ON YOUR URINE-SOAKED MATTRESS TRYING TO TAKE CARE OF YOU?
YEAH, I'M SORRY.
THAT NIGHT I LET HIM SLEEP ON MY COUCH TO DRY OUT. OUR FRIENDSHIP ENDED SHORTLY AFTER.
DO YOU REMEMBER WHAT YOU SAID TO ME YESTERDAY?
I DO. I DON'T KNOW WHY I SAID THAT ABOUT YOUR HAIR THOUGH. YOUR HAIR IS FINE.
WHAT THE FUCK.

I ALSO RESOLVED TO ATTEND MORE PARTIES, AN ENDEAVOR THAT HAD MIDDLING SUCCESS.

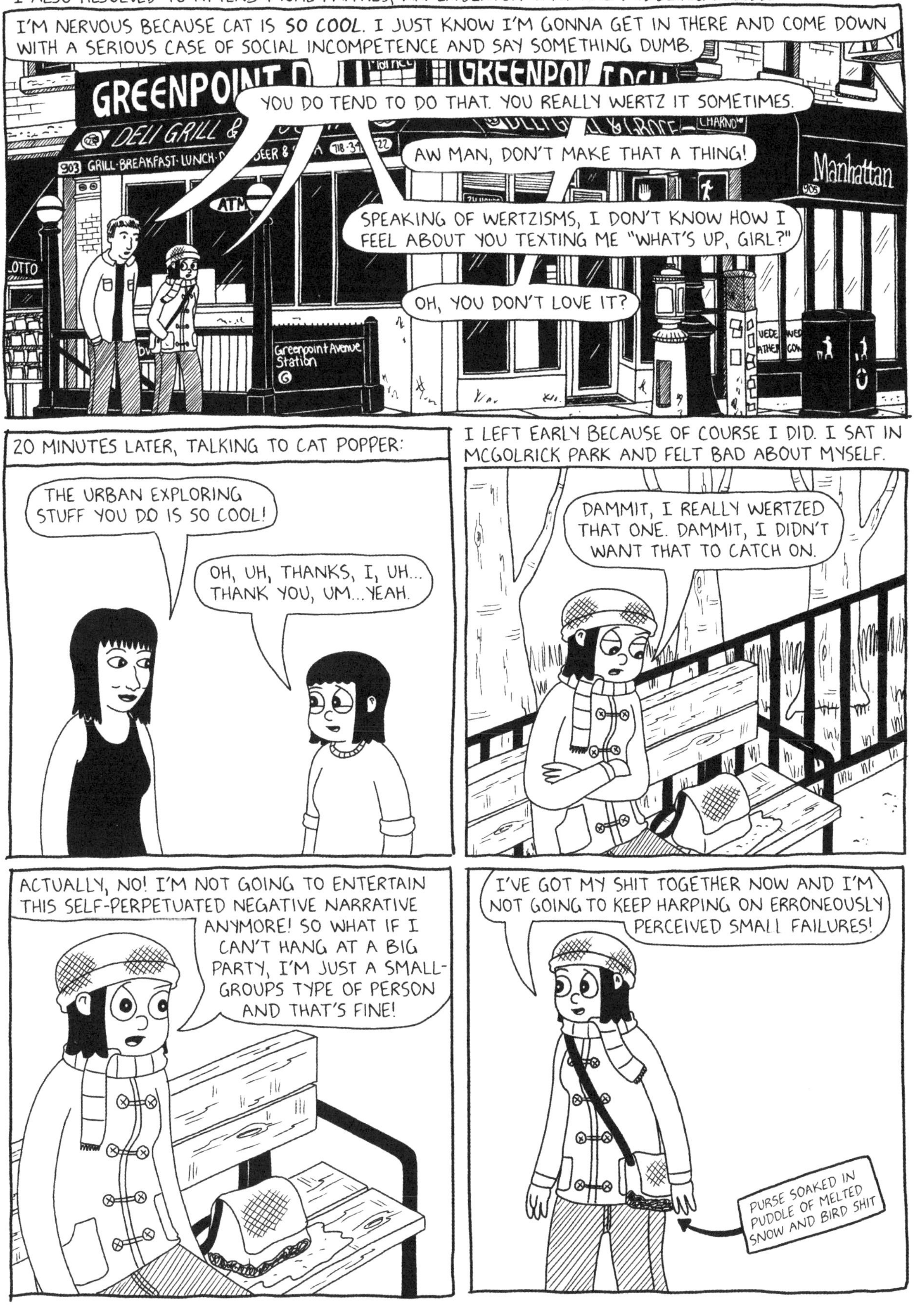
I'M NERVOUS BECAUSE CAT IS **SO COOL**. I JUST KNOW I'M GONNA GET IN THERE AND COME DOWN WITH A SERIOUS CASE OF SOCIAL INCOMPETENCE AND SAY SOMETHING DUMB.
YOU DO TEND TO DO THAT. YOU REALLY WERTZ IT SOMETIMES.
AW MAN, DON'T MAKE THAT A THING!
SPEAKING OF WERTZISMS, I DON'T KNOW HOW I FEEL ABOUT YOU TEXTING ME "WHAT'S UP, GIRL?"
OH, YOU DON'T LOVE IT?
GREENPOINT
DELI GRILL &
Manhattan
ATM
Greenpoint Avenue Station
20 MINUTES LATER, TALKING TO CAT POPPER:
THE URBAN EXPLORING STUFF YOU DO IS SO COOL!
OH, UH, THANKS, I, UH... THANK YOU, UM... YEAH.
I LEFT EARLY BECAUSE OF COURSE I DID. I SAT IN MCGOLRICK PARK AND FELT BAD ABOUT MYSELF.
DAMMIT, I REALLY WERTZED THAT ONE. DAMMIT, I DIDN'T WANT THAT TO CATCH ON.
ACTUALLY, NO! I'M NOT GOING TO ENTERTAIN THIS SELF-PERPETUATED NEGATIVE NARRATIVE ANYMORE! SO WHAT IF I CAN'T HANG AT A BIG PARTY, I'M JUST A SMALL-GROUPS TYPE OF PERSON AND THAT'S FINE!
I'VE GOT MY SHIT TOGETHER NOW AND I'M NOT GOING TO KEEP HARPING ON ERRONEOUSLY PERCEIVED SMALL FAILURES!
PURSE SOAKED IN PUDDLE OF MELTED SNOW AND BIRD SHIT

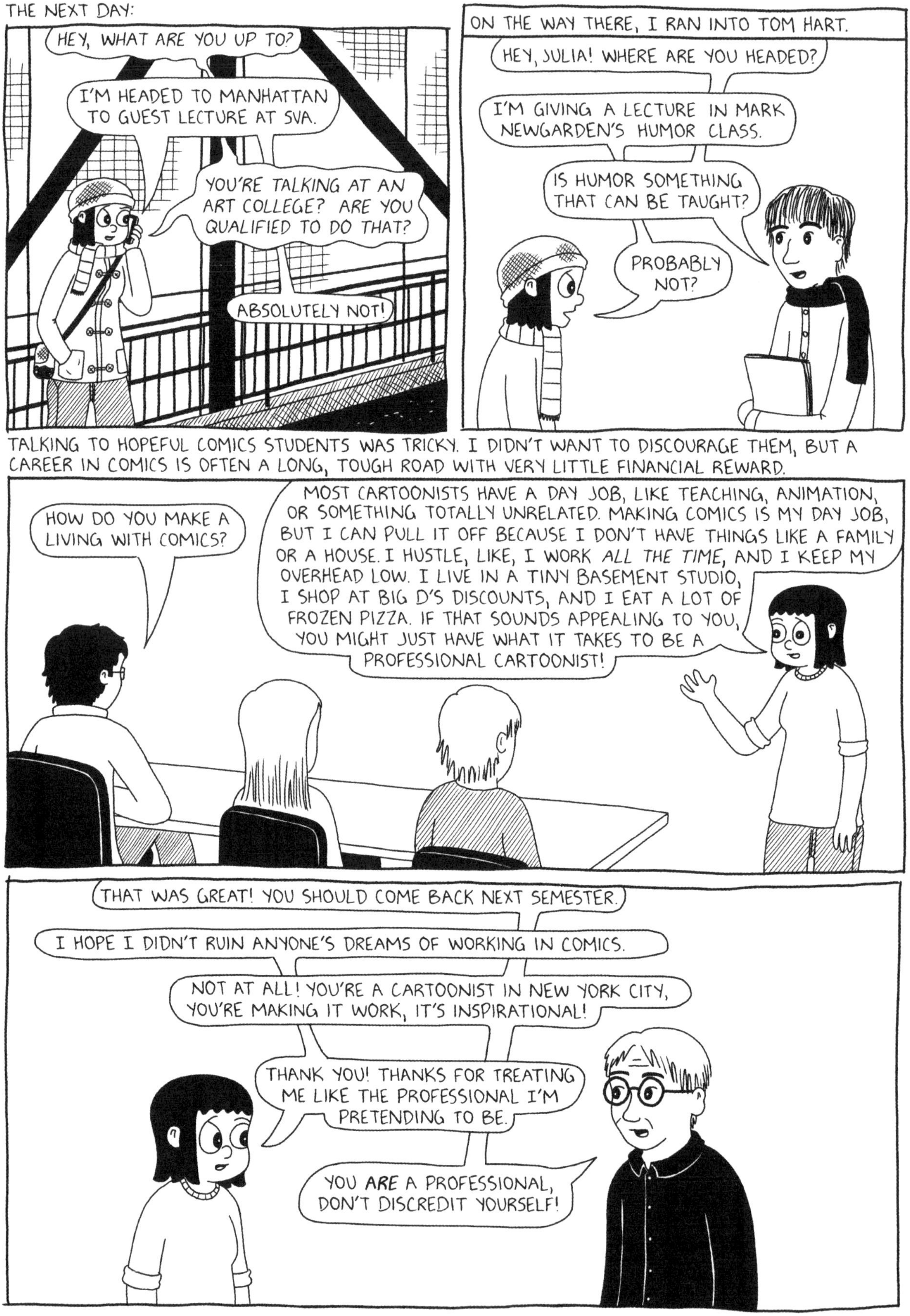
THE NEXT DAY:
HEY, WHAT ARE YOU UP TO?
I'M HEADED TO MANHATTAN TO GUEST LECTURE AT SVA.
YOU'RE TALKING AT AN ART COLLEGE? ARE YOU QUALIFIED TO DO THAT?
ABSOLUTELY NOT!
ON THE WAY THERE, I RAN INTO TOM HART.
HEY, JULIA! WHERE ARE YOU HEADED?
I'M GIVING A LECTURE IN MARK NEWGARDEN'S HUMOR CLASS.
IS HUMOR SOMETHING THAT CAN BE TAUGHT?
PROBABLY NOT?
TALKING TO HOPEFUL COMICS STUDENTS WAS TRICKY. I DIDN'T WANT TO DISCOURAGE THEM, BUT A CAREER IN COMICS IS OFTEN A LONG, TOUGH ROAD WITH VERY LITTLE FINANCIAL REWARD.
HOW DO YOU MAKE A LIVING WITH COMICS?
MOST CARTOONISTS HAVE A DAY JOB, LIKE TEACHING, ANIMATION, OR SOMETHING TOTALLY UNRELATED. MAKING COMICS IS MY DAY JOB, BUT I CAN PULL IT OFF BECAUSE I DON'T HAVE THINGS LIKE A FAMILY OR A HOUSE. I HUSTLE, LIKE, I WORK *ALL THE TIME*, AND I KEEP MY OVERHEAD LOW. I LIVE IN A TINY BASEMENT STUDIO, I SHOP AT BIG D'S DISCOUNTS, AND I EAT A LOT OF FROZEN PIZZA. IF THAT SOUNDS APPEALING TO YOU, YOU MIGHT JUST HAVE WHAT IT TAKES TO BE A PROFESSIONAL CARTOONIST!
THAT WAS GREAT! YOU SHOULD COME BACK NEXT SEMESTER.
I HOPE I DIDN'T RUIN ANYONE'S DREAMS OF WORKING IN COMICS.
NOT AT ALL! YOU'RE A CARTOONIST IN NEW YORK CITY, YOU'RE MAKING IT WORK, IT'S INSPIRATIONAL!
THANK YOU! THANKS FOR TREATING ME LIKE THE PROFESSIONAL I'M PRETENDING TO BE.
YOU **ARE** A PROFESSIONAL, DON'T DISCREDIT YOURSELF!

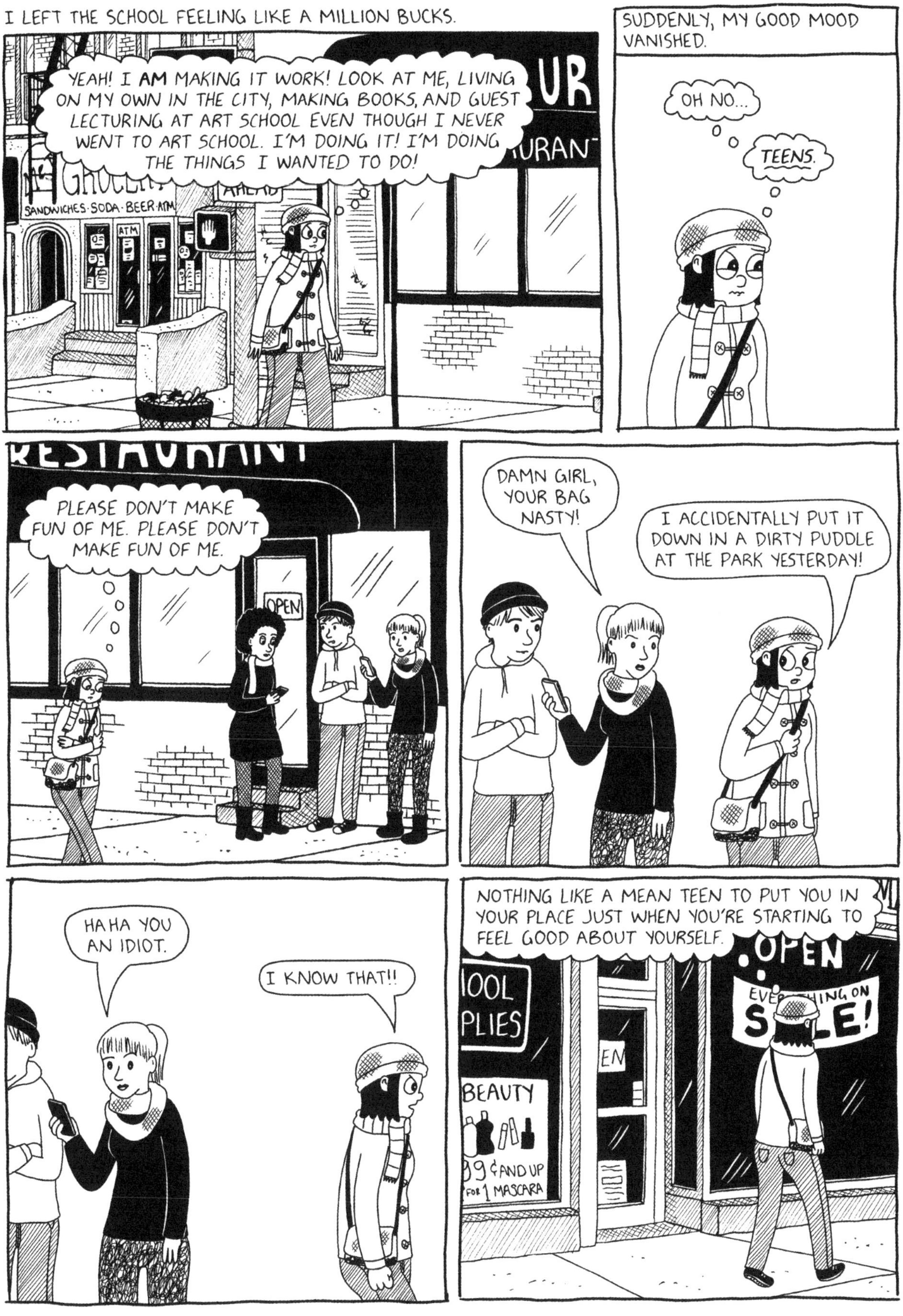
I LEFT THE SCHOOL FEELING LIKE A MILLION BUCKS.
YEAH! I AM MAKING IT WORK! LOOK AT ME, LIVING ON MY OWN IN THE CITY, MAKING BOOKS, AND GUEST LECTURING AT ART SCHOOL EVEN THOUGH I NEVER WENT TO ART SCHOOL. I'M DOING IT! I'M DOING THE THINGS I WANTED TO DO!
SANDWICHES·SODA·BEER·ATM
ATM
SUDDENLY, MY GOOD MOOD VANISHED.
OH NO...
TEENS.
PLEASE DON'T MAKE FUN OF ME. PLEASE DON'T MAKE FUN OF ME.
OPEN
DAMN GIRL, YOUR BAG NASTY!
I ACCIDENTALLY PUT IT DOWN IN A DIRTY PUDDLE AT THE PARK YESTERDAY!
HA HA YOU AN IDIOT.
I KNOW THAT!!
NOTHING LIKE A MEAN TEEN TO PUT YOU IN YOUR PLACE JUST WHEN YOU'RE STARTING TO FEEL GOOD ABOUT YOURSELF.
OPEN
BEAUTY
99¢ AND UP FOR 1 MASCARA

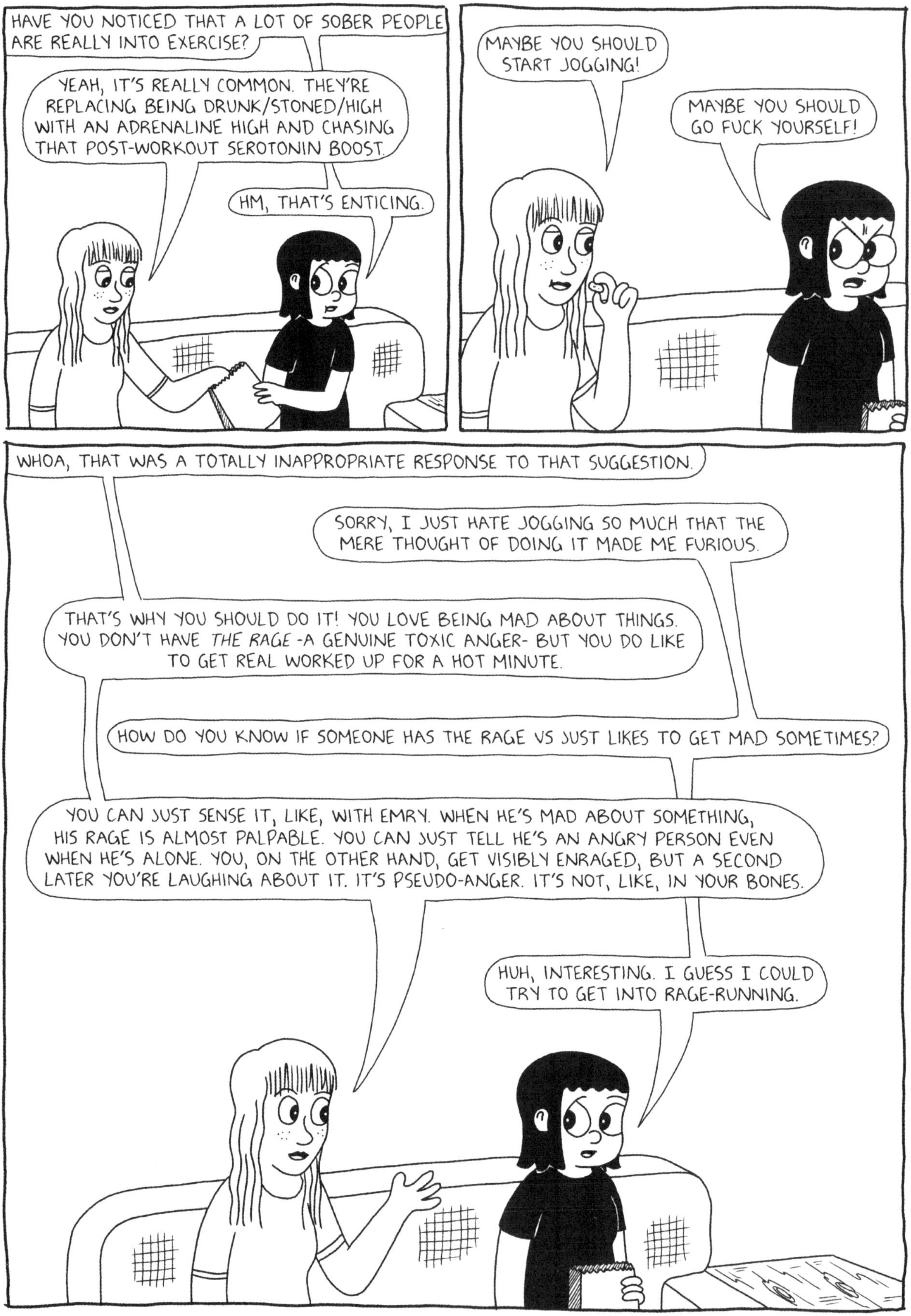
HAVE YOU NOTICED THAT A LOT OF SOBER PEOPLE ARE REALLY INTO EXERCISE?
YEAH, IT'S REALLY COMMON. THEY'RE REPLACING BEING DRUNK/STONED/HIGH WITH AN ADRENALINE HIGH AND CHASING THAT POST-WORKOUT SEROTONIN BOOST.
HM, THAT'S ENTICING.
MAYBE YOU SHOULD START JOGGING!
MAYBE YOU SHOULD GO FUCK YOURSELF!
WHOA, THAT WAS A TOTALLY INAPPROPRIATE RESPONSE TO THAT SUGGESTION.
SORRY, I JUST HATE JOGGING SO MUCH THAT THE MERE THOUGHT OF DOING IT MADE ME FURIOUS.
THAT'S WHY YOU SHOULD DO IT! YOU LOVE BEING MAD ABOUT THINGS. YOU DON'T HAVE *THE RAGE* -A GENUINE TOXIC ANGER- BUT YOU DO LIKE TO GET REAL WORKED UP FOR A HOT MINUTE.
HOW DO YOU KNOW IF SOMEONE HAS THE RAGE VS JUST LIKES TO GET MAD SOMETIMES?
YOU CAN JUST SENSE IT, LIKE, WITH EMRY. WHEN HE'S MAD ABOUT SOMETHING, HIS RAGE IS ALMOST PALPABLE. YOU CAN JUST TELL HE'S AN ANGRY PERSON EVEN WHEN HE'S ALONE. YOU, ON THE OTHER HAND, GET VISIBLY ENRAGED, BUT A SECOND LATER YOU'RE LAUGHING ABOUT IT. IT'S PSEUDO-ANGER. IT'S NOT, LIKE, IN YOUR BONES.
HUH, INTERESTING. I GUESS I COULD TRY TO GET INTO RAGE-RUNNING.

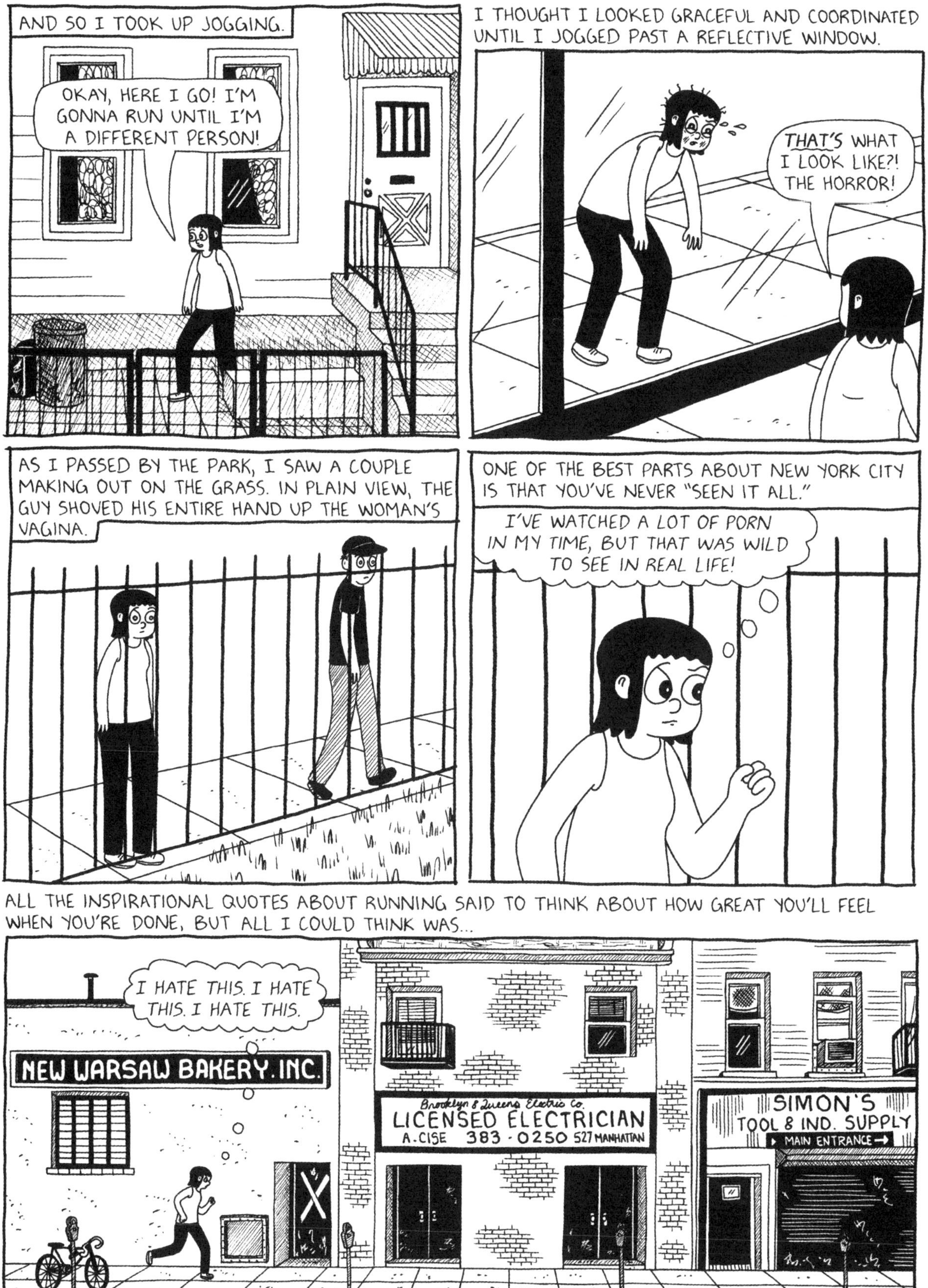
AND SO I TOOK UP JOGGING.
OKAY, HERE I GO! I'M GONNA RUN UNTIL I'M A DIFFERENT PERSON!
I THOUGHT I LOOKED GRACEFUL AND COORDINATED UNTIL I JOGGED PAST A REFLECTIVE WINDOW.
THAT'S WHAT I LOOK LIKE?! THE HORROR!
AS I PASSED BY THE PARK, I SAW A COUPLE MAKING OUT ON THE GRASS. IN PLAIN VIEW, THE GUY SHOVED HIS ENTIRE HAND UP THE WOMAN'S VAGINA.
ONE OF THE BEST PARTS ABOUT NEW YORK CITY IS THAT YOU'VE NEVER "SEEN IT ALL."
I'VE WATCHED A LOT OF PORN IN MY TIME, BUT THAT WAS WILD TO SEE IN REAL LIFE!
ALL THE INSPIRATIONAL QUOTES ABOUT RUNNING SAID TO THINK ABOUT HOW GREAT YOU'LL FEEL WHEN YOU'RE DONE, BUT ALL I COULD THINK WAS...
I HATE THIS. I HATE THIS. I HATE THIS.
NEW WARSAW BAKERY. INC.
Brooklyn & Queens Electric Co.
LICENSED ELECTRICIAN
A. CISE 383-0250 527 MANHATTAN
SIMON'S
TOOL & IND. SUPPLY
MAIN ENTRANCE

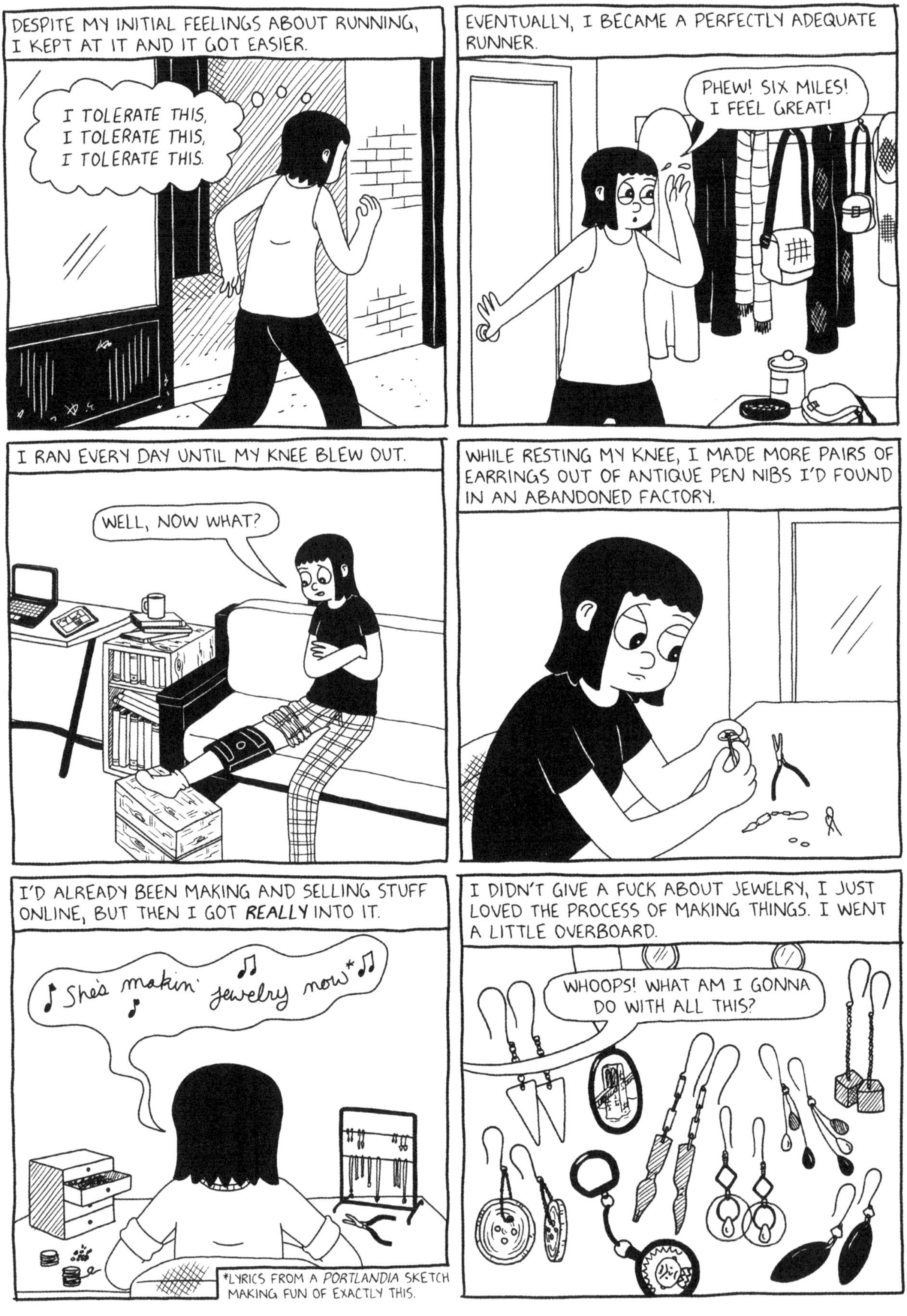
DESPITE MY INITIAL FEELINGS ABOUT RUNNING, I KEPT AT IT AND IT GOT EASIER.
I TOLERATE THIS, I TOLERATE THIS, I TOLERATE THIS.
EVENTUALLY, I BECAME A PERFECTLY ADEQUATE RUNNER.
PHEW! SIX MILES! I FEEL GREAT!
I RAN EVERY DAY UNTIL MY KNEE BLEW OUT.
WELL, NOW WHAT?
WHILE RESTING MY KNEE, I MADE MORE PAIRS OF EARRINGS OUT OF ANTIQUE PEN NIBS I'D FOUND IN AN ABANDONED FACTORY.
I'D ALREADY BEEN MAKING AND SELLING STUFF ONLINE, BUT THEN I GOT **REALLY** INTO IT.
♪ She's makin' ♪ jewelry now* ♫
*LYRICS FROM A *PORTLANDIA* SKETCH MAKING FUN OF EXACTLY THIS.
I DIDN'T GIVE A FUCK ABOUT JEWELRY, I JUST LOVED THE PROCESS OF MAKING THINGS. I WENT A LITTLE OVERBOARD.
WHOOPS! WHAT AM I GONNA DO WITH ALL THIS?

WHILE OUT EXPLORING ABANDONED PLACES, I BEGAN TO, SHALL WE SAY, "RESCUE" ANTIQUE OBJECTS FROM LOCATIONS I KNEW WERE GOING TO BE DEMOLISHED.

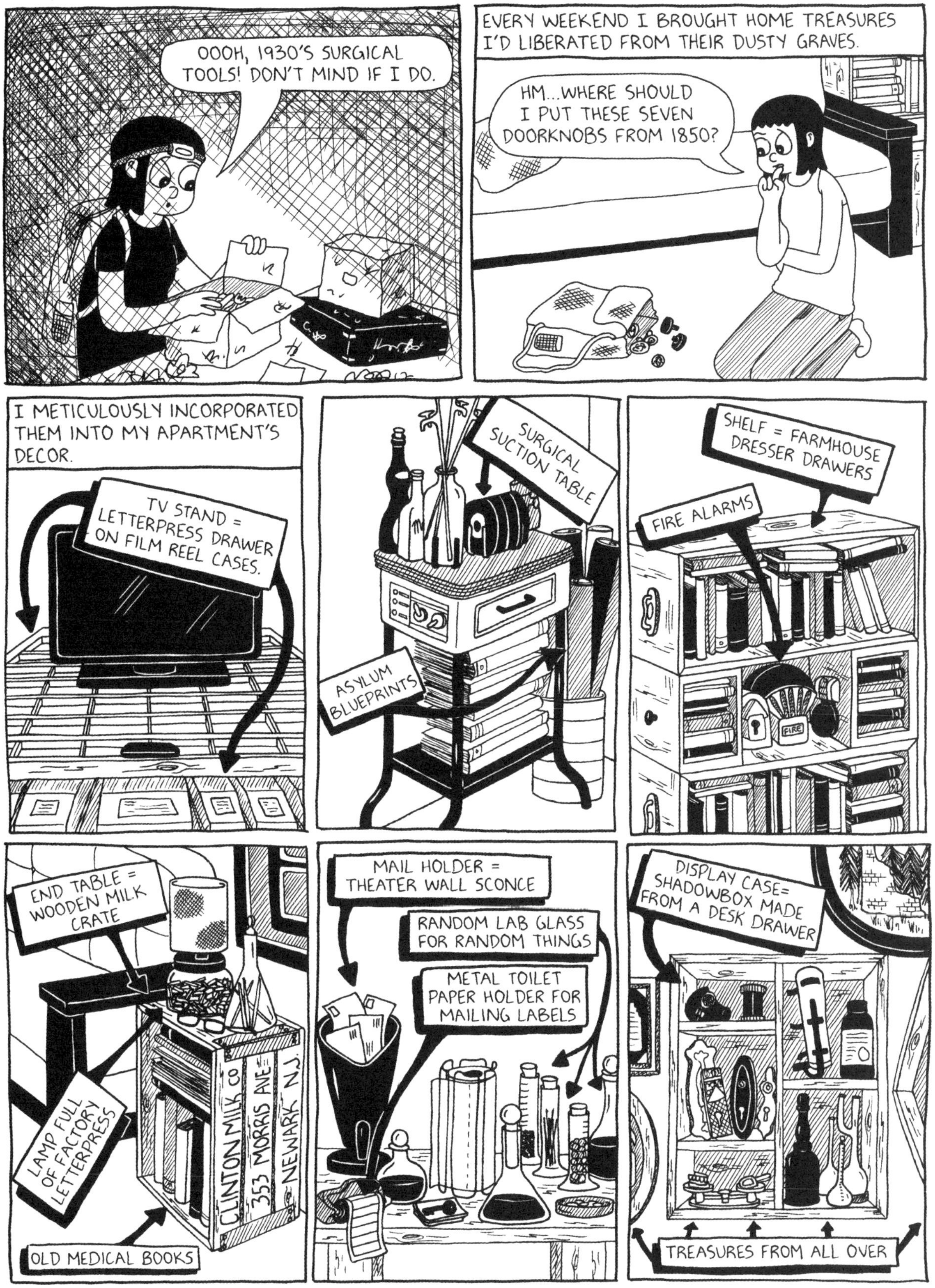

OOOH, 1930'S SURGICAL TOOLS! DON'T MIND IF I DO.
EVERY WEEKEND I BROUGHT HOME TREASURES I'D LIBERATED FROM THEIR DUSTY GRAVES.
HM...WHERE SHOULD I PUT THESE SEVEN DOORKNOBS FROM 1850?
I METICULOUSLY INCORPORATED THEM INTO MY APARTMENT'S DECOR.
TV STAND = LETTERPRESS DRAWER ON FILM REEL CASES.
SURGICAL SUCTION TABLE
ASYLUM BLUEPRINTS
SHELF = FARMHOUSE DRESSER DRAWERS
FIRE ALARMS
FIRE
END TABLE = WOODEN MILK CRATE
LAMP FULL OF FACTORY LETTERPRESS
CLINTON MILK CO
353 MORRIS AVE
NEWARK N.J.
OLD MEDICAL BOOKS
MAIL HOLDER = THEATER WALL SCONCE
RANDOM LAB GLASS FOR RANDOM THINGS
METAL TOILET PAPER HOLDER FOR MAILING LABELS
DISPLAY CASE= SHADOWBOX MADE FROM A DESK DRAWER
TREASURES FROM ALL OVER

READING WERNER MUENSTERBERGER'S COLLECTING: AN UNRULY PASSION: PSYCHOLOGICAL PERSPECTIVES

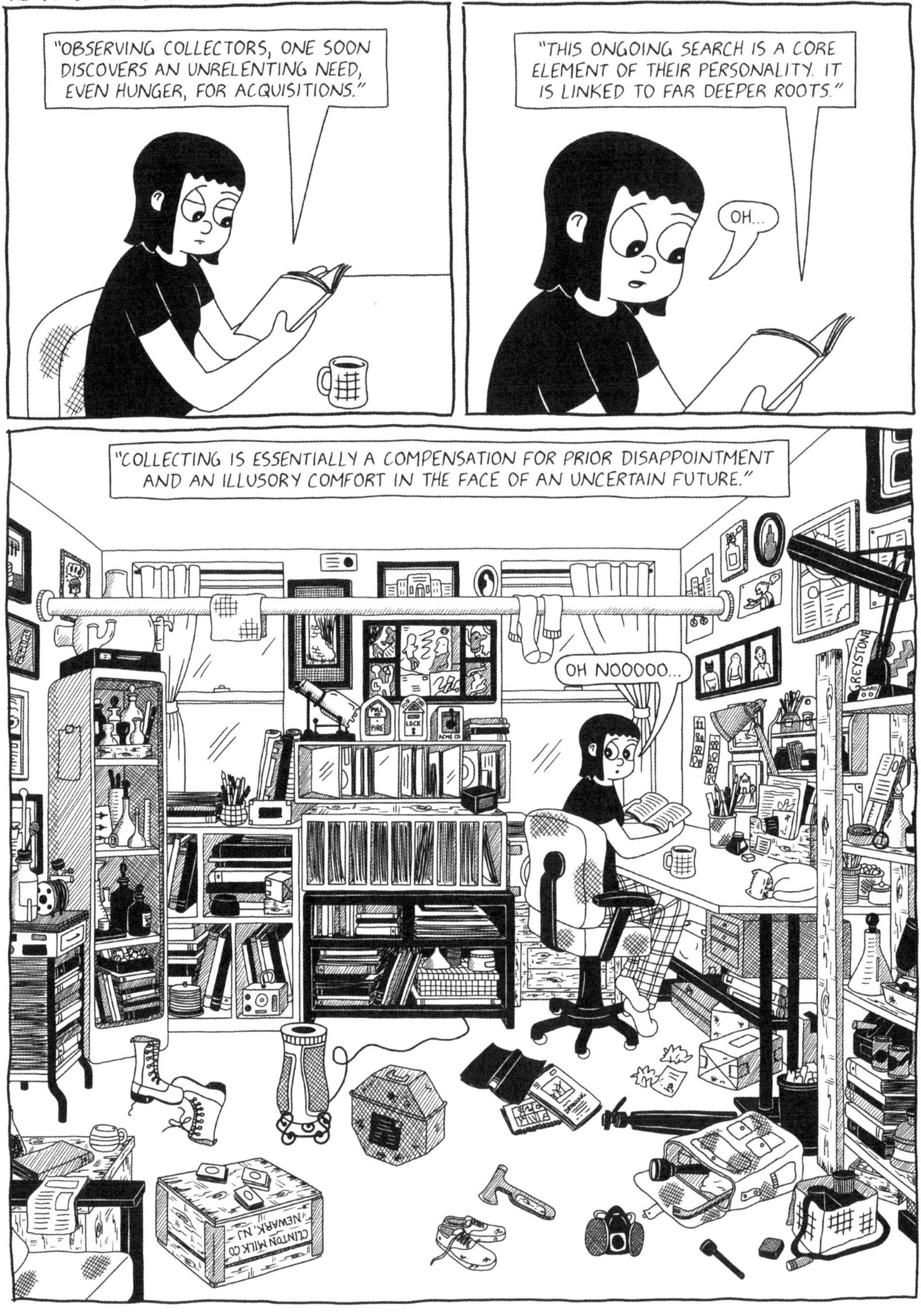

"OBSERVING COLLECTORS, ONE SOON DISCOVERS AN UNRELENTING NEED, EVEN HUNGER, FOR ACQUISITIONS."
"THIS ONGOING SEARCH IS A CORE ELEMENT OF THEIR PERSONALITY. IT IS LINKED TO FAR DEEPER ROOTS."
OH...
"COLLECTING IS ESSENTIALLY A COMPENSATION FOR PRIOR DISAPPOINTMENT AND AN ILLUSORY COMFORT IN THE FACE OF AN UNCERTAIN FUTURE."
OH NOOOOO...
GREYSTONE
CLINTON MILK CO
NEWARK, N.J.

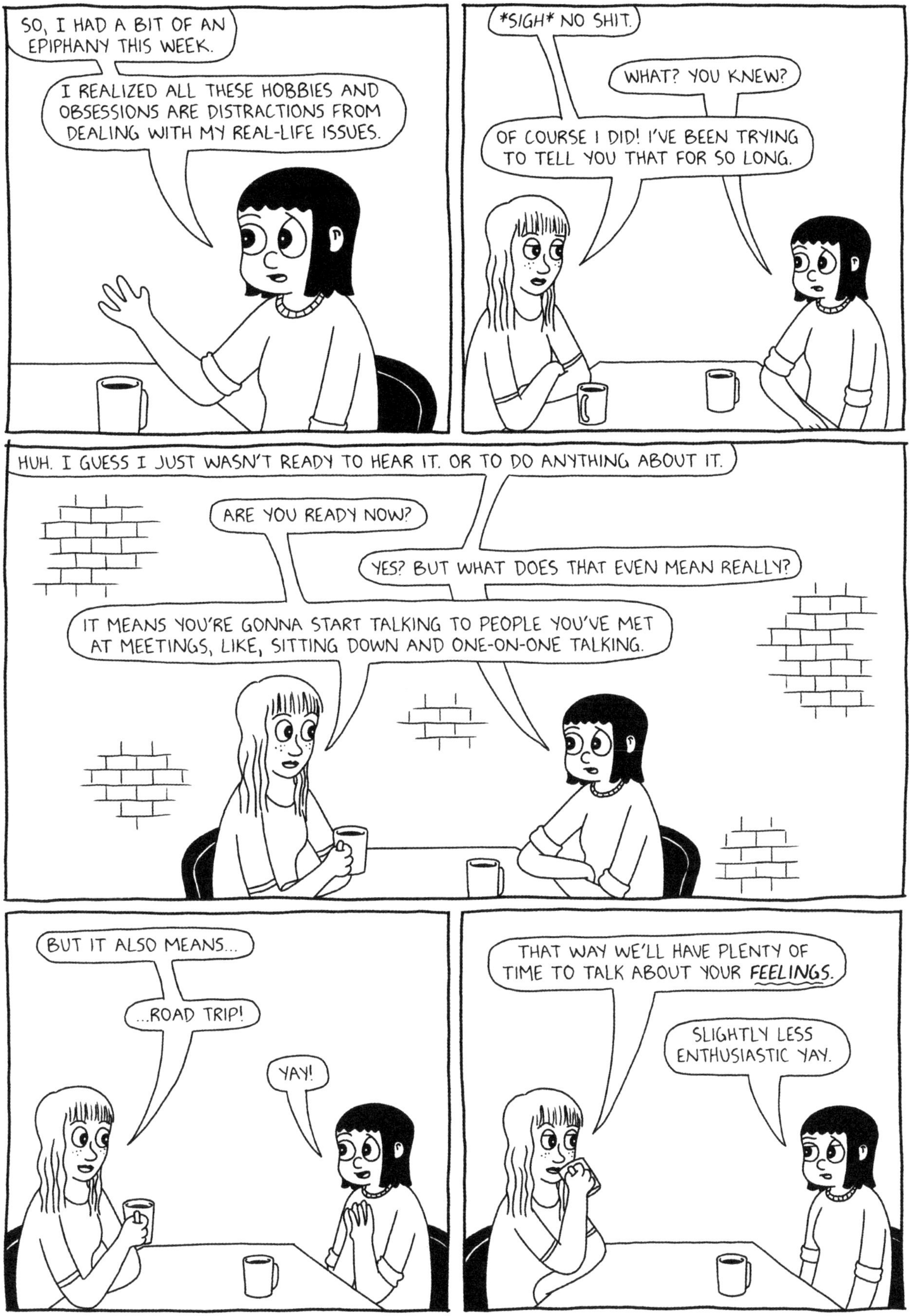
SO, I HAD A BIT OF AN EPIPHANY THIS WEEK.
I REALIZED ALL THESE HOBBIES AND OBSESSIONS ARE DISTRACTIONS FROM DEALING WITH MY REAL-LIFE ISSUES.
SIGH NO SHIT.
WHAT? YOU KNEW?
OF COURSE I DID! I'VE BEEN TRYING TO TELL YOU THAT FOR SO LONG.
HUH. I GUESS I JUST WASN'T READY TO HEAR IT. OR TO DO ANYTHING ABOUT IT.
ARE YOU READY NOW?
YES? BUT WHAT DOES THAT EVEN MEAN REALLY?
IT MEANS YOU'RE GONNA START TALKING TO PEOPLE YOU'VE MET AT MEETINGS, LIKE, SITTING DOWN AND ONE-ON-ONE TALKING.
BUT IT ALSO MEANS...
...ROAD TRIP!
YAY!
THAT WAY WE'LL HAVE PLENTY OF TIME TO TALK ABOUT YOUR FEELINGS.
SLIGHTLY LESS ENTHUSIASTIC YAY.

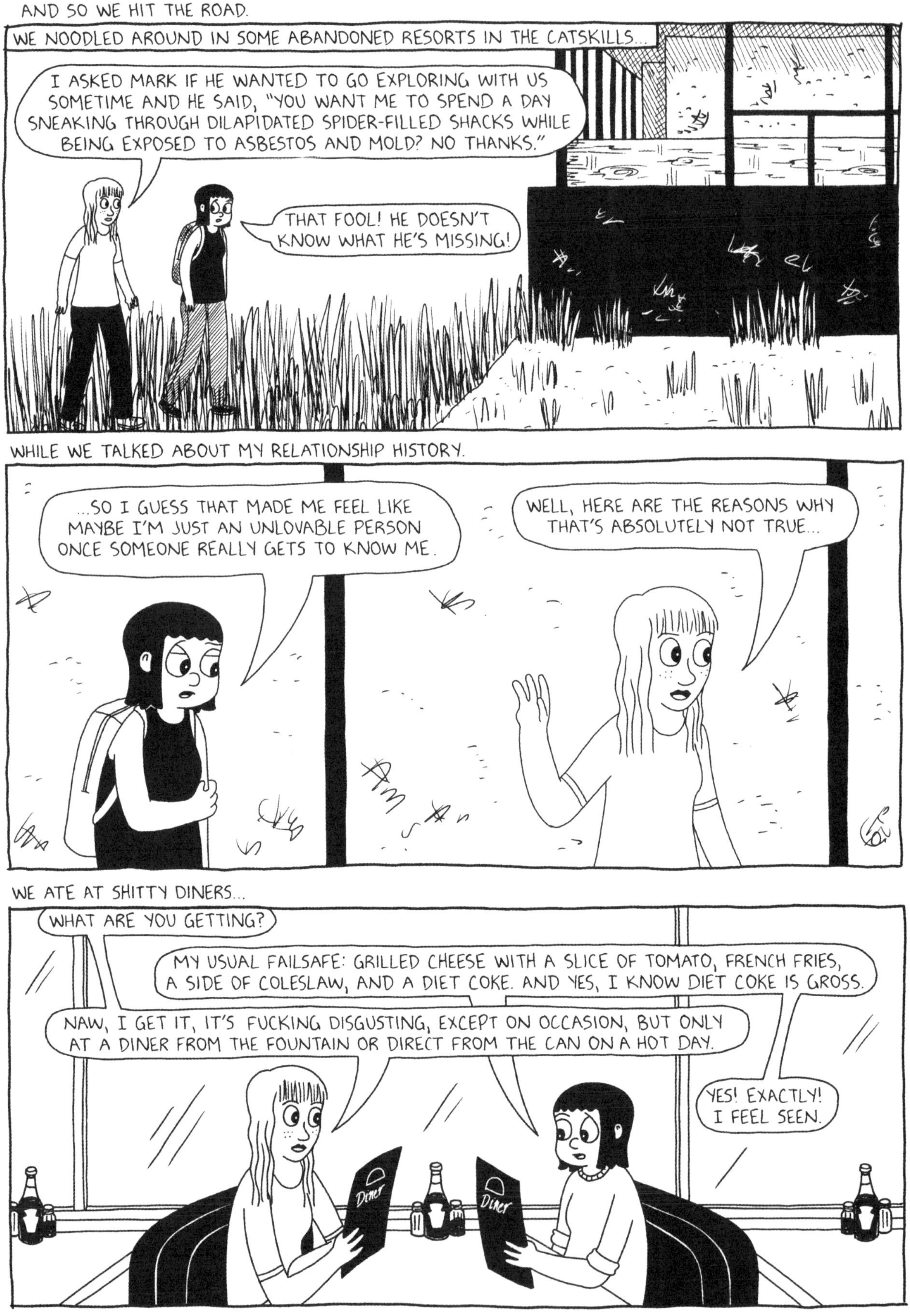

AND SO WE HIT THE ROAD.
WE NOODLED AROUND IN SOME ABANDONED RESORTS IN THE CATSKILLS...
I ASKED MARK IF HE WANTED TO GO EXPLORING WITH US SOMETIME AND HE SAID, "YOU WANT ME TO SPEND A DAY SNEAKING THROUGH DILAPIDATED SPIDER-FILLED SHACKS WHILE BEING EXPOSED TO ASBESTOS AND MOLD? NO THANKS."
THAT FOOL! HE DOESN'T KNOW WHAT HE'S MISSING!
WHILE WE TALKED ABOUT MY RELATIONSHIP HISTORY.
...SO I GUESS THAT MADE ME FEEL LIKE MAYBE I'M JUST AN UNLOVABLE PERSON ONCE SOMEONE REALLY GETS TO KNOW ME.
WELL, HERE ARE THE REASONS WHY THAT'S ABSOLUTELY NOT TRUE...
WE ATE AT SHITTY DINERS...
WHAT ARE YOU GETTING?
MY USUAL FAILSAFE: GRILLED CHEESE WITH A SLICE OF TOMATO, FRENCH FRIES, A SIDE OF COLESLAW, AND A DIET COKE. AND YES, I KNOW DIET COKE IS GROSS.
NAW, I GET IT, IT'S FUCKING DISGUSTING, EXCEPT ON OCCASION, BUT ONLY AT A DINER FROM THE FOUNTAIN OR DIRECT FROM THE CAN ON A HOT DAY.
YES! EXACTLY! I FEEL SEEN.
Diner
Diner

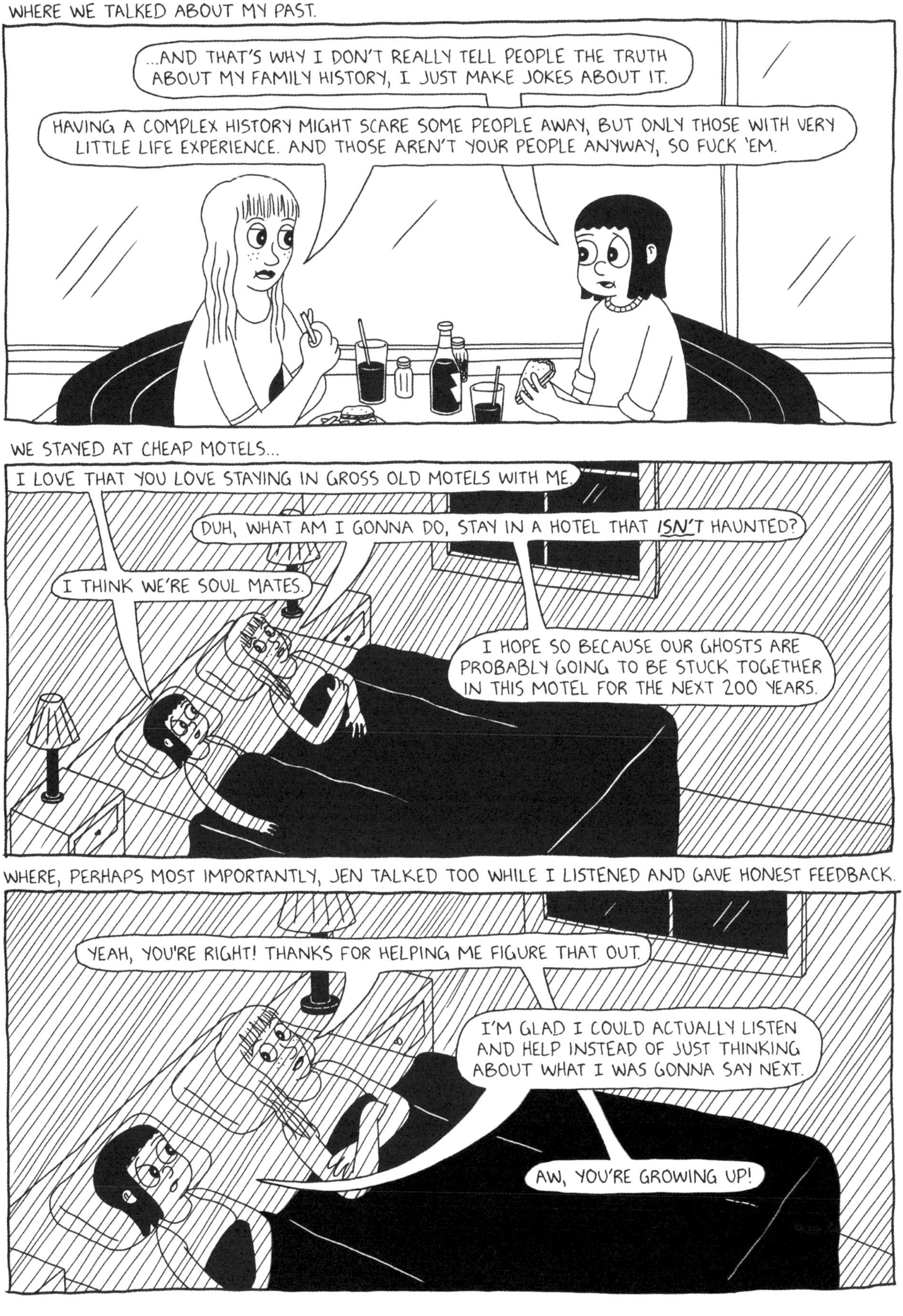
WHERE WE TALKED ABOUT MY PAST.
...AND THAT'S WHY I DON'T REALLY TELL PEOPLE THE TRUTH ABOUT MY FAMILY HISTORY, I JUST MAKE JOKES ABOUT IT.
HAVING A COMPLEX HISTORY MIGHT SCARE SOME PEOPLE AWAY, BUT ONLY THOSE WITH VERY LITTLE LIFE EXPERIENCE. AND THOSE AREN'T YOUR PEOPLE ANYWAY, SO FUCK 'EM.
WE STAYED AT CHEAP MOTELS...
I LOVE THAT YOU LOVE STAYING IN GROSS OLD MOTELS WITH ME.
DUH, WHAT AM I GONNA DO, STAY IN A HOTEL THAT ISN'T HAUNTED?
I THINK WE'RE SOUL MATES.
I HOPE SO BECAUSE OUR GHOSTS ARE PROBABLY GOING TO BE STUCK TOGETHER IN THIS MOTEL FOR THE NEXT 200 YEARS.
WHERE, PERHAPS MOST IMPORTANTLY, JEN TALKED TOO WHILE I LISTENED AND GAVE HONEST FEEDBACK.
YEAH, YOU'RE RIGHT! THANKS FOR HELPING ME FIGURE THAT OUT.
I'M GLAD I COULD ACTUALLY LISTEN AND HELP INSTEAD OF JUST THINKING ABOUT WHAT I WAS GONNA SAY NEXT.
AW, YOU'RE GROWING UP!

A SUMMER WALK

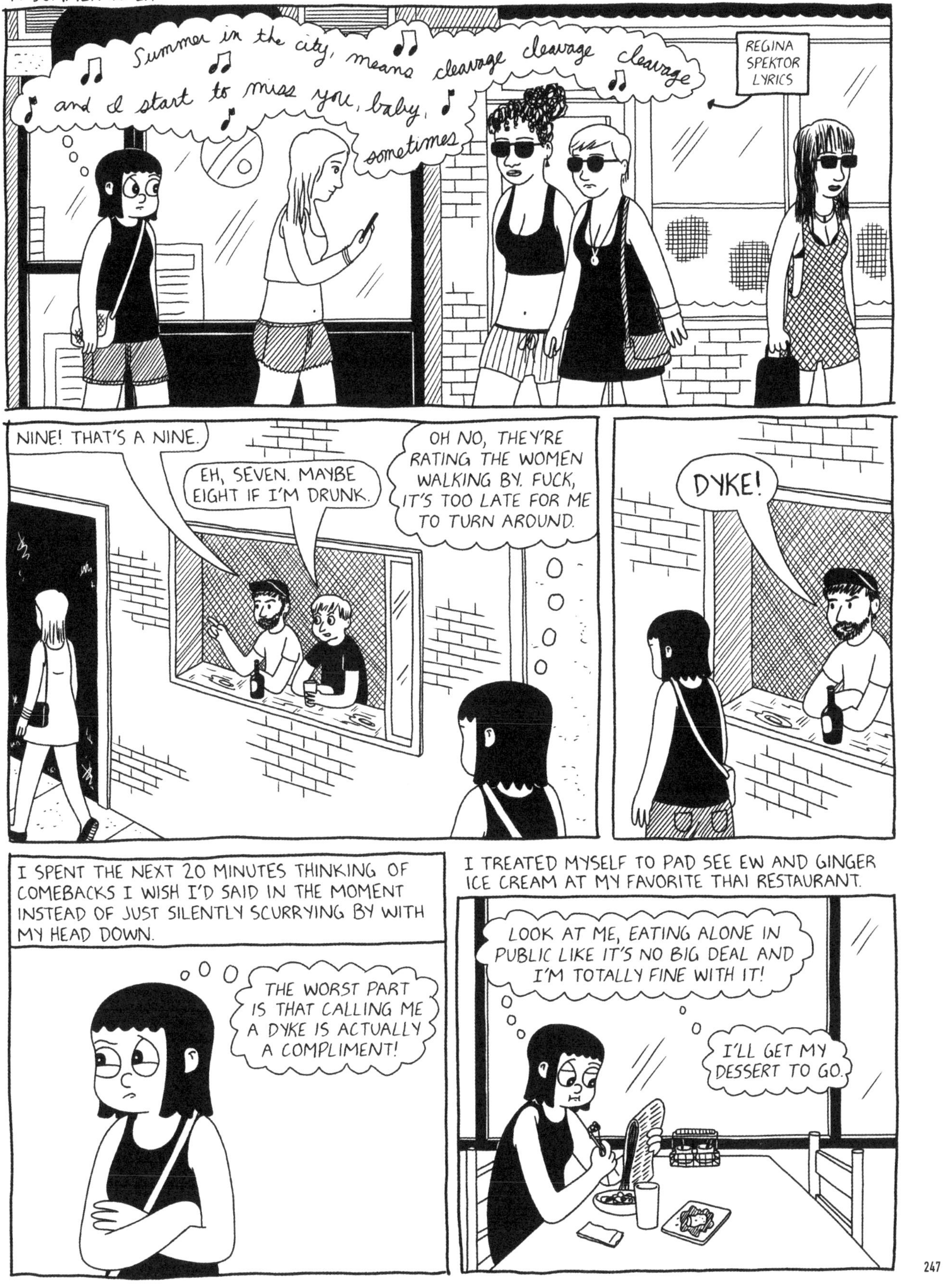
Summer in the city, means cleavage cleavage cleavage
and I start to miss you, baby, sometimes
REGINA SPEKTOR LYRICS
NINE! THAT'S A NINE.
EH, SEVEN. MAYBE EIGHT IF I'M DRUNK.
OH NO, THEY'RE RATING THE WOMEN WALKING BY. FUCK, IT'S TOO LATE FOR ME TO TURN AROUND.
DYKE!
I SPENT THE NEXT 20 MINUTES THINKING OF COMEBACKS I WISH I'D SAID IN THE MOMENT INSTEAD OF JUST SILENTLY SCURRYING BY WITH MY HEAD DOWN.
THE WORST PART IS THAT CALLING ME A DYKE IS ACTUALLY A COMPLIMENT!
I TREATED MYSELF TO PAD SEE EW AND GINGER ICE CREAM AT MY FAVORITE THAI RESTAURANT.
LOOK AT ME, EATING ALONE IN PUBLIC LIKE IT'S NO BIG DEAL AND I'M TOTALLY FINE WITH IT!
I'LL GET MY DESSERT TO GO.

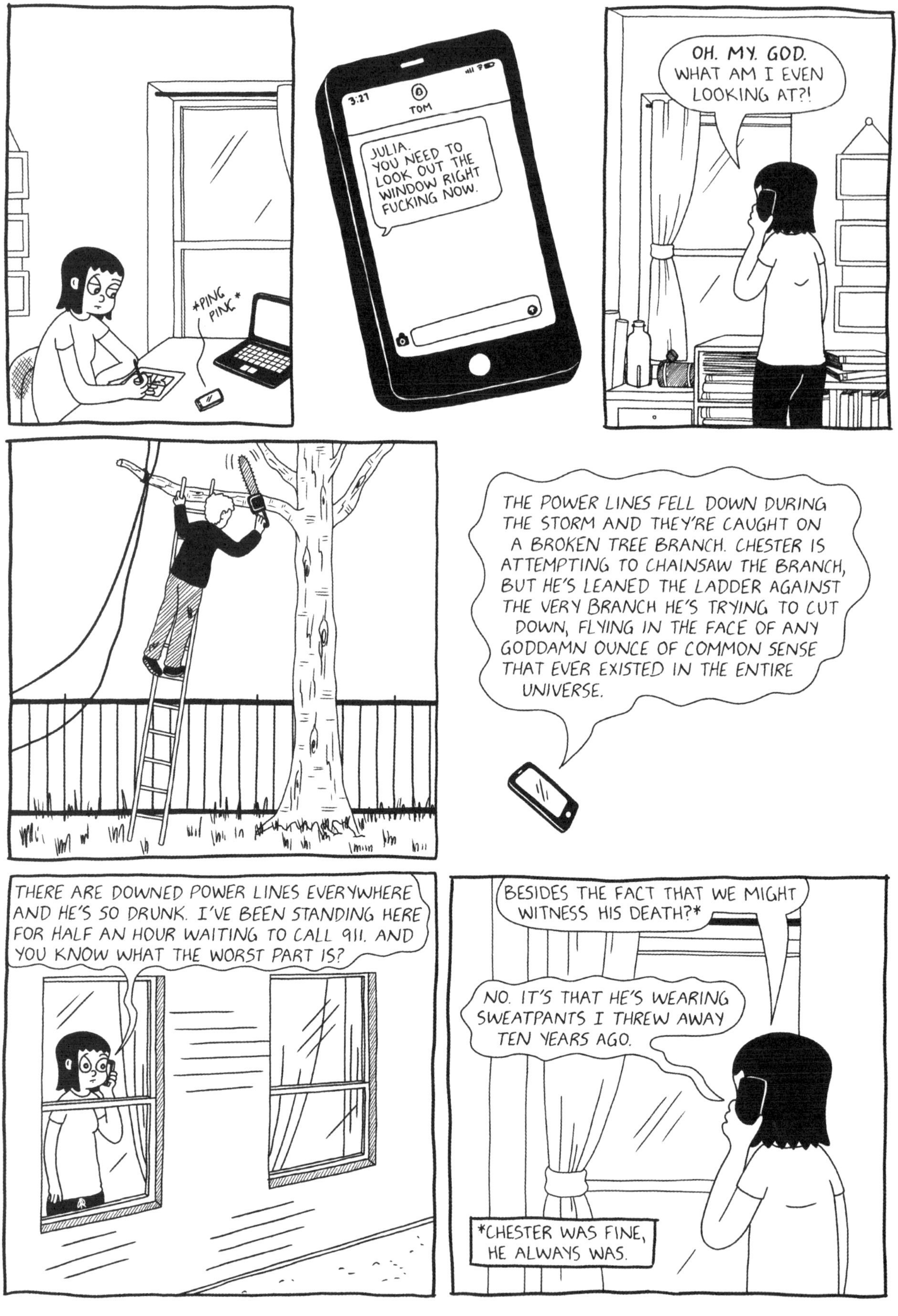
PING PING.
3:27
TOM
JULIA. YOU NEED TO LOOK OUT THE WINDOW RIGHT FUCKING NOW.
OH. MY. GOD. WHAT AM I EVEN LOOKING AT?!
THE POWER LINES FELL DOWN DURING THE STORM AND THEY'RE CAUGHT ON A BROKEN TREE BRANCH. CHESTER IS ATTEMPTING TO CHAINSAW THE BRANCH, BUT HE'S LEANED THE LADDER AGAINST THE VERY BRANCH HE'S TRYING TO CUT DOWN, FLYING IN THE FACE OF ANY GODDAMN OUNCE OF COMMON SENSE THAT EVER EXISTED IN THE ENTIRE UNIVERSE.
THERE ARE DOWNED POWER LINES EVERYWHERE AND HE'S SO DRUNK. I'VE BEEN STANDING HERE FOR HALF AN HOUR WAITING TO CALL 911. AND YOU KNOW WHAT THE WORST PART IS?
BESIDES THE FACT THAT WE MIGHT WITNESS HIS DEATH?*
NO. IT'S THAT HE'S WEARING SWEATPANTS I THREW AWAY TEN YEARS AGO.
*CHESTER WAS FINE, HE ALWAYS WAS.

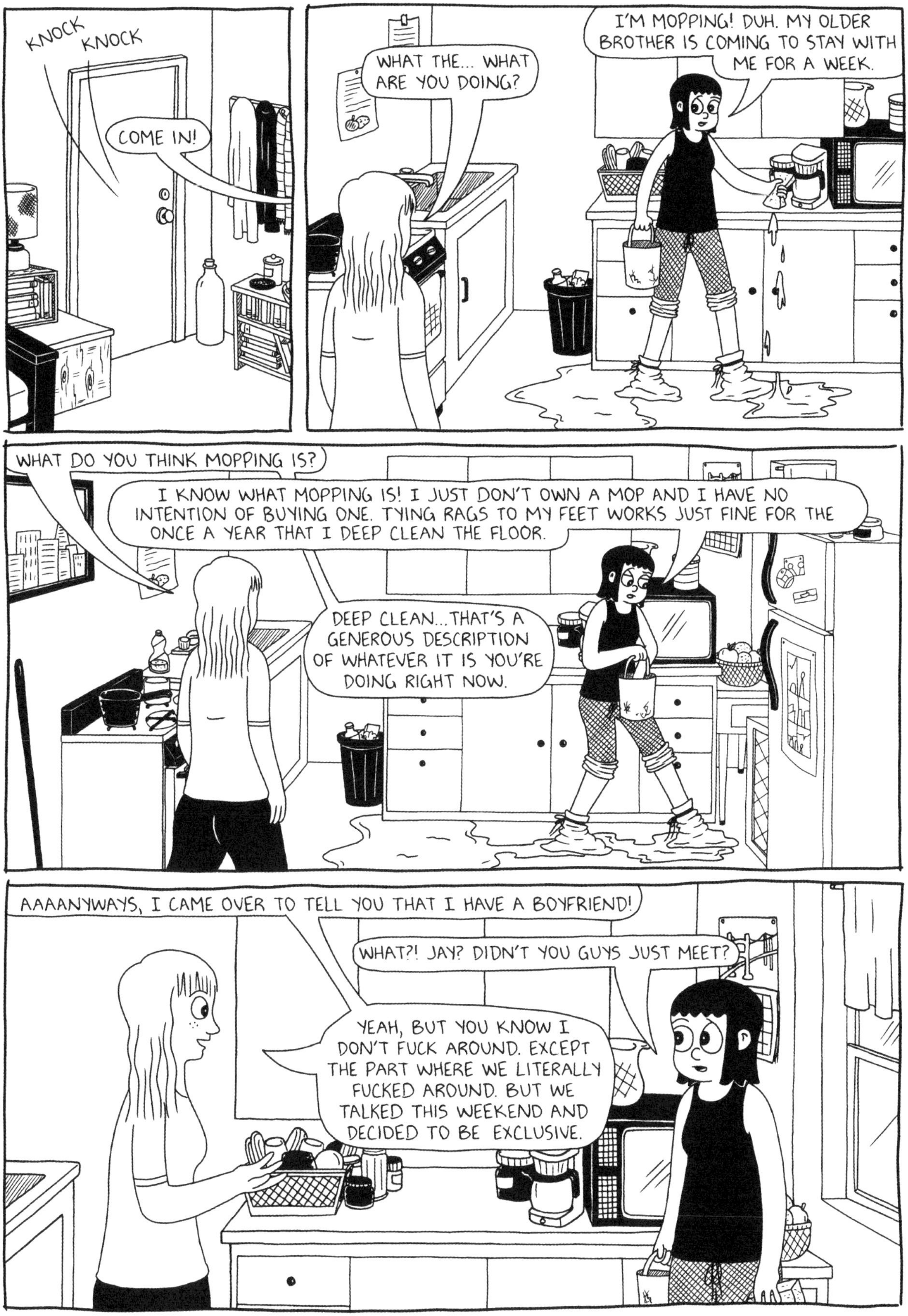
KNOCK KNOCK
COME IN!
WHAT THE... WHAT ARE YOU DOING?
I'M MOPPING! DUH. MY OLDER BROTHER IS COMING TO STAY WITH ME FOR A WEEK.
WHAT DO YOU THINK MOPPING IS?
I KNOW WHAT MOPPING IS! I JUST DON'T OWN A MOP AND I HAVE NO INTENTION OF BUYING ONE. TYING RAGS TO MY FEET WORKS JUST FINE FOR THE ONCE A YEAR THAT I DEEP CLEAN THE FLOOR.
DEEP CLEAN...THAT'S A GENEROUS DESCRIPTION OF WHATEVER IT IS YOU'RE DOING RIGHT NOW.
AAAANYWAYS, I CAME OVER TO TELL YOU THAT I HAVE A BOYFRIEND!
WHAT?! JAY? DIDN'T YOU GUYS JUST MEET?
YEAH, BUT YOU KNOW I DON'T FUCK AROUND. EXCEPT THE PART WHERE WE LITERALLY FUCKED AROUND. BUT WE TALKED THIS WEEKEND AND DECIDED TO BE EXCLUSIVE.

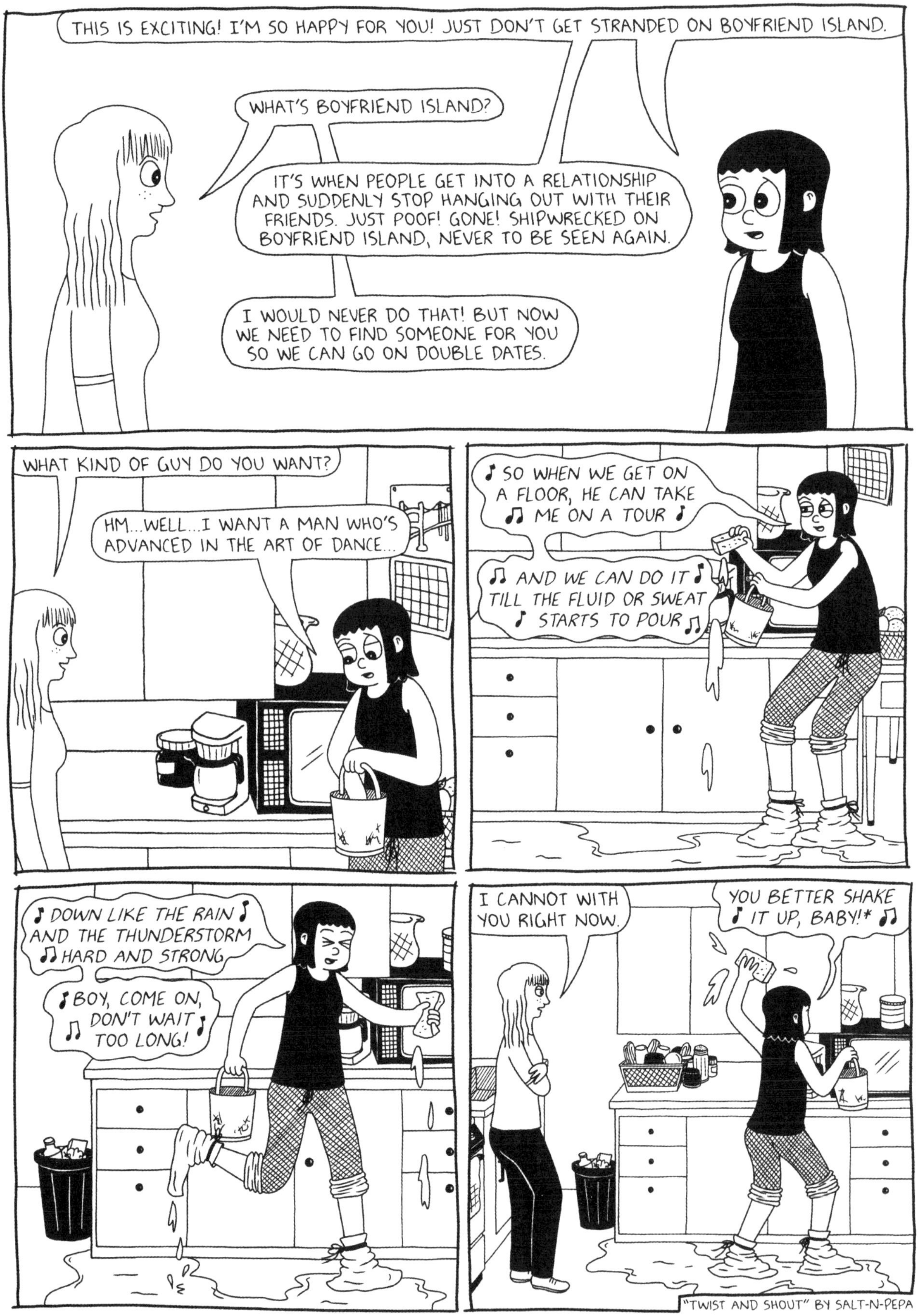
THIS IS EXCITING! I'M SO HAPPY FOR YOU! JUST DON'T GET STRANDED ON BOYFRIEND ISLAND.
WHAT'S BOYFRIEND ISLAND?
IT'S WHEN PEOPLE GET INTO A RELATIONSHIP AND SUDDENLY STOP HANGING OUT WITH THEIR FRIENDS. JUST POOF! GONE! SHIPWRECKED ON BOYFRIEND ISLAND, NEVER TO BE SEEN AGAIN.
I WOULD NEVER DO THAT! BUT NOW WE NEED TO FIND SOMEONE FOR YOU SO WE CAN GO ON DOUBLE DATES.
WHAT KIND OF GUY DO YOU WANT?
HM...WELL...I WANT A MAN WHO'S ADVANCED IN THE ART OF DANCE...
♪ SO WHEN WE GET ON A FLOOR, HE CAN TAKE ♫ ME ON A TOUR ♪
♫ AND WE CAN DO IT ♪ TILL THE FLUID OR SWEAT ♪ STARTS TO POUR ♫
♪ DOWN LIKE THE RAIN ♪ AND THE THUNDERSTORM ♫ HARD AND STRONG
♪ BOY, COME ON, ♫ DON'T WAIT ♪ TOO LONG!
I CANNOT WITH YOU RIGHT NOW.
YOU BETTER SHAKE ♪ IT UP, BABY!* ♫

*"TWIST AND SHOUT" BY SALT-N-PEPA

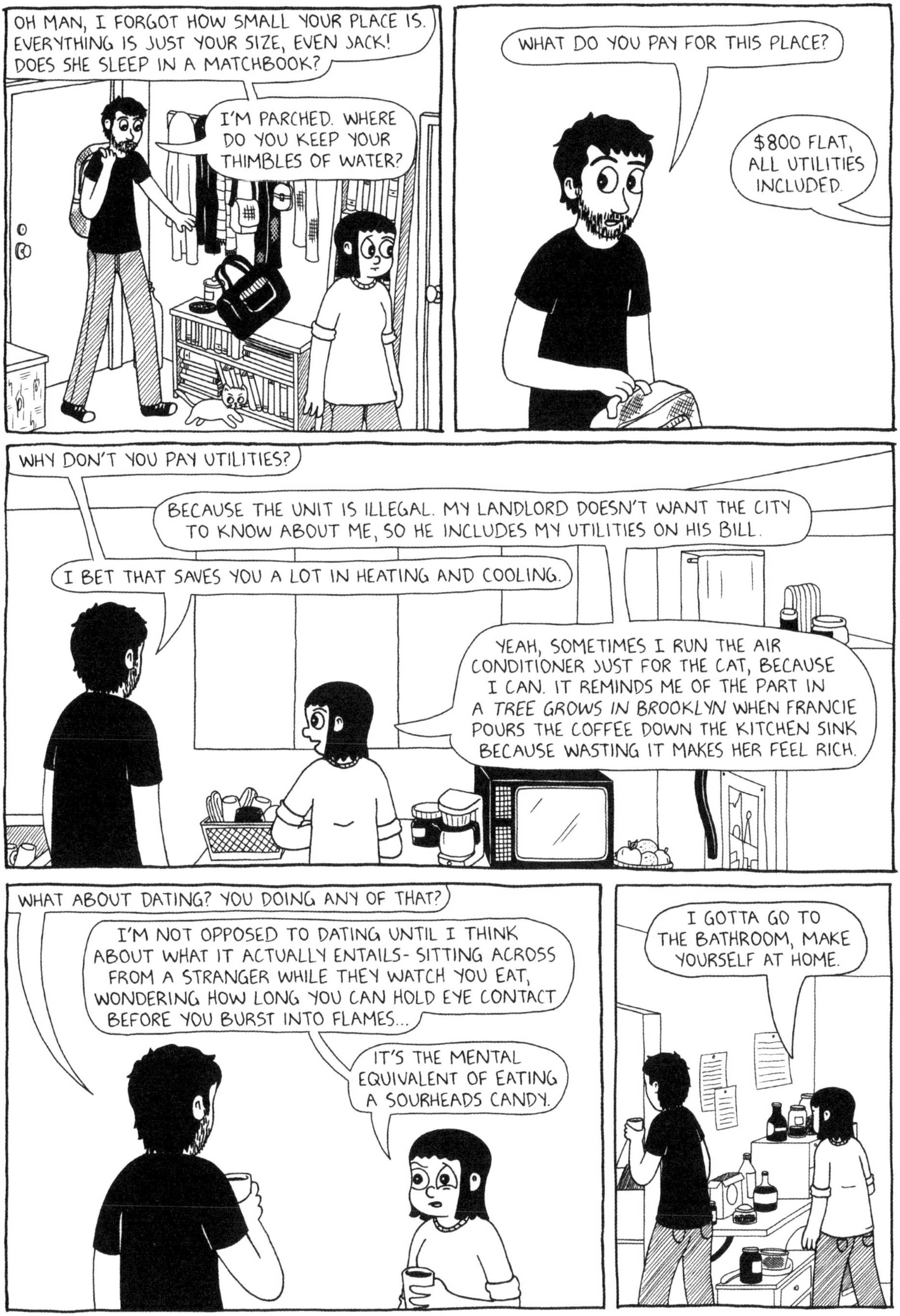

OH MAN, I FORGOT HOW SMALL YOUR PLACE IS. EVERYTHING IS JUST YOUR SIZE, EVEN JACK! DOES SHE SLEEP IN A MATCHBOOK?
I'M PARCHED. WHERE DO YOU KEEP YOUR THIMBLES OF WATER?
WHAT DO YOU PAY FOR THIS PLACE?
$800 FLAT, ALL UTILITIES INCLUDED.
WHY DON'T YOU PAY UTILITIES?
BECAUSE THE UNIT IS ILLEGAL. MY LANDLORD DOESN'T WANT THE CITY TO KNOW ABOUT ME, SO HE INCLUDES MY UTILITIES ON HIS BILL.
I BET THAT SAVES YOU A LOT IN HEATING AND COOLING.
YEAH, SOMETIMES I RUN THE AIR CONDITIONER JUST FOR THE CAT, BECAUSE I CAN. IT REMINDS ME OF THE PART IN A *TREE GROWS IN BROOKLYN* WHEN FRANCIE POURS THE COFFEE DOWN THE KITCHEN SINK BECAUSE WASTING IT MAKES HER FEEL RICH.
WHAT ABOUT DATING? YOU DOING ANY OF THAT?
I'M NOT OPPOSED TO DATING UNTIL I THINK ABOUT WHAT IT ACTUALLY ENTAILS- SITTING ACROSS FROM A STRANGER WHILE THEY WATCH YOU EAT, WONDERING HOW LONG YOU CAN HOLD EYE CONTACT BEFORE YOU BURST INTO FLAMES...
IT'S THE MENTAL EQUIVALENT OF EATING A SOURHEADS CANDY.
I GOTTA GO TO THE BATHROOM, MAKE YOURSELF AT HOME.

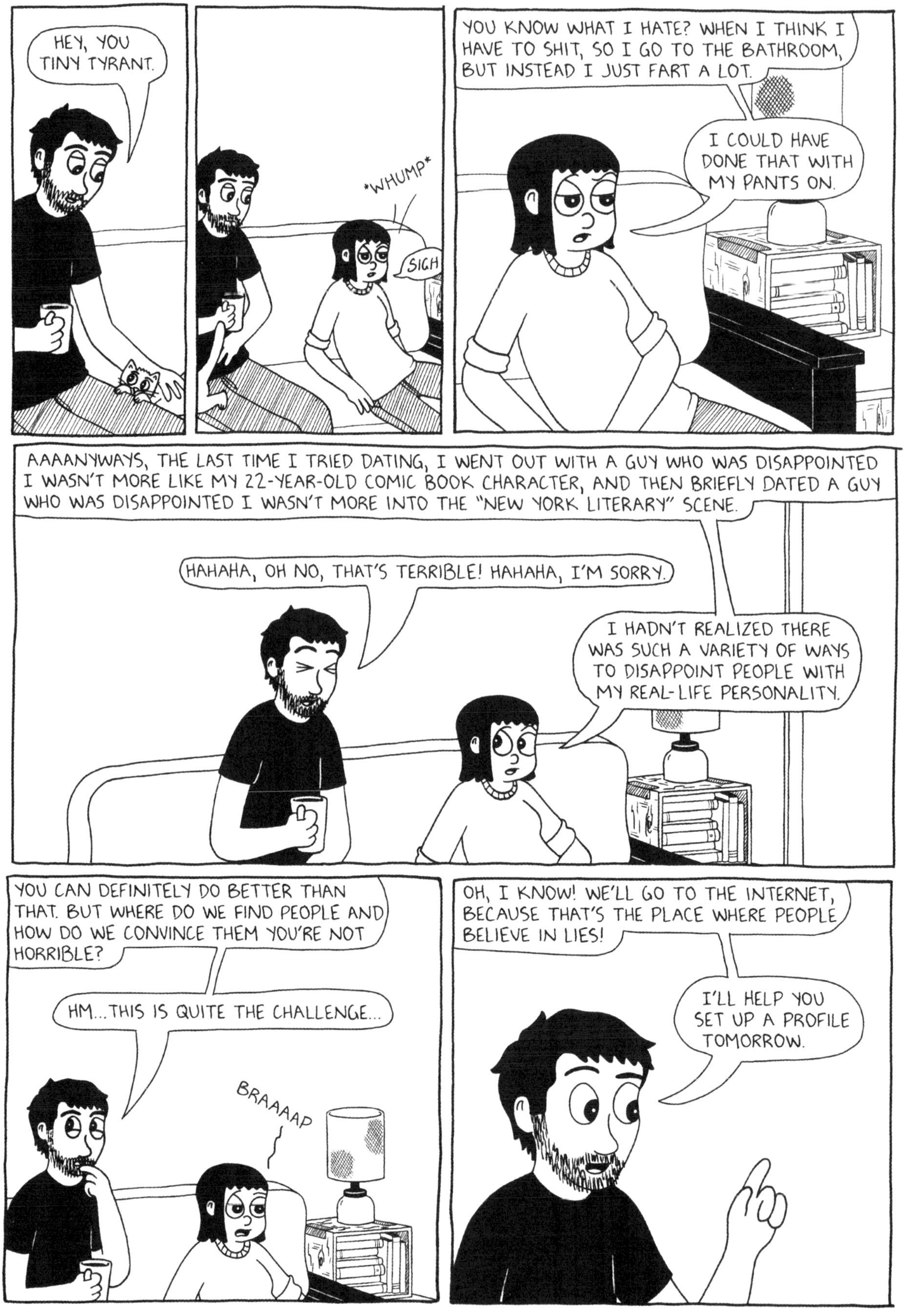
HEY, YOU TINY TYRANT.
WHUMP
SIGH
YOU KNOW WHAT I HATE? WHEN I THINK I HAVE TO SHIT, SO I GO TO THE BATHROOM, BUT INSTEAD I JUST FART A LOT.
I COULD HAVE DONE THAT WITH MY PANTS ON.
AAAANYWAYS, THE LAST TIME I TRIED DATING, I WENT OUT WITH A GUY WHO WAS DISAPPOINTED I WASN'T MORE LIKE MY 22-YEAR-OLD COMIC BOOK CHARACTER, AND THEN BRIEFLY DATED A GUY WHO WAS DISAPPOINTED I WASN'T MORE INTO THE "NEW YORK LITERARY" SCENE.
HAHAHA, OH NO, THAT'S TERRIBLE! HAHAHA, I'M SORRY.
I HADN'T REALIZED THERE WAS SUCH A VARIETY OF WAYS TO DISAPPOINT PEOPLE WITH MY REAL-LIFE PERSONALITY.
YOU CAN DEFINITELY DO BETTER THAN THAT. BUT WHERE DO WE FIND PEOPLE AND HOW DO WE CONVINCE THEM YOU'RE NOT HORRIBLE?
HM... THIS IS QUITE THE CHALLENGE...
BRAAAAP
OH, I KNOW! WE'LL GO TO THE INTERNET, BECAUSE THAT'S THE PLACE WHERE PEOPLE BELIEVE IN LIES!
I'LL HELP YOU SET UP A PROFILE TOMORROW.

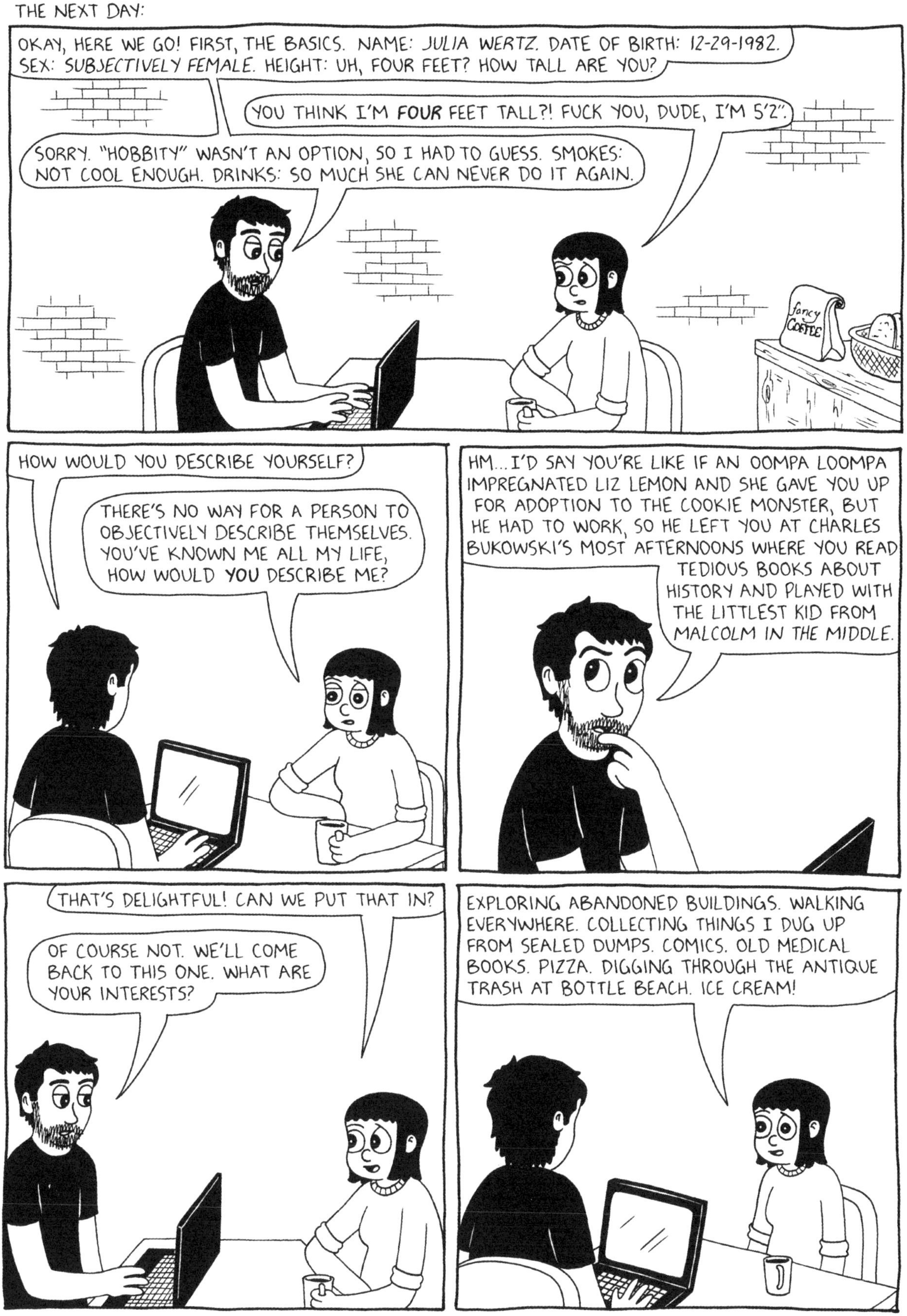
THE NEXT DAY:
OKAY, HERE WE GO! FIRST, THE BASICS. NAME: JULIA WERTZ. DATE OF BIRTH: 12-29-1982. SEX: SUBJECTIVELY FEMALE. HEIGHT: UH, FOUR FEET? HOW TALL ARE YOU?
YOU THINK I'M **FOUR** FEET TALL?! FUCK YOU, DUDE, I'M 5'2".
SORRY. "HOBBITY" WASN'T AN OPTION, SO I HAD TO GUESS. SMOKES: NOT COOL ENOUGH. DRINKS: SO MUCH SHE CAN NEVER DO IT AGAIN.
fancy COFFEE
HOW WOULD YOU DESCRIBE YOURSELF?
THERE'S NO WAY FOR A PERSON TO OBJECTIVELY DESCRIBE THEMSELVES. YOU'VE KNOWN ME ALL MY LIFE, HOW WOULD **YOU** DESCRIBE ME?
HM...I'D SAY YOU'RE LIKE IF AN OOMPA LOOMPA IMPREGNATED LIZ LEMON AND SHE GAVE YOU UP FOR ADOPTION TO THE COOKIE MONSTER, BUT HE HAD TO WORK, SO HE LEFT YOU AT CHARLES BUKOWSKI'S MOST AFTERNOONS WHERE YOU READ TEDIOUS BOOKS ABOUT HISTORY AND PLAYED WITH THE LITTLEST KID FROM MALCOLM IN THE MIDDLE.
THAT'S DELIGHTFUL! CAN WE PUT THAT IN?
OF COURSE NOT. WE'LL COME BACK TO THIS ONE. WHAT ARE YOUR INTERESTS?
EXPLORING ABANDONED BUILDINGS. WALKING EVERYWHERE. COLLECTING THINGS I DUG UP FROM SEALED DUMPS. COMICS. OLD MEDICAL BOOKS. PIZZA. DIGGING THROUGH THE ANTIQUE TRASH AT BOTTLE BEACH. ICE CREAM!

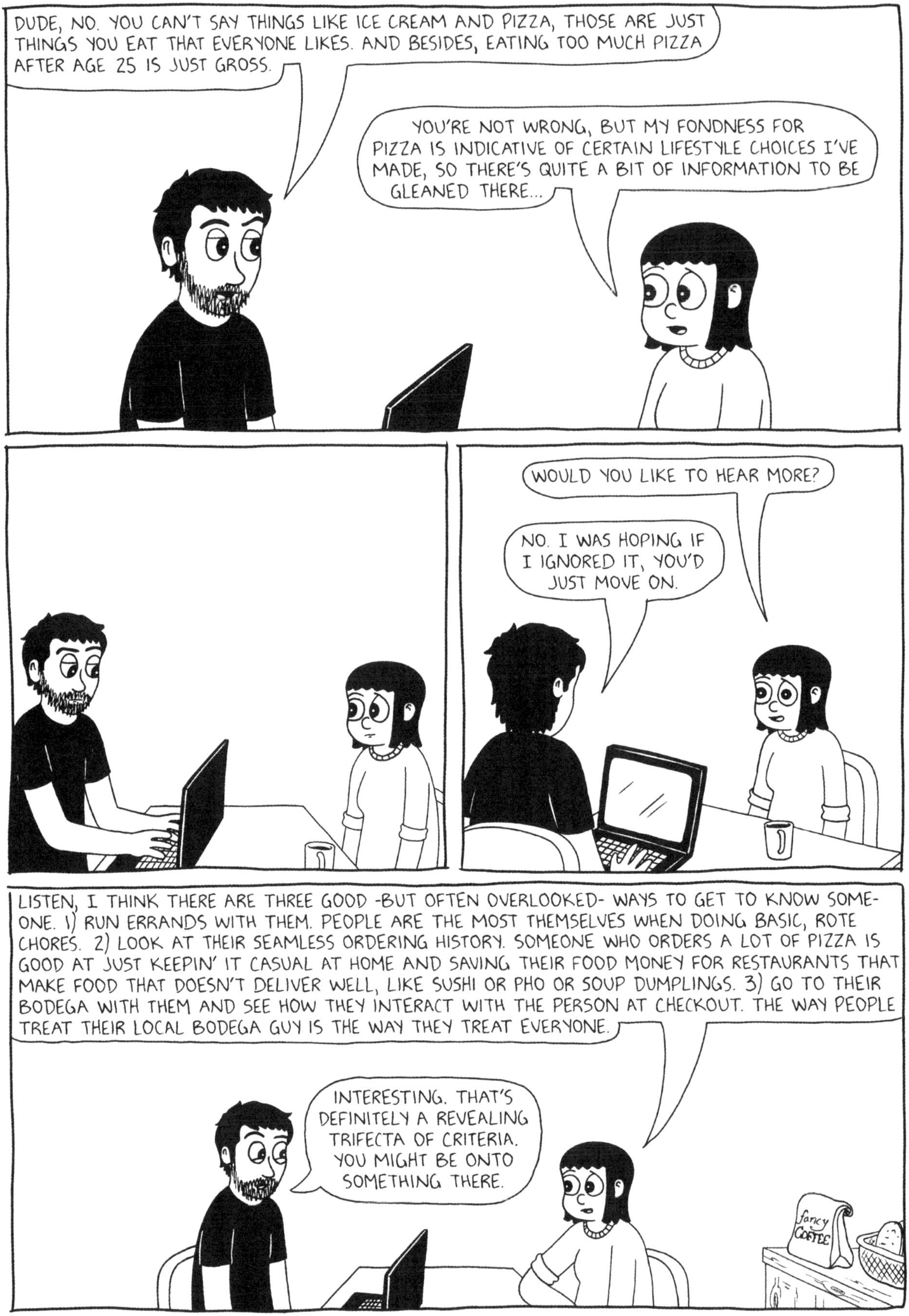
DUDE, NO. YOU CAN'T SAY THINGS LIKE ICE CREAM AND PIZZA, THOSE ARE JUST THINGS YOU EAT THAT EVERYONE LIKES. AND BESIDES, EATING TOO MUCH PIZZA AFTER AGE 25 IS JUST GROSS.
YOU'RE NOT WRONG, BUT MY FONDNESS FOR PIZZA IS INDICATIVE OF CERTAIN LIFESTYLE CHOICES I'VE MADE, SO THERE'S QUITE A BIT OF INFORMATION TO BE GLEANED THERE...
WOULD YOU LIKE TO HEAR MORE?
NO. I WAS HOPING IF I IGNORED IT, YOU'D JUST MOVE ON.
LISTEN, I THINK THERE ARE THREE GOOD -BUT OFTEN OVERLOOKED- WAYS TO GET TO KNOW SOMEONE. 1) RUN ERRANDS WITH THEM. PEOPLE ARE THE MOST THEMSELVES WHEN DOING BASIC, ROTE CHORES. 2) LOOK AT THEIR SEAMLESS ORDERING HISTORY. SOMEONE WHO ORDERS A LOT OF PIZZA IS GOOD AT JUST KEEPIN' IT CASUAL AT HOME AND SAVING THEIR FOOD MONEY FOR RESTAURANTS THAT MAKE FOOD THAT DOESN'T DELIVER WELL, LIKE SUSHI OR PHO OR SOUP DUMPLINGS. 3) GO TO THEIR BODEGA WITH THEM AND SEE HOW THEY INTERACT WITH THE PERSON AT CHECKOUT. THE WAY PEOPLE TREAT THEIR LOCAL BODEGA GUY IS THE WAY THEY TREAT EVERYONE.
INTERESTING. THAT'S DEFINITELY A REVEALING TRIFECTA OF CRITERIA. YOU MIGHT BE ONTO SOMETHING THERE.
fancy COFFEE

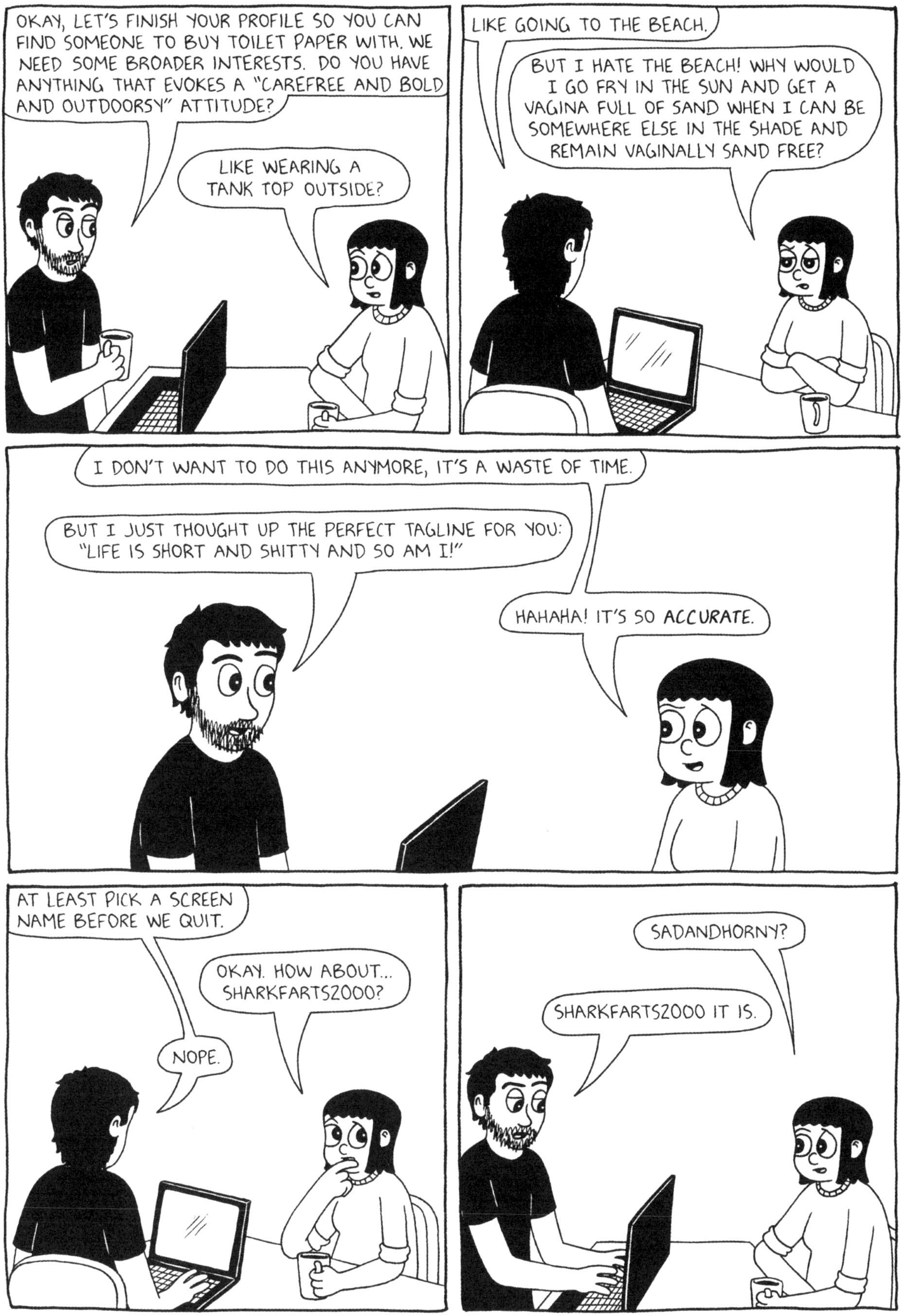
OKAY, LET'S FINISH YOUR PROFILE SO YOU CAN FIND SOMEONE TO BUY TOILET PAPER WITH. WE NEED SOME BROADER INTERESTS. DO YOU HAVE ANYTHING THAT EVOKES A "CAREFREE AND BOLD AND OUTDOORSY" ATTITUDE?
LIKE WEARING A TANK TOP OUTSIDE?
LIKE GOING TO THE BEACH.
BUT I HATE THE BEACH! WHY WOULD I GO FRY IN THE SUN AND GET A VAGINA FULL OF SAND WHEN I CAN BE SOMEWHERE ELSE IN THE SHADE AND REMAIN VAGINALLY SAND FREE?
I DON'T WANT TO DO THIS ANYMORE, IT'S A WASTE OF TIME.
BUT I JUST THOUGHT UP THE PERFECT TAGLINE FOR YOU: "LIFE IS SHORT AND SHITTY AND SO AM I!"
HAHAHA! IT'S SO ACCURATE.
AT LEAST PICK A SCREEN NAME BEFORE WE QUIT.
OKAY. HOW ABOUT... SHARKFARTS2000?
NOPE.
SADANDHORNY?
SHARKFARTS2000 IT IS.

FOR TWO WEEKS, JOSH AND I RAN AROUND NEW YORK CITY, GOOFING OFF AND HAVING LITTLE ADVENTURES. WE PROBABLY WALKED HUNDREDS OF MILES, COLLECTIVELY.

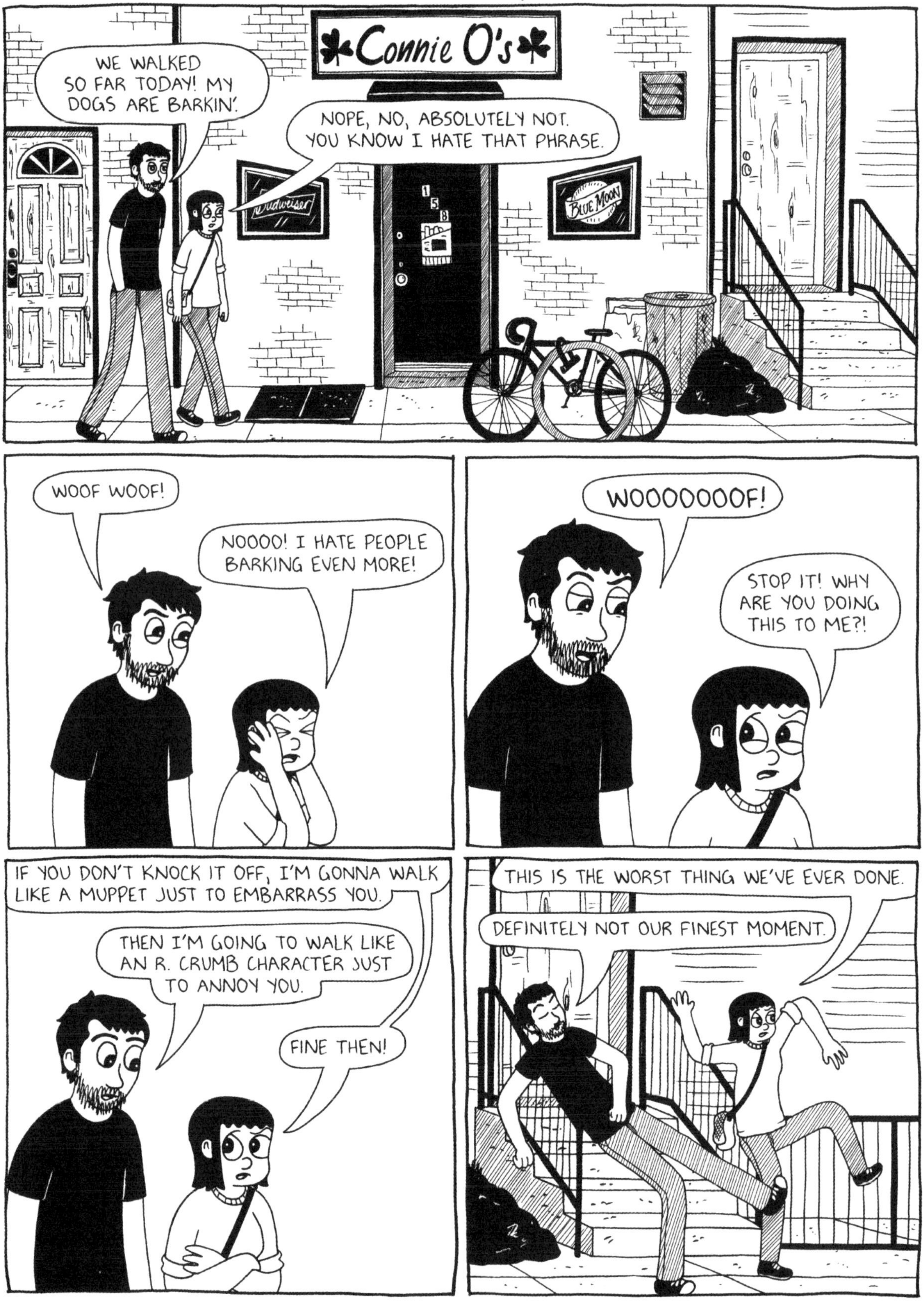

Connie O's
WE WALKED SO FAR TODAY! MY DOGS ARE BARKIN'.
NOPE, NO, ABSOLUTELY NOT. YOU KNOW I HATE THAT PHRASE.
Budweiser
BLUE MOON
158
WOOF WOOF!
NOOOO! I HATE PEOPLE BARKING EVEN MORE!
WOOOOOOOF!
STOP IT! WHY ARE YOU DOING THIS TO ME?!
IF YOU DON'T KNOCK IT OFF, I'M GONNA WALK LIKE A MUPPET JUST TO EMBARRASS YOU.
THEN I'M GOING TO WALK LIKE AN R. CRUMB CHARACTER JUST TO ANNOY YOU.
FINE THEN!
THIS IS THE WORST THING WE'VE EVER DONE.
DEFINITELY NOT OUR FINEST MOMENT.

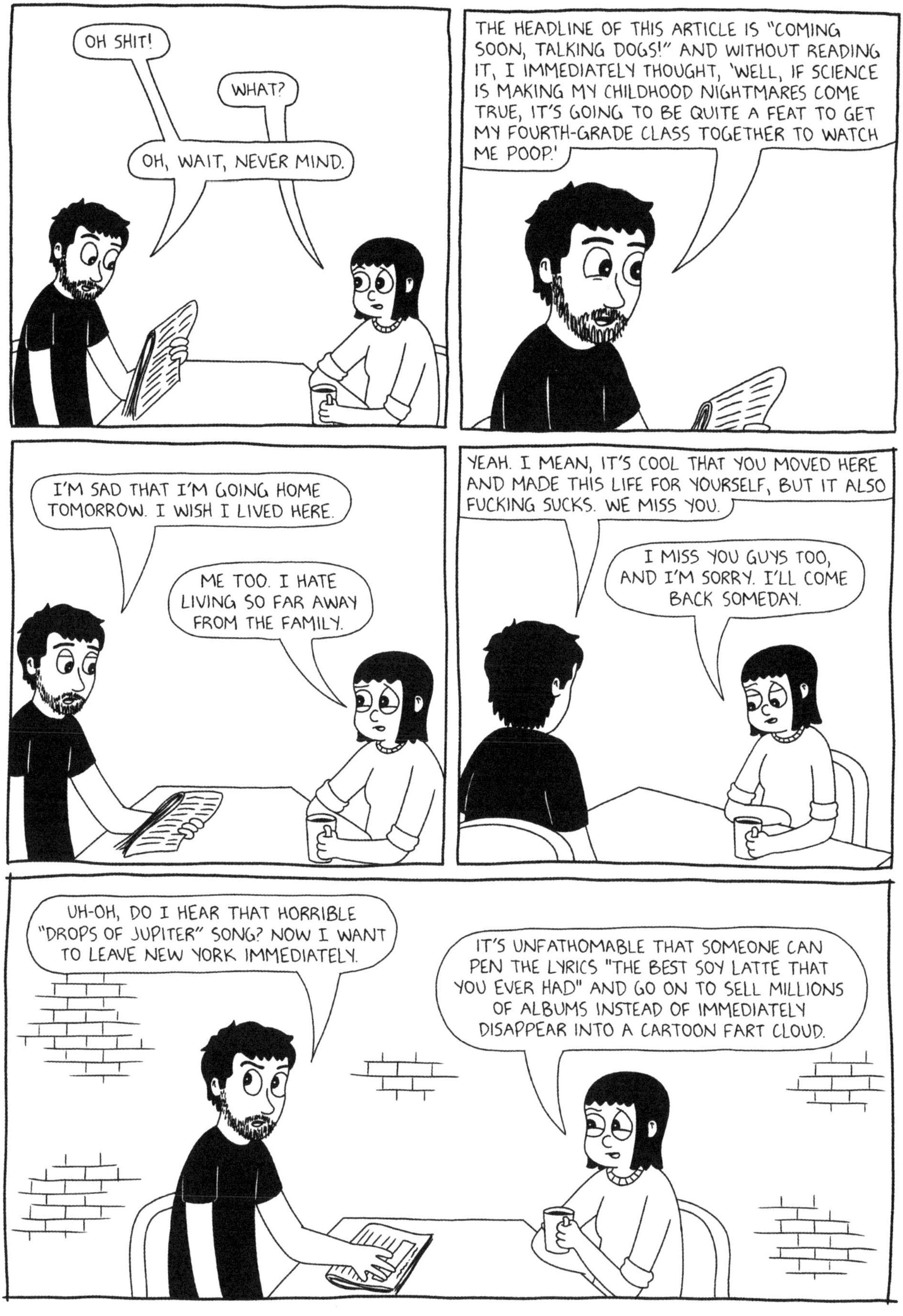
OH SHIT!
WHAT?
OH, WAIT, NEVER MIND.
THE HEADLINE OF THIS ARTICLE IS "COMING SOON, TALKING DOGS!" AND WITHOUT READING IT, I IMMEDIATELY THOUGHT, 'WELL, IF SCIENCE IS MAKING MY CHILDHOOD NIGHTMARES COME TRUE, IT'S GOING TO BE QUITE A FEAT TO GET MY FOURTH-GRADE CLASS TOGETHER TO WATCH ME POOP.'
I'M SAD THAT I'M GOING HOME TOMORROW. I WISH I LIVED HERE.
ME TOO. I HATE LIVING SO FAR AWAY FROM THE FAMILY.
YEAH. I MEAN, IT'S COOL THAT YOU MOVED HERE AND MADE THIS LIFE FOR YOURSELF, BUT IT ALSO FUCKING SUCKS. WE MISS YOU.
I MISS YOU GUYS TOO, AND I'M SORRY. I'LL COME BACK SOMEDAY.
UH-OH, DO I HEAR THAT HORRIBLE "DROPS OF JUPITER" SONG? NOW I WANT TO LEAVE NEW YORK IMMEDIATELY.
IT'S UNFATHOMABLE THAT SOMEONE CAN PEN THE LYRICS "THE BEST SOY LATTE THAT YOU EVER HAD" AND GO ON TO SELL MILLIONS OF ALBUMS INSTEAD OF IMMEDIATELY DISAPPEAR INTO A CARTOON FART CLOUD.

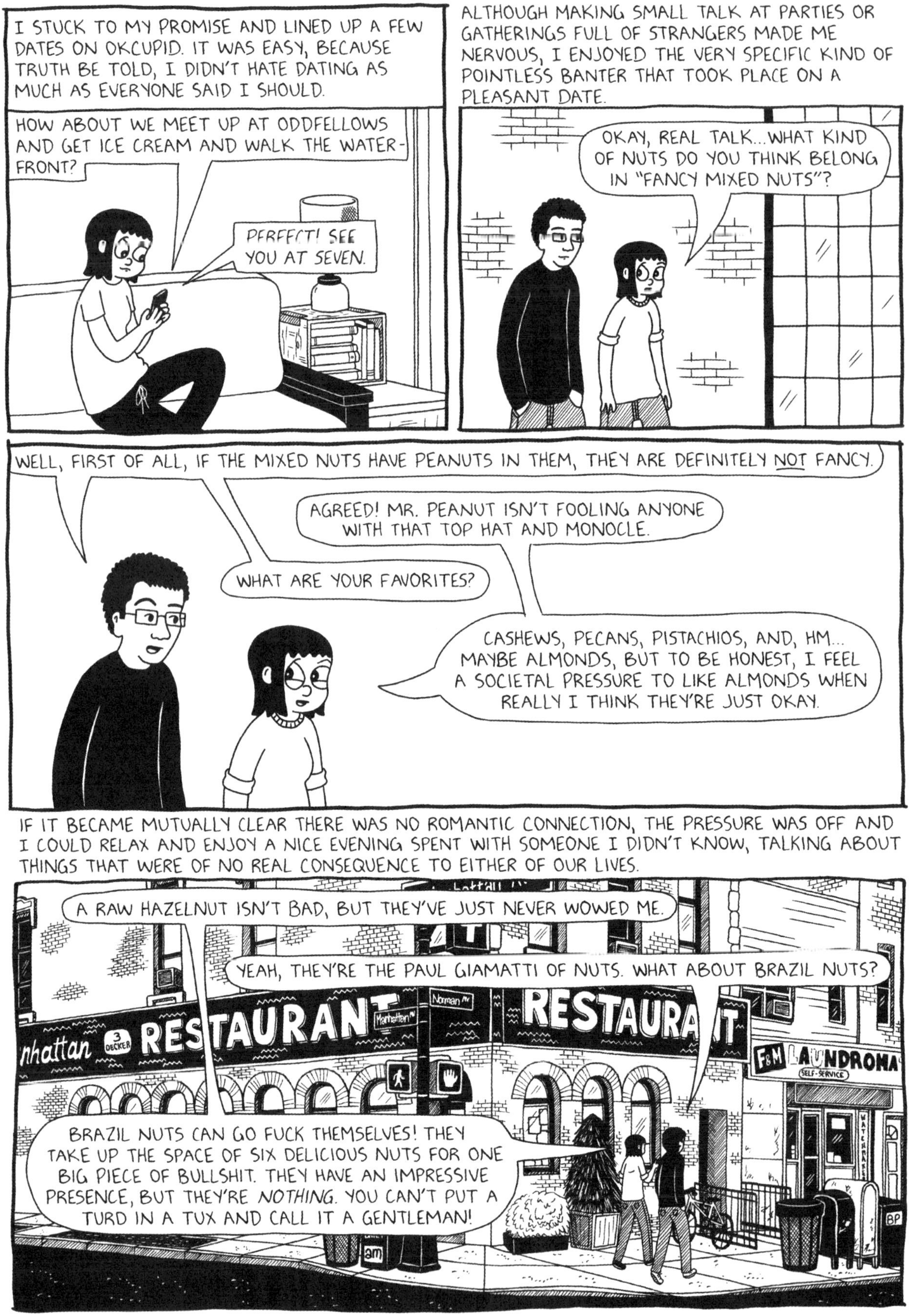
I STUCK TO MY PROMISE AND LINED UP A FEW DATES ON OKCUPID. IT WAS EASY, BECAUSE TRUTH BE TOLD, I DIDN'T HATE DATING AS MUCH AS EVERYONE SAID I SHOULD.
HOW ABOUT WE MEET UP AT ODDFELLOWS AND GET ICE CREAM AND WALK THE WATER-FRONT?
PERFECT! SEE YOU AT SEVEN.
ALTHOUGH MAKING SMALL TALK AT PARTIES OR GATHERINGS FULL OF STRANGERS MADE ME NERVOUS, I ENJOYED THE VERY SPECIFIC KIND OF POINTLESS BANTER THAT TOOK PLACE ON A PLEASANT DATE.
OKAY, REAL TALK...WHAT KIND OF NUTS DO YOU THINK BELONG IN "FANCY MIXED NUTS"?
WELL, FIRST OF ALL, IF THE MIXED NUTS HAVE PEANUTS IN THEM, THEY ARE DEFINITELY NOT FANCY.
AGREED! MR. PEANUT ISN'T FOOLING ANYONE WITH THAT TOP HAT AND MONOCLE.
WHAT ARE YOUR FAVORITES?
CASHEWS, PECANS, PISTACHIOS, AND, HM... MAYBE ALMONDS, BUT TO BE HONEST, I FEEL A SOCIETAL PRESSURE TO LIKE ALMONDS WHEN REALLY I THINK THEY'RE JUST OKAY.
IF IT BECAME MUTUALLY CLEAR THERE WAS NO ROMANTIC CONNECTION, THE PRESSURE WAS OFF AND I COULD RELAX AND ENJOY A NICE EVENING SPENT WITH SOMEONE I DIDN'T KNOW, TALKING ABOUT THINGS THAT WERE OF NO REAL CONSEQUENCE TO EITHER OF OUR LIVES.
A RAW HAZELNUT ISN'T BAD, BUT THEY'VE JUST NEVER WOWED ME.
YEAH, THEY'RE THE PAUL GIAMATTI OF NUTS. WHAT ABOUT BRAZIL NUTS?
BRAZIL NUTS CAN GO FUCK THEMSELVES! THEY TAKE UP THE SPACE OF SIX DELICIOUS NUTS FOR ONE BIG PIECE OF BULLSHIT. THEY HAVE AN IMPRESSIVE PRESENCE, BUT THEY'RE NOTHING. YOU CAN'T PUT A TURD IN A TUX AND CALL IT A GENTLEMAN!
RESTAURANT
3 DECKER
RESTAURANT
Norman Av
Manhattan Av
F&M LAUNDROMA
SELF-SERVICE

A FEW DATES LED TO ONE OR TWO MORE DATES...

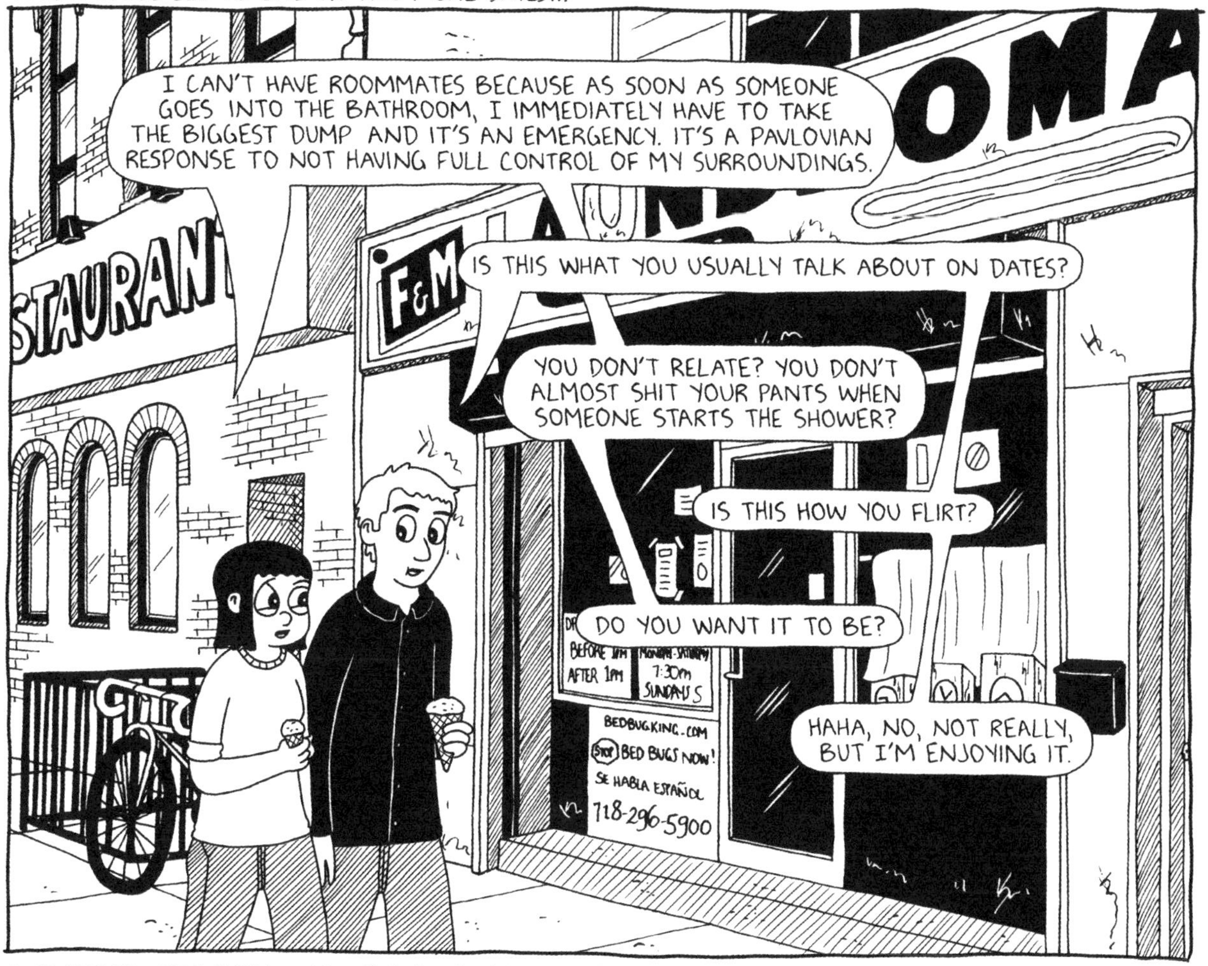
I CAN'T HAVE ROOMMATES BECAUSE AS SOON AS SOMEONE GOES INTO THE BATHROOM, I IMMEDIATELY HAVE TO TAKE THE BIGGEST DUMP AND IT'S AN EMERGENCY. IT'S A PAVLOVIAN RESPONSE TO NOT HAVING FULL CONTROL OF MY SURROUNDINGS.
IS THIS WHAT YOU USUALLY TALK ABOUT ON DATES?
YOU DON'T RELATE? YOU DON'T ALMOST SHIT YOUR PANTS WHEN SOMEONE STARTS THE SHOWER?
IS THIS HOW YOU FLIRT?
DO YOU WANT IT TO BE?
HAHA, NO, NOT REALLY, BUT I'M ENJOYING IT.
STAURANT
F&M
OMA
BEFORE 1PM
AFTER 1PM
7:30PM
SUNDAYS
BEDBUGKING.COM
STOP BED BUGS NOW!
SE HABLA ESPAÑOL
718-296-5900

AND THERE WERE EVEN A FEW PLEASANT SHORT-LIVED FLINGS THAT GOT JUST FAR ENOUGH TO WATCH MOVIES TOGETHER...

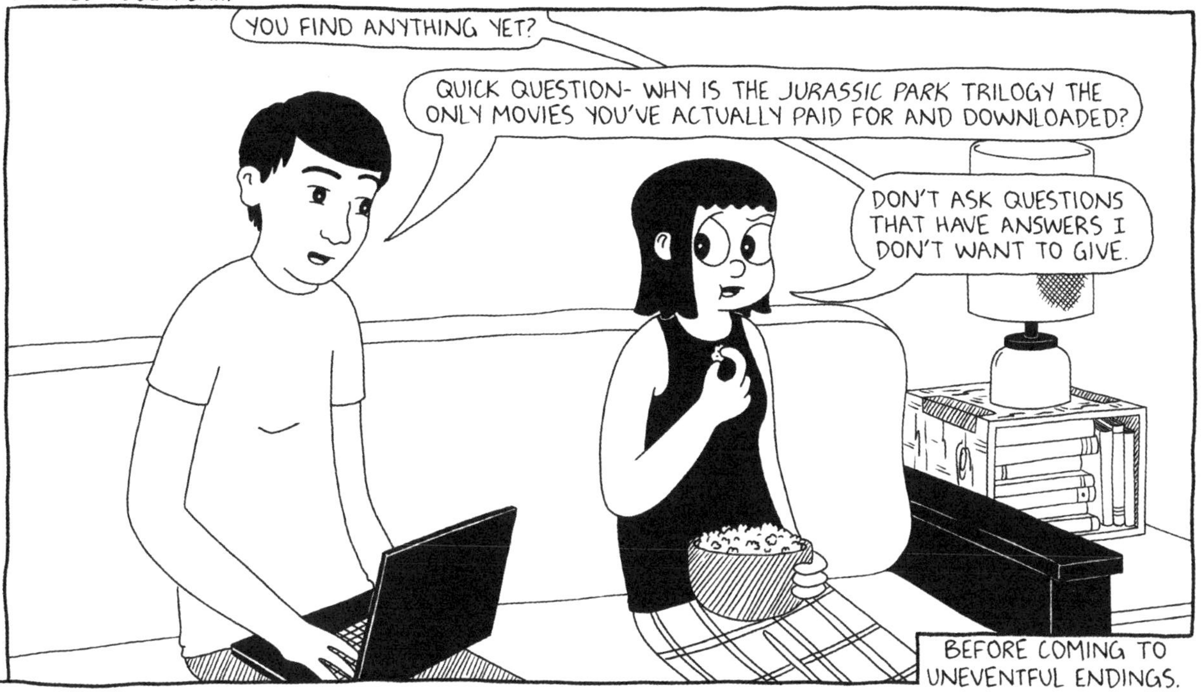
YOU FIND ANYTHING YET?
QUICK QUESTION- WHY IS THE *JURASSIC PARK* TRILOGY THE ONLY MOVIES YOU'VE ACTUALLY PAID FOR AND DOWNLOADED?
DON'T ASK QUESTIONS THAT HAVE ANSWERS I DON'T WANT TO GIVE.
BEFORE COMING TO UNEVENTFUL ENDINGS.

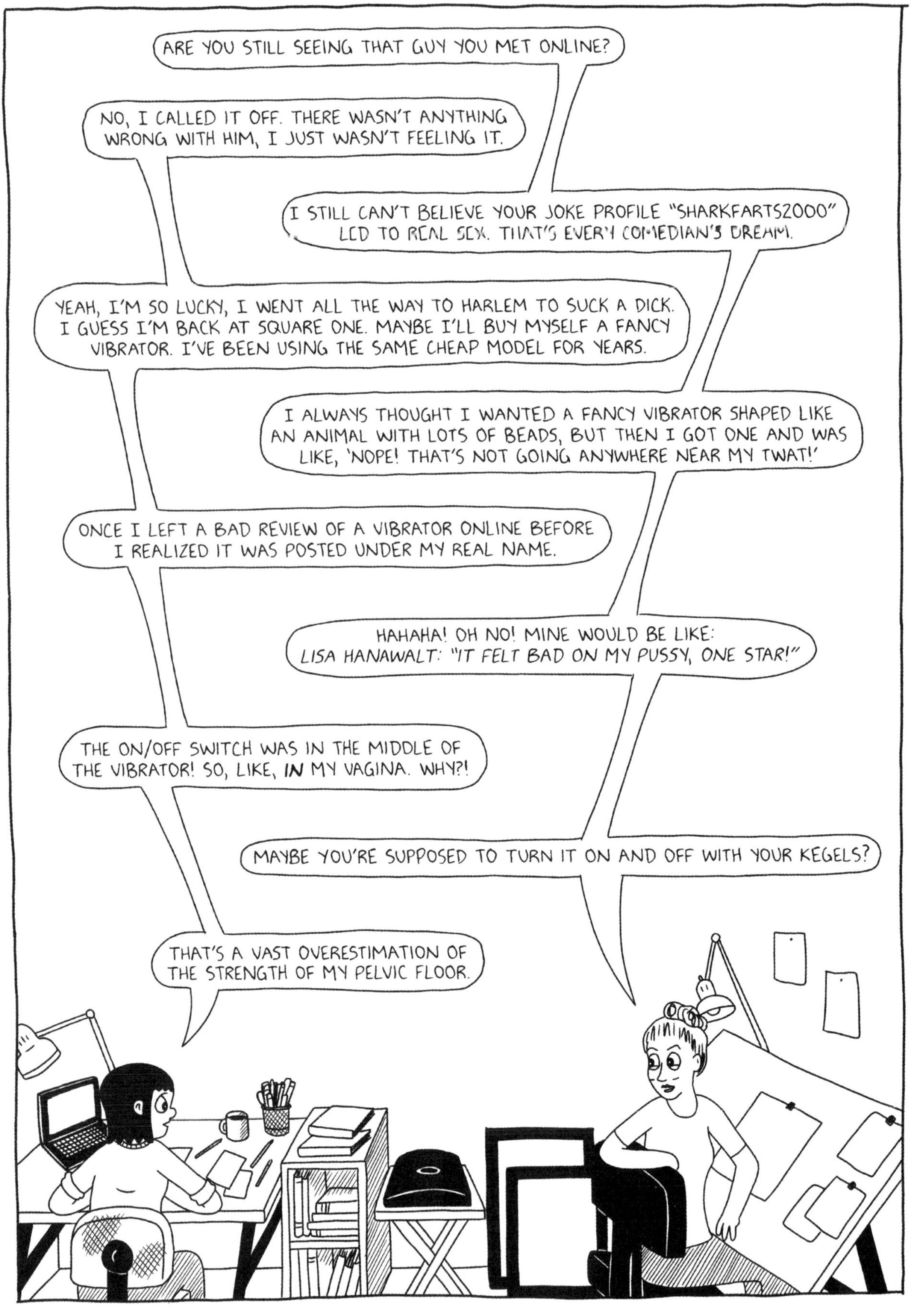
ARE YOU STILL SEEING THAT GUY YOU MET ONLINE?
NO, I CALLED IT OFF. THERE WASN'T ANYTHING WRONG WITH HIM, I JUST WASN'T FEELING IT.
I STILL CAN'T BELIEVE YOUR JOKE PROFILE "SHARKFARTS2000" LED TO REAL SEX. THAT'S EVERY COMEDIAN'S DREAM.
YEAH, I'M SO LUCKY, I WENT ALL THE WAY TO HARLEM TO SUCK A DICK. I GUESS I'M BACK AT SQUARE ONE. MAYBE I'LL BUY MYSELF A FANCY VIBRATOR. I'VE BEEN USING THE SAME CHEAP MODEL FOR YEARS.
I ALWAYS THOUGHT I WANTED A FANCY VIBRATOR SHAPED LIKE AN ANIMAL WITH LOTS OF BEADS, BUT THEN I GOT ONE AND WAS LIKE, 'NOPE! THAT'S NOT GOING ANYWHERE NEAR MY TWAT!'
ONCE I LEFT A BAD REVIEW OF A VIBRATOR ONLINE BEFORE I REALIZED IT WAS POSTED UNDER MY REAL NAME.
HAHAHA! OH NO! MINE WOULD BE LIKE: *LISA HANAWALT: "IT FELT BAD ON MY PUSSY, ONE STAR!"*
THE ON/OFF SWITCH WAS IN THE MIDDLE OF THE VIBRATOR! SO, LIKE, **IN** MY VAGINA. WHY?!
MAYBE YOU'RE SUPPOSED TO TURN IT ON AND OFF WITH YOUR KEGELS?
THAT'S A VAST OVERESTIMATION OF THE STRENGTH OF MY PELVIC FLOOR.

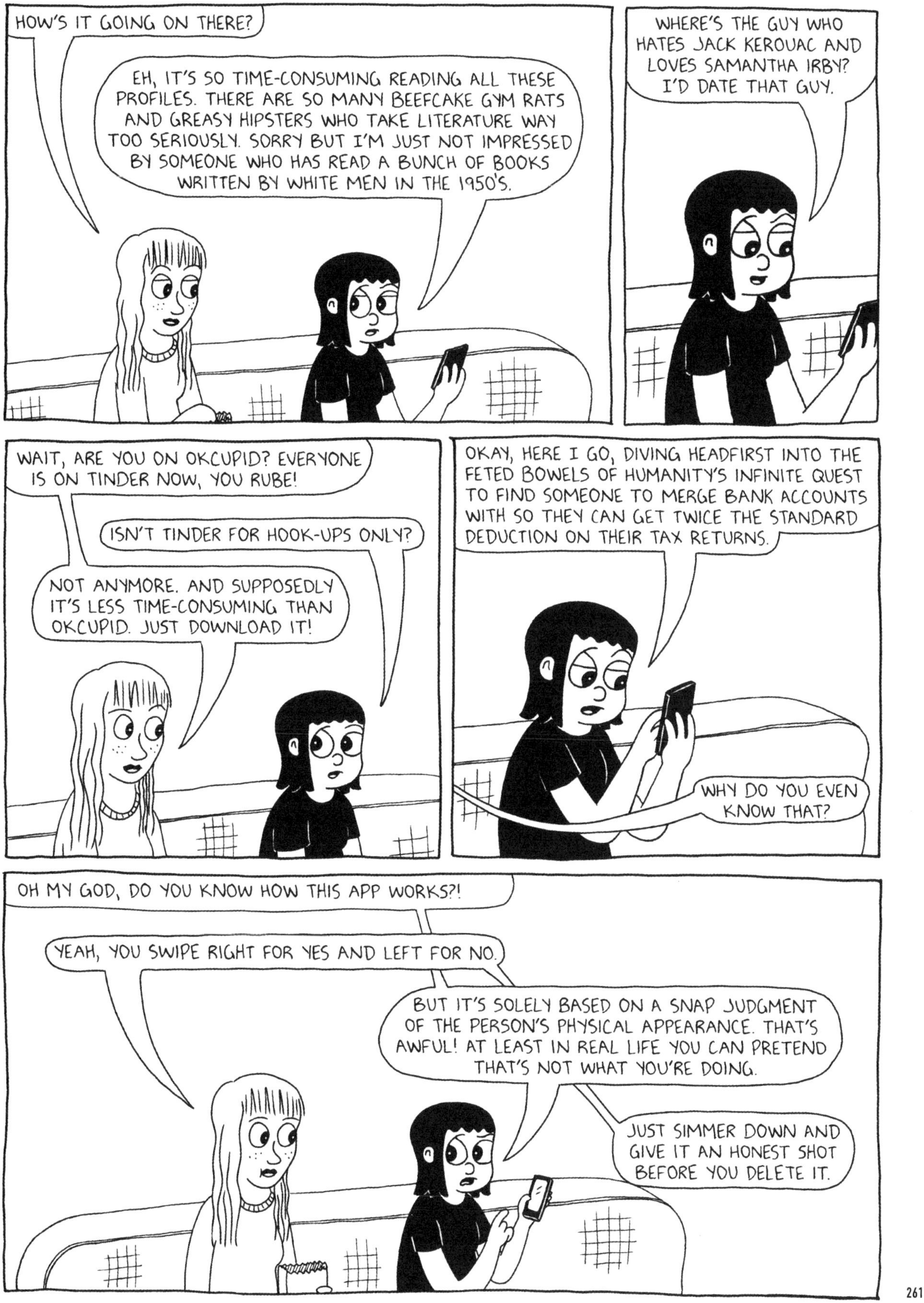
HOW'S IT GOING ON THERE?
EH, IT'S SO TIME-CONSUMING READING ALL THESE PROFILES. THERE ARE SO MANY BEEFCAKE GYM RATS AND GREASY HIPSTERS WHO TAKE LITERATURE WAY TOO SERIOUSLY. SORRY BUT I'M JUST NOT IMPRESSED BY SOMEONE WHO HAS READ A BUNCH OF BOOKS WRITTEN BY WHITE MEN IN THE 1950'S.
WHERE'S THE GUY WHO HATES JACK KEROUAC AND LOVES SAMANTHA IRBY? I'D DATE THAT GUY.
WAIT, ARE YOU ON OKCUPID? EVERYONE IS ON TINDER NOW, YOU RUBE!
ISN'T TINDER FOR HOOK-UPS ONLY?
NOT ANYMORE. AND SUPPOSEDLY IT'S LESS TIME-CONSUMING THAN OKCUPID. JUST DOWNLOAD IT!
OKAY, HERE I GO, DIVING HEADFIRST INTO THE FETED BOWELS OF HUMANITY'S INFINITE QUEST TO FIND SOMEONE TO MERGE BANK ACCOUNTS WITH SO THEY CAN GET TWICE THE STANDARD DEDUCTION ON THEIR TAX RETURNS.
WHY DO YOU EVEN KNOW THAT?
OH MY GOD, DO YOU KNOW HOW THIS APP WORKS?!
YEAH, YOU SWIPE RIGHT FOR YES AND LEFT FOR NO.
BUT IT'S SOLELY BASED ON A SNAP JUDGMENT OF THE PERSON'S PHYSICAL APPEARANCE. THAT'S AWFUL! AT LEAST IN REAL LIFE YOU CAN PRETEND THAT'S NOT WHAT YOU'RE DOING.
JUST SIMMER DOWN AND GIVE IT AN HONEST SHOT BEFORE YOU DELETE IT.

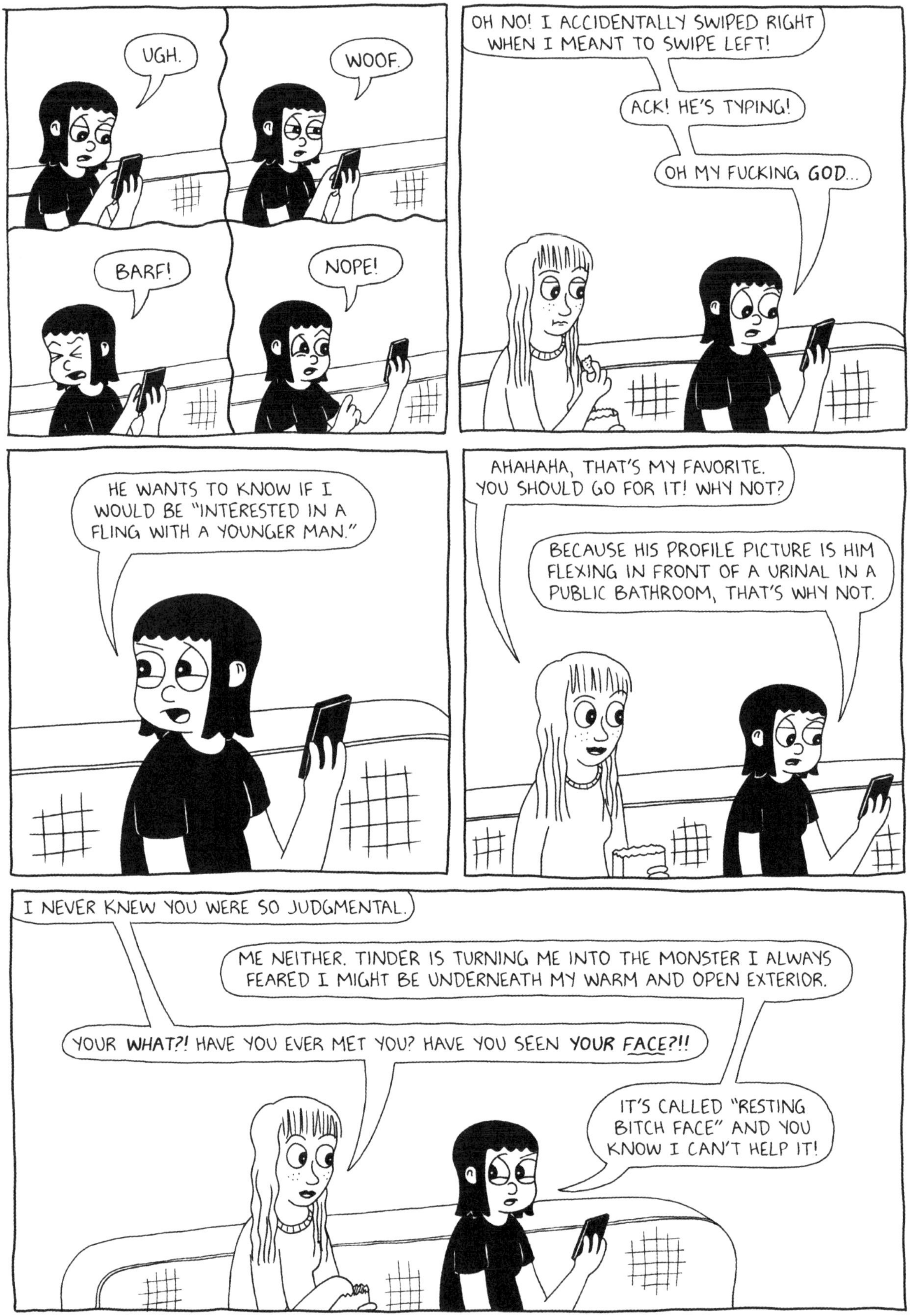
UGH.
WOOF.
BARF!
NOPE!
OH NO! I ACCIDENTALLY SWIPED RIGHT WHEN I MEANT TO SWIPE LEFT!
ACK! HE'S TYPING!
OH MY FUCKING GOD...
HE WANTS TO KNOW IF I WOULD BE "INTERESTED IN A FLING WITH A YOUNGER MAN."
AHAHAHA, THAT'S MY FAVORITE. YOU SHOULD GO FOR IT! WHY NOT?
BECAUSE HIS PROFILE PICTURE IS HIM FLEXING IN FRONT OF A URINAL IN A PUBLIC BATHROOM, THAT'S WHY NOT.
I NEVER KNEW YOU WERE SO JUDGMENTAL.
ME NEITHER. TINDER IS TURNING ME INTO THE MONSTER I ALWAYS FEARED I MIGHT BE UNDERNEATH MY WARM AND OPEN EXTERIOR.
YOUR WHAT?! HAVE YOU EVER MET YOU? HAVE YOU SEEN YOUR FACE?!!
IT'S CALLED "RESTING BITCH FACE" AND YOU KNOW I CAN'T HELP IT!

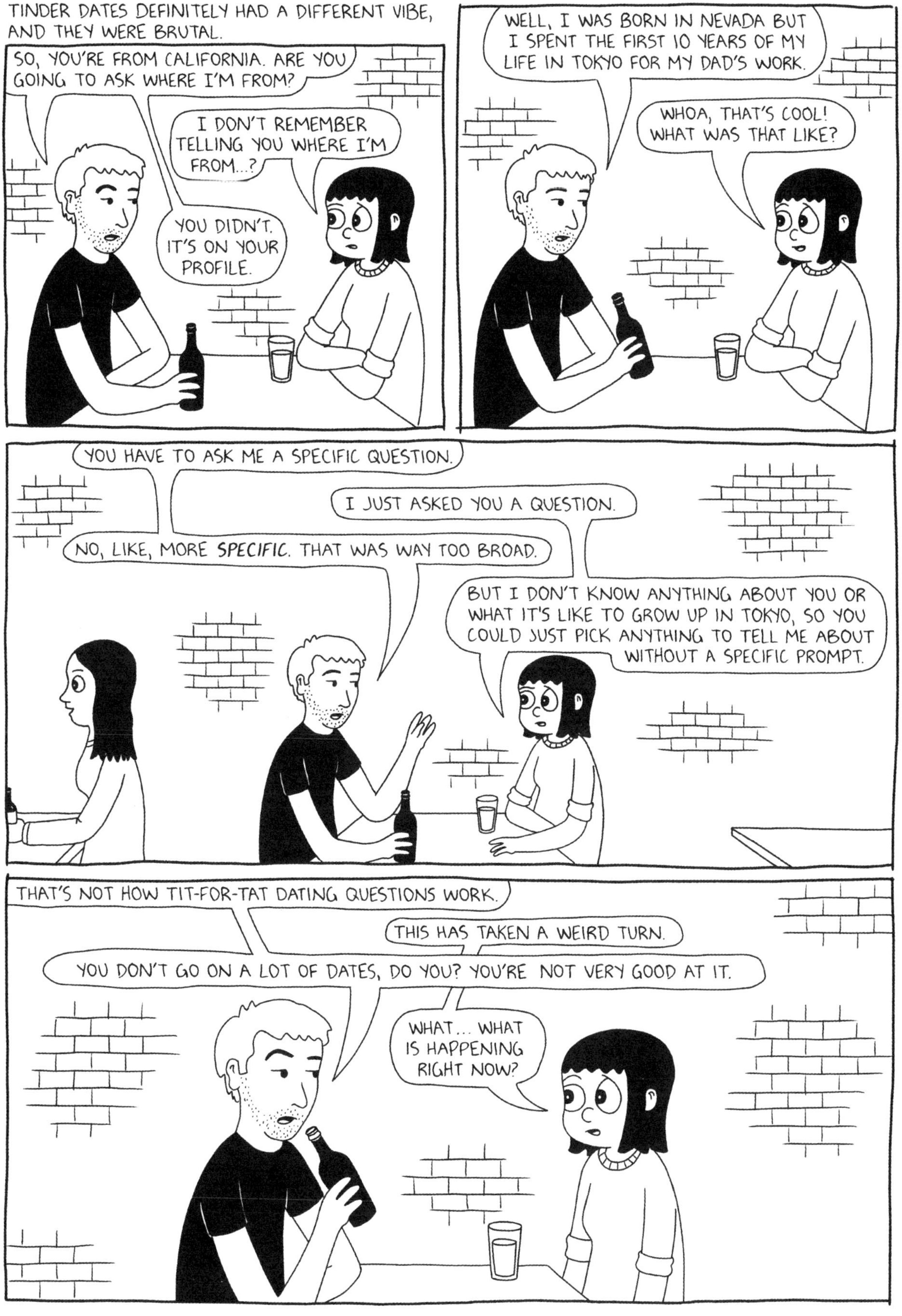
TINDER DATES DEFINITELY HAD A DIFFERENT VIBE, AND THEY WERE BRUTAL.
SO, YOU'RE FROM CALIFORNIA. ARE YOU GOING TO ASK WHERE I'M FROM?
I DON'T REMEMBER TELLING YOU WHERE I'M FROM...?
YOU DIDN'T. IT'S ON YOUR PROFILE.
WELL, I WAS BORN IN NEVADA BUT I SPENT THE FIRST 10 YEARS OF MY LIFE IN TOKYO FOR MY DAD'S WORK.
WHOA, THAT'S COOL! WHAT WAS THAT LIKE?
YOU HAVE TO ASK ME A SPECIFIC QUESTION.
I JUST ASKED YOU A QUESTION.
NO, LIKE, MORE SPECIFIC. THAT WAS WAY TOO BROAD.
BUT I DON'T KNOW ANYTHING ABOUT YOU OR WHAT IT'S LIKE TO GROW UP IN TOKYO, SO YOU COULD JUST PICK ANYTHING TO TELL ME ABOUT WITHOUT A SPECIFIC PROMPT.
THAT'S NOT HOW TIT-FOR-TAT DATING QUESTIONS WORK.
THIS HAS TAKEN A WEIRD TURN.
YOU DON'T GO ON A LOT OF DATES, DO YOU? YOU'RE NOT VERY GOOD AT IT.
WHAT... WHAT IS HAPPENING RIGHT NOW?

A FEW GUYS ATTEMPTED THE TRENDY (AND EMOTIONALLY ABUSIVE) DATING METHOD OF NEGGING.*

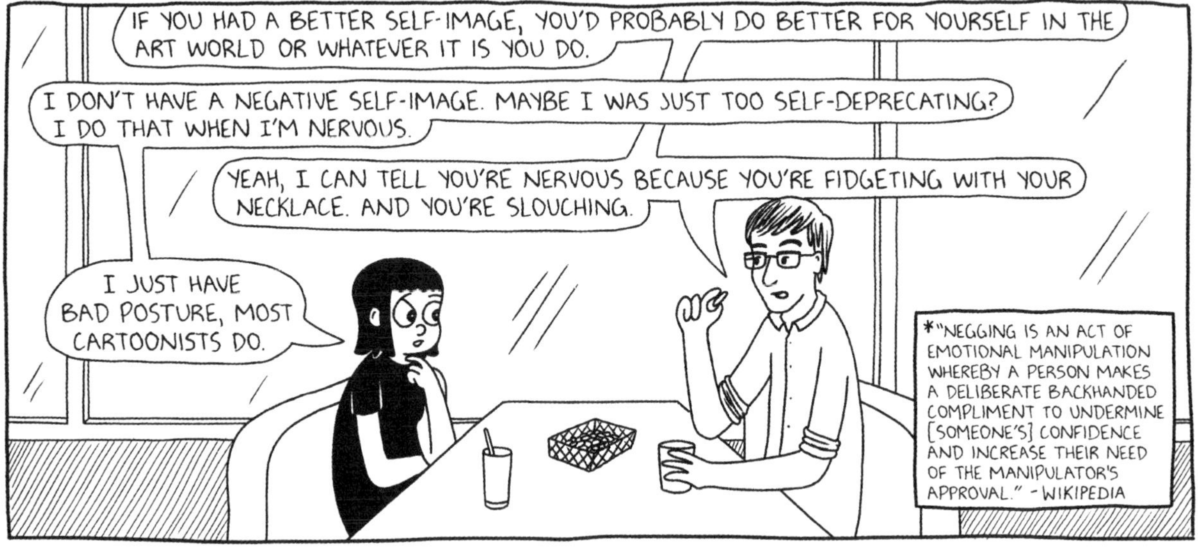
IF YOU HAD A BETTER SELF-IMAGE, YOU'D PROBABLY DO BETTER FOR YOURSELF IN THE ART WORLD OR WHATEVER IT IS YOU DO.
I DON'T HAVE A NEGATIVE SELF-IMAGE. MAYBE I WAS JUST TOO SELF-DEPRECATING? I DO THAT WHEN I'M NERVOUS.
YEAH, I CAN TELL YOU'RE NERVOUS BECAUSE YOU'RE FIDGETING WITH YOUR NECKLACE. AND YOU'RE SLOUCHING.
I JUST HAVE BAD POSTURE, MOST CARTOONISTS DO.
*"NEGGING IS AN ACT OF EMOTIONAL MANIPULATION WHEREBY A PERSON MAKES A DELIBERATE BACKHANDED COMPLIMENT TO UNDERMINE [SOMEONE'S] CONFIDENCE AND INCREASE THEIR NEED OF THE MANIPULATOR'S APPROVAL." - WIKIPEDIA

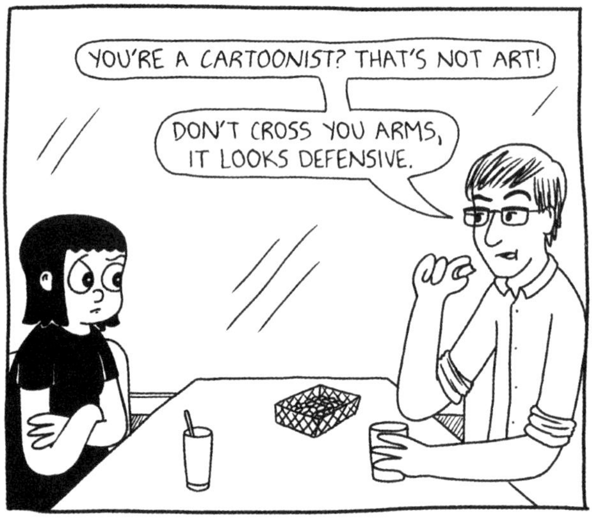
YOU'RE A *CARTOONIST*? THAT'S NOT ART!
DON'T CROSS YOU ARMS, IT LOOKS DEFENSIVE.

OTHER DATES WERE JUST DIFFICULT TO NAVIGATE AS A SOBER PERSON.

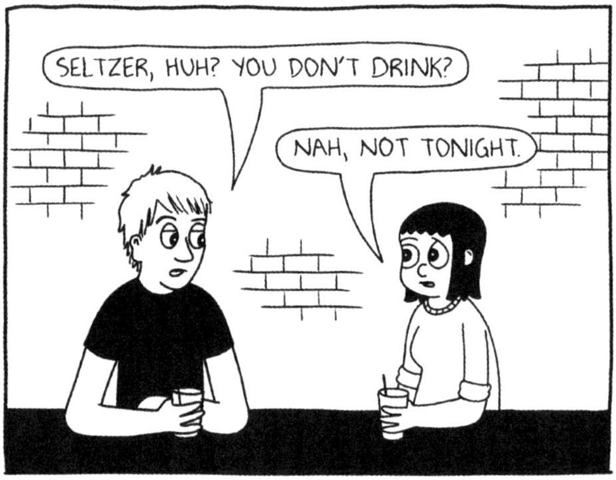
SELTZER, HUH? YOU DON'T DRINK?
NAH, NOT TONIGHT.

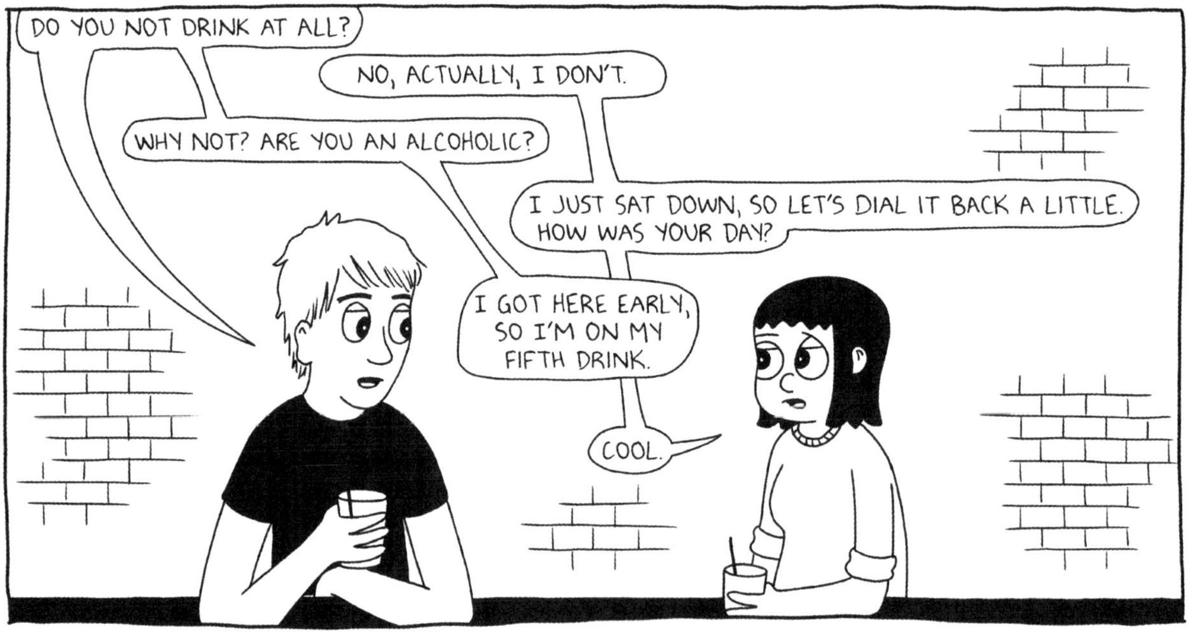
DO YOU NOT DRINK AT ALL?
NO, ACTUALLY, I DON'T.
WHY NOT? ARE YOU AN ALCOHOLIC?
I JUST SAT DOWN, SO LET'S DIAL IT BACK A LITTLE. HOW WAS YOUR DAY?
I GOT HERE EARLY, SO I'M ON MY FIFTH DRINK.
COOL.

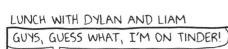
LUNCH WITH DYLAN AND LIAM

GUYS, GUESS WHAT, I'M ON TINDER!

GOOD GOD, WHY?

BECAUSE THERE'S NOTHING WRONG WITH WANTING TO WATCH TV AND EAT THAI DELIVERY WITH SOMEONE INSTEAD OF EATING LEFTOVERS ALONE WHILE FILLING MY COUCH WITH FARTS.

I DON'T KNOW IF I'LL LAST LONG ON IT THOUGH. IT'S ALL BATHROOM SELFIES, "WACKY" COSTUMES, BRO-FACE, AND GUYS IN BUTTON-UP SHIRTS STANDING NEXT TO HOUSE-PLANTS.

BUT I'M GONNA GIVE IT A SHOT. I'M ENTERING "CUFFING SEASON."

IS THAT A REAL THING OR A WERTZ THING?

IT'S REAL! IT'S WHEN FALL ARRIVES AND PEOPLE WHO NORMALLY PREFER TO BE SINGLE TRY TO GET "CUFFED," LIKE, TIED DOWN IN A RELATIONSHIP FOR THE COLD, LONELY WINTER AHEAD.

I MEAN, I'M NOT OPPOSED TO FINDING SOMEONE TO SETTLE DOWN WITH FOR A LONGER STINT, BUT COME SPRING, I'VE GOT A LOT TO DO. I WANT TO EXPLORE THE ABANDONED RESORTS UP IN THE CATSKILLS.

I DON'T THINK YOU'RE LOOKING FOR SOMEONE TO SETTLE DOWN WITH- I THINK YOU WANT SOMEONE TO GO EXPLORING AND CRAWL THROUGH SEPTIC TUNNELS WITH YOU.

YUP, AND THAT SEPTIC TUNNEL IS MY VAGINA.

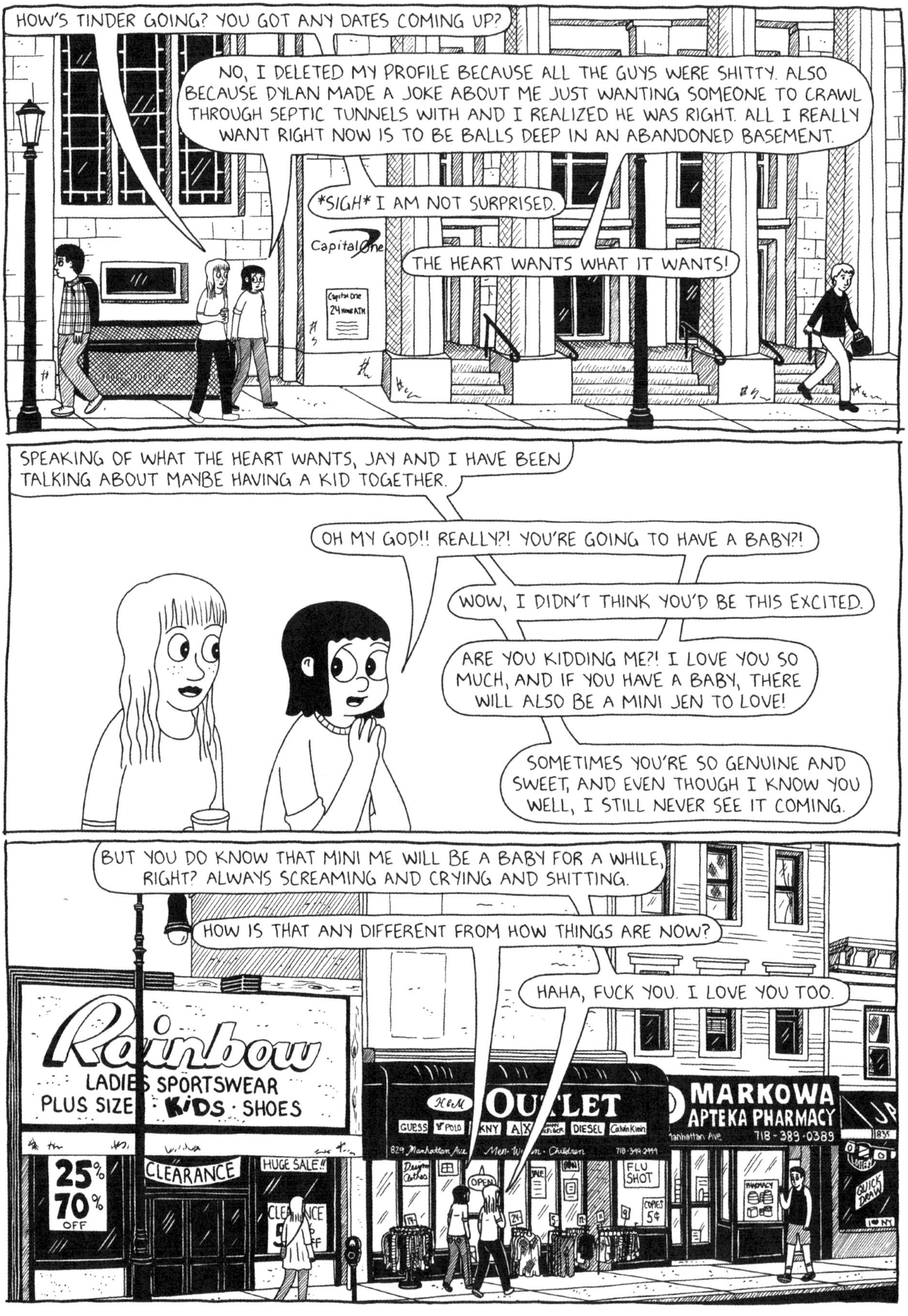
HOW'S TINDER GOING? YOU GOT ANY DATES COMING UP?
NO, I DELETED MY PROFILE BECAUSE ALL THE GUYS WERE SHITTY. ALSO BECAUSE DYLAN MADE A JOKE ABOUT ME JUST WANTING SOMEONE TO CRAWL THROUGH SEPTIC TUNNELS WITH AND I REALIZED HE WAS RIGHT. ALL I REALLY WANT RIGHT NOW IS TO BE BALLS DEEP IN AN ABANDONED BASEMENT.
SIGH I AM NOT SURPRISED.
THE HEART WANTS WHAT IT WANTS!
Capital One
SPEAKING OF WHAT THE HEART WANTS, JAY AND I HAVE BEEN TALKING ABOUT MAYBE HAVING A KID TOGETHER.
OH MY GOD!! REALLY?! YOU'RE GOING TO HAVE A BABY?!
WOW, I DIDN'T THINK YOU'D BE THIS EXCITED.
ARE YOU KIDDING ME?! I LOVE YOU SO MUCH, AND IF YOU HAVE A BABY, THERE WILL ALSO BE A MINI JEN TO LOVE!
SOMETIMES YOU'RE SO GENUINE AND SWEET, AND EVEN THOUGH I KNOW YOU WELL, I STILL NEVER SEE IT COMING.
BUT YOU DO KNOW THAT MINI ME WILL BE A BABY FOR A WHILE, RIGHT? ALWAYS SCREAMING AND CRYING AND SHITTING.
HOW IS THAT ANY DIFFERENT FROM HOW THINGS ARE NOW?
HAHA, FUCK YOU. I LOVE YOU TOO.
Rainbow
LADIES SPORTSWEAR
PLUS SIZE · KIDS · SHOES
25% 70% OFF
CLEARANCE
HUGE SALE!!
OUTLET
GUESS POLO DKNY A|X DIESEL Calvin Klein
829 Manhattan Ave Men · Women · Children 718-349-2444
OPEN
FLU SHOT
COPIES 5¢
MARKOWA
APTEKA PHARMACY
718-389-0389
QUICK DRAW

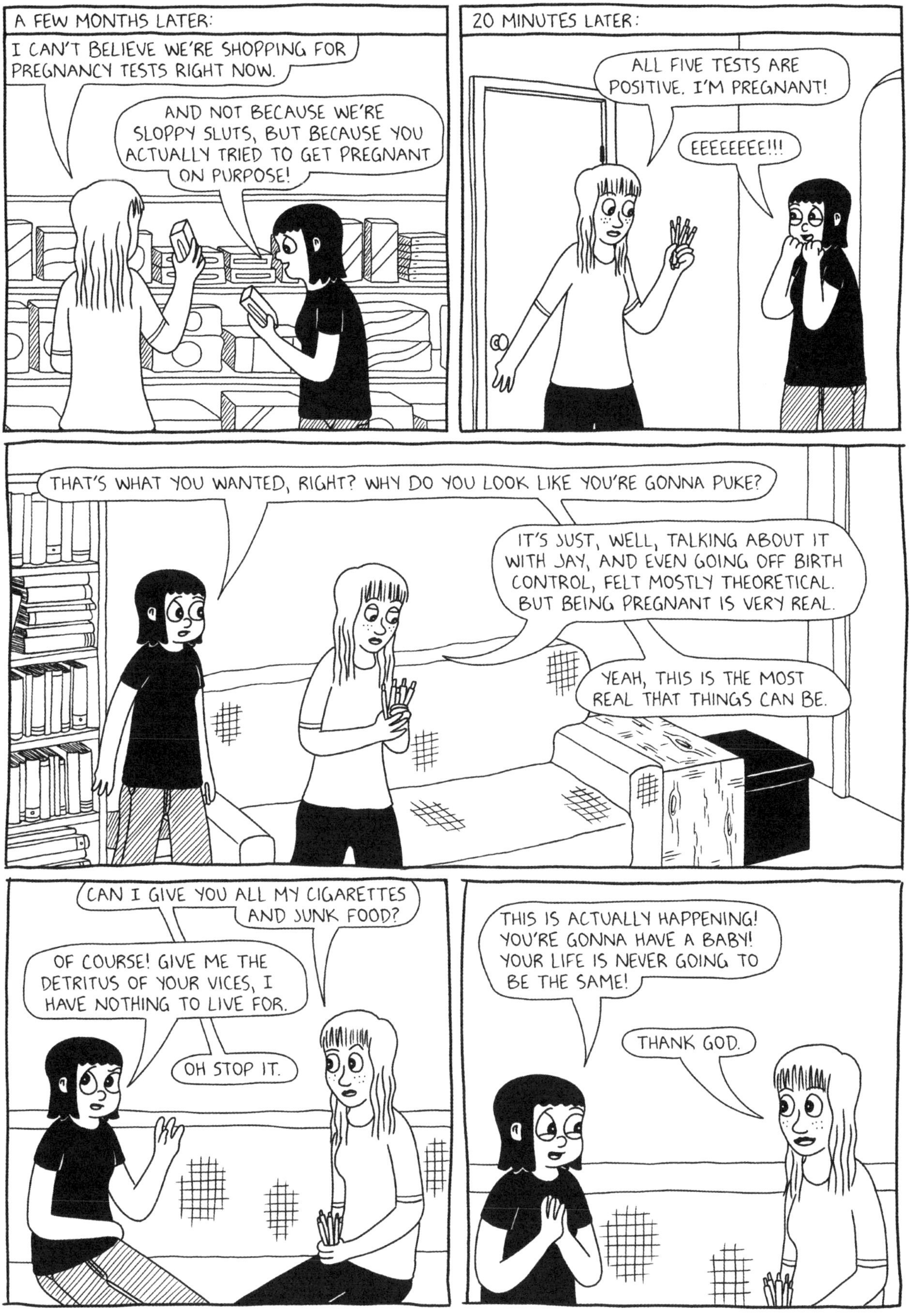
A FEW MONTHS LATER:
I CAN'T BELIEVE WE'RE SHOPPING FOR PREGNANCY TESTS RIGHT NOW.
AND NOT BECAUSE WE'RE SLOPPY SLUTS, BUT BECAUSE YOU ACTUALLY TRIED TO GET PREGNANT ON PURPOSE!
20 MINUTES LATER:
ALL FIVE TESTS ARE POSITIVE. I'M PREGNANT!
EEEEEEEE!!!
THAT'S WHAT YOU WANTED, RIGHT? WHY DO YOU LOOK LIKE YOU'RE GONNA PUKE?
IT'S JUST, WELL, TALKING ABOUT IT WITH JAY, AND EVEN GOING OFF BIRTH CONTROL, FELT MOSTLY THEORETICAL. BUT BEING PREGNANT IS VERY REAL.
YEAH, THIS IS THE MOST REAL THAT THINGS CAN BE.
CAN I GIVE YOU ALL MY CIGARETTES AND JUNK FOOD?
OF COURSE! GIVE ME THE DETRITUS OF YOUR VICES, I HAVE NOTHING TO LIVE FOR.
OH STOP IT.
THIS IS ACTUALLY HAPPENING! YOU'RE GONNA HAVE A BABY! YOUR LIFE IS NEVER GOING TO BE THE SAME!
THANK GOD.

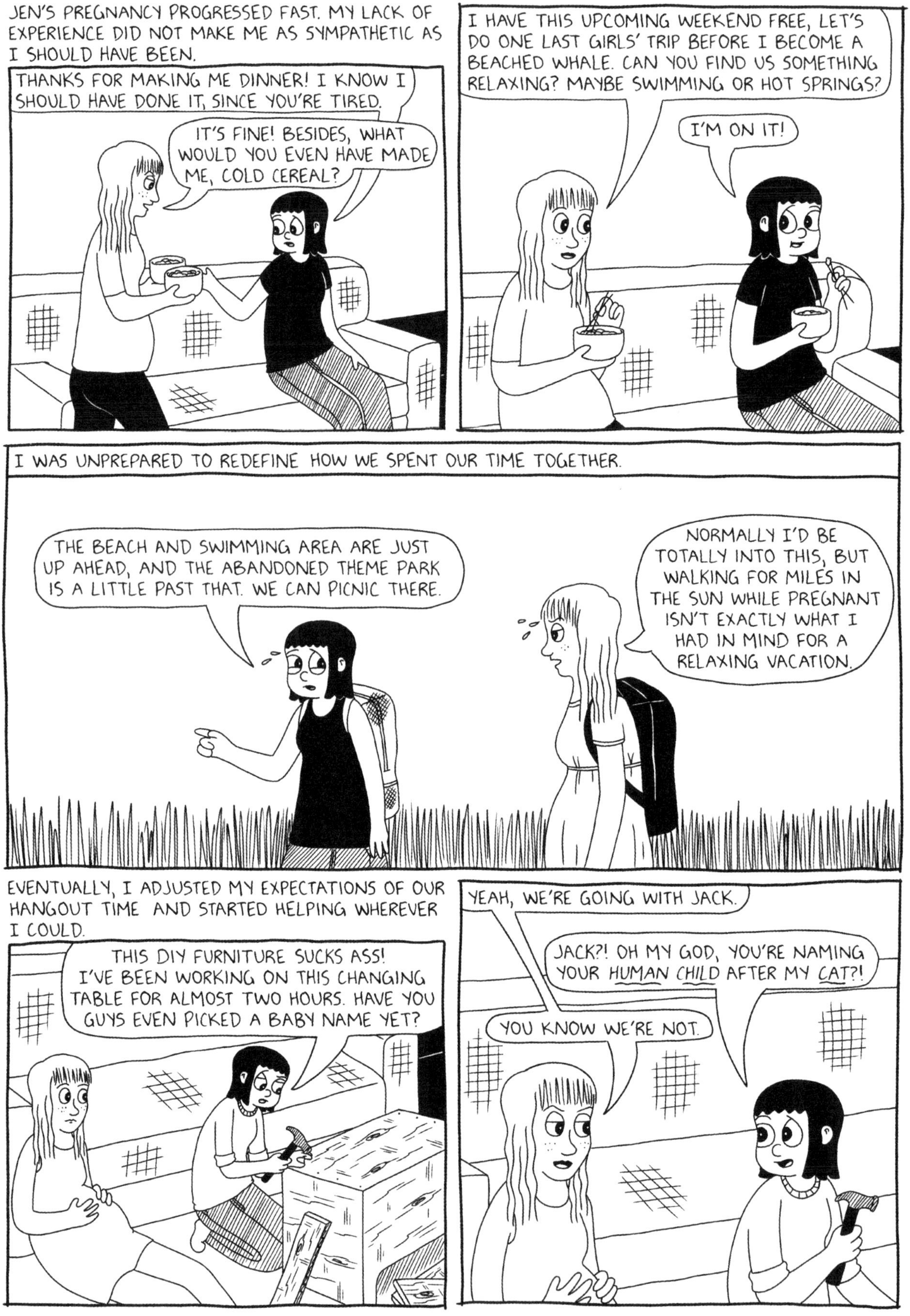
JEN'S PREGNANCY PROGRESSED FAST. MY LACK OF EXPERIENCE DID NOT MAKE ME AS SYMPATHETIC AS I SHOULD HAVE BEEN.
THANKS FOR MAKING ME DINNER! I KNOW I SHOULD HAVE DONE IT, SINCE YOU'RE TIRED.
IT'S FINE! BESIDES, WHAT WOULD YOU EVEN HAVE MADE ME, COLD CEREAL?
I HAVE THIS UPCOMING WEEKEND FREE, LET'S DO ONE LAST GIRLS' TRIP BEFORE I BECOME A BEACHED WHALE. CAN YOU FIND US SOMETHING RELAXING? MAYBE SWIMMING OR HOT SPRINGS?
I'M ON IT!
I WAS UNPREPARED TO REDEFINE HOW WE SPENT OUR TIME TOGETHER.
THE BEACH AND SWIMMING AREA ARE JUST UP AHEAD, AND THE ABANDONED THEME PARK IS A LITTLE PAST THAT. WE CAN PICNIC THERE.
NORMALLY I'D BE TOTALLY INTO THIS, BUT WALKING FOR MILES IN THE SUN WHILE PREGNANT ISN'T EXACTLY WHAT I HAD IN MIND FOR A RELAXING VACATION.
EVENTUALLY, I ADJUSTED MY EXPECTATIONS OF OUR HANGOUT TIME AND STARTED HELPING WHEREVER I COULD.
THIS DIY FURNITURE SUCKS ASS! I'VE BEEN WORKING ON THIS CHANGING TABLE FOR ALMOST TWO HOURS. HAVE YOU GUYS EVEN PICKED A BABY NAME YET?
YEAH, WE'RE GOING WITH JACK.
JACK?! OH MY GOD, YOU'RE NAMING YOUR HUMAN CHILD AFTER MY CAT?!
YOU KNOW WE'RE NOT.

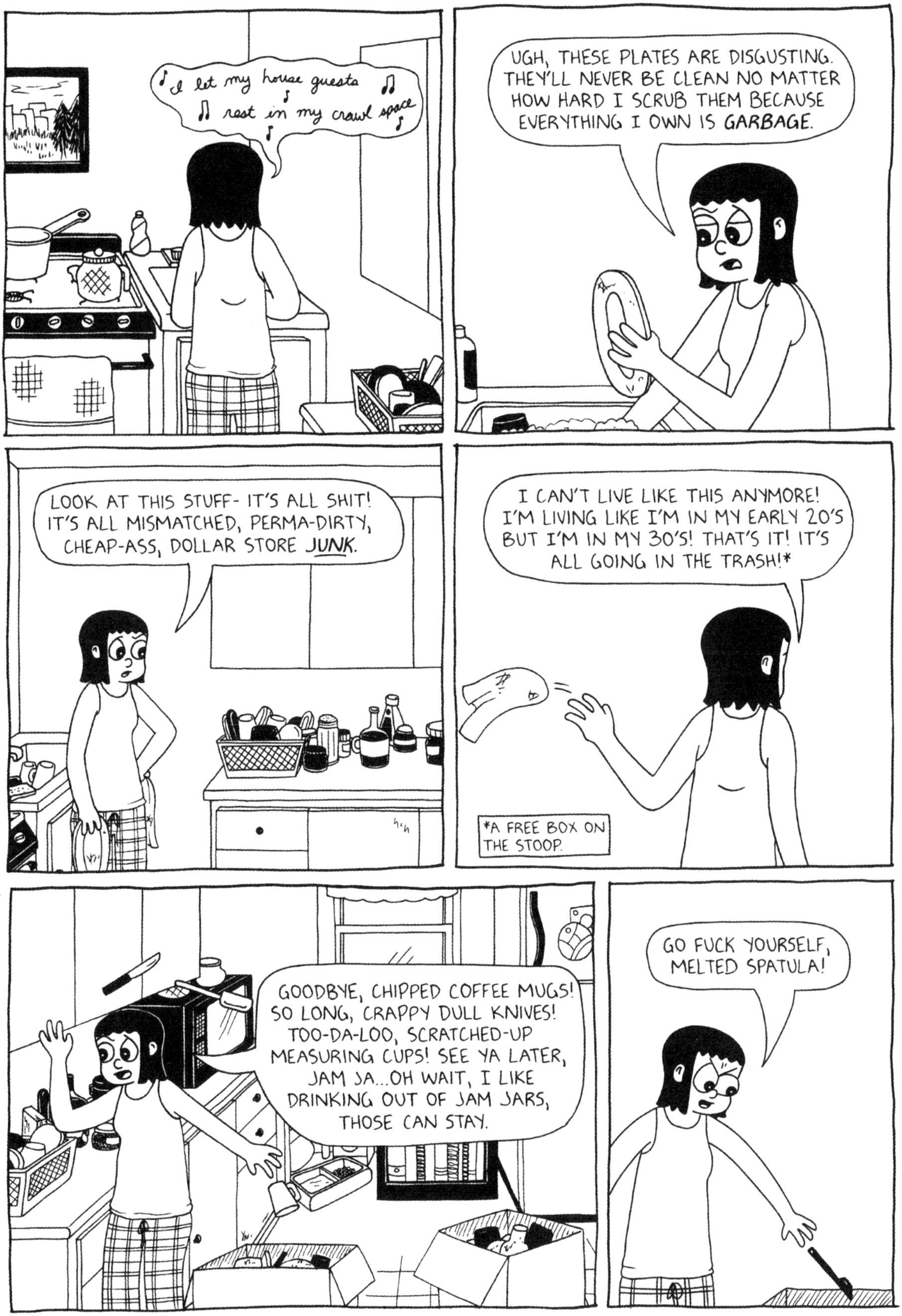
I let my house guests rest in my crawl space
UGH, THESE PLATES ARE DISGUSTING. THEY'LL NEVER BE CLEAN NO MATTER HOW HARD I SCRUB THEM BECAUSE EVERYTHING I OWN IS GARBAGE.
LOOK AT THIS STUFF- IT'S ALL SHIT! IT'S ALL MISMATCHED, PERMA-DIRTY, CHEAP-ASS, DOLLAR STORE JUNK.
I CAN'T LIVE LIKE THIS ANYMORE! I'M LIVING LIKE I'M IN MY EARLY 20'S BUT I'M IN MY 30'S! THAT'S IT! IT'S ALL GOING IN THE TRASH!*
*A FREE BOX ON THE STOOP.
GOODBYE, CHIPPED COFFEE MUGS! SO LONG, CRAPPY DULL KNIVES! TOO-DA-LOO, SCRATCHED-UP MEASURING CUPS! SEE YA LATER, JAM JA...OH WAIT, I LIKE DRINKING OUT OF JAM JARS, THOSE CAN STAY.
GO FUCK YOURSELF, MELTED SPATULA!

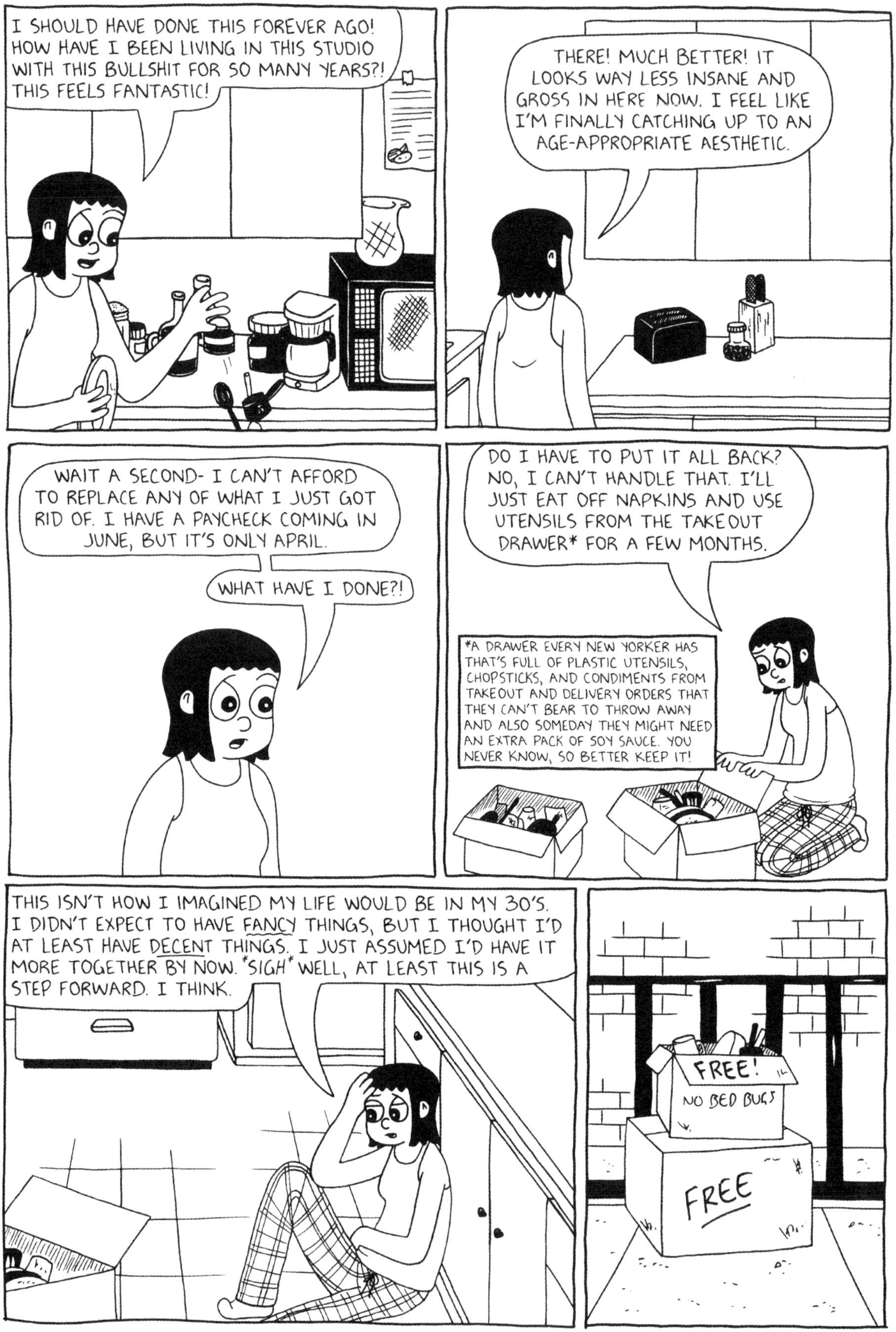
I SHOULD HAVE DONE THIS FOREVER AGO! HOW HAVE I BEEN LIVING IN THIS STUDIO WITH THIS BULLSHIT FOR SO MANY YEARS?! THIS FEELS FANTASTIC!
THERE! MUCH BETTER! IT LOOKS WAY LESS INSANE AND GROSS IN HERE NOW. I FEEL LIKE I'M FINALLY CATCHING UP TO AN AGE-APPROPRIATE AESTHETIC.
WAIT A SECOND- I CAN'T AFFORD TO REPLACE ANY OF WHAT I JUST GOT RID OF. I HAVE A PAYCHECK COMING IN JUNE, BUT IT'S ONLY APRIL.
WHAT HAVE I DONE?!
DO I HAVE TO PUT IT ALL BACK? NO, I CAN'T HANDLE THAT. I'LL JUST EAT OFF NAPKINS AND USE UTENSILS FROM THE TAKEOUT DRAWER* FOR A FEW MONTHS.
*A DRAWER EVERY NEW YORKER HAS THAT'S FULL OF PLASTIC UTENSILS, CHOPSTICKS, AND CONDIMENTS FROM TAKEOUT AND DELIVERY ORDERS THAT THEY CAN'T BEAR TO THROW AWAY AND ALSO SOMEDAY THEY MIGHT NEED AN EXTRA PACK OF SOY SAUCE. YOU NEVER KNOW, SO BETTER KEEP IT!
THIS ISN'T HOW I IMAGINED MY LIFE WOULD BE IN MY 30'S. I DIDN'T EXPECT TO HAVE FANCY THINGS, BUT I THOUGHT I'D AT LEAST HAVE DECENT THINGS. I JUST ASSUMED I'D HAVE IT MORE TOGETHER BY NOW. *SIGH* WELL, AT LEAST THIS IS A STEP FORWARD. I THINK.
FREE!
NO BED BUGS
FREE

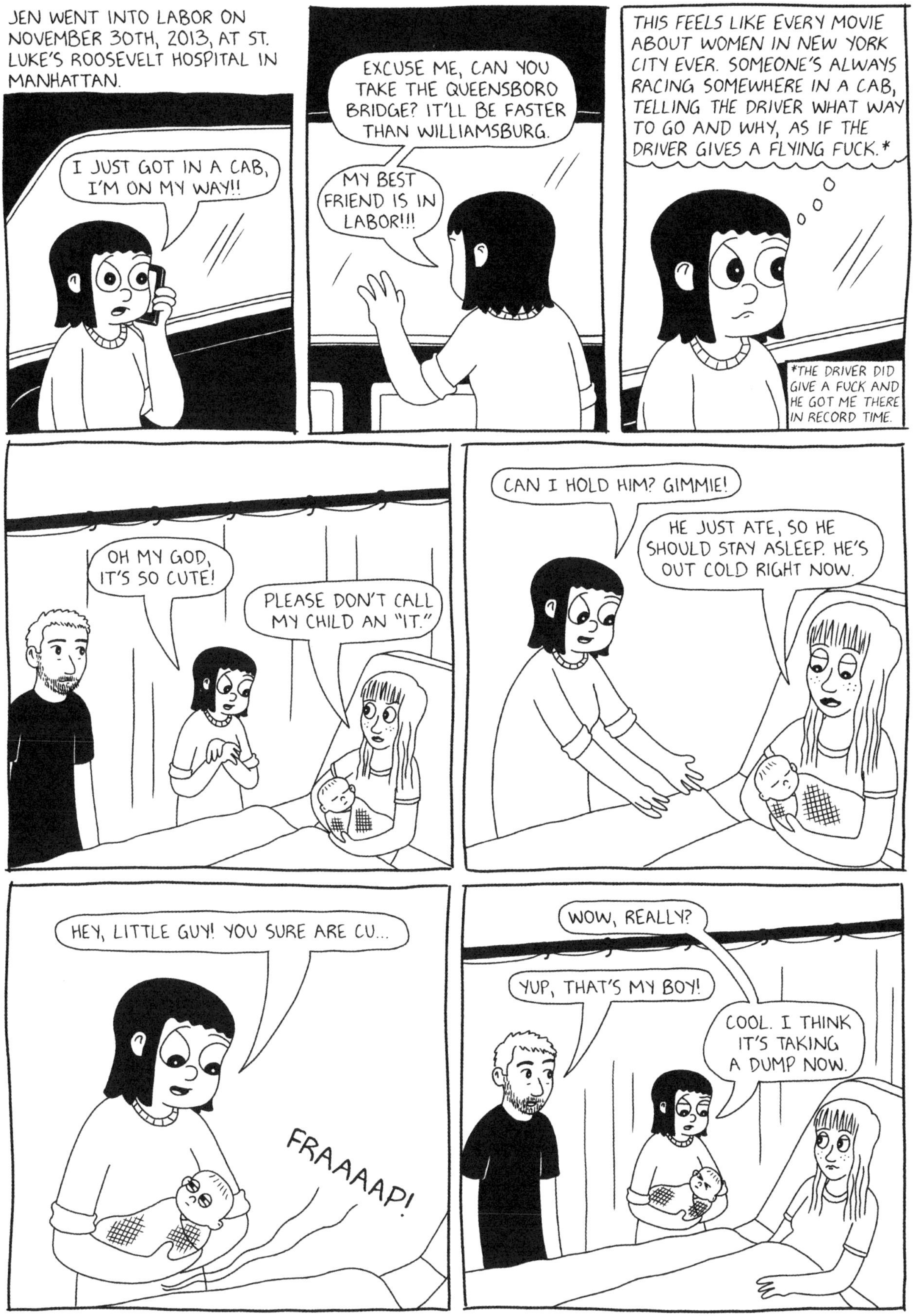
JEN WENT INTO LABOR ON NOVEMBER 30TH, 2013, AT ST. LUKE'S ROOSEVELT HOSPITAL IN MANHATTAN.
I JUST GOT IN A CAB, I'M ON MY WAY!!
EXCUSE ME, CAN YOU TAKE THE QUEENSBORO BRIDGE? IT'LL BE FASTER THAN WILLIAMSBURG.
MY BEST FRIEND IS IN LABOR!!!
THIS FEELS LIKE EVERY MOVIE ABOUT WOMEN IN NEW YORK CITY EVER. SOMEONE'S ALWAYS RACING SOMEWHERE IN A CAB, TELLING THE DRIVER WHAT WAY TO GO AND WHY, AS IF THE DRIVER GIVES A FLYING FUCK.*
*THE DRIVER DID GIVE A FUCK AND HE GOT ME THERE IN RECORD TIME.
OH MY GOD, IT'S SO CUTE!
PLEASE DON'T CALL MY CHILD AN "IT."
CAN I HOLD HIM? GIMMIE!
HE JUST ATE, SO HE SHOULD STAY ASLEEP. HE'S OUT COLD RIGHT NOW.
HEY, LITTLE GUY! YOU SURE ARE CU...
FRAAAAP!
WOW, REALLY?
YUP, THAT'S MY BOY!
COOL. I THINK IT'S TAKING A DUMP NOW.

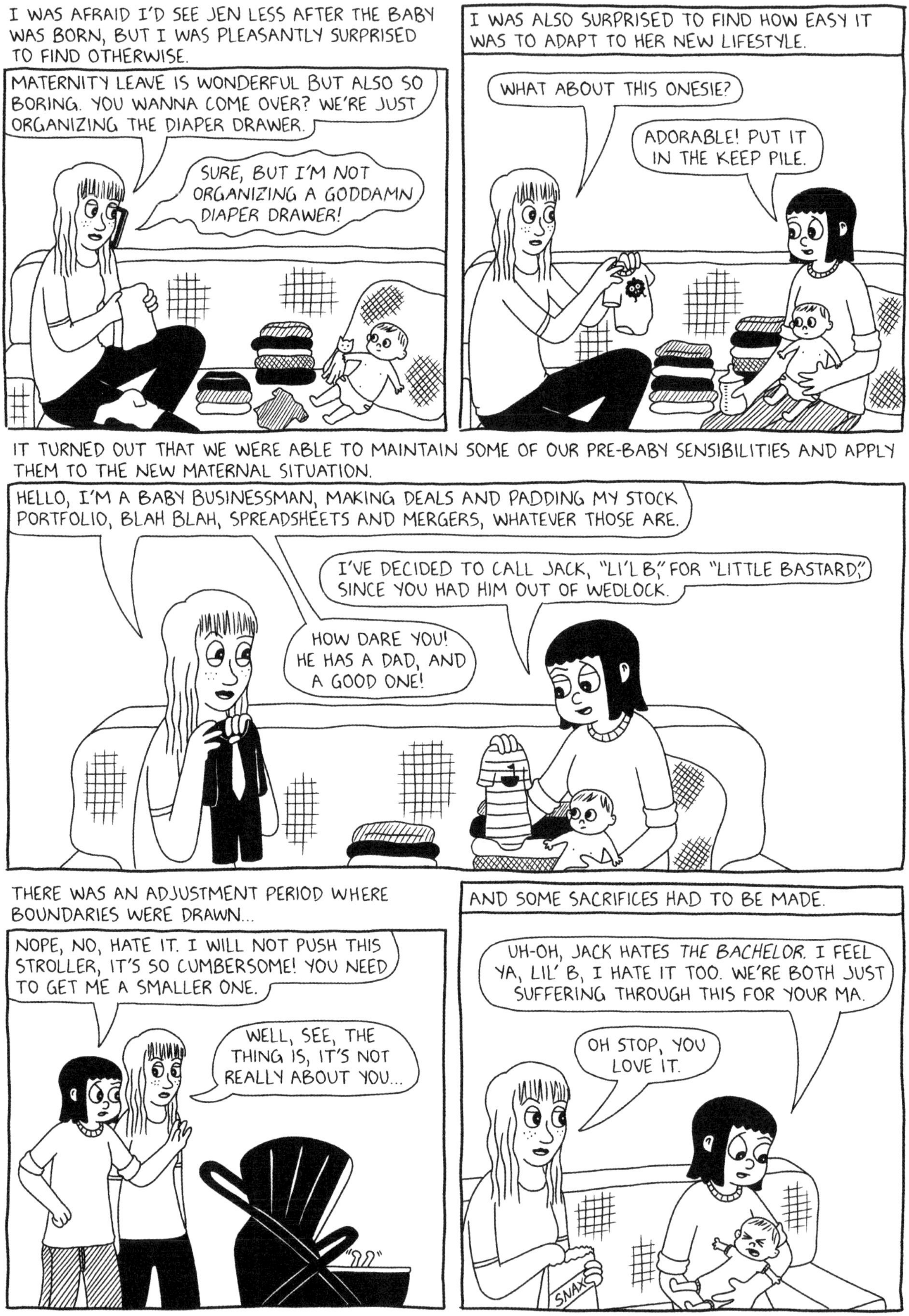

I WAS AFRAID I'D SEE JEN LESS AFTER THE BABY WAS BORN, BUT I WAS PLEASANTLY SURPRISED TO FIND OTHERWISE.
MATERNITY LEAVE IS WONDERFUL BUT ALSO SO BORING. YOU WANNA COME OVER? WE'RE JUST ORGANIZING THE DIAPER DRAWER.
SURE, BUT I'M NOT ORGANIZING A GODDAMN DIAPER DRAWER!
I WAS ALSO SURPRISED TO FIND HOW EASY IT WAS TO ADAPT TO HER NEW LIFESTYLE.
WHAT ABOUT THIS ONESIE?
ADORABLE! PUT IT IN THE KEEP PILE.
IT TURNED OUT THAT WE WERE ABLE TO MAINTAIN SOME OF OUR PRE-BABY SENSIBILITIES AND APPLY THEM TO THE NEW MATERNAL SITUATION.
HELLO, I'M A BABY BUSINESSMAN, MAKING DEALS AND PADDING MY STOCK PORTFOLIO, BLAH BLAH, SPREADSHEETS AND MERGERS, WHATEVER THOSE ARE.
I'VE DECIDED TO CALL JACK, "LI'L B," FOR "LITTLE BASTARD," SINCE YOU HAD HIM OUT OF WEDLOCK.
HOW DARE YOU! HE HAS A DAD, AND A GOOD ONE!
THERE WAS AN ADJUSTMENT PERIOD WHERE BOUNDARIES WERE DRAWN...
NOPE, NO, HATE IT. I WILL NOT PUSH THIS STROLLER, IT'S SO CUMBERSOME! YOU NEED TO GET ME A SMALLER ONE.
WELL, SEE, THE THING IS, IT'S NOT REALLY ABOUT YOU...
AND SOME SACRIFICES HAD TO BE MADE.
UH-OH, JACK HATES *THE BACHELOR*. I FEEL YA, LIL' B, I HATE IT TOO. WE'RE BOTH JUST SUFFERING THROUGH THIS FOR YOUR MA.
OH STOP, YOU LOVE IT.
SNAX

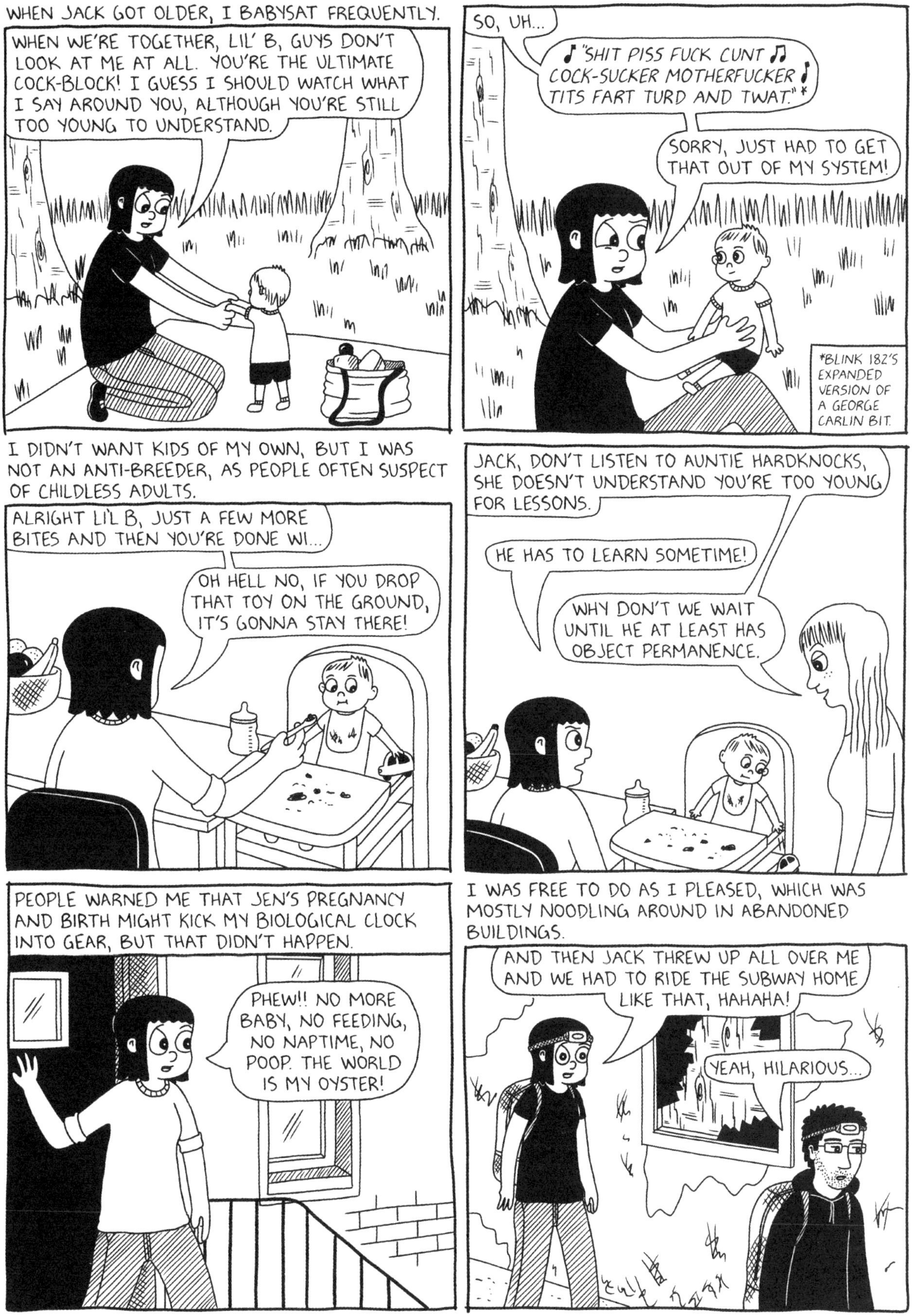
WHEN JACK GOT OLDER, I BABYSAT FREQUENTLY.
WHEN WE'RE TOGETHER, LIL' B, GUYS DON'T LOOK AT ME AT ALL. YOU'RE THE ULTIMATE COCK-BLOCK! I GUESS I SHOULD WATCH WHAT I SAY AROUND YOU, ALTHOUGH YOU'RE STILL TOO YOUNG TO UNDERSTAND.
SO, UH...
♪ "SHIT PISS FUCK CUNT ♫ COCK-SUCKER MOTHERFUCKER ♪ TITS FART TURD AND TWAT." *
SORRY, JUST HAD TO GET THAT OUT OF MY SYSTEM!
*BLINK 182'S EXPANDED VERSION OF A GEORGE CARLIN BIT.
I DIDN'T WANT KIDS OF MY OWN, BUT I WAS NOT AN ANTI-BREEDER, AS PEOPLE OFTEN SUSPECT OF CHILDLESS ADULTS.
ALRIGHT LI'L B, JUST A FEW MORE BITES AND THEN YOU'RE DONE WI...
OH HELL NO, IF YOU DROP THAT TOY ON THE GROUND, IT'S GONNA STAY THERE!
JACK, DON'T LISTEN TO AUNTIE HARDKNOCKS, SHE DOESN'T UNDERSTAND YOU'RE TOO YOUNG FOR LESSONS.
HE HAS TO LEARN SOMETIME!
WHY DON'T WE WAIT UNTIL HE AT LEAST HAS OBJECT PERMANENCE.
PEOPLE WARNED ME THAT JEN'S PREGNANCY AND BIRTH MIGHT KICK MY BIOLOGICAL CLOCK INTO GEAR, BUT THAT DIDN'T HAPPEN.
PHEW!! NO MORE BABY, NO FEEDING, NO NAPTIME, NO POOP. THE WORLD IS MY OYSTER!
I WAS FREE TO DO AS I PLEASED, WHICH WAS MOSTLY NOODLING AROUND IN ABANDONED BUILDINGS.
AND THEN JACK THREW UP ALL OVER ME AND WE HAD TO RIDE THE SUBWAY HOME LIKE THAT, HAHAHA!
YEAH, HILARIOUS...

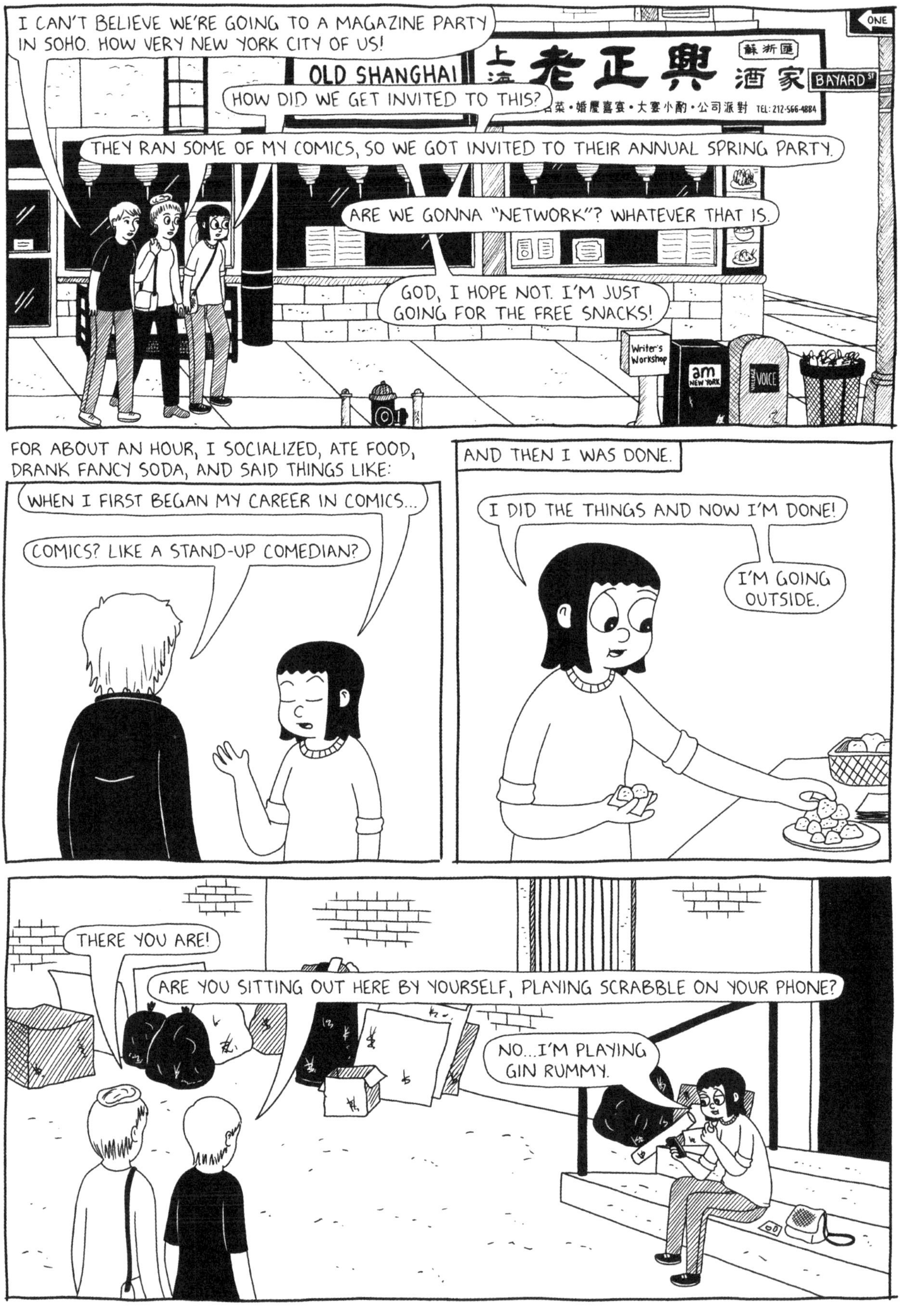
I CAN'T BELIEVE WE'RE GOING TO A MAGAZINE PARTY IN SOHO. HOW VERY NEW YORK CITY OF US!
OLD SHANGHAI
上海 老正興 蘇浙匯 酒家
BAYARD ST
ONE
TEL: 212-566-4884
HOW DID WE GET INVITED TO THIS?
THEY RAN SOME OF MY COMICS, SO WE GOT INVITED TO THEIR ANNUAL SPRING PARTY.
ARE WE GONNA "NETWORK"? WHATEVER THAT IS.
GOD, I HOPE NOT. I'M JUST GOING FOR THE FREE SNACKS!
Writer's Workshop
am NEW YORK
VOICE
FOR ABOUT AN HOUR, I SOCIALIZED, ATE FOOD, DRANK FANCY SODA, AND SAID THINGS LIKE:
WHEN I FIRST BEGAN MY CAREER IN COMICS...
COMICS? LIKE A STAND-UP COMEDIAN?
AND THEN I WAS DONE.
I DID THE THINGS AND NOW I'M DONE!
I'M GOING OUTSIDE.
THERE YOU ARE!
ARE YOU SITTING OUT HERE BY YOURSELF, PLAYING SCRABBLE ON YOUR PHONE?
NO...I'M PLAYING GIN RUMMY.

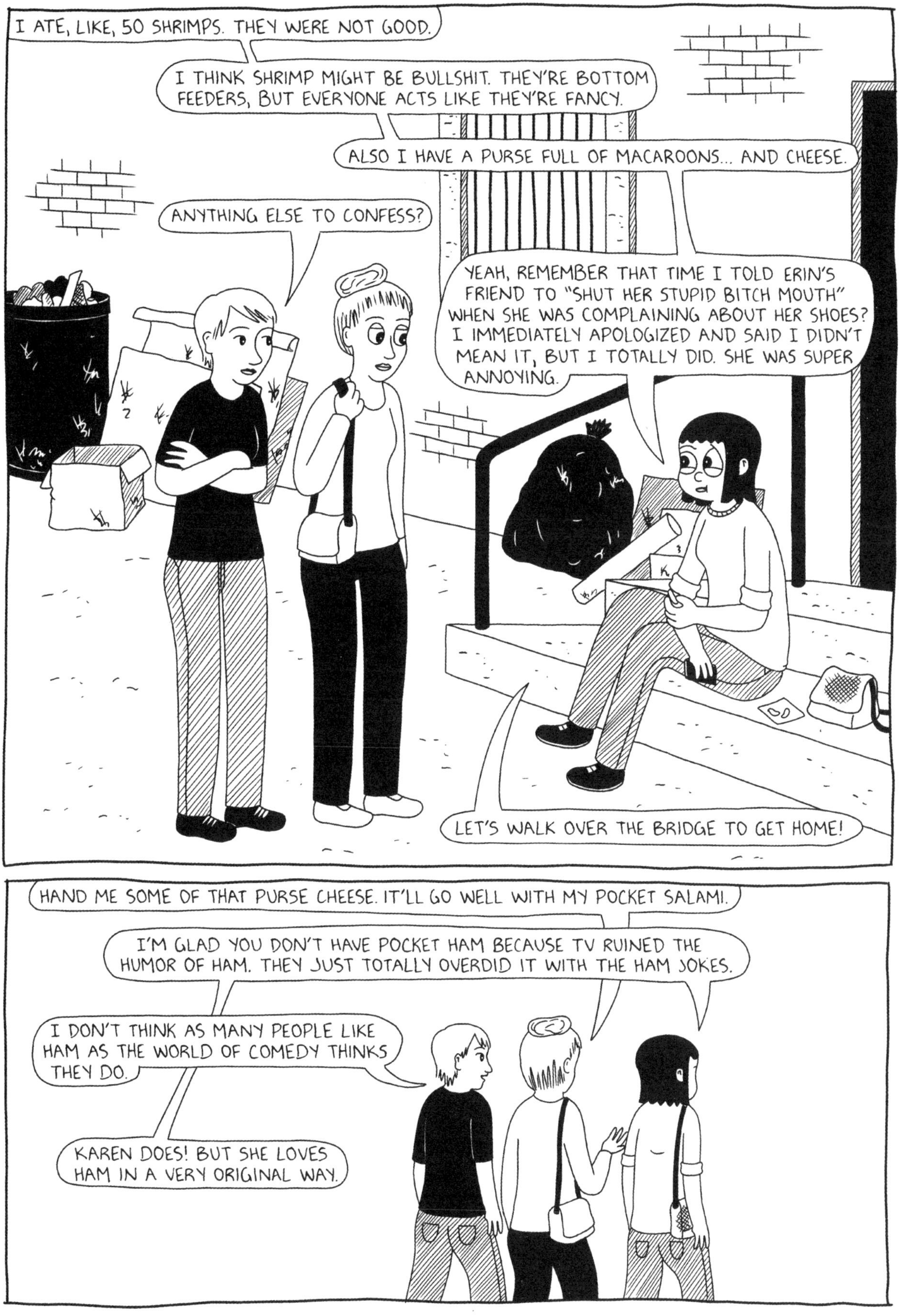

I ATE, LIKE, 50 SHRIMPS. THEY WERE NOT GOOD.
I THINK SHRIMP MIGHT BE BULLSHIT. THEY'RE BOTTOM FEEDERS, BUT EVERYONE ACTS LIKE THEY'RE FANCY.
ALSO I HAVE A PURSE FULL OF MACAROONS... AND CHEESE.
ANYTHING ELSE TO CONFESS?
YEAH, REMEMBER THAT TIME I TOLD ERIN'S FRIEND TO "SHUT HER STUPID BITCH MOUTH" WHEN SHE WAS COMPLAINING ABOUT HER SHOES? I IMMEDIATELY APOLOGIZED AND SAID I DIDN'T MEAN IT, BUT I TOTALLY DID. SHE WAS SUPER ANNOYING.
LET'S WALK OVER THE BRIDGE TO GET HOME!
HAND ME SOME OF THAT PURSE CHEESE. IT'LL GO WELL WITH MY POCKET SALAMI.
I'M GLAD YOU DON'T HAVE POCKET HAM BECAUSE TV RUINED THE HUMOR OF HAM. THEY JUST TOTALLY OVERDID IT WITH THE HAM JOKES.
I DON'T THINK AS MANY PEOPLE LIKE HAM AS THE WORLD OF COMEDY THINKS THEY DO.
KAREN DOES! BUT SHE LOVES HAM IN A VERY ORIGINAL WAY.

A SPRING WALK

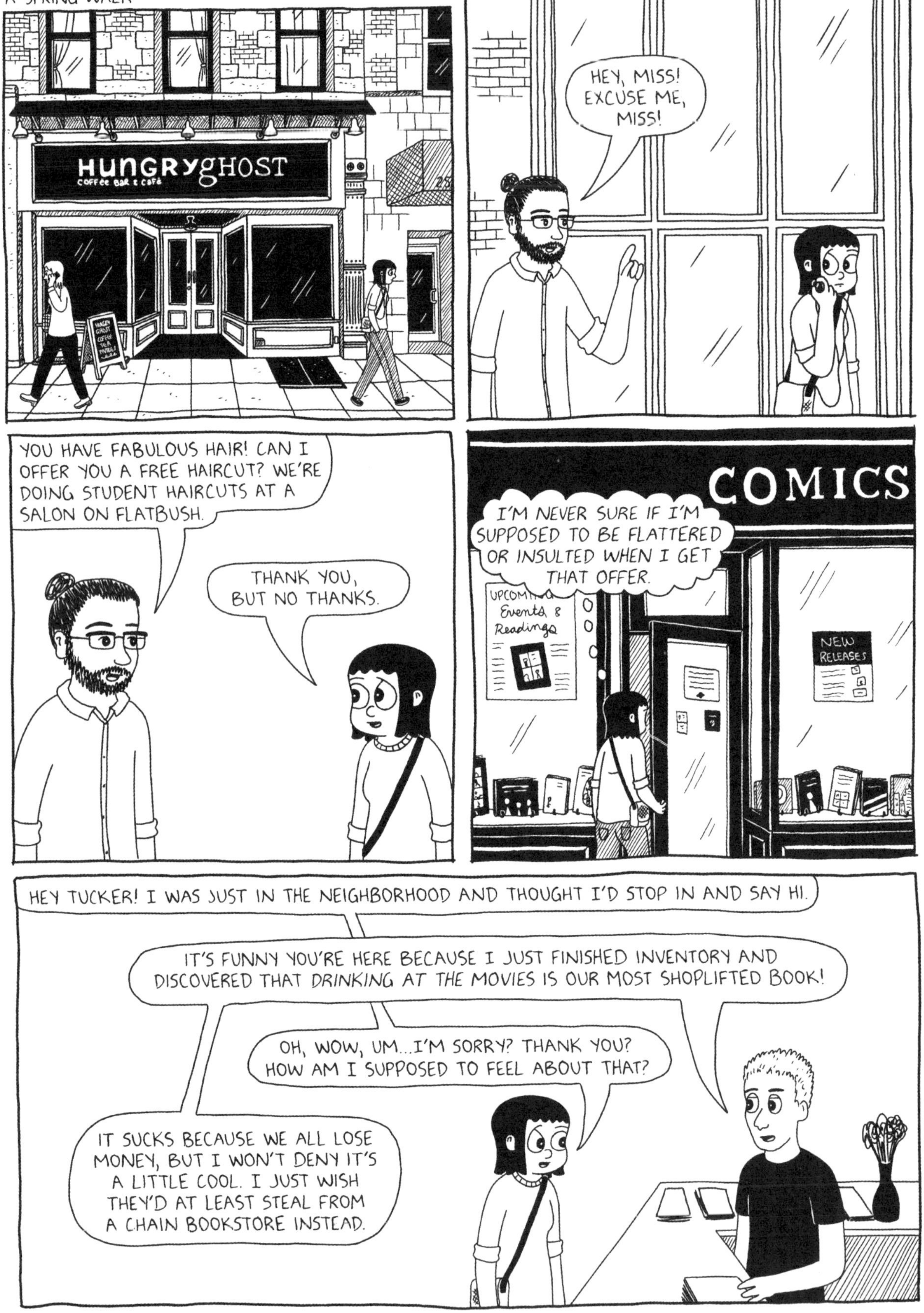
HUNGRYGHOST
COFFEE BAR & CAFÉ
HEY, MISS! EXCUSE ME, MISS!
YOU HAVE FABULOUS HAIR! CAN I OFFER YOU A FREE HAIRCUT? WE'RE DOING STUDENT HAIRCUTS AT A SALON ON FLATBUSH.
THANK YOU, BUT NO THANKS.
COMICS
I'M NEVER SURE IF I'M SUPPOSED TO BE FLATTERED OR INSULTED WHEN I GET THAT OFFER.
Events & Readings
NEW RELEASES
HEY TUCKER! I WAS JUST IN THE NEIGHBORHOOD AND THOUGHT I'D STOP IN AND SAY HI.
IT'S FUNNY YOU'RE HERE BECAUSE I JUST FINISHED INVENTORY AND DISCOVERED THAT *DRINKING AT THE MOVIES* IS OUR MOST SHOPLIFTED BOOK!
OH, WOW, UM...I'M SORRY? THANK YOU? HOW AM I SUPPOSED TO FEEL ABOUT THAT?
IT SUCKS BECAUSE WE ALL LOSE MONEY, BUT I WON'T DENY IT'S A LITTLE COOL. I JUST WISH THEY'D AT LEAST STEAL FROM A CHAIN BOOKSTORE INSTEAD.

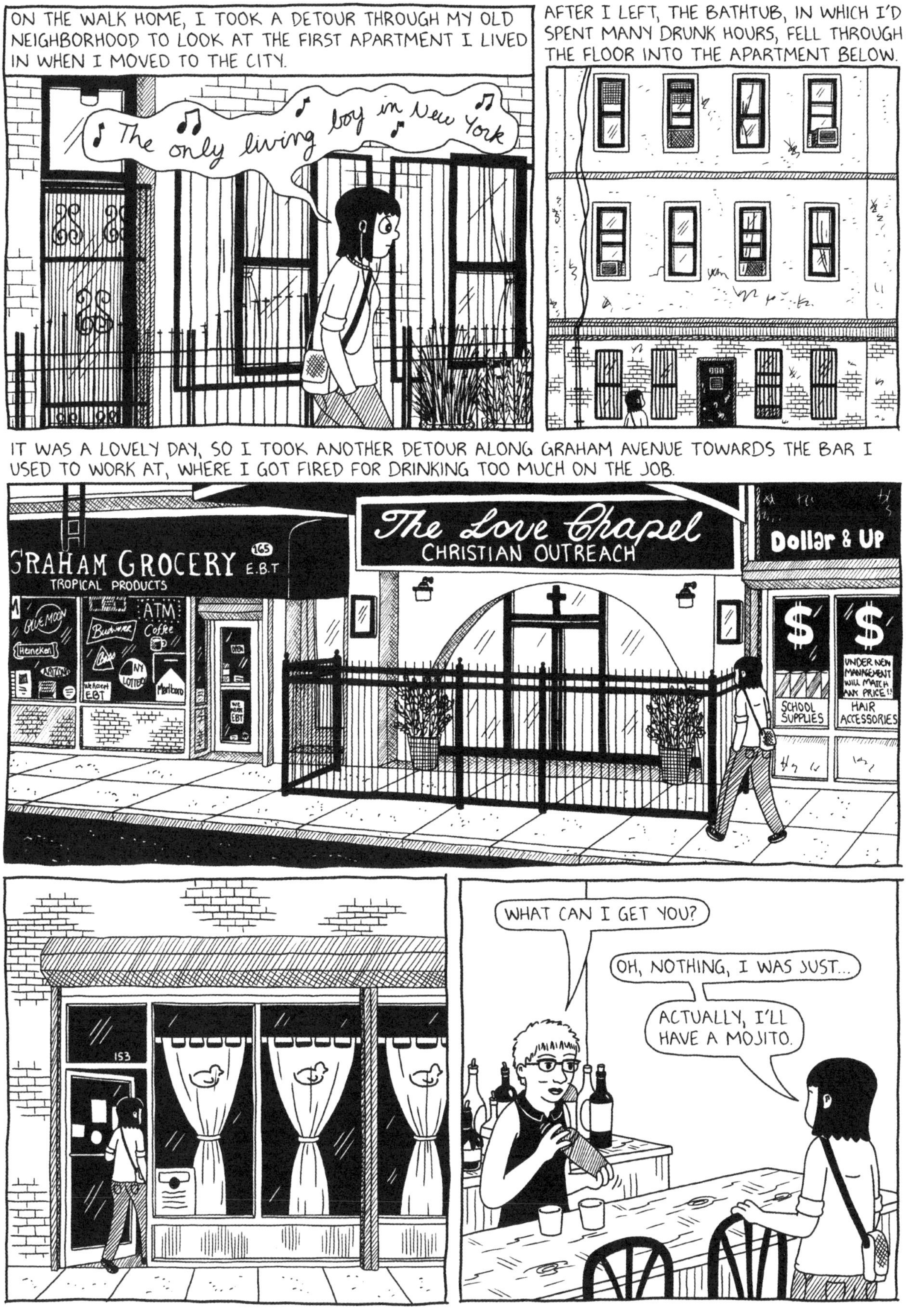
ON THE WALK HOME, I TOOK A DETOUR THROUGH MY OLD NEIGHBORHOOD TO LOOK AT THE FIRST APARTMENT I LIVED IN WHEN I MOVED TO THE CITY.
The only living boy in New York
AFTER I LEFT, THE BATHTUB, IN WHICH I'D SPENT MANY DRUNK HOURS, FELL THROUGH THE FLOOR INTO THE APARTMENT BELOW.
IT WAS A LOVELY DAY, SO I TOOK ANOTHER DETOUR ALONG GRAHAM AVENUE TOWARDS THE BAR I USED TO WORK AT, WHERE I GOT FIRED FOR DRINKING TOO MUCH ON THE JOB.
GRAHAM GROCERY 165 E.B.T
TROPICAL PRODUCTS
ATM
Coffee
The Love Chapel
CHRISTIAN OUTREACH
Dollar & UP
$ $
UNDER NEW MANAGEMENT WILL MATCH ANY PRICE!!
SCHOOL SUPPLIES
HAIR ACCESSORIES
153
WHAT CAN I GET YOU?
OH, NOTHING, I WAS JUST...
ACTUALLY, I'LL HAVE A MOJITO.

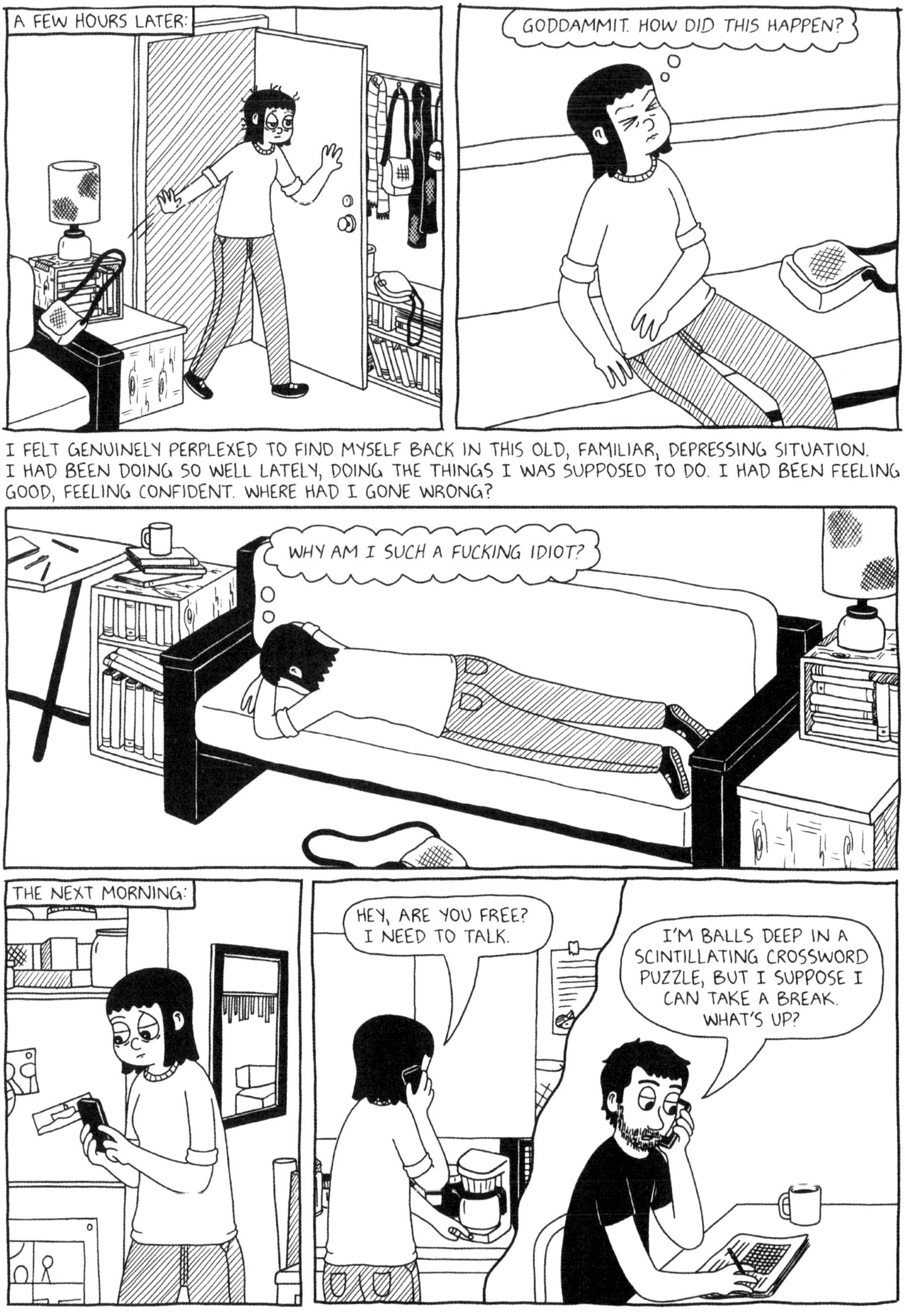
A FEW HOURS LATER:
GODDAMMIT. HOW DID THIS HAPPEN?
I FELT GENUINELY PERPLEXED TO FIND MYSELF BACK IN THIS OLD, FAMILIAR, DEPRESSING SITUATION. I HAD BEEN DOING SO WELL LATELY, DOING THE THINGS I WAS SUPPOSED TO DO. I HAD BEEN FEELING GOOD, FEELING CONFIDENT. WHERE HAD I GONE WRONG?
WHY AM I SUCH A FUCKING IDIOT?
THE NEXT MORNING:
HEY, ARE YOU FREE? I NEED TO TALK.
I'M BALLS DEEP IN A SCINTILLATING CROSSWORD PUZZLE, BUT I SUPPOSE I CAN TAKE A BREAK. WHAT'S UP?

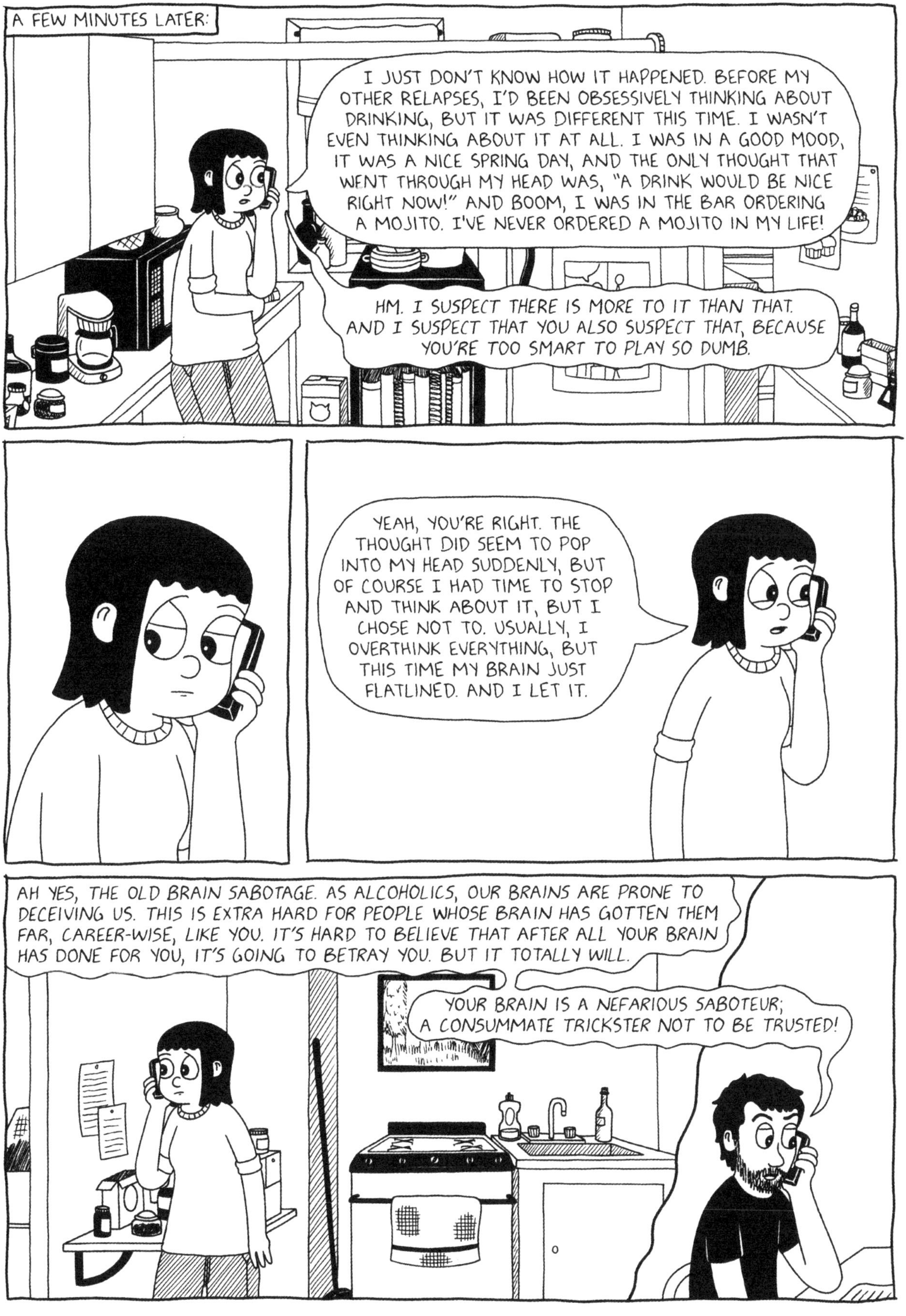
A FEW MINUTES LATER:
I JUST DON'T KNOW HOW IT HAPPENED. BEFORE MY OTHER RELAPSES, I'D BEEN OBSESSIVELY THINKING ABOUT DRINKING, BUT IT WAS DIFFERENT THIS TIME. I WASN'T EVEN THINKING ABOUT IT AT ALL. I WAS IN A GOOD MOOD, IT WAS A NICE SPRING DAY, AND THE ONLY THOUGHT THAT WENT THROUGH MY HEAD WAS, "A DRINK WOULD BE NICE RIGHT NOW!" AND BOOM, I WAS IN THE BAR ORDERING A MOJITO. I'VE NEVER ORDERED A MOJITO IN MY LIFE!
HM. I SUSPECT THERE IS MORE TO IT THAN THAT. AND I SUSPECT THAT YOU ALSO SUSPECT THAT, BECAUSE YOU'RE TOO SMART TO PLAY SO DUMB.
YEAH, YOU'RE RIGHT. THE THOUGHT DID SEEM TO POP INTO MY HEAD SUDDENLY, BUT OF COURSE I HAD TIME TO STOP AND THINK ABOUT IT, BUT I CHOSE NOT TO. USUALLY, I OVERTHINK EVERYTHING, BUT THIS TIME MY BRAIN JUST FLATLINED. AND I LET IT.
AH YES, THE OLD BRAIN SABOTAGE. AS ALCOHOLICS, OUR BRAINS ARE PRONE TO DECEIVING US. THIS IS EXTRA HARD FOR PEOPLE WHOSE BRAIN HAS GOTTEN THEM FAR, CAREER-WISE, LIKE YOU. IT'S HARD TO BELIEVE THAT AFTER ALL YOUR BRAIN HAS DONE FOR YOU, IT'S GOING TO BETRAY YOU. BUT IT TOTALLY WILL.
YOUR BRAIN IS A NEFARIOUS SABOTEUR; A CONSUMMATE TRICKSTER NOT TO BE TRUSTED!

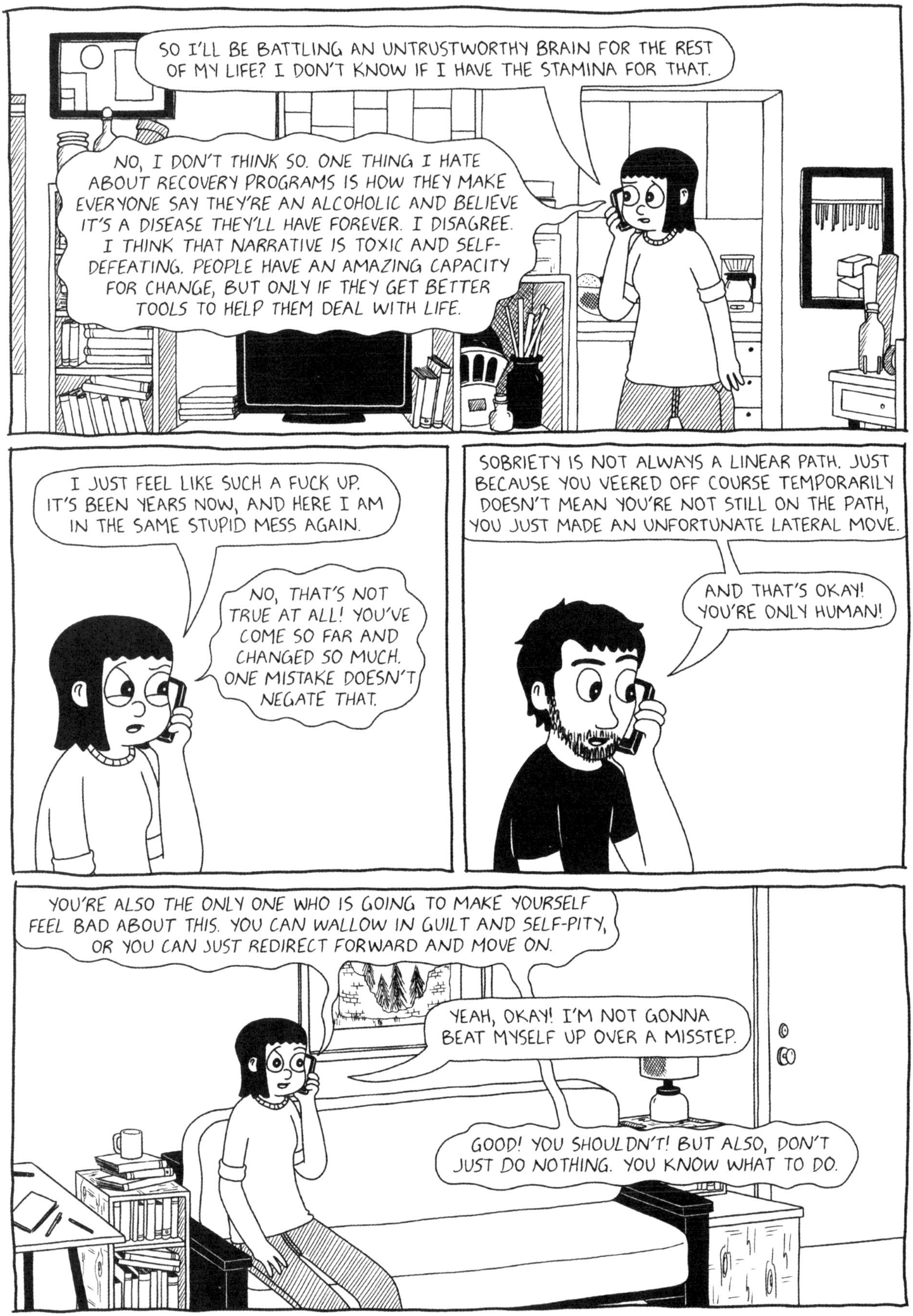
SO I'LL BE BATTLING AN UNTRUSTWORTHY BRAIN FOR THE REST OF MY LIFE? I DON'T KNOW IF I HAVE THE STAMINA FOR THAT.
NO, I DON'T THINK SO. ONE THING I HATE ABOUT RECOVERY PROGRAMS IS HOW THEY MAKE EVERYONE SAY THEY'RE AN ALCOHOLIC AND BELIEVE IT'S A DISEASE THEY'LL HAVE FOREVER. I DISAGREE. I THINK THAT NARRATIVE IS TOXIC AND SELF-DEFEATING. PEOPLE HAVE AN AMAZING CAPACITY FOR CHANGE, BUT ONLY IF THEY GET BETTER TOOLS TO HELP THEM DEAL WITH LIFE.
I JUST FEEL LIKE SUCH A FUCK UP. IT'S BEEN YEARS NOW, AND HERE I AM IN THE SAME STUPID MESS AGAIN.
NO, THAT'S NOT TRUE AT ALL! YOU'VE COME SO FAR AND CHANGED SO MUCH. ONE MISTAKE DOESN'T NEGATE THAT.
SOBRIETY IS NOT ALWAYS A LINEAR PATH. JUST BECAUSE YOU VEERED OFF COURSE TEMPORARILY DOESN'T MEAN YOU'RE NOT STILL ON THE PATH, YOU JUST MADE AN UNFORTUNATE LATERAL MOVE.
AND THAT'S OKAY! YOU'RE ONLY HUMAN!
YOU'RE ALSO THE ONLY ONE WHO IS GOING TO MAKE YOURSELF FEEL BAD ABOUT THIS. YOU CAN WALLOW IN GUILT AND SELF-PITY, OR YOU CAN JUST REDIRECT FORWARD AND MOVE ON.
YEAH, OKAY! I'M NOT GONNA BEAT MYSELF UP OVER A MISSTEP.
GOOD! YOU SHOULDN'T! BUT ALSO, DON'T JUST DO NOTHING. YOU KNOW WHAT TO DO.

OF COURSE I KNEW WHAT TO DO, AND I DID IT. I KEPT GOING TO MEETINGS AND I STARTED HAVING MORE LONG AND GENUINE CONVERSATIONS WITH WOMEN I MET THERE. I HEARD MANY DIFFERENT STORIES ABOUT DIFFERENT LIFE PATHS, ALL OF WHICH AFFIRMED THAT I WAS ON THE RIGHT ONE AT THE RIGHT TIME, DESPITE THE MISTAKES I HAD MADE.

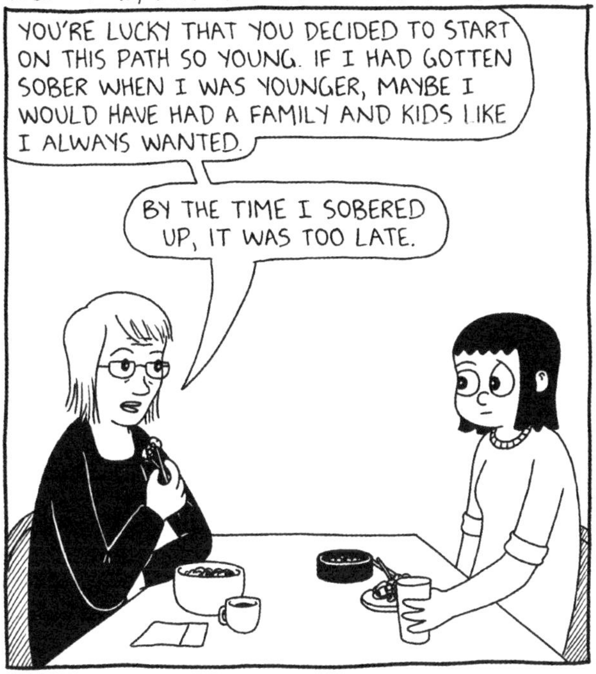
YOU'RE LUCKY THAT YOU DECIDED TO START ON THIS PATH SO YOUNG. IF I HAD GOTTEN SOBER WHEN I WAS YOUNGER, MAYBE I WOULD HAVE HAD A FAMILY AND KIDS LIKE I ALWAYS WANTED.
BY THE TIME I SOBERED UP, IT WAS TOO LATE.

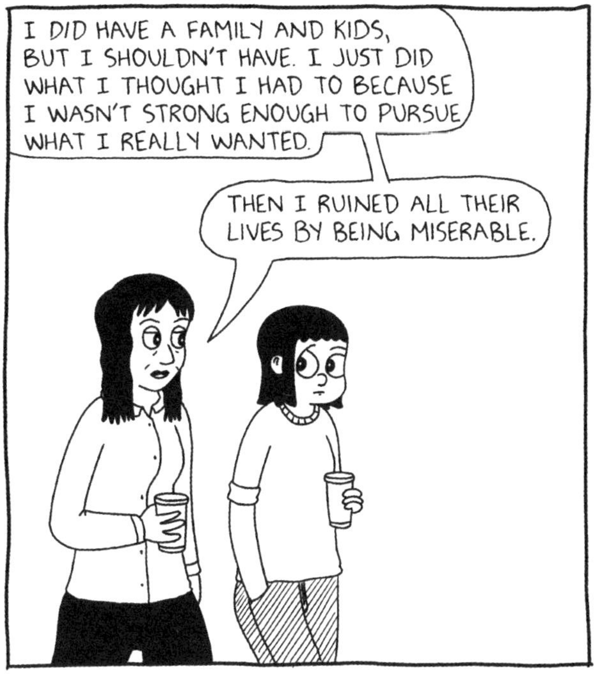
I *DID* HAVE A FAMILY AND KIDS, BUT I SHOULDN'T HAVE. I JUST DID WHAT I THOUGHT I HAD TO BECAUSE I WASN'T STRONG ENOUGH TO PURSUE WHAT I REALLY WANTED.
THEN I RUINED ALL THEIR LIVES BY BEING MISERABLE.

I ALSO TALKED MORE OPENLY WITH THE PEOPLE WHO WERE ALREADY IN MY LIFE.

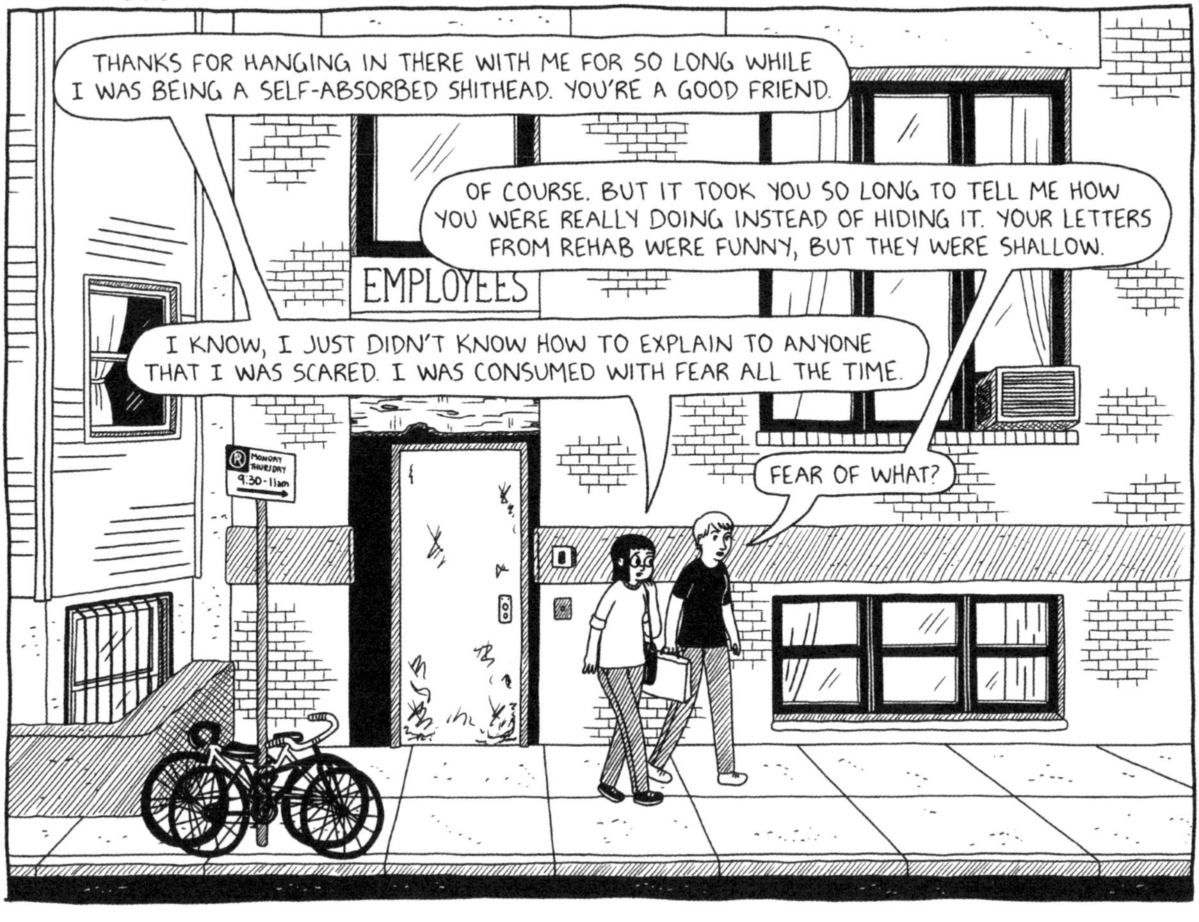
THANKS FOR HANGING IN THERE WITH ME FOR SO LONG WHILE I WAS BEING A SELF-ABSORBED SHITHEAD. YOU'RE A GOOD FRIEND.
OF COURSE. BUT IT TOOK YOU SO LONG TO TELL ME HOW YOU WERE REALLY DOING INSTEAD OF HIDING IT. YOUR LETTERS FROM REHAB WERE FUNNY, BUT THEY WERE SHALLOW.
EMPLOYEES
I KNOW, I JUST DIDN'T KNOW HOW TO EXPLAIN TO ANYONE THAT I WAS SCARED. I WAS CONSUMED WITH FEAR ALL THE TIME.
FEAR OF WHAT?

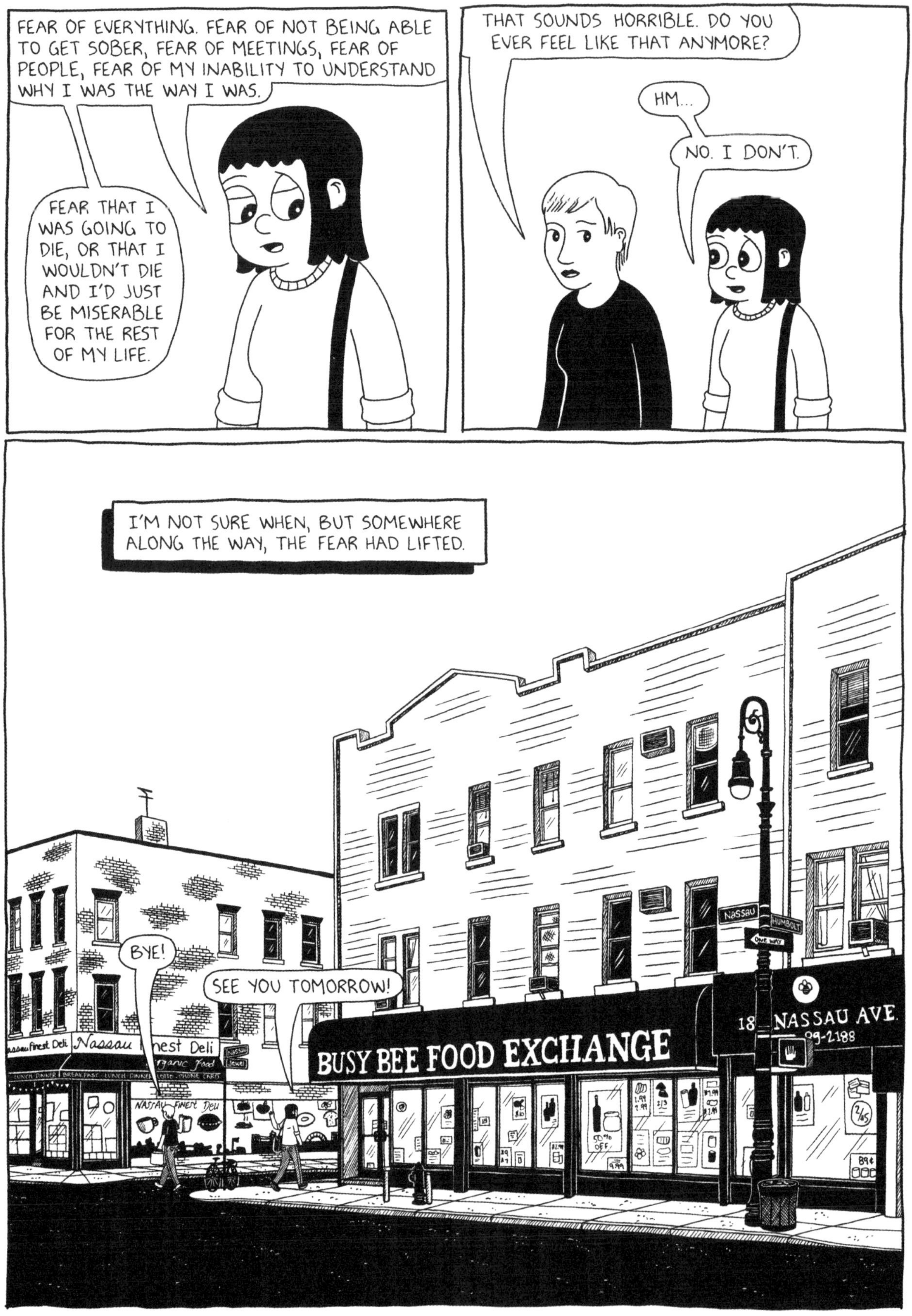
FEAR OF EVERYTHING. FEAR OF NOT BEING ABLE TO GET SOBER, FEAR OF MEETINGS, FEAR OF PEOPLE, FEAR OF MY INABILITY TO UNDERSTAND WHY I WAS THE WAY I WAS.
FEAR THAT I WAS GOING TO DIE, OR THAT I WOULDN'T DIE AND I'D JUST BE MISERABLE FOR THE REST OF MY LIFE.
THAT SOUNDS HORRIBLE. DO YOU EVER FEEL LIKE THAT ANYMORE?
HM...
NO. I DON'T.
I'M NOT SURE WHEN, BUT SOMEWHERE ALONG THE WAY, THE FEAR HAD LIFTED.
NASSAU
HUMBOLT
ONE WAY
BYE!
SEE YOU TOMORROW!
Nassau Finest Deli
BUSY BEE FOOD EXCHANGE
NASSAU AVE.

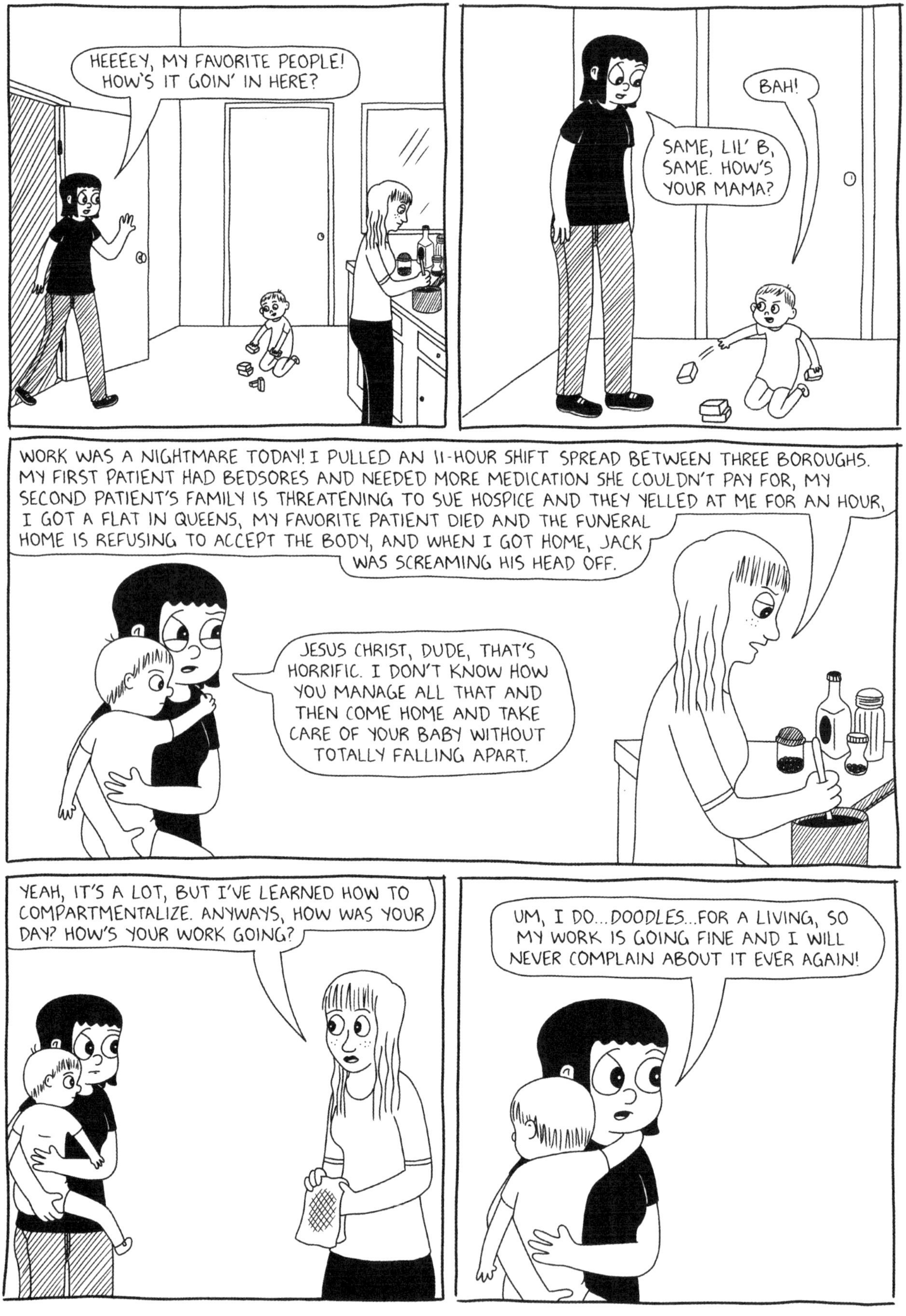
HEEEEY, MY FAVORITE PEOPLE! HOW'S IT GOIN' IN HERE?
BAH!
SAME, LIL' B, SAME. HOW'S YOUR MAMA?
WORK WAS A NIGHTMARE TODAY! I PULLED AN 11-HOUR SHIFT SPREAD BETWEEN THREE BOROUGHS. MY FIRST PATIENT HAD BEDSORES AND NEEDED MORE MEDICATION SHE COULDN'T PAY FOR, MY SECOND PATIENT'S FAMILY IS THREATENING TO SUE HOSPICE AND THEY YELLED AT ME FOR AN HOUR, I GOT A FLAT IN QUEENS, MY FAVORITE PATIENT DIED AND THE FUNERAL HOME IS REFUSING TO ACCEPT THE BODY, AND WHEN I GOT HOME, JACK WAS SCREAMING HIS HEAD OFF.
JESUS CHRIST, DUDE, THAT'S HORRIFIC. I DON'T KNOW HOW YOU MANAGE ALL THAT AND THEN COME HOME AND TAKE CARE OF YOUR BABY WITHOUT TOTALLY FALLING APART.
YEAH, IT'S A LOT, BUT I'VE LEARNED HOW TO COMPARTMENTALIZE. ANYWAYS, HOW WAS YOUR DAY? HOW'S YOUR WORK GOING?
UM, I DO...*DOODLES*...FOR A LIVING, SO MY WORK IS GOING FINE AND I WILL NEVER COMPLAIN ABOUT IT EVER AGAIN!

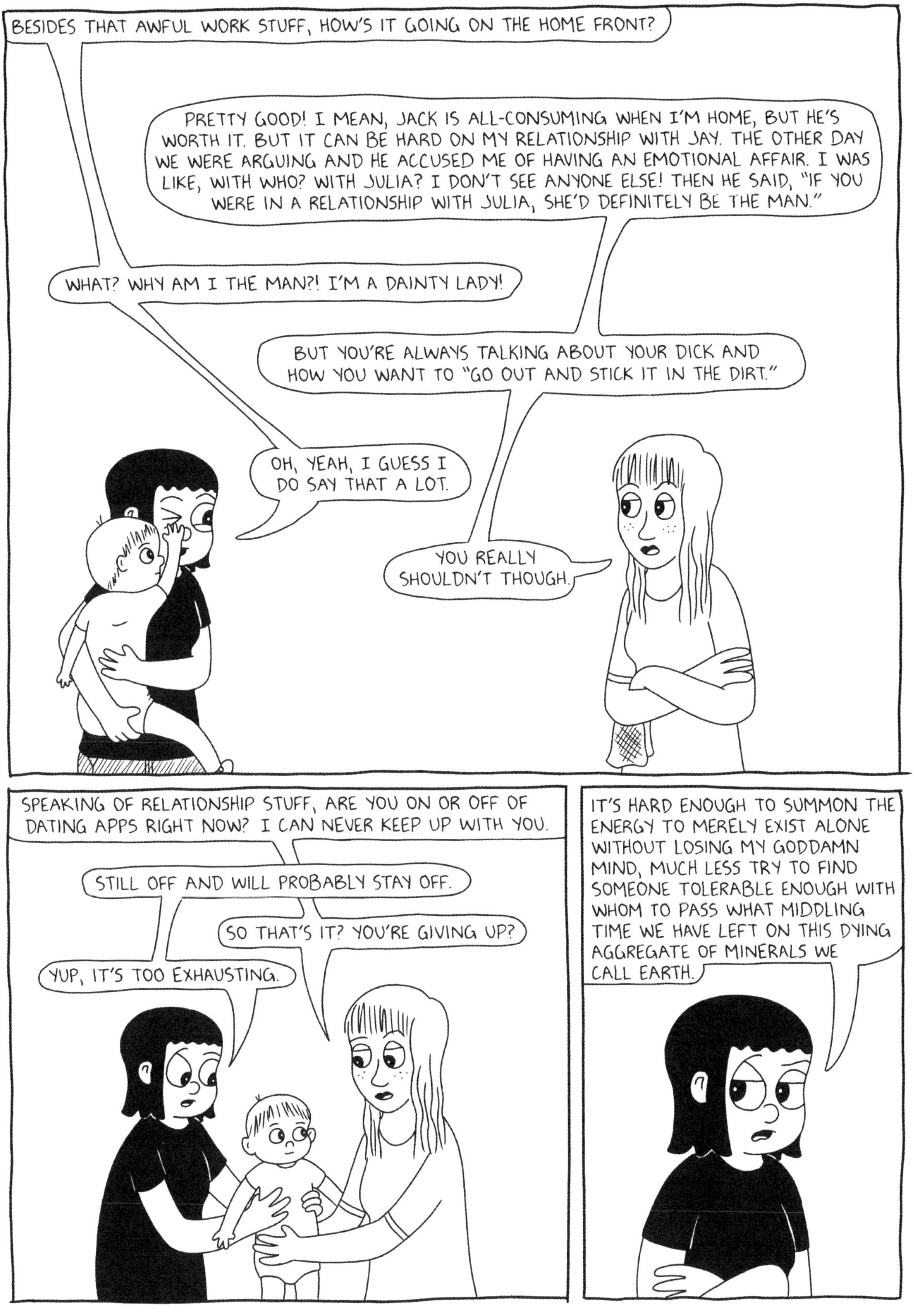
BESIDES THAT AWFUL WORK STUFF, HOW'S IT GOING ON THE HOME FRONT?
PRETTY GOOD! I MEAN, JACK IS ALL-CONSUMING WHEN I'M HOME, BUT HE'S WORTH IT. BUT IT CAN BE HARD ON MY RELATIONSHIP WITH JAY. THE OTHER DAY WE WERE ARGUING AND HE ACCUSED ME OF HAVING AN EMOTIONAL AFFAIR. I WAS LIKE, WITH WHO? WITH JULIA? I DON'T SEE ANYONE ELSE! THEN HE SAID, "IF YOU WERE IN A RELATIONSHIP WITH JULIA, SHE'D DEFINITELY BE THE MAN."
WHAT? WHY AM I THE MAN?! I'M A DAINTY LADY!
BUT YOU'RE ALWAYS TALKING ABOUT YOUR DICK AND HOW YOU WANT TO "GO OUT AND STICK IT IN THE DIRT."
OH, YEAH, I GUESS I DO SAY THAT A LOT.
YOU REALLY SHOULDN'T THOUGH.
SPEAKING OF RELATIONSHIP STUFF, ARE YOU ON OR OFF OF DATING APPS RIGHT NOW? I CAN NEVER KEEP UP WITH YOU.
STILL OFF AND WILL PROBABLY STAY OFF.
SO THAT'S IT? YOU'RE GIVING UP?
YUP, IT'S TOO EXHAUSTING.
IT'S HARD ENOUGH TO SUMMON THE ENERGY TO MERELY EXIST ALONE WITHOUT LOSING MY GODDAMN MIND, MUCH LESS TRY TO FIND SOMEONE TOLERABLE ENOUGH WITH WHOM TO PASS WHAT MIDDLING TIME WE HAVE LEFT ON THIS DYING AGGREGATE OF MINERALS WE CALL EARTH.

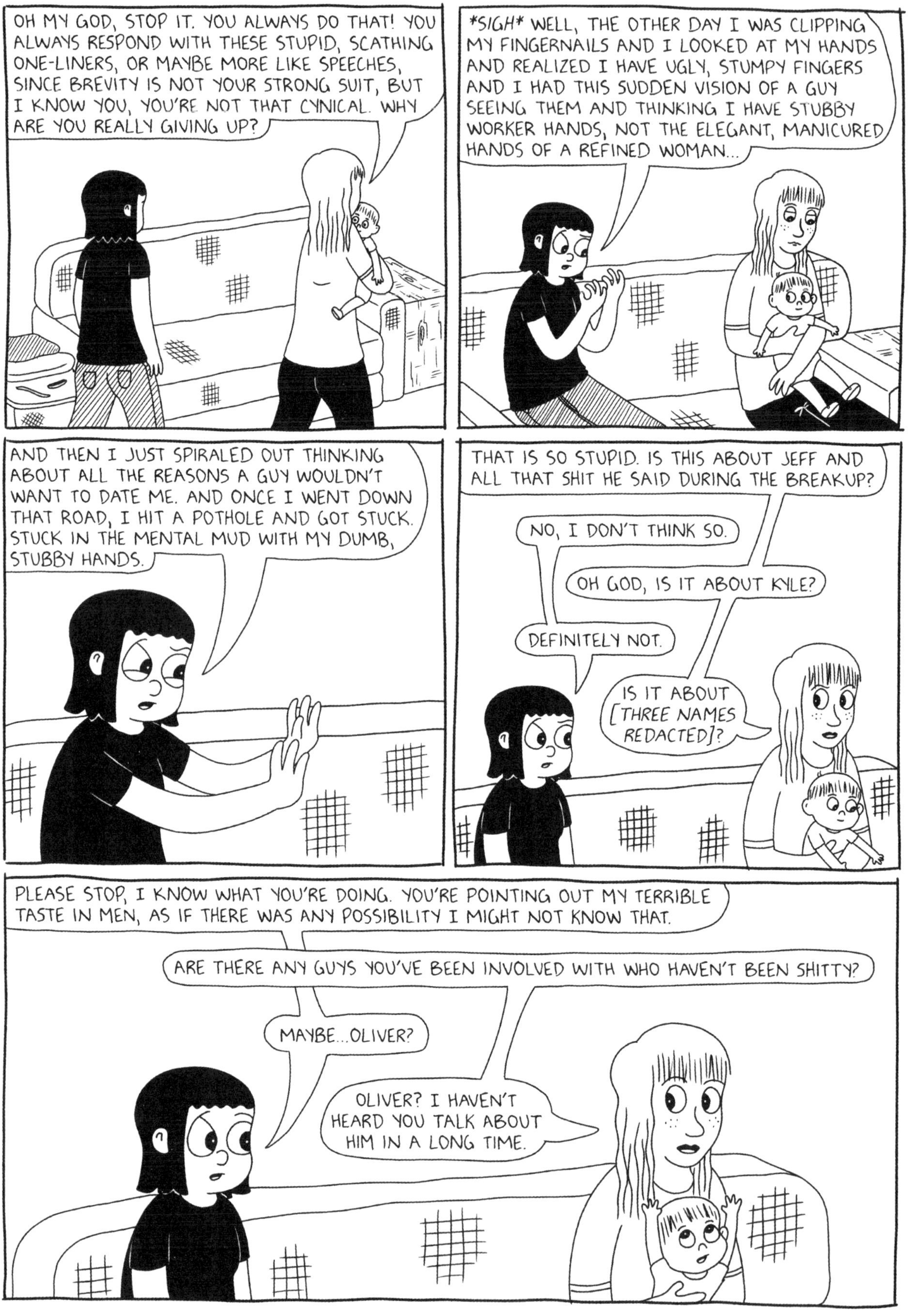
OH MY GOD, STOP IT. YOU ALWAYS DO THAT! YOU ALWAYS RESPOND WITH THESE STUPID, SCATHING ONE-LINERS, OR MAYBE MORE LIKE SPEECHES, SINCE BREVITY IS NOT YOUR STRONG SUIT, BUT I KNOW YOU, YOU'RE NOT THAT CYNICAL. WHY ARE YOU REALLY GIVING UP?
SIGH WELL, THE OTHER DAY I WAS CLIPPING MY FINGERNAILS AND I LOOKED AT MY HANDS AND REALIZED I HAVE UGLY, STUMPY FINGERS AND I HAD THIS SUDDEN VISION OF A GUY SEEING THEM AND THINKING I HAVE STUBBY WORKER HANDS, NOT THE ELEGANT, MANICURED HANDS OF A REFINED WOMAN...
AND THEN I JUST SPIRALED OUT THINKING ABOUT ALL THE REASONS A GUY WOULDN'T WANT TO DATE ME. AND ONCE I WENT DOWN THAT ROAD, I HIT A POTHOLE AND GOT STUCK. STUCK IN THE MENTAL MUD WITH MY DUMB, STUBBY HANDS.
THAT IS SO STUPID. IS THIS ABOUT JEFF AND ALL THAT SHIT HE SAID DURING THE BREAKUP?
NO, I DON'T THINK SO.
OH GOD, IS IT ABOUT KYLE?
DEFINITELY NOT.
IS IT ABOUT [THREE NAMES REDACTED]?
PLEASE STOP, I KNOW WHAT YOU'RE DOING. YOU'RE POINTING OUT MY TERRIBLE TASTE IN MEN, AS IF THERE WAS ANY POSSIBILITY I MIGHT NOT KNOW THAT.
ARE THERE ANY GUYS YOU'VE BEEN INVOLVED WITH WHO HAVEN'T BEEN SHITTY?
MAYBE...OLIVER?
OLIVER? I HAVEN'T HEARD YOU TALK ABOUT HIM IN A LONG TIME.

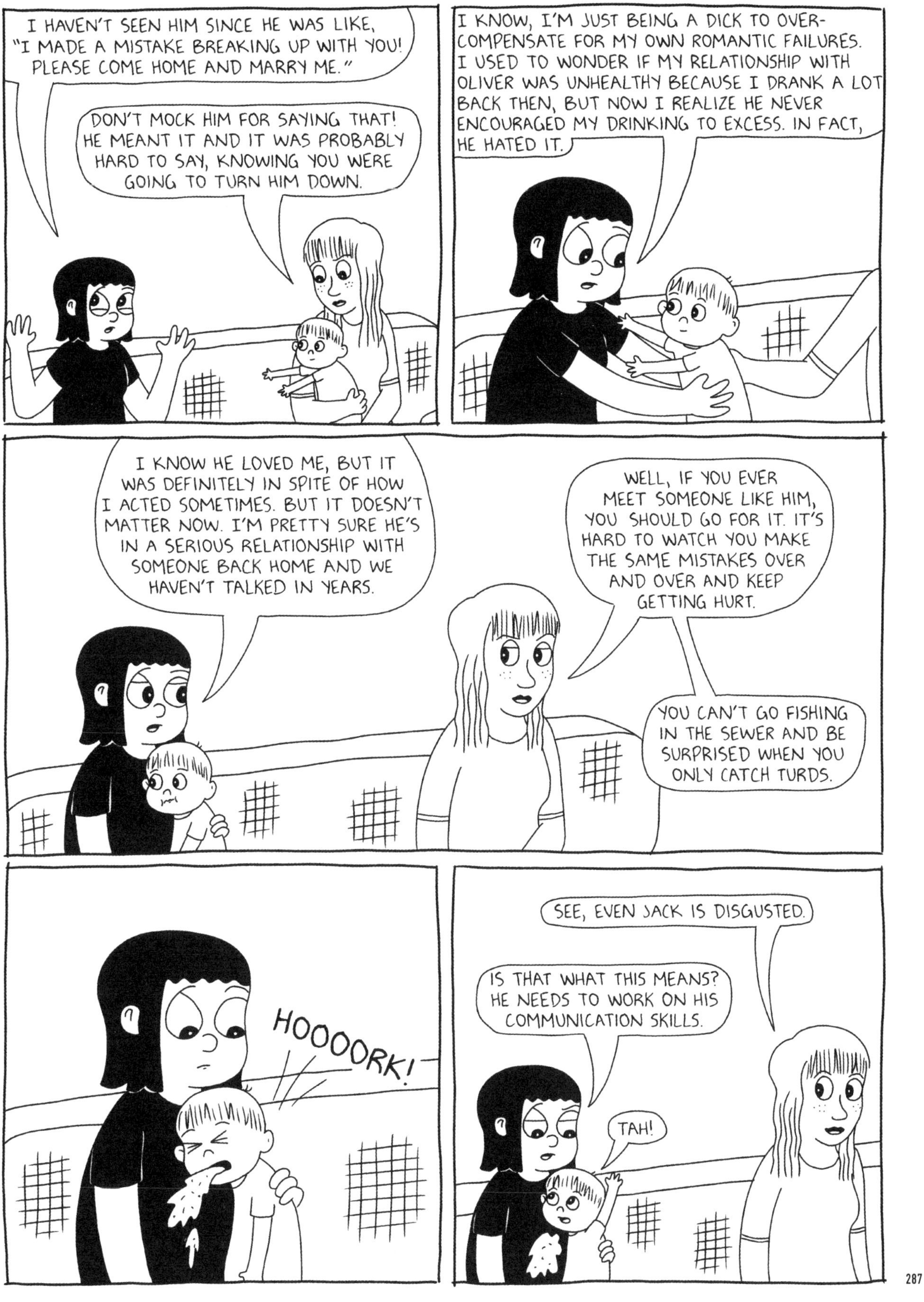

I HAVEN'T SEEN HIM SINCE HE WAS LIKE, "I MADE A MISTAKE BREAKING UP WITH YOU! PLEASE COME HOME AND MARRY ME."
DON'T MOCK HIM FOR SAYING THAT! HE MEANT IT AND IT WAS PROBABLY HARD TO SAY, KNOWING YOU WERE GOING TO TURN HIM DOWN.
I KNOW, I'M JUST BEING A DICK TO OVER-COMPENSATE FOR MY OWN ROMANTIC FAILURES. I USED TO WONDER IF MY RELATIONSHIP WITH OLIVER WAS UNHEALTHY BECAUSE I DRANK A LOT BACK THEN, BUT NOW I REALIZE HE NEVER ENCOURAGED MY DRINKING TO EXCESS. IN FACT, HE HATED IT.
I KNOW HE LOVED ME, BUT IT WAS DEFINITELY IN SPITE OF HOW I ACTED SOMETIMES. BUT IT DOESN'T MATTER NOW. I'M PRETTY SURE HE'S IN A SERIOUS RELATIONSHIP WITH SOMEONE BACK HOME AND WE HAVEN'T TALKED IN YEARS.
WELL, IF YOU EVER MEET SOMEONE LIKE HIM, YOU SHOULD GO FOR IT. IT'S HARD TO WATCH YOU MAKE THE SAME MISTAKES OVER AND OVER AND KEEP GETTING HURT.
YOU CAN'T GO FISHING IN THE SEWER AND BE SURPRISED WHEN YOU ONLY CATCH TURDS.
HOOOORK!
SEE, EVEN JACK IS DISGUSTED.
IS THAT WHAT THIS MEANS? HE NEEDS TO WORK ON HIS COMMUNICATION SKILLS.
TAH!

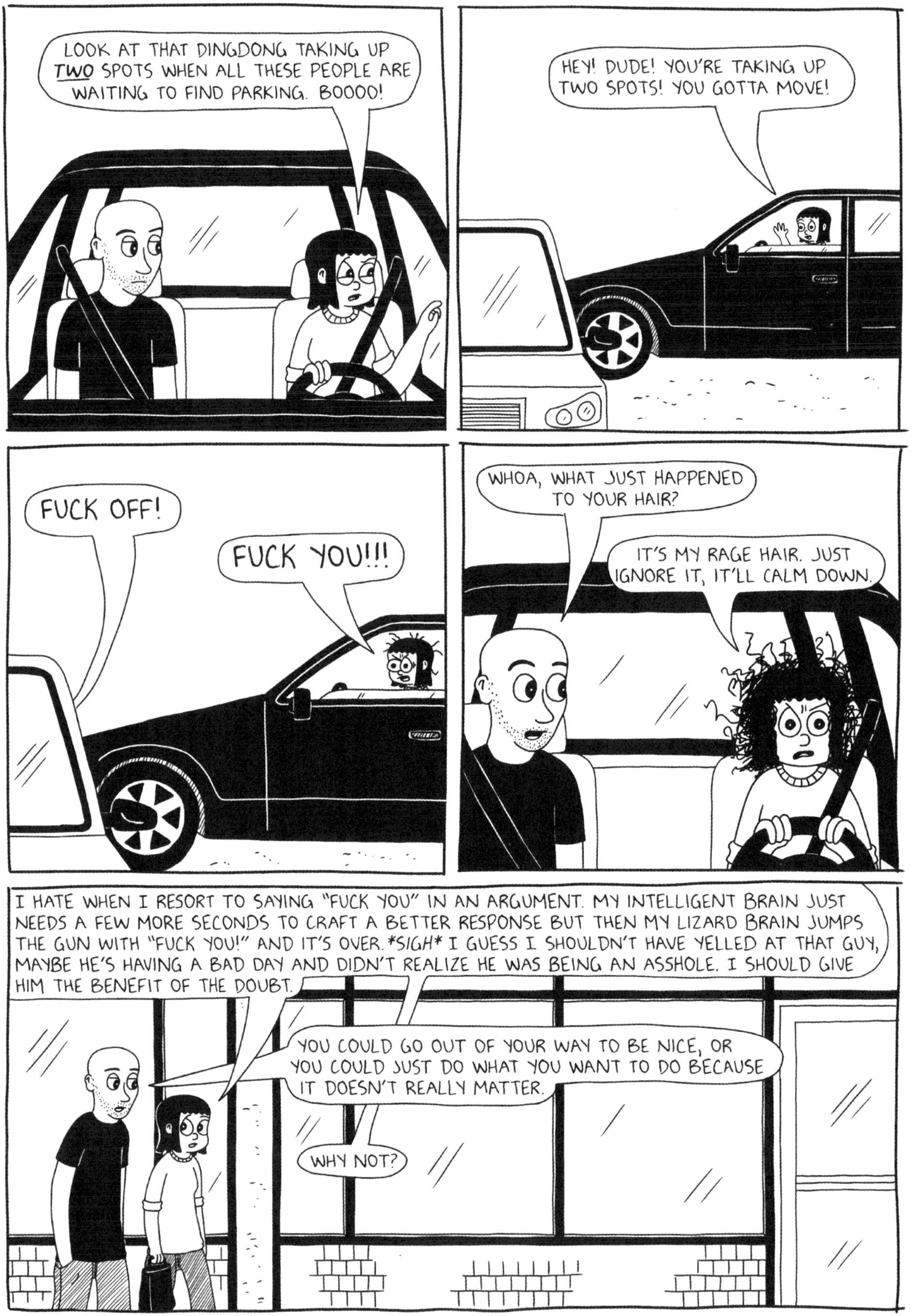
LOOK AT THAT DINGDONG TAKING UP TWO SPOTS WHEN ALL THESE PEOPLE ARE WAITING TO FIND PARKING. BOOOO!
HEY! DUDE! YOU'RE TAKING UP TWO SPOTS! YOU GOTTA MOVE!
FUCK OFF!
FUCK YOU!!!
WHOA, WHAT JUST HAPPENED TO YOUR HAIR?
IT'S MY RAGE HAIR. JUST IGNORE IT, IT'LL CALM DOWN.
I HATE WHEN I RESORT TO SAYING "FUCK YOU" IN AN ARGUMENT. MY INTELLIGENT BRAIN JUST NEEDS A FEW MORE SECONDS TO CRAFT A BETTER RESPONSE BUT THEN MY LIZARD BRAIN JUMPS THE GUN WITH "FUCK YOU!" AND IT'S OVER. *SIGH* I GUESS I SHOULDN'T HAVE YELLED AT THAT GUY, MAYBE HE'S HAVING A BAD DAY AND DIDN'T REALIZE HE WAS BEING AN ASSHOLE. I SHOULD GIVE HIM THE BENEFIT OF THE DOUBT.
YOU COULD GO OUT OF YOUR WAY TO BE NICE, OR YOU COULD JUST DO WHAT YOU WANT TO DO BECAUSE IT DOESN'T REALLY MATTER.
WHY NOT?

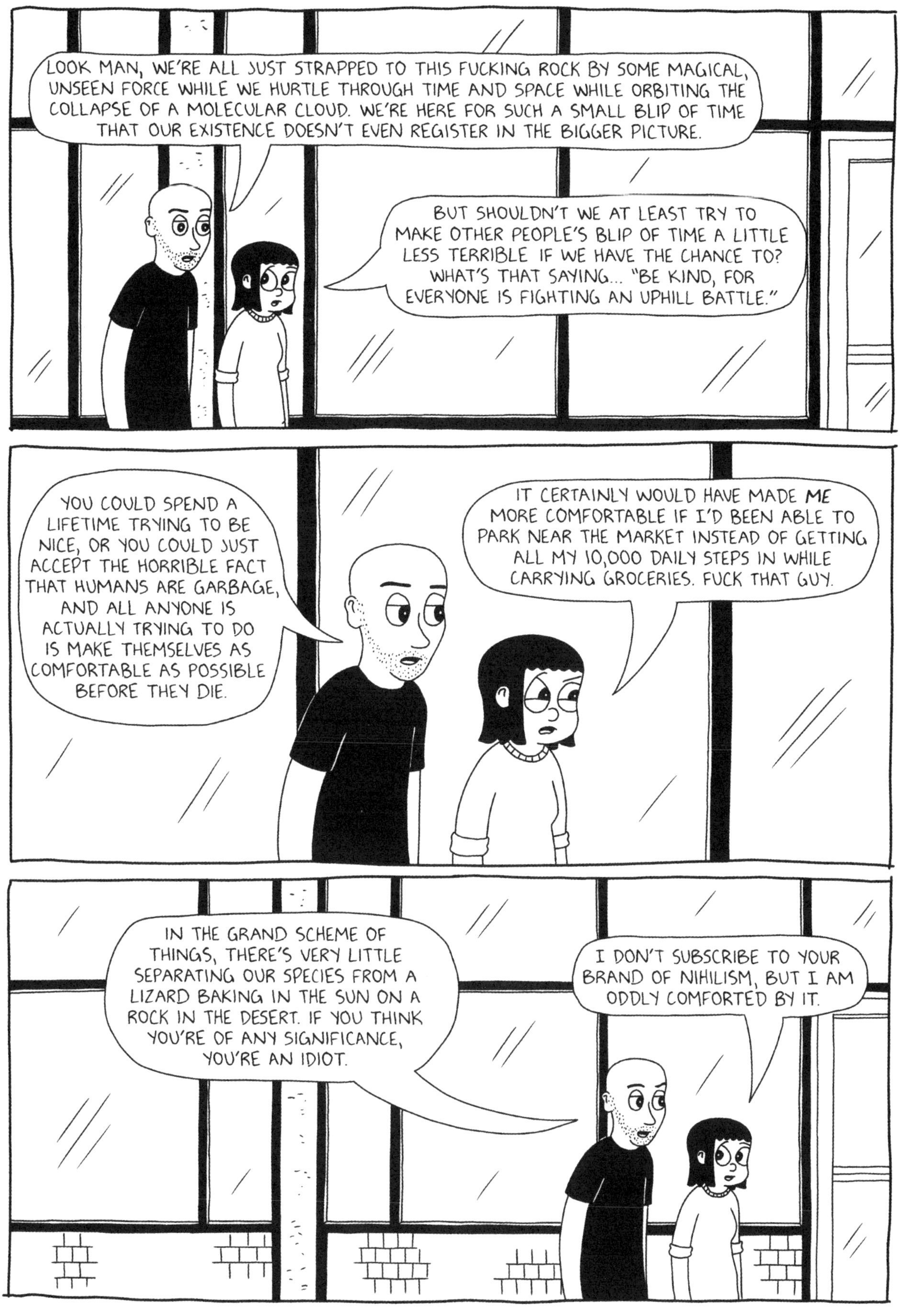
LOOK MAN, WE'RE ALL JUST STRAPPED TO THIS FUCKING ROCK BY SOME MAGICAL, UNSEEN FORCE WHILE WE HURTLE THROUGH TIME AND SPACE WHILE ORBITING THE COLLAPSE OF A MOLECULAR CLOUD. WE'RE HERE FOR SUCH A SMALL BLIP OF TIME THAT OUR EXISTENCE DOESN'T EVEN REGISTER IN THE BIGGER PICTURE.
BUT SHOULDN'T WE AT LEAST TRY TO MAKE OTHER PEOPLE'S BLIP OF TIME A LITTLE LESS TERRIBLE IF WE HAVE THE CHANCE TO? WHAT'S THAT SAYING... "BE KIND, FOR EVERYONE IS FIGHTING AN UPHILL BATTLE."
YOU COULD SPEND A LIFETIME TRYING TO BE NICE, OR YOU COULD JUST ACCEPT THE HORRIBLE FACT THAT HUMANS ARE GARBAGE, AND ALL ANYONE IS ACTUALLY TRYING TO DO IS MAKE THEMSELVES AS COMFORTABLE AS POSSIBLE BEFORE THEY DIE.
IT CERTAINLY WOULD HAVE MADE **ME** MORE COMFORTABLE IF I'D BEEN ABLE TO PARK NEAR THE MARKET INSTEAD OF GETTING ALL MY 10,000 DAILY STEPS IN WHILE CARRYING GROCERIES. FUCK THAT GUY.
IN THE GRAND SCHEME OF THINGS, THERE'S VERY LITTLE SEPARATING OUR SPECIES FROM A LIZARD BAKING IN THE SUN ON A ROCK IN THE DESERT. IF YOU THINK YOU'RE OF ANY SIGNIFICANCE, YOU'RE AN IDIOT.
I DON'T SUBSCRIBE TO YOUR BRAND OF NIHILISM, BUT I AM ODDLY COMFORTED BY IT.

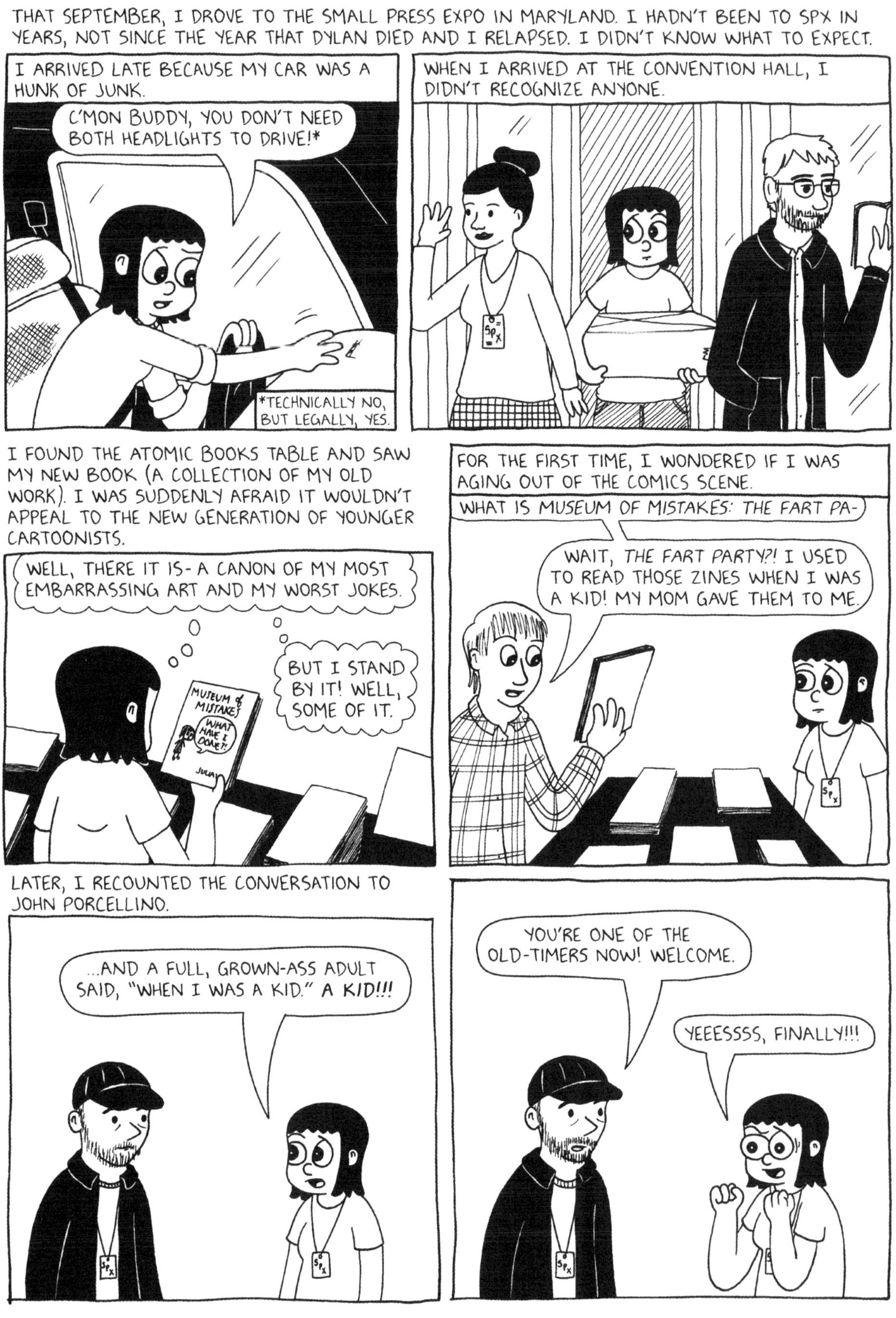
THAT SEPTEMBER, I DROVE TO THE SMALL PRESS EXPO IN MARYLAND. I HADN'T BEEN TO SPX IN YEARS, NOT SINCE THE YEAR THAT DYLAN DIED AND I RELAPSED. I DIDN'T KNOW WHAT TO EXPECT.
I ARRIVED LATE BECAUSE MY CAR WAS A HUNK OF JUNK.
C'MON BUDDY, YOU DON'T NEED BOTH HEADLIGHTS TO DRIVE!*
*TECHNICALLY NO, BUT LEGALLY, YES.
WHEN I ARRIVED AT THE CONVENTION HALL, I DIDN'T RECOGNIZE ANYONE.
I FOUND THE ATOMIC BOOKS TABLE AND SAW MY NEW BOOK (A COLLECTION OF MY OLD WORK). I WAS SUDDENLY AFRAID IT WOULDN'T APPEAL TO THE NEW GENERATION OF YOUNGER CARTOONISTS.
WELL, THERE IT IS- A CANON OF MY MOST EMBARRASSING ART AND MY WORST JOKES.
MUSEUM of MISTAKES
WHAT HAVE I DONE?!
BUT I STAND BY IT! WELL, SOME OF IT.
FOR THE FIRST TIME, I WONDERED IF I WAS AGING OUT OF THE COMICS SCENE.
WHAT IS MUSEUM OF MISTAKES: THE FART PA-
WAIT, THE FART PARTY?! I USED TO READ THOSE ZINES WHEN I WAS A KID! MY MOM GAVE THEM TO ME.
LATER, I RECOUNTED THE CONVERSATION TO JOHN PORCELLINO.
...AND A FULL, GROWN-ASS ADULT SAID, "WHEN I WAS A KID." A KID!!!
YOU'RE ONE OF THE OLD-TIMERS NOW! WELCOME.
YEEESSSS, FINALLY!!!

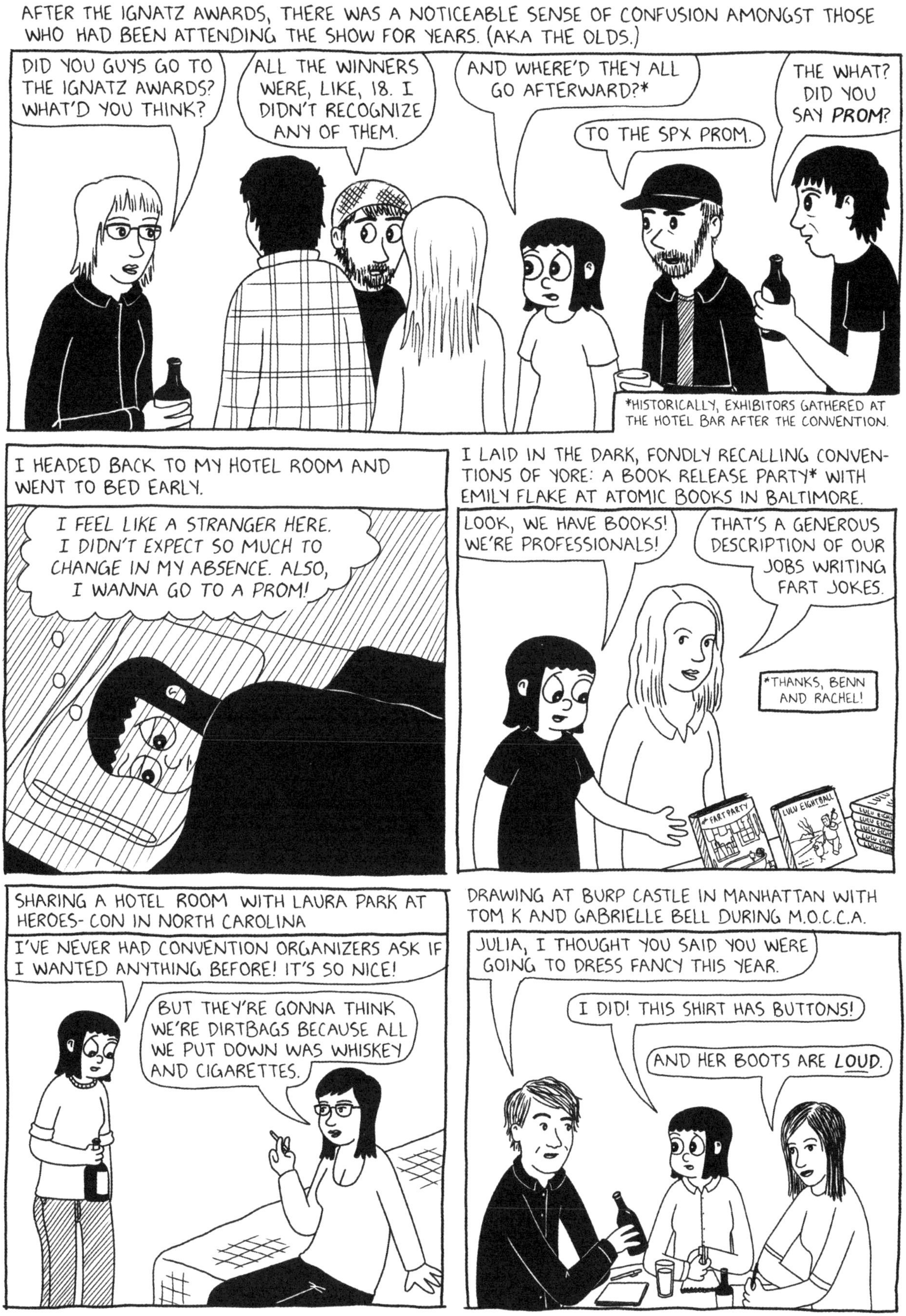

AFTER THE IGNATZ AWARDS, THERE WAS A NOTICEABLE SENSE OF CONFUSION AMONGST THOSE WHO HAD BEEN ATTENDING THE SHOW FOR YEARS. (AKA THE OLDS.)
DID YOU GUYS GO TO THE IGNATZ AWARDS? WHAT'D YOU THINK?
ALL THE WINNERS WERE, LIKE, 18. I DIDN'T RECOGNIZE ANY OF THEM.
AND WHERE'D THEY ALL GO AFTERWARD?*
TO THE SPX PROM.
THE WHAT? DID YOU SAY **PROM**?
*HISTORICALLY, EXHIBITORS GATHERED AT THE HOTEL BAR AFTER THE CONVENTION.
I HEADED BACK TO MY HOTEL ROOM AND WENT TO BED EARLY.
I FEEL LIKE A STRANGER HERE. I DIDN'T EXPECT SO MUCH TO CHANGE IN MY ABSENCE. ALSO, I WANNA GO TO A PROM!
I LAID IN THE DARK, FONDLY RECALLING CONVENTIONS OF YORE: A BOOK RELEASE PARTY* WITH EMILY FLAKE AT ATOMIC BOOKS IN BALTIMORE.
LOOK, WE HAVE BOOKS! WE'RE PROFESSIONALS!
THAT'S A GENEROUS DESCRIPTION OF OUR JOBS WRITING FART JOKES.
*THANKS, BENN AND RACHEL!
FART PARTY
LULU EIGHTBALL
SHARING A HOTEL ROOM WITH LAURA PARK AT HEROES-CON IN NORTH CAROLINA
I'VE NEVER HAD CONVENTION ORGANIZERS ASK IF I WANTED ANYTHING BEFORE! IT'S SO NICE!
BUT THEY'RE GONNA THINK WE'RE DIRTBAGS BECAUSE ALL WE PUT DOWN WAS WHISKEY AND CIGARETTES.
DRAWING AT BURP CASTLE IN MANHATTAN WITH TOM K AND GABRIELLE BELL DURING M.O.C.C.A.
JULIA, I THOUGHT YOU SAID YOU WERE GOING TO DRESS FANCY THIS YEAR.
I DID! THIS SHIRT HAS BUTTONS!
AND HER BOOTS ARE LOUD.

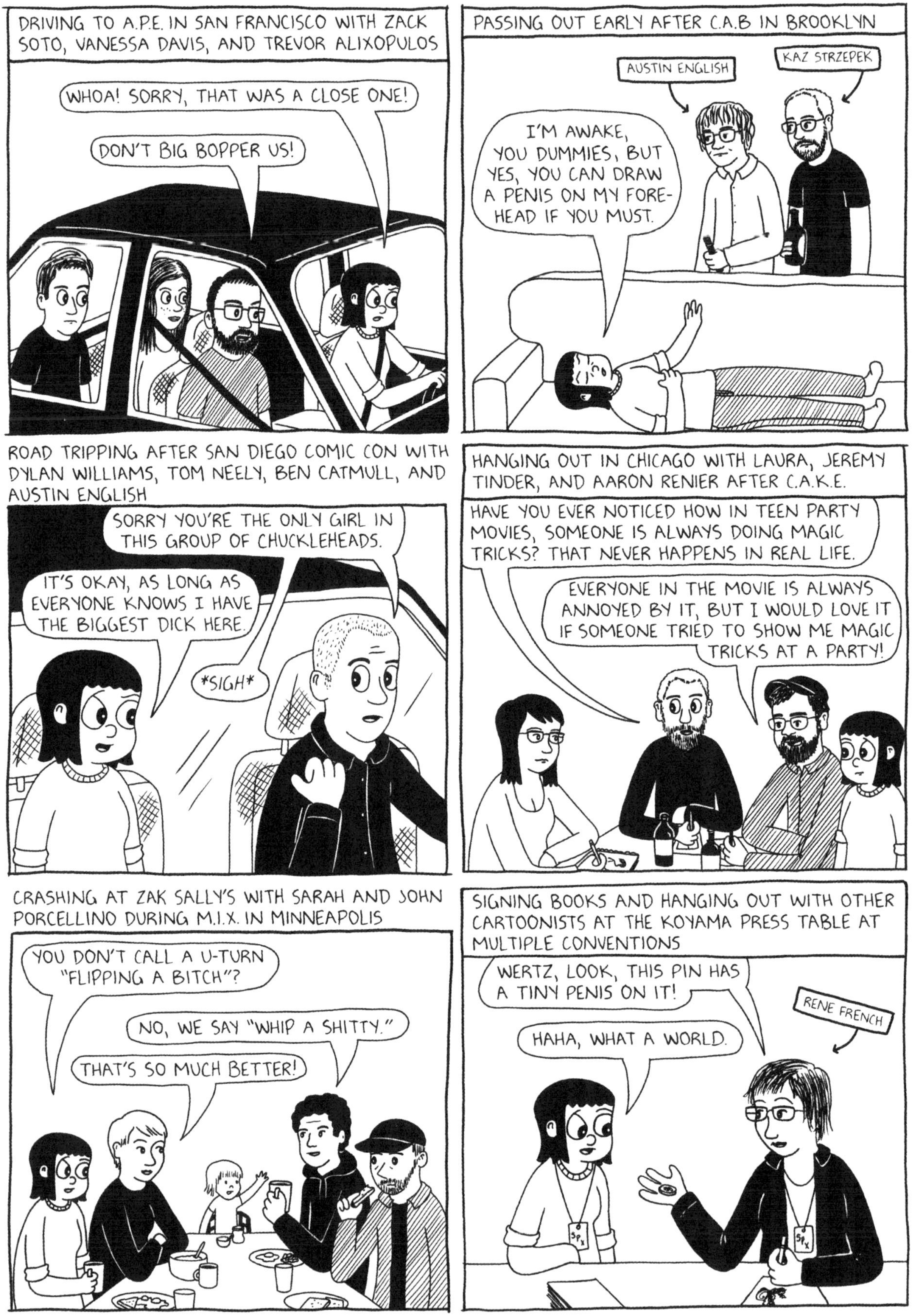
DRIVING TO A.P.E. IN SAN FRANCISCO WITH ZACK SOTO, VANESSA DAVIS, AND TREVOR ALIXOPULOS
WHOA! SORRY, THAT WAS A CLOSE ONE!
DON'T BIG BOPPER US!
PASSING OUT EARLY AFTER C.A.B IN BROOKLYN
AUSTIN ENGLISH
KAZ STRZEPEK
I'M AWAKE, YOU DUMMIES, BUT YES, YOU CAN DRAW A PENIS ON MY FOREHEAD IF YOU MUST.
ROAD TRIPPING AFTER SAN DIEGO COMIC CON WITH DYLAN WILLIAMS, TOM NEELY, BEN CATMULL, AND AUSTIN ENGLISH
SORRY YOU'RE THE ONLY GIRL IN THIS GROUP OF CHUCKLEHEADS.
IT'S OKAY, AS LONG AS EVERYONE KNOWS I HAVE THE BIGGEST DICK HERE.
SIGH
HANGING OUT IN CHICAGO WITH LAURA, JEREMY TINDER, AND AARON RENIER AFTER C.A.K.E.
HAVE YOU EVER NOTICED HOW IN TEEN PARTY MOVIES, SOMEONE IS ALWAYS DOING MAGIC TRICKS? THAT NEVER HAPPENS IN REAL LIFE.
EVERYONE IN THE MOVIE IS ALWAYS ANNOYED BY IT, BUT I WOULD LOVE IT IF SOMEONE TRIED TO SHOW ME MAGIC TRICKS AT A PARTY!
CRASHING AT ZAK SALLY'S WITH SARAH AND JOHN PORCELLINO DURING M.I.X. IN MINNEAPOLIS
YOU DON'T CALL A U-TURN "FLIPPING A BITCH"?
NO, WE SAY "WHIP A SHITTY."
THAT'S SO MUCH BETTER!
SIGNING BOOKS AND HANGING OUT WITH OTHER CARTOONISTS AT THE KOYAMA PRESS TABLE AT MULTIPLE CONVENTIONS
WERTZ, LOOK, THIS PIN HAS A TINY PENIS ON IT!
RENE FRENCH
HAHA, WHAT A WORLD.

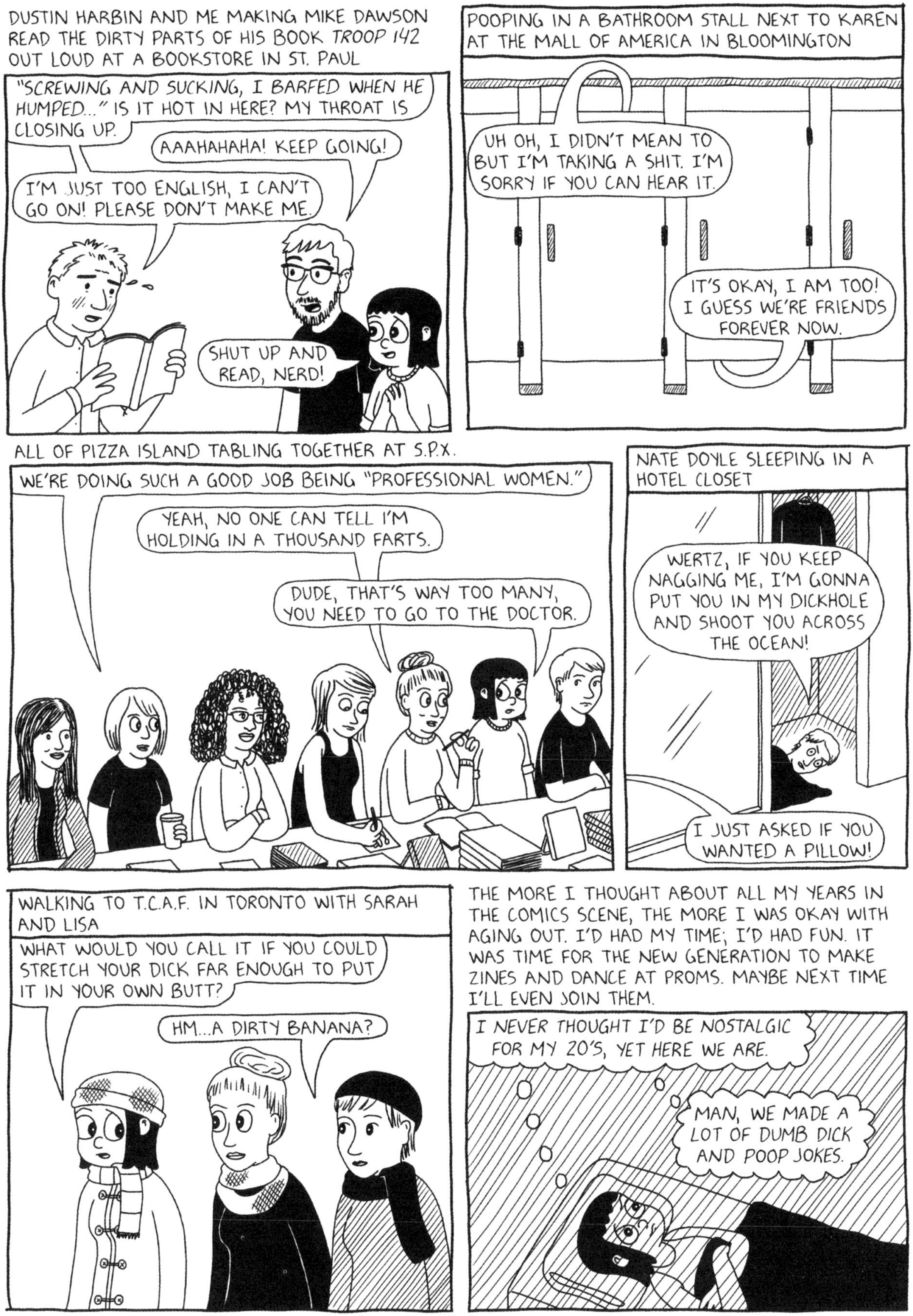
DUSTIN HARBIN AND ME MAKING MIKE DAWSON READ THE DIRTY PARTS OF HIS BOOK *TROOP 142* OUT LOUD AT A BOOKSTORE IN ST. PAUL
"SCREWING AND SUCKING, I BARFED WHEN HE HUMPED..." IS IT HOT IN HERE? MY THROAT IS CLOSING UP.
AAAHAHAHA! KEEP GOING!
I'M JUST TOO ENGLISH, I CAN'T GO ON! PLEASE DON'T MAKE ME.
SHUT UP AND READ, NERD!
POOPING IN A BATHROOM STALL NEXT TO KAREN AT THE MALL OF AMERICA IN BLOOMINGTON
UH OH, I DIDN'T MEAN TO BUT I'M TAKING A SHIT. I'M SORRY IF YOU CAN HEAR IT.
IT'S OKAY, I AM TOO! I GUESS WE'RE FRIENDS FOREVER NOW.
ALL OF PIZZA ISLAND TABLING TOGETHER AT S.P.X.
WE'RE DOING SUCH A GOOD JOB BEING "PROFESSIONAL WOMEN."
YEAH, NO ONE CAN TELL I'M HOLDING IN A THOUSAND FARTS.
DUDE, THAT'S WAY TOO MANY, YOU NEED TO GO TO THE DOCTOR.
NATE DOYLE SLEEPING IN A HOTEL CLOSET
WERTZ, IF YOU KEEP NAGGING ME, I'M GONNA PUT YOU IN MY DICKHOLE AND SHOOT YOU ACROSS THE OCEAN!
I JUST ASKED IF YOU WANTED A PILLOW!
WALKING TO T.C.A.F. IN TORONTO WITH SARAH AND LISA
WHAT WOULD YOU CALL IT IF YOU COULD STRETCH YOUR DICK FAR ENOUGH TO PUT IT IN YOUR OWN BUTT?
HM...A DIRTY BANANA?
THE MORE I THOUGHT ABOUT ALL MY YEARS IN THE COMICS SCENE, THE MORE I WAS OKAY WITH AGING OUT. I'D HAD MY TIME; I'D HAD FUN. IT WAS TIME FOR THE NEW GENERATION TO MAKE ZINES AND DANCE AT PROMS. MAYBE NEXT TIME I'LL EVEN JOIN THEM.
I NEVER THOUGHT I'D BE NOSTALGIC FOR MY 20'S, YET HERE WE ARE.
MAN, WE MADE A LOT OF DUMB DICK AND POOP JOKES.

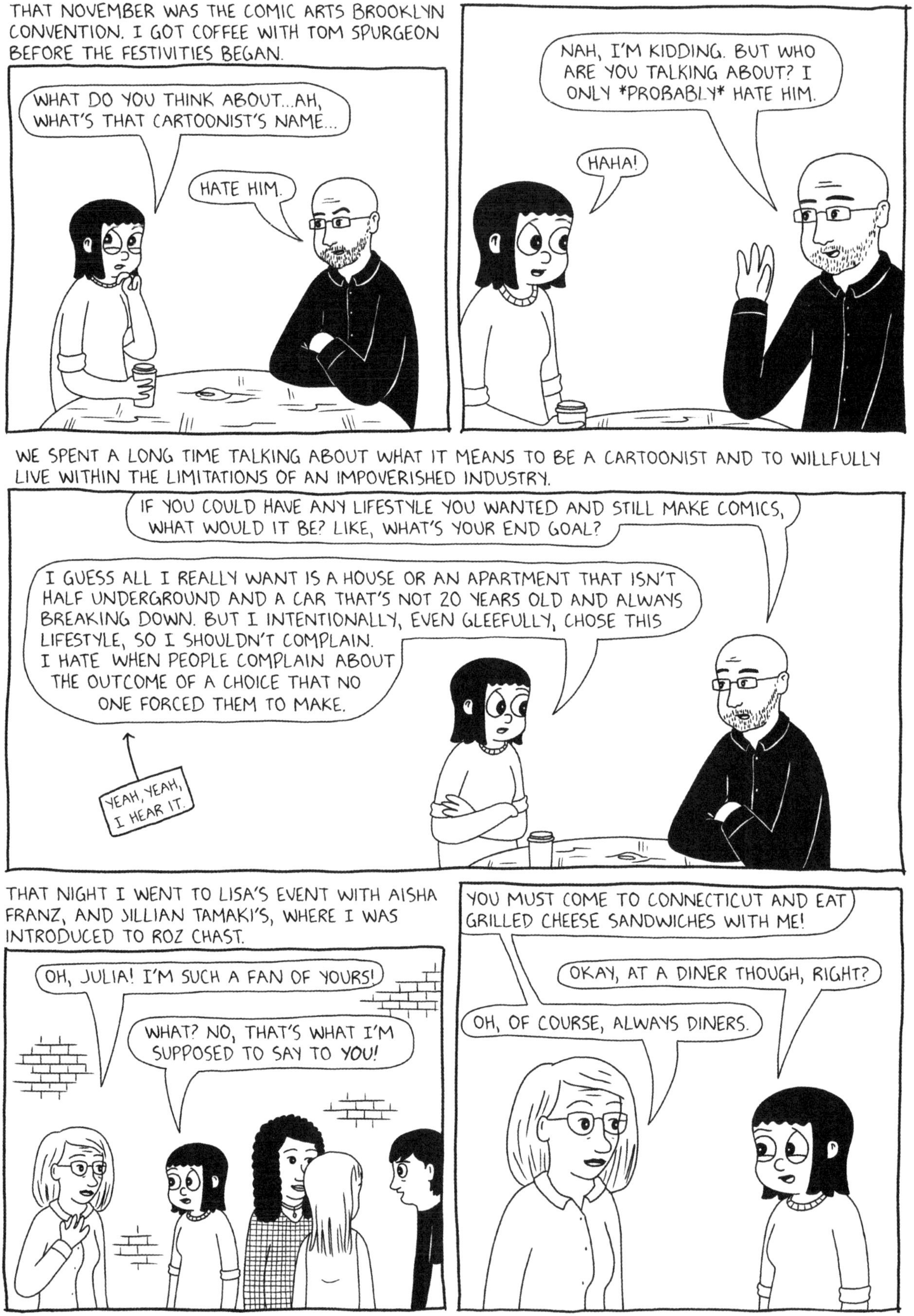
THAT NOVEMBER WAS THE COMIC ARTS BROOKLYN CONVENTION. I GOT COFFEE WITH TOM SPURGEON BEFORE THE FESTIVITIES BEGAN.
WHAT DO YOU THINK ABOUT...AH, WHAT'S THAT CARTOONIST'S NAME...
HATE HIM.
HAHA!
NAH, I'M KIDDING. BUT WHO ARE YOU TALKING ABOUT? I ONLY *PROBABLY* HATE HIM.
WE SPENT A LONG TIME TALKING ABOUT WHAT IT MEANS TO BE A CARTOONIST AND TO WILLFULLY LIVE WITHIN THE LIMITATIONS OF AN IMPOVERISHED INDUSTRY.
IF YOU COULD HAVE ANY LIFESTYLE YOU WANTED AND STILL MAKE COMICS, WHAT WOULD IT BE? LIKE, WHAT'S YOUR END GOAL?
I GUESS ALL I REALLY WANT IS A HOUSE OR AN APARTMENT THAT ISN'T HALF UNDERGROUND AND A CAR THAT'S NOT 20 YEARS OLD AND ALWAYS BREAKING DOWN. BUT I INTENTIONALLY, EVEN GLEEFULLY, CHOSE THIS LIFESTYLE, SO I SHOULDN'T COMPLAIN. I HATE WHEN PEOPLE COMPLAIN ABOUT THE OUTCOME OF A CHOICE THAT NO ONE FORCED THEM TO MAKE.
YEAH, YEAH, I HEAR IT.
THAT NIGHT I WENT TO LISA'S EVENT WITH AISHA FRANZ, AND JILLIAN TAMAKI'S, WHERE I WAS INTRODUCED TO ROZ CHAST.
OH, JULIA! I'M SUCH A FAN OF YOURS!
WHAT? NO, THAT'S WHAT I'M SUPPOSED TO SAY TO YOU!
YOU MUST COME TO CONNECTICUT AND EAT GRILLED CHEESE SANDWICHES WITH ME!
OKAY, AT A DINER THOUGH, RIGHT?
OH, OF COURSE, ALWAYS DINERS.

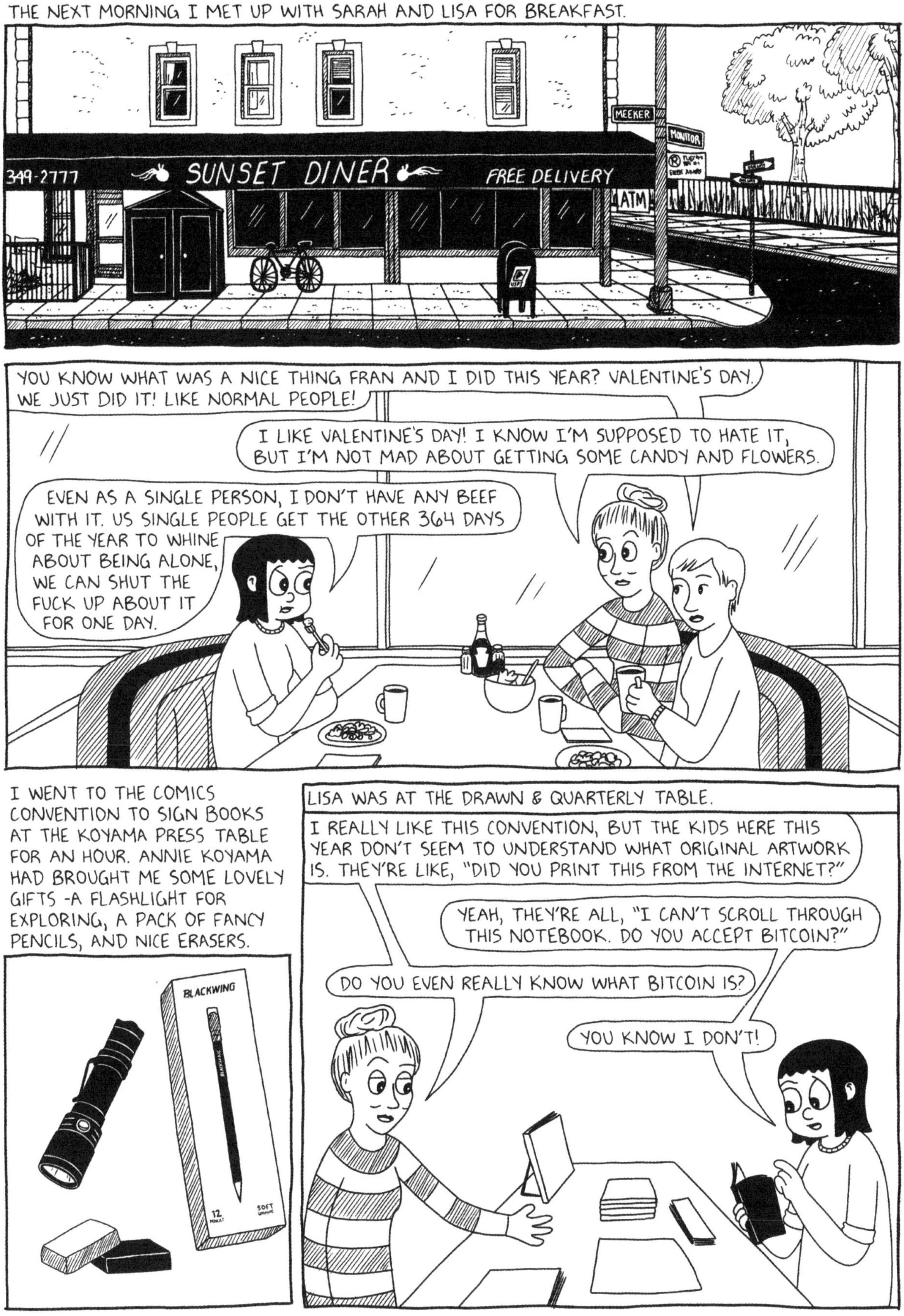
THE NEXT MORNING I MET UP WITH SARAH AND LISA FOR BREAKFAST.
349-2777
SUNSET DINER
FREE DELIVERY
MEEKER
MONITOR
ATM
YOU KNOW WHAT WAS A NICE THING FRAN AND I DID THIS YEAR? VALENTINE'S DAY. WE JUST DID IT! LIKE NORMAL PEOPLE!
I LIKE VALENTINE'S DAY! I KNOW I'M SUPPOSED TO HATE IT, BUT I'M NOT MAD ABOUT GETTING SOME CANDY AND FLOWERS.
EVEN AS A SINGLE PERSON, I DON'T HAVE ANY BEEF WITH IT. US SINGLE PEOPLE GET THE OTHER 364 DAYS OF THE YEAR TO WHINE ABOUT BEING ALONE, WE CAN SHUT THE FUCK UP ABOUT IT FOR ONE DAY.
I WENT TO THE COMICS CONVENTION TO SIGN BOOKS AT THE KOYAMA PRESS TABLE FOR AN HOUR. ANNIE KOYAMA HAD BROUGHT ME SOME LOVELY GIFTS -A FLASHLIGHT FOR EXPLORING, A PACK OF FANCY PENCILS, AND NICE ERASERS.
BLACKWING
LISA WAS AT THE DRAWN & QUARTERLY TABLE.
I REALLY LIKE THIS CONVENTION, BUT THE KIDS HERE THIS YEAR DON'T SEEM TO UNDERSTAND WHAT ORIGINAL ARTWORK IS. THEY'RE LIKE, "DID YOU PRINT THIS FROM THE INTERNET?"
YEAH, THEY'RE ALL, "I CAN'T SCROLL THROUGH THIS NOTEBOOK. DO YOU ACCEPT BITCOIN?"
DO YOU EVEN REALLY KNOW WHAT BITCOIN IS?
YOU KNOW I DON'T!

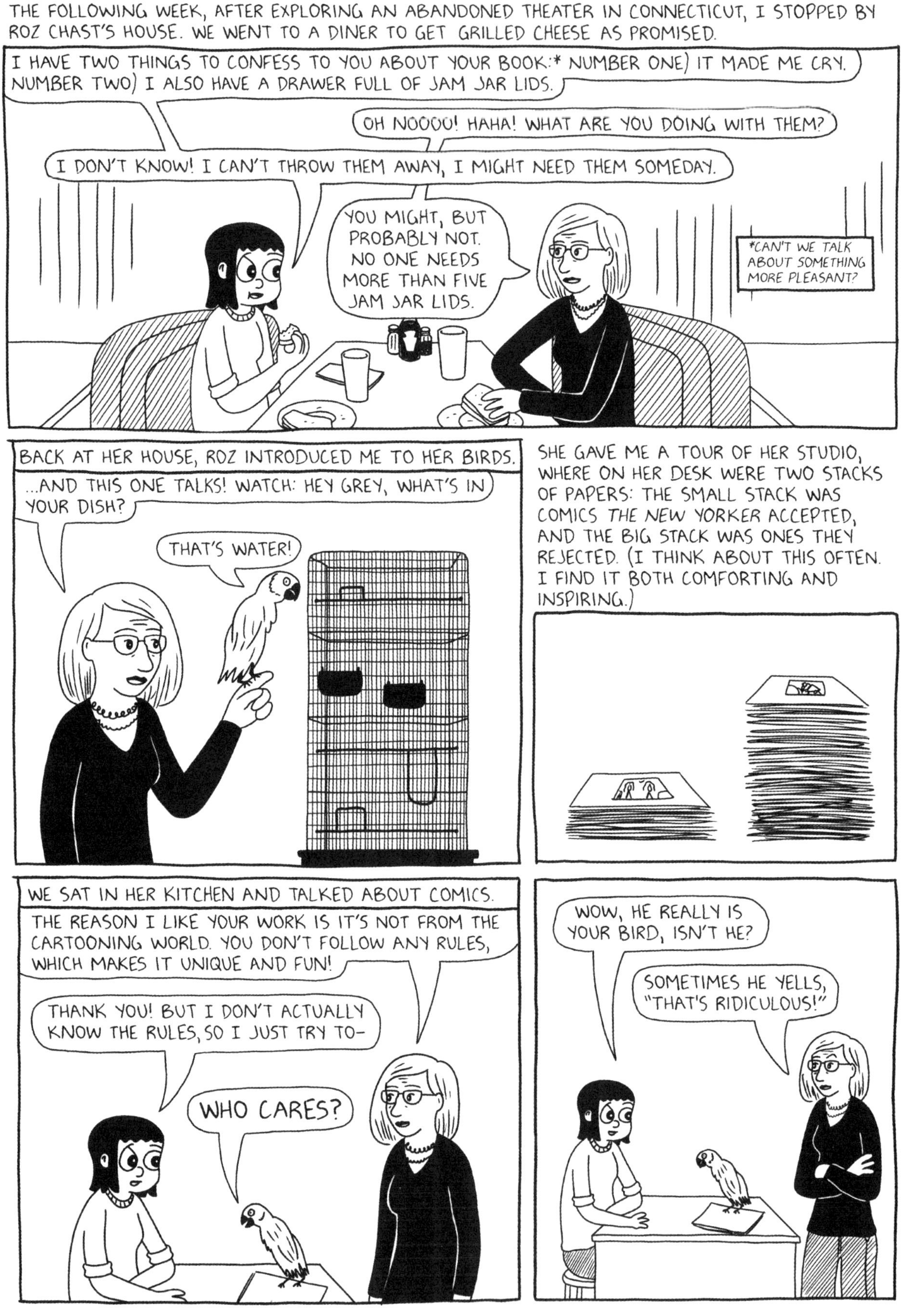
THE FOLLOWING WEEK, AFTER EXPLORING AN ABANDONED THEATER IN CONNECTICUT, I STOPPED BY ROZ CHAST'S HOUSE. WE WENT TO A DINER TO GET GRILLED CHEESE AS PROMISED.
I HAVE TWO THINGS TO CONFESS TO YOU ABOUT YOUR BOOK:* NUMBER ONE) IT MADE ME CRY. NUMBER TWO) I ALSO HAVE A DRAWER FULL OF JAM JAR LIDS.
OH NOOOO! HAHA! WHAT ARE YOU DOING WITH THEM?
I DON'T KNOW! I CAN'T THROW THEM AWAY, I MIGHT NEED THEM SOMEDAY.
YOU MIGHT, BUT PROBABLY NOT. NO ONE NEEDS MORE THAN FIVE JAM JAR LIDS.
*CAN'T WE TALK ABOUT SOMETHING MORE PLEASANT?
BACK AT HER HOUSE, ROZ INTRODUCED ME TO HER BIRDS.
...AND THIS ONE TALKS! WATCH: HEY GREY, WHAT'S IN YOUR DISH?
THAT'S WATER!
SHE GAVE ME A TOUR OF HER STUDIO, WHERE ON HER DESK WERE TWO STACKS OF PAPERS: THE SMALL STACK WAS COMICS THE NEW YORKER ACCEPTED, AND THE BIG STACK WAS ONES THEY REJECTED. (I THINK ABOUT THIS OFTEN. I FIND IT BOTH COMFORTING AND INSPIRING.)
WE SAT IN HER KITCHEN AND TALKED ABOUT COMICS.
THE REASON I LIKE YOUR WORK IS IT'S NOT FROM THE CARTOONING WORLD. YOU DON'T FOLLOW ANY RULES, WHICH MAKES IT UNIQUE AND FUN!
THANK YOU! BUT I DON'T ACTUALLY KNOW THE RULES, SO I JUST TRY TO-
WHO CARES?
WOW, HE REALLY IS YOUR BIRD, ISN'T HE?
SOMETIMES HE YELLS, "THAT'S RIDICULOUS!"

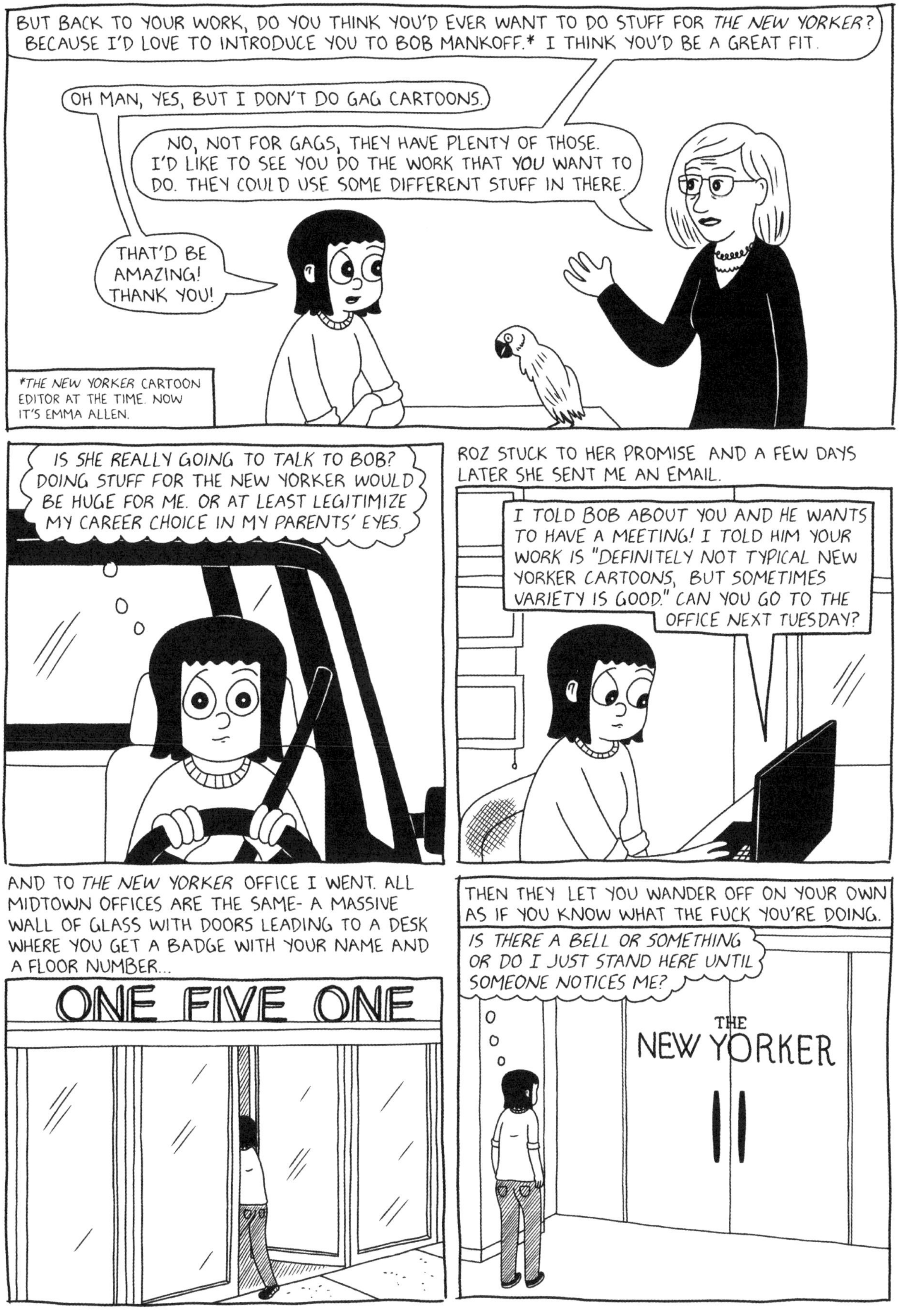
BUT BACK TO YOUR WORK, DO YOU THINK YOU'D EVER WANT TO DO STUFF FOR *THE NEW YORKER*? BECAUSE I'D LOVE TO INTRODUCE YOU TO BOB MANKOFF.* I THINK YOU'D BE A GREAT FIT.
OH MAN, YES, BUT I DON'T DO GAG CARTOONS.
NO, NOT FOR GAGS, THEY HAVE PLENTY OF THOSE. I'D LIKE TO SEE YOU DO THE WORK THAT *YOU* WANT TO DO. THEY COULD USE SOME DIFFERENT STUFF IN THERE.
THAT'D BE AMAZING! THANK YOU!
*THE NEW YORKER CARTOON EDITOR AT THE TIME. NOW IT'S EMMA ALLEN.
IS SHE REALLY GOING TO TALK TO BOB? DOING STUFF FOR THE NEW YORKER WOULD BE HUGE FOR ME. OR AT LEAST LEGITIMIZE MY CAREER CHOICE IN MY PARENTS' EYES.
ROZ STUCK TO HER PROMISE AND A FEW DAYS LATER SHE SENT ME AN EMAIL.
I TOLD BOB ABOUT YOU AND HE WANTS TO HAVE A MEETING! I TOLD HIM YOUR WORK IS "DEFINITELY NOT TYPICAL NEW YORKER CARTOONS, BUT SOMETIMES VARIETY IS GOOD." CAN YOU GO TO THE OFFICE NEXT TUESDAY?
AND TO *THE NEW YORKER* OFFICE I WENT. ALL MIDTOWN OFFICES ARE THE SAME- A MASSIVE WALL OF GLASS WITH DOORS LEADING TO A DESK WHERE YOU GET A BADGE WITH YOUR NAME AND A FLOOR NUMBER...
ONE FIVE ONE
THEN THEY LET YOU WANDER OFF ON YOUR OWN AS IF YOU KNOW WHAT THE FUCK YOU'RE DOING.
IS THERE A BELL OR SOMETHING OR DO I JUST STAND HERE UNTIL SOMEONE NOTICES ME?
THE NEW YORKER

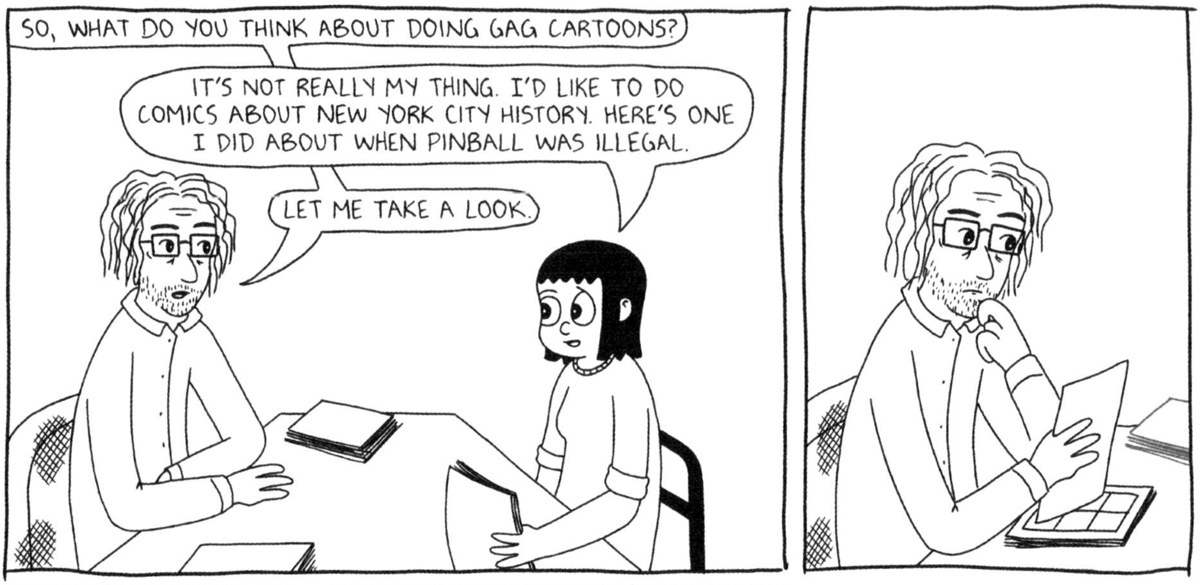
SO, WHAT DO YOU THINK ABOUT DOING GAG CARTOONS?
IT'S NOT REALLY MY THING. I'D LIKE TO DO COMICS ABOUT NEW YORK CITY HISTORY. HERE'S ONE I DID ABOUT WHEN PINBALL WAS ILLEGAL.
LET ME TAKE A LOOK.

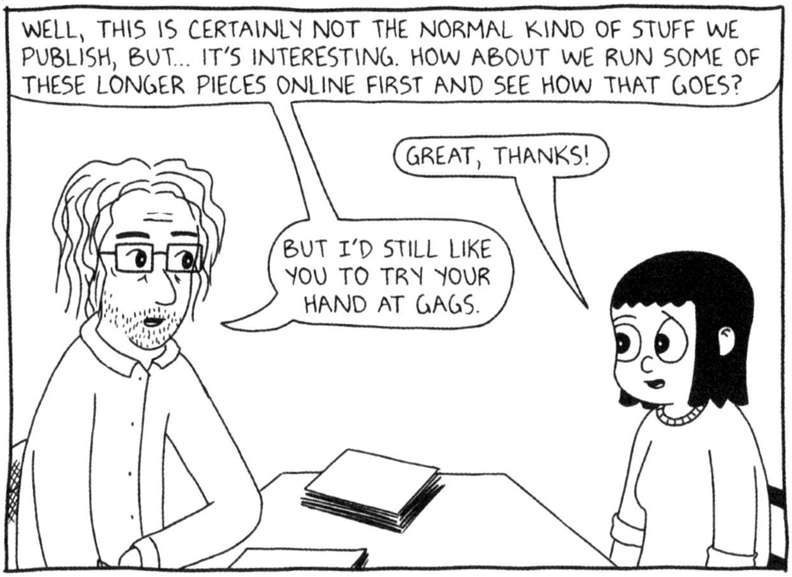
WELL, THIS IS CERTAINLY NOT THE NORMAL KIND OF STUFF WE PUBLISH, BUT... IT'S INTERESTING. HOW ABOUT WE RUN SOME OF THESE LONGER PIECES ONLINE FIRST AND SEE HOW THAT GOES?
GREAT, THANKS!
BUT I'D STILL LIKE YOU TO TRY YOUR HAND AT GAGS.

FOR TWO MONTHS, I WROTE, DREW, AND PITCHED GAG CARTOONS TO BOB, BUT I COULDN'T WITHSTAND THE PERPETUAL REJECTION PROCESS. IT WASN'T THE REJECTION OF MY WORK THAT I COULDN'T HANDLE, IT WAS THE AMOUNT OF TIME IT TOOK TO MAKE THAT WORK, ONLY TO GET REJECTED AND HAVE TO START OVER. I HAD RENT TO PAY AND ILLUSTRATION GIGS TO COMPLETE. EVENTUALLY I THREW IN THE TOWEL, BUT NOT BEFORE BOB ACCEPTED AND PUBLISHED ONE GAG CARTOON I WROTE WITH MY OLDER BROTHER.

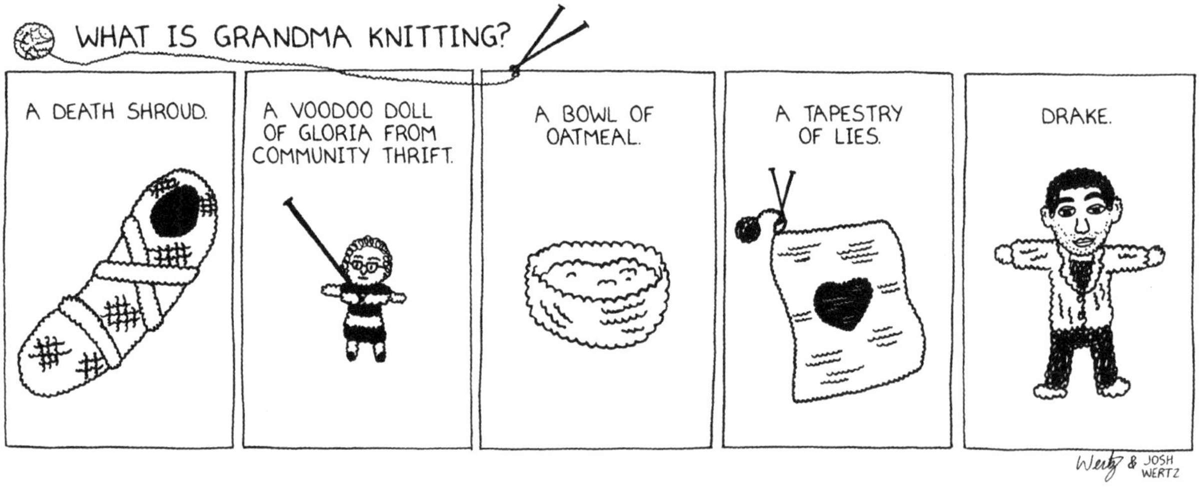
WHAT IS GRANDMA KNITTING?
A DEATH SHROUD.
A VOODOO DOLL OF GLORIA FROM COMMUNITY THRIFT.
A BOWL OF OATMEAL.
A TAPESTRY OF LIES.
DRAKE.
Wertz & JOSH WERTZ

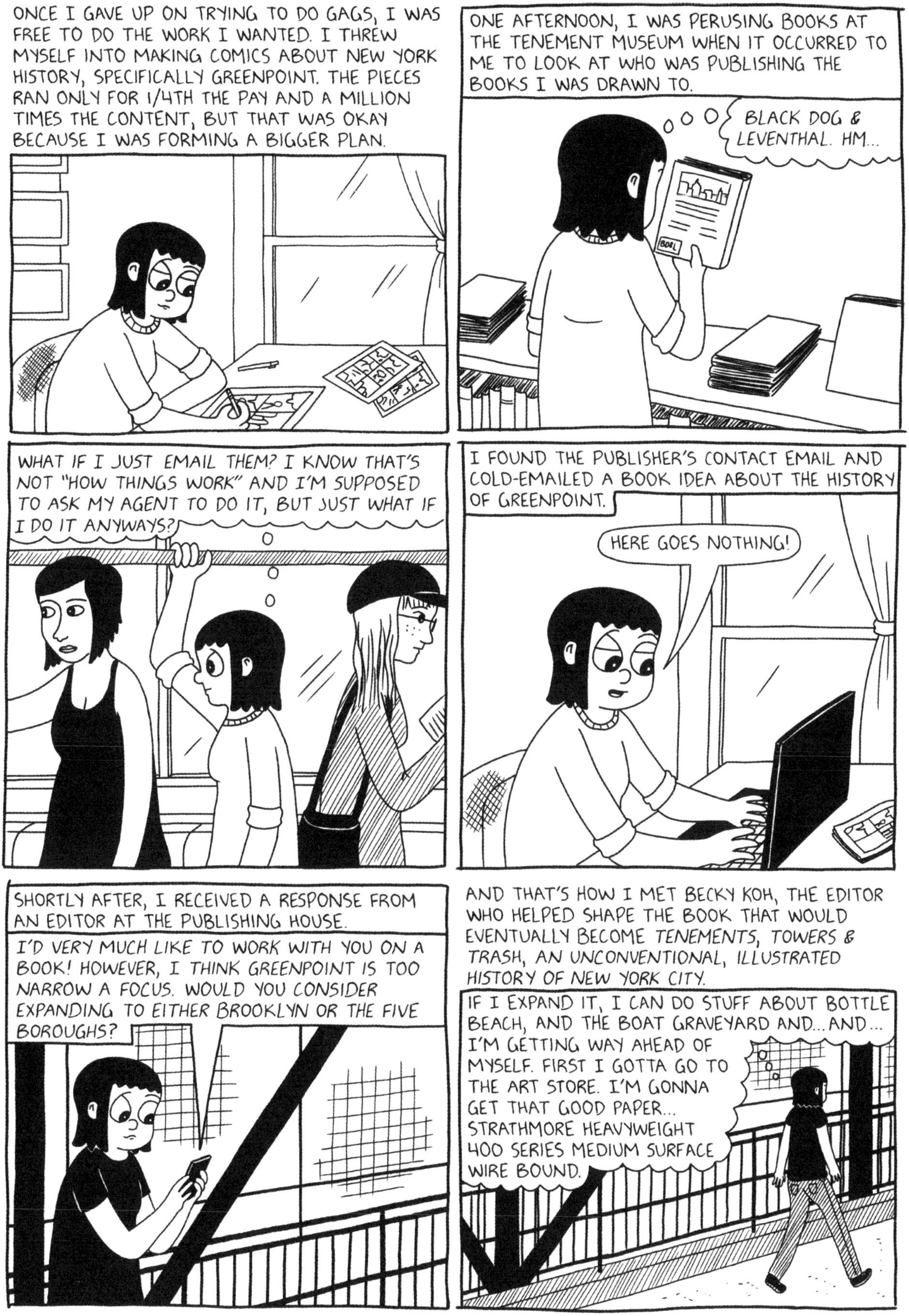
ONCE I GAVE UP ON TRYING TO DO GAGS, I WAS FREE TO DO THE WORK I WANTED. I THREW MYSELF INTO MAKING COMICS ABOUT NEW YORK HISTORY, SPECIFICALLY GREENPOINT. THE PIECES RAN ONLY FOR 1/4TH THE PAY AND A MILLION TIMES THE CONTENT, BUT THAT WAS OKAY BECAUSE I WAS FORMING A BIGGER PLAN.
ONE AFTERNOON, I WAS PERUSING BOOKS AT THE TENEMENT MUSEUM WHEN IT OCCURRED TO ME TO LOOK AT WHO WAS PUBLISHING THE BOOKS I WAS DRAWN TO.
BLACK DOG & LEVENTHAL. HM...
BD&L
WHAT IF I JUST EMAIL THEM? I KNOW THAT'S NOT "HOW THINGS WORK" AND I'M SUPPOSED TO ASK MY AGENT TO DO IT, BUT JUST WHAT IF I DO IT ANYWAYS?
I FOUND THE PUBLISHER'S CONTACT EMAIL AND COLD-EMAILED A BOOK IDEA ABOUT THE HISTORY OF GREENPOINT.
HERE GOES NOTHING!
SHORTLY AFTER, I RECEIVED A RESPONSE FROM AN EDITOR AT THE PUBLISHING HOUSE.
I'D VERY MUCH LIKE TO WORK WITH YOU ON A BOOK! HOWEVER, I THINK GREENPOINT IS TOO NARROW A FOCUS. WOULD YOU CONSIDER EXPANDING TO EITHER BROOKLYN OR THE FIVE BOROUGHS?
AND THAT'S HOW I MET BECKY KOH, THE EDITOR WHO HELPED SHAPE THE BOOK THAT WOULD EVENTUALLY BECOME *TENEMENTS, TOWERS & TRASH*, AN UNCONVENTIONAL, ILLUSTRATED HISTORY OF NEW YORK CITY.
IF I EXPAND IT, I CAN DO STUFF ABOUT BOTTLE BEACH, AND THE BOAT GRAVEYARD AND... AND... I'M GETTING WAY AHEAD OF MYSELF. FIRST I GOTTA GO TO THE ART STORE. I'M GONNA GET THAT GOOD PAPER... STRATHMORE HEAVYWEIGHT 400 SERIES MEDIUM SURFACE WIRE BOUND.

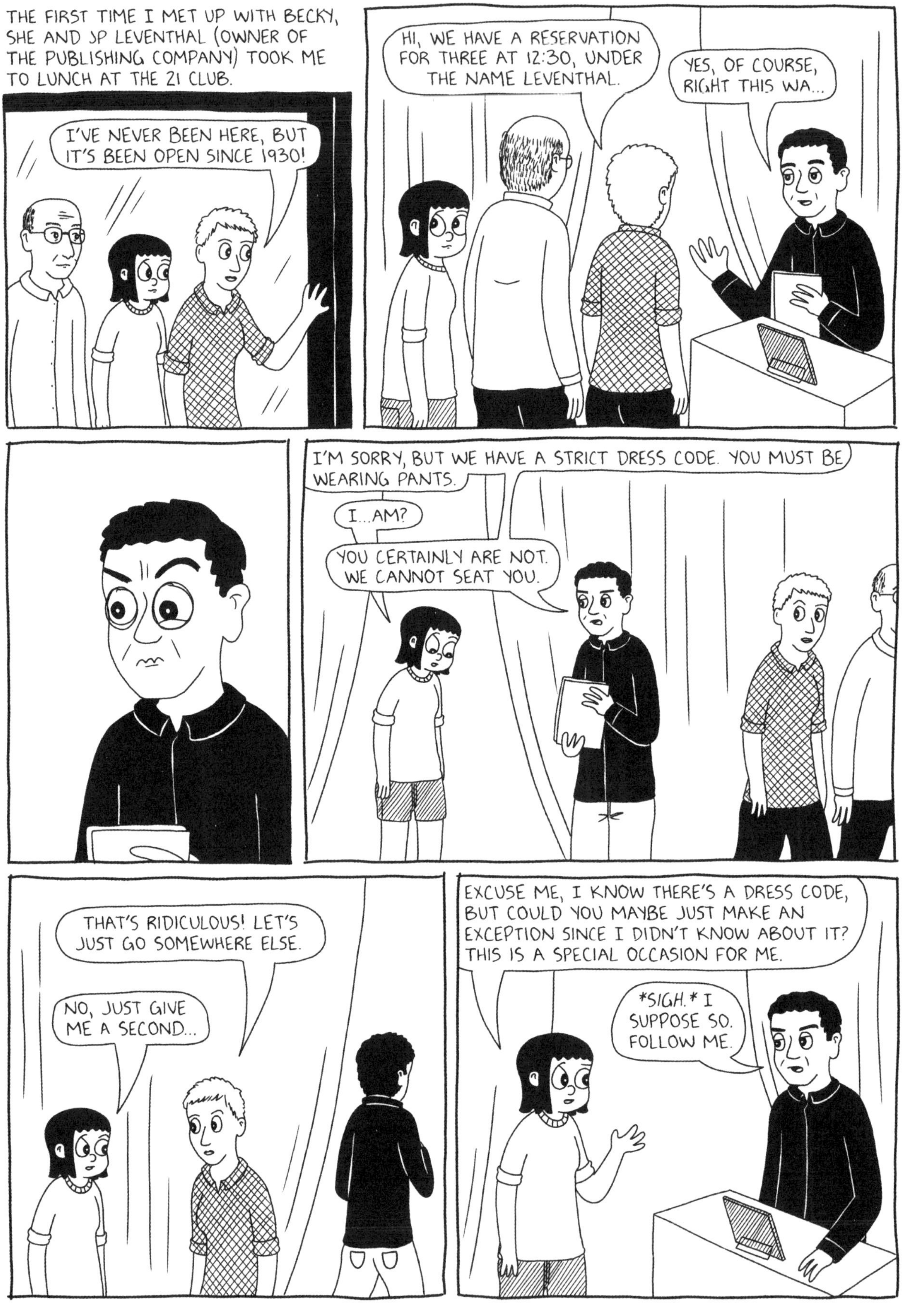
THE FIRST TIME I MET UP WITH BECKY, SHE AND JP LEVENTHAL (OWNER OF THE PUBLISHING COMPANY) TOOK ME TO LUNCH AT THE 21 CLUB.
I'VE NEVER BEEN HERE, BUT IT'S BEEN OPEN SINCE 1930!
HI, WE HAVE A RESERVATION FOR THREE AT 12:30, UNDER THE NAME LEVENTHAL.
YES, OF COURSE, RIGHT THIS WA...
I'M SORRY, BUT WE HAVE A STRICT DRESS CODE. YOU MUST BE WEARING PANTS.
I...AM?
YOU CERTAINLY ARE NOT. WE CANNOT SEAT YOU.
THAT'S RIDICULOUS! LET'S JUST GO SOMEWHERE ELSE.
NO, JUST GIVE ME A SECOND...
EXCUSE ME, I KNOW THERE'S A DRESS CODE, BUT COULD YOU MAYBE JUST MAKE AN EXCEPTION SINCE I DIDN'T KNOW ABOUT IT? THIS IS A SPECIAL OCCASION FOR ME.
SIGH. I SUPPOSE SO. FOLLOW ME.

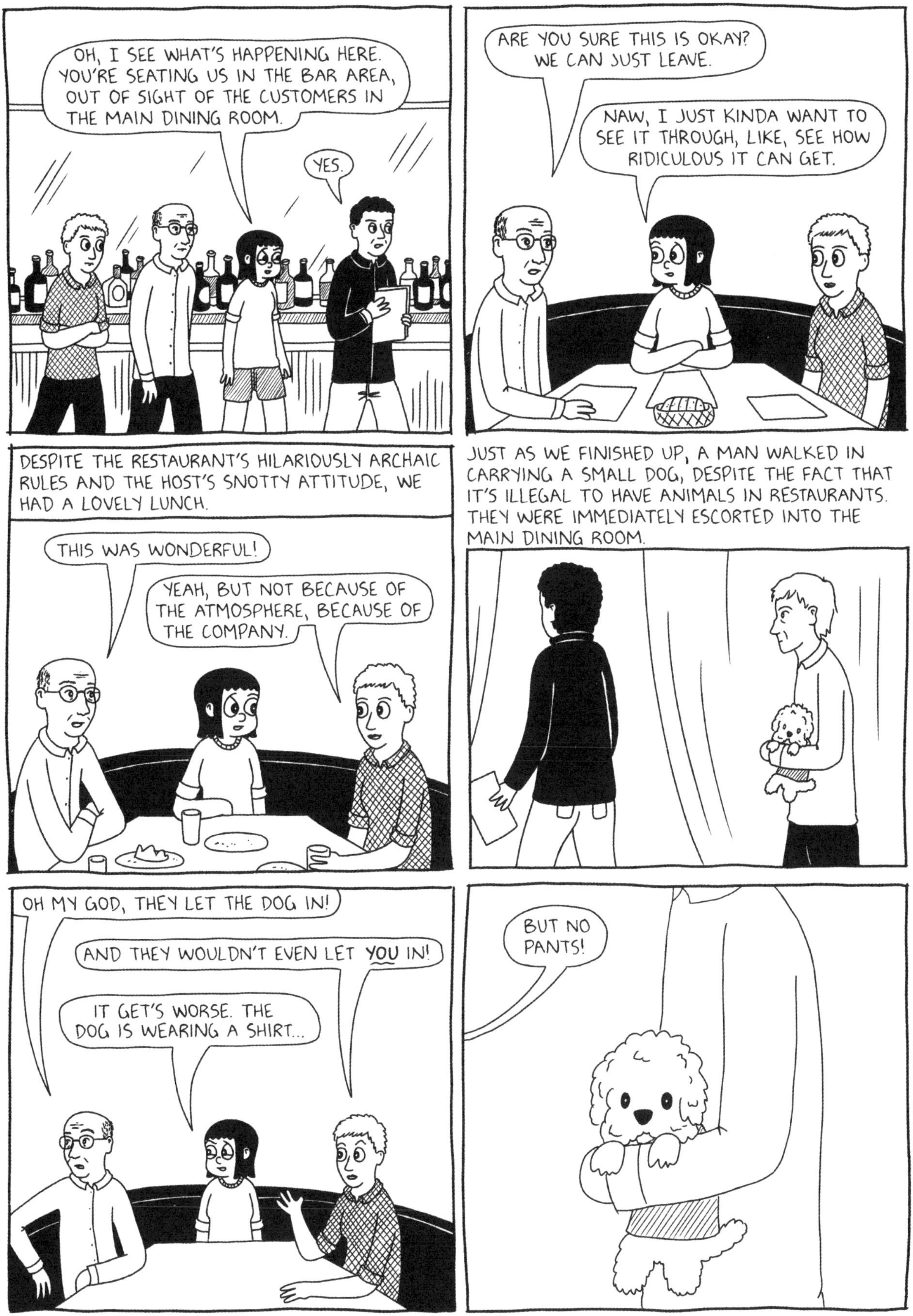
OH, I SEE WHAT'S HAPPENING HERE. YOU'RE SEATING US IN THE BAR AREA, OUT OF SIGHT OF THE CUSTOMERS IN THE MAIN DINING ROOM.
YES.
ARE YOU SURE THIS IS OKAY? WE CAN JUST LEAVE.
NAW, I JUST KINDA WANT TO SEE IT THROUGH, LIKE, SEE HOW RIDICULOUS IT CAN GET.
DESPITE THE RESTAURANT'S HILARIOUSLY ARCHAIC RULES AND THE HOST'S SNOTTY ATTITUDE, WE HAD A LOVELY LUNCH.
THIS WAS WONDERFUL!
YEAH, BUT NOT BECAUSE OF THE ATMOSPHERE, BECAUSE OF THE COMPANY.
JUST AS WE FINISHED UP, A MAN WALKED IN CARRYING A SMALL DOG, DESPITE THE FACT THAT IT'S ILLEGAL TO HAVE ANIMALS IN RESTAURANTS. THEY WERE IMMEDIATELY ESCORTED INTO THE MAIN DINING ROOM.
OH MY GOD, THEY LET THE DOG IN!
AND THEY WOULDN'T EVEN LET YOU IN!
IT GET'S WORSE. THE DOG IS WEARING A SHIRT...
BUT NO PANTS!

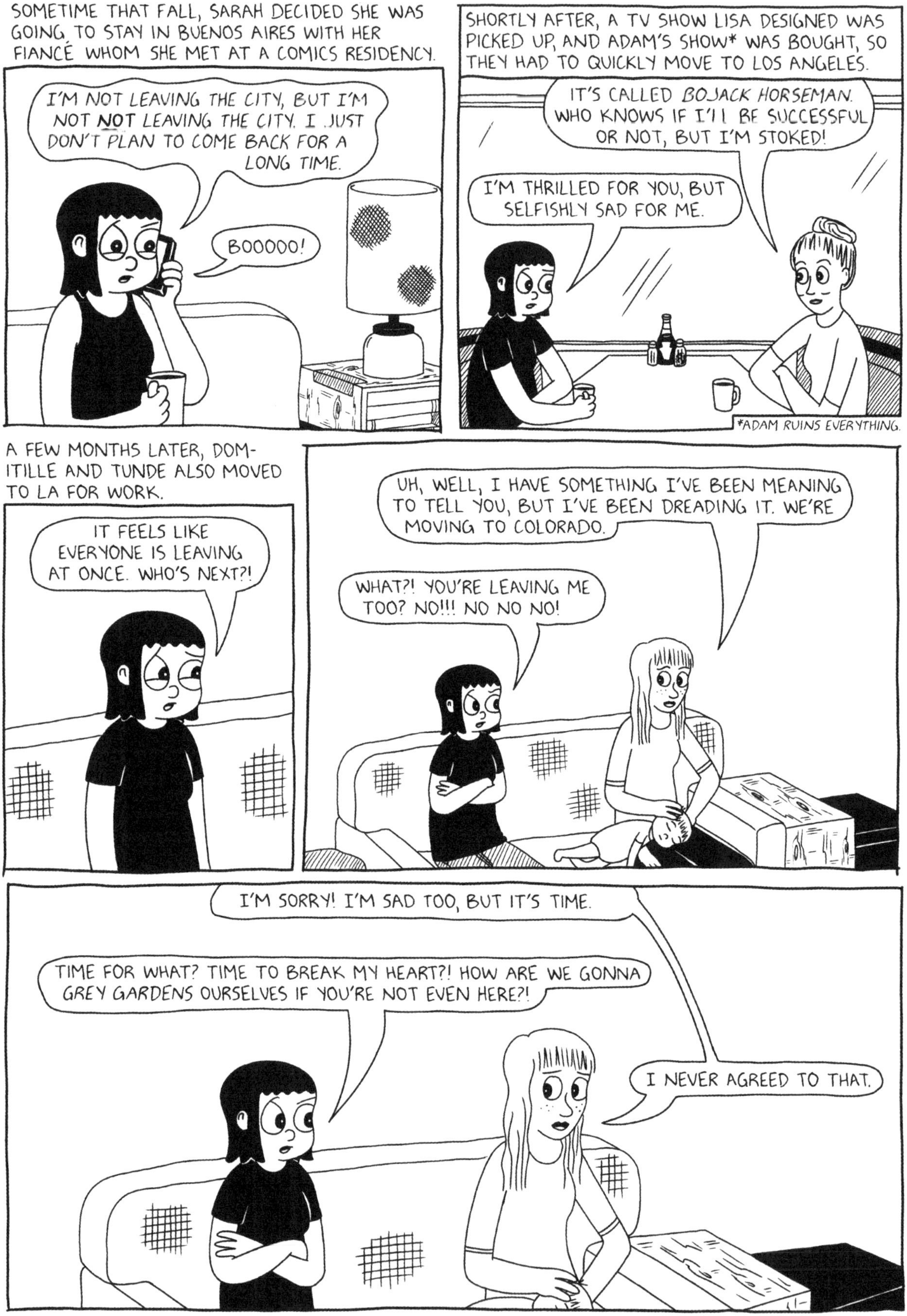
SOMETIME THAT FALL, SARAH DECIDED SHE WAS GOING TO STAY IN BUENOS AIRES WITH HER FIANCÉ WHOM SHE MET AT A COMICS RESIDENCY.
I'M NOT LEAVING THE CITY, BUT I'M NOT **NOT** LEAVING THE CITY. I JUST DON'T PLAN TO COME BACK FOR A LONG TIME.
BOOOOO!
SHORTLY AFTER, A TV SHOW LISA DESIGNED WAS PICKED UP, AND ADAM'S SHOW* WAS BOUGHT, SO THEY HAD TO QUICKLY MOVE TO LOS ANGELES.
IT'S CALLED *BOJACK HORSEMAN*. WHO KNOWS IF I'LL BE SUCCESSFUL OR NOT, BUT I'M STOKED!
I'M THRILLED FOR YOU, BUT SELFISHLY SAD FOR ME.
*ADAM RUINS EVERYTHING.
A FEW MONTHS LATER, DOM-ITILLE AND TUNDE ALSO MOVED TO LA FOR WORK.
IT FEELS LIKE EVERYONE IS LEAVING AT ONCE. WHO'S NEXT?!
UH, WELL, I HAVE SOMETHING I'VE BEEN MEANING TO TELL YOU, BUT I'VE BEEN DREADING IT. WE'RE MOVING TO COLORADO.
WHAT?! YOU'RE LEAVING ME TOO? NO!!! NO NO NO!
I'M SORRY! I'M SAD TOO, BUT IT'S TIME.
TIME FOR WHAT? TIME TO BREAK MY HEART?! HOW ARE WE GONNA GREY GARDENS OURSELVES IF YOU'RE NOT EVEN HERE?!
I NEVER AGREED TO THAT.

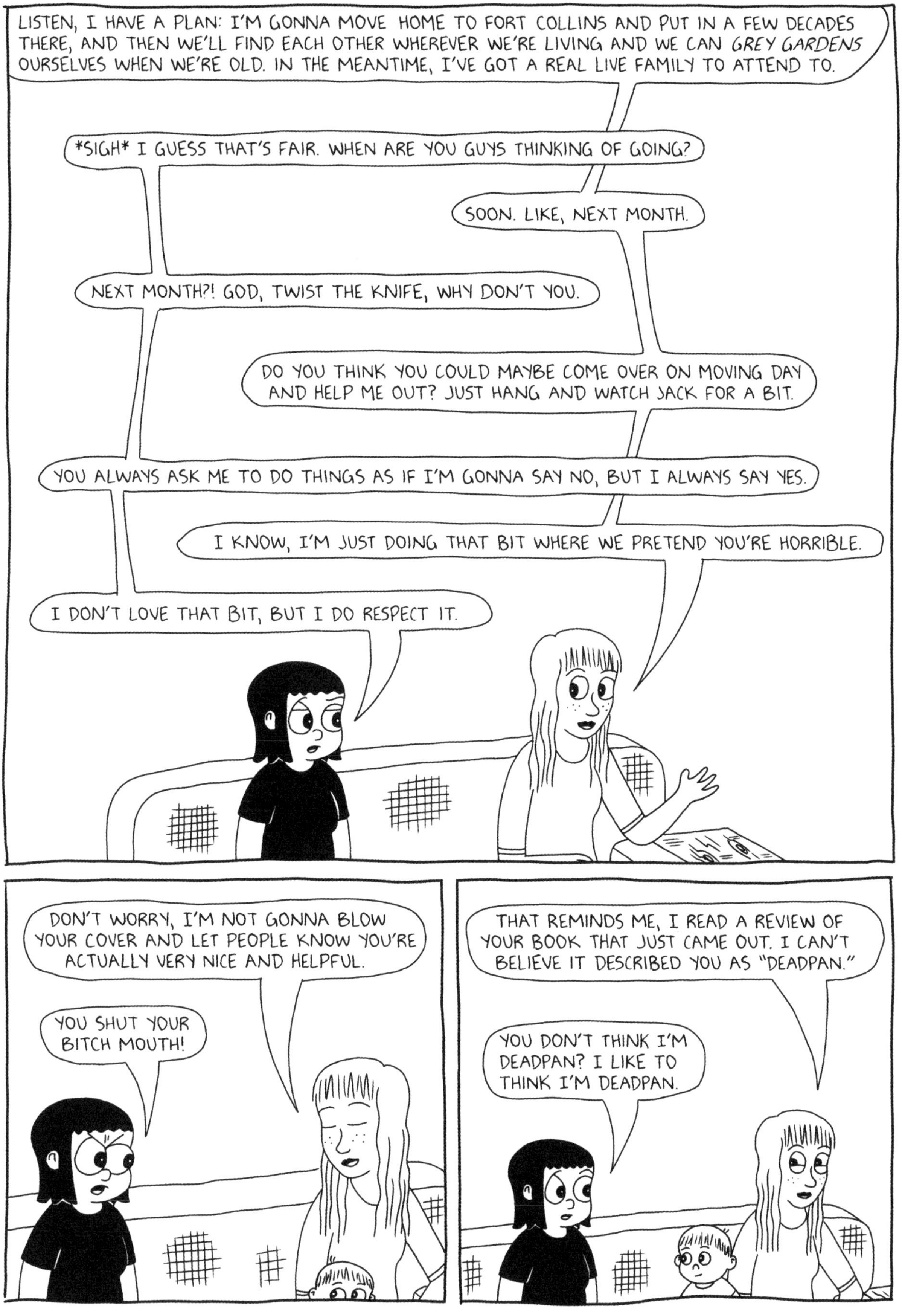
LISTEN, I HAVE A PLAN: I'M GONNA MOVE HOME TO FORT COLLINS AND PUT IN A FEW DECADES THERE, AND THEN WE'LL FIND EACH OTHER WHEREVER WE'RE LIVING AND WE CAN *GREY GARDENS* OURSELVES WHEN WE'RE OLD. IN THE MEANTIME, I'VE GOT A REAL LIVE FAMILY TO ATTEND TO.
SIGH I GUESS THAT'S FAIR. WHEN ARE YOU GUYS THINKING OF GOING?
SOON. LIKE, NEXT MONTH.
NEXT MONTH?! GOD, TWIST THE KNIFE, WHY DON'T YOU.
DO YOU THINK YOU COULD MAYBE COME OVER ON MOVING DAY AND HELP ME OUT? JUST HANG AND WATCH JACK FOR A BIT.
YOU ALWAYS ASK ME TO DO THINGS AS IF I'M GONNA SAY NO, BUT I ALWAYS SAY YES.
I KNOW, I'M JUST DOING THAT BIT WHERE WE PRETEND YOU'RE HORRIBLE.
I DON'T LOVE THAT BIT, BUT I DO RESPECT IT.
DON'T WORRY, I'M NOT GONNA BLOW YOUR COVER AND LET PEOPLE KNOW YOU'RE ACTUALLY VERY NICE AND HELPFUL.
YOU SHUT YOUR BITCH MOUTH!
THAT REMINDS ME, I READ A REVIEW OF YOUR BOOK THAT JUST CAME OUT. I CAN'T BELIEVE IT DESCRIBED YOU AS "DEADPAN."
YOU DON'T THINK I'M DEADPAN? I LIKE TO THINK I'M DEADPAN.

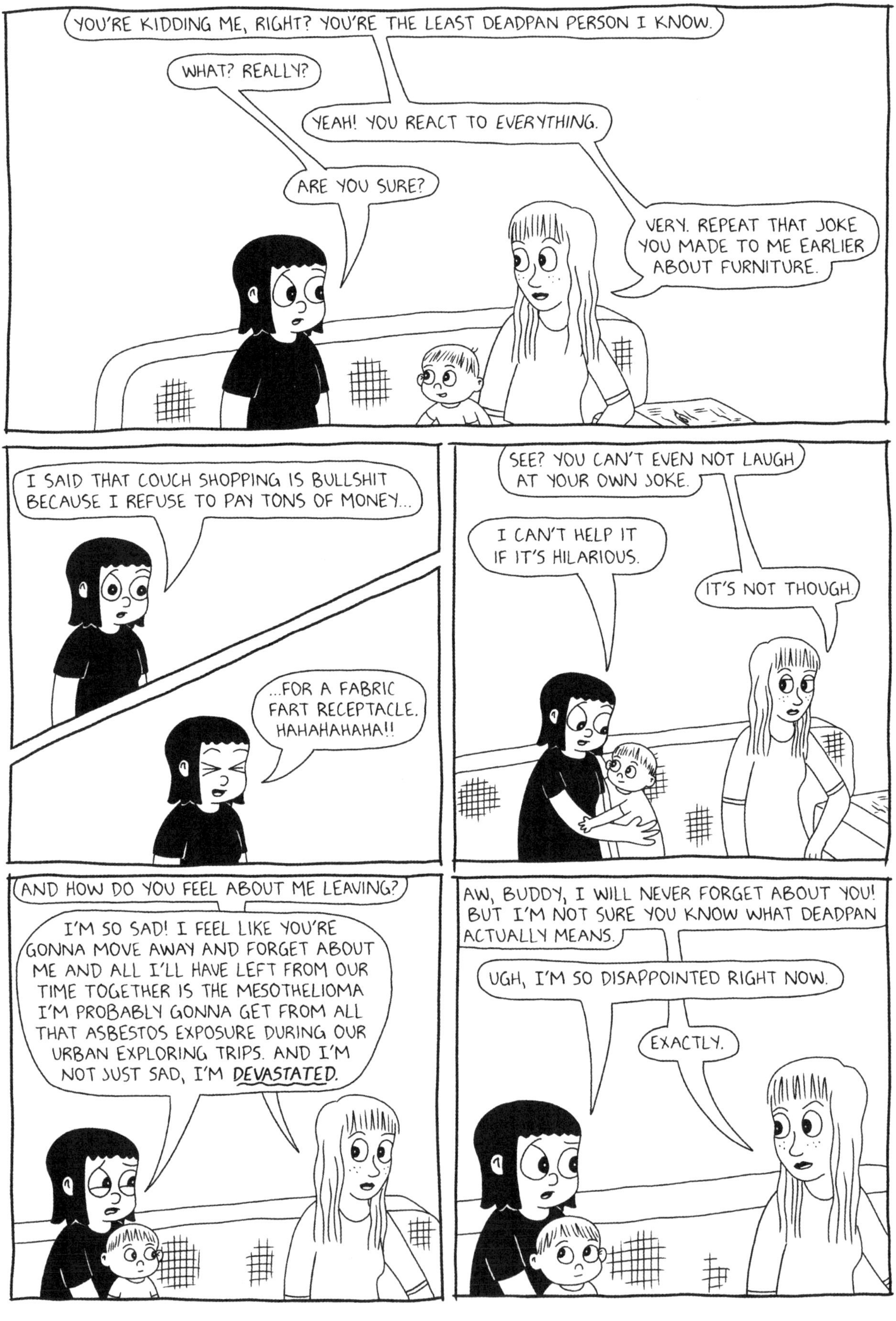
YOU'RE KIDDING ME, RIGHT? YOU'RE THE LEAST DEADPAN PERSON I KNOW.
WHAT? REALLY?
YEAH! YOU REACT TO EVERYTHING.
ARE YOU SURE?
VERY. REPEAT THAT JOKE YOU MADE TO ME EARLIER ABOUT FURNITURE.
I SAID THAT COUCH SHOPPING IS BULLSHIT BECAUSE I REFUSE TO PAY TONS OF MONEY...
...FOR A FABRIC FART RECEPTACLE. HAHAHAHAHA!!
SEE? YOU CAN'T EVEN NOT LAUGH AT YOUR OWN JOKE.
I CAN'T HELP IT IF IT'S HILARIOUS.
IT'S NOT THOUGH.
AND HOW DO YOU FEEL ABOUT ME LEAVING?
I'M SO SAD! I FEEL LIKE YOU'RE GONNA MOVE AWAY AND FORGET ABOUT ME AND ALL I'LL HAVE LEFT FROM OUR TIME TOGETHER IS THE MESOTHELIOMA I'M PROBABLY GONNA GET FROM ALL THAT ASBESTOS EXPOSURE DURING OUR URBAN EXPLORING TRIPS. AND I'M NOT JUST SAD, I'M DEVASTATED.
AW, BUDDY, I WILL NEVER FORGET ABOUT YOU! BUT I'M NOT SURE YOU KNOW WHAT DEADPAN ACTUALLY MEANS.
UGH, I'M SO DISAPPOINTED RIGHT NOW.
EXACTLY.

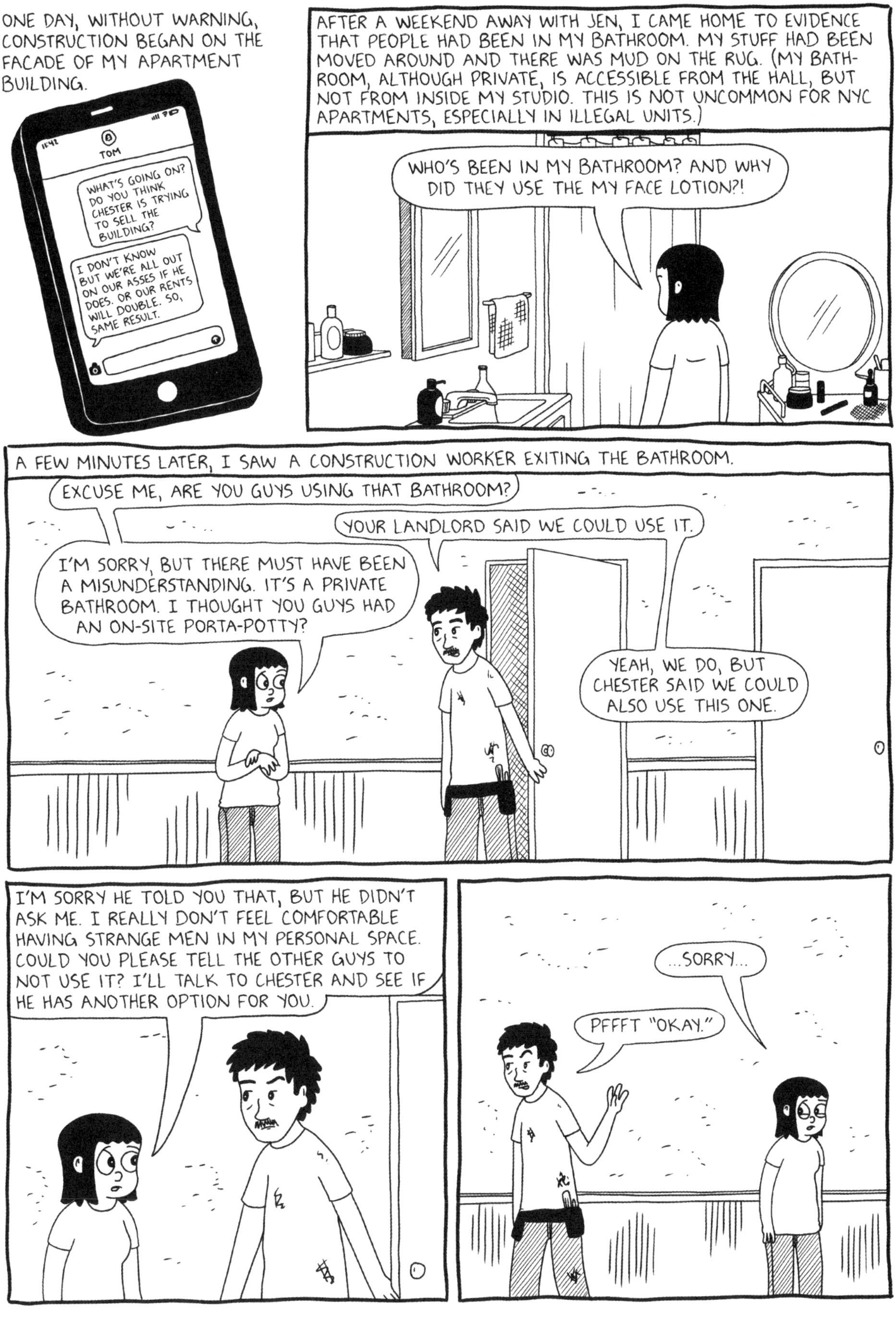
ONE DAY, WITHOUT WARNING, CONSTRUCTION BEGAN ON THE FACADE OF MY APARTMENT BUILDING.
TOM
WHAT'S GOING ON? DO YOU THINK CHESTER IS TRYING TO SELL THE BUILDING?
I DON'T KNOW BUT WE'RE ALL OUT ON OUR ASSES IF HE DOES. OR OUR RENTS WILL DOUBLE. SO, SAME RESULT.
AFTER A WEEKEND AWAY WITH JEN, I CAME HOME TO EVIDENCE THAT PEOPLE HAD BEEN IN MY BATHROOM. MY STUFF HAD BEEN MOVED AROUND AND THERE WAS MUD ON THE RUG. (MY BATHROOM, ALTHOUGH PRIVATE, IS ACCESSIBLE FROM THE HALL, BUT NOT FROM INSIDE MY STUDIO. THIS IS NOT UNCOMMON FOR NYC APARTMENTS, ESPECIALLY IN ILLEGAL UNITS.)
WHO'S BEEN IN MY BATHROOM? AND WHY DID THEY USE THE MY FACE LOTION?!
A FEW MINUTES LATER, I SAW A CONSTRUCTION WORKER EXITING THE BATHROOM.
EXCUSE ME, ARE YOU GUYS USING THAT BATHROOM?
YOUR LANDLORD SAID WE COULD USE IT.
I'M SORRY, BUT THERE MUST HAVE BEEN A MISUNDERSTANDING. IT'S A PRIVATE BATHROOM. I THOUGHT YOU GUYS HAD AN ON-SITE PORTA-POTTY?
YEAH, WE DO, BUT CHESTER SAID WE COULD ALSO USE THIS ONE.
I'M SORRY HE TOLD YOU THAT, BUT HE DIDN'T ASK ME. I REALLY DON'T FEEL COMFORTABLE HAVING STRANGE MEN IN MY PERSONAL SPACE. COULD YOU PLEASE TELL THE OTHER GUYS TO NOT USE IT? I'LL TALK TO CHESTER AND SEE IF HE HAS ANOTHER OPTION FOR YOU.
...SORRY...
PFFFT "OKAY."

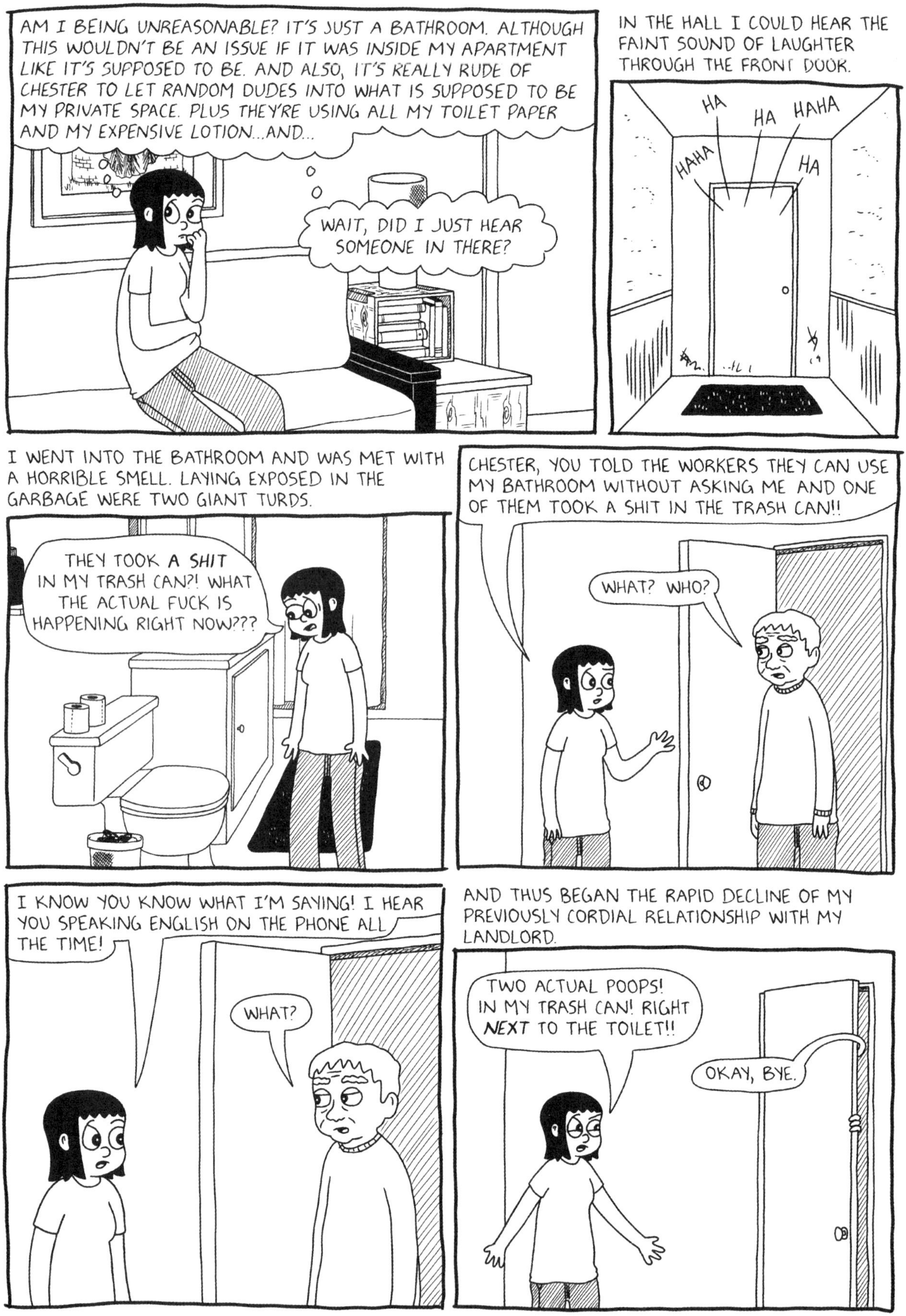
AM I BEING UNREASONABLE? IT'S JUST A BATHROOM. ALTHOUGH THIS WOULDN'T BE AN ISSUE IF IT WAS INSIDE MY APARTMENT LIKE IT'S SUPPOSED TO BE. AND ALSO, IT'S REALLY RUDE OF CHESTER TO LET RANDOM DUDES INTO WHAT IS SUPPOSED TO BE MY PRIVATE SPACE. PLUS THEY'RE USING ALL MY TOILET PAPER AND MY EXPENSIVE LOTION...AND...
WAIT, DID I JUST HEAR SOMEONE IN THERE?
IN THE HALL I COULD HEAR THE FAINT SOUND OF LAUGHTER THROUGH THE FRONT DOOR.
HA
HA
HAHA
HAHA
HA
I WENT INTO THE BATHROOM AND WAS MET WITH A HORRIBLE SMELL. LAYING EXPOSED IN THE GARBAGE WERE TWO GIANT TURDS.
THEY TOOK A SHIT IN MY TRASH CAN?! WHAT THE ACTUAL FUCK IS HAPPENING RIGHT NOW???
CHESTER, YOU TOLD THE WORKERS THEY CAN USE MY BATHROOM WITHOUT ASKING ME AND ONE OF THEM TOOK A SHIT IN THE TRASH CAN!!
WHAT? WHO?
I KNOW YOU KNOW WHAT I'M SAYING! I HEAR YOU SPEAKING ENGLISH ON THE PHONE ALL THE TIME!
WHAT?
AND THUS BEGAN THE RAPID DECLINE OF MY PREVIOUSLY CORDIAL RELATIONSHIP WITH MY LANDLORD.
TWO ACTUAL POOPS! IN MY TRASH CAN! RIGHT NEXT TO THE TOILET!!
OKAY, BYE.

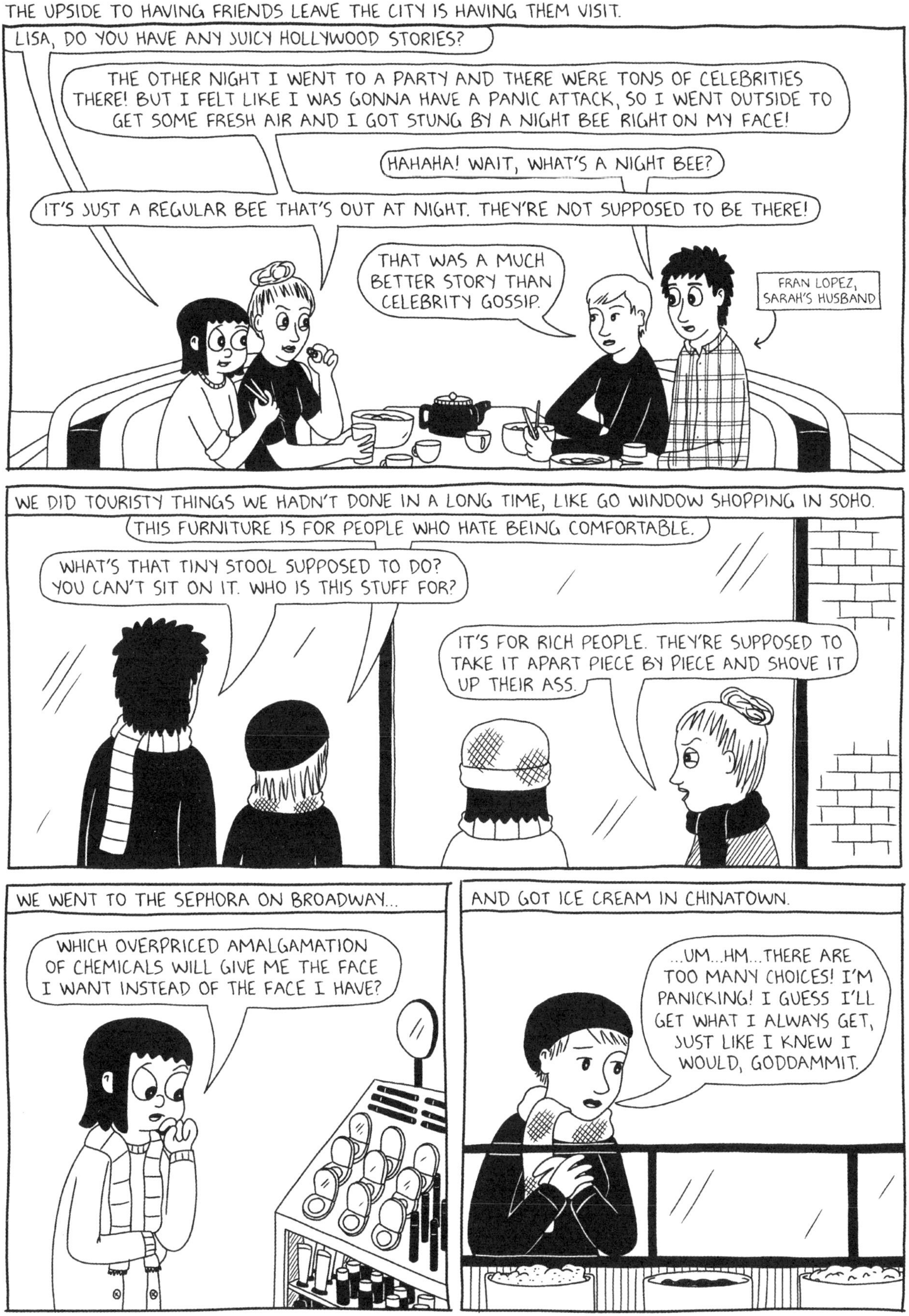
THE UPSIDE TO HAVING FRIENDS LEAVE THE CITY IS HAVING THEM VISIT.
LISA, DO YOU HAVE ANY JUICY HOLLYWOOD STORIES?
THE OTHER NIGHT I WENT TO A PARTY AND THERE WERE TONS OF CELEBRITIES THERE! BUT I FELT LIKE I WAS GONNA HAVE A PANIC ATTACK, SO I WENT OUTSIDE TO GET SOME FRESH AIR AND I GOT STUNG BY A NIGHT BEE RIGHT ON MY FACE!
HAHAHA! WAIT, WHAT'S A NIGHT BEE?
IT'S JUST A REGULAR BEE THAT'S OUT AT NIGHT. THEY'RE NOT SUPPOSED TO BE THERE!
THAT WAS A MUCH BETTER STORY THAN CELEBRITY GOSSIP.
FRAN LOPEZ, SARAH'S HUSBAND
WE DID TOURISTY THINGS WE HADN'T DONE IN A LONG TIME, LIKE GO WINDOW SHOPPING IN SOHO.
THIS FURNITURE IS FOR PEOPLE WHO HATE BEING COMFORTABLE.
WHAT'S THAT TINY STOOL SUPPOSED TO DO? YOU CAN'T SIT ON IT. WHO IS THIS STUFF FOR?
IT'S FOR RICH PEOPLE. THEY'RE SUPPOSED TO TAKE IT APART PIECE BY PIECE AND SHOVE IT UP THEIR ASS.
WE WENT TO THE SEPHORA ON BROADWAY...
WHICH OVERPRICED AMALGAMATION OF CHEMICALS WILL GIVE ME THE FACE I WANT INSTEAD OF THE FACE I HAVE?
AND GOT ICE CREAM IN CHINATOWN.
...UM...HM...THERE ARE TOO MANY CHOICES! I'M PANICKING! I GUESS I'LL GET WHAT I ALWAYS GET, JUST LIKE I KNEW I WOULD, GODDAMMIT.

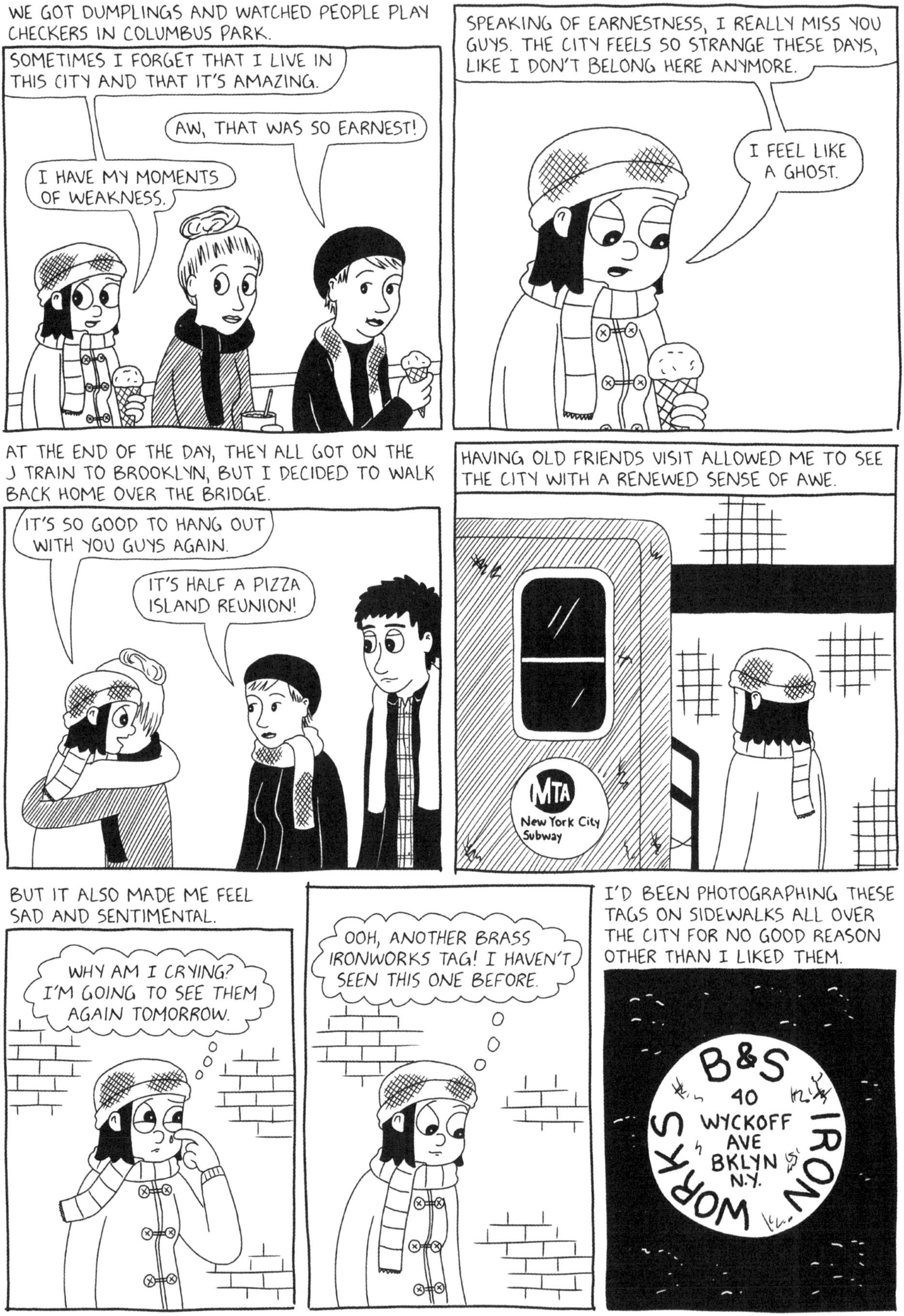
WE GOT DUMPLINGS AND WATCHED PEOPLE PLAY CHECKERS IN COLUMBUS PARK.
SOMETIMES I FORGET THAT I LIVE IN THIS CITY AND THAT IT'S AMAZING.
AW, THAT WAS SO EARNEST!
I HAVE MY MOMENTS OF WEAKNESS.
SPEAKING OF EARNESTNESS, I REALLY MISS YOU GUYS. THE CITY FEELS SO STRANGE THESE DAYS, LIKE I DON'T BELONG HERE ANYMORE.
I FEEL LIKE A GHOST.
AT THE END OF THE DAY, THEY ALL GOT ON THE J TRAIN TO BROOKLYN, BUT I DECIDED TO WALK BACK HOME OVER THE BRIDGE.
IT'S SO GOOD TO HANG OUT WITH YOU GUYS AGAIN.
IT'S HALF A PIZZA ISLAND REUNION!
HAVING OLD FRIENDS VISIT ALLOWED ME TO SEE THE CITY WITH A RENEWED SENSE OF AWE.
MTA
New York City Subway
BUT IT ALSO MADE ME FEEL SAD AND SENTIMENTAL.
WHY AM I CRYING? I'M GOING TO SEE THEM AGAIN TOMORROW.
OOH, ANOTHER BRASS IRONWORKS TAG! I HAVEN'T SEEN THIS ONE BEFORE.
I'D BEEN PHOTOGRAPHING THESE TAGS ON SIDEWALKS ALL OVER THE CITY FOR NO GOOD REASON OTHER THAN I LIKED THEM.
B&S
40
WYCKOFF
AVE
BKLYN
N.Y.
IRON
WORKS

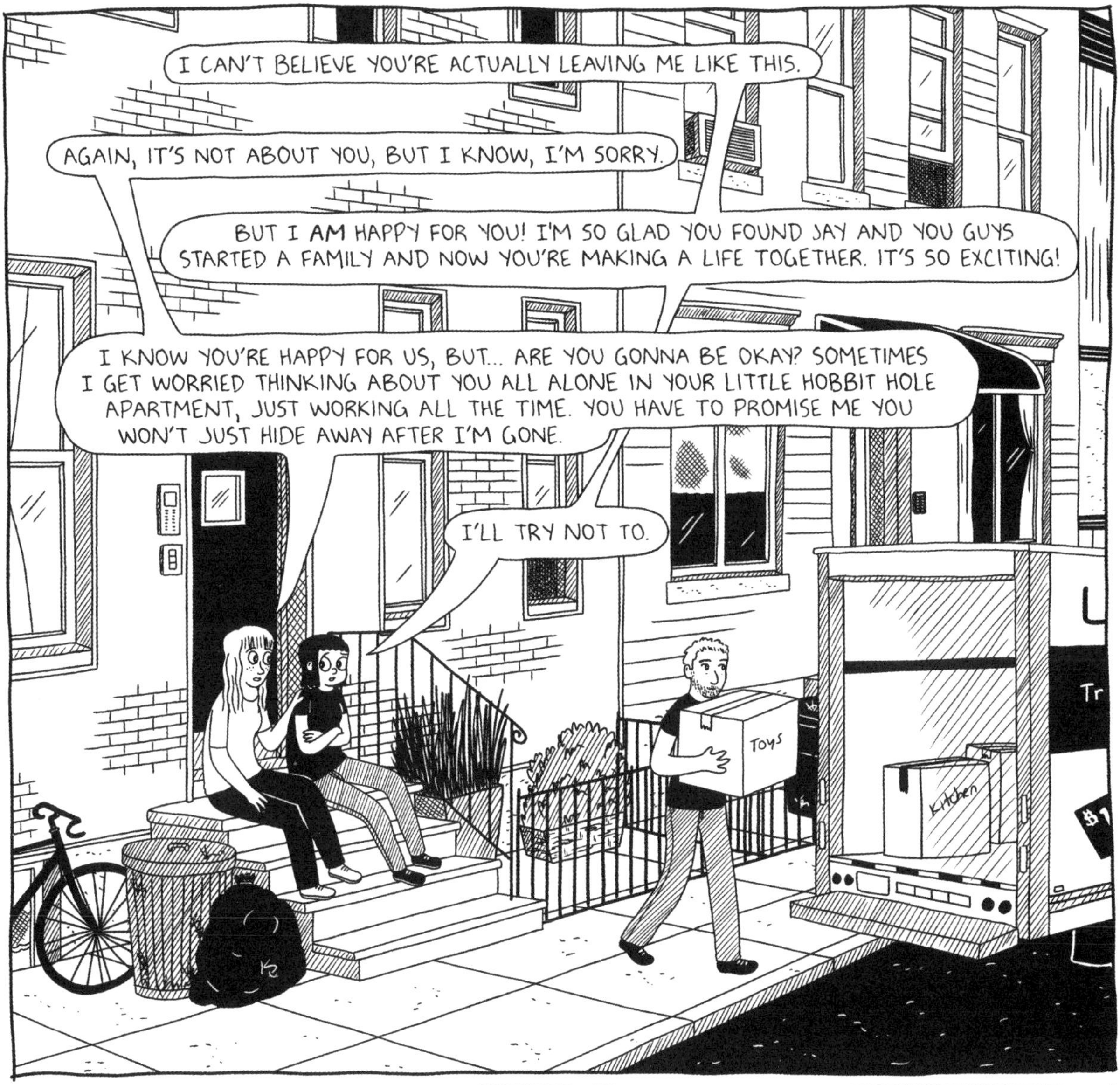
I CAN'T BELIEVE YOU'RE ACTUALLY LEAVING ME LIKE THIS.
AGAIN, IT'S NOT ABOUT YOU, BUT I KNOW, I'M SORRY.
BUT I **AM** HAPPY FOR YOU! I'M SO GLAD YOU FOUND JAY AND YOU GUYS STARTED A FAMILY AND NOW YOU'RE MAKING A LIFE TOGETHER. IT'S SO EXCITING!
I KNOW YOU'RE HAPPY FOR US, BUT... ARE YOU GONNA BE OKAY? SOMETIMES I GET WORRIED THINKING ABOUT YOU ALL ALONE IN YOUR LITTLE HOBBIT HOLE APARTMENT, JUST WORKING ALL THE TIME. YOU HAVE TO PROMISE ME YOU WON'T JUST HIDE AWAY AFTER I'M GONE.
I'LL TRY NOT TO.
Toys
Kitchen

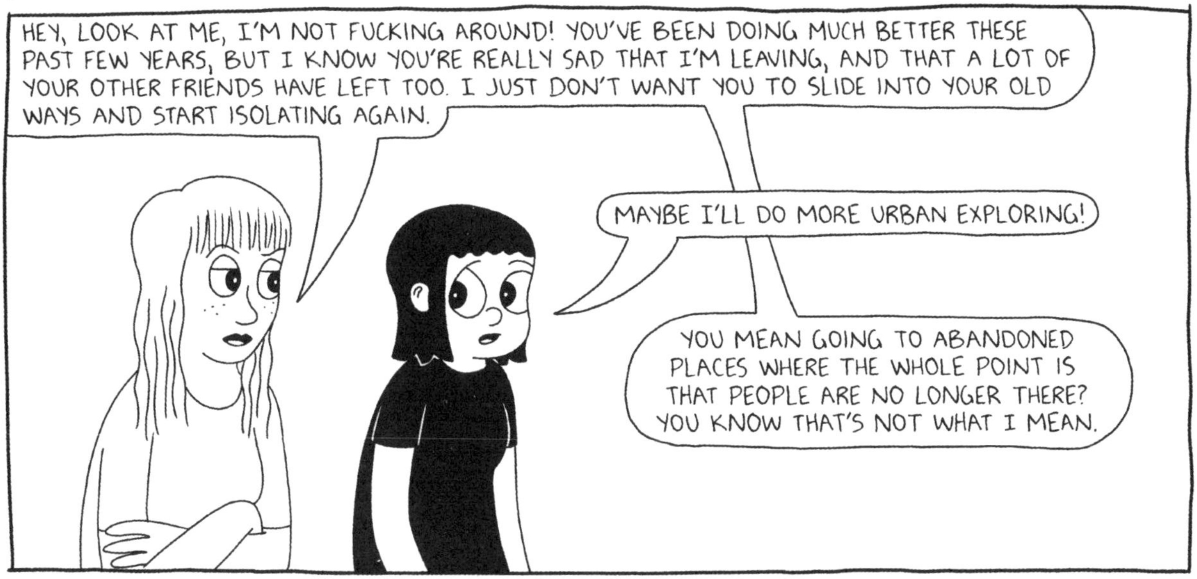
HEY, LOOK AT ME, I'M NOT FUCKING AROUND! YOU'VE BEEN DOING MUCH BETTER THESE PAST FEW YEARS, BUT I KNOW YOU'RE REALLY SAD THAT I'M LEAVING, AND THAT A LOT OF YOUR OTHER FRIENDS HAVE LEFT TOO. I JUST DON'T WANT YOU TO SLIDE INTO YOUR OLD WAYS AND START ISOLATING AGAIN.
MAYBE I'LL DO MORE URBAN EXPLORING!
YOU MEAN GOING TO ABANDONED PLACES WHERE THE WHOLE POINT IS THAT PEOPLE ARE NO LONGER THERE? YOU KNOW THAT'S NOT WHAT I MEAN.

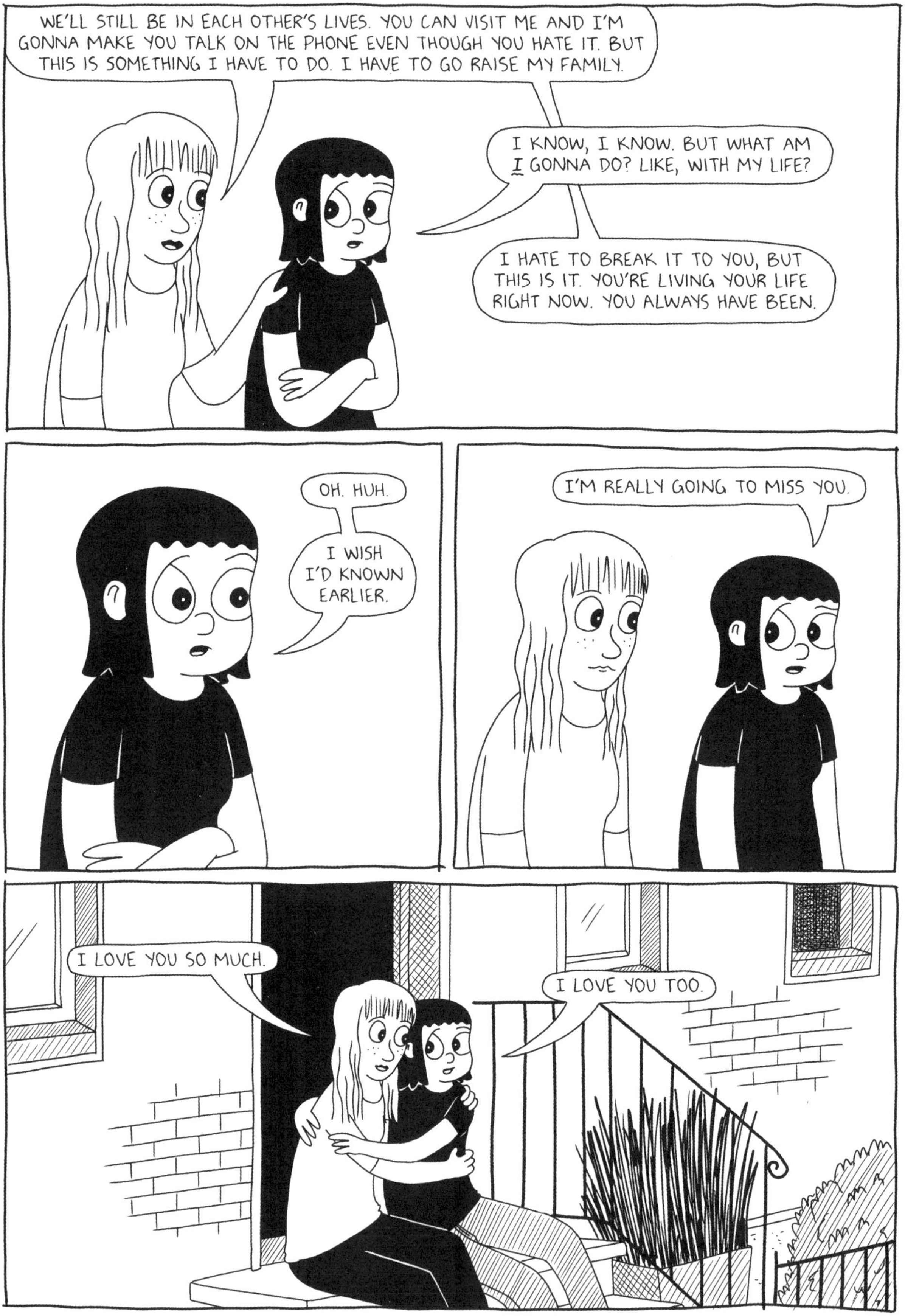
WE'LL STILL BE IN EACH OTHER'S LIVES. YOU CAN VISIT ME AND I'M GONNA MAKE YOU TALK ON THE PHONE EVEN THOUGH YOU HATE IT. BUT THIS IS SOMETHING I HAVE TO DO. I HAVE TO GO RAISE MY FAMILY.
I KNOW, I KNOW. BUT WHAT AM I GONNA DO? LIKE, WITH MY LIFE?
I HATE TO BREAK IT TO YOU, BUT THIS IS IT. YOU'RE LIVING YOUR LIFE RIGHT NOW. YOU ALWAYS HAVE BEEN.
OH. HUH.
I WISH I'D KNOWN EARLIER.
I'M REALLY GOING TO MISS YOU.
I LOVE YOU SO MUCH.
I LOVE YOU TOO.

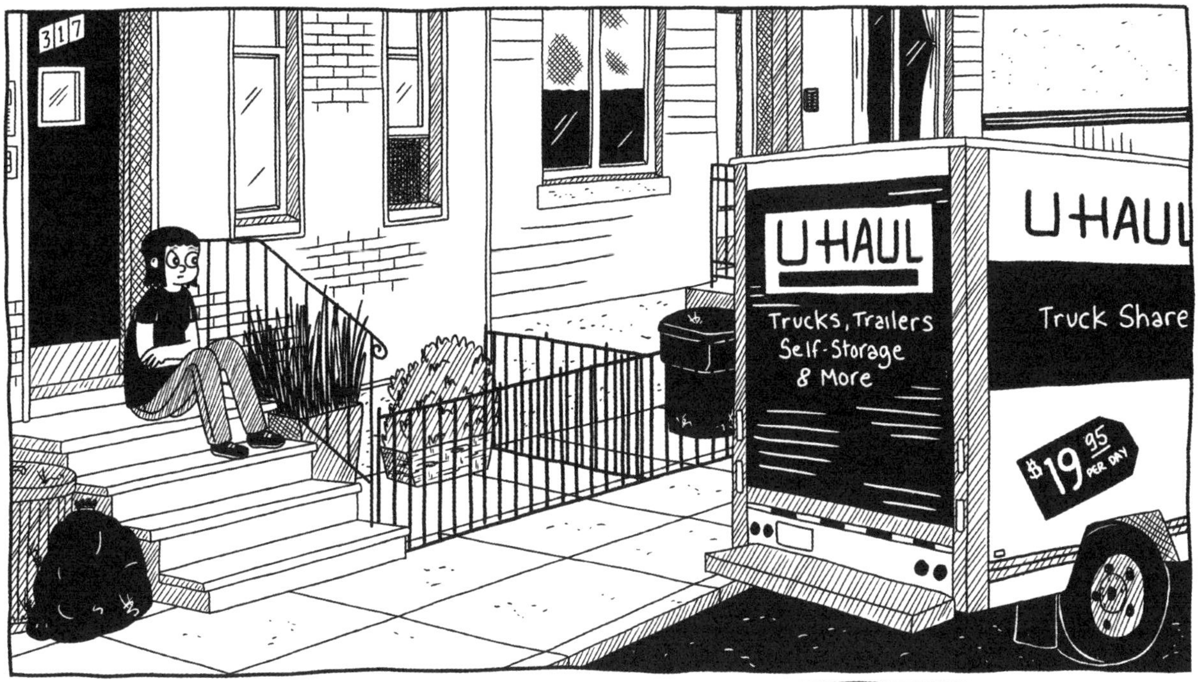
317
U-HAUL
Trucks, Trailers
Self-Storage
& More
U-HAUL
Truck Share
$19 95 PER DAY

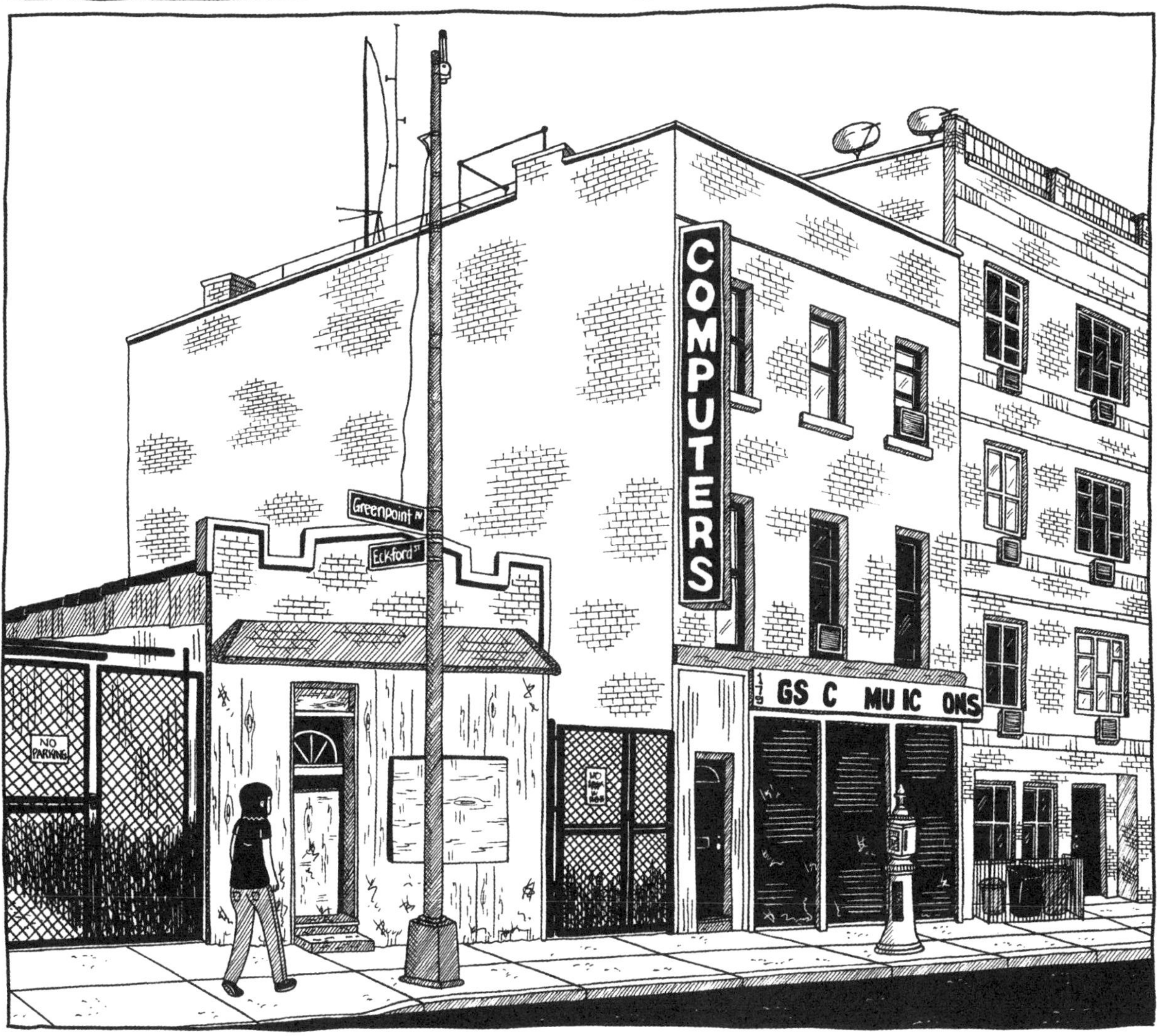
COMPUTERS
Greenpoint AV
Eckford ST
NO PARKING
GS C MU IC ONS

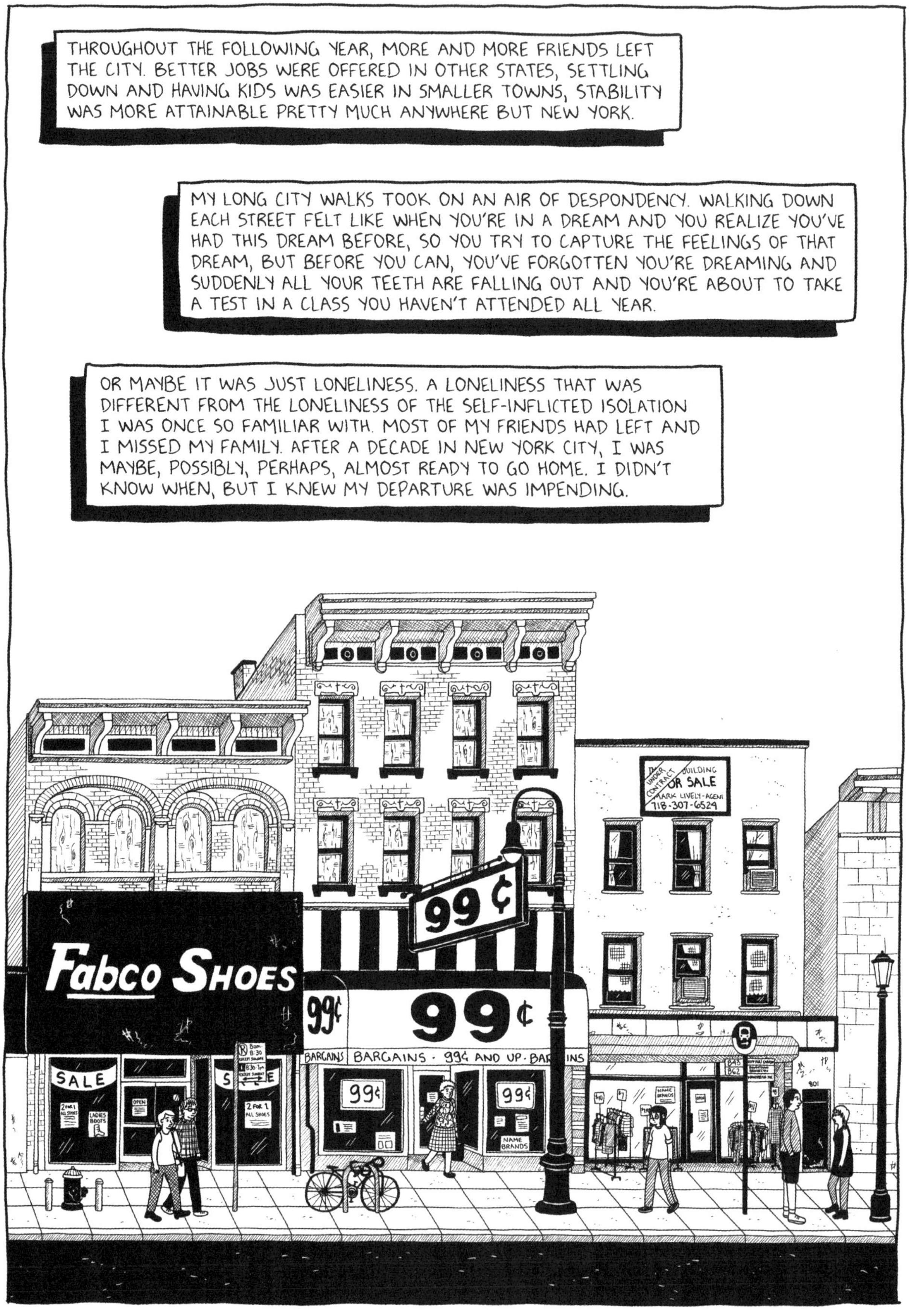
THROUGHOUT THE FOLLOWING YEAR, MORE AND MORE FRIENDS LEFT THE CITY. BETTER JOBS WERE OFFERED IN OTHER STATES, SETTLING DOWN AND HAVING KIDS WAS EASIER IN SMALLER TOWNS, STABILITY WAS MORE ATTAINABLE PRETTY MUCH ANYWHERE BUT NEW YORK.
MY LONG CITY WALKS TOOK ON AN AIR OF DESPONDENCY. WALKING DOWN EACH STREET FELT LIKE WHEN YOU'RE IN A DREAM AND YOU REALIZE YOU'VE HAD THIS DREAM BEFORE, SO YOU TRY TO CAPTURE THE FEELINGS OF THAT DREAM, BUT BEFORE YOU CAN, YOU'VE FORGOTTEN YOU'RE DREAMING AND SUDDENLY ALL YOUR TEETH ARE FALLING OUT AND YOU'RE ABOUT TO TAKE A TEST IN A CLASS YOU HAVEN'T ATTENDED ALL YEAR.
OR MAYBE IT WAS JUST LONELINESS. A LONELINESS THAT WAS DIFFERENT FROM THE LONELINESS OF THE SELF-INFLICTED ISOLATION I WAS ONCE SO FAMILIAR WITH. MOST OF MY FRIENDS HAD LEFT AND I MISSED MY FAMILY. AFTER A DECADE IN NEW YORK CITY, I WAS MAYBE, POSSIBLY, PERHAPS, ALMOST READY TO GO HOME. I DIDN'T KNOW WHEN, BUT I KNEW MY DEPARTURE WAS IMPENDING.
UNDER CONTRACT
MARK LIVELY-AGENT
718-307-6524
99¢
Fabco SHOES
99¢
99¢
BARGAINS · BARGAINS · 99¢ AND UP · BARGAINS
SALE
2 FOR 1 ALL SHOES
LADIES BOOTS
OPEN
99¢
99¢
NAME BRANDS
NAME BRANDS
801

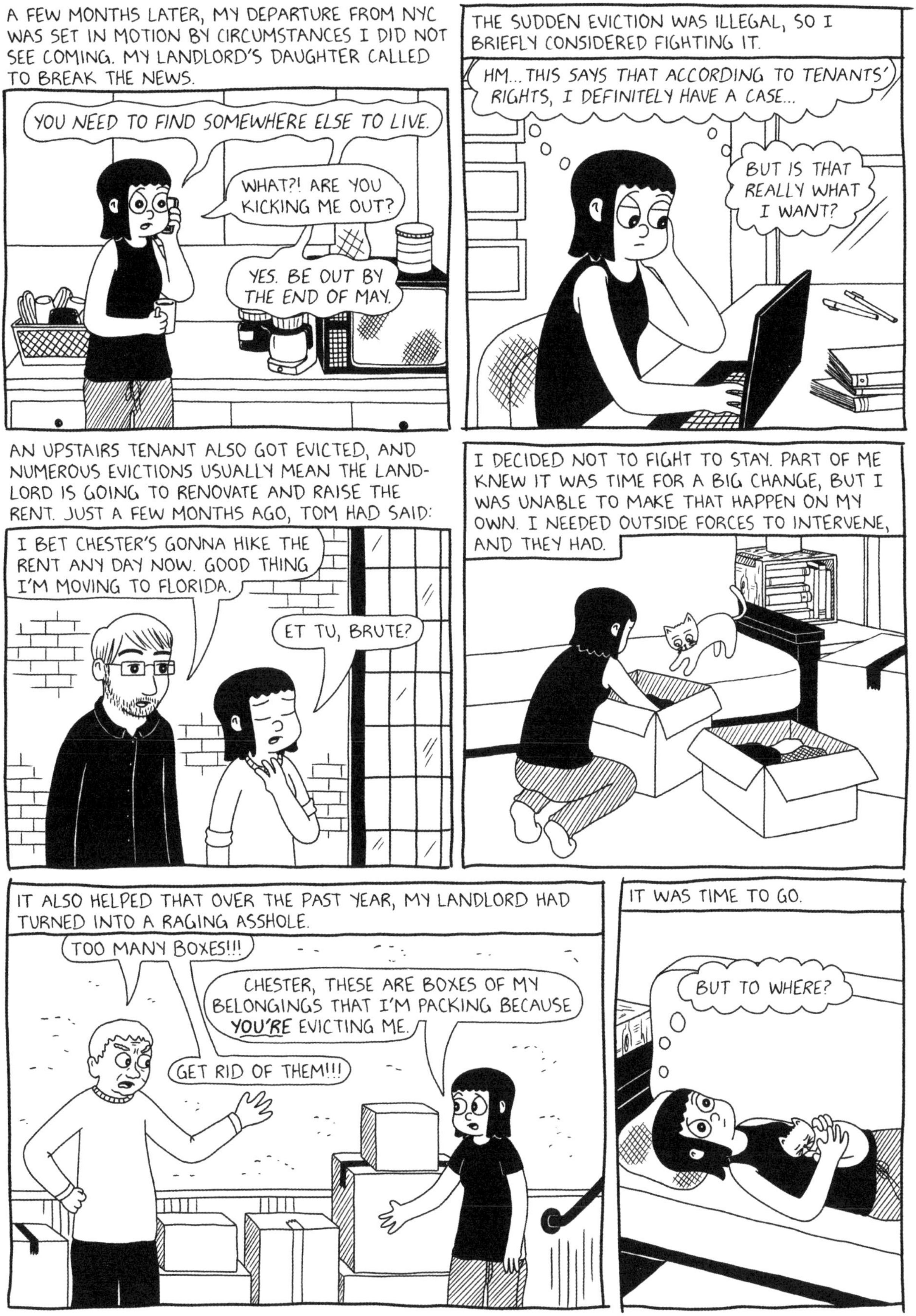
A FEW MONTHS LATER, MY DEPARTURE FROM NYC WAS SET IN MOTION BY CIRCUMSTANCES I DID NOT SEE COMING. MY LANDLORD'S DAUGHTER CALLED TO BREAK THE NEWS.
YOU NEED TO FIND SOMEWHERE ELSE TO LIVE.
WHAT?! ARE YOU KICKING ME OUT?
YES. BE OUT BY THE END OF MAY.
THE SUDDEN EVICTION WAS ILLEGAL, SO I BRIEFLY CONSIDERED FIGHTING IT.
HM... THIS SAYS THAT ACCORDING TO TENANTS' RIGHTS, I DEFINITELY HAVE A CASE...
BUT IS THAT REALLY WHAT I WANT?
AN UPSTAIRS TENANT ALSO GOT EVICTED, AND NUMEROUS EVICTIONS USUALLY MEAN THE LANDLORD IS GOING TO RENOVATE AND RAISE THE RENT. JUST A FEW MONTHS AGO, TOM HAD SAID:
I BET CHESTER'S GONNA HIKE THE RENT ANY DAY NOW. GOOD THING I'M MOVING TO FLORIDA.
ET TU, BRUTE?
I DECIDED NOT TO FIGHT TO STAY. PART OF ME KNEW IT WAS TIME FOR A BIG CHANGE, BUT I WAS UNABLE TO MAKE THAT HAPPEN ON MY OWN. I NEEDED OUTSIDE FORCES TO INTERVENE, AND THEY HAD.
IT ALSO HELPED THAT OVER THE PAST YEAR, MY LANDLORD HAD TURNED INTO A RAGING ASSHOLE.
TOO MANY BOXES!!!
CHESTER, THESE ARE BOXES OF MY BELONGINGS THAT I'M PACKING BECAUSE YOU'RE EVICTING ME.
GET RID OF THEM!!!
IT WAS TIME TO GO.
BUT TO WHERE?

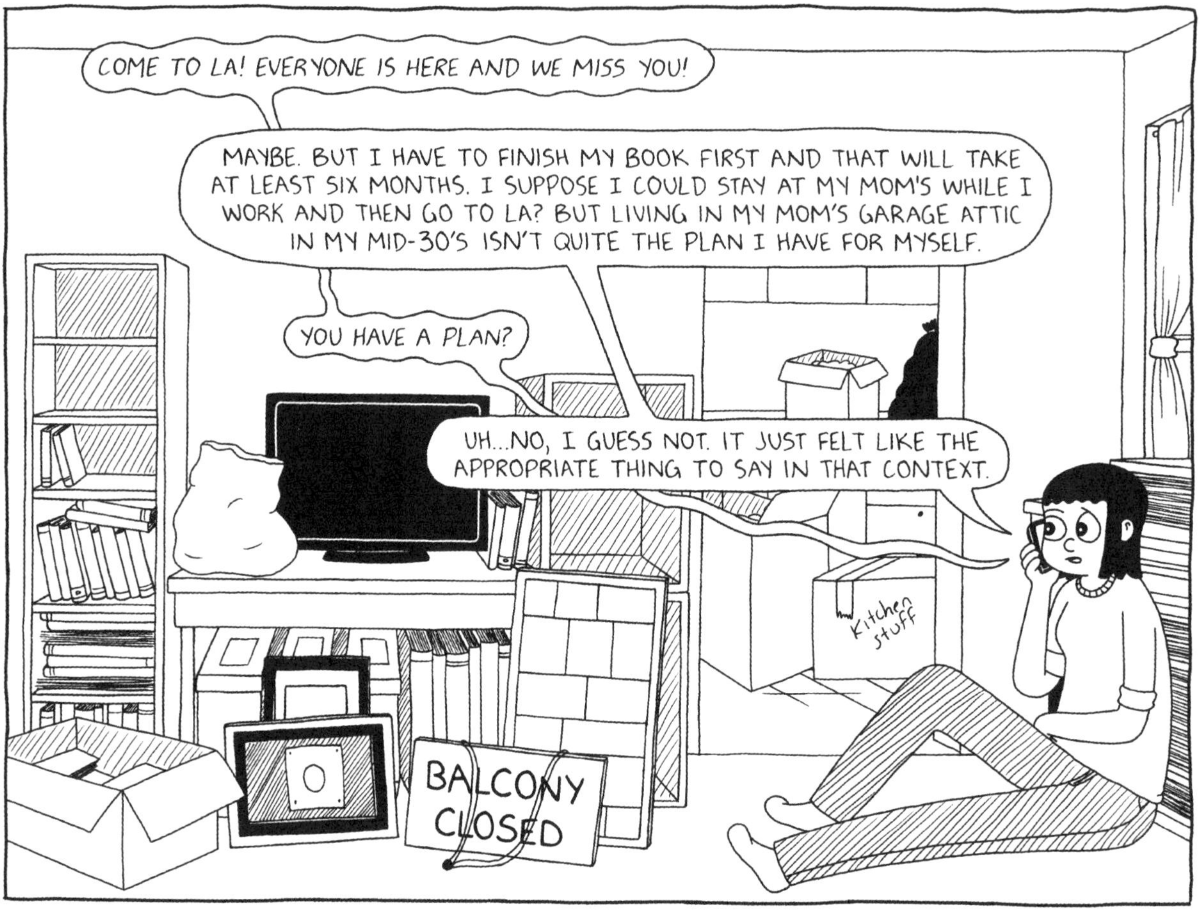
COME TO LA! EVERYONE IS HERE AND WE MISS YOU!
MAYBE. BUT I HAVE TO FINISH MY BOOK FIRST AND THAT WILL TAKE AT LEAST SIX MONTHS. I SUPPOSE I COULD STAY AT MY MOM'S WHILE I WORK AND THEN GO TO LA? BUT LIVING IN MY MOM'S GARAGE ATTIC IN MY MID-30'S ISN'T QUITE THE PLAN I HAVE FOR MYSELF.
YOU HAVE A PLAN?
UH...NO, I GUESS NOT. IT JUST FELT LIKE THE APPROPRIATE THING TO SAY IN THAT CONTEXT.
Kitchen stuff
BALCONY CLOSED

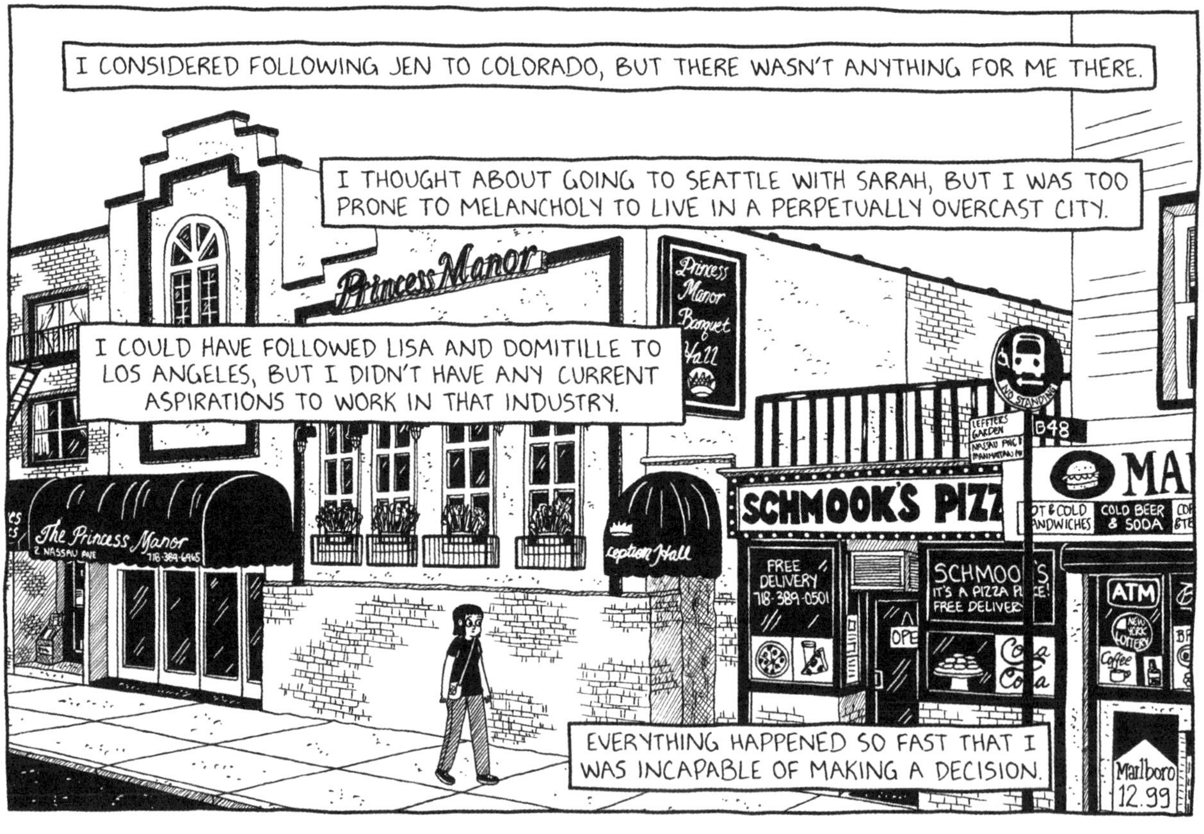
I CONSIDERED FOLLOWING JEN TO COLORADO, BUT THERE WASN'T ANYTHING FOR ME THERE.
I THOUGHT ABOUT GOING TO SEATTLE WITH SARAH, BUT I WAS TOO PRONE TO MELANCHOLY TO LIVE IN A PERPETUALLY OVERCAST CITY.
Princess Manor
Princess Manor Banquet Hall
I COULD HAVE FOLLOWED LISA AND DOMITILLE TO LOS ANGELES, BUT I DIDN'T HAVE ANY CURRENT ASPIRATIONS TO WORK IN THAT INDUSTRY.
NO STANDING
B48
The Princess Manor
2 NASSAU AVE 718-389-6965
SCHMOOK'S PIZZ
FREE DELIVERY 718-389-0501
SCHMOO S IT'S A PIZZA PL E! FREE DELIVER
COLD BEER & SODA
ATM
Coffee
EVERYTHING HAPPENED SO FAST THAT I WAS INCAPABLE OF MAKING A DECISION.
Marlboro 12.99

THE EVICTION HAD BEEN ABRUPT AND THERE WAS NO TIME TO PROCESS THE FACT THAT I WAS REALLY, TRULY LEAVING NEW YORK CITY.

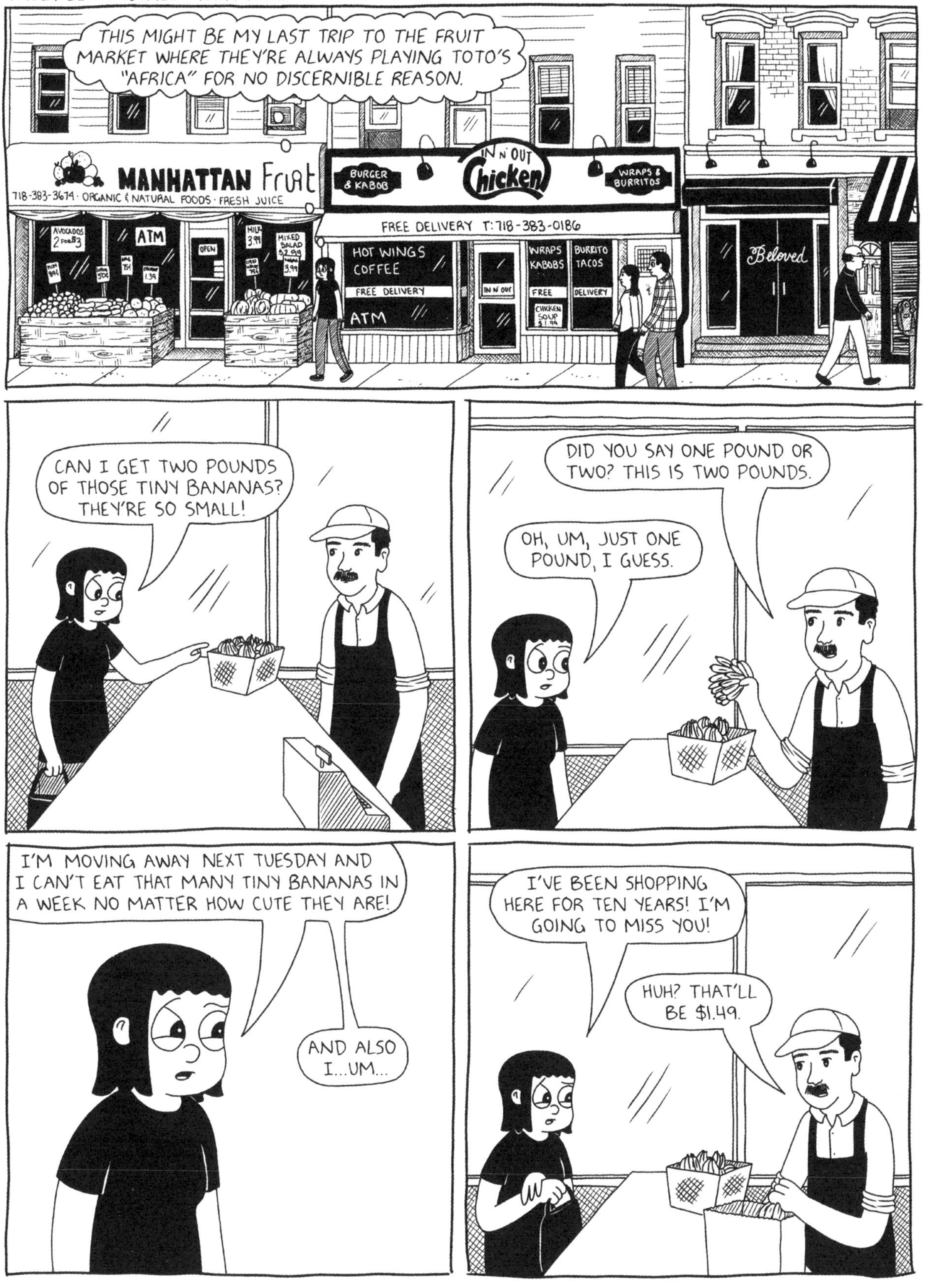
THIS MIGHT BE MY LAST TRIP TO THE FRUIT MARKET WHERE THEY'RE ALWAYS PLAYING TOTO'S "AFRICA" FOR NO DISCERNIBLE REASON.
MANHATTAN Fruit
718-383-3674 · ORGANIC & NATURAL FOODS · FRESH JUICE
AVOCADOS 2 FOR $3
ATM
OPEN
MILK 3.99
MIXED SALAD $2.99
IN N' OUT Chicken
BURGER & KABOB
WRAPS & BURRITOS
FREE DELIVERY T: 718-383-0186
HOT WINGS COFFEE
FREE DELIVERY
ATM
IN N' OUT
WRAPS KABOBS
BURRITO TACOS
FREE
DELIVERY
CHICKEN SOUP $1.99
Beloved
CAN I GET TWO POUNDS OF THOSE TINY BANANAS? THEY'RE SO SMALL!
DID YOU SAY ONE POUND OR TWO? THIS IS TWO POUNDS.
OH, UM, JUST ONE POUND, I GUESS.
I'M MOVING AWAY NEXT TUESDAY AND I CAN'T EAT THAT MANY TINY BANANAS IN A WEEK NO MATTER HOW CUTE THEY ARE!
AND ALSO I...UM...
I'VE BEEN SHOPPING HERE FOR TEN YEARS! I'M GOING TO MISS YOU!
HUH? THAT'LL BE $1.49.

IN THE END, I KNEW WHERE I HAD TO GO.

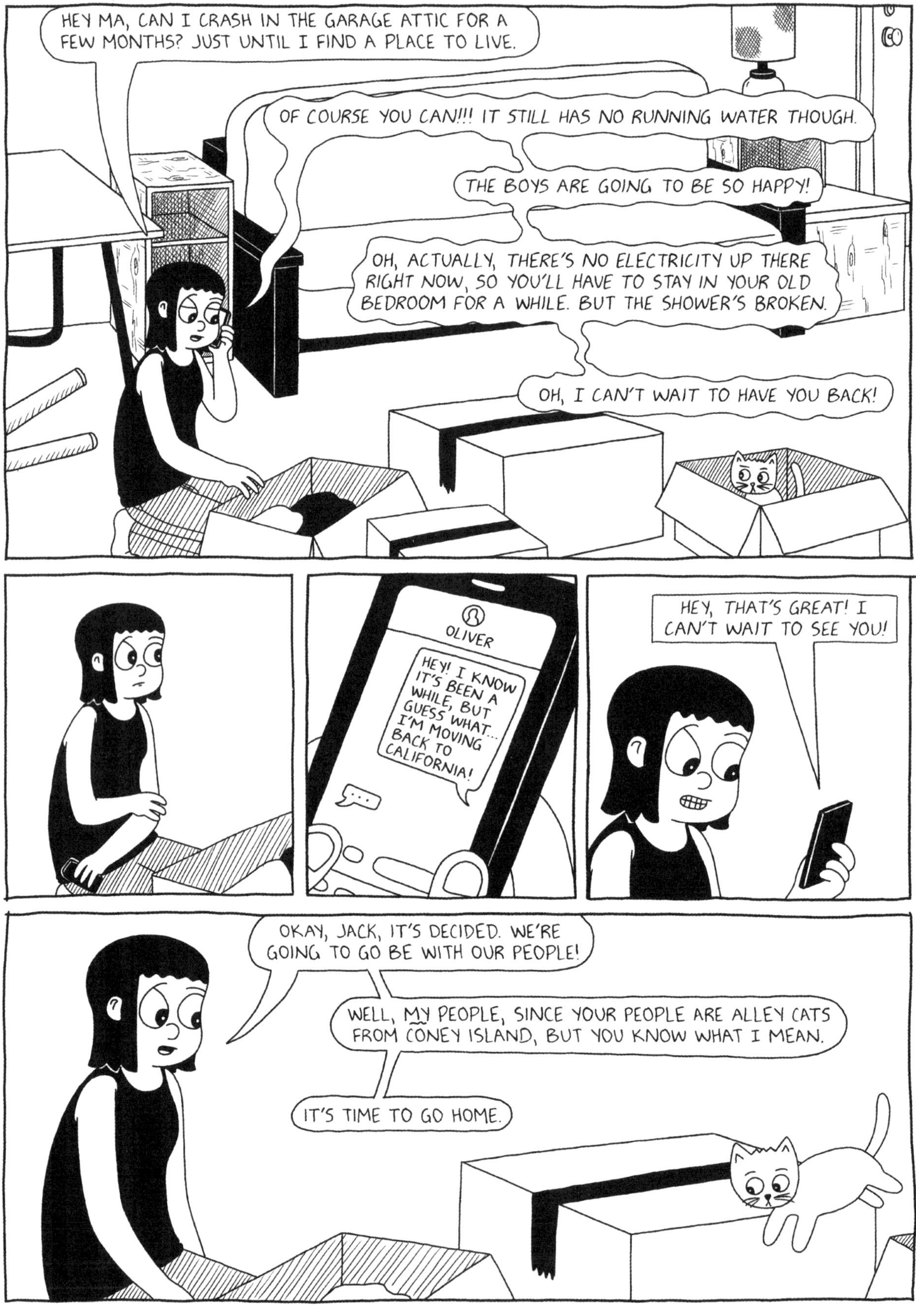

HEY MA, CAN I CRASH IN THE GARAGE ATTIC FOR A FEW MONTHS? JUST UNTIL I FIND A PLACE TO LIVE.
OF COURSE YOU CAN!!! IT STILL HAS NO RUNNING WATER THOUGH.
THE BOYS ARE GOING TO BE SO HAPPY!
OH, ACTUALLY, THERE'S NO ELECTRICITY UP THERE RIGHT NOW, SO YOU'LL HAVE TO STAY IN YOUR OLD BEDROOM FOR A WHILE. BUT THE SHOWER'S BROKEN.
OH, I CAN'T WAIT TO HAVE YOU BACK!
OLIVER
HEY! I KNOW IT'S BEEN A WHILE, BUT GUESS WHAT... I'M MOVING BACK TO CALIFORNIA!
HEY, THAT'S GREAT! I CAN'T WAIT TO SEE YOU!
OKAY, JACK, IT'S DECIDED. WE'RE GOING TO GO BE WITH OUR PEOPLE!
WELL, MY PEOPLE, SINCE YOUR PEOPLE ARE ALLEY CATS FROM CONEY ISLAND, BUT YOU KNOW WHAT I MEAN.
IT'S TIME TO GO HOME.

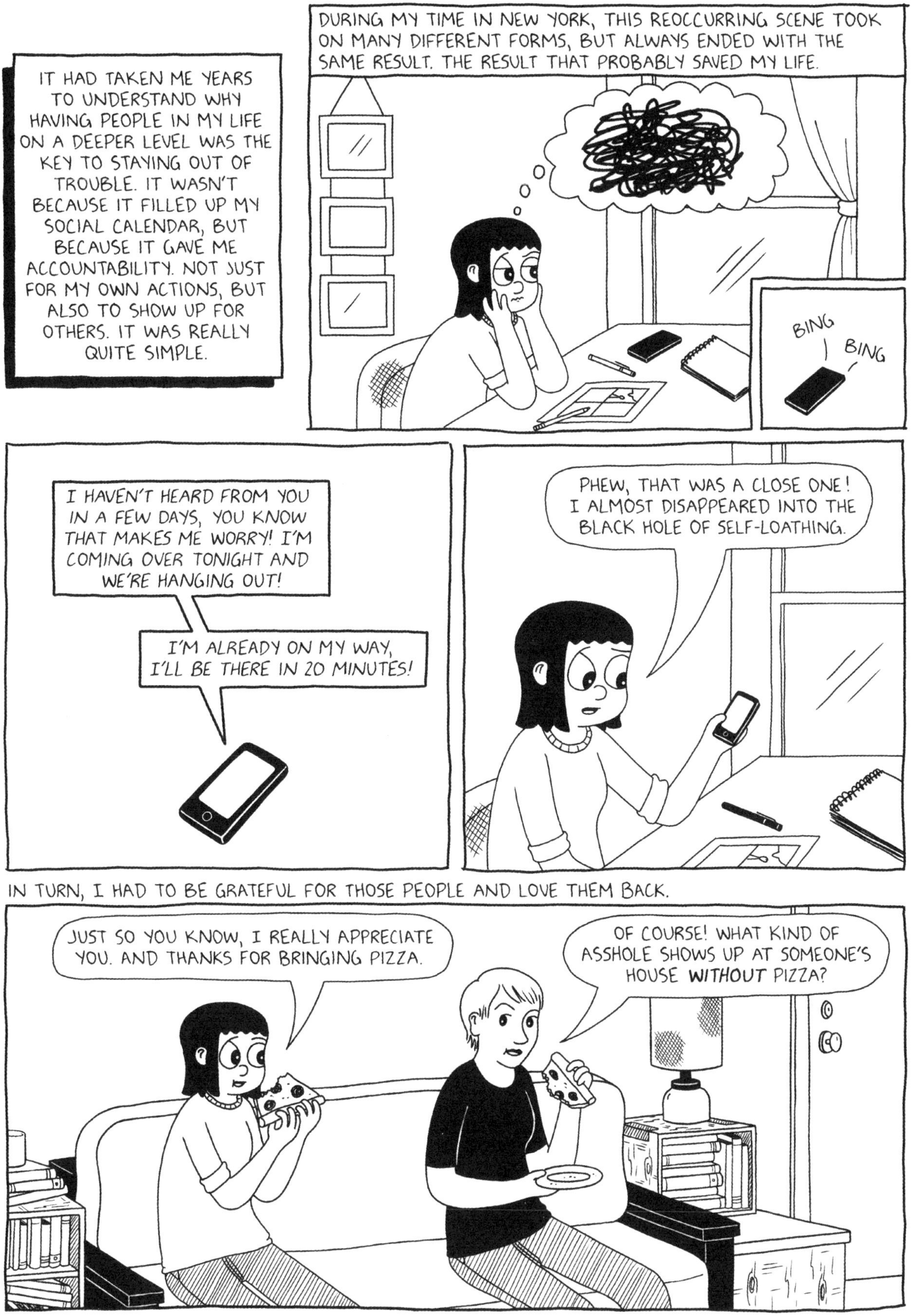
IT HAD TAKEN ME YEARS TO UNDERSTAND WHY HAVING PEOPLE IN MY LIFE ON A DEEPER LEVEL WAS THE KEY TO STAYING OUT OF TROUBLE. IT WASN'T BECAUSE IT FILLED UP MY SOCIAL CALENDAR, BUT BECAUSE IT GAVE ME ACCOUNTABILITY. NOT JUST FOR MY OWN ACTIONS, BUT ALSO TO SHOW UP FOR OTHERS. IT WAS REALLY QUITE SIMPLE.
DURING MY TIME IN NEW YORK, THIS REOCCURRING SCENE TOOK ON MANY DIFFERENT FORMS, BUT ALWAYS ENDED WITH THE SAME RESULT. THE RESULT THAT PROBABLY SAVED MY LIFE.
BING
BING
I HAVEN'T HEARD FROM YOU IN A FEW DAYS, YOU KNOW THAT MAKES ME WORRY! I'M COMING OVER TONIGHT AND WE'RE HANGING OUT!
I'M ALREADY ON MY WAY, I'LL BE THERE IN 20 MINUTES!
PHEW, THAT WAS A CLOSE ONE! I ALMOST DISAPPEARED INTO THE BLACK HOLE OF SELF-LOATHING.
IN TURN, I HAD TO BE GRATEFUL FOR THOSE PEOPLE AND LOVE THEM BACK.
JUST SO YOU KNOW, I REALLY APPRECIATE YOU. AND THANKS FOR BRINGING PIZZA.
OF COURSE! WHAT KIND OF ASSHOLE SHOWS UP AT SOMEONE'S HOUSE **WITHOUT** PIZZA?

IT'S OFTEN SAID THAT FOR SOMEONE TO REMAIN SOBER, THEY HAVE TO WANT IT FOR THEMSELVES. THAT SIMPLY HAVING ACCOUNTABILITY TO OTHERS IS NOT ENOUGH.

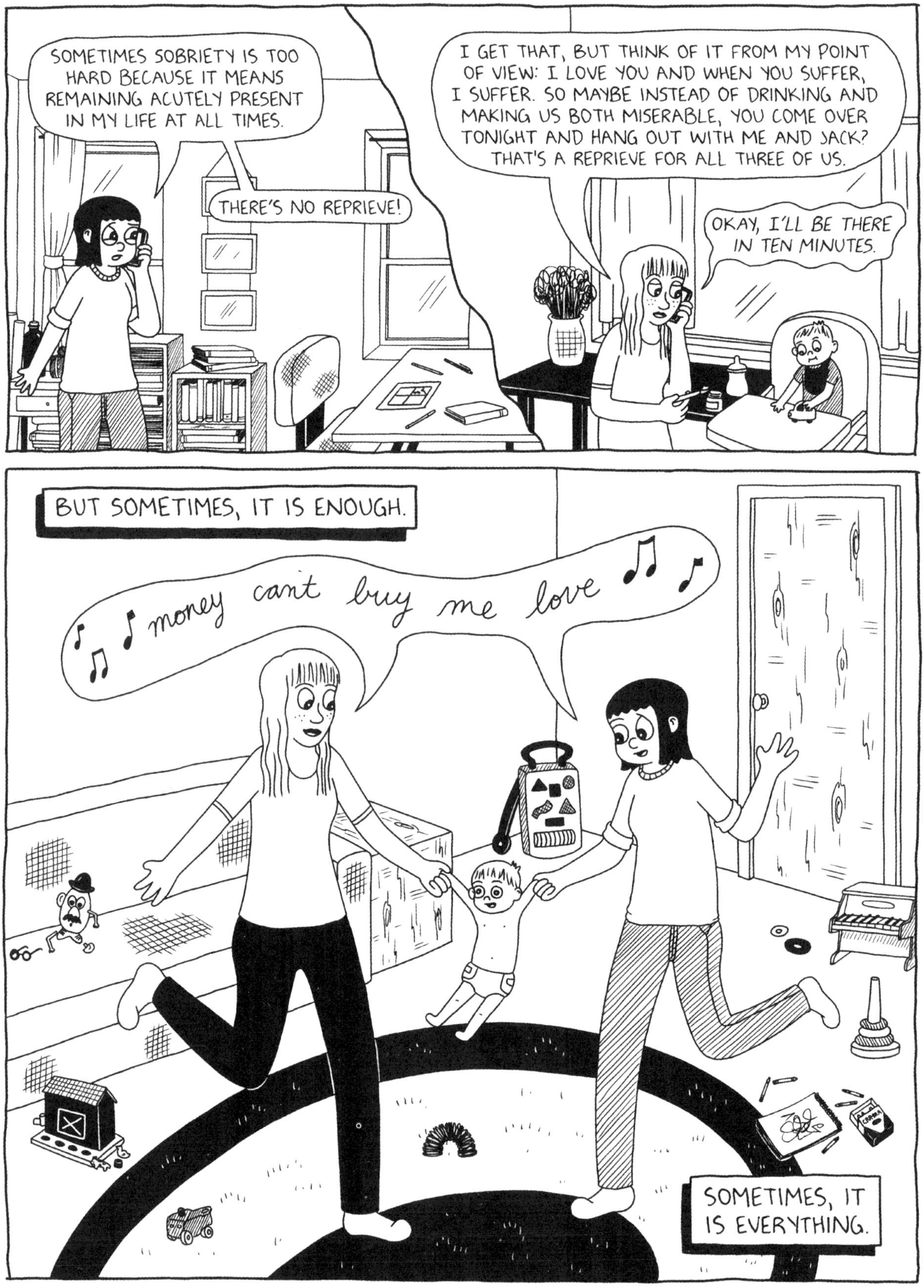
SOMETIMES SOBRIETY IS TOO HARD BECAUSE IT MEANS REMAINING ACUTELY PRESENT IN MY LIFE AT ALL TIMES.
THERE'S NO REPRIEVE!
I GET THAT, BUT THINK OF IT FROM MY POINT OF VIEW: I LOVE YOU AND WHEN YOU SUFFER, I SUFFER. SO MAYBE INSTEAD OF DRINKING AND MAKING US BOTH MISERABLE, YOU COME OVER TONIGHT AND HANG OUT WITH ME AND JACK? THAT'S A REPRIEVE FOR ALL THREE OF US.
OKAY, I'LL BE THERE IN TEN MINUTES.
BUT SOMETIMES, IT IS ENOUGH.
money can't buy me love
SOMETIMES, IT IS EVERYTHING.

THE END
(SORT OF)

ACKNOWLEDGMENTS

MY UTMOST GRATITUDE TO JENNIFER PHIPPEN AND SARAH GLIDDEN FOR BEING THE BEST FRIENDS ANYONE COULD EVER HAVE. THANK YOU TO THE LADIES OF PIZZA ISLAND FOR PUTTING UP WITH ME THEN (AND NOW). THANK YOU TO MY FAMILY WHO HAVE ALWAYS BEEN THERE FOR ME AND CONTINUE TO PROVIDE ENDLESS FODDER. THANK YOU TO MY AGENT MICHELLE BROWER AND EDITOR BECKY KOH, BOTH OF WHOM WERE VERY UNDERSTANDING WHILE I TOOK WAY TOO LONG TO FINISH THIS BOOK. THANK YOU TO OLIVER FOR SUPPORTING AND ENCOURAGING ME DURING THE PROCESS, AND THANK YOU TO FELIX WHO WAS INCONVENIENTLY BORN RIGHT IN THE MIDDLE OF IT. I LOVE YOU ALL.

ABOUT THE AUTHOR

JULIA WERTZ IS A PROFESSIONAL CARTOONIST, AMATEUR HISTORIAN, AND PART-TIME URBAN EXPLORER. HER BOOKS INCLUDE *THE FART PARTY, MUSEUM OF MISTAKES, DRINKING AT THE MOVIES, THE INFINITE WAIT AND OTHER STORIES,* AND *TENEMENTS, TOWERS, & TRASH: AN UNCONVENTIONAL, ILLUSTRATED HISTORY OF NEW YORK CITY.* SHE DOES MONTHLY COMICS AND DOODLES FOR THE *NEW YORKER* AND THE *NEW YORK TIMES.* AFTER LEAVING NEW YORK CITY, SHE SETTLED DOWN IN NORTHERN CALIFORNIA WITH OLIVER (YES, *THAT* OLIVER) AND THEIR SON, FELIX.